SECOND EDITION

A LONE STAR READER

Edited by

KIRK BANE
Blinn College
CHARLES SWANLUND
Blinn College
SCOTT SOSEBEE
Stephen F. Austin State University

Kendall Hunt
publishing company

Kendall Hunt
publishing company

www.kendallhunt.com
Send all inquiries to:
4050 Westmark Drive
Dubuque, IA 52004-1840

Copyright © 2010, 2015 by Kendall Hunt Publishing Company

ISBN 978-1-4652-7744-2

Kirk Bane: For M.B., J.B., and P.W.B., with much love.

Charles Swanlund: For Gail, Kevin, and Kelsey for their patience
and understanding, and to my father, Cliff, who believed in me.

Scott Sosebee: For Don Walker and Paul Carlson,
two mentors who taught me how to be a historian.

"It is admitted by all, that cultivated mind is the guardian genius of Democracy, and while guided and controlled by virtue, the noblest attribute of man. It is the only dictator that freemen acknowledge, and the only security which freemen desire."

PRESIDENT MIRABEAU B. LAMAR, FIRST MESSAGE TO CONGRESS, DECEMBER 21, 1838

Contents

INTRODUCTION AND ACKNOWLEDGMENTS

We are excited to introduce the second edition of *A Lone Star Reader*. To begin, we are delighted to welcome aboard an additional editor, Professor Scott Sosebee. A fine scholar, Dr. Sosebee serves as Executive Director of the East Texas Historical Association, based at Stephen F. Austin State University in Nacogdoches. His insight and energy have greatly strengthened the new edition. Second, readers will notice that we have substantially overhauled our anthology. New contributions may be found from Lone Star historians Gregory W. Ball, Judy Gentry, Daniel Hickerson, Ken Howell, Diana Compton Fisher, Bradley Folsom, Brandon Franke, Rick Koster, James Smallwood, Scott Sosebee, Leland Turner, and Don Worcester. Finally, while we received many compliments on the first edition, we believe that the revised volume of *A Lone Star Reader* is significantly improved. Like the earlier work, this book is intended for both students and general readers interested in the rich history of our state. Every article in the new edition, we believe, is well written, reliable, and engaging. Hopefully, you will agree.

We wish to thank our families for their love and support; we dedicate this new edition to them, with gratitude and affection. A number of individuals helped us complete this project, and a hearty "thank you" is in order. We are especially indebted to Jon Alston, Christine Bochniak, Tom Britten, Clayton Brown, Paul Carlson, Gary Cartwright, Ty Cashion, Brandon Franke, Bruce Glasrud, Ken Howell, Alex Hunt, Tai Kreidler, Diane Lovell, Carrie Maro, Jeff Mitchell, Phoebe Procter, Ken Stevens, Mark L. Thomas, John Troesser, Kate Wong Troesser, Don Walker, Robert Weaver, and Harris Worcester.

Kirk Bane
Charles Swanlund
Scott Sosebee

March 2, 2015

About the Editors

Kirk Bane, Professor of History at Blinn College—Bryan, holds degrees from Texas A&M University (B.A.—1987; M.A.—1989) and Texas Christian University (Ph.D.—1993). At TCU, his professors included Don Worcester and Ben Procter, both of whom are represented in this anthology. Dr. Bane has written for such scholarly publications as the *Southwestern Historical Quarterly*, the *Panhandle-Plains Historical Review*, the *East Texas Historical Journal*, the West Texas Historical Association *Year Book*, and the *Great Plains Quarterly*. He also contributes reviews to the popular online magazine, *Texas Escapes*. A former Board Member of the West Texas Historical Association, Bane is presently Managing Editor for the journal of the Central Texas Historical Association.

Charles Swanlund, Professor of History at Blinn College—Bryan, holds degrees from Lake Superior State University (B.A. –1981) and Sam Houston State University (M.A.—1998). At Sam Houston State, his professors included Caroline Castillo-Crimm and Gregg Cantrell. With Kenneth Howell, he is coeditor of the forthcoming *Single Star of the West* (University of North Texas Press), an anthology on the Texas Republic. Professor Swanlund has also contributed to the *East Texas Historical Journal*, the West Texas Historical Association *Year Book*, and the *Journal of South Texas*. He presently serves as Community Liaison for the Central Texas Historical Association.

Scott Sosebee, Executive Director of the East Texas Historical Association and Associate Professor of History at Stephen F. Austin State University in Nacogdoches, holds three degrees from Texas Tech University (B.A—1997; M.A.—2000; and Ph.D.—2004). At Tech, his professors included Paul Carlson, who is represented in this volume, Don Walker, and Alwyn Barr. Dr. Sosebee serves as editor for the *East Texas Historical Journal*. His publications have appeared in the West Texas Historical Association *Year Book*, the *Journal of Southern History*, and the anthology, *West Texas: A History of the Giant Side of the State* (University of Oklahoma Press, 2014).

Hasinai–European
Interaction, 1694–1715

DANIEL A. HICKERSON

Independent scholar Daniel A. Hickerson specializes in the history of the Hasinai Confederacy, a loosely organized Caddo group living along the Neches and Angelina Rivers in eastern Texas. His research on the Hasinai has also appeared in the journal, *Ethnohistory*.

In this selection, Dr. Hickerson analyzes how the Hasinai Indians and European newcomers forged an uneasy, yet somewhat accommodating, relationship on the early Texas frontier. ✍

SPANISH WITHDRAWAL AND RETRENCHMENT, 1694–1709

The first Spanish missionary effort in East Texas began in 1690 with the arrival of a small party that left among the Hasinai Indians three Franciscan priests, accompanied by three soldiers. The missionization of the Hasinai was undertaken as a reaction to the occupation of the Texas Gulf coast by the French explorer Rene Robert Cavelier, Sieur de La Salle during the 1680s. Despite an optimistic beginning, the Spaniards were forced to abandon their mission only three years later when the hostility of the Hasinai compelled them to flee. The Hasinai, who initially welcomed the Europeans, had suffered a series of severe epidemics for which they correctly blamed the Spaniards. They were further angered by the priests' persistent attempts to convert them to Catholicism, as well as the failure of the Spanish soldiers to aid them in battles against the Apaches and other enemies.

After the retreat from the East Texas mission in 1693, the Spanish had little direct documented contact with the Hasinai for more than two decades. For most of this period there is little evidence of what was taking place in eastern Texas. After their initial failures, both Spain and France seem to have lost interest in Texas temporarily. This lack of activity has led to the perception that these were, in the words of historian Carlos Castaneda, "silent years" in the history of Texas. It was not until after 1715, when the French trader and adventurer Louis Juchereau de St. Denis appeared unexpectedly at a Spanish settlement on the Rio Grande, that the territory of the Hasinai was reoccupied officially by Europeans.

This appearance of inactivity from eastern Texas is deceiving. Although the historical record may contain little direct documentation of the Hasinai during this period, these two decades were anything but silent. Contact did take place between the Hasinai and Europeans, although on a less official, and thus less well documented, level. The French, in particular, began to make exploring and trading forays into Texas during this period. Far-reaching political and economic changes continued to take place, changes to which the Hasinai undoubtedly tried to adjust, to react, and to turn in their favor.

During the seventeenth century, the Hasinai had acquired Spanish goods and horses through trade. The primary source of these commodities was the Jumano Indians, traders who made regular journeys from the Spanish colonial settlements along the Rio Grande to the Hasinai villages of eastern Texas. These regular trade connections to the south and west were broken sometime after the withdrawal of the Spanish missions, although it is likely that some goods and horses continued to make their way to the territory of the Hasinai from that direction through members of other Indian groups. After 1699, when the French constructed a fort at the mouth of the Mississippi River, new opportunities for trade were opened to the east because of French settlement, exploration, and trading activity in western Louisiana. When the Spanish returned to eastern Texas in 1715, they found the Hasinai trading animal skins, Indian slaves, corn, horses, and livestock to the French in return for rifles and other goods, a commerce that the Spanish authorities attempted to eradicate, without success, for most of the eighteenth century.

Exactly when the trade connections with the Jumanos were broken is not certain. The last time that Jumanos are noted at or near the Hasinai territory in the historical record is in 1693, during the Salinas Varona expedition that travelled to eastern Texas to resupply the Spanish missions shortly before their abandonment. Shortly after this time, Apache dominance of the southern plains apparently increased to the point that the annual trading expeditions became too hazardous to continue. The Jumanos' support of the Hasinai in their uprising against the Spanish soldiers and missionaries may also have strained their relationship with the Spaniards at Nueva Vizcaya, making problematic their access to, and subsequent trade in, Spanish goods.

These factors combined to cut off the Hasinai from the trade network of which they had been a part, probably by 1695, and almost certainly by 1700. The Jumano disappear completely from the historical record for several years. They eventually realigned themselves with their old enemies; when they reappear in the historical record two decades later, in 1716, they are described as allies of the Apaches and enemies of the Spaniards and the Hasinai.

This is not to say that the Hasinai were left completely without a source of Spanish horses and trade goods, as well as information on happenings among the Spanish settlements. Even without the Jumanos, the Hasinai maintained their long-time alliances with many of the hunting and gathering tribes who lived to their south and southwest. These alliances were still in place more than two decades later. In a declaration given to Spanish authorities in 1715, St. Denis noted that to the south of the Hasinai "there is a multiplicity of nations allied with this one, which are well-governed according to the relationship that these Indians have with them. And at the time of the reestablishment of the Spanish missions in 1716, Domingo Ramon noted that in addition to the Hasinai, the missions could "attract various and innumerable nations of Indians, friends of the Tejas, that I have had notice are in these parts."

Following the setback created by the failure of their initial efforts in Texas, the Franciscans established several missions in northern Mexico, at or near the Rio Grande, beginning in 1698. A few of the Spanish priests working in these missions maintained an interest in returning to the Hasinai. Principal among these was Father Francisco Hidalgo, who was among the missionaries who had fled East Texas in 1693. Hidalgo's efforts to bring about a return of the Spanish to eastern Texas proved pivotal in the reestablishment of the missions in 1716.

Hidalgo and his colleagues in the Rio Grande missions remained informed of events among the Hasinai and probably maintained a sporadic communication with them, primarily through their contact with members of the Coahuiltecan tribes who lived and wandered in the territory from northeastern Mexico to central Texas. Many of these were among the groups that had accompanied the Jumano on their journeys to the Hasinai during the previous decades. By 1700, the Hasinai evidently had direct interaction with French traders, who already had made inroads into their territory, and were in more indirect communication with the Spanish priests, who maintained an active interest in the Hasinai from their base at the missions along the Rio Grande.

French forays into eastern Texas began almost immediately after their occupation of the mouth of the Mississippi River in 1699. These expeditions had the initial purpose of making treaties of friendship with the Indian tribes and discovering the locations of mineral deposits that could be exploited. In March 1700, a party of twenty-two Canadians and seven Indians commanded by Jean Baptiste Le Moyne de Bienville and Louis de St. Denis reached the village of the Yatasi, Caddoan Indians who lived on the Red River, who told them where they could find the Hasinai and the closest Spanish settlements. Later the same year, a second expedition reached the Natchitoches and Kadohadachos on the Red River. More expeditions followed, and, according to Vito Alessio Robles, it is likely that the French of Louisiana had established regular contact with the Hasinai by 1704 or 1705. St. Denis probably had spent several months among the Hasinai shortly before, according to his own account, he had made his initial journey to the Rio Grande.

Spanish records suggest that such contact had been made several years before this time. In 1700 Father Diego de San Buenaventura y Salazar, the Franciscan priest in charge of the newly-founded Rio Grande missions, travelled from the Mission Santa Maria de los Dolores, in northern Nuevo Leon, to Mexico City to request aid and military protection for the Rio Grande missions. Salazar was accompanied on this expedition by two Hasinai Indians who had come to the missions with news of French advances into Spanish territory for the purpose of establishing trade with the Indians. These two Hasinai Indians were to testify to the French intrusions before the Spanish authorities.

The Indians testified that Frenchmen had come to the village of the Nasoni, located at the northern end of Hasinai territory, and had given two rifles to the chief of the village in exchange for two horses. More ominously, from the point of view of the Spaniards, the French seemed prepared to settle permanently among the Kadohadacho on the Red River. They had built houses, and had brought with them "religious who are dressed like those of San Francisco [Franciscans]." The two Hasinai stated that they had been sent to the Rio Grande missions by their uncle, the "Governor of the Tejas," to ask the Spanish to send priests and soldiers to settle at a place they called "The Three Crosses," which was on the banks of the San Marcos River, close to, but not within, Hasinai territory. Salazar's requests for aid for the missions were approved by the Junta, or council, that heard his petition. Undoubtedly, the indication of French advances into the area had some impact on this decision. The request of the Indians for soldiers and missionaries was put off with a provision for an investigation into their claims. Just as importantly, the presence of the two Indians on this expedition demonstrates that contact between the Hasinai and the Spanish could not have been completely cut off during this period.

There is little doubt that, as a result of their regular contact with the Spanish, the hunting-and-gathering tribes of central Texas and the Rio Grande valley were able to carry on some trade with the Hasinai in Spanish goods, horses, and livestock. As suggested by the testimony of the two Hasinai who accompanied Father Salazar, it was probably these horses and cattle, as well as grain and Indian slaves, that served as the principal commodities that the Hasinai traded to the French colonists in Louisiana during the first two decades of the eighteenth century. St. Denis noted in 1715 that the Hasinai possessed huge herds of "thousands of cows, bulls, horses, and mares, with which their fields are entirely covered." While this claim was almost certainly an exaggeration, the herds of the Hasinai probably were sizeable. It was in part due to the need for livestock for the Louisiana colony that the governor of French Louisiana established contact with the Spanish on the Rio Grande. It is likely that as the French colonial establishment grew, the colonists feared that their need for cattle and horses would outgrow the ability of the Hasinai and other Indians of the area to supply them. The colonial settlements of New Spain seemed to be a more direct source of these commodities as well as a potentially profitable trading partner for the French colonists.

The extent of the contact, direct or indirect, that took place between Spanish religious agents and the Hasinai in the years after the missions were abandoned is not clear, although it was almost certainly more frequent that the official documents indicate. Rumors of French activity in Louisiana, including occasional forays into Texas, reached the Franciscans, who made certain that they were passed on to Spanish political authorities in the hope that the East Texas missions would be reactivated, this time with a more effective military presence to protect them against both the French and hostile Indians. The missionaries evidently believed that the Hasinai would once again welcome them into their territory, despite the hostility that had forced the earlier retreat. The presence of the two Hasinai on Salazar's expedition to Mexico City suggests that they provided some degree of cooperation to the Spaniards. Some of the Coahuiltecans who frequented the Rio Grande missions also probably had suggested that the Caddoans would be receptive to a Spanish reoccupation of their lands.

THE 1709 OLIVARES-ESPINOSA-AGUIRRE EXPEDITION TO THE COLORADO RIVER

Thus it was with some optimism that Spanish authorities approved, and the priests planned, an expedition into Texas in 1709. The expedition was commanded by Pedro de Aguirre, with the assistance of Father Antonio de San Buenaventura y Olivares and Father Isidro Felix de Espinosa. This expedition, like most of those undertaken by Spain in its colonial territory, had both a military and religious purpose. Reports of French forays into Texas once again increased, creating renewed fears of a threat to Spain's colonial borders. At the same time, the expectation that the Hasinai again would receive missionaries willingly is reflected in the preparation for this expedition. It had been rumored that the Hasinai had moved from their homeland along the Neches and Angelina rivers to the banks of what the Spanish called the San Marcos River, by which they probably meant the Colorado, to be closer to the Spanish settlements along the Rio Grande, presumably to persuade them to reestablish the missions. The source of these rumors is not clear; they could have come from any of the Indians who frequented the Rio Grande missions. Whatever the source, the Spaniards almost certainly recalled the two Hasinai in Mexico City nine years earlier, who asked them to send priests to the banks of the same river.

The Spaniards were disappointed in the results of this expedition. The party, consisting of the two priests and fifteen soldiers, departed on April 5 from the San Juan Bautista mission, located on the southern bank of the Rio Grande at present-day Guerrero, Coahuila. On April 19, having reached the Colorado River where they hoped to find the Hasinai, the Spaniards instead were met by a party of approximately forty Yojuan Indians and a few individuals of other tribes. This group was led by the Yojuan chief Cantona, who according to Espinosa was "an Indian who knew the Spanish very well." A larger group of Yojuan Indians camped several miles away.

Cantona was known to have been among the Hasinai, and was questioned closely concerning their whereabouts and intentions. Asked by the Spaniards "if it was true that they had abandoned their territory and come to the San Marcos [Colorado] River to settle it," Cantona responded "that the Hasinai Indians (also known as Tejas) were in their land where they always had lived and that they had not departed to settle in the place of which we had asked; that only some of them departed from it to hunt for bison meat on these banks of the Colorado River and its vicinity." And he said "that the Indian named Bernardino, who is a Tejas Indian who speaks Spanish, and who has been in Mexico and spent many years among the Spanish, was Governor of all the Tejas," and that Bernardino "is known to be very hostile to all matters of the faith, and could never be reduced to it." It seemed clear to the Spaniards that they would not be welcomed by the Hasinai leader and his people.

Faced with this disappointing news, the Spanish party did not press any further toward the territory of the Hasinai, despite having been told by the Yojuanes that they were only three days' travel from their territory. Discouraged, running short on supplies, and lacking orders from their superiors that would have been necessary to advance further into Texas, they returned to Mission San Juan Bautista, arriving there on April 28. Before retreating the missionaries made one last attempt to contact the Hasinai. They persuaded Cantona to deliver to Bernardino a paper cross painted with ink that they had made, a symbol that they knew would be recognized by the Hasinai leader. Cantona was then to tell Bernardino and his people "that we had gone to seek them, and they they should come to the Rio Grande to our missions, since they knew where they were." It is clear that the priests never received a response to this invitation.

The motives of Cantona and the veracity of his statements about the Hasinai and their chief are not clear, although historians have never questioned the truth of the information he gave to the Spaniards. For example, both Carlos Castaneda and, more recently, Donald Chipman note this incident briefly with little comment. This may be in part because little is known about the Yojuanes. They seem to have been a fairly large group. According to the account of Espinosa, the Yojuanes that several members of the Spanish party encountered during a side trip to their main camp were quite numerous. However, although their presence is noted several times in the historical record, their identity or ethnic affiliation has not been determined satisfactorily.

Nevertheless, the possibility should be noted that the Yojuan chief was trying to steer the Spaniards away from the Hasinai and that he may have been attempting to court the favor of the Spaniards toward his own people in the hope of establishing a military alliance and a source of trade goods. Although this is speculation, the circumstances of the encounter provide at least some support for it. Although the priests were in error about the move of the Hasinai to the Colorado River, they probably had cause to think the Hasinai would be receptive to their overtures of renewed friendship. As previously noted, there was almost certainly some contact between the Spanish and the Caddoans. Even the last line of the message entrusted to Cantona reminding Bernardino that the Hasinai "knew where [the Rio Grande missions] were" suggests familiarity, given that those missions had been established several years after the Franciscans' abandonment of eastern Texas.

The actions of Cantona and his followers also suggest that they were hoping to establish an amicable relationship with the Spaniards. The Yojuanes and their companions were clearly well prepared for their encounter with the Franciscan priests, and seem to have anticipated the meeting. Father Espinosa noted in his diary that in their initial encounter near the banks of the Colorado River, Cantona and a group of the Indians arrived:

> with a cross of cane, well crafted, and behind this Indian crucifix, three Indians, each one with an image of Our Lady of Guadalupe, two of these painted, and the other an old print. And upon their arrival, they all made demonstrations of peace, some kneeling, and approaching the Spaniards and embracing them, which is their means of demonstrating their happiness with meeting those of whom they are fond.

It was just after this demonstration of friendship and faith, which was designed to win the favor of the priests, that Cantona delivered to the Spaniards his report detailing the continued hostility of the Hasinai, and particularly their leader, toward the Spanish and the Catholic religion. The Spaniards responded by presenting Cantona with a baton "with a tip of silver" to reward his demonstration of friendship, to encourage his peoples' conversion to Catholicism, and to symbolize his leadership. He made a prominent display of this baton upon his return to the camp where most of his people had remained to show "his Indians that the priests and Spaniards esteemed him much."

The possibility that the Yojuanes were attempting to court the favor of the Spaniards does not necessarily imply that they were trying to deflect this favor from the Hasinai, or that they were in competition with them for trade and alliance with the Spanish. But it does seem apparent that Cantona and his followers were attempting to demonstrate a clear contrast between their own friendship and receptivity toward the Catholic religion and the hostility and faithlessness of the Hasinai. It should be noted also that when the Yojuanes next appear in the historical record, upon the return of the Spanish to the Hasinai in 1716, they are listed as being among the enemies who "encircled to the north" and harassed the Hasinai, as well as the newly reestablished Spanish missions. Franciscan missionary priest and historian Father Isidro Felix de Espinosa later noted that around 1714, the Yojuanes, who he also now describes as enemies of the Hasinai, had attacked and burned the fire temple and the house of the Conenesi, or spirit children, to whom the Hasinai regularly gave offerings and made petitions. The possibility should be noted that the Yojuanes, by 1709, were in competition with the Hasinai for access to trade goods, for political and military alliances, and for a favored position in the regional political and economic system. If this is the case, then it is also likely that the Hasinai chief Bernardino never received the painted cross and message that Fathers Olivares and Espinosa expected Cantona to carry to him.

HIDALGO, SAN DENIS, AND THE RETURN TO THE HASINAI

Two individuals, one a Spanish missionary priest, Father Francisco Hidalgo, and the other a French explorer and trader, Louis Juchereau de St. Denis, have been credited as the principal figures who engineered the return of the Spanish to eastern Texas. Numerous historical accounts of this fascinating episode in the colonial period of this region have described in detail the actions of these two persons and the effect that they had on the policies of Spain and France on the frontier between the two colonial territories. In these accounts, the territory of the Hasinai is always mentioned as part of the setting for this historical drama. The actual role played by the Hasinai rarely receives more than a few sentences in these accounts, but without the influence and cooperation of the Hasinai, the goals of the French traders and the Spanish priests almost certainly could not have been realized.

After the Espinosa-Olivares expedition of 1709 failed to locate and reestablish contact with the Hasinai, the two priests involved in that journey left the Rio Grande missions for other duties, leaving Father Francisco Hidalgo to continue to lobby the Spanish religious and political authorities for a return to eastern Texas. Hidalgo almost certainly had been in contact with the Hasinai—indirect contact through members of other tribes, and probably at least sporadic direct contact as well. When St. Denis arrived at the Rio Grande accompanied by four Hasinai Indians, Diego Ramon, captain of the Presidio de San Juan Bautista, wrote to Father Hidalgo, noting that one of the Hasinai was "he who came to see Your Reverence in past years." Robert Weddle notes that some sources have indicated, although without clear documentation, that while at San Juan Bautista, Hidalgo made periodic journeys, alone and without official permission, to the territory of the Hasinai. Regardless of whether this is true, he certainly knew of the French activity in Louisiana and their forays into eastern Texas to trade with the Hasinai and their neighbors.

On January 17, 1711, Hidalgo wrote to the French governor of Louisiana, Lamothe Cadillac, to inquire about the well being of the Hasinai and ask for his cooperation in reestablishing a Spanish mission for the Indians. He sent three copies of the letter by separate routes to Louisiana. One of the copies reached the French governor more than two years later, on May 2, 1713. It was at just this time that Cadillac was attempting to establish a commercial enterprise in Louisiana, with the primary goals of finding sources of minerals to mine, increasing the Indian trade, and establishing a regular commerce with the Spanish colonial settlements. Hidalgo's letter created the possibility of bringing about the third of these goals by bringing the Spanish closer to the colonial frontier.

Almost immediately an expedition composed of twenty-four Canadian soldiers was dispatched from Mobile late in September 1713 under the command of St. Denis. The expedition was to seek out Father Hildago, and purchase cattle and horses for the French colony. Certainly, an additional purpose was to make the Spanish authorities aware of the French presence at the frontier of Texas and Louisiana to oblige the Spaniards to establish a presence on that frontier as well. It was hoped that such a presence would open up a line of communication and, more importantly, of commerce, between the two colonies.

Setting out from Mobile, St. Denis travelled by the Mississippi and Red rivers to the village of the Natchitoches Indians, who he described as "people with whom the French have traded for fourteen years in this place." From there he and his party travelled overland about forty leagues to the territory of the Hasinai. There he found the eleven villages of the Hasinai confederacy united under their leader, the Xinesi (chief or high priest) Bernardino, "who all obey." This was the same Bernardino the Spaniards had known two decades earlier as the nephew of the Caddi (village chief) of the Hasinai village of Nabedachi, and whose hostility toward the Spaniards had been described by the Yojuan chief in 1709. From the Hasinai, St. Denis sent twenty-one of the soldiers back to Mobile. After a stay of undetermined length among the Hasinai, St. Denis, his three remaining soldiers, and a party of twenty-five Indians led by Bernardino set out for the Presidio de San Juan Bautista on the Rio Grande. Along the way the group was attacked "by some two hundred thieving Indians from the coast," probably Karankawa. After a six-hour battle, in which at least twelve of the enemy group were killed, peace was made, and twenty-one of the Hasinai returned to their villages. St. Denis and his party finally arrived at the Spanish presidio on July 19, 1714.

St. Denis presented himself to the commander of the Presidio de San Juan Bautista, Diego Ramon, showing his passport and explaining that he wished to purchase supplies for the French settlements in Louisiana. He also asked for Father Hidalgo, who had some time earlier returned to his *Colegio* at Queretaro. St. Denis and his three companions were arrested by Ramon and confined to the commander's own household. After an "imprisonment" of several months, during which St. Denis lived comfortably, charmed and befriended the entire Ramon household, and became engaged to Captain Diego Ramon's granddaughter, he was sent to Mexico City. There he appeared several times before the Viceroy, the Duke of Linares, to account for his illegal entrance into Spanish territory and describe the route that he had taken. St. Denis' official statement regarding his journey was recorded on June 22, 1715.

The report that St. Denis gave the Spaniards concerning his voyage was calculated to stimulate their interest in returning to the land of the Hasinai. Noting the cultivated fields and vast herds of the Hasinai, he also described the fertility of the land, on which, he said, are found "fruits of every kind, very rich and most noble, with the most prolific vines that he has seen, of distinct qualities and colors, and in such quantity that the countryside is covered with bunches of grapes which are of the size of a ball of 28 or 30 pounds each, as also such vast fields, covered with hemp so fine that it could provide the rigging for all the ships of Europe." His report on the inhabitants of this land was no less positive. Many of the Hasinai, including Bernardino, he reported, had maintained the Catholic faith even without priests in residence among them. Furthermore, the Indians had asked St. Denis to find Father Hidalgo, "who had lived among them with singular knowledge of their customs and language," and persuade him to return to East Texas. The Hasinai, said St. Denis, "have always retained a firm veneration for the Spanish, which they express even unto death, with the hope of their restitution."

St. Denis' testimony contained numerous exaggerations and even some outright falsehoods. His description of the land and its resources seems to have been designed to remind the Spaniards of the most positive features of the environment while judiciously omitting more negative features and conditions, such as the dense forest, the unpredictable rainfall, and the periodic flooding of the rivers that had caused them difficulty during their first occupation. St. Denis' report was particularly deceptive concerning the supposed devotion of the Hasinai to the Catholic faith. There is no evidence that any of the Indians had remained practicing Catholics or even maintained an interest in the religion after the departure of the Franciscans in 1693. There is little reason to believe that any conversions had been made, even during the first Spanish occupation, except perhaps a few among those who were dying of disease. According to some accounts, Father Hidalgo had won some genuine converts among the Hasinai, who had begged him not to abandon them in 1693. The devotion of these converts presumably accounted for Hidalgo's long-time dedication to bringing about the return of the Franciscans to eastern Texas. However, this scenario probably is based more on romantic fantasy than genuine documentation. Whatever conversions had been achieved were few and far between. Nor would the priests have any greater success in converting the Hasinai after 1716 when they returned to eastern Texas.

Nevertheless, St. Denis' statement had its intended effect. The following month, the Spanish *Fiscal* directed the Viceroy to order the establishment of a mission among the Hasinai, and soon the number of missions to be established was increased to four. St. Denis was released from prison, appointed to guide the expedition to establish these missions, and was given a salary. The reasons for this decision to reoccupy Texas were numerous. The Spanish authorities certainly had been aware of French activity in the area for some years, having no doubt been reminded by Fathers Hidalgo and Salazar time and again, but it apparently took the appearance of St. Denis to shake them out of their complacency and to make them aware of the "pernicious consequences" that the Spanish could suffer from the French forays into their domain. The continuous lobbying of the priests must have had some effect, as well as did the glowingly positive report of St. Denis on the land and on the desires of the Indians to once again receive missionaries. But the other major figures in this episode, the Hasinai Indians themselves, played a part, as well. What were their goals during this period, and what were their strategies in bringing them about?

THE HASINAI AND THE REOCCUPATION OF EAST TEXAS

Unfortunately, there are only two accounts of first-hand encounters with the Hasinai that pertain to this period: the documents detailing Salazar's expedition to Mexico City, on which he was accompanied by two Hasinai Indians; and St. Denis' report, which contains a few sentences designed primarily to spark the interest of the Spaniards in a reoccupation of eastern Texas. So it is necessary, to an even greater degree that for other periods, to infer what may have been the motives and strategies of the Hasinai in dealing with Europeans in their land. There are a number of points that seem relevant to this endeavor.

First, although, as noted, St. Denis' report of the Catholic zeal of the Hasinai was an obviously calculated deception, the Hasinai nevertheless were interested in having the Spanish return to their territory. The reason was not their desire for religious instruction or the salvation of their souls, but rather an opportunity to benefit from the increase in trade that would result from the presence of both Spaniards and Frenchmen in their vicinity. Thus, the Hasinai were probably just as eager to see San Denis' mission succeed as was St. Denis himself. The last segment of St. Denis' journey, from the Hasinai to the Rio Grande, may have been undertaken partly at the urging of Bernardino. St. Denis indicates, as quoted in a letter written to Father Hidalgo by Diego Ramon, that he initially had intended to contact Hidalgo by letter from the territory of the Hasinai. The Hasinai individual who at first had agreed to carry the letter then made an excuse not to do so. As St. Denis noted in another letter, this one written by himself to Hidalgo, "it is Bernardo [Bernardino], a Hasinai, who wanted to guide us here, with three others of his countrymen." Apparently at Bernardino's urging, St. Denis and his small party "departed from his land without supplies . . . living on the road on whatever we could hunt.

Bernardino was instrumental in bringing about St. Denis' contact with the Spanish, or at least in encouraging the French party in making their journey to the Rio Grande. As the most powerful political leader among the Hasinai, it would have been among Bernardino's duties and prerogatives to mediate between the Hasinai and the French and Spanish outsiders and to arrange trading relationships with those outsiders. The arrangement of such relationships by a political leader also would have been a means of reinforcing and consolidating his power. Bernardino no doubt hoped that his relationship with St. Denis would give him access to an exclusive source of European goods, a source that would allow him to strengthen his network of allies and sources among the Hasinai and with surrounding tribes.

While Bernardino certainly remembered the disastrous outcome of the first Spanish occupation of his territory and the anger with which he and his uncle had evicted the Spaniards, it should not be considered unusual that he would welcome them back. In the social world of the Southeast and the Southern Plains during this period, friendships, alliances, and trade relationships constantly shifted, and an enemy one year might be an ally the next. In this unstable social climate, the willingness of the Hasinai to overlook past conflicts with other groups probably accounted in part for the large network of alliances and exchange partnerships they enjoyed. If an amicable relationship with the Spaniards could bring material or political benefits to the Hasinai, past grievances would be forgotten readily.

There was one group with whom there was little or no chance of arranging an alliance or a regular trading relationship. The Apaches were still mortal and irrevocable enemies of the Hasinai and all of their neighbors. In 1716, Captain Domingo Ramon, the son of Diego Ramon, who led the military arm of the party that reestablished the missions among the Hasinai, reported that he was unable to carry out a planned exploration of the surrounding territory because of the presence of Apaches and Yojuanes, who were enemies of the Hasinai. And the following year, Don Juan de Olivan Rebolledo proposed the building of a presidio on the bank of the Red River to Guard "against the invasions of the Apaches, who are enemies of one and all."

It was the hostility of the Apaches that had made the development of an amicable relationship with the French of Louisiana all the more important to the Hasinai. This is true because the French were the source of a commodity, previously unavailable to the Hasinai, that gave them a distinct advantage over their enemies. Beginning around 1700 the French colonists of Louisiana began to bring firearms to the Hasinai and their neighbors. At first guns were obtained in such small numbers that they were almost certainly a prestige item, available only to individuals who held high social status and political authority. In addition to their utilitarian value, firearms would be displayed by elites as symbols of their status and distributed selectively to allies and supporters.

In 1700, one of the two Hasinai who accompanied Father Salazar to Mexico City reported that the Frenchmen who had come to the province of the Hasinai had met the "Captain of the Nazones [Nasoni]," and had presented to him two rifles in exchange for two horses. Sixteen years later, the Spaniards found firearms among the Hasinai in slightly greater numbers that had been noted in 1700. Domingo Ramon reported in a letter written shortly after the Spanish reoccupation of East Texas in 1716, "I have found that the Tejas have eighteen or twenty long rifles, all French," in addition to beads, knives, and clothing that the French had traded to them for livestock. At this time, firearms still appear to be primarily a prestige item. In his diary of the 1716 expedition, Domingo Ramon described a Hasinai welcoming procession in which the Indians marched in three columns, the middle of which included "the Captains, who carried shotguns as they approached."

The introduction of guns would give the Hasinai and their allies the advantage of being better armed than their enemies. The Apaches did not have a reliable source to obtain firearms in trade, and thus were unable to acquire guns and ammunition in sufficient numbers to be useful in warfare." Access to a reliable source of guns, ammunition, and other trade goods would enable elites among the Hasinai, such as Bernardino, to attract allies and supporters hoping to take advantage of those goods. St. Denis must have made clear to Bernardino and the other Hasinai leaders that if the Spaniards were to settle among them, more Frenchmen would settle nearby, and the flow of trade goods, including the valuable firearms, would increase. The request for missionaries made by the two Hasinai Indians who took part in the Salazar expedition almost fifteen years earlier suggests that Bernardino may have been aware of this implication for quite some time before St. Denis' journey of 1715.

A further clue as to what the Hasinai expected from their relationship with the French may be found in the speech given by a chief of the Kadohadacho on the occasion of the establishment of a French post in their territory of the Red River The Kadohadacho had suffered heavy losses in war, and the chief, who was described as "a venerated old man and the most eloquent talker of his nation," told his people that:

> the time had come to change their tears into happiness, even though it was true that most their comrades had been killed or made slaves by their adversaries, and that they were no longer numerous. The arrival of he Canouches [the name given to the French] would prevent their total destruction; and their enemies, becoming their allies, would no longer make war upon them.

The Hasinai do not seem to have suffered as heavily in war as the Red River Caddo. The Kadohadacho were more exposed than the Hasinai to attack by parties of Osage and Chickasaw from the north and east, who went well-armed with French and English guns. However, the Hasinai had certainly taken some losses in warfare over the years, and the expectation of protection from enemies by their relationship with Europeans must have been much the same. Earlier experiences had taught the Hasinai not to expect the Spaniards to come to their aid in warfare, and they knew of the Spanish policy not to give or trade firearms to the Indians. But now the French, and their guns, presented a new advantage over their enemies, as well as a source of political power for Hasinai leaders. If a Spanish occupation of their territory would help to bring more French goods to them, then the Hasinai would not hesitate to welcome Spaniards back into their territory.

La Salle's Grand Dream

JAMES E. BRUSETH AND TONI S. TURNER

James E. Bruseth is Director of the Archaeology Division at the Texas Historical Commission. In 1996–1997, Dr. Bruseth headed the excavation of La Salle's lost ship, *La Belle*. Freelance writer and fundraiser Toni S. Turner assisted in the vessel's recovery.

In 1685, courageous French explorer Robert Cavelier, Sieur de La Salle, planted a small colony, Fort St. Louis, on Garcitas Creek, several miles upstream from Lavaca Bay. His endeavor, however, was doomed to fail. In this selection, Bruseth and Turner discuss La Salle's ambitious vision of founding a French base on the Gulf of Mexico. ◄

★ ★

In the name of the most high, powerful, invincible, and victorious Prince, Louis the Great, by the grace of God, King of France and Navarre, fourteenth of the name, I, this ninth day of April one thousand six hundred and eighty-two, do now take, in the name of His Majesty and of his successors to the crown, possession of this country of Louisiana, its seas, harbors, ports, bays, adjacent straits, and all nations, peoples, provinces, cities, towns, villages, mines, minerals, fisheries, streams, and rivers.

—ROBERT CAVELIER, SIEUR DE LA SALLE, APRIL, 1682

Less than four years before *La Belle* was lost on the Texas coast, La Salle, in a vast marshland with no one to hear him but a small band of followers and some curious local Indians, had claimed possession of one-third of the North American continent for France. After a long and arduous journey, he had finally discovered where the mouth of the Mississippi River emptied into the Gulf of Mexico.

The French claim in the New World now extended from the upper reaches of Canada to the shores of the Gulf of Mexico, encompassing savannas, forests, deserts, and plains. The land was watered by innumerable rivers, streams, and creeks and populated by thousands of American Indians who knew nothing of this moment or its implications.

A DRIVEN MAN

Scion of a wealthy family of merchants, La Salle was born in 1643, baptized a short time later, and grew up in Rouen, a major port on the River Seine in Normandy. Early in his life, La Salle joined the Jesuit priesthood, as did many French boys from well-to-do families. Entering the monastery meant La Salle must relinquish his share of the family's fortune, for he was expected to make the church paramount. Trained in the Jesuit Order, he became a teacher.

La Salle's quiet and introspective temperament, however, did not suit the vocation of teaching unruly schoolboys. He appealed to his Father Superior to be sent to a mission in China, where he could experience the excitement of remote parts of the world. His request was denied. Undaunted, he then petitioned to go to Portugal to teach mathematics; this request was also refused. With this rejection and after twelve years as a Jesuit, La Salle submitted his resignation.

La Salle then decided to travel to New France, or today's eastern Canada, to join his elder brother, the Abbé Cavelier, a priest of St. Sulspice in Montreal. In the spring of 1666, at the age of 23, La Salle thus made his first journey to the New World. Despite its unforgiving climate, the colony of New France was a bustling place, though its remoteness often weakened the rule of law. Opportunities for entrepreneurs were abundant. European powers had long sought a water passage through the New World to China and the East Indies for trade. The St. Lawrence River, leading to the Great Lakes and beyond, seemed a likely route. There was even talk of a great river that might traverse the continent and discharge into the Gulf of California.

The young La Salle was intrigued by the wealth and prestige that awaited the explorer who might discover such a route across North America. The conditions would be harsh, to be sure: there would be hostile Indians, severe winters, and uncertain food supplies. Nevertheless, he began to devise a plan—and met considerable opposition. The Jesuits, who had built a series of missions in the Upper Great Lakes, controlled the region through their religious emissaries and profited from the fur trade with the Indians, although they could not admit that profit was a motive in their endeavors. La Salle appeared to be a threat to the Jesuits' monopoly over trade.

The merchants of New France were even more alarmed at his intentions. Discovery of a new water route through the continent might interrupt the trade in furs and hides that flowed through Montreal and Quebec. The merchants did not wish to see their rewarding enterprise disrupted by this brash young Norman with grandiose ideas. These two groups, Jesuits and merchants, were to become the "enemies" about whom La Salle lamented many times during moments of despair: "I am utterly tired of this business; for I see that it is not enough to put property and life in constant peril, but it requires more pains to answer envy and distraction than to overcome the difficulties inseparable from my undertaking."

North American rivers and lakes were the seventeenth-century equivalent of modern highways, and knowledge of their locations could be turned into great monetary gain. Louis Joliet and Father Marquette, who had discovered the Mississippi River in 1673, were the first to understand the relationship of that river to the Great Lakes. They observed that the Mississippi, flowing southward, probably emptied into the Gulf of Mexico, rather than the Gulf of California. However, Joliet and Marquette never reached the Mississippi's mouth.

La Salle, who by this time had already begun searching for a transcontinental water route, received news of the Joliet-Marquette expedition with great interest. He formulated a plan to chart this potential watercourse through North America. If the Mississippi flowed into the Gulf of Mexico, it might be possible to establish a warm-water port at the mouth of the river. Furs and hides could be transported downstream, allowing the riches of Canada and the Great Lakes to be transported to France year-round. Traders could avoid the cold climate of eastern Canada and the icebound streams and lakes that made commerce impossible in winter. Moreover, France could control the land along the Mississippi, creating a vast empire that would keep the English and Dutch in the east and the Spanish in Mexico.

The realization of this grand dream would require a new series of forts along the river and substantial financial backing. La Salle had previously secured private funding to establish forts at various points along Lakes Michigan, Erie, and Ontario. But he was a poor manager, and each time a series of mishaps had eliminated the profits he promised his backers. Adding to his difficulties, his Jesuit detractors constantly undermined his credibility in Montreal and Quebec.

There was another problem: La Salle's own personality. He often lapsed into a mysterious sickness, described as a "moral malady." He probably suffered from periods of depression and might today be diagnosed as manic-depressive. This chronic debilitation fed La Salle's arrogant and demanding nature, which in turn created a recurring inability to inspire and direct his men amid the challenges of exploring the wilderness. His failings were so severe that during a trip along the Ohio River in 1679 one of his servants tried to kill him by mixing hemlock into his salad. La Salle was sick for more than forty days. From that time on, he carried an antidote with him to protect against poisonings.

Though in 1682 he had traveled down the Mississippi River and found its mouth, La Salle knew his plan would be met with skepticism in France. His only choice was to present his case to the king himself. He traveled back to France in 1683 and petitioned Louis XIV to establish a colony where the Mississippi River met the Gulf of Mexico. In an effort to foil his plan, La Salle's enemies had written to France that he was unfit for future explorations in the New World. La Salle tried to get support from merchants in Rochefort and La Rochelle, but his reputation for leading failed enterprises in New France preceded him. Finally, he headed to

Paris to enlist the support of two abbés, Claude Bernou and Eusèbe Renaudot, who enjoyed the favor of the French court. They agreed to lobby on La Salle's behalf.

Spain had declared war on France the preceding October, and tensions between the two countries could not have been higher. La Salle was counseled that an expedition through the Gulf of Mexico would attract more royal support than a return to the Mississippi River mouth by way of New France and the St. Lawrence River. The French king was angry with Spanish opposition to foreign ships traveling in the Gulf of Mexico. French vessels violating this zone were captured and their crews imprisoned. La Salle's effort would be a bold statement against Spain's efforts to control the gulf.

Thus, from the point of view of the French monarch, the timing was just right for such a mission, but it was even more propitious when one considered Spain's current role in the New World. Spain had ignored Nueva Vizcaya, what is now northern Mexico, since the early explorations of Pineda, Cabeza de Vaca, and De Soto had failed to find gold, silver, or other wealth there. Spain had also lost control of the seas with England's defeat of the Spanish Armada in 1588 and had difficulty monitoring significant portions of its territorial claims. This was especially true of territories north of today's Mexico between Florida and New Mexico.

It was against this backdrop of international incident and intrigue that La Salle presented his plan to the king in 1683. He proposed a three-pronged approach. First, he would establish a fort at the mouth of the Mississippi River to maintain the French claim to Louisiana. Second, he would establish trade with thousands of Indians and convert them to Christianity. Finally, he would establish a permanent colony, a base from which the future invasion of Spain's Nueva Vizcaya could be launched.

For the French Crown, the colony was a critical part of La Salle's plan. While Spain had been shipping gold, silver, and other treasures from the New World, France had been forced to content itself with beaver pelts from its Canadian colonies. Louis saw his opportunity to capture some of Spanish King Charles II's wealth.

Several variations on La Salle's proposal were discussed, some involving the use of French buccaneers to help invade Nueva Vizcaya and seize control of the silver mines. The king finally granted La Salle the authority to "command . . . all the lands of North America that may hereafter be submitted to our [French] rule, from Fort St. Louis on the Illinois River to Nueva Vizcaya." Louis also gave La Salle substantial support for the expedition, including two ships rather than the one he had originally requested. Specifically, La Salle was granted the naval gunship *Le Joly* and a *barque longue* (light frigate) christened *La Belle*. As it turned out, these two ships did not possess enough cargo space for such a venture, and La Salle was forced to lease two other vessels, the frigate *l'Aimable* from La Rochelle ship owner Jean Massiot and a small ketch, *Le Saint-François*, from François Duprat, also of La Rochelle. The king's grant included full crews, a hundred soldiers, and funds to hire carpenters, masons, coopers, and other skilled workers to establish his colony. The expedition included about three hundred persons in all.

Some supplies, such as goods to trade with the Indians, were not provided by the king, which meant that La Salle and his men had to buy them. The explorer had persuaded twenty thousand Shawnee, Illinois, and Miami Indians to settle around Fort St. Louis des Illinois, which he had established in 1682. La Salle's plan was that these Indians would hunt and trap in the northern Great Plains and Great Lakes and bring the furs and hides to the fort for trade, where he would ship them down the Mississippi River to the settlement he envisioned on the Gulf of Mexico, and then onward to France. From the warm gulf port, France could import goods year-round, a distinct advantage over the ports of Montreal and Quebec, where the St. Lawrence River was iced over half the year. The medium of exchange that would drive all this would be the glass beads, brass pins, finger rings, iron knives, and hatchets they purchased to trade to the Indians.

DESTINATION: A NEW WORLD

La Salle set sail from La Rochelle, France, on July 24, 1684, to fulfill his dream of a colony at the mouth of the Mississippi River—and to enrich himself.

On January 1, 1685, after a long and difficult journey across the ocean, La Salle's expedition sighted land along the Gulf Coast, somewhere in today's Louisiana west of the Mississippi. By this time, only three vessels remained: *Le Joly, l'Aimable,* and *La Belle.* The *Saint-François* had been captured by Spanish privateers off the western coast of Hispaniola as the ship traveled from Port de Paix to Petit Goàve.

La Salle had been warned about strong easterly currents that carried ships towards the Bahamian Channel. Upon sighting land, he concluded that they had not made enough westward progress and were in fact east of the Mississippi. He decided to travel west, following the Gulf Coast as closely as possible.

For the next two and a half weeks the ships continued to sail westward, turning toward the southwest as they progressed. La Salle remained certain that the Mississippi lay in this direction. Measurements of latitude were taken daily to help chart their progress, but longitude—a time-dependent measurement—could not be accurately calculated until the eighteenth century. Consequently, there was no accurate method to determine exactly how far west they were traveling—a problem La Salle recognized. In addition, an astrolabe La Salle suspected to be faulty had hampered measurements of latitude during his 1682 journey down the Mississippi River, so those earlier calculations were erroneous as well. To complicate the situation further, some period maps showed the Mississippi flowing into the Gulf of Mexico through what is now central Texas. Despite these problems, La Salle believed the Mississippi River lay farther to the west, and he instructed Captain Beaujeu to continue sailing in this direction.

Finally, they noticed that they were moving more southwest than west, and suspected they might have passed the Mississippi. La Salle and Beaujeu quarreled about their location, but La Salle remained resolute that they were near one of the western branches of the great river. The relationship between the two men had deteriorated to the point that they were communicating only through official letters couriered back and forth; their deep mutual antipathy may be seen in a letter La Salle wrote when Beaujeu wished to return to France rather than assist in landing the colonists:

[Y]our longboat does not give me time to reply to your letter with so much consideration as you have devoted to writing it, though the way in which you vent your spleen in the letter suggests that you wrote it rather more hastily than its length would require.

It is no fault of mine, Monsieur, if you have not already provided for the safety of His Majesty's ship; but I know on what grounds you ask me for pilots to take it into this river which I never intended that it should enter, and more than I wished to stop it at this shore. You may take it where you think fit.

On January 17, 1685, La Salle determined it was time to land his men, explore the coast, find the river, and locate a place to establish the colony. He was probably near Cedar Bayou and the western end of today's Matagorda Island in Texas. After several days of surveying the surrounding countryside, the expedition's chronicler Henri Joutel noted, "The country did not seem very favorable to me. It was flat and sandy but did nevertheless produce grass. There were several salt pools. We hardly saw any wild fowl except some cranes and Canadian geese which were not expecting us."

Early in February, La Salle ordered Joutel to disembark with 120 to 130 men and march up the coast to find a large river that he was convinced would be the west branch of the Mississippi. Joutel complained that the men had little or no military experience: "Truthfully, although we had 120 to 130 men with us, 30 good men would have been better and would have done more and perforce eaten less, to which end they were without rival . . . these were all men who had been taken by force or deceit. In a way, it was almost like Noah's Ark where they were all sorts of animals. We likewise had men of different nationalities. The soldiers had been recruited by the lower ranking officers of the navy, who received a half pistole [five francs] for each man, by whatever means possible."

The party eventually encountered what they thought was a large river, which was actually Pass Cavallo, today's name for the entrance into Matagorda Bay. The three vessels arrived shortly afterward, and La Salle came ashore to inspect the terrain. He found a location on the western side of Pass Cavallo suitable for establishing a temporary camp, called the Grand Camp, and ordered *La Belle* and *l'Aimable* to come through the pass. On February 16, the ship's pilots made a sounding and determined that the two vessels could enter. They marked the entrance with buoys to guide the two ships away from hazardous sandy shoals.

La Belle came through the pass without difficulty about two in the afternoon and anchored inside Matagorda Bay. La Salle ordered that cargo be unloaded from *l'Aimable*, the expedition's main supply ship, which was five times larger than *La Belle*, so that she could also enter the pass. Eight iron cannons were removed from the ship and taken ashore to the temporary camp. On February 19 *l'Aimable*'s Captain Aigron was satisfied that adequate cargo had been unloaded, although much remained on board. According to Joutel, "On the 20th, La Salle ordered the captain to approach the bar, adding that when the sea was high, he should signal to him to be towed. La Salle also ordered the pilot of *La Belle* to help the captain of the *Aimable* with what he had to do as that ship had already entered. But the captain sent the pilot back, telling him that he was capable of bringing the ship in without him."

When the water level was sufficiently high, La Salle signaled for the ship to enter the pass. At about the same time, he was told that local Karankawa Indians had taken some of his men hostage. La Salle was now compelled to go search for them. He traveled about a league and a half (about three miles) until he found the Indian village, but before entering it he could see *l'Aimable*'s sails, indicating that she was beginning to enter the pass. She appeared to do so incorrectly, however, running too close to the shoals. La Salle was greatly concerned, but he was powerless to influence the situation. Soon a cannon was fired, indicating distress aboard the ship. Next *l'Aimable*'s sails were furled, confirming his fear that a disaster had occurred. La Salle met with the Indians, retrieved his men, and returned to assess the damage to his supply ship.

L'Aimable was grounded hard against a sandbank. Upon questioning the captain and crew, La Salle grew suspicious that the captain, Aigron, had intentionally run the ship aground. Aigron was unhappy with La Salle's efforts to find the Mississippi, believing that the explorer had missed the river and was taking the expedition into uncharted areas that would result in failure of the colony. La Salle concluded that Aigron had deliberately steered the ship past the buoys marking the safe entry and directly onto a sandbank. Once the ship was stuck, the captain could have thrown out an anchor and freed the vessel. Witnesses stated that, instead, the captain ordered the ship to sail forward until she was firmly grounded on the shallow sandy bottom. There was now no hope of saving the ship.

According to Joutel, "we learned how the captain had disgraced himself. The incident made one conclude that the mischief must have been by design or premediated act. Four buoys had been placed and one only had to steer by them. Moreover, a sailor was in the topmast for seeing better. Although the sailor continually called out 'to luff sail,' the ill-intentioned captain called out to the contrary and gave the command to bear down until he saw he was on the sandbanks."

L'Aimable, a large private merchant vessel, contained much of the planned colony's provisions. La Salle prepared to unload as much cargo as possible, but the ship was far from shore and he had only small longboats. The crew could remove cargo when the waters were calm. But *l'Aimable* broke apart one night during a period of heavy seas, and in the morning the buoyant cargo was found floating in the water.

In early March *Le Joly*'s captain, Beaujeu, decided to return to France. He had orders only to accompany La Salle to the New World and unload his ship's cargo. Once this had been accomplished, his job was done. Beaujeu was impatient to leave the wild country and the arrogant explorer with whom he often quarreled, and a number of the colonists decided to join him. La Salle asked Beaujeu to ensure that supplies would be sent back to assist his colony. On March 14, *Le Joly* departed with 120 of the original 300 colonists, leaving La Salle with a diminished number of men and greatly compromised provisions for building a settlement. La Salle's request for more supplies was delivered to officials in France, but it was never honored.

With only *La Belle* and 180 colonists, La Salle began to seek a more permanent location for his fort. He sought a safe site where he could leave many of the colonists while he searched overland for the Mississippi. When he found the river, he would build his second and final settlement. La Salle and a few men left the temporary camp near Pass Cavallo in late March, 1685, and began searching along the western side of Matagorda Bay for a more suitable site for a fort. He found a creek that he called "the River of the Bison" (now known as Garcitas Creek) flowing into the north-western part of today's Lavaca Bay. On a high, flat rise on the western side of the creek, about four miles upriver from the bay, he began construction of the temporary settlement, Fort St. Louis, where he would begin colonizing the Gulf Coast.

Provisions from *l'Aimable* and *Le Joly*, together with cargo from *La Belle*, were moved to a supply depot about midway between the pass and the Grand Camp. From the depot they were transported by canoe upriver to the fort. Wood suitable for buildings was not readily available, so La Salle commanded his men to travel a league inland and bring back trees of suitable size. This proved difficult work, and several men died from the exertion. Finally La Salle resorted to salvaging timbers from *l'Aimable* to build the fort.

A two-story structure similar to buildings La Salle had constructed in Canada was erected. It was divided into four rooms: one for La Salle, another for the priests, a third for the officers of the expedition, and a fourth, the upper story, for supplies. Smaller structures were erected to house other members of the expedition. *L'Aimable's* eight cannons would help fight off Karankawa Indian attacks.

With the settlement established, La Salle again concentrated on finding the Mississippi. Now realizing that the river almost certainly had to be toward the east, he organized an exploration party. He left supplies for the colony on *La Belle*, along with all of his personal possessions and those of his men. He instructed her captain to proceed as far up the bay as possible, where he should lay anchor and wait for La Salle's return. The exploration party, meanwhile, would travel along the shore and head east to find the Mississippi.

La Salle expected to be gone about ten days; instead he was absent for more than two frustrating months. The Indians he encountered along the way knew nothing of the great river. In fact, these native peoples did not even speak the languages he had heard along the Mississippi on his earlier travels. La Salle traded for horses and food with the Caddo Indians and returned to Fort St. Louis, where he was devastated to discover that his sole remaining ship had been lost in a storm.

Le Belle had contained all the remaining supplies to build his final New World colony. With his grand dream of a French settlement on the Gulf of Mexico in great jeopardy, La Salle's only recourse now was to go overland to his settlement at Fort St. Louis des Illinois and up to Canada to get supplies—a journey of twelve hundred miles.

MURDER ON THE TRAIL

On January 12, 1687, La Salle and sixteen men departed the small settlement on Garcitas Creek to obtain supplies from Canada. It was to be the explorer's last expedition.

Remaining at Fort St. Louis were twenty men, women, and children—a meager fragment of the more than 180 who had stayed to help build the settlement. Disease and Indian attacks had taken the rest. The survivors would be stranded on Garcitas Creek for two years, waiting in vain for La Salle's return with the desperately needed provisions. In late 1688 or early 1689, the Karankawas would launch a final attack on the vulnerable outpost, killing almost all the remaining colonists and kidnapping several children.

In March, 1687, La Salle and his overland party reached a spot near today's Navasota, Texas, where they crossed the River of the Canoes and camped. During La Salle's previous trip, he had buried food supplies at a crossing a short distance downstream. He gave orders for some of his men to go and recover the stores because hunting was lean this time of the year. The men found the food, but it was spoiled. Luckily, La Salle's trusted Shawnee Indian hunter, Nika, shot two buffalo while returning to their leader. The men stopped to smoke the meat and sent word to La Salle.

As the men prepared to eat the portions that could not be smoked, La Salle's nephew, Colin Morenger, instructed them that he would control the remaining food and would decide who would eat what portion. For the dispirited men who had endured countless hardships and depredations, this was the final insult, and they plotted to kill Morenger. Revenge was planned by five men: Duhaut, Liotot (the expedition surgeon), Hiems, Tessier, and L'Archevêque. Later that night, they murdered Morenger, Nika, and La Salle's servant, Saget.

The murderers had accomplished their immediate plan, but they knew that La Salle, still at the other camp and waiting for the buffalo meat, would exact punishment. The five planned yet another murder: the assassination of Robert Cavelier, Sieur de la Salle. They knew that La Salle would soon come looking for them, and they waited in ambush.

Within a few days, a gunshot warned the men that La Salle was nearby. Duhaut and L'Archevêque crossed the river on a trail that La Salle would follow and waited in the bushes. As the explorer approached, L'Archevêque stepped into view. La Salle asked where Morenger was, and L'Archevêque replied that he had drifted away. Before La Salle could respond, Duhaut, who was hidden from view, fired a musket shot into the explorer's head, killing him.

At the age of 43, after twenty years of conquering and colonizing the wilderness of North America, the great explorer lay dead. La Salle's killers took his possessions, even his clothing, and left his body "to the discretion of the wolves and other wild animals."

Trinidad de Salcedo: A Forgotten Villa in Colonial Texas, 1806–1813

BRADLEY FOLSOM

B radley Folsom, a specialist in the late Spanish colonial period, serves as a Teaching Fellow at the University of North Texas in Denton.

In this selection, Dr. Folsom discusses the important, though forgotten, settlement of Trinidad de Salcedo, which was situated on the Trinity River between San Antonio and Nacogdoches. Because of its strategic location, he asserts, "Trinidad was at the epicenter of an ideological and military struggle for control of North America." ✷

★ ★

From 1806 to 1813, soldiers and civilians of different races, nationalities, and professions lived in a small Spanish villa in East Texas known as Trinidad de Salcedo. Trinidad rested on the east bank of the Trinity River between San Antonio de Béxar, the capital of Spanish Texas, and Nacogdoches, which bordered the expansionist United States. This location made Trinidad strategically important to Spain during a time when warfare in Europe, insurgency in New Spain, and United States aggression threatened the nation's hold on Texas. Trinidad was at the epicenter of an ideological and military struggle for control of North America, and its residents witnessed a number of historical events.

In spite of this, historians have written little on Trinidad. Donald Chipman and Harriet Denise Joseph's otherwise excellent *Spanish Texas, 1519–1821* devoted only one line to Trinidad, declaring the villa not "destined for permanency." David J. Weber's assessment of Trinidad in *The Spanish Frontier in North America* is friendlier but equally fleeting. In a single line, the historian referred to Trinidad as the most successful settlement on Spain's northern frontier in the early years of the nineteenth century. Perhaps the best scholarly Texas history survey, Randolph Campbell's *Gone to Texas*, does not even mention Trinidad.

References to Trinidad are rare or absent in popular history, as well. Texas history textbooks explain the importance of San Antonio, La Bahia, and Nacogdoches in the colonial era, but say nothing of Trinidad. Although a historical marker in the city of Madisonville, Texas, indentifies the believed location of Trinidad, the sign is only five sentences long, and it contains factual inaccuracies.

Historians have not ignored Trinidad entirely. In 1927, Mattie Austin Hatcher, an archivist and translator for the University of Texas, published *The Opening of Texas to Foreign Settlement*, an exhaustive study of Spain's attempt to populate its northern frontier. Hatcher's work placed Trinidad in the larger context of Spain's struggle to maintain control of Texas in the face of Anglo expansion. To Hatcher, Trinidad was a small part of a greater effort to populate Texas. More recently, Jean L. Epperson included a chapter about Trinidad in her privately published work, *Lost Spanish Towns: Atascosito and Trinidad de Salcedo*. Unlike Hatcher, Epperson focused almost exclusively on Trinidad and ignored the town's place in Spain's larger frontier strategy. Although well researched, Epperson's work was more a calendar of important events in Trinidad than a scholarly study.

This paper will combine Epperson and Hatcher's approaches in telling a local and political history of Trinidad de Salcedo. Who lived in the villa? Why did they settle in Trinidad? What role did Trinidad play in important historical events in colonial Texas? The article begins with a synopsis of the troubles that Spain faced at the beginning of the nineteenth century. A detailed account of the founding of Trinidad and the first years of its existence follow. Included next is a brief demographic study of the population of the villa—with a focus on the inhabitants' nationalities, ethnicities, professions, and ages. The history of the final years of human habitation of Trinidad follows. The study concludes by tracking Trinidad's settlers after the villa's destruction.

Trinidad came to life following almost a century of Spanish settlement in Texas. Because Texas was home to hostile, difficult to subdue Indians and it lacked easily extracted wealth, the Spanish largely ignored the region until the late seventeenth century. In order to form a human barrier between the French, who had begun to settle in Louisiana, and the silver-rich provinces of northern New Spain, the Spanish sent missionaries, presidio soldiers, and civilians to settle Texas in the early eighteenth century. Progress was slow, as few wanted to move to an underdeveloped region inhabited by dangerous Indians. In spite of this arrested growth, Spanish settlers established San Antonio de Béxar in Central Texas, La Bahía near the Gulf Coast, and later Nacogdoches on the border with Louisiana.

Outside events changed Spain's attitude towards Texas in the late eighteenth and early nineteenth centuries. When France ceded control of Louisiana to Spain in 1763, it placed Texas firmly within the Spanish empire. With no foreign threat on its border, Spain saw little reason to continue funding missionaries and soldiers, and so colonization efforts slowed. By 1800, Texas could claim only 4,000 Spanish citizens. That year, Spain returned Louisiana to France in exchange for land concessions in Europe. Three years later in 1803, France sold the Louisiana territory to the burgeoning United States, a development that worried Spanish officials in Texas. At the start of the nineteenth century, the United States was growing in population, geography, and economic power based, in part, on the profitable expansion of cotton cultivation in the South. The acquisition of Louisiana meant more land for cotton, and tens of thousands of Americans moved into the new territory to grow the crop. Soon, over 75,000 Americans lived in Louisiana, dwarfing the 4,000 Spanish residents of Texas.

Nemesio Salcedo, the Commandant General of the Internal Provinces—a military subdivision of New Spain that included Texas—was responsible for ensuring that these Americans did not encroach on Spanish territory. Salcedo recognized that a Texas populated with loyal Spanish citizens would be the only effective countermeasure to U.S. expansion, so he offered incentives to residents of New Spain who would move to the frontier. Unfortunately for Salcedo, few people within New Spain were willing to move to an undersupplied frontier largely controlled by Indians.

Although Salcedo would eventually muster enough Spanish citizens to found the small villa of San Marcos de Neve in 1808, without a large military presence, this settlement fell victim to constant Indian depredations and was soon abandoned. Salcedo also tried to create a military encampment at Atascosito near the Gulf Coast, but this proved to be a drain on the Spanish treasury. The Commandant General needed another approach and more settlers and settlements to stop Americans from entering Texas.

Although citizens from within New Spain were hard to come by, there was no shortage of Louisianans asking to settle in Texas. As soon as the United States acquired Louisiana in 1803, petitions from individuals who had lived under the Spanish flag from 1763 to 1800 began to arrive on Salcedo's desk. Their reasons for wanting to live in Texas varied. Having lived under Catholic Spain and France, some feared persecution under the predominantly Protestant United States. Some of those born in Spanish-controlled Louisiana maintained loyalty to the nation of their birth. Still others, like Bernardo Despallier, had made enemies in Louisiana and wanted a fresh start in Texas. In addition to these reasons, former Spanish citizens from Louisiana wanted to make money. They had not been blind to the profit that cotton had brought the incoming Americans, and they recognized that Texas had plenty of arable farmland suitable for cotton cultivation. If the Commandant General would grant them free land in Texas, they could have plantations of their own.

It would seem that the settlers from Louisiana would be a perfect solution to Salcedo's dilemma. They had lived under the Spanish Crown, and they wanted to live in Texas. Salcedo, however, harbored a strong distrust of Louisianans. He saw them as more French than

Spanish and believed that their brief time under the United States flag had corrupted them. Because of this, Salcedo would only allow the Louisianans to settle in Coahuila or Nueva Vizcaya, far from the border with the United States. He would not authorize their colonization plans for Texas.

The Governor of Texas in 1803, Juan Bautista de Elguezabal, did not share Salcedo's distrust of Louisianans. Elguezabal wanted to create a civilian settlement on the Trinity River in order to facilitate trade between San Antonio and Nacogdoches, but he knew that he would have a difficult time finding settlers from New Spain to carry through with the plan. Upon receiving a letter from former Spanish subject Bernardo Despallier asking to settle himself and other families from Louisiana in Texas, Elguezabal slyly passed the petition on to both Commandant General Salcedo and the Spanish King. Salcedo would allow Despallier to settle only if he met certain conditions, but the Crown approved the plan without such restrictions on September 9, 1805.

Elguezabal died before he could carry through with his civilian settlement plan. Antonio Cordero relieved him as governor in 1805. Cordero shared his predecessor's desire to establish a settlement on the Trinity, but he believed that a joint civilian-military garrison could accomplish the goal without colonists from Louisiana. Stationing soldiers on the frontier would protect civilians from Indians, which would decrease the risks of frontier life and make recruitment from within New Spain easier. Civilians would then provide food for soldiers and promote trade between San Antonio and Nacogdoches while the military garrison could guard the border against an invasion from the United States and stop contraband trade. In Cordero's plan, a local military commandant would have judicial authority over both civilians and soldiers. He would also be responsible for divvying up land and overseeing construction of the town. Cordero would send the soldiers to the Trinity, and then recruit families in San Antonio to join them later.

Acting before Commandant General Salcedo could approve of the plan, on September 17, 1805, Cordero nominated Pedro Nolasco Carrasco as the settlement's commandant and ordered him and 120 soldiers from San Antonio to the east bank of the Trinity River. They departed two days later and arrived on the Trinity by December. Once there, Carrasco ordered his men to construct a barracks and small chapel, and he parceled out two rectangular plots of land for use by the civilians. One plot was to be divided into private property for the settlement's first residents; the other plot was for communal pasture, water, and lumber. At one point, someone, probably Governor Cordero, gave the outpost the name Trinidad de Salcedo, demarking its location on the Trinity and as homage to Commandant General Salcedo.

While the soldiers were on their way to the Trinity, Cordero offered free land to any civilians in San Antonio who would move to the soon-to-be-founded settlement. He especially needed ranchers and farmers to provide soldiers with meat, eggs, milk, and other foodstuffs. Likely influenced by the security the military garrison would afford, five families accepted the governor's offer and departed San Antonio for the Trinity on December 20. This group consisted of Pedro Cruz, his wife, and three children; José Luis Durán, his wife, and two sons; José Manuel Casanova and his wife; Francisco Travieso and his son; and José Aldrete.

When the San Antonio families arrived in Trinidad early the next year, they found not only Spanish soldiers but also Bernardo Despallier and twenty-three settlers from Louisiana. Apparently informed that the Crowns had approved former governor Elguezabal's plan to settle Louisiana families on the Trinity, Despallier and his fellow settlers had crossed into Texas late in 1805. They arrived on the Trinity around the same time as Carrasco and his soldiers. Carrasco seems to have welcomed these unplanned visitors, allotting them land alongside the San Antonio settlers. The first Louisiana families included Despallier, his wife, and two sons; Irishman John McCann, his wife, two daughters, and two sons; German Enrique Sheridan, his wife, two sons, and three daughters; and Irishmen Miguel Quin and Hugo Coyle.

The soldiers, Louisianans, and San Antonio families worked together to build Trinidad. The soldiers finished their barracks and chapel, stocking the latter building with an altar, lectern, various silver vessels, and candles. The Spanish and Louisiana civilians plowed their allotted properties for crops, chopped down trees for lumber, and erected wooden homes, granaries, and barns. Because the area lacked usable rock, all buildings in Trinidad were of either wooden or jacal construct. It seems that settlers primarily used the latter material, as one callous American observer would later remark that the town consisted of "twenty five or thirty miserable mud cabins." No maps or drawings of Trinidad survive today, but Carrasco used the Villa de Pitic in Sonora as its model. Likewise, there is no official date for the founding of Trinidad, but it likely occurred sometime in January 1806. Trinidad's construction cost Spain 1,652 pesos.

This investment paid off later in 1806 when Spain almost went to war with the United States. When the United States purchased Louisiana from France, it believed that the territory extended west to the Sabine River and possibly to the Rio Grande. This would mean that all, or at least some, of Texas would belong to the United States. Spain balked at these claims and insisted that Texas's eastern border was the Arroyo Hondo, west of Natchitoches. In 1806, Commandant General Salcedo stationed Spanish soldiers east of the Sabine River as a means of staking Spain's claim to the territory. In response to what it perceived as an aggressive maneuver, the United States placed part of its own army just east of the Arroyo Hondo in Natchitoches. For nearly a year, Spain and the United States stood ready for war.

In preparation for conflict, officials in Mexico City sent supplies and soldiers to the Texas frontier. Far enough from the disputed territory to avoid being caught in a surprise attack but close enough to react to an American invasion, Trinidad served as a sort of forward operating base for Spain. As such, the nation increased the numbers of soldiers stationed at Trinidad's military garrison from 120 to some 400 men. More soldiers meant more mouths to feed, so civilian farmers likely profited from the increased demand for food.

In September 1806, tensions eased along the border when General Salcedo withdrew his troops west of the Sabine and reached an unofficial agreement with United States officials. Both sides approved a plan creating a neutral area between the Sabine River and the Arroyo Hondo, where neither nation could build settlements or send soldiers without first informing the neighboring country. This Neutral Ground Agreement averted a potential war, which diminished Trinidad's strategic importance and allowed Spain to reduce the number of soldiers at the villa's military garrison to pre-crisis levels.

In spite of the military drawdown, the people of Trinidad continued to witness history. In 1807, for example, explorer Zebulon Pike stayed overnight in the villa. The year before, United States President Thomas Jefferson had sent Pike and a survey team to explore the Arkansas and Red rivers in the nation's newly acquired Louisiana Territory. If possible, Pike was also to report on Spanish military strength in the Internal Provinces. While carrying out Jefferson's orders, Pike wandered into Spanish territory and became lost. Spanish soldiers located the wayward explorer, arrested him and his men for trespassing, and delivered them to Commandant Salcedo in Saltillo for interrogation. Because tensions with the United States had eased following the Neutral Ground Agreement, Salcedo ordered his soldiers to escort Pike and his men to the United States border and set them free.

This return trip took Pike and his escorts through Trinidad. They arrived in the villa on June 21, 1807, and stayed overnight. During the stopover, Pike met some Irishmen and a Frenchman—probably Miguel Quin, John McCann, and Pedro Lartigue. He also encountered runaway slaves from the United States who had taken refuge in Trinidad. Although the explorer observed that Trinidad's seven officers and nearly one hundred soldiers were all suffering from a debilitating illness, the post's military commander seems to have been well enough to make the American's acquaintance. When Pike and his escorts left Trinidad, the commandant lent them horses to finish their journey. After reaching the United States, Pike put Trinidad on the map, literally. His map of the Western Territories showed Trinidad on the eastern shore of the Trinity, with the simple label "Presidio."

Escaped slaves like those reported by Pike were a common sight at Trinidad. The United States acquisition of Louisiana and the expansion of plantation agriculture meant more slaves on the New Spain-Louisiana border. Hoping for refuge in Spanish territory, many of these bondsmen ran away and crossed into Texas. Blaming Spain for an inability to protect its borders, American slave owners called on the Spanish government to return their bondsmen. Although Spain and the United States were at peace, Commandant General Salcedo did not want to go out of his way to help the expansionist Americans. Continuing to view the United States as a threat and realizing that every escaped slave meant one less laborer on a Louisiana plantation, Salcedo not only ignored the Americans' requests, he helped escaped slaves once they were in Texas.

Trinidad played a small role in this practice. On May 31, 1808, Salcedo ordered that military officials at Nacogdoches should transfer a group of escaped slaves to Trinidad. Ostensibly, the move was to protect the slaves from Indians. In reality, Salcedo knew that the further slaves were from the United States border, the less likely that their owners could retrieve them. Under these orders, Spanish officer Jaime Mirlan arrived in Trinidad in December 1808 with the fugitive slaves from Nacogdoches. More escaped bondsmen arrived in Trinidad in 1809, but by this time Salcedo had conceded to pressure from Louisiana slaveowners and had begun ordering his men to return slaves to the border. Once this second group of fugitive slaves realized that they would not find refuge in Trinidad, they ran away in the direction of La Bahía and disappeared from history.

What was the ultimate fate of the escaped slaves seen by Pike and those delivered to Trinidad in 1808? It is possible that some of the bondsmen remained in Trinidad, but evidence supporting this conclusion is scant. Although at least two free persons of African ancestry called Trinidad home, neither were escaped slaves. There is also the prospect that the escaped slaves were re-enslaved. Two of Trinidad's families owned slaves, and the 1809 census lists four African laborers. Although the origins of these bondsmen are unknown, there is no evidence to indicate that they were re-enslaved refugees. The escaped slaves likely stopped in Trinidad and moved on. Overall, slavery does not seem to have been an important part of Trinidad's daily life and economy.

The Trinidad settler's relationship with local American Indians, on the other hand, both hindered and helped the fiscal wellbeing of the frontier town. Resenting the construction of a town on their hunting grounds and looking to profit from their new neighbors, Tawakoni and the Tahuayace Indians stole horses and cattle from ranches on the outskirts of Trinidad. They also attacked small parties of settlers and soldiers traveling outside of the villa. Other Indian tribes preyed on Trinidad's citizens. In one instance, Chickasaws kidnapped a daughter of the Sheridan family. Subsequent attempts to locate the young girl yielded no results.

Not all Indian tribes were hostile to the residents of Trinidad, however, and many came to trade and converse with the villa's settlers. In 1809, a Quichai Chief named Castor warned the soldiers of Trinidad that Tawakonis were planning to raid the settlement. A year later, Asescio Arreola went to a Quichai village to purchase corn and beans. In 1811, an Orocoquisa Indian leader asked the Spanish to open an official trading post in his town. The settlers of Trinidad also appear to have traded with the Tejas, but these Indians also raided the villa.

The people of Trinidad had the most contact with Coushatta Indians. Forced west by encroaching Americans, the Coushattas had petitioned the governor of Texas for permission to settle in his province. The governor granted their request, and the tribe established a village of 150 warriors near Trinidad sometime before 1809. With the exception of one settler complaining that a group of young Coushattas stole from his herd, the relationship between Trinidad's citizens and the Indians was mutually beneficial. In an 1810 report, a resident of Trinidad remarked that the Coushattas were "naturally pacific," "industrious," and that they "get along well with Spaniards." He also lauded the Indians' houses, farming ability, and their exquisite cow and buffalo leathercraft. The people of the Spanish villa and Coushattas got along so well that in 1810, ten men set out from Trinidad to clear a path to the Indians' village in order to facilitate trade between the two towns.

To communicate with the various Indian tribes, the residents of Trinidad employed interpreters. One interpreter, Gerónimo Hernández, however, ran off to join the Indians, briefly leaving his family behind at Trinidad. A second interpreter, Francisco Lacosta, fled Trinidad less than a year later. Yet a third interpreter not only left Trinidad, but also began inciting Indians to attack the settlement. Trinidad had little luck keeping its interpreters.

Indians and escaped slaves did not worry Spanish officials, however. They were more concerned about American influence on the Trinidad settlers from Louisiana, as smuggling had become prevalent in East Texas. Because of this, on March 24, 1809, newly installed Texas Governor Manuel Salcedo traveled from San Antonio to Trinidad in order to conduct an inspection and to assess the loyalty of the villa's foreign population. Salcedo found over one hundred civilians in Trinidad. This included the original colonists from San Antonio and Louisiana as well as new arrivals. Some of the newcomers were from the United States and had settled in Trinidad without the government's authorization. Instead of ordering these immigrants to leave, as Salcedo's uncle Commandant General Nemesio Salcedo may have done, the governor interrogated the newcomers, found them to be loyal to Spain, and allowed them to stay in Trinidad. He did require the villa's residents to sign an oath of loyalty to Spain, which they did. When Governor Salcedo departed for San Antonio, he felt confident that the people of Trinidad would remain faithful to the Crown. The new settlers included Vicente Micheli, an Italian farmer who had moved from Nacogdoches to Trinidad in 1806; Pedro Lartigue, a French surgeon, and his two sons; Santiago Fierr, his wife, son, and daughter; and Elisha Nelson and his family of six.

As a part of his 1809 tour, Salcedo ordered an official census of Trinidad. The resulting documents reveal that the small town was home to a diverse group of people. An American named Zedoc Harman was 63, making him the villa's oldest citizen. The youngest resident was one month old; one of six children listed as having been born in Trinidad. Children made up almost forty-four percent of the total civilian population of the villa. Sixty-nine percent of Trinidad's adult population was married. Some of those listed as being single, however, like Hugo Coyle, were in fact married to women outside of Texas. Males outnumbered females in Trinidad by a ratio of three to two. At least three people had died in Trinidad since the villa's founding.

As the Spanish government was well aware, Trinidad was home to a number of foreigners. Indeed, only eighteen percent of the villa's civilian population was born within the 1809 borders of New Spain. Sixty percent, however, were born within the 1803 border that included the Louisiana territory. Of the remaining, only Gerónimo Hernández from Havana could claim Spanish citizenship by birth. Three Germans called Trinidad home, as did four Irish, two Italians, at least one French, and one Canadian. This entire group had lived in Louisiana or Nacogdoches prior to their arrival in Trinidad. Eighteen persons born in the United States called Trinidad home, around twenty percent of the total population. None of the Americans, however, had moved directly from the United States to Texas. Like the other foreigners, they had lived in Louisiana prior to settling in Trinidad.

The people of Trinidad were also racially diverse. Indian males served as ranch hands and at least one Indian woman, Maria del Carmen Casanova, lived in Trinidad in 1809. Although there are only four mulatto slaves listed on the census, it is possible that some of the runaway slaves previously seen in Trinidad remained in the town yet were not listed on the census for unspecified reasons. At least one person in Trinidad, Zadoc Harman, was a free person of African descent, although there were likely more. Harman was a mulatto from North Carolina, who had previously lived in the Ouachita Parish of Louisiana. There, Harman had become wealthy trading horses with local Indians, but his success had brought legal disputes with white residents, possibly leading to his relocation to Trinidad.

There were approximately twenty homesteads in Trinidad on land of varying sizes. Most citizens lived on their personal property or in the households of their families. Some, like Carlos Dupon, lived on their employers' homesteads. Lots varied in size, but most families had 60 × 60 varas of land. Because many of Trinidad's residents lacked titles to their property before 1809, disputes arose over land ownership. In one such disagreement, Maria Juana Tijerina claimed that Vicente Micheli had stolen her house and land. To prevent such disagreements in the future, in 1810 the Spanish government approved Irishman Hugo Coyle's petition to become Trinidad's land surveyor, a job that he had previously held in Louisiana. In addition to their homes, barns, mills, the chapel, and the barracks, Trinidad settlers had also built a school by 1809. Shortly after its construction, Martin Martínez began teaching class for the children of Trinidad.

The people of Trinidad were farmers and ranchers, with over eighty percent of male heads of households listing these as their primary professions. Women and children joined men in growing wheat, maize, beans, watermelon, pumpkins, and a variety of other fruits and vegetables. Sometimes harvests were bountiful. For example, one year John McGee needed to enlarge his flourmill to accommodate an abundance of wheat. Trinidad farmers also grew cotton, which they worked in their homes. The quality of thread this process produced, however, was unfit for use in clothing.

Ranching arrived with Trinidad's first settlers and was an important part of its economy. Three of the villa's Spanish founders—Pedro Cruz, José Borrego, and José Manuel Casanova—were ranchers, as evidenced by the registration of their cattle brands. Like most ranchers in Texas, herdsmen in Trinidad raised horses, cattle, sheep, and goats. Although only one person listed their profession as "herdsman" on the 1809 census, at least eighteen additional Trinidad settlers had registered brands with the Spanish government. This accounts for the fifty percent of families that owned livestock on the census.

Soldiers also raised horses and cattle, but they kept their stock separate from the civilians' to avoid conflict. In 1809, Commandant General Salcedo supplemented the military's herd with horses from San Antonio. Hoping to limit the amount of time spent at pasture, Salcedo ordered that San Antonio's soldiers could only keep two horses. Those with more than this count were to send their horses to Trinidad. In the hopes of helping the villa economically, in 1810 Salcedo proposed that Trinidad ranchers provide cattle and horses for the citizens of San Antonio. He quickly abandoned this idea, however, when he found that the animals of Trinidad were so sickly that they could not survive the trip to the capital.

Skilled workers lived in Trinidad, yet they made up less than twenty percent of the total workforce. The town had at least three carpenters and multiple blacksmiths. The carpenters made use of the nearby white oak and other deciduous trees to construct new buildings and repair wooden equipment like wagon wheels. Trinidad was also home to a surgeon, Pedro Lartigue, although he listed his primary profession as a farmer on the census. In 1806 Trinidad had a barber, but he fled the villa after Spanish officials accused him of stealing a soldier's horse. The 1809 census also listed one man as being a stonemason and Hugo Coyle as a surveyor. It is likely that, in addition to these men, a number of Trinidad's settlers had multiple professions but listed farming on the census because it was their primary form of employment.

From 1806 to 1813, three persons served as priests in Trinidad's small chapel, where both soldiers and civilians worshipped. The first priest to minister to Trinidad was Father Jesus Sosa, who had previously served in Nacogdoches. In August 1809, a Spanish secular priest named Francisco Maynes replaced Sosa and ministered to Trinidad for the next year. After Maynes left Trinidad for a post in Nacogdoches in 1811, Father Juan José Guerra assumed his duties. During his time in Trinidad, Father Maynes described the majority of the villa's people as Catholic and noted that the villa's few Protestants were at least respectful of Catholicism's holy ceremonies. Another observer remarked that these non-Catholics were "so poorly instructed in their beliefs that under the influence of a priest, it would not be difficult to convert them to our faith."

Many Trinidad citizens engaged in contraband trading to supplement their income. Although direct trade with the United States from Texas was illegal and violators faced harsh penalties, disheartened Spanish officials found it difficult to stop contrabanders. The province's distance from the more populated regions of New Spain and the reluctance of traders to travel through Indian-controlled territories meant that manufactured goods were difficult to procure through legal avenues. Therefore, many desired items came from unscrupulous American traders who had little issue setting up shop in the difficult-to-patrol neutral zone between Texas and the United States.

Because of their previous residence in Louisiana, Spanish officials suspected that foreigners in Trinidad were engaged in illegal trade. They were right. On June 2, 1807, Commandant General Salcedo placed Louisianan Sedecias Armand on trial for contraband trade at Trinidad. Spanish soldiers caught another smuggler in the villa in September 1807. Officials later arrested John Magee and Miguel Quin, two Irish settlers, for contraband trading. Although Quin managed to break out of jail and escape Texas, he lost all of his possessions when Spanish officials sold the confiscated goods at auction. In 1809, Pedro Lartigue faced imprisonment for contraband trading, but in exchange for clemency, he promised to practice medicine in Trinidad free of charge. Because there was an epidemic in Trinidad at the time, officials approved Lartigue's request. One of Trinidad's civilian founders, Bernardo Despallier, was not so fortunate. Spanish officials exiled Despallier in 1809 for contraband trading.

In addition to guarding against Indians and an invasion from the United States, it was the job of Spanish soldiers at Trinidad to halt this contraband trade. Although it would be impossible to determine how successful they were in this duty, soldiers accomplished something. In October 1808, for example, nine Trinidad soldiers snuck up on a group of horse smugglers, bound them, and delivered them to Nacogdoches. The military, however, also smuggled. For example, Officer Pedro Lopez Prieto was dismissed from his position for engaging in the contraband trade with a civilian in the settlement.

That soldiers would engage in illegal trade is understandable, as military service along the Texas frontier was unrewarding, unprofitable, and it often served as punishment for a crime. Frontier assignment in a place like Trinidad meant the possibility of dying in an Indian attack, less contact with women, unstable pay, and poor health. Sickness, as seen by Zebulon Pike, was an ever-present occupational hazard. The humidity, sweltering heat, and frequent flooding of the

Trinity created an excellent breeding ground for malaria-carrying mosquitoes. While civilians could take refuge from the insalubrious environment inside their homes, soldiers sat exposed to insects and the environment while on guard duty. They also slept in the close confines of the barracks, where diseases could more easily transfer from one host to another. The first report of illness among the soldiers of Trinidad occurred within a month of the town's establishment. Subsequent reports of epidemics among the troops appeared in 1808 and 1809. There was an attempt to drain the swamps around Trinidad to reduce the mosquito population, but it is unknown if this task was ever completed.

Continuous changes in command further weakened the Spanish military presence at Trinidad. Carrasco had left his post as commandant of Trinidad shortly after the villa's founding. In 1810, Commandant General Salcedo placed Captain Agabo de Ayala in charge of Trinidad, but he promptly became too ill to perform his duties. A few months later, the governor replaced the ailing Ayala with Felipe de Garza. Garza remained at Trinidad until July 18, 1812, when he turned over command to Trinidad's final commandant Isidro de la Garza. Perhaps owing to this persistent change in leadership, discipline and morale suffered and fighting among soldiers was common. In January 1812, for example, two soldiers got into a fight, with one José Navarro beating José del Toro so badly that the man was unable to perform his duties. In addition to fighting, desertion was rampant.

Military members at Trinidad also often went hungry. Although soldiers raised their own crops and livestock for food, they were never self-sufficient. Food and supply shipments from San Antonio were rare, leaving soldiers to depend on Trinidad's civilians for sustenance. Although citizens offered fair prices and occasionally provided food to soldiers free of charge, this was often insufficient to feed the men of the post. In January 1811, for example, Felipe de la Garza complained to the governor that his soldiers had completely exhausted their meat supply. Instances like this led hungry frontier troops to steal in order to satiate their hunger. This seems to have been the case on February 24, 1809, when civilian William Barr accused the soldiers of Trinidad of stealing his cattle.

A shortage of paper also caused problems for Trinidad's military men. In 1810, Commandant Bonavia informed Governor Salcedo that he was unable to file his reports because he had nothing on which to write. His request for three reams went unanswered, and when his replacement made an identical appeal, he was compensated for the cost of only one and one-half reams. Although a lack of paper may seem to be a tertiary issue, it caused problems. For example, a military commander at Trinidad was unable to report on rebel activity because he lacked the paper to do so.

An even more pressing concern to the military at Trinidad was a lack of weapons, horses, and ammunition. In a February 1810 report, Trinidad's military commander claimed that most of his 150-man detachment had no firearms. When Governor Salcedo ordered Deputy Commandant General Bonavía to expel a group of Americans that had taken up residence in the neutral zone, Bonavia replied that the soldiers at Trinidad lacked the guns, ammo, and horses needed to do so. Later in 1810, the commander of Trinidad remarked that it would require 291 flints and 4,776 cartridges to arm his men properly. When Salcedo reassigned fifty cavalrymen from

Nacogdoches to Trinidad, the post's commander replied that Governor Salcedo must provide flour and mounts for the new arrivals. There were not enough of these items for the soldiers already stationed in Trinidad.

It is unknown if Salcedo fulfilled the request, but it is very possible that he could not. Owing to distance from population centers and the poor condition of the *Camino Real*, supplying Trinidad was difficult. Compounding the problem was the uncertain water line of the Trinity River. Rainfall could flood the river, making crossing almost impossible. In April 1809, for example, the river carried off a barge used for ferrying personnel and supplies. Making matters worse, Indians frequently raided shipments sent to East Texas, making it difficult to travel outside of towns. The supply problem eventually got so bad that at one point Commandant General Salcedo considered abandoning Trinidad.

The supply shortage also resulted from political and social changes in Spain and New Spain. In 1808, Napoleon Bonaparte invaded Spain and installed his brother, Joseph, on the Spanish throne. Liberal reformers in Spain's American colonies used Joseph's ascension as an opportunity to bring about social change. In New Spain, Father Miguel Hidalgo called for more rights for Indians, a republican government, and an overthrow of the political leadership of New Spain, which he claimed answered to the illegitimate Bonaparte. After Hidalgo issued his famous *Grito de Dolores* on September 16, 1810, many disenfranchised people throughout New Spain took up arms against the colonial government in Mexico City.

In order to combat Hidalgo and his followers, officials in Mexico City diverted supplies and personnel meant for Texas, leaving Trinidad undersupplied and undermanned. Local Indians took advantage of the situation, began to siphon from Trinidad's herds, and increased attacks on those traveling outside of town. Mail deliverers came under such frequent assault that in May 1812, the commandant required them to have a military escort. Fearing that Indians were preparing for a direct assault on Trinidad, the commander begged the governor of Texas for funds for construction of a fort.

The trouble went beyond Indians. In January 1811, Juan Bautista de las Casas arrested Governor Salcedo in San Antonio and assumed command of Texas in the name of Hidalgo's revolution. News of the De las Casas Revolt reached Trinidad's military post in February 1811. Informed that other areas of Texas had acquiesced to De las Casas's command, Trinidad's commander, Felipe de la Garza, chose not to resist the change in government. The villa's civilians actively supported De las Casas and even imprisoned priest Francisco Maynes because of his Spanish birth. Fortunately for Maynes, the De las Casas Revolt did not last long. Two months after De las Casas's takeover, royalists in San Antonio retook control of Texas and executed the perpetrators of the rebellion.

In 1812, revolution once again came to Texas. A supporter of Hidalgo's revolution, José Bernardo Gutiérrez de Lara wanted an independent, republican New Spain and believed that he could achieve this goal with assistance from the United States. After unsuccessfully petitioning that government for aid, Gutiérrez de Lara traveled to Louisiana where he planned an invasion of Texas as the first step in expelling Spain from New Spain. With the assistance of an experienced lieutenant in the United States Army named Augustus Magee, Gutiérrez de Lara recruited an army of Americans by promising free land in Texas once it was free of Spanish control. In the coming months, Indians, revolutionaries from New Spain, and others dissatisfied with the government in Mexico City would also join Gutiérrez de Lara's invasion force.

He also enlisted two former residents of Trinidad. The first was Bernardo Despallier, who had been among Trinidad's first settlers but had been exiled from the town for contraband trading. After his expulsion, Despallier and his wife Candida Grande relocated to Natchitoches, across the United States border, where they had a child. When Gutiérrez de Lara passed through the town in 1812 on his way to Texas, Despallier joined him. The exile even authored pamphlets explaining the purpose of Gutiérrez de Lara's expedition, hoping that residents of Trinidad and Texas would support the invasion. Candida Grande's brother and former resident of Trinidad, Luis Grande, joined Despallier.

Apprised of Gutiérrez de Lara's activities on the United States-Texas border, Spanish officials prepared to repel the invasion. Owing to its location on the road from Louisiana to San Antonio, Trinidad was integral to their planning. In April 1812, Governor Salcedo reassigned the men of the nearby military encampment at Atascosito to Trinidad. Once there, the men and the villa's civilian population erected defensive fortifications, including a stockade and two sentry boxes.

These additional defenses and the Atascosito soldiers meant little in the end. When Gutiérrez de Lara's republican army entered Texas, the outnumbered Spanish soldiers in Nacogdoches fled in the face of likely defeat. Liberal-minded residents of Nacogdoches joined the invaders. News of the retreat and defection, apathy toward the government in Mexico City, and fear of death caused the majority of Trinidad's disheartened soldiers to abandon their post. When a contingent of Gutierrez de Lara's cavalry rushed ahead to take Trinidad, they found only thirty-seven soldiers remaining at the garrison. These outnumbered men quickly laid down their arms.

The remainder of the republican army left Nacogdoches on September 13, 1812, arriving in Trinidad shortly thereafter. They stayed in Trinidad for the next month, discussing their upcoming plans and waiting until the weather cooled. During this time, Gutierrez de Lara and Despallier attempted to lure the villa's residents to the revolutionary cause. Although it is unclear how effective the men were in this effort, at least some of Trinidad's soldiers joined with the insurgents. One of the soldiers was so enthusiastic that Gutiérrez de Lara placed him in charge of distributing Despallier's pamphlets to other areas of Texas. It is unclear if any civilians joined with the revolutionaries, but based on their reaction to the De las Casas Revolt, it is probable some of the younger men did. Older residents likely offered material and moral support to the expedition.

Although Gutiérrez de Lara's forces spent only one month in Trinidad, the villa drastically affected the expedition in one major way: a contagion infected American leader Augustus Magee while in the town. Magee reported contracting a fever—probably from malaria—in Trinidad, and he died of the illness a few months later. Magee had played an important part in keeping the American and New Spain troops focused on fighting the Spanish, not each other. After his death, infighting between the two ethnic groups increased, limiting the army's effectiveness.

It is unclear what happened to Trinidad in the year after Gutierrez de Lara's departure, but it appears that most of the civilians of Trinidad carried on as they had since the villa's founding. Volunteers from the United States looking to join the Republican Army of the North likely passed through the town on a regular basis, and Trinidad's sympathetic citizens probably provided them with goods and services.

From Trinidad, Gutierrez de Lara's Republican Army of the North—as the invasion force had begun to call itself—proceeded to La Bahía, which they successfully captured after enduring a long siege. The revolutionaries then defeated Spanish forces at the Battle of Rosillo and captured San Antonio in March 1813. They would remain in the Spanish capital for the next six months. During this time, volunteers from the United States and within New Spain flocked to join Gutiérrez de Lara's army, swelling its ranks to some 1,400 men.

In June 1813, the government in Mexico City ordered the new Commandant General of the Eastern Internal Provinces, Joaquin de Arredondo, to retake Texas. Arredondo marched into Texas shortly thereafter and on August 18, 1813, his forces defeated the revolutionaries south of San Antonio in what is known as the Battle of Medina. Thirteen-hundred of 1,400 insurgents died in the battle and its immediate aftermath. Spanish troops followed up their victory by entering San Antonio, where they rounded up and executed anyone suspected of aiding the revolutionary cause. The few rebel sympathizers that managed to escape San Antonio headed in the direction of Trinidad and the safety of the United States. On August 21, Arredondo ordered his subordinate Ignacio Elizondo and 500 mounted troops in pursuit of these escapees. Elizondo was to clear both Trinidad and Nacogdoches of rebel sympathizers. Elizondo made quick time, stopping only to sleep and round up a group of some 200 rebels fleeing from San Antonio. It appeared as if Elizondo's army would reach Trinidad before its residents had a chance to flee.

Somewhat ironically, something that had made life difficult for the residents of Trinidad halted the royalists: the Trinity River. Heavy rains had recently caused the river to swell, forcing Elizondo to set up camp on the river's west bank until the water calmed and it was safe for his army to cross. Impatient, Elizondo dispatched forty men to cross the river at a different location. Once across, the men were to swing back towards Trinidad and prevent anyone from escaping to Nacogdoches. Although Elizondo's troops found a suitable location to traverse the turbulent river, a hail of arrows met them when they attempted to cross it. Sympathetic to the republicans, Xaraname Indians had taken up a position on the opposite bank of the river and it was their arrows that prevented Elizondo's men from traversing the Trinity. Elizondo sent a second set of soldiers to ford the Trinity at a place called El Salto, but this crossing was also flooded. Out of options, Elizondo had to wait until the Trinity subsided before crossing into Trinidad.

Survivors of the Battle of Medina and refuges from San Antonio had reached Trinidad before the river became unnavigable. They likely informed the villa's residents of the royalist victory and warned of the harsh reprisals that faced anyone who had not actively fought against the revolutionary army. This sent almost everyone in Trinidad into a mad scramble to gather his or her belongings. Owing to its foreign population, the Spanish government had always been wary of Trinidad, the town had supported the De las Casas revolt, and it had hosted Gutiérrez de Lara's army for a month. Realizing that this would not look good to Elizondo and his men, most residents of Trinidad decided to leave their homes for the United States. On September 3, the Trinity River subsided enough for Elizondo and his men to cross into Trinidad. They found the villa deserted but for a few loyalist families. The Trinity had given the rest of the town enough time to escape to the United States.

Elizondo used Trinidad as his base of operations for the next four days. As one of his first orders of business, he sent three members of the remaining families to scout Nacogdoches for rebel activity. Unwilling to betray their neighbors, the three scouts reached Nacogdoches and helped people escape to the United States. The scouts then returned to Elizondo and reported that Nacogdoches was abandoned. While the scouts were away, Elizondo executed seventy-one of the prisoners he had captured on his way to Trinidad. Elizondo also reported that he gave some foreigners money and allowed them to return to the United States. Trinidad resident and professed loyalist Vicente Micheli was one such person. It is unclear why Elizondo provided Micheli with money, but it may have been as payment for what he was preparing to do. On September 6, 1813, Elizondo burned Trinidad to the ground and left for San Antonio with his remaining prisoners in tow. He would not complete the trip, as one of his men— enraged by the wonton killing and destruction of the previous days— gashed Elizondo's torso with a saber.

Elizondo's demolition meant an end to Trinidad as a physical location, but many of the villa's residents survived. Exactly how many escaped the revolutionary violence of 1812 and 1813 is difficult to ascertain with current data, but at least a few of Trinidad's civilians were among the refugees who made it to safety in Louisiana. In an 1813 letter to James Monroe, Louisiana Governor William C. C. Claiborne reported that the "ascendancy of the Royalists in the Province of Texas, have thrown upon this frontier, many distressed Spanish families." He estimated the number of refugees to be 1,200 persons. Claiborne furthered commented that the refugees were "wholly destitute of the comforts, & the necessaries of life." However, he proudly reported that the citizens of Louisiana eagerly offered aid to the refugees. Although most of the refugees described by Claiborne were from Nacogdoches, at least a few had lived in Trinidad.

As indicated by parish and census records, many Trinidad residents settled in Natchitoches, just across the border from Texas. For example, parish records indicate that Miquel Quin married Celeste Sheridan in Natchitoches. Quin had resided in Trinidad, as had Celeste, who was likely one of three Sheridan daughters, aged 17–22 in the 1809 census. When the couple had a boy in July 1816, they listed another Natchitoches resident, A. Sheridan, as the child's godmother. This was likely Celeste's sister Ana Sheridan, another former Trinidad resident. Rebecca Sheridan also survived. Although she lived with her husband Juan Lunn in the 1809 Trinidad census, Rebecca was likely Ana and Celeste's older sister. Natchitoches parish records list Rebecca Sheridan and Jean Lom— probably her husband Juan Lunn from the Trinidad census—as having had a child on March 27, 1815. Elisha Nelson, who lived in Trinidad in 1809 with his wife and five daughters, resided in Natchitoches in 1820, and it seems that most of his daughters remained with him. José Leal, who appeared on the supplemental census of Trinidad, was possibly the same José Leal who married Maria Alexandra in October 1813 in Natchitoches.

Former Trinidad residents moved outside of Natchitoches, and some returned to the area of their original homes in Louisiana. The 1820 U.S. Census, for example, lists Charles Trahan and his family as residing in Saint Martin County near their pre-Trinidad home in Opelousas.

Residents of Trinidad of Spanish descent also settled in the United States. Pedro and Juana Cruz and their children had been among the original colonists from San Antonio. They settled in Natchitoches in spite of having no Louisiana ties. Jose Luis Duran, wife Guadalupe Travieso, and their two children were also among the first San Antonio settlers, and they too moved to Natchitoches in 1813. Jose Luis Duran died of "a pain" in January 1814. Born in Havana, Cuba, Geronimo Hernández moved to Natchitoches early in life and married Isabelle Rachal. In 1808, the couple resettled in Trinidad where they had two children. Likely fleeing royalists, the Hernandez family returned to Natchitoches in 1813. A José Leal listed on the 1809 census may also be the same José Leal from San Antonio in an 1813 parish record.

Although a number of Trinidad's civilians successfully fled to Louisiana, many disappeared from history. Early nineteenth century data keeping and human error may be to blame for this. Although Louisiana parish records and Spanish censuses are often detailed and historians have done an excellent job of compiling these records, no central database of these records yet exists. This leaves researches to pour through thousands of pages of documents in an attempt to locate one hundred names that one source spells differently from another. Oversight is likely to occur. Although the 1820 United States census is digitally searchable, it lists only heads of households by name. If any of Trinidad's females escaped and remarried, they would not appear on the census. Likewise, the 1820 census does not list children's names, meaning a child from Trinidad living with an uncle or stepfather would be untraceable. Additionally, because residents of Trinidad had French, Spanish, and English names, one person's name may appear differently from one census to another, making searching difficult.

The disappearance of some of Trinidad's population could also mean that some of the villa's residents died in the Battle of Medina or the royalist purge that followed. No male residents of Trinidad of fighting age in 1813 appear on later Spanish or United States censuses. This may indicate that some of Trinidad's young men joined Gutiérrez de Lara's army and were among the 1,300 men who died at the Battle of Medina. Historian Charles Schwarz reported that Spanish soldiers shot Despallier's brother-in-law and former Trinidad resident, Luis Grande, while he was passing out insurgent propaganda. Although there is no evidence to dispute this conclusion, Schwarz's contention that Trinidad founder Bernardo Despallier died during the Battle of Medina is inaccurate, as Louisiana parish records indicate that Despallier survived. Trinidad resident Vicente Micheli would claim that he lost his son, who would have been nineteen, due to revolutionary violence but it is unclear when or how this happened. The names José Leal, Francisco Travieso, and possible distortions of other Trinidad residents' names appear in Spanish records of individuals who had their property confiscated after the Battle of Medina. Although this has led some historians to conclude that these individuals died, it may instead indicate that the Spanish confiscated the residents' property after they fled to Louisiana.

Some historians have reported that Elizondo captured and executed many of Trinidad's residents. According to one early Texas history, the Spanish army found rebel-sympathizers in the town, took them to a nearby hill, and executed them. One report holds that some of Trinidad's civilians crossed the Trinity before Elizondo's arrival in the hopes of receiving leniency by surrendering to the Spanish commander but were instead executed. Elizondo never mentions these events. According to his reports, the people executed near Trinidad were those fleeing from San Antonio. Likewise, the only people Elizondo recorded as luring across a river were from San Antonio, and it was the Brazos River, not the Trinity. Earlier historians probably mistranslated Elizondo. It is still possible, because the Spanish officer tended to blur his words, that some of the town's untraceable residents are untraceable because they met an untimely end in 1813.

Only two people from Trinidad returned to Texas following the villa's destruction: Vicente Micheli and his wife Maria. Micheli had remained in Trinidad when Elizondo arrived but had traveled to the United States on Elizondo's request. Micheli wanted to return to Texas, however, so in a letter to Commandant General Arredondo that is both poetic and pathetic, the exile begged Arredondo to absolve him of accusations that he had supported the rebellion. Micheli indicated that he lost everything— including his oldest son—in the revolutionary turmoil. On March 8, 1814, Vicente Micheli received the pardon he sought. Micheli appears on an 1820 census of San Antonio married to fifty-year-old Indian woman Maria Susana Moron, whom he had married in Trinidad. They are listed as having an eighteen-year-old son who was not listed on the 1809 Trinidad census.

At least some Spanish officials who served at Trinidad went on to prominence. Felipe de Garza, who was commander of Trinidad's military garrison from 1811 to 1812 later served as Commandant General of the Eastern Internal provinces after Mexican Independence. In this capacity, he worked to assist *empresario* Stephen F. Austin in his colonization efforts. Austin's colony "San Felipe de Austin" bore Garza's name.

Father Francisco Maynes became a priest in Natchitoches following his service at Trinidad's church in from 1809 to 1811. There, he presided over the funerals and marriages of Trinidad's former residents who moved to Natchitoches after the events of 1813. Maynes's popularity in Natchitoches prompted Stephen F. Austin to request his service as the Catholic priest of his colony. Although Maynes did not accept Austin's proposal, he would remain an important figure on the Louisiana-Texas frontier for years to come.

The actual physical location of Trinidad has been lost to time. The settlement contained no stone structures, and Elizondo burned everything in the town that was made of wood. The lead archeologist of San Marcos de Neve—another settlement founded in the last years of Spanish Texas—believes that this destructive conflagration and the likelihood of the site being located on private property are to blame for archeologists' failure to locate Trinidad.

Although the site of Trinidad remains a mystery, the town's legacy should not be forgotten. The people of Trinidad played an important role in the political, diplomatic, and military events of the last years of colonial Texas. Although it did not survive, Trinidad was Spain's most successful attempt at populating Texas in the final years of colonial rule. Unlike the civilian settlement San Marcos de Neve, which collapsed under the constant threat of Indian depredations, Trinidad had a military garrison that offered protection from most Indians. Unlike the military post Atascosito, which had to rely on Spain for most of its food and supplies, under good conditions Trinidad's civilians were self-reliant. In peaceful years, the people of Trinidad even thrived. Had Spain adopted the joint military-civilian model earlier, it is possible that they could have provided a counter balance to American expansion.

Los Tejanos:

Mexican Texans in the Revolution

PAUL D. LACK

P aul D. Lack is Executive Vice President for Academic Affairs and Dean at Stevenson University in Maryland. Prior to accepting this position, he taught history at McMurry University in Abilene, Texas. Dr. Lack authored the pioneering study, *The Texas Revolutionary Experience: A Political and Social History, 1835–1836.*

In 1835, more than 4,000 Tejanos lived in Texas. They resided chiefly in four settlements: Nacogdoches, Victoria, Bexar, and Goliad. The Texas Revolution of 1835–1836 divided Mexican Texans and brought them substantial hardship. Some Tejanos remained neutral while others supported Mexico. Many Tejanos, though, actively aided the Texian cause, including such men as Juan Seguin, Victor Loupy, and Placido Benavides. In this selection, Dr. Lack examines the Tejano role in the Texas Revolution. ✥

★ ★

The experience of Tejanos in the Texas Revolution, while distinctive from that of any other group, was not characterized by uniformity. Numbering over 4,000 on the eve of the conflict, the Texas Mexican population resided mostly in four communities. Except in Nacogdoches, with a Tejano population of over 600, they found themselves engulfed by the war. The approximately 450 De León colonists from in and around Victoria felt the effects less severely at first than did the 1,600 in the Béxar area and the 1,350 in the Goliad region, where the people suffered from living in the war zone. Essentially, the Tejano experience centered around problems of military occupation, with the victorious side changing four times in less than a year. Almost any behavior, even that designed to protect themselves from the ravages of war, made the Tejanos seem like traitors from the perspective of one army, if not both, which in any case ravaged the people's food and other resources.

From October, 1835, until the end of March, 1836, the war took place in the Tejano homeland. The conflict not only ended the physical distance between Anglo and Mexican Texans but threw the two peoples together in an atmosphere of extreme tension. Initially, though they had not themselves begun the hostilities, Tejanos volunteered for the Texas side in substantial numbers, but enthusiasm for the war soon declined, and for significant reasons. The bitter experiences of living in occupied territory caused disillusionment. Political factors also led to growing doubts, as the cause changed from federalism within the Mexican nation, which many Tejanos supported, to independence, which left them in a minority status. These influences evolved in different ways, depending on circumstances unique to each community.

Tejanos serving in the Texas cause came mostly from the town of San Antonio de Béxar in the fall of 1835. Names and numbers of volunteers cannot be determined with precision because of the absence of muster rolls for them for this period, but several sources indicate substantial recruitment early in the war. Years later San Antonio citizens claimed that 160 Tejanos had participated in the siege, service for which, as local resident Sam J. Smith wrote in 1874, "they got no pay or credit." Juan Seguín, who commanded one of the native companies, identified the origins and numbers of the Tejano recruits of 1835: his company of thirty-seven men had entered at Salado Creek in October; Salvador Flores and Manuel Leal together raised forty-one volunteers from area ranches; fourteen (mostly Bexareños) deserted from Cos's forces in the city. Plácido Benavides brought a company of twenty-eight from Victoria, and an additional Tejano detachment of about twenty from the forces at Goliad later arrived along with a similar number of isolated enlistments from there.

From a variety of other sources, most especially bounty and donation grant records, the names of ninety-one Tejanos who served in the fall of 1835 have been ascertained. Biographical information on these men reveals the following profile: most were young, the average age being 27.5 (25 when measured by the median figure), about four to six years younger, in fact, than the Anglo volunteers of this period. Nevertheless, a majority of them had already married. Native-born Texans (85 percent) naturally dominated the ranks, and the few who had come north to settle from Mexico had done so seven to fifteen years earlier. The place of residence of these volunteers becomes even more difficult to establish; however, Bexareños clearly outnumbered any other group. Only fifteen of those who saw service in 1835 can be identified as from outside of the Béxar municipality, and the census records suggest that town residents were twice as numerous as those from the ranches. As Seguín recalled, his company was the largest, and it "was made up of men from this city [San Antonio]."

Bexareño soldiers made contributions commensurate with their numbers. From his initial meeting with General Austin at Camp Salado on October 22, Captain Seguín energetically executed a number of varied responsibilities. Recruitment continued up to the storming of the city on December 5, but the unit became active from its inception. As the commander in chief wrote on November 24, the company of "native Mexicans . . . was very efficient in the cause." On the fourteenth of that month Austin dispatched a unit under Salvador Flores on an "important" mission away from the scene of the siege. Primarily sent to scout for centralist reinforcements south of the Nueces River, its orders also involved capturing horses and burning the grasslands to inhibit enemy movement. The Tejanos seemed especially adept in this kind of service, no doubt because of their knowledge of the countryside. Austin praised them for capturing expresses directed to the centralist forces in Béxar, but he also made it clear that "Cap. Seguín and his men were at all times ready and willing to go on any service they were ordered. They uniformly acquited themselves to their credit as patriots and soldiers."

This service included participation in battle. Seguín's men saw action with Bowie at missions San José and Concepción in November, and Tejanos answered the call for volunteers to storm the city on December 5. Antonio Cruz, of the Béxar company, so distinguished himself in the fighting at the Veramendi house as to attract commendation by no less of an anti-Mexican than Travis. Nonsoldiers also got into the action as the conflict came literally into their homes. Among these María Jesusa de García stood out, because, in the words of an act subsequently passed by the Texas Congress, she "was wounded and permanently disabled in rendering extraordinary services to the army of Texas at San Antonio." García had attempted to carry water to the Texans on December 5 in spite of the heavy Mexican barrage. These acts of individual valor gained particular recognition, but one veteran of the campaign extended the plaudits to the community as a whole. "Our army owe[s] many thanks to the brave inhabitants" of the city, he wrote on Christmas day, for they "ranked themselves on the side of liberty, and fought bravely with the Texan forces. Were all the Mexicans such ardent lovers of liberty, as the citizens of San Antonio, we should not now be left to fight our battles alone."

That a sizable force of Bexareños turned out for the Texas cause came as no great surprise to the leaders of the rebellion, for the city had acquired a reputation of opposition to the military-centralist party. The more remarkable feature of the high level of volunteering was that those from town found sufficient opportunity to participate despite a form of martial law imposed by General Cos. On October 15, a full week before the Texas army arrived at Salado Creek near the town, he ordered Political Chief Angel Navatro to devise and administer a passport system. Essentially, this edict forbid anyone from leaving without a pass from either Cos or Navarro. The civil authority complied, periodically supplying a list of persons who had been given exit permits, but the commander expressed dissatisfaction with enforcement. The system had been in place but a few days when local resident Zeferino Ruiz boldly left town with no pass and even more brazenly returned with a note from one of the rebel leaders. According to further correspondence from Cos, only "a few inhabitants among this population have heeded the policy"; therefore, he informed Navarro, beginning November 18 and "without exception" anyone caught violating the passport rule would be sentenced to forced labor. This level of noncompliance occurred in the face of a strong night patrol, staffed by both infantry and cavalry.

The Texas forces expected to benefit from the enemy's problems in controlling the town population. Before the army had even arrived one observer predicted that the number of Cos's troops required "to keep down the citizens" would be a significant advantage. In fact, several residents managed to leave town to join the Texas cause. Austin indicated that these included both "deserters" from the Mexican army and "inhabitants who have connected with us." Movement between Béxar and the rebel lines seems to have occurred almost constantly. Macedonio Arocha, one of the recruits, recalled later that he went back and forth at night from town to Seguín's company several times, to visit his family and to obtain extra provisions. Friendly Bexareños even helped the Texas artillery overcome its ammunition shortage by returning used cannon balls. Perhaps most importantly, the people of the city provided information on the centralist army and through intermediaries like rancher José María Solmas sent out confidential communications.

Those who left the town brought complaints about the military rule of General Cos. According to reports made to Bowie and Fannin at Espada mission on October 22, "a large number of the citizens of Bexar and of this place, are now *laying out*, to prevent being forced to perform the most servile duties." Erasmo Seguín "and others of the most respectable citizens" were reputedly to be made "to sweep the public square, and in case [Cos] whiped [*sic*] us, to make their Ladies, grind tortias for his soldiers." The general eventually forced the elder Seguín to walk to his son's ranch, leaving behind the remainder of the family to endure the Texas barrage for the rest of the siege. Cos also impressed mules and drivers and perhaps other property, and he reportedly razed houses on the outskirts of town to provide a more favorable field of fire in case of a rebel assault.

Hearing these reports, the Texas leaders came to expect more support from the Bexareños. Following a month of loosely conducted siege warfare, Austin issued a "Proclamation to the Inhabitants of Bexar" that amounted to an invitation for them somehow to make peace. This document enumerated an eight-point set of terms, half of which concerned capitulation and withdrawal, matters more appropriately directed to Cos or his superiors. Remaining provisions promised fair representation for Béxar and a kind of amnesty: "No Citizen will be persecuted nor molested in any way in either their persons or property on account of their political opinions." Finally, Austin indicated that all who sought the protection of his plan should present themselves to the army of Texas. After this pronouncement the besieging forces increasingly considered the remaining residents to be enemies and suspected those who moved back and forth between the town and the Texan lines as potential spies rather than useful informants. Naturally, this changing opinion led to increased tensions between Béxar civilians and the Texans.

Relations also worsened because of the army's growing demands for supplies. Actually, from the date of their arrival in October the Texas forces had but a meager commissary and little cash with which to make purchases. Even officers who attempted to respect private property had difficulty in establishing ownership of the corn, beans, and beef they needed; further they could not always determine the genuine needs of the local population, some of whom they suspected of intending to withhold from the Texans in order to sell to the centralists in town. As late as November 16 Austin had to explain to Antonio de la Garza why he would not be permitted to transport his maize and beans to the plaza while it remained in enemy hands. The commander assured his correspondent that war's end would bring restoration of civil authority and payment for properties confiscated from patriotic citizens (not enemies).

Soon after their arrival in the neighborhood it became obvious that, lacking the money with which to make purchases, the Texans would resort to impressment. Responding to queries regarding dealings with the recalcitrant *mayordomo* of Espada mission, Austin ordered Bowie and Fannin to use persuasion, give certificates of credit, and keep an accurate accounting: "In the event this arrangement will not satisfy him there is no resource left but to follow the Law of necessity, and take what you want." However oppressive this policy might have been in these matters Austin showed more patience and restraint than did most other members of the army. One of the first assignments given Seguín was contracting with area ranch owners for corn and beans to be paid for in bank bills or on public credit. On November 17 Austin ordered Quartermaster Patrick C. Jack to organize a food-gathering expedition. This officer received authority to take charge of all wagons and oxen, employ loyal teamsters, and oversee the harvesting of the grain. Austin also attempted to prevent soldiers from killing beef and to exempt certain fields from being ravaged by the army.

Despite these efforts, the Texas commander obviously knew that much property had been taken without attention to any form of payment. A week after his resignation Austin reminded the provisional government of its responsibility "to ascertain the amount of property thus [by compulsion] made use of, and to provide for a Just compensation." Nevertheless, over four years later Josefa Jiménez still had not settled the account for the corn "that during the storming of Bexar was taken from her by the volunteer army of Texas," as her claim read. These contributions burdened both poor and affluent. In 1840 a congressional resolution awarded Erasmo Seguín $3,004 for the oxen, mules, corn, beans, beef, and other supplies he had furnished in 1835.

Had it not been for the moderating presence of Austin the impact of the war on the Tejano population of Béxar might well have been far worse. Many other officers like Fannin favored a more concerted scorched earth policy. On November 5 the general wrote his thoughts on military strategy to the Consultation. While he agreed basically that circumstances of war had undercut the middle ground, Austin opposed "laying waste the country round Bexar. I think [that] too hard on the inhabitants who are our friends." For some time this issue was a source of internal disaffection in the Texas army, but the general continued to order his subordinates to discriminate between friend and foe in raiding area ranches.

These divisions on treatment of civilians still existed among the soldiers as they stormed the city and battled house-to-house between December 5 and 10. Consequently, one unit shot a boy who tried to escape from a captured dwelling and arrested three women and a priest. Another company stormed a stone house and shot inside until it heard the "screams of women & children" and then paroled the men who laid down their arms, allowing all of them to flee to an area away from the fighting. In making peace General Edward Burleson agreed to restore private property "to its proper owners," to protect the citizens of Béxar "in their persons," and not to molest civilian or soldier "on account of his political opinions hitherto expresed."

The question of the war's impact on civilian life in Béxar had not greatly distracted either of the armies as they pursued the laws of necessity and confiscated, consumed, or destroyed property. The people of Béxar endured a battle that literally reached into their homes. The Texas tactics of turning houses into strongholds involved forced entries, tearing holes out of walls and ceilings, and reinforcing doors and windows with dirt and furniture. These methods left the city marked by heaps of ruins. Further, the siege created shortages for civilians trapped in the town; even those in farming areas controlled by Texans found that the army used up staples at an alarming rate. At the time of arrival in the outskirts of Béxar no less qualified an observer than West Point-trained Fannin described the provisions as virtually inexhaustible. Yet, less than a month later he reported to Austin, "We have nearly consumed all the corn &c near here." These shortages translated into privation for Tejano civilians. Their sacrifices of liberty and property were substantial if only because the armies were large and more stationary than at any other time in the war.

The people of the Goliad area also experienced the traumas of military rule in the fall of 1835. The size and character of the occupation differed from that of Béxar in that the Texans triumphed there very early in the war, on October 9, and held the post with a garrison that seldom exceeded one hundred men. However, commander Dimitt asserted absolute control over both resources and the civil authorities, resulting in a form of domination at least equal to that suffered by the Bexareños. By late in the year, as Texas forces gathered in and around Goliad for a projected assault against Matamoros, the Tejanos of this region had to endure the pressure of a large, hostile army in their midst. In early spring, 1836, centralist troops arrived and added the hardships of battle to the sufferings of the people.

Not all these problems could have been predicted. The entire region acquired a reputation for lukewarmness toward the Texas cause; yet, Tejanos from both Victoria and Goliad volunteered initially in support of the rebellion. When Texans from Matagorda arrived at the de León colony on their way to conquer the Mexican fortress, Alcalde Juan Antonio Padilla, who considered it "disgraceful to live under the military yoke," joined the expedition. He brought into the ranks other prominent Victorians, including the empresario's son Silvestre de León and son-in-law Plácido Benavides. Austin described Padilla as "a true friend to Texas and to Liberty." Miguel Galán, from Goliad, volunteered on October 10, the day after the fort capitulated, to be joined soon by Paulino de la Garza, Agustín Bernal, and some of the men who had been serving in the Mexican garrison. Controversy soon developed, as Col. Benjamin Fort Smith wrote to his friend Austin, over what to do with "the Mexican Volunteers." "We know Not as yet how far they may be relied upon," he opined. Dimitt resolved the issue by sending Padilla "with a Small detachment of creole troops" under Benavides to Béxar for Austin to deal with personally. This company of about thirty men remained for the duration of the siege and participated with distinction in some of the fiercest fighting in December.

What Dimitt apparently intended, and clearly achieved, amounted to a purging of Mexicans from his force. Although rancher Miguel Aldrete remained affiliated with this unit, even signing the controversial declaration of December 22, and men like Tomás Amador served as a messenger, Anglo and Irish colonists dominated the Goliad command for the of 1835. Lacking the potentially moderating influence of "native" troops, the Texa an army of occupation pitted against the people of the region. Perhaps the command believe that he needed a Tejano perspective because, as one veteran later wrote, Di a Mexican wife and was, for all practical purposes, a Mexican." Undoubtedly, the Goliad would not have concurred in this conclusion.

Even though a sizable body of centralist supplies fell into Texas hands with the capitulation of the fort, Dimitt immediately began to impress the property of local citizens. On October 10 he seized "into the public service" $120 worth of beef belonging to C. [J.] E. Vasquez. A few days later Domingo Falcón and A. Volors forcibly surrendered some of their cattle to the Texas army, and other residents of the vicinity furnished twenty horses for the use of the soldiers. Through the month of November the people continued to make more forced contributions—animals, corn, wagon wheels, a rifle, a string of ponies, even a crowbar—nothing seemed to escape the army's clutches. Dimitt's grasp reached one hundred miles north to the ranch of Erasmo Seguín, who lost five hundred dollars worth of mules to impressment.

The garrison's most insatiable need seemed not to be food but transportation. In order to move Irish colonists out of the war zone and send provisions to Béxar. Dimitt seized both carts and teamsters. On November 13 Alcalde Galán enumerated the sufferings of the Goliad residents in a letter to Austin: "[The soldiers are] breaking into houses, ravaging the corn without the consent of property owners, killing cows randomnly without making an effort to know who they belong to, impressing servants without the consent of their masters, and then letting them loose without supervision . . . [or] paying them for their labor." The commander also made the people work on fortifying the plaza and perform other forms of manual labor.

The citizens of Goliad responded in several ways. As Dimitt himself explained, "immediately after the place was taken," they began to seek refuge in the countryside. Some fled from the section altogether. On October 25 he continued to affect surprise at this reaction, claiming "I have done, and have said, every thing which I could do, or say, to pacify and inspire them with confidence." Dimitt attributed the people's conduct to awe of the military display earlier made by the centralists. Other observers assigned responsibility to the policies of the Texas military in general and its local leader in particular. John J. Linn complained to Austin of the many "acts of tireney" of Dimitt, "a great enimey of the Mexicans." All but twenty had left town; "the people are afraid to come [back] as they do not want to be made hewers of wood and Drawers of water."

Having left their homes in search of security, in early November the Tejanos sought to rectify their situation through politics. Many enthusiastically welcomed the arrival of Governor Viesca, who came with an armed guard on November 11 in his flight from the centralists; as a legally constituted federalist leader, he must have seemed a potential deliverer. But Dimitt's refusal to receive the governor "in an official capacity" incited what the Texas officer called "insubordination, . . . discontent, and . . . a spirit of opposition, both in and out of the fort." Tejanos held a public meeting on the twelfth and protested military usurpation of democratically elected authority. All but one of the thirty-two who signed this document were Tejanos, but they gained some support among soldiers.

Dimitt promptly declared martial law. His order proclaimed: "All persons manifesting an opposition dangerous to the cause espoused by the People of Texas—All who oppose, or threaten to oppose, the observance of order, of discipline, and subordination, or who endeavour to excite discontent wither in the Fortress, or within the Town, will be regarded as public enemies, arrested as such, and dealt with accordingly." Specifically, no one could arrive or leave without reporting and obtaining a passport. This policy brought on an additional set of protests, mostly directed to Austin and seeking replacement of the Goliad commander. Thomas G. Western, who had as the post's adjutant opposed Dimitt on the Viesca matter, explained that the inhabitants had not only "flown to the country for Security . . . [but also] prepared hiding places to which to escape at the very sound of the name Dimitt." The alcalde catalogued the various infringements on popular liberry and pointed out the irony of these being committed in the name of the liberal cause. Austin promptly ordered Dimitt's ouster and informed Galán that the replacement would respect civil authority; however, the Goliad garrison kept Dimitt in power. A public meeting at Texana renewed the Tejanos' request for protection by the provisional government, but by then their fate more than ever rested with the increasingly powerful and antagonistic Texas army. Many area Tejanos continued to hide.

These inherited tensions, combined with newer aggravations, poisoned Tejano-military relations during that period. Considerable underground support existed for the centralists, and the U.S. volunteers and other troops who swelled in numbers between December and February held militantly anti-Mexican attitudes. Fannin reported from the fort in February that "no aid need be expected from Mexicans." Recruits from the United States likewise expressed skepticism about Tejano trustworthiness. As one wrote, the citizens of La Bahía "professed to be hearty in the cause of the revolution" but actually fled from town in order to hedge their fate. This perceived vacillation, which the people attributed to a desire to escape the unruly behavior of the Texas troops, led the soldier to doubt both words and deeds of support. He did admit that "the absconded citizens of Goliad . . . received us kindly, and treated us with hospitality, professed the warmest hospitality to our cause, and denied having any communication with the Mexican army."

Residents of this region provided several kinds of service to Texas. Juan A. Zambrano went to Matamoros as a spy for Austin and fell prisoner to Urrea. Plácido Benavides, shortly after leading a company in the storming of Béxar, likewise set out on an intelligence-gathering mission to centralist-held territory near the Rio Grande. In early February he returned with news of an impending invasion, information that Fannin ignored, to his later grief. Other Tejanos made less spectacular contributions. Miguel Benítez, also a veteran of the siege, along with other drivers carried ammunition and other stores from the coast. Victor Loupy probably filled as many roles as any Texan in the Revolution. He volunteered for the army at Goliad on October 9 and subsequently acted as soldier, interpreter, and contractor, supplying Fannin's troops with more than four hundred head of cattle. The centralists captured and imprisoned him; after the Revolution a Texas secretary of war endorsed Loupy's application for back pay with a commendation for his "long and meritorious service."

One mercantile enterprise involving Tejanos from this region resulted in a substantial loss of property. José María Carbajal and his brother-in-law Fernando de León, of Victoria, chartered the *Hannah Elizabeth* in November to carry arms and other goods from New Orleans to the Texas forces. The vessel and proprietors fell prey to a centralist ship operating near the coast in December; their goods ended up in the hands of a group of Matagordans who had commissioned a coastal raider that recaptured the *Hannah*. Despite their vigorous protest, the Victorianos received none of the proceeds from the auction of the salvaged supplies. Nevertheless, Acting Governor Robinson appointed de León as aide-de-camp to organize the militia of Victoria, "believing that you are willing to serve your country in any way that you can be useful."

The Tejano masses lost their property in the conflict not through business dealings but by the continuing impressment policies of the Texas army. Once again in early 1836 as in the previous year the most sought-after of their possessions were draft animals. To some extent earlier and then especially during the attempted retreat in March, A. C. Horton and other press gangs rounded up every yoke of oxen, team of mules, or stray horse they could find. Leg-weary infantrymen also attempted spur-of-the-moment appropriations from Tejano corrals, but they sometimes found the mounts too wild to be handled.

Most of the people of La Bahía stayed in their rural sanctuaries. Troops new to the town found little but "empty streets," as one wrote. "All of the inhabitants had kept indoors, and only a few aged Mexicans deigned to look at us from the small air-holes which form the windows of their cabins." For Tejanos even flight to ranches no longer provided protection from the more numerous and disorderly recruits who conducted frequent forays in search of provisions and enemies.

When hostilities came to this region in February and March, more Tejanos fought on for the invaders than for Fannin. The wonder is that any sided with Texas at all, given the state of military-civilian relations. About ten Mexican Texans saw action in the Nueces River area, of whom two were killed and the others captured. As the action came closer to Refugio, Tejano participation on the side of the Revolution dwindled, although Mariano Carbajal and one other perished at Goliad. Either from simple charity or in support of the Texas cause, several Tejanas aided the few soldiers who had managed to escape the fate of Fannin and his men. These acts of mercy included tips about the locations of Urrea's soldiers as well as provisions of food and clothing.

Whether they welcomed the invasion or opposed it, the coming of the war into their homeland devastated the lives of many Tejanos. Some who considered themselves noncombatants died in the guerrilla-like fighting around Refugio from March 11–13. They also lost equipment, horses, cattle, and other property; especially devastated were those who resided in the town, which rebel forces under William Ward burned on March 13. That same fate befell La Bahía, as Fannin set it ablaze just before beginning his tardy retreat. Santa Anna later used the fact that the Texas brand of warfare had "reduced [the Tejanos] to the most dreadful situation" to justify the vengeful treatment of Urrea's captives. At Victoria, which of all the Mexican-dominated communities of this area had shown the greatest loyalty to the Texas cause, the authorities had reserved twenty yoke of oxen to assist civilian evacuation in case of a centralist victory. Fannin impressed these at the last minute, depriving the people of the means of flight. Ironically, the Texas army later used their failures to evacuate as evidence of Tory sentiment.

However harsh his policies toward the enemy, Urrea promised not "'to molest the inhabitants of the country who remained at their homes and took no part in the war.'" Yet, according to an official who carried this message, "'the general would depend on the citizens for much subsistence.'" This included a measure of cooperation as well as material support. Urrea forced the principal leaders of Victoria to report and perform certain duties. Fernando de León had to turn over hidden contraband goods. His brother-in-law Manuel Escalera served under compulsion as a courier for Urrea.

In this period between December and April, 1836, the community of Béxar had as before lent more voluntary support to the Texas cause than had the areas to the south. Still, many of the problems experienced by Goliad also characterized the situation in the departmental capital. In the fall hostilities had been more intense and thus destruction greater in Béxar, and the people continued to supply an army of occupation after the surrender of Cos. For the entire period from December to April this community continued to feel in innumerable ways the burden of war.

Like other Texans, a majority of the Tejano soldiers returned to civilian life as soon after the December 5 victory over the centralists as possible, and most of those who served in 1835 did not join the army again in the spring of 1836. Instead, Anglo and Tejano veterans alike looked first to the care of their families in the belief that those who had not yet gone to war should do so. Though few at the time saw this retirement as anything but natural, some critics subsequently cited it as evidence of a lack of patriotic zeal. A substantial number of Bexareños in fact remained militarily active, albeit in a somewhat irregular fashion. Captain Seguín led a body of cavalry which tracked the movement of Cos's forces to scout their threatened return from south of the Rio Grande. Company commander Salvador Flores and a few others risked themselves in "spy" work north of that river to detect centralist troop movement, but throughout most of early 1836 the military authorities did not actually seek Tejano participation.

During the month of December Tejanos of the town and the surrounding area still lived under military rule, as General Ed Burleson's successor, Francis W. Johnson, made no attempt to reestablish civil authority. The masses of people, though "greatly impoverished" in Neill's words, had to share their provisions with the military. Much of the burden of feeding the army of occupation still rested on area farmers. One such group living near San José mission resisted impressment of six wagon loads of corn with such "pitiful pleas" that the press gang leader consulted his superiors about returning the grain. Eventually, he decided that the farmers had been deceitful in claiming that this "was their only food until the next harvest" because they had actually intended to sell part of their holdings in town. The profit motive and dislike of Americans, not "dread of famine kept them from sharing their surplus with us." It seems not to have occurred to him that the impressed corn comprised the people's only asset in acquiring other goods from town because most of the farmers received certificates of credit, not negotiable currency, for the commodities taken by Seguín, Johnson, and other officers in December and January.

By contrast to what he considered the grim behavior of the rural people. Herman Ehrenberg perceived a more light-hearted spirit in town. Residents who had fled during the siege returned soon after the peace of December 11 so that "bustle and animation again filled the streets, where Texans and Mexicans walked about their business without fear or resentment." Most of the native people seemed content to pursue their traditional pleasures and welcomed as "guests" the American volunteers who made up the bulk of the local garrison. Without the displays of protest that had occurred at the mission, merchants like Francisco A. Ruiz and José A. Navarro sold on credit a variety of supplies ranging from beef, corn, and other food to horses, mules, and cooking utensils. Nevertheless, the burden of having supplied armies since October had exhausted the area economy by January. Neill reported that even the ubiquitous cattle had come into short supply, and he received authorization to employ vaqueros at twenty dollars per month to drive in beef from the range. This promise of employment on credit hardly improved the economy. According to the acting governor, "the unfortunate inhabitants [were] reduced by the war, from opulence and ease, to penury and want."

This material suffering did not lead to overwhelming disaffection by the people, as seen by a consensus of the military leaders stationed in Béxar. Only Travis seemed to fear Tejano treachery. In contrast, Neill wrote emphatically to Houston on January 14, "I can say to you with Confidence, that we can rely on great aid from the citizens of this town, in case of an attack." He cited the voluntary contribution of supplies by Gaspar Flores and Luciano Navarro as evidence of this genuine support. Within the next two weeks Bowie and G. B. Jameson confirmed Neill's assessment, with the latter giving praise to Seguín and others of "the most wealthy and influential citizens." This account also noted the problem of "loose [military] discipline" that led to soldier-civilian tensions.

Neill had restored civil authority when he became head of the post at the end of 1835, but disorder associated with the struggle to succeed him threatened to undo the amicable relations he had created. The elevation of Bowie over Travis in this contest in February, as the latter wrote, made "everything topsy turvey." Bowie began interfering with private property, preventing citizens from carting their goods to the country, and in effect he abrogated civil government by releasing prisoners from jail. This act brought on conflict. Judge Seguín angrily resigned in protest, and Bowie retaliated by calling an armed parade of the Alamo troops, all of whom acted in what the post adjutant described as "a rumultously and disorderly manner," attributable to the drunkenness of the Texas forces.

Part of these tensions grew out of the awareness of many Bexareños of the impending centralist invasion and their reaction to this threat. As the above episode revealed, a large number of citizens had been fleeing the town since mid-January. Knowledge of centralist plans did not indicate treason; rather, the local population simply took seriously the reports of those who had been dispatched to the Laredo area to gather intelligence. The Texas commanders also had access to this information but refused to retreat from the Alamo fortress.

When Santa Anna's men began arriving on February 22, they found the town reduced in population but not entirely abandoned. Some of the people stayed at home in support of the invading force, but more often they had hopes of maintaining an undeclared neutrality. In part this waning of support for Texas may have been the result of the growing tensions between civilians and the Texas army; however, the most significant influence on local Tejano behavior was the failure of the military to prevent the centralist reoccupation. Like many Anglo colonists, Bexareños who supported the cause often chose to provide for the welfare of their families first before joining or reenrolling in the service. In fact, when the ranks of the Alamo defenders are defined to include all those who served under Neill in early February as well as Travis and Bowie later in the month, the number of Tejanos becomes nineteen rather than the three cited by Travis. Mostly from Béxar, this Tejano contingent of defenders ranked next to Gonzales in number of recruits and represented nearly twenty percent of the Texans who served in the army at San Antonio in the first two months of 1836. Many of the Bexareños received discharges from commander Neill and left to help evacuate their families, or like Seguín became messengers in one of the many last-ditch efforts to bring reinforcements to the fortress. Some, as historian Walter Lord suggests, may also have chosen to retire from what obviously had become a losing cause. The list of those who braved the assault in the Alamo should also include four or five Bexareñas and nine dependent children who had accompanied their husband-father-protectors into the fort.

Generally, Santa Anna seemed determined to demonstrate restraint in his relations with the local population. A few Béxar homeowners had to quarter Mexican officers, and the Mexican president eventually confiscated and auctioned property belonging to "colonists" in the town, but his army apparently paid for more commodities than did the impressment-prone Texans, who once again had herded local cattle and seized corn and other property in their hasty flight into the fortress. Townspeople had considerable freedom of movement, some even managing to wander into and out of the fort after the siege had begun. In battle, too, most of the destruction of local property emanated from the Texans—Travis's men burned many houses in La Villita in an attempt to reduce the cover of the attackers.

The day after the final assault the victorious general ordered Bexareños to return home where they would be protected in their domestic life. Actually, they did not easily or quickly resume normal routines. Alcalde Francisco Antonio Ruiz led a delegation of citizens forced to identify corpses, cart off Mexican bodies for burial, and prepare the funeral pyre for the defenders. Other leaders, including political chief Ramón Músquiz, established hospitals and attended the wounded before and after the battle. For the next two months civilians and soldiers suffered from scarcity of food and high prices. Nevertheless, the people endured these sufferings and still managed to display courtesy and kindheartedness, according to an American physician stationed there in April and May.

A large number of Béxar residents fled before the invading force came onto the scene. Having placed their families in some rural sanctuary or on the road to the east and presumed safety, many of the men rallied to one of the military units forming in the vicinity of the Colorado River. Seguín, after failing to stir movement from Fannin, went to the neighborhood of Gonzales and organized some of these recruits into a company. Houston used this command as a rear guard during the long retreat and proposed similar duty for it at San Jacinto. At the insistence of its leader and men like Antonio Menchaca the Tejano company engaged in the battle as part of the left wing of the Texas army and behaved with suitable gallantry. Most estimates give the number in this unit at twenty-two to twenty-four (Seguín's recollection placed the figure at forty-six, including those who served in the rear baggage detail); adding those from Nacogdoches and other parts of Texas, thirty-two Tejanos can be identified by name as having served at this decisive battle. Most of them were young, averaging but twenty-five years in age, and 60 percent were single, characteristics that reflected the fact that family men had been diverted from service by the need to provide for their dependents. Thirteen others besides Seguín had also served in the Béxar siege of the previous fall. Far more Bexareños had turned out for the Texas cause in the spring of 1836 than served in the battle of San Jacinto. Among those who gathered at Gonzales in early March, General Houston sent a company of twenty-five to forty under the command of Salvador Flores to defend families that had remained on their farms. Another body of about thirty soldiers escorted civilians from Béxar to Nacogdoches.

Whichever destination they decided on, the fleeing civilians confronted substantial risks. Siege veteran Agustín Bernal took his family forty miles from town to the ranch of Tía Calvilla on the San Antonio River. He "was obliged to remain at that place," as he recalled years later, "to protect his wife and young child against the Indians and some parties of Mexican outlaws." Some of the women and children set off to the east with neither protectors not adequate equipment. The Tejana wife of Erastus (Deaf) Smith loaded her two sets of twins and personal possessions in a bulky cart but had no draft animals. She borrowed a team from her fellow refugees on her one-leg-at-a-time journey. The more affluent Seguín family attempted to save three thousand sheep and a herd of cattle by driving them past the Colorado River, in the common but mistaken notion that Texas forces would stop Santa Anna's advance at that point. Slowed by their possessions and by the snarl of other families on the miserable roads, most of the Seguín animals fell to the pursuing division of General Joaquín Ramírez y Sesma. The family members managed to get away to San Augustine and then to Nacogdoches, but without their assets they had to sell personal property, including even clothing, just to avoid starving. Illness as well as poverty beset the Seguíns during their brief stay in east Texas.

Their experience may have been particularly unpleasant because they entered an isolated and suspect Tejano community in Nacogdoches, where the Revolution engaged the Hispanic people politically—invariably in opposition—but not militarily and had less impact socially than elsewhere. Leaders of the Texas cause had attempted at the outset "to try and Rase the Maxacans" as a group, in the words of George A. Nixon, but repeatedly failed. Tejano militiamen did agree to serve as a home guard unit; however, this same official later wrote, "they Seeme Not to under Stand the Busi[-]ness." This ruse of feigned ignorance allowed the masses to stay at home, but individuals made contributions to the war effort. In early November the Nacogdoches vigilance committee head informed Thomas J. Rusk that "the most wealthy" of the Tejanos have "furnished horses and money for the equipment" of a company of U.S. volunteers that came through town on the way to Béxar. These contributors included Miguel Cortines, "one of the few Mexicans whose energies have been used in our cause," Rusk later wrote. The supplies included a horse and four rifles valued at $210. In December Bernard Pantallion provided nearly one thousand eight hundred pounds of beef and pork to another of these companies, and others gave horses or worked as cooks, couriers, or servants.

Although the Tejanos of east Texas refused to form into a single body and march to the front as a unit, individually they did join the army, Anglo-American criticisms notwithstanding. Most of this volunteering occurred in fall of 1835, before the cause had become independence, when at least six "natives" from the region served in the siege of Béxar. Squite Cruse enlisted at Jasper on October 14; the remainder were from Nacogdoches. They came from a variety of personal circumstances, some of them being young and single, while Esteban Mora, forty-eight years old, had a wife and four children living at home. Juan José Ybarbo, another married man in his forties, received an honorable discharge that testified also to his bravery and his financial contributions to the Texas forces. Casimiro García fell prisoner to General Cos during the siege while serving in Rusk's company.

Despite these examples of individual participation, the Tejanos as a whole remained a separate community in Nacogdoches. When newcomer William F. Gray arrived there in early February, he observed that "there is no social intercourse between them [Anglo Americans] and the Mexicans." The latter impressed him as "a quiet, orderly, and cheerful people, . . . unthrifty and unambitious," though some seemed atypically "intelligent and respectable." His own experience indicated a less than absolute segregation, in that Anglos frequented the Tejano gambling houses, but a high degree of separation clearly characterized both political and social behavior.

Anglo-Tejano tensions continued well beyond the battle of San Jacinto. In June military authorities still considered the issue of drafting Nacogdoches Tejanos, and the local vigilance group discussed using force to make them join the revolutionary cause. At the end of the month Houston wrote to the head of that committee urging him "not to adopt any harsh measures towards the Mexicans in the neighborhood of Nacogdoches. Treat them kindly and pass them as tho' there was no difficulty or differences of opinion. *By no means* treat them with *violence*." Though the General's advice apparently forestalled an immediate conflict, his argument rested on a flimsy public relations reasoning: "The world would damn our cause if we shed blood at home" before defeating the invader decisively. Thus, the future boded ill for the Tejanos as a group, and individually they began to suffer loss of liberty even during the summer of 1836. Local Mexicans found themselves detained illegally by private citizens, and the courts sentenced a Tejano to a whipping and a term of forced labor for a six-dollar fraud case.

Residents of the other Tejano communities continued to face the problems of living in occupied Texas during the entire summer of 1836. Though centralist armies retreated to the Rio Grande in May, all of the west remained an insecure area for several months. Many Tories evacuated southward with the army as it left Béxar on May 25. "The remaining citizens," as a U.S. soldier-physician there reported in his journal, "seem to be much relieved at the departure of the troops, with which they have been oppressed for three months. Some of them broke out into transports that made them out quite ludicrously. . . . Navarro was seen capering about the streets like a boy in perfect ecstasy of glee. He said that now he should recover his health; that nothing but the impure air occasioned by the residence of the Mexican troops had made him sick." Unfortunately, this celebration proved to be premature both for Navarro, who died two weeks later, and for the community as a whole, which continued to experience the difficulties of wartime occupation. Worries about reinvasion kept refugees in east Texas or in their rural hideaways, leaving the town depopulated. Some of the people of the municipality faced dire enough conditions that they set out to plunder the retreating army of Vicente Filisola as it retreated beyond the Nueces. Seguín arrived in Béxar in early June with such a small company that he felt insecure from a potential attack by Tories and from marauding Indians who threatened to rob, murder, and otherwise ravage the entire area.

These various forces of disorder meant that the Bexareños would live under military rule for the remainder of the year, and army measures were often harsh. Initially, at least, the commander operated from a vision of restraint. Rusk specifically ordered Col. James Smith, head of a force dispatched to relieve Seguín at Béxar on June 8, that "you will be careful on going to San Antonio to prevent any unnecessary interruption to the citizens there. Such conduct as entering their homes and taking their property you will certainly forbid [as] improper" in that the people who remained in town had demonstrated friendship toward the Texas cause. Unfortunately, according to reports that reached Mexico that summer, the soldiers did exactly what the General had forbidden. Perhaps in response to this treatment, several townspeople joined those who had earlier given themselves over to centralist protection. This resumed flight renewed army fears of Toryism. Further, some of the people evidently drove their cattle southward with them, thus exacerbating fears of a reinvasion force being fed by Texas beef. Army-civilian relations had become a vicious cycle.

When Seguín departed the town on June 21, he ordered the people of the region to herd their animals eastward, out of potential enemy use, as evidence of loyalty to Texas. Their subsequent conduct failed to satisfy the military leaders. A month later Rusk wrote, "I wish in a few days to give Bejar a shake." This general's earlier goal of a civilian-army accord had largely vanished by August. Residents protested about their treatment, but Rusk could only express "eternal regret . . . that the distress of War should fall upon families of women and children." He promised that "in no case will they be injured by our Troops." His letter to Miguel Arciniega held out little hope for relief: "Bejar being the frontier however must be for some time the Theatre of War and as such will be exposed to many hardships & inconvenience." At the end of August he ordered Col. Francisco Ruiz to visit the town and use his knowledge to ferret our disloyal persons. To the friends of Texas the general offered scant relief: personal protection and promises to pay for the articles they furnished to the army. Property that the military claimed to be public would be repossessed from private hands; those who drove off their cattle toward the Rio Grande would be treated as enemies. Even in the early fall a harsh regimen continued to dominate the community. On September 17 Seguín received orders to recruit a full brigade and a militia force to replace the small regular company previously stationed in the town. His instructions allowed use of military justice to preserve order "provided that sever[e] punishment does not extend to loss of life or limb."

Refugees hiding in the east fared hardly better than the Bexareños remaining closer to home. Seguín and Antonio Menchaca did not gain leave to retrieve their families from Nacogdoches until mid-July. The effects of a fever epidemic still lingered a month later when they set out for home on what proved a traumatic journey. For much of the time only Menchaca felt well enough either to lead the wagon train or attend to the sick. They arrived home to find the town still largely deserted and, "to crown their misfortunes," as Seguín recalled years later, "their fields laid waste, and their cattle destroyed or dispersed." His own ranch had been "despoiled" either "by the retreating enemy, [or] had been wasted by our own army; ruin and misery met me on my return."

The devastation may have seemed like a sudden transformation to the refugees, but it had in fact begun months earlier and affected all property owners whether they stayed home or fled. Seguín should not have been much surprised, for he had issued receipts for goods offered to or impressed by the army from other affluent Tejanos like the Navarros and José Antonio de la Garza. Life and property continued to be in danger as late as mid-October 1836 when a raiding party from Mexico entered San Antonio in search of plunder and perhaps revenge. Seguín, then a Colonel, still offered the local population little in the way of security other than the lame advice of driving their cattle out of the war zone. Those who clung to their homes in contravention of this policy were even regarded as "pretended friends" of Texas by the leading newspaper of the Republic.

In the communities of Victoria, Goliad, and Refugio, the people experienced problems similar to those of the Bexareños but made worse by several factors. When the centralists troops arrived in the spring of 1836, most of the Mexican residents had stayed at home and made their peace with the new order. Since Urrea sought to win support from the local population and left but a small force of occupation behind as he marched east, the inhabitants lived under a relatively light-handed rule through the late spring. In contrast to the situation in Béxar, few of the natives celebrated the retreat of the centralist army in the second half of May. The withdrawal occurred in two phases, first by the division under Filisola, followed closely by that of Urrea.

These generals agreed that the retreat left the people in desperate position but launched into a protracted debate about who should be held responsible. Urrea blamed Filisola for ordering the evacuation and leaving the locals behind in a state of such depravity that no army could possibly subsist there, much less offer protection. Filisola claimed that he had attempted to prepare Goliad as a base for operations, a policy that Urrea had undermined by spreading panic as he passed through on the road to Matamoros. Further, the latter general allegedly had impressed so many draft animals and carts that the people had no means of fulfilling his advice to accompany the centralist army in retreat. However vigorously they debated the matter of blame, the two leaders agreed that many Tejanos had fled with the Mexican army and that those who stayed behind had been left defenseless to cope with a mean-spirited, vengeful Texas force. Neither general bothered to record popular responses, but one other officer did. The people, he wrote in his diary, expressed surprise at being compelled to abandon their property and retreat with the army: "The residents of Goliad, who had suffered much, became quite angry with us and insulted us, saying that we were fleeing as cowards from a handful of adventurers."

Many of the area Tejanos remained on their homelands, either because they lacked the means to flee, chose to resist, or felt themselves safe because they had never voluntarily supported the centralist cause. However, their previous loyalties counted for little in the summer of 1836. The doomsayers had been right; the Texas army arrived on the scene in a vindictive mood, already disposed to hate Mexicans. Their attitude worsened with the discovery of the grisly remains of the victims of the Goliad massacre.

Poor discipline added to the indiscriminate nature of army policies, as did the weakness of the commissary, which forced commanders to rely on local provisions. Limited in power at first by its small numbers, the army soon grew from four hundred to two thousand. An advanced unit under Col. Sidney Sherman camped near Victoria on May 23, looking for provisions and spies among the citizens, thus setting the tone for subsequent army policies. Rusk arrived there before the end of the month and extended the military influence to Goliad and San Patricio by sending out companies to forage for more supplies and probe for traitors. The commander of one such expedition reported on May 30 that he had found few arms and no documentary evidence to implicate the inhabitants of the ranches he had raided. Nevertheless, he impressed horses and intended to arrest enough family heads to serve as "examples" but not so many as to leave the women entirely defenseless.

His and other groups of soldiers continued these forays in the next few days, reaching all the way to the Nueces River. On June 2 Captains H. Teal and H. W. Karnes reported an adverse response to these activities. Some "Mexicans citizens . . . stated that they was at there Ranch and some of our scouts came up and took them prisoner with some others and robed of there guns and there horses," threatening to remove them to Victoria. The officers protested these attacks for undermining support among the inhabitants, who had responded by fleeing with their cattle. The "rascooly" civilians had used army outrages to convince many of the "old settlers" that "they wood all be killed and they think that you are after them as hard as you can march."

Many of these arrests, insults, and property confiscations resulted from the excesses of soldiers acting outside of army control. Several observers shared this conclusion. John J. Linn's account of the outrages against area Tejanos attributed them to soldiers, especially new recruits from the United States, who operated from a "creed [of] the total extermination of the Mexican race and the appropriation of their property to the individual use of the exterminators." He praised the commander for attempting to control these attacks against civilians and for offering "asylum" to Fernando de León. This head of the Victoria family that had lent so much support to the Texas cause suffered a bushwhacking while at army headquarters. A veteran of this period concurred in absolving Rusk of blame for these disgraceful attacks against the persons and property of the De Leones; he attributed the outrages to adventurers who excused their plundering by false allegations of their victims' unfriendliness. Yet, this account made it clear that the general had failed either to obtain a return of stolen goods or to control the band of army outlaws.

Further, army leaders also seized civilian property in large quantities. Wealthier ranchers and merchants turned over not only cattle but also wagons, mules, oxen, rum, salt, and tobacco. The quartermaster, other officers, and even the commander himself issued some receipts for these goods, but much of what they took went undocumented and thus uncompensated. María Antonio de la Garza, of Victoria, surrendered around sixty head of cattle to the Texas army and received no certificate of impressment for over a year. Luckily, she managed to gain Rusk's endorsement of her claim, with an inscription that revealed much about the process. She had, in fact, "placed her cattle at the disposition of the army and many of them were used," wrote the general, "what number or quality I am unable to say."

Rusk's policy may have been haphazard at first, but it soon became purposeful: throughout the western frontier the people would be removed and their land despoiled of its most valuable property, cattle. This strategy would provision the Texas army, deny support to a threatened enemy reinvasion, and remedy the irritant of civilian-military conflict. Tejanos, who comprised virtually all the people of this broad region, would suffer loss of their possessions, livelihood, and liberty so that the Revolution might be furthered. The Tory behavior of the area hardly served to excuse this oppressive policy, since a majority of that persuasion had already fled with the centralist forces or in response to attacks by the army of occupation in early summer. Most who remained and suffered from this forced evacuation had been loyal to the Texas Revolution. As in Béxar, Rusk's strategy was not implemented in a coherent fashion, but the army did compel substantial numbers to leave their homes.

On June 19 Rusk informed the secretary of war of the issuance of orders "to all the Families Mexicans and all to fall back at once and clear the Country." He offered residents of the entire region between the Guadalupe and Nueces rivers a grim choice—to flee either to Mexico or to a part of Texas out of the war zone, driving out their herds or surrendering them to the control of the army. In actuality, the Tejanos could not protect their properties because they lacked means or opportunity to remove possessions and must leave lands and homes to the mercy of the military. Feigning ignorance of the policy did not provide an effective shield. "Some of the Mexican families," in Rusk's words, "are pretending that they have no orders to remove," but he handled this ploy by reiterating his policy and sending cavalry units to enforce it. He paid particular attention to forcing the evacuation of the leading family of Victoria, the De Leones, by boarding them under guard onto vessels routed to New Orleans. The ranks of evacuees included Benavides, whose revolutionary service had most recently included fighting against Urrea, and José María Carbajal, also a staunch and early supporter of the federalist cause. The army loaded about eighty members of this extended family on the *Durango* at Matagorda Bay on June 26, bringing a large measure of success to Rusk's orders to "dispose of the Families."

He intended to make a complete evacuation of all the Tejano-dominated areas, but enforcement became less rigorous away from Victoria. Carlos de la Garza gave no response to the soldiers who brought the removal orders to his ranch near Refugio and thus led his people into successful resistance. This act capped his thorough and consistent opposition to the Texas cause. In spite of this glaring exception, Rusk's otherwise ruthless policy allowed him to police the region more successfully for the remainder of the summer. Into the fall Texas authorities continued to issue orders to drive the livestock belonging to unfriendly citizens out of the valleys of the San Antonio and Nueces rivers.

The ravages of the war and immediate postwar period left a permanent mark on the entire area. For years the De Leones remained in exile in Louisiana while their Anglo neighbors or newcomers to the area piled up legal claims to Tejano property. Exparriates Bei Carbajal never resettled in Texas; others in the family came back only after much had been taken over by others and the cattle had been long-since lost. Poverty de once-powerful clan both during and after their exile. The population centers of tl also underwent transformation. Victoria became what one historian has described a. Anglo-American town, dominated by an army and many newcomers that distrusted ar. the Mexicans." Goliad and Refugio were largely destroyed during the fighting of the spring of 1836. Some of the Tejano residents were killed in the war, and many more became exiles south of the Rio Grande or exiles from their native land under the unrelenting pressure of the Texas army of occupation. Though exceptional ones like Carlos de la Garza remained to keep the Tejano heritage alive, the area as a whole suffered large-scale depopulation.

Many Tejanos attempted to save their birthrights and perform their patriotic duties by volunteering for military service in the summer of 1836. Near the end of the year the *Telegraph and Texas Register* reported that "Col. Seguín, the untiring friend of Texas," commanded a force of about eighty "Americans" in the regular army and two hundred "Mexican citizen volunteers." Not nearly that number received the bounty grants due for service for the period May to December, 1836. Of those who did, about 40 percent had participated in earlier campaigns and tended to be young (in the mid-twenties, on the average) and single (62 percent). Virtually all of these veterans had followed Seguín into the army from the Béxar municipality. The Tejanos who joined for the first time in this period possessed as a group much less uniformity. Though the largest number volunteered in the Company "B" Cavalry of Bexareños led by Seguín's lieutenant, Manuel Flores, many served in one of the other units, usually some kind of mounted rangers, formed at various times and places in the summer and fall of 1836. Next to Béxar, Nacogdoches yielded the largest number; the region from Victoria to San Patricio, at that time being largely depopulated by Rusk, produced scarcely any soldiers. In personal characteristics these first-time volunteers showed more variety—they were older by an average of five years, some being in their fifties, and were more likely to be married than were the earlier Tejano recruits. These attributes suggest a powerful and broad compulsion to demonstrate loyalty to Texas during this time of growing ethnic tensions.

Service of various kinds may have helped to advance the cause of the Tejanos individually or even as a community, as in the case of Béxar, but as a whole Texas policy toward citizens of Mexican descent had become capricious by the summer of 1836. Their problems steammed mostly from living in a year-long war zone where they suffered from military policies of harsh material exploitation and ruthless denial of liberty. Well before the end of summer sweeping anti-Mexican prejudice had largely triumphed over restraint. Army-enforced deportations and property confiscations had become indiscriminate under General Rusk, with the burden falling as heavily on the patriotic Bexareños and Victorianos as on the defiant Tories of Refugio. For Tejanos the Revolution established a tradition of trouble and portended a future of overwhelming governmental discrimination and societal prejudice.

Determined Valor and Desperate Courage

STEPHEN L. HARDIN

S tephen L. Hardin teaches at McMurry University in Abilene. His books include *Texian Iliad: A Military History of the Texas Revolution, 1835–1836* (1994) and *Texian Macabre: The Melancholy Tale of a Hanging in Early Houston* (2007). Dr. Hardin served as history consultant for John Lee Hancock's 2004 film, *The Alamo*.

The battle of the Alamo will never be forgotten. In this selection, Hardin discusses the resolute Texian defense of the old Spanish mission, which fell to Santa Anna's forces on the morning of March 6, 1836. ✎

★ ★

Alamo defenders watched their adversaries pour into Béxar in what seemed an unending stream. So that the rebels would not misunderstand their intent, Mexicans hoisted the red flag of no quarter atop San Fernando Church. Then in accordance with established procedures of siege warfare, they offered the garrison an opportunity to surrender and made their requirements known: "The Mexican army cannot come to terms under any conditions with rebellious foreigners to whom there is no other recourse left, if they wish to save their lives, than to place themselves immediately at the disposal of the Supreme Government from whom alone they may expect clemency after some considerations are taken up." Travis informed the enemy courier that a response would be forthcoming. And it was—a single shot hurled from the eighteen-pounder. There could be no mistaking the meaning of such a succinct reply.

With the formalities out of the way, the Mexican cannoneers set about reducing the adobe walls. Once they had knocked down the walls, the garrison would have to surrender in the face of overwhelming odds. Although Jameson had once referred to the works as "Fortress Alamo," he had clearly done so in jest. "The Alamo never was built by a military people for a fortress," he had explained to Houston, "tho' it is strong, there is not a redoubt that will command the whole line of the fort, all is in the plain wall and intended to take advantage with a few pieces of artillery."

Jameson had detected a major drawback; all was, indeed, "in the plain wall." Unfortunately, the advent of heavy cannon had rendered the curtain wall obsolete four centuries earlier, necessitating a complete transformation of defensive positions and siege craft. The most important developments in both were the work of French engineer Marquis Sébastien Le Prestre de Vauban. By the nineteenth century, it was accepted that one would storm a fortress only if no other option were available. Rather, a careful siege with sufficiently powerful artillery placed in prepared trenches would eventually breach a wall, whereupon the garrison would surrender, defeat being a foregone conclusion.

By the standards of its day, the Alamo was certainly no fortress. It lacked mutually supporting strong points—demilunes, bastions, hornworks, ravelines, sally ports, and the like. There were simply no strong points from which its defenders could oppose an assault. Nor was it logistically self-sustaining; the defenders could not hope to outlast the besiegers. Although the fort contained a good water well, the food supply might have lasted four weeks at most. It did not even command a significant terrain feature, such as a vital pass or port. A perceptive Texian, Dr. J. H. Barnard, identified the chief disadvantage of both La Bahía and the Alamo: "Situated in an open prairie country, they controlled no passes, nor obstructed any route that could check or impede the march of an enemy army. They simply defended what ground they stood upon, and what their guns could reach, and no more, and were from fifty to seventy miles distant from any settlers upon which they could rely for supplies and succor."

Of course, the Spanish priests and presidial troopers who had constructed Mission San Antonio de Valero in 1718 never intended it to function as a fortress. The adobe walls were more than sufficient to stop the arrows of the hostile Indians and to keep friendly neophytes from escaping. The abandoned mission had served as the barracks for the dragoons of the Flying Company of San José y Santiago del Alamo de Parras, who gave it the unit's name. For convenience, locals shortened the post's name to the Alamo. Presidial troopers rested easily behind those thick walls; the Comanches did not have artillery.

But Santa Anna did. The chances are remote that any Texian inside the Alamo, including the lawyer-turned-engineer Green Jameson, was aware of Vauban's system of fortification. They were not, however, blind to the obvious. Travis and Bowie were firm in their determination to defend the Alamo, but both understood it would be only a matter of days before the enemy artillery breached the walls; they were well aware that their survival depended on the speed with which Texians rallied to their aid. They made that clear on the first day of the siege when the co-commanders wrote Fannin in Goliad: "We have but little Provisions, but enough to serve us till you and your men arrive. We deem it unnecessary to repeat to a brave officer, who knows his duty, that we call on him for assistance." Despite all the hyperbole about preferring to "die in these ditches" and "victory or death," Bowie and Travis were not suicidal. They simply could not imagine that fellow Texians, once aware of their perilous position, would not rush to their aid.

Neither could Santa Anna. He was more concerned about Texian reinforcements coming to break the siege than the meager force bottled up inside the fort. He did not intend to be caught in Béxar as Cós had been. When he heard rumors that two hundred men from Goliad were on the march to relieve the Alamo, Santa Anna ordered General Ramírez y Sesma to intercept them with his cavalry. In addition to sending Ramírez y Sesma's horsemen, he also dispatched the Jiménez infantry battalion out in search of the enemy.

Mexican officers never seemed to worry about the Alamo itself; when its food was exhausted, its fall was certain. His Excellency dismissed the post as an "irregular fortification hardly worthy of the name." Never missing a chance to criticize Santa Anna, de la Peña described the Alamo as "an irregular fortification without flank fires which a wise general would have taken with insignificant losses." Filisola agreed: "By merely placing twenty artillery pieces properly, that poor wall could not have withstood one hour of cannon fire without being reduced to rubble."

Perhaps, but the Mexicans did not have twenty pieces of artillery. They had brought fewer than ten light fieldpieces. Artillerymen customarily relied upon heavy siege guns to reduce enemy fortifications; such weapons were on the way but could not arrive until March 7 or 8. Lacking heavy ordnance, the gunners had to place their smaller cannon closer to the walls, but venturing within two hundred yards of the fort in daylight was an invitation to the deadly Texian riflemen. Working after dark, therefore, the Mexicans began digging a series of entrenchments that grew nearer to the old walls each night.

Inside the Alamo, Bowie's health continued to decline. On the second day of the siege, he collapsed completely. The malady must have been a form of respiratory ailment, for it was variously described as "hasty consumption" and "typhoid pneumonia." (Contrary to persistent legend, Bowie did *not* fall from a gun platform.) Whatever his affliction, Bowie could no longer function as commander, so he instructed his volunteers to obey Travis.

Now in full command, Travis prepared to meet the enemy. If the Mexicans made a frontal assault with infantry, the defenders could inflict heavy losses with rifles and artillery. Anglo-Celtic frontiersmen reared on stories of the victory of Jackson's riflemen over British regulars at New Orleans were naturally drawn to the thick walls around the Alamo. The high adobe ramparts would be as impenetrable as the cotton bales that had shielded their forebears a generation before. Far from being bent on self-sacrifice, Travis and the garrison remained in the fort because they were convinced that they could hold it until reinforcements arrived.

Texian rifles continued to take their toll on the enemy. Atop walls that were in some places twelve feet high, defenders could easily hit unwary Mexicans at two hundred yards. The Mexicans' Brown Bess muskets, on the other hand, were ineffective at ranges of more than seventy yards. The "mountaineers" and "hunters," for whom Tornell had expressed such contempt, soon proved their worth as marksmen, dropping men at ranges the Mexicans thought impossible.

Travis wisely placed Crockett and a unit of skilled riflemen at what seemed the weakest link in the fort's defensive perimeter, the low picket barricade between the chapel and the south wall. The Mexicans soon had reason to avoid the area opposite Crockett's post.

Crockett and his riflemen could kill at long range, but in the event of an enemy assault, the defenders greatest assets would be their cannon. Neill had scrounged some twenty-one pieces of ordnance, but Jameson had not mounted all of them by the time the siege began. Sutherland recalled that "not more than about twenty were put to use during the siege." That figure was confirmed by a number of Mexican reports. In a diagram of the fort, Sánchez-Navarro depicted tubes lying on the ground, supporting Sutherland's testimony that the defenders had not mounted all their artillery.

Best estimates are that Jameson had judiciously mounted nineteen pieces at various points. He placed the eighteen-pounder on the south-west corner to cover the town. Travis commanded a battery of nine-pounders on the north wall. In the chapel, three twelve-pounders covered the area east of the fort. One of the guns was a gunade, a stubby, short-range naval gun of the period. No one has ever determined why a ship's gunade had been taken to a post 150 miles from the nearest coast, but Jameson did not stop to question Providence and reportedly mounted the seagoing ordnance on the west wall.

Despite its fortunate supply of artillery, the garrison nevertheless faced some serious disadvantages. The fort was much too large for so few men to defend. The main plaza contained almost three acres, making the defensive perimeter almost a quarter of a mile long. The small number of Texians could not possibly defend a perimeter that large; it was a case of too much space and too few riflemen. It was also a matter of too few cannoneers for all the cannon. Prevailing doctrine allotted a six-man crew to each piece of ordnance. Travis began the siege with about 150 men; if he had followed that rule and manned all available cannon, 114 of his men would have been assigned as gunners. Travis, of course, did no such thing. Fewer men could fire a cannon if necessary, just not so quickly. In fact, it is unlikely that more than three gunners manned any piece of Alamo artillery. Even at that, rifles along the 440-yard perimeter were spread pitifully thin.

Both riflemen and gunners were vulnerable to enemy counterfire. The Alamo, built as a mission, did not have firing ports. Jameson seemed to have constructed makeshift catwalks, but when the Mexicans approached within the seventy-yard range of their muskets, the defender's upper bodies were exposed. Those men who fired from atop the small rooms along the west wall were even more exposed. Most of the cannon were positioned to fire not through the breastworks but over them. The men had constructed gun emplacements by piling dirt against the inside of the walls, but this arrangement left artillery and artillerymen silhouetted against the sky. Colonel Juan Almonte recorded that on the second day of the siege, Mexican artillery fire dismounted two pieces of Alamo ordnance, including the prized eighteen-pounder. Texians soon had the guns back in operation, but the incident revealed their precarious position.

Once the Mexicans had their artillery in place, they maintained an almost constant fire upon the Alamo. On February 24, in his famous letter addressed to the "People of Texas & all Americans in the world," Travis reported, "I have sustained a continual Bombardment & cannonade for 24 hours & have not lost a man." Although the Texians were lucky not to have suffered any casualties, that happy consequence likely stemmed from the fact that the enemy was directing most of its fire against the wall. Almonte recorded that during the night of February 25 the Mexicans erected two more batteries. Prudence demanded they work at night; that day "in random firing the [Texians] wounded 4 of the Cazadores de Matamoros battalion, and 2 of the battalion of Jimenes, and killed one corporal and a soldier of the battalion of Matamoros."

At first Travis had matched the enemy shot for shot, but by day four he realized how much powder and ball that policy was consuming. The defenders needed to conserve ammunition in the event of an assault. Crockett's men were the exception. Their long rifles wasted less powder with better results. The deadly rifles rarely missed their marks. The remainder of the garrison, frustrated by a growing feeling of impotence, could only sit and endure.

Exhausted defenders grew steadily weaker. Travis did not have enough men to rotate sentries, so each of them slept at his post. Conditions worsened as a blue norther swept through, dropping the temperature to thirty-nine degrees. A party of defenders sallied out of the fort to forage for firewood but were repulsed by Mexican skirmishers equipped with the Baker rifle that could kill at 170 yards. Texians accorded these enemy riflemen more respect than they did the line infantry with smoothbore muskets and so scurried back to the safety of the fort.

Both Suzanna Dickenson, wife of Artillery Captain Almeron Dickenson, and Colonel Travis noted Crockett's efforts to bolster the flagging morale of the garrison. Mrs. Dickenson recalled that he often cheered the troops with his fiddle. Travis reported in a letter to Houston that "the Hon. David Crockett was seen at all points, animating the men to their duty." Even the stricken Bowie had his cot brought out in the open, where he attempted to encourage the men from his sickbed. Despite all efforts, the strain began to tell. Arkansas artilleryman Henry Warnell bitterly expressed their anxieties: "I'd much rather be out on that open prairie. . . . I don't like to be penned up like this." But in more thoughtful moments, others realized that without cover they could not last an hour against vastly superior Mexican numbers. By the seventh day, the men could see through the desperate attempts to boost their spirits. Only reinforcements could do that.

At least a few were on their way. On February 24 Travis had dispatched Captain Albert Martin to the settlements with his "Victory or Death" letter. The courier rode all night and most of the next day to reach his hometown of Gonzales, some seventy miles away. To his commander's plea for assistance, he added one of his own: "Since the above was written I heard a very heavy

Canonade during the whole day [and] think there must have been an attack made upon the alamo[.] We were short of Ammunition when I left[.] Hurry on all the men you can in haste[.]" Alamo messengers John W. Smith and Dr. John Sutherland had reached the town earlier, and Martin's arrival heightened the sense of urgency. The proud men of Gonzales had been the first to shoulder their rifles against centralist oppression; how could they refuse now when fellow Texians needed their help.

The Gonzales Ranging Company of Mounted Volunteers boasted a grandiose title but only twenty-two effectives. With news of the fighting, a few others joined up. The company was a frontier porpourri: New York hatter George Kimball; nineteen-year-old newlywed Johnnie Kellogg; and Béxar carpenter John W. Smith, eager to rejoin his Alamo comrades. The oldest, at forty-one, was Isaac Millsaps; the youngest, William P. King, was only sixteen. By the time of their departure on February 27, their ranks had increased to twenty-five, and another eight joined on the march. Travis had made it clear that a "thousand or more" Mexicans surrounded the fort; fully aware of the disparity of numbers these thirty-two men gamely rode on. Numbers did not always decide a fight; in October, eighteen Gonzales men had held off a hundred Mexican dragoons until their neighbors arrived. Now the fighting men of Gonzales were riding to repay their debt.

The Gonzales volunteers reached the outskirts of Béxar on the night of February 29. They had been fortunate; Santa Anna was expecting Fannin's relief force to come from La Bahía and had therefore detailed Ramírez y Sesma to patrol the Béxar-Goliad road to the southeast. Approaching from the northeast, the Gonzales contingent encountered little opposition. They could see the clusters of Mexican campfires and hear the calls of the sentries. Stealthily making their way through the brush, the men felt their way toward the walls looming ahead in the darkness. Just before three o'clock, they were nearing the fort when a skittish Alamo sentry fired, wounding one of the Gonzales men in the foot. The rest called out to stop shooting. The defenders eagerly swung open the gates to welcome the long-awaited reinforcements. Their spirits must have fallen when they saw how few there were.

March 1 was, nevertheless, a day of celebration inside the Alamo. Travis, of course, had hoped for many more than thirty-two men, but the Gonzales contingent had at least shown that a determined force could make it through the Mexican cordon, and surely more were on the way. The irrepressible Crockett played his fiddle, and Scotsman John McGregor joined in on the bagpipes. In honor of the new arrivals, Travis even allowed the gunners two precious shots to let Santa Anna know that they had not forgotten him. Knowing ammunition was in short supply, the men sighted carefully. The first ball crashed into the town's Military Plaza; the next tore through the roof of an adjoining house. The gunners had no way of knowing it, but the building served as Santa Anna's head-quarters. That shot might have produced propitious results had His Excellency been there to receive it.

March 2 saw a return to siege routine. The Mexicans continued their cannonading, and the defenders observed that the enemy artillery edged even closer to the walls. Travis could not imagine why Fannin and his four hundred men had not arrived. It had been nine days since he and Bowie had summoned him, plenty of time for the ninety-five-mile journey.

The next day, Travis poured out his feelings in a letter to the Independence Co[...]ing at Washington-on-the-Brazos:

> *Col. Fannin is said to be on the march to this place with reinforcements, bu[...]*
> *not true, as I have repeatedly sent to him for aid without receiving any. . . . [...]*
> *colonies alone for aid; unless it arrives soon, I shall have to fight the enemy[...]*
> *terms. I will, however, do the best I can under the circumstances; and I fe[...]*
> *that the determined valor and desperate courage, heretofore exhibited by m[...]*
> *not fail them in the last struggle; and although they may be sacrificed to the vengeance*
> *of a Gothic enemy, the victory will cost the enemy dear, that it will be worse for him*
> *than defeat.*

Travis had begun to accept the fall of the Alamo as a distinct likelihood, but he was not a man with a death wish. He never stopped calling on Texians to rally to his aid. "I hope your honorable body will hasten on reinforcements, ammunition, and provisions to our aid as soon as possible. We have provisions for twenty days for the men we have. Our supply of ammunition is limited." In his letters to the Convention, Travis continued to stress the vital importance of Béxar, which he described as the "great and decisive ground." Better to fight Santa Anna on the frontier, he argued, than "to suffer a war of devastation to rage in our settlements."

Travis also wrote his close friend Jesse Grimes, revealing more of his true feelings. Now as always, he asserted, the men of the Alamo were staunch supporters of Texas Independence:

> *Let the Convention go on and make a declaration of independence, and we will then*
> *understand, and the world will understand, what we are fighting for. If independence is*
> *not declared, I shall lay down my arms, and so will the men under my command. But*
> *under the flag of independence, we are ready to peril our lives a hundred times a day, and*
> *to drive away the monster who is fighting under a blood-red flag, threatening to murder*
> *all prisoners and make Texas a waste desert. . . . If my countrymen do not rally to my*
> *relief, I am determined to perish in the defense of this place, and my bones shall reproach*
> *my country for her neglect.*

Travis's fiery words were in vain. On March 3, courier James Butler Bonham arrived from Goliad with the grim news that Fannin would not be coming. He had received the messages from Travis and Bowie calling for his assistance and on February 28 had actually begun the march to Béxar. But Fannin had never been personally committed to the relief of the Alamo, and when an ox cart broke down less than a mile from Goliad, his resolve evaporated. Accepting the advice of a council of his officers, he called off the expedition and led his men back to La Bahía.

That same evening, Fannin explained his decision in a letter to Acting Governor James W. Robinson. Some have criticized Fannin's failure to relieve the Alamo, but from a strategic standpoint his reasons were valid: "It is now obvious that the Enemy have entered Texas at two points, for the purpose of attacking Béxar & this place—The first has been attacked and we may expect the enemy here momentarily—Both places are important—and at this time particularly so."

ed that his supplies were running short: "We have not in the garrison supplies of Bread
for a single day and as yet but little Beef and should our Supplies be cut off our situation
ll be, to say the least—disagreeable." He expressed sympathy for the valiant "volunteers now
shut in Béxar" but concluded that permitting his command to be cut off with them would ill-
serve the interests of Texas. Abandoning Goliad would leave the eastern door open to Urrea's
advance. Travis and his men would have to manage without Fannin's help.

By day eleven of the siege, the constant battering by Mexican artillery had weakened the walls.
Santa Anna had established a battery within "musket shot" of the north wall. At that range, he
did not need siege guns; each round shot hammered the crumbling adobe until a portion of
the wall collapsed. Jameson directed work parties throughout the night, buttressing the wall
with odd pieces of timber. The chief engineer realized that these were only stop-gap measures.
In the event of a determined attack, the north wall could not hold.

On March 5, day twelve of the siege, Santa Anna called a meeting of his officers to discuss the
possibility of an assault. Most of the officers present were amazed that the question was even
being considered. The walls were already crumbling, and in two or three days the siege guns
would arrive. Many argued that, surrounded by such a superior force, the defenders were no real
threat. No Texian relief column had been sighted, so there was no reason for haste. They needed
only to wait until the garrison's provisions ran out, when Travis would have no choice but to
yield. Lieutenant Colonel de la Peña recorded that the majority of officers "were of the opinion
that victory over a handful of men concentrated in the Alamo did not call for a great sacrifice."

Despite these reasonable objections, Santa Anna stubbornly insisted on attacking. He cited
morale as a factor, claiming that "an assault would infuse our soldiers with that enthusiasm of
the first triumph that would make them superior in the future to those of the enemy." General
Ramírez y Sesma—no doubt still fancying himself as Murat—eagerly agreed with His Excellency. Oddly, so did Colonel Almonte, who normally demonstrated better judgment. It became
obvious that Santa Anna had already decided; the meeting had merely been a matter of form.
De la Peña recalled that most of the officers were horrified at Santa Anna's decision but "chose
silence, knowing that he would not tolerate opposition."

Inside the Alamo, Travis had also assembled his men for a conclave. According to legend, he
drew a line in the dust with his saber, inviting all who were resolved to stay and die with him
to cross. Evidence does not support the tale, but apparently Travis did gather the men for a
conference. Mrs. Dickenson remembered that he "asked the command that if any desired
to escape, now was the time to let it be known, and to step out of ranks." Shortly thereafter
Frenchman Louis Rose is said to have escaped, which may mean that Travis told each man to
decide for himself whether to stay or go.

Reliable Mexican accounts, however, suggest a different story. According to them, a *bexareña*
left the fort after the meeting. She told Santa Anna that morale was low and that defenses were
crumbling. De la Peña recounted:

> *Travis's resistance was on the verge of being overcome; for several days his followers had*
> *been urging him to surrender, giving the lack of food and the scarcity of munitions as*

reasons, but he had quieted their restlessness with hope of quick relief, something not difficult for them to believe since they had seen some reinforcements arrive. Nevertheless, they had pressed him so hard that on the 5th he promised them that if no help arrived on that day they would surrender the next day or would try to escape under the cover of darkness; these facts were given to us by a lady from Bejar, a Negro who was the only male who escaped, and several women who were inside and were rescued by Colonels Morales and Minion.

General Filisola also recalled that the garrison had considered the possibility of surrender:

On that same evening [March 5] about nightfall it was reported that Travis Barnet [William Barret Travis], commander of the enemy garrison, through the intermediary of a woman, proposed to the general in chief that they would surrender arms and fort with everybody in it with the only condition of saving his life and that of all his comrades in arms. However, the answer had come back that they should surrender unconditionally, without guarantees, not even for life itself, since there should be no guarantees for traitors. With this reply it is clear that all were determined to lose their existence, selling it as dearly as possible.

The prospects of an honorable surrender seemed to have alarmed Santa Anna. De la Peña speculated that the general was determined to precipitate an assault before the garrison could yield. A capitulation would not create a favorable "sensation"; the president-general "would have regretted taking the Alamo without clamor and without bloodshed, for some believe that without these there is no glory." There was no need for concern. There would be clamor and bloodshed aplenty.

The Mexican army would assault in Bonaparte's column formation. The self-proclaimed Napoleon of the West intended to hurl his troops toward the Alamo like irresistible missiles, terrify the rebels with overwhelming mass, and win a glorious victory to add to his laurels. Santa Anna organized his force into five units; four columns would attack from every point of the compass, while he personally commanded the reserves. The lancers would form a cordon around the fort "to prevent the possibility of escape."

The attack orders of March 5 set the onslaught for five o'clock the next morning. The Mexican artillery fell silent later that afternoon. Officers told soldiers to get plenty of rest, for they would be called to arms at midnight to take their positions. The general hoped that weary rebels would also take advantage of the lull to get some sleep. He intended to surprise the garrison. If the Mexicans approached the fort silently, they could be over the walls before the bleary-eyed defenders reached their stations.

The men of the Alamo welcomed the silence, ominous though it was. For twelve days, they had endured an almost constant bombardment. Travis posted a few men in listening posts outside the fort and dispatched sixteen-year-old Jim Allen with his last request for assistance. Then, succumbing to lack of sleep, he turned the watch over to Adjutant John Baugh and collapsed on his cot. All was quiet inside the fort as the stroke of midnight heralded the beginning of day thirteen of the siege: March 6, 1836.

At that same moment, the Mexican camp came alive, contrasting sharply with the stillness of the Alamo. Sergeants tapped their sleeping men awake with the wooden staffs that were the symbols of their rank; when that failed, the toe of their boots roused groggy recruits. Sappers distributed ladders and crowbars; noncoms saw that all shako straps were firmly fastened; officers made sure that all men were wearing shoes or sandals—proper footgear would be crucial when scaling walls. And, of course, weapons were inspected. The general's order had been specific: "The arms, principally the bayonets, should be in perfect order."

By 5:00 A.M. all was in readiness. The morning was chilly and many of the troops had been shivering in place for hours. Column commanders informed His Excellency that the men were becoming restless. Finally at 5:30, Santa Anna gave the word to move out.

All went smoothly as the Mexicans moved silently through the early morning moonlight. A massed column provided an excellent target, but it was a necessary formation for controlling recruits who were boxed in by steadier veterans. Cós, commanding the lead column, marched toward the northwest corner. Colonel Francisco Duque, at the head of the second column, angled from the northwest toward the patched breach in the north wall. Colonel José María Romero came in behind the fort from the east. Colonel Juan Morales led his column toward the low parapet by the chapel, supposedly the fort's soft spot. Lines of light infantry skirmishers fanned out several yards in advance of the columns; armed with Baker rifles, it was their assignment to pick off any defenders who showed their heads. They caught the snoozing Texian sentinels outside the walls; an efficient bayonet thrust, a blade drawn across the throat, and they died quickly—but more critical, silently. Unopposed and undetected, the columns approached inexorably nearer to the walls.

Bathed in bright moonlight that cast eerie, unearthly shadows across the landscape, the Alamo loomed ahead. The tension finally became unbearable. A soldier deep within one of the columns shouted, "Viva Santa Anna!" "Viva la Republica!" another countered. Soon hundreds of voices filled the air. Santa Anna was incensed by these "imprudent huzzas," for he knew the noise would alert the slumbering rebels.

It did. John Baugh heard the clamor and then saw the columns, already within musket range of the walls. The adjutant raced across the plaza, adding his voice to the cacophony from outside. "Colonel Travis! The Mexicans are coming." Joe, Travis's slave, slept in the same room with his master, and each staggered from his cot, grabbed his weapons, and rushed to the north wall battery. Travis shouted as he ran: "Come on, boys, the Mexicans are upon us and we'll give them Hell!" He must have wondered why the sentries outside the walls had not sounded the alarm. When he reached the battery and saw how far the enemy had advanced, he knew the answer.

Texian gunners had loaded their cannon. Lacking proper canister shot, they had crammed their ordnance with chopped-up horseshoes, links of chain, nails, bits of door hinges— every piece of jagged scrap metal they could scavenge. Packing that lethal load, the artillery doubled as giant shotguns. In that light and at that range, they could not miss their massed targets.

A gust of metal fragments swept the columns like a "terrible shower." The close-packed bodies of the soldiers soaked up the force of the scatter shot. Rusty shards slammed home, slowed as they plowed through the ranks, and finally stopped, lodged in flesh.

Then came round shot. Nine-pound iron balls probed further into the mass, gouging great swaths of destruction. Far worse than the roar of cannon was the sickening thud of iron striking flesh. The attackers were frightfully exposed; de la Peña watched in horror as "a single cannon volley did away with half the company of chasseurs from Toluca." Huddled together as they were in tight formation, even those untouched by enemy fire were splattered with blood and bits of flesh torn from their less fortunate friends. Bashing bodies, round shot paid multiple dividends; flying bone fragments proved as lethal as grapeshot. Those trapped inside the column could see little, but they heard the bedlam—the anguished screams of mangled comrades.

But Texians were also suffering losses. Rebel riflemen had to reveal themselves in order to fire on the attackers; the accurate Baker rifles swept the parapets, and at this range even Brown Bess could kill. The fort was lit from within by gunfire. Outlined against the light, the men atop the walls "could not remain for a single second without being killed." Travis was among the first to fall. He had just emptied both barrels of his shotgun into a column when a slug smacked into his forehead, sending him tumbling down the earthen ramp. With his master down and dying, Joe took refuge within one of the rooms along the west wall.

The Mexicans, shattered by grape and round shot, took scant notice of Texian casualties. Facing this deadly welter of fire, some demoralized recruits faltered, but the officers and noncoms stood firm. Sergeants beat the men back into ranks with their thick staffs, the officers with the flat of their swords. The men could not retreat far, for at their rear were the lancers Santa Anna had posted to prevent the escape of his own troops as well as the Texians.

The Mexican assault troops were taking heavy casualties, but ragged formations regrouped and drove forward. Viewing the debacle, Santa Anna committed the reserves, but stayed out of rifle range himself. Once more, the brave Mexican infantry charged into the maelstrom.

The devastating fire savaged Mexican ranks. Ordered columns were ripped asunder, but still they came. Unit integrity broke down as the columns of Cós and Duque swirled together at the base of the north wall. Advancing from the east, Romero's formation was swept by artillery fire from atop the chapel. To avoid effects of the deadly grapeshot, the column performed a right oblique toward the north wall, where it ran into the intermingled mob of Duque and Cós. Morales's attack against the palisade faltered as well. Contrary to expectations, that portion of the perimeter was anything but weak. In the face of direct fire from a cannon and Crockett's riflemen, the column angled to the left toward the southwest corner and the eighteen-pounder.

Once the surviving Mexicans reached the base of the wall, their problem became one of climbing over. They concentrated their main effort on the north wall and Jameson's makeshift repairs. Travis's nine-pounders, however, had taken a heavy toll. "The few poor ladders that we were bringing had not arrived," a Mexican officer reported, "because their bearers had either perished on the way or escaped." Yet the rough-hewn repairs to the north wall had left numerous gaps and toeholds. Realizing the time had come to conquer or die, the Mexicans began hoisting each other over the jerry-built barricade.

Desperation and sheer mass finally supplanted careful planning. General Juan Amador began the difficult twelve-foot climb over the north wall, challenging his soldiers to follow. The general and his men grappled up and over the parapet and dropped into the plaza below. Amador and his men inside the Alamo located the north wall postern and swung it open. Their comrades flooded through, penetrating the Alamo's defensive perimeter. From that moment, the outcome of the assault was never in doubt.

The Texians abandoned the north wall. As they fell back, Alamo gunners turned their cannon toward the wave of Mexicans rushing through the postern. Combined rifle and artillery fire ripped into the uniformed soldiers pinned against the inside of the wall. But now, when rapid fire was essential, rifles were a disadvantage; the long grooved barrels that rendered them so accurate also made them slow to load. When the fort's guns were swung northward to counter the enemy pouring through the postern, the Morales column, which had taken refuge behind some nearby stone huts, rallied and charged up and over the south wall. The cannoneers were slain before they had time to spike their gun. Seeing the enemy on the front and rear walls, outflanked Texians in the courtyard fell back to the final defensive line inside the long barracks. At the same time, Crockett's riflemen withdrew into the chapel.

Jameson had prepared well. The barracks doors facing the courtyard were buttressed by semicircular parapets of dirt secured with cowhides. From windows and loopholes, the defenders shot down Mexicans in the plaza. But in their haste to fall back to the long barracks, the crews on the northwest battery had failed to spike their guns. Mexicans loaded the captured cannon, swung them around, and systematically blasted each door. Realizing the utter hopelessness of their situation, a few of the rebels tried to surrender. De la Peña remembered their pathetic attempts: "Some . . . desperately cried, 'Mercy, valiant Mexicans,' others poked the points of their bayonets through a hole or a door with a white cloth, the symbol of ceasefire, and some even used their socks." There was a brief lull as Mexicans advanced, but as they entered the quarters they were ruthlessly gunned down by other Texians who "had no thought of surrendering."

Angry Mexicans charged through the shattered openings to finish the work begun by the captured cannon. In the darkened rooms of the long barracks, the adversaries grappled with Bowie knife and bayonet. Having seen their men shot down after flags of truce had been raised, the *soldados* took no prisoners, slaughtering even the wounded. A few Texians sought to escape by bounding over the east wall and running for cover, but the lancers made short work of them. The butchering was repeated in the rooms along the south wall; even the delirious Bowie, too weak to rise from his sickbed, found no mercy. But then, neither would he have asked for it.

The chapel was the last to fall. The Mexicans swung the eighteen-pounder, blew down the sandbags guarding the main entrance, and pushed through by the dozens. Bonham and Dickenson fell beside their cannon on the battery at the rear of the church. Crockett and six of his men fought on until they were literally overwhelmed. This was no longer war; it was wanton slaughter; and General Manuel Fernández Castrillón ordered his soldiers to spare these helpless men.

Even after all the defenders had been killed or captured, dazed Mexicans continued to shoot at shadows. As a cat scurried among the ruins, a superstitious *soldado* shouted: "It is not a cat, but an American!" The feline was immediately killed. One can easily appreciate this wanton blood lust; these men had seen friends mangled by artillery, riddled by rifles, gutted by Bowie knives. Having survived the slaughter themselves, they were taking no chances.

Upon being informed that the Alamo had fallen, Santa Anna ventured into the fort. As he was surveying the carnage, General Castrillón brought forward Crockett and the others. The chivalrous Castrillón attempted to intercede on behalf of the defenseless prisoners, but Santa Anna answered with a "gesture of indignation" and ordered their immediate execution. De la Peña reported that several officers were outraged at the murder of helpless men and refused to enforce the command. But "in order to flatter their commander," nearby staff officers who had not taken part in the assault fell upon Crockett and the others with their swords and hacked them to pieces. De la Peña recorded that "these unfortunates died without complaining and without humiliating themselves before their torturers."

How true to pattern. Crockett's motto—or at least the one attributed to him—had been, "Be sure you're right, then go ahead." Once in Congress, his colleagues had urged him to support President Andrew Jackson's Indian bill. To do otherwise, they assured him, was political suicide. He replied in genuine Crockett style: "I told them I believed it was a wicked, unjust measure, and that I should go against it, let the cost to myself be what it might; . . . that I would sooner be honestly and politically d_____nd, than hypocritically immortalized. . . . I voted against this Indian bill, and my conscience yet tells me that I gave a good honest vote, and one that I believe will not make me ashamed in the day of judgement."

He was, of course, soundly walloped in the next election, but satisfied that he had taken the honorable course, Crockett stubbornly ignored the consequences. Most of those who had fallen alongside him readily understood that brand of righteous bullheadedness. To remain loyal to their upbringing and the legacy of their rebel forebears, resistance to Santa Anna could be their only recourse. Behind the walls of the Alamo, they cast their final vote against centralism, a system they believed "wicked" and "unjust." March 6 was judgment day for them all; like Crockett, none had reason to be ashamed.

Once Upon a Time in Matagorda: The Death of Samuel Rhoads Fisher

DIANA COMPTON FISHER

An attorney and independent historian, Diana Compton Fisher is the great-great-great granddaughter of prominent early Texan Samuel Rhoads Fisher (1794–1839), after whom Fisher County is named.

In this selection, Fisher examines the murder of her ancestor, a signer of the Texas Declaration of Independence and Secretary of the Texas Navy during the Republic. She also provides a fascinating account of the tumultuous era when Texas was a nation. ⊷

★ ★

"This is the West, sir. When the legend becomes fact, print the legend."

—*THE MAN WHO SHOT LIBERTY VALANCE*

Although Texas' raucous beginnings have never been a secret, it is easy to forget or inadvertently downplay how wild the West really was. Hordes of settlers, squatters, and scoundrels poured into the frontier Republic during the years 1835–1840, leading one cynical missionary to find Texas "the great receptacle of our surplus population." Bitter British investor N. Doran Maillard warned potential emigrants away from this insolent new country "filled with habitual liars, drunkards . . . sanguinary gamesters and cold-blooded assassins," while back in Texas, Dr. Francis W. Moore Jr., the editor of the *Telegraph and Texas Register*, scolded the ruffians "fighting in duels and swaggering at fandangos." Texas' embryonic justice system depended on social pressure to enforce a veneer of order in its rowdy, often dangerous, little towns. Murders were relatively common but rarely prosecuted; instead, disruptive elements were literally run out of town, or worse. When a shooting feud broke out among neighbors, however, there was little that respectable society could do but duck, pray, and wait.

Given the lawless times, it is not that surprising that a stranger shot and killed Samuel Rhoads Fisher in Matagorda, Texas on March 14, 1839. However, Fisher's violent end has remained unusually opaque for someone so well-known. One of the proprietors of colonial Matagorda, a tiny coastal community whose main street is still called "Fisher Street," Rhoads Fisher was a leader in the Texas Revolution whose influential and vocal supporters seemed to fall silent after his shocking death. Although most relevant records have been lost or destroyed, the evidence that has survived suggests that politics and/or slave trading could have played a role in Fisher's death.

Albert G. Newton, a mysterious recurring visitor to Matagorda who described his occupation on ship passenger lists as "gentleman," surrendered immediately after Fisher's death and posted $3,000 bail. *The Matagorda Bulletin* subsequently noted that a "fatal encounter" had occurred between the two men, without elaborating further. About a year later, on March 3, 1840, Newton was no-billed for Fisher's murder by an elite Matagorda grand jury made up of county commissioners, aldermen, a former judge, the port collector, a former Senator, and other power brokers. Newton had returned to Matagorda months before his grand jury appearance and had apparently resumed conducting his business there.

There is no evidence that Fisher and Newton knew each other prior to the shooting, nor any indications about what had happened between the two that had led to Fisher's death. Newton's exoneration also raises questions. A duel seems the most likely possibility, but Fisher's daughter, Annie P. Harris, claimed that her father was shot in the back, which appears inconsistent with dueling as well as theories of self-defense or justifiable homicide. No other named suspects have ever been connected to Fisher's case, and no other official actions appear to have been taken to resolve the matter. Although Fisher's passing was publicly mourned in Houston, the capital of Texas at the time, and was memorialized in the Texas Senate, the silence that continues to surround how Fisher died hints that something more than a tragic accident had transpired between the two men.

Historical inquiry into Rhoads Fisher's death is virtually non-existent, despite the fact that the public eulogy in Houston called his death a "deep calamity" and an "irreparable loss" to the Republic. This lack of information might seem to foreclose an understanding of what had happened between the two men, but there are deeper truths hidden within the decontextualized list of names of the members of Newton's grand jury. A long and bitter public feud between Fisher and former Matagorda Senator Albert C. Horton suddenly becomes potentially relevant, since the grand jury that exonerated Newton included Horton, Horton's business partner, and at least eight others with connections to Horton.

While Newton and Horton are not known to have been acquainted, either, reinvestigation reveals that the two men apparently were involved in slave trading, as were a substantial proportion of the others caught up in this tangle of events, except for Fisher. Newton and Horton also shared at least one close mutual friend: William Douglass Wallach, the gregarious editor of the *Matagorda Bulletin*. Wallach, a political junkie from Washington, DC, has documented ties to Horton, and his links to Newton are even stronger: he married Newton's sister, Margaret, just six months after Newton's acquittal. As a proven connection between someone who was tried for Fisher's murder and someone with longstanding animus toward Fisher, Wallach merits additional scrutiny along with Horton and Newton.

The only name associated with Fisher's death historically has been Newton's, but in addition to Wallach and Horton, others deserve a closer look. One recently uncovered Republic claim hints that a George Robinson was indicted alongside Newton, as do the Matagorda County District Court Minutes. More new evidence is possibly contained in a controversial unpublished letter written by Fisher's daughter, Annie P. Harris, stating that her father was assassinated by "Houston's crowd" in a Newton-related altercation. Although Fisher's falling-out with Houston in 1837 has been well-documented, Harris' startling allegation could never be properly evaluated because Republic of Texas records do not shed any light on Albert G. Newton. The enigmatic stranger is only mentioned in the court minutes and in contemporary newspaper articles by name, without other identifying information. Finding Albert G. Newton was an essential first step in figuring out what had actually happened to Samuel Rhoads Fisher.

Advances in the digital humanities, including specialized software, internet search engines, and databases of primary sources, have now enabled the accurate identification of Albert G. Newton. Surprisingly, Sam Houston turns out to have been well acquainted with Newton's influential Washington, D.C. family, and Newton's brother-in-law Doug was President Houston's "great friend, Mr. Wallach" according to Houston himself. While there is no indication that Sam Houston personally played any part in Fisher's death, this paper will argue that, whether for political, slave-trading, or other reasons, at least one of "Houston's crowd" was involved in the death of Rhoads Fisher.

Rhoads Fisher, the second son in a wealthy Philadelphia Quaker merchant family, was in touch with Texas *empresario* Stephen F. Austin by 1830 regarding emigration to his colony. In 1832, Fisher settled his wife and children in Matagorda, a small outpost located south of Galveston on the banks of the Colorado River. A friend and kinsman of Austin, Fisher owned the *Champion*, a schooner with which he planned to trade tobacco and hides. The town prospered as the most important port in the area, and Fisher was soon invited to join Matagorda's original proprietors as a shareholder, and later served the town in other civic capacities, including the appointed office of *alcalde*.

Between the time when Fisher visited Matagorda in 1830 and when he finally settled his family there in 1832, traditional Texas historian John Henry Brown noted that a "self-organized colony of kinsmen and friends" from Decatur and Tuscumbia, Alabama, had settled along the Colorado River near Matagorda. One important member of this Alabama-Matagorda cohort, Richard R. Royall from Tuscumbia, would later become a Fisher opponent. Royall is also one candidate for the intriguing claim by pioneer Noah Smithwick that Austin's colony fell "under the domination of a ring" with a leader from Alabama.

Another candidate for Smithwick's Alabama ringleader besides Royall is Albert Clinton Horton, who emigrated to Matagorda from Alabama in 1835. Horton had been an Alabama state representative for the Tuscumbia area in 1829 and 1830, thus the Alabama cohort were likely Horton's former constituents, including Royall. With an influential voting bloc already in place, it seems inevitable that the seasoned politician Albert Horton, along with his associates, would eventually move to take over Matagorda, which appears to be exactly what happened.

One demonstration of the changeover of power in Matagorda can be seen in the fate of an 1838 public bequest by original settler and town proprietor Mayor Ira Ingram, which vanished during this period. The $75,000 gift, an enormous sum at the time, decreed the establishment of schools and "seminaries of learning" in Matagorda and had a specific directive to assist "the children of the poor of Matagorda". As documented by historian John Columbus Marr in 1928, Matagorda elder Judge W. E. McNabb voiced his regret that thousands of acres of land belonging to the Ingram school fund had disappeared into private hands. Marr described an 1838 editorial in the *Matagorda Bulletin* which complained that the town had elected five commissioners to administer the Ingram fund, but that the commissioners had only met once. Three of those five would meet again in 1840 at the grand jury considering the case against Albert G. Newton.

The disappearance of the school fund would not be Matagorda's only loss. Although Matagorda to this day celebrates its illustrious past, its fortunes began to falter when it lost its port in 1841. The decline of this historic town, one of the most important in colonial Texas and the Republic, is sometimes attributed to hurricanes and the devastation that followed the Civil War, although Galveston and other coastal communities bounced back from these disasters. The final blow occurred when Matagorda lost its status as county seat in the late 1800s to the paper town of Bay City at the hands of a group led by G. M. Magill, a developer from Caney Creek, where Horton had settled. This formerly thriving locus of Texas culture, which one Matagorda founding pioneer, Ira Lewis, described as Texas' "glass of fashion and mold of form," and by original settler Mary Maverick as the "most cultivated society" in Texas, eventually dwindled to "just a wide place in the road" in 1912, and is today a beach village situated downstream from a nuclear reactor.

Though other factors may have played a role in Matagorda's fall, the Fisher-Horton feud arguably had a lasting negative impact on the community. Fisher's dispute with Horton was contemporaneously noted and included a dueling challenge, yet for some reason Horton's presence on the jury that freed Newton has never drawn attention. While Newton remains the prime suspect, and Wallach becomes a person of interest, Albert Horton is a logical starting point for the reinvestigation of the death of Samuel Rhoads Fisher.

Fisher's problems with Horton seem to have begun with the *Hannah Elizabeth* dispute between Fisher and James W. Fannin, which arose during the beginnings of the Texas Revolution. From

1832 through 1835, settlers from the various colonies in the Mexican state of Coahuila y Tejas formed a common resistance to attempts by the Mexican authorities to centralize the government and better enforce tax collection and antislavery laws. Only a minority of colonists had advocated independence at the beginning, but after the brutal suppression of Tejano federalist allies at Zacatecas in May 1835, even moderates like Stephen F. Austin were resigned to severing ties with Mexico.

On November 15, 1835, the General Council chosen by the colonists to helm these resistance efforts was alerted that an American schooner, the *Hannah Elizabeth*, had been hired by Fernando De León, José María Jesús Carbajál, and Peter Kerr, to smuggle contraband munitions from New Orleans to Texas. De León and Carbajál were prominent Tejano residents of the De León Colony near Victoria, where Kerr operated a mercantile business, and the three men had driven a herd of horses from their colony to New Orleans to pay for the supplies. Unfortunately, the *Hannah Elizabeth* was captured by a Mexican centralist ship, the *Bravo*, off the coast of Matagorda, and the passengers scuttled the precious munitions to try to avoid arrest. But the captive *Hannah Elizabeth* with its remaining cargo was left near Matagorda with a Mexican prize crew and Peter Kerr still aboard, while the *Bravo* sailed away with De León, Carbajál, and other *Hannah Elizabeth* passengers as prisoners.

About November 21, the Texian privateer *William Robbins*, outfitted by the Matagorda Committee of Safety to protect their port from Mexican centralist blockaders, swooped in after the *Bravo* left, recaptured the *Hannah Elizabeth*, and took the Mexican navy crew prisoner and the cargo of the *Hannah Elizabeth* as a prize. The prize crew from the *Bravo* surrendered the *Hannah Elizabeth* without a struggle, and Rhoads Fisher, President of the Matagorda Committee of Safety, acted as agent of Captain Norman Hurd of the *William Robbins* and participated in an emergency auction of the cargo. Fisher claimed the auction was held because the ship was breaking up and the Matagordans feared the *Bravo* might return.

Captain James W. Fannin requested and received an honorable discharge from the Texian Army on November 22, then was appointed an Army requisition officer on December 10. In the meantime, Fisher had notified the General Council about the *Hannah Elizabeth* and the auction on December 6. However, Fannin filed an official complaint with the General Council on December 11, accusing Fisher and Hurd of profiteering. Fannin was not at the auction; his complaint was based on information he had gathered afterward in Matagorda. Fisher responded that the General Council must not have received his letter of December 6, which was sent in care of Richard R. Royall.

Since the auction proceeds were going to be delivered to the General Council anyway, Fannin's injection of himself into the situation seems puzzling. Nor was Fannin's the only protest in the *Hannah Elizabeth* affair. The commission merchant house of Horton & Clements, whose partners were Albert C. Horton and Abner L. Clements, was a guarantor of the *William Robbins*, as were Fisher and other Matagordans. Fannin was Horton's neighbor on Caney Creek, and according to J. Harbert Davenport, a noted Fannin scholar, Horton was "Fannin's personal acquaintance and friend." Whether because they were friends, neighbors, or for other reasons, Horton & Clements signed Fannin's petition against Fisher.

The squabble escalated in January 1836, when Fisher was given a copy of Fannin's allegations by a helpful Richard Royall. Fisher struck back with a scathing broadside defending the recapture of the *Hannah Elizabeth*, wherein he also accused Fannin of African slave-trading, a capital offense under Mexican law. At the time Fisher made his accusation Fannin was already a well-known slave-trader, while Fisher accepted the reality of slavery even as he advocated for its eventual elimination. Interestingly, one Fannin biographer claims Fannin used the *Hannah Elizabeth* in an African slave-trading venture just a few months prior to the November voyage, which was the same undertaking to which Fisher referred in his broadside.

Fisher's public attack not only left Fannin vulnerable to prosecution but probably discomfited Fannin's clientele. Horton eventually became one of the top five slaveholders in Texas and was head of a commission merchant house, entities which often loaned money on cotton crops using slaves as collateral, and which financed purchases of slaves by giving mortgages. Horton could well have had pecuniary reasons for signing Fannin's petition in addition to neighborly ones. Given Fannin's history and reputation, it becomes reasonable to wonder if the *Hannah Elizabeth* were not also carrying slaves again in November 1835, and if this were not the real reason why Fannin and Horton became so enraged with Fisher over the auction of other people's salvaged flour, liquor, soap, and shoes.

The re-examination of the *Hannah Elizabeth* evidence also demonstrates that it has never been clear which items Fannin was claiming were improperly auctioned. De León and Carbajál's cargo of munitions, presumably of interest to Fannin as requisition agent, was scuttled before the *William Robbins* arrived on the scene. Kerr requested and was allowed to buy back, on his own terms, everything that he identified as his prior to the auction without being required to show a bill of lading. Kerr was also allowed by the auctioneers to give a note for his purchases and could have done the same for his compatriots De León and Carbajál. Merchants Horton & Clements made no claim to any cargo on board the *Hannah Elizabeth*, nor did Fannin on their behalf.

But Fannin's complaint that "the vessel was sold" to Captain Norman Hurd at the end of the auction "with all on board, without going on board and exposing the goods to the public eye" could apply just as easily to human cargo as to barrels of soap. "The official inquiry into the incident contains telling comments, such as "some of the persons elected as officers in the army of Texas have safer and more profitable business than fighting." When a Matagorda judge inquired regarding the disposition of prisoners from the *Hannah Elizabeth* confrontation, whom he had ordered quartered among the citizens, the investigating official sarcastically noted that "as your committee is ignorant to what class of animals the eleven prisoners belong, whether biped or quadruped, cannot advise this body the nature of the counsel, which would aid the Judge in his present quandary."

Both Fannin's and the investigator's statements are arguably consistent with the presence of slaves on board the *Hannah Elizabeth* in November 1835, as is the timing of Fannin's comings and goings, as well as the prolonged dispute between Fisher, Fannin, and Horton. More potential support for slaves aboard the *Hannah Elizabeth* is found in the disallowed claim for restitution later submitted to the State of Texas by Fernando De León. According to this claim, unenumerated cargo with a "first cost" of $9000 was on board the "*Elizabeth*," with one "Chain" as master, a rare reference to the *Hannah Elizabeth's* captain. A search for Master "Chain" has proved fruitless, but the name bears intriguing written and aural similarities to "Chattin," who later was master of the slave ship *Hermosa*, which made regular trips to Texas, and, at least once, carried as passengers Albert G. Newton and William Douglass Wallach.

Since Captain Hurd bought the wrecked vessel and its remaining cargo outright, and since the *Bravo* sailed away with unnamed passengers from the *Hannah Elizabeth* while others were quartered in Matagorda, a slavery angle in the *Hannah Elizabeth* dispute cannot be ruled out. Fisher apparently purchased De León's horse and carriage at the auction, but this hardly seems a basis for his feud with Fannin and Horton. On the other hand, Fisher's interference in a slave-trading scheme could certainly have enraged anyone who lost out financially as a result.

Fisher was no abolitionist, but as a town proprietor and the highest local authority at the time of the *Hannah Elizabeth* incident, he still had a duty to ensure that Matagorda was law-abiding. The town's growing reputation as a slave trading port could account for its being targeted by the Mexican blockaders, which interfered with legitimate trade and threatened the town's survival. Provisional Governor Henry Smith issued his own condemnation of Fisher's actions without waiting to hear Fisher's side; Smith's biographer explained that Smith's pique arose from the plundering of a wrecked vessel, although the breaking up of the ship was a legitimate reason to hold an on-the spot auction. Whatever Smith's initial animus, the fallout from the *Hannah Elizabeth* would have a disastrous effect on Fisher's subsequent relations with Smith as well as those with Fannin and Horton. In 1838, Fisher won a defamation suit in the *Hannah Elizabeth* case, and the unnamed losing defendants were presumably Fannin and those who had ratified Fannin's accusations, including the merchant house of Horton & Clements.

As shown by his ongoing lawsuit, Fisher's dispute with Fannin and Horton continued on through March 1836 and the Battle of Goliad, where Fannin was executed by Mexican troops just a few months after the *Hannah Elizabeth* fiasco. The Matagorda community had been emotionally invested in the Goliad area since the beginning of the Texas Revolution. Fort La Bahia, near the town of Goliad, was captured on October 9, 1835, by Matagordan George Morse Collinsworth and a company of volunteers, most of whom were from Matagorda. The volunteers signed the "Matagorda and Bay Prairie Company Pledge of Protection" for Goliad, and later issued the "Goliad Declaration of Independence." This first Battle of Goliad in 1835 proved to be a major victory of the Texas Revolution, for which Collinsworth was rewarded with the Matagorda District port collectorship on December 11, 1835, the same day of Fannin's letter to the General Council about the *Hannah Elizabeth*. At the time, Matagorda was the largest port in Texas, and Collinsworth, entitled to a percentage of what he collected, and with jurisdiction over all maritime trade with Matagorda, was suddenly a very wealthy, very powerful man.

Under the General Council's "organic law," Collinsworth's official duties included collecting customs fees on legally imported slaves and intercepting illegal slave trading throughout an area that not only included the port of Matagorda but all the waterways in the Matagorda District, an area well known for slave smuggling. Important to the understanding of the growth of the powerful Horton faction is the fact that Collinsworth was nominated for his new position by

Richard Royall of the Alabama-Matagorda cohort, the friend and neighbor of both Horton and Fannin, and whose courier abilities were unreliable when it came to Rhoads Fisher. Royall was a documented slave-trading associate of Fannin, while Collinsworth eventually married Susan Kendrick, daughter of another Fannin slave-trading associate, Harvey Kendrick, from whom Fannin had purchased a slave-trading boat in Havana, Cuba in 1834.

The Goliad command was assumed from Collinsworth by Fannin in January 1836, as Mexico moved to control its rebellious settlers. By March 16, with the Mexican Army nearing Goliad, Horton had arrived with oxen, carts, and a company of mounted Matagorda volunteers to help his friend Fannin evacuate Fort La Bahia. A few days later, Horton was commanding his cavalry as a vanguard near Coleto Creek when Fannin and his men, marching on foot about a half-mile back, were surrounded by Mexican troops, and the second Battle of Goliad began. The greatly outnumbered Fannin eventually surrendered while under the mistaken impression that his command would be treated as prisoners of war. Some of Fannin's men apparently expected Horton to return to help them, but viewing the rout from a distance, Horton ordered his cavalry to retreat to Victoria. According to the one member of Horton's cavalry who returned to fight with Fannin, Herman Ehrenberg, Horton justified his decision by saying, "If Fannin had so far forgotten his duty as to surrender, we were obliged to save ourselves for the Republic."

Mexico's President, General Antonio Lopez de Santa Anna, chose to execute the approximately 340 men who surrendered with Fannin at the second Battle of Goliad, but the memory of Fannin's martyrs would help to catalyze the lopsided Texas victory at the Battle of San Jacinto a few weeks later. While some who had managed to flee the battle were caught and executed along with the others, Horton and the majority of his command escaped. Some Goliad survivors, who were in the best position to judge, claimed Horton had had no choice but to flee, while others remained unconvinced. Many Matagordans must have supported Horton's hard decision, which did save the lives of most of his command, but they probably also remained defensive about whispers of cowardice. Others would stoke the growing feud between Fisher and Horton for reasons of their own.

A General Convention had been set for March 1, 1836, to address the problems settlers were having with Mexican authorities. The February election for convention delegates saw Richard Royall, friend to Fannin, Horton, and Collinsworth, vying with Rhoads Fisher for the privilege of representing Matagorda. Royall was initially thought to have won by four votes, but Fisher presented evidence showing many of Royall's votes to be invalid, including some cast by volunteer soldiers from Goliad. The Convention agreed with Fisher and seated him in Royall's place, which would be one more mark against Fisher for those with Alabama and Goliad ties.

Fannin, Horton, and Royall were not Rhoads Fisher's only adversaries. In fact, Fisher is probably best known for his 1837 dispute with President Sam Houston. The feisty Philadelphian was appointed Secretary of the Texas Navy by President Houston in October 1836 in a well-intentioned gesture meant to bring warring factions together for the sake of Texas unity. Unfortunately, patriotism could not overcome politics. A desire to assure other nations of Texas' sovereignty led to President Houston's controversial strategy of absorbing sporadic Mexican attacks, while asserting that war with Mexico had ended through a treaty that Mexico had actually rejected. Rhoads Fisher was one of many who did not agree with Houston's passive stance towards Mexico, even though it may well have been an effective diplomatic strategy.

Matters came to a head in April 1837, when Fisher personally witnessed the capture of the Texas Navy flagship *Independence*, with a crew of 31, by Mexican warships *Vencedor del Alamo* (Conqueror of the Alamo), with a crew of 140, and *Libertad*, with a crew of 120. The Mexican ships had been blockading the port of Velasco. Though President Houston had relented and instructed Fisher to defend Velasco, his change of heart came too late for the *Independence*, all of whose passengers were taken prisoner by Mexico, including former minister to the United States William H. Wharton, a Houston supporter who by this time had become an opponent.

The public humiliation of the Texas Navy convinced Fisher that an extreme response was justified, as did a concurrent anti-Houston House proposal for heightened naval defense. Fisher eventually wrangled a furlough from Houston by claiming health problems, then set sail in June 1837 with the navy's two remaining ships, the *Invincible* and the *Brutus*, on a daring mission to decoy the Mexican blockade away from the Texas coast. During Fisher's three month "cruise" to the Yucatan, the tiny Texas Navy captured six Mexican vessels as prizes, burned a number of Mexican villages, claimed several Mexican islands from bemused but obliging local officials, and seized the British merchant vessel *Eliza Russell* for carrying Mexican contraband. Houston was furious at the serious negative diplomatic consequences caused by the Texas Navy, not to mention his being publicly misled and upstaged by his uncontrollable Secretary.

However, Fisher's exploits on the Yucatan "cruise" were wildly popular with the public, with the Congress, and with the press, and Houston was forced to publicly acknowledge that Mexico was still committing acts of war. Through an invitation published in the *Telegraph and Texas Register* on September 9, 1837, a committee of prominent Houston citizens pointedly invited Fisher to a public dinner honoring his "gallant exploits" that was set in Sam Houston's own backyard. But on September 4, 1837, Houston had informed Fisher that an acting Secretary of the Navy, Dr. William Shepherd, had been appointed in Fisher's place. Houston had struck back, and now Fisher had one more foe on his hands. Within days, Albert Horton and others would join forces with Sam Houston against Samuel Rhoads Fisher.

The beleaguered Secretary was not without powerful friends of his own, however, including David G. Burnet, interim President of Texas, the General Council's Lt. Governor James W. Robinson, as well as the most dominant media figure of his day, Dr. Francis W. Moore Jr., editor of the *Telegraph and Texas Register*. The influential brothers, Senator William H. Wharton and Representative John A. Wharton, were also staunch Fisher allies, and most of the Texas Congress appeared to take great offense at Houston's unilateral action against Fisher.

On September 29, the House sent Fisher, not Shepherd, a request for information on the Navy, and would remain intensely interested in Fisher's predicament. On the Senate's side, Houston was required by the Constitution to obtain the Senate's consent when appointing and removing cabinet officers, and the Senate was united when protecting its constitutional prerogatives. During the called special session on October 6, when the Senate demanded an explanation for Fisher's replacement, Houston responded in a letter that the Senate found "disrespectful" and "dictatorial." The Senate demanded that Houston reinstate Fisher, but Houston stalled. The Senate then ordered Fisher back to post, but Houston's acting Secretary refused to give up his appointment. Even Senate threats to get the House further involved did not faze Houston. The furious President successfully held up the Senate's request for specific charges against Secretary Fisher until November 7, 1837, the day after the regular session of Congress began.

Houston eventually publicly charged Fisher with plotting to smuggle tobacco to Mexico, taking the unauthorized "cruise," and committing acts of insubordination and financial misconduct. The financial allegations were particularly damaging, as they were reminiscent of Fannin's similar charges of misappropriation. In a formal hearing, the Senate considered the President's best evidence, but ultimately they found that Houston had not proven any of his claims against Fisher. By the end of November, the weary Senate reached a compromise that Fisher should resign because of incompatibility with Houston and not because of any wrongdoing on Fisher's part.

Fisher's defense attorneys David G. Burnet, General Thomas J. Rusk, and Hon. John A. Wharton were somehow able to convince the Senate that the unauthorized "cruise" and Fisher's admissions of insubordination did not rise to the level of official misconduct, even though these acts undeniably took place. As for the remaining charges, the Lamar Papers contain a highly suggestive counterargument that the army was engaged in tobacco smuggling with the approval of the executive. Some feel the evidence for the charges of financial misconduct against Fisher is the strongest. However, the Secretary of the Treasury during Fisher's brief tenure was Houston ally Henry Smith, who had taken Fannin's side against Fisher in the *Hannah Elizabeth* dispute. Smith's involvement in Houston's campaign against Fisher is suggested by letters published in the Lamar Papers indicating that the official charged with examining navy funds, Second Auditor John G. Welschmeyer, had embezzled with Smith's knowledge during the summer of 1837. Smith stated that Welschmeyer was the acting Treasurer in the summer of 1837, close in time when Fisher said he paid $545.05 "to the Treasurer" on June 6, 1837.

In a re-examination of existing evidence and claims, it becomes reasonable to wonder if the money Fisher said he had given to Welschmeyer had not also been embezzled and if Fisher were not meant to take the fall for Welschmeyer's misdeeds. It does seem suspicious that part of Fisher's payment to the government on November 4, 1837, was converted that same day into Welschmeyer's salary, by Welschmeyer. Although Lamar removed Welschmeyer from office, the errant auditor was never prosecuted for defrauding the Republic; on the contrary, all of Welschmeyer's official actions were made legal retroactively by February 1840. Welschmeyer died a few weeks after Fisher and is buried in an unmarked grave in Houston's Founder's Cemetery.

Matagorda Senator Albert C. Horton was one of the few in Congress to join Smith and Welschmeyer in helping President Houston bring down their mutual adversary. From November 9 through November 29, 1837, Horton made resolutions against Fisher and in support of Houston, voted against Fisher and for Houston, and requested and received the honor of reading the Senate resolution asking for Fisher's resignation. In support of a fresh take on Horton's activities during the fall of 1837, it should be noted that Houston gave Horton $1000 that November to pass on to *Matagorda Bulletin* editor J.W.J. Niles, in a failed attempt to purchase the newspaper. Allegations of an abandoned dueling challenge between Horton and Fisher during this time frame also seem relevant to Fisher's case.

As Fisher's star began to fall, Horton's began to rise. By private act dated May 24, 1838, Horton was appointed procurement agent for the Texas Navy, and his large monthly salary of $350, retroactive to the previous December, was to be deducted from unspecified sums that Horton was said to owe the Republic. Horton was not a navy man and lacked qualifications for such a post; the somewhat retaliatory timing suggests that an arrangement for Horton's benefit was possibly worked out after the Senate consented to dismiss Fisher. Because the *Hannah Elizabeth* decision in Fisher's favor was rendered in April 1838, it is possible that the Republic paid Fisher's claims against Horton and Fannin from the lawsuit, and then sought reimbursement from Horton, especially since a similar act for Fannin's relief was passed at around the same time. Between December 1838 and August 1839, President Lamar noted that Horton had "returned" to the Treasury of the Republic (not Houston) the exact sum of $1000.00.

The *Matagorda Bulletin*, under J.W.J. Niles, and the *Telegraph and Texas Register*, under Dr. Francis W. Moore Jr., were the two most important papers in Texas during the period 1837–1839, and both were initially pro-Fisher. For instance, on September 20, 1837, the *Bulletin* reprinted parts of the glowing *Telegraph* account of Fisher's public reception after the "cruise," as well as a pro-Fisher editorial. Moore's *Telegraph*, never a Houston supporter, essentially remained in Fisher's corner throughout his ordeal. But, although Houston was unsuccessful in his bid for the *Bulletin*, Matagorda's hometown newspaper did make an editorial about-face.

In late November 1835, around the time of the Fisher Senate hearings and Houston's transfer of $1000 to Horton for Niles, one James S. Jones acquired an interest in the *Bulletin*, and attacks against Fisher in that paper began. After Fisher had resigned, a December 13, 1837, editorial in the *Bulletin*, apparently in response to reader pleas for fairness, stated:

> S. Rhoads Fisher, the former secretary of the navy, who was arraigned before the senate for malfeasance in office, has been tried, condemned, and removed from his station as a public delinquent. We are ignorant of the facts 'upon which his resignation is founded, and must forbear expressing an opinion upon the justice of his sentence.

The next week, Niles sought to disassociate himself from his co-editor, Jones, reminding readers that he, Niles, "has ceased to exercise any control, whatever, over the editorial content of this paper." The Niles-Jones partnership would dissolve two months later in February 1838, and Jones disappeared from the masthead. After Jones' departure, the *Bulletin* became a Fisher supporter again, at least until Niles sold the paper to its next owner.

Matagorda Bulletin editor James S. Jones was the younger brother of Judge William Jefferson Jones, who would preside over the Fisher grand jury hearing in 1840. The Jones brothers were from Mobile, Alabama, where William Jones had edited the *Mobile Morning Chronicle*, and were well acquainted with former Alabama legislator Horton. The brothers were also very close to Georgia native Mirabeau Lamar, who had lived for several years in Alabama. William Jones acted as Lamar's campaign manager during Lamar's campaign for President in 1838, warning him not to provoke Horton or his supporters, and he wrote Lamar's speeches, including his inauguration speech. William Jones had also worked on Lamar's newspaper in Columbus, Georgia, when Columbus was also the home of another close friend of Lamar's, James W. Fannin. Though Fisher supported Lamar, other Lamar supporters apparently joined forces with the Fannin/Horton faction to attack Fisher and consolidate Horton's influence.

As Lamar sought the Presidential nomination, Fisher's feud with Horton persisted through surrogates throughout 1838, during Horton's concurrent campaign for the Vice-Presidency. Horton won his home county of Matagorda against Fisher ally and eventual overall winner David G. Burnet, 153–103, the election returns providing an indication of the split in the county. One scholar has interpreted the press of the day as indicating Horton's campaign in Matagorda "degenerated into a personal conflict between [Horton's] friends and those of S. Rhodes (*sic*) Fisher." Another characterized the campaign as "effectively splitting Matagorda County into the friends of Horton and those of Fisher." Horton's feud with Fisher contributed to Horton's loss of the Vice-Presidency. The feud may also have cost Fisher his life.

Samuel Rhoads Fisher's descendants have preserved an account of Fisher's death on March 14, 1839, written by Fisher's daughter, Annie P. Harris. Sixteen when her father died, Harris claimed that Fisher was assassinated by strangers on the eve of a duel with Albert G. Newton. According to Harris, Fisher was at a tavern when he was asked by an unknown by stander if he planned to proceed with a duel against Newton that was scheduled for the next day. As Harris explained in a letter to her niece Margaret, Fisher replied, "Yes, I am going to kill a damn fool, or get killed myself." Harris continued, "The words were scarcely uttered when a shot rang out, fired from the front door. Grandpa was hit in the back, killed instantly by one of Houston's crowd, who had been put there to kill him." During the commotion that followed, Harris said, both bystander and shooter escaped in a waiting boat and were "never seen again."

Annie P. Harris' account of her father's death is compelling, but confusing as to whether Newton himself was present at the shooting or was merely implicated because of the alleged upcoming duel. Her version of the story also has Fisher's death happening on a Sunday, but March 14, 1839 was a Thursday. It also is clear from her letter that Harris had mixed emotions about her father, and it was written more than 40 years after the murder took place. For these and other reasons, Harris' narrative should be treated with both respect and caution.

Harris' version of events is supported by those of the descendants of her brother Samuel William Fisher, who was twenty years old when his father died; that branch's genteel tradition is that Fisher was shot "on the courthouse steps." Court prior to 1845 was held in George Collinsworth's territory, the Matagorda custom-house located on Cedar Street, which terminated at Matagorda Bay. The Matagorda House hotel, which had a bar, was located on the corner of Fisher and Cedar Streets, just a block from Matagorda Bay and the custom-house. Similarly, the descendants of Rhoads Fisher, Harris' other surviving brother, were told that Fisher was shot while "riding past" the tavern.

Harris' allegation that several people were involved in Fisher's death is also not congruent with the vague report in the *Matagorda Bulletin*, which stated simply that a "fatal encounter" between Fisher and Newton took place on March 14, 1839. However, the three separate Fisher family traditions, taken together, claim that Rhoads Fisher died in or near a tavern that was near the Matagorda courthouse/customhouse and that he was shot intentionally. The tradition's location of the shooting, within a few blocks of both Matagorda Bay and the Colorado River, also shows that Fisher's assailants could have escaped by waiting boat, as Harris alleged. These internal consistencies between traditions and with known geography, while not conclusive, do support Harris' version of the location of Fisher's shooting.

Some historians have also hinted that Fisher's death was related to dueling, and there is other evidence suggestive of dueling, including the grand jury records. Although duels and murders were relatively common during the Republic, prosecutions for them were not, since convictions of even obvious murders were rare. Weighing against a duel is the fact that, historically, no second for either man has ever been mentioned, although seconds were always present in a formal duel. Had Newton pre-emptively murdered Fisher to avoid dueling with him, which is implied by Harris' account, then Fisher's second would have been honor bound to retaliate, yet Newton died in 1889.

That dueling is mentioned across the spectrum of what little evidence exists in Fisher's shooting weighs in its favor as a consideration. On the other hand, the fact that Newton was indicted suggests that the prosecution either had compelling evidence against him over and above a threatened duel or was politically pressured to proceed. But no matter how convincing any evidence could have been for the prosecution, Albert G. Newton's acquittal was assured. At least ten of the Newton jurors were somehow tied to Goliad, whether under juror George M. Collinsworth in 1835 or under juror Albert C. Horton in 1836. A reconstruction of Matagorda's jury list, assembled in 1841 by the successor to the District Clerk who handled the Newton indictment, and augmented by the Fisher grand jurors, shows 237 freeholders formed the pool of qualified jurors in 1840–41. Of these 237, thirty were either known Goliad veterans, brothers of veterans, or potentially related to Fannin's men. In other words, thirty is a generous estimate of the Goliad veterans eligible and available to serve on a Matagorda jury in 1840. The probability that ten of those thirty would be randomly selected out of a pool of 237 to serve on a jury of thirteen (twelve plus an alternate) is approximately 1/100,000[th] of one percent.

During the days of the Republic, jurors were selected from a list that had been generated by a random public drawing held the preceding term, but this system was easily gamed. Matagorda's District Court records for the 1838 Fall Term show a list of veniremen for the 1839 Spring Term, a list that ironically included Rhoads Fisher, but no court was held in 1839, Spring or Fall, nor was any drawing for Spring 1840 noted in the minutes. Some of the jurors who sat on Newton's grand jury during the Spring 1840 term were chosen from the Fall 1838 list, but not all. The minutes merely state that Judge Jefferson ordered the jurors to participate and names the jurors. It is possible that a balanced jury was intended, but that certain veniremen were absent, and the judge was forced to make do with whoever was available. With incomplete records, the means of selecting the jury in Fisher's case cannot be determined with certainty, but for whatever reason and by whatever means, the regular procedure was not followed and the jury that resulted was not random. The show of force from Goliad in the Fisher case is an unmistakable tie to Fisher's dispute with Fannin and Horton, which had nothing do with the Goliad massacre, but which appears to have been successfully linked to it by the Horton faction. In its appeal to the outrage over Goliad, the makeup of this jury also suggests that Newton would have been convicted of Fisher's murder, had Fisher's best known enemy not ridden to Newton's defense.

It is no surprise that jurors in the Fisher murder case shared social and business relationships; nonetheless, a close examination of these relationships can reveal the unexpected. For example, Jurors Cook, McKinstry, and Mayor Harvey Kendrick were some of those to whom Collinsworth gave patronage positions at the customhouse. Many jurors were Masonic brothers. Some of the closest juror ties appear connected with Matagorda's Christ Episcopal Church.

Rhoads Fisher, a Quaker, was the first person buried by Reverend Caleb Ives of Christ Episcopal Church, the first Episcopal congregation in Texas. Albert Horton had helped to bring his friend Reverend Ives to Matagorda from Mobile, and Horton & Clements had donated the land for the new church. However, after going to the trouble and expense of helping found Christ Church and bringing the Reverend Ives to Matagorda, Horton began gravitating to the Baptist church around 1841.

As it turns out, five of Newton's grand jurors were also vestrymen of Christ Episcopal Church, as was Matagorda Sheriff and Ingram fund commissioner Isaac Vandorn. Judge William Jefferson Jones was baptized at Christ Church in June of 1840, "he thinking he was soon to die," although Jones did not die until 1897. Juror Hamilton Cook's son was baptized at Christ Church in July of 1840, with Albert Horton serving as godfather, and *Matagorda Bulletin* editor William Douglass Wallach's firstborn was also baptized at Christ Church in March of 1842.

Lamar had good reasons for wanting a trusted ally like William Jefferson Jones in Matagorda's volatile Second Judicial District. Jones assumed the bench in February 1840, when factions were well entrenched and tensions high. Special Judge J. W. Robinson, a Fisher ally but no follower, had felt compelled to flee the county in April 1838, before letting the citizenry know of his decision in Fisher's favor in the *Hannah Elizabeth* case. Newton should have been prosecuted during the Fall Term of 1839, but the District Judge, Benjamin C. Franklin, had left Texas in January for personal reasons. H. W. Fontaine was selected to take Franklin's place, but Fontaine resigned prior to the Fall Term. The judge who did serve out the remainder of 1839, John Scott, did not hear any Matagorda cases; as previously noted, there was no court held in Matagorda in 1839, and the Matagorda District Clerk's paperwork through 1839 was submitted through the Colorado County District Court. Newton's case is missing from that paperwork. Two of Lamar's nominations for District Attorney also resigned or refused to serve from 1839 through 1840, the respected John R. Reid (twice), as well as Governor-to-be E.M. Pease. Judge Jones eventually selected William Delap to serve as a special District Attorney pro tern, "[i]n the absence of the District Attorney. . . ." These substitutions and resignations suggest that the Fisher murder case was very controversial, while a defiant public notice posted by Fisher's son Samuel in 1857, accusing Judge William Jefferson Jones of stealing from Fisher's estate, provides another troubling hint at the forces tearing Matagorda apart.

But the most surprising of all the unexpected ties in the Fisher case come from the *Matagorda Bulletin*, which J.W.J. Niles sold in June 1838 to Alabama lawyer John G. Davenport, who gave as his references Albert C. Horton of Matagorda and William J. Jones of Mobile. William Douglass Wallach contributed anonymous columns to the *Bulletin* during 1838 and bought the newspaper outright in late 1839. Wallach was a civil engineer from a prominent political Washington, DC family, whose younger brother Richard became mayor of that city. Wallach arrived in Matagorda late in 1837, and was subsequently provided entree to Lamar's inner circle through Lamar's closest childhood friend, and the Republic's future Secretary of State, Samuel A. Roberts from Mobile, Alabama. Wallach's being the editor of the only paper in town would be a stroke of luck for his future brother-in-law, Albert G. Newton.

Wallach was hired in 1839 by the town of Matagorda to remove the Colorado River raft, a series of logjams seven miles long located about 12 miles above Matagorda. Elimination of the raft would allow navigation of the Colorado River all the way to the new capital of Texas, Austin. At least five of the jurors in the Fisher murder case were associated with the Colorado Navigation Company, which was set up to fund and administer the removal of the raft. Juror William C, McKinstry was especially associated with the project and Wallach; McKinstry surveyed the Colorado River and its raft in August 1839 before publishing a short book on his findings, a work which not only referenced Wallach, but was also printed through Wallach's newspaper offices.

Horton and Collinsworth were members of the Board of Directors for the Colorado Navigation Company, and were also commissioners appointed to manage the sale of the stock. President Lamar was given five shares of stock in the Colorado Navigation Company by Horton on December 3, 1839. Horton claimed he wanted Lamar's prestige in order to help the Colorado Navigation Company's chances for success, but the savvy politician also might have wanted to tie Lamar to the venture as political insurance. Hedging his bets, Horton helped host a dinner honoring Sam Houston within a few weeks of the time Lamar received his stock.

There is another potential link between Horton and Wallach. President Lamar had appointed Horton as one of five commissioners to select a new site for the permanent capital in January 1839. Horton's final report of April 1839 on the new site is similar to a report written by Wallach analyzing the Pass Cavallo Bay for the Matagorda Board of Aldermen. The writing styles are both erudite, even flowery, and both reports contain hydrological jargon such as "debouche". Stylometric examination of the two texts would provide more information as to the probability that Wallach wrote Horton's report.

The dates of the Austin site expedition, January to April 1839, might seem to preclude any involvement by Horton or Wallach in Fisher's death, which occurred in March 1839, but the commissioners only met periodically during their assignment. Wallach spoke at a public meeting in Matagorda about the Colorado Navigation Company just five days before Fisher's murder. A month after Fisher's death, Wallach used Horton as a reference for his new engineering business, which he located at the corner of Fisher & Cedar Streets, near Horton & Clements, and possibly even in the same building. Unfortunately for Matagorda, however, Wallach never made any headway on the Colorado River raft, and his report on the Pass Cavallo may have supported the economically devastating removal of Matagorda's port to a different location in 1841.

Wallach's brother, Charles S. Wallach, who was appointed U.S. Consul to Matagorda on April 16, 1840, resigned in 1842 and returned to the United States. Doug Wallach's attentions had shifted by that time, also, away from Lamar to the new Presidential election and to Sam Houston. Historians have noted the devoted friendship between Houston and Wallach, and Houston refers to Wallach as "my great friend, Mr. Wallach" in a letter to his wife. By 1844, Doug Wallach had followed his brother back to Washington, DC, and in 1846, Wallach would visit Senator Sam Houston of Texas in Houston's lodgings at Washington's famous National Hotel, long associated with the family of Albert G. Newton.

Bert Newton was a privileged, wealthy bachelor of 26 when he was accused of murdering Samuel Rhoads Fisher. Newton's father, Augustine Newton, and grandfather, John Gadsby, were the most prominent hoteliers in Washington, DC and had catered for years to the politicians, diplomats, and others doing business at the seat of government, including Presidents Washington, Jefferson, Adams, and Jackson. Gadsby's O'Neale's Tavern and, later, his National Hotel were the physical headquarters of the Jacksonians and, for a while, of Old Hickory himself. Sam Houston had lived at O'Neale's Tavern from 1824–1828 when he was a Congressman from Tennessee, exactly during the time John Gadsby had run O'Neale's. John Gadsby ran the National Hotel from 1828 to 1836, after which he handed over the reins to his son-in-law Augustine Newton. Albert Newton and his siblings had grown up in his family's hotels, and he had, in all likelihood, known both Jackson and Houston since boyhood. When Houston was living at Gadsby's O'Neale's Tavern, Albert Newton would have been about 12 years old.

At the time of Fisher's death, Newton's grandfather John Gadsby had made a fortune, not only with his hotels, but also with slave trading. All of Gadsby's hotels were staffed with slave labor. Gadsby purchased the magnificent Decatur House in Washington, DC in 1836, and, to the dismay of his neighbors, held slave auctions in the courtyard behind his mansion. Gadsby and his family are implicated in cases of kidnapping of free black men and selling them into slavery, including the celebrated case of Solomon Northup, a National Hotel guest who was drugged and abducted directly from his room. Augustine Newton is cited in a similar case along with Newton's brother-in-law, William Gadsby, where both men are identified as associates of the notorious slave trader and private jail owner William H. Williams, whose quarters were conveniently located near the National Hotel. Albert G. Newton was most likely in faraway Matagorda on family slave trading business when he shot Rhoads Fisher. The National Hotel was no stranger to scandal, duels, and intrigue.

Because of their age disparity, Newton's 26 to Fisher's 45, their unequal life experience, their lack of known interactions, and Newton's status as a visitor, it is hard to imagine what could have provoked a "fatal encounter" between the two men. Disputes over politics and/or slave trading seem reasonable possibilities given Fisher's history, local dynamics, and the known metrics of the case. However, our fresh re-examination of the evidence also reveals that Second Auditor J. G. Welschmeyer's firing, in late February 1839, or Doug Wallach's speech to Matagorda about the Colorado Navigation Company on March 9, 1839, are close enough in time to Fisher's murder, and related enough to events surrounding Fisher, to deserve closer scrutiny.

The Albert G. Newton who was tried for the murder of Samuel Rhoads Fisher is unquestionably Albert G. Newton of Alexandria and Norfolk, VA and Washington, DC. A notice in Wallach's *Colorado Gazette and Weekly Advertiser* shows Newton and Wallach arriving together in Galveston in November 1839 on the slave ship *Hermosa*. Wallach married Newton's sister Margaret in September 1840, six months after Newton's release. Obviously, these two young scions of elite Washington, DC families had either known each other before coming to Texas, or had befriended and assisted each other in Matagorda; in fact, after the National Hotel was sold in 1844, one of Wallach's kinsmen appears to have been an investor. Horton's ties to Wallach, forged during Horton's campaign for Vice President, and later with the Colorado Navigation Company and the Austin expedition, reasonably explain Horton's mustering of the Goliad troops to rescue Newton. Or, perhaps Horton was doing an important political favor for someone who was close to Newton's family.

Harris' controversial letter describing the murder of her father alleges that at least two men were involved in Fisher's shooting. Taking Harris' allegation as true for the sake of generating new leads and theories, the never-examined claim submitted to the Republic by William L. Delap, the District Attorney who drew up Newton's indictment, takes on new importance. Delap's claim mentions two other defendants along with Newton, George Robinson and Ben H. Mordecai, and the claim's ambiguous wording appears to connect at least Robinson to Newton. Robinson and Newton appear to have been added onto Delap's claim for prosecuting Mordecai. The brackets that connect Newton and Robinson to a central lower-case ampersand do appear to designate them, or even point to them, as co-defendants. In view of the biased makeup of the jury of Goliad veterans, it seems particularly striking Mordecai and perhaps Robinson were survivors of the Goliad massacre.

There were several George Robinsons in the Republic, including George Washington Robinson, wounded at San Jacinto, and George Robinson, Galveston printer and founder of the *Huntsville Item*. Even more confusingly, there were two George Robinsons in Matagorda County, one of whom was one of Austin's original 300 colonists, an older settler who lived in a rural part of the county and was well known in Matagorda. The other was George N. Robinson, a volunteer soldier who came to Texas in 1836 from Kentucky. George N. Robinson was also a clerk for Horton & Clements, who served under Horton at Goliad and escaped the massacre along with his commanding officer. Although George N. Robinson seems a likelier suspect because of his connection to Horton, the older George Robinson could also have been the one indicted.

A review of the Matagorda District Court Minutes shows that the attempted murder case against George Robinson was indeed connected to that of Albert Newton. Though Delap's claim seems to implicate all three men, Newton, Mordecai, and Robinson, the dates that Mordecai was in custody predate Fisher's death, and Mordecai is shown in the Minutes as having been accused of murdering someone else. The man Robinson is accused of trying to murder is noted in the minutes as "Rowland Rickey," or Rowland Richey, who appears in Republic of Texas scrip claims for 1836, and as a litigant in another case in Matagorda.

Thus, what little documentary evidence has survived from Fisher's era supports, to a greater or lesser degree, either a duel between Newton and Fisher, with Robinson and Richey as seconds, or Fisher's daughter's shoot-out scenario. Robinson could have been helping either Newton or Fisher and taken a shot at Richey; unfortunately, this new evidence does not suggest any motives for Fisher's death nor clarify how it took place. However, the multiple ties to slave-trading that have appeared in this case, as well as Newton's and Wallach's connections to Sam Houston, are new leads for future historians to follow, as are the names of the other participants in the crime, George Robinson and Rowland Richey, in the search for the how and why Newton shot Fisher.

The chronology of the power change in Matagorda is a silent witness to Fisher's passing, but perhaps not the only one. By January 1840, Dr. Francis Moore Jr., editor of the *Telegraph and Texas Register* and Mayor of Houston, was elected to the Senate, where he almost single-handedly organized and passed anti-dueling legislation that essentially stopped the practice. For a hundred years thereafter, all who aspired to hold any public employment in Texas had to swear they had never been involved in or enabled a duel. If Fisher did die in a duel, perhaps his friend Francis Moore, long a vocal opponent of the practice, had felt personally compelled to take action. Moreover, Fisher's main adversaries were office-holders, and public knowledge of any involvement in a duel would have meant the end of their careers.

During the years of the Fisher-Horton feud, Rhoads Fisher tried at least three times to calm the hostilities roiling his beloved Matagorda. First, he publicly appealed to patriotic feelings of unity in an article in the *Telegraph* during his dispute with Houston in 1837, where he urged that "the love of Texas make us a band of *Brothers*," (emphasis in original). Later that fall, Fisher publicly either turned away from or disavowed a dueling challenge with Horton, which under dueling conventions risked social disgrace. Most poignantly, in a large public ceremony held in Matagorda on February 3, 1839, Fisher, a non-Mason, donated a lot to the Matagorda Masons for their lodge. Fisher said that, in doing so, he hoped to encourage others to join with him and "individually commence the great work by individual charity and forbearance" as "the most rational means of advocating and fostering universal benevolence. According to the *Bulletin*, also present at the Masonic ceremony were Harvey Kendrick, Charles Howard, George Collinsworth, and the members of Matagorda Lodge No. 7 A.F. & A.M., which included William McKinstry, Hamilton Cook, and William Douglass Wallach.

Fisher's peacemaking attempts hint at one last possible scenario in his death. Historian emeritus William Ransom Hogan noted that a gang of hundreds of Army mercenaries and outlaws calling themselves the "Band of Brothers" had preyed for years on the Victoria area near Goliad, and that a "lawless band" had plagued Matagorda beginning in 1836. The Lamar Papers contain two separate statements corroborating Hogan, letters that complain in September 1839 about the increasing boldness of this horde of predatory outlaws. Perhaps this "lawless band" was related to the combination alluded to by Noah Smithwick, or referred to obliquely by Fisher in his "band of *Brothers*" speech. Fisher's remark raises a possibility that some of the actors in Fisher's death were allied to this "Band of Brothers," and that the Fisher-Horton feud could have been something more complicated than a personal dispute.

There are few published contemporary accounts of Fisher's death. The *Telegraph and Texas Register* published a stunning eulogy for both Fisher and William Wharton, who had died of tetanus the same day as Fisher was shot, calling their deaths "a deep calamity" and an "irreparable loss" to the Republic, but the article did not go into any details about Fisher's shooting. *The Matagorda Bulletin's* story was predictably brief. The New Orleans press possibly carried the story, if the dubious *Jonathan Sharpe: the Adventures of a Kentuckian* can be believed, while Texas bane N. Doran Maillard used "The assassination of Judge Fisher, Matagorder (*sic*)" as an example of a "Texas Atrocity" in his polemic against the new Republic. Although Maillard is often discounted as a source because of his skepticism of Texas, he was in the Republic at the time of the Fisher grand jury hearing and became a member of the Texas bar, and thus was in a position to know details about Fisher's death and the case against Newton. Interestingly, Maillard exempted the officers of the Texas Navy from his otherwise scathing criticism of the Republic, saying he had "never met a more liberal, high-minded, and gentlemanly set of men in any part of the world."

Reading between the lines of other anecdotes might also be instructive. According to Judge Alex W. Terrell, Sam Houston slandered a political opponent named Oldham in a speech, causing Oldham to exclaim to Terrell that Houston was trying to have him (Oldham) assassinated. Terrell, a respected historian and Houston intimate, goes on to say, somewhat smugly, that "Oldham knew the devotion of Houston's friends and how a personal difficulty would terminate." "Difficulty" was a well-known euphemism at the time for a duel.

Based on the evidence found in this investigation, it appears that Fisher was killed by "one of Houston's crowd," just as his daughter Annie had claimed, but for reasons that remain unknown, at least for now. The Fisher case also demonstrates what many others have already pointed out: the overly mythologized history of the Republic of Texas remains fertile ground for historical excavation and revision. Not only have entire populations been left out of traditional Texas history, but archives of primary sources such as the Lamar Papers cannot be read for long without realizing that early Texas frequently veered closer to Sergio Leone's vision of the West than it did to our often idealized traditions. Leone's violent and picaresque deconstruction of early Texas in his "Dollar" movies could be more accurate representations than heretofore realized. Leone's favorite Western, John Ford's *The Man Who Shot Liberty Valance*, also called into question the conventional acceptance of a sanitized and mythologized West. Leone loved *Liberty Valance* because it showed "the conflict between political forces and the single solitary hero of the West. A conflict and a more attentive eye looking at the implications of the conflict. And in the end a pessimistic look at the conflict."

As historians review and revise the historiography of early Texas, they could do worse than reconsider the implications of known conflicts, teasing apart their hidden subtleties through attentive and skeptical probing. Fisher's fortunes mirrored those of Matagorda, and his revised history seems almost Leone-like in his inevitable fall from favor. Whether Samuel Rhoads Fisher died because of a duel, fell victim to lawless elements in power, or simply crossed the wrong people, at least one thing seems undisputable: the whole story of Texas has yet to be told.

A Great Captain and a New Weapon

CHARLES M. ROBINSON, III

Charles M. Robinson, III (1949–2012) taught history at South Texas College in McAllen. His many studies include *Bad Hand: A Biography of General Ranald S. Mackenzie* (1993), *The Buffalo Hunters* (1995), *A Good Year to Die: The Story of the Great Sioux War* (1995), *Satanta: The Life and Death of a War Chief* (1997), and *The Men Who Wear the Star: The Story of the Texas Rangers* (2000).

In this selection, Professor Robinson discusses the Texas Rangers during the Captain Jack Hays era. Republic of Texas President Sam Houston lauded the fearless Indian fighter. "The frontier of our country would have been defenseless but for his gallantry and vigilance," Houston asserted. Robinson also recounts the significance of the new Colt's revolver, a weapon favored by Captain Hays. ✍

★ ★

Jack Hays was only one of several outstanding Ranger captains during the Republic, but he is the most famous because he was the type of frontiersman who inspires legends. Barely an adult when he rose to command, he nevertheless won the admiration of Sam Houston himself, who observed, "The frontier of our country would have been defenceless but for his gallantry and vigilance united With fine capacity." Indeed, he was so widely known by reputation that people were surprised when they saw him for the first time. Pioneer John W. Lockhart, who met Hays in a hotel lobby in Washington-on-the-Brazos, said:

> *I thought that my eyes had deceived me. Could that Small, Boyish Looking Youngster, not a particle of beard on his face, homely palefaced young man, be the veritable Jack Hays, the celebrated Indian fighter, the man whose name was sung with praise by all Texians? It could not be, I thought, but I soon found out that it was the veritable "Captain Jack."*

John Coffee Hays had the right credentials to achieve greatness in Texas. Like Sam Houston, he was a Tennessean, born on his family's plantation near Nashville on January 28, 1817. His father, Harmon Hays, was related to Andrew Jackson's wife, Rachel, and named his son for longtime family friend and Jackson protégé Col. John Coffee. The areas's social life centered around the Hermitage, which the Jacksons had built on land purchased from Harmon Hays. Here Jack and his brothers met the great men of the frontier and nation, including the up-and-coming Houston, who numbered Harmon among his friends.

Harmon Hays died when Jack was fifteen years old, and he was placed with a well-meaning uncle who urged him to try for West Point. Not liking the prospect of military regimentation, he left his uncle's home and worked his way westward over the next four years. He arrived in Texas shortly after the Battle of San Jacinto and, finding the new republic's rough-and-tumble army suited him better than the spit and polish of the American military, promptly enlisted as a scout and surveyor. After a stint in the army, he joined a Ranger company commanded by Henry Karnes, distinguishing himself in fights against Indians and Mexicans and developing a reputation for cool, daring leadership.

Besides being an outstanding leader, Hays more than any other individual is responsible for arming the Rangers with another great Texas legend—the Colt's revolver.

Hays achieved his reputation as a leader in the 1840s, a decade unusually rife with bloodshed, for the Texans were beset by both Comanches and Mexicans. Despite several peace treaties, Comanche raids had stepped up during the second half of the 1830s, and the number of captive women and children had grown.

Hostilities opened with a seemingly innocuous event. On January 9, 1840, three Comanches brought a Mexican captive to San Antonio, saying they had been delegated to negotiate a peace. Their message was passed on to Secretary of War Albert Sidney Johnston (later a noted Confederate general), who instructed Lt. Col. William S. Fisher of the First Infantry to meet with the Indians in San Antonio. If the Comanches brought their white captives, it would be considered a pledge of good faith, and they could depart unmolested after the treaty conference. If, however, they did not bring the captives, the chiefs would be detained as hostages.

The Comanches returned on March 19. The party consisted of sixty-five men, women, and children, but only one captive, fifteen-year-old Matilda Lockhart, who had been taken two years earlier. She obviously had been tortured during much of her captivity; her nose was almost completely burned off, her hair had been singed to the scalp, and she was covered with fresh bruises and sores.

Twelve of the main chiefs were escorted into the "Council House," as the old Spanish government house was sometimes known, while the other Indians passed the time in the courtyard. A quick conversation with Matilda Lockhart determined the other white prisoners were held at the main Comanche camp and would be brought in one or two at a time in hopes of large and continuous ransom payments.

Assembling his troops around the building, Colonel Fisher told the chiefs they would remain as hostages while the Comanche women, children, and warriors returned to their camp for the captives. Troops were brought into the room, and the chiefs drew knives and strung their bows. Fisher told the soldiers to fire if the Indians did not surrender calmly. At that moment, one chief stabbed a sentry and was shot. The others attacked the troops, who opened fire. Within moments all twelve chiefs were dead.

Hearing the commotion, the warriors and soldiers outside began fighting. Some Comanches headed toward the nearby San Antonio River, while others barricaded themselves into out-buildings around the Council House. When the shooting stopped, thirty chiefs and warriors, three women, and two children were dead, and twenty-seven women and children and two old men were prisoners. Among the Texans, seven soldiers and bystanders were killed and eight wounded.

During the weeks following the Council House Fight, an uneasy truce prevailed while the two sides negotiated and exchanged prisoners. The death of the twelve chiefs left the Comanches temporarily demoralized, and it took them time to recover. By early summer, however, they had retreated into the hills west of Austin and San Antonio and begun planning a revenge raid. They were encouraged by Gen. Valentín Canalizo, the Mexican commandant in Matamoros, near the mouth of the Rio Grande. As word of the Mexican involvement filtered north into Texas, Dr. Branch Archer, who succeeded Johnston as secretary of war, called up volunteer units against a potential raid. But when the weeks passed and nothing happened, the volunteers were mustered out and allowed to return home.

The Great Comanche Raid of August 1840 took the Texans completely by surprise. Mexican agents in Texas had kept in touch with the Indians and apparently convinced them to delay until the volunteers disbanded. On August 4, a war party consisting of about six hundred Comanches and Kiowas moved out of the hills and descended onto a relatively uninhabited area of the coastal plains. By the afternoon of August 6, they were spotted on the outskirts of Victoria, where the citizens prepared a defense. Avoiding the town itself, the Indians spent that day and the next in the immediate vicinity, stealing horses, burning and killing, and taking some women and children prisoner.

From Victoria, the raiders rode on to the small coastal settlement of Linnville. They struck that town on the morning of August 8, taking the citizens completely by surprise. Most fled in boats to the steamer *Mustang*, anchored in the bay. Those who didn't make it were captured or killed. The refugees on the steamer spent the rest of the day watching as the Indians burned and plundered the town. When they finally retreated, they carried several hundred horses and mules loaded with plunder taken from warehouses at the port.

Even before the sack of Linnville, the Texans were gathering their forces. Early reports of Indian movement had prompted two ad hoc Ranger units, under Capts. Adam Zumwalt and Ben McCulloch, to head out in pursuit. The two units came together on the morning of August 7. By noon they were joined by the old Indian-fighting Ranger John Tumlinson with sixty-five men from Victoria and Cuero, who, unaware of the raiding around Victoria, were returning from a scouting expedition.

As word of the attack on the towns spread, more soldiers, Rangers, and militia assembled, and Maj. Gen. Felix Huston assumed command. Guided by Tonkawa scouts under their veteran Chief Placido, the Texans moved inland and on August 12 intercepted the returning Comanches at Plum Creek, about twenty-seven miles southeast of Austin. Huston sent Ranger Robert Hall ahead with five men to reconnoiter. The Indians were strung out along the prairie, and to Hall the column "looked to be seven miles long." Skirting the column to the Comanche rear, the Texans could see warriors decked out in the plunder of Linnville.

Many of them put on cloth coats and buttoned them behind. Most of them had on stolen shoes and hats. They spread the calico over their horses, and tied hundreds of yards of ribbon in their horses' manes and to their tails.

By the condition of their fighting equipment and tribal regalia. Hall surmised they had been preparing for the raid for a long time.

At that moment, an officer and a private inexplicably blundered into the Indian line and were surrounded. The officer managed to break free and escape, but the private was killed in sight of the Rangers. Hall told his men to keep back a safe distance and fire whenever they had a target. The men obeyed, and they skirmished for about two miles until they got back to the main body of Texans, and the battle opened in earnest.

The cautious General Huston ordered the Texans to dismount, form into line, and open fire, but the bullets glanced off the tough rawhide of the Comanche shields. Seeing this, veteran fighters waited until the Indians wheeled about on their ponies, then shot them as they turned. As their losses mounted, the Comanches began pulling back out of range. Pressed by Ben McCulloch and Edward Burleson, Huston ordered a charge.

The sudden Texas assault startled the Comanches, but some fought back. A load of buckshot hit Ranger Nelson Lee near his elbow. He dropped his reins and his uncontrolled horse carried him straight into the Indians. Other members of his company rode after him and rescued him.

Hall took a bullet in his thigh. "It made a terrible wound and the blood ran until it sloshed out of my boots." He fell off his horse, but managed to stagger to his feet just as an Indian rode up. Hall raised his rifle, but the Indian threw up his hands and shouted, "Tonkaway!"—identifying himself as one of old Placido's scouts.

The Comanches were routed, and the Texans chased them until their horses gave out. In the confusion, the Comanches left behind their plunder and captives. Some of the captives were recovered alive, but several had been killed when the Comanches realized they were defeated. One woman was seriously wounded but saved from death because her steel corset had deflected her captor's arrow. A considerable amount of Mexican equipment was found, indicating the Comanches had been supplied from that quarter.

Two months later, on October 14, an ad hoc Ranger company under Capt. John Moore with Lipan scouts attacked a large Comanche camp on the upper Colorado River. The Indians were completely routed, bringing public demand for more campaigns. These were the last major expeditions for the time being, however. The Republic was completely penniless.

Jack Hays was in the Battle of Plum Creek, although not a key participant; the day really belonged to veteran Rangers Ben McCulloch and Ed Burleson. Nevertheless, Hays had already earned a solid reputation with a military expedition against Laredo under Col. Eurastus "Deaf" Smith in 1837, returned on two separate occasions in 1839 with Ranger expeditions of his own, and was in several Indian fights with Henry Karnes's Rangers. His prestige was such that when the Texas Congress reorganized the frontier defense forces in January 1841, the twenty-three-year-old Hays was appointed to command one of three new Ranger companies. Records of these units are sketchy, but apparently Hays and the other two captains. John Price and Antonio Pérez, were responsible for enlisting the men.

Nelson Lee, who had recovered sufficiently from his buckshot wound to join Hays's company, recalled:

> He was a slim, slight, smooth-faced boy . . . and looking younger than he was in fact. In his manners he was unassuming in the extreme, a stripling of few words, whose quiet demeanor stretched quite to the verge of modesty. Nevertheless, it was this youngster whom the tall, huge-framed brawny-armed campaigners hailed unanimously as their chief and leader when they assembled together in their uncouth garb in the grand plaza of Bexar [San Antonio] . . . for young as he was, he had already exhibited abundant evidence that, though a lamb in peace, he was a lion in war. . . .

Hays's calculated aggressiveness inspired frontiersmen to say an enemy fled "as if Jack Hays, himself, were after them."

Yet to say he was a daring youth amid grizzled pioneers does injustice to his men. The frontier drew people from all walks of life, and Hays's Rangers were no exception. One of the company, Benjamin Highsmith, remembered many of them as "men of education and refinement. Around the campfire at night it was not uncommon to hear men quoting from the most popular poets and authors, and talking learnedly on ancient and modern history."

In addition to Highsmith, who had carried messages out of the Alamo for Travis, Hays's Rangers at various times included such men as Samuel Walker, who, while not an intellectual, would help design the first purely military Colt's revolver; Ben McCulloch; P. H. Bell, a future governor of Texas; and Creed Taylor, around whom would one day center the most vicious blood feud in Texas history. As Rangers, however, they were young men looking for excitement.

"Discipline is almost wholly lacking," a visiting German naturalist observed, "but this lack is made up for by the unconditional devotion to the leader, who by example leads all in the privations and hardships they usually endure. No one is punished. The coward or incompetent must face the disgrace of dismissal. A uniform is not prescribed and everyone dresses to suit his taste and needs."

Creed Taylor remembered that before one fight, "[w]e dismounted and tightened up our saddle girths belts and etc, and while doing this I was struck with the spirit of dare-devil levity that seemed to have siezed every man."

When the new company organized, Hays's salary was set at $75 a month, later raised to $150. The men were listed at $30 a month, although at first no one was paid because the Republic was in the process of stabilizing its badly inflated currency. It was not a terribly critical problem, however, because the militia acts that governed the Rangers initially allowed only fifteen men. They furnished their own arms, horses, and equipment. The government supplied ammunition and, officially at least, provisions. In reality, the Rangers in the field were cut off from supply and so lived by hunting or on provisions seized from Mexican trains. As a long arm, most carried single-shot muzzle-loading Jaeger rifles across the pommels of their saddles. Hays and a handful of others carried Col. Samuel Colt's revolver.

Colt was not the first to invent a multishot revolving firearm, and he undoubtedly was inspired after seeing British attempts. Nevertheless, the Colt handgun, patented on February 25, 1836, was the first practical revolver, and by the end of that year, Colt was producing revolving pistols and rifles in his newly established factory in Paterson, New Jersey. The handguns included a pocket model in .28 caliber, and two .31-caliber belt models. The No. 5 (actually the fourth model produced) was a holster pistol in .36 caliber. Colt's Patent No. 5 had a total production of a thousand, many of which went to Texas, and for that reason it is known as the Texas Paterson.

By almost any later standard, the Texas Paterson was a crude, clumsy weapon. It was a cap-and-ball arm, with the five chambers in the cylinder charged from the front, the powder and ball being loaded separately. Each chamber had a nipple in the rear for a percussion cap that, when struck by the hammer, flashed directly into the chamber and ignited the powder charge. Once the chambers were loaded, they were sealed with grease, so that the powder blast from one would not ignite the others and cause the cylinder to explode in the hand of the user. The trigger normally folded into the frame and popped out when the gun was cocked; there was no trigger guard. The single-action mechanism required the hammer to be pulled back manually in order to turn the cylinder and cock the gun.

Yet for all its faults, the Texas Paterson was revolutionary. It fired five times before it was empty, compared to other contemporary handguns that had to be reloaded after each shot. And it was wonderfully uncomplicated, with only three basic components—frame, cylinder, and barrel. When it was empty, one simply removed the barrel, charged the chambers in the cylinder simultaneously from a five-spout powder flask, inserted the bullets, sealed the chambers, capped each nipple, replaced the barrel, and resumed firing. Paterson boxed sets often included an extra cylinder, doubling the amount of firepower before reloading. For its time, it was a brutally efficient weapon, and on the frontier, it could be used with devastating effect. J. W. Wilbarger, who was familiar with the arm, later wrote, "With these improved fire arms in their hands, then unknown to the Indians and Mexicans . . . one ranger was a fair match for five or six Mexicans or Indians."

Oddly enough, the advantages of the Colt's Patent Revolver were not immediately evident in Texas. The War of Independence had left the country penniless and enormously in debt. Given Houston's peace policy and his aversion to a standing army, such weapons as remained after the war were deemed sufficient for the Republic's needs. But President Lamar's decision to take the offensive against the Indians and maintain a state of preparedness against Mexico required new arms purchases from abroad.

In the spring of 1839, Lamar received a visit from an old friend, John Fuller, owner of a successful Washington, D.C., hotel. Before embarking on his trip, Fuller had obtained several samples of the company's products, including the No. 5 pistol. Upon arriving in Texas, Fuller demonstrated the arms to Col. George W. Hockley of Texas's Bureau of Ordnance. A conservative officer who preferred the old-fashioned single-shot flintlock pistols and muskets, Hockley was unimpressed. The expanding Texas Navy, however, was delighted with the Colt's revolver, and on April 29, 1839, Navy captain Edward Moore, on a procuring mission to the United States, was instructed to negotiate purchase of 180 of these handguns for use by naval boarding and landing parties. According to Moore, "The Colt's pistols used by the Texas Rangers before annexation were all supplied from the Navy, after they had been in constant use by that arm of the service for upwards of four years. . . . "

Thus Colt's Texas Paterson revolver, ancestor of the gun that became synonymous with the American West, originally went west as navy surplus!

Jack Hays apparently obtained his first Colt's revolver in 1839, not long after it appeared in Texas. He may have purchased it through David K. Torrey, a prominent Waco trader, who wrote him from New York about Colt's "beautiful pattern of belt pistol." At the time, Colt's revolvers were almost unknown outside government circles, scarce, and very expensive for private citizens on the frontier, so several years would pass before they became commonplace among either citizens or Rangers.

With or without Colt's revolvers, the Rangers still had to contend with Indians. The Comanches had begun to recover from the shock of Plum Creek and were moving back down toward the settlements. By the summer of 1841, they once again were raiding ranches and driving off cattle in the vicinity of San Antonio. On June 24, Hays led an expedition that struck a trail that led northwest to Uvalde Canyon. The command consisted of Hays's own company, now made up of sixteen Texans, and a company of twenty *tejano* Rangers under a captain identified as "Flores" but who probably was Antonio Pérez.

About two miles from the entrance to the canyon, they encountered a raiding party of ten Indians bound for San Antonio. The Rangers charged, pushing the Indians into a thicket. The Comanches gave ground grudgingly, forcing the Rangers to fight the distance. The thicket was too dense for a charge, so Hays had it surrounded while he and two others slipped in. Fighting broke out, and a fourth Ranger joined. Eight of the Indians were killed, and a wounded warrior and woman were captured. A Ranger named Miller was slightly wounded.

Hays reckoned that the main Comanche camp was within striking range, but when he followed the trail he realized it was farther than he had thought. His horses were becoming jaded, so he returned to San Antonio.

Still determined to find the main camp, Hays took a company of fifty Rangers and ten Lipan scouts under the war chief Flacco and headed back toward Uvalde Canyon. The Comanches, meanwhile, had retreated westward, deep into the Hill Country, "where the white men had never before made a track."

As the Rangers and Lipans neared the camp, they ran into a Comanche hunting party, which turned about and rushed back to alert the others. Taking twenty-five of his best riders on fast horses, Hays chased them eight miles, catching the main band as the women were packing to flee. About a hundred warriors rode out to block the Rangers and lead them away from the camp, and a running fight ensued for about ninety minutes. Hays's exhausted horses finally forced him to abandon the chase. Several Rangers were wounded. Hays could not determine Indian losses, because they recovered their dead and wounded.

The search for the Comanche camp had taken the Rangers so far west of the line of settlement that they were completely out of provisions. On their return trip, they slaughtered and ate their worn-out horses. Nevertheless, the expedition had carried the Texans into an area the Comanches had previously believed secure, and they abandoned their depredations around San Antonio.

Part of Hays's success in these early expeditions was attributable to his skill as a tracker who could find an enemy trail that was almost invisible. John W. Lockhart observed:

> In the dry and rocky portions of West Texas a squad of fifteen or twenty Indians could go through the country without leaving much sign, consequently a trailer was considered a very effective man. This faculty Captain Hays had to a very marked degree, it almost amounted to instinct with him; he could ride along at a good pace and see the signs where other men could see nothing, hence his great tact in overhauling and finishing Indians. It is said that often he would dismount and observe the small pebbles, and by noticing the slightest displacement made by the horses, could, in a moment, tell in what direction they had gone.

In the field, Hays would halt his men a couple of hours before sunset, preferably near fresh water. Some were sent to hunt game for supper, while others tended the horses and built fires. After dark, when they had finished eating, they mounted up and rode until they found a secluded spot for camp. The object was to get far away from their cooking fire, whose telltale curl of smoke could be seen for miles. Two hours before dawn, they were in the saddle again. "Thus we passed day after day, and night after night, scouring in all directions the wide plains of Texas," Nelson Lee wrote.

Given the historical record of Hays's daring and audacity, it is not surprising that he inspired legend as well. The most famous story concerns a single-handed stand against a band of Comanches atop Enchanted Rock near Fredericksburg, some seventy miles west of Austin. The story first appeared in Samuel C. Reid's *The Scouting Expeditions of McCulloch's Texas*

Rangers, published in Philadelphia in 1847. It was among the Hays exploits that Reid picked up around Ranger camps during the Mexican War.

According to Reid, the incident occurred about 1841 or 1842, when Hays and his men were attacked by Indians near the base of the "hill." Separated from his men, Hays retreated "to the top of the hill. Reaching the 'Enchanted Rock,' he there intrenched himself, and determined to sell his life dearly, for he had scarcely a gleam of hope left to escape."

For almost an hour, he held them off by bluff, the mere act of raising his rifle enough to keep the Indians under cover. Finally, they grew bolder, and started to rush his position. Hays discharged his rifle, "and then seizing his five-shooter, he felled them on all sides." After three more hours, his men finally made their way through the horde of warriors and rescued their leader.

> *"This," said the Texian, who told us the story, "was one of 'Jack's' most narrow escapes, and he considers it one of the tightest little places that he ever was in. The Indians who had believed for a long time that he bore a charmed life, were then more than ever convinced of the fact."*

Reid himself obviously never saw Enchanted Rock, because he described it as "forming the apex of a high, round hill, very rugged and difficult of ascent. In the center there is a hollow, in the shape of a bowel, and sufficiently large to allow a small party of men to lie in it, thus forming a small fort, the projecting and elevated sides serving as a protection." In fact, Enchanted Rock is the hill itself, a giant granite dome, formed by a volcanic upheaval about a billion years ago, and one of the oldest geological features of North America. Eons of rain and wear have pitted the top with shallow depressions ranging from a few inches to hundreds of feet across, but scarcely deep enough to protect a man against attackers. But the slopes of the rock are broken by rifts and caves that could shelter a man in a fight. Thus, like many legends, the Enchanted Rock Fight probably was based on an actual event that was embroidered in Ranger camps over the passage of time. Whatever the case, it illustrates the nerve and imagination that made Hays the great captain of the 1840s.

While Hays and his men dealt with Indians, the government struggled to keep afloat. Lamar's term expired, and on December 13, 1841, Sam Houston resumed the presidency with the finances in shambles. Nine days later, Dr. Anson Jones, the brilliant, Machiavellian secretary of state, bluntly told the cabinet, "The country is *absolutely* without present means of any kind: her resources are large, though *prospective*, but her credit is utterly prostrate." The government's entire annual revenue, he continued, would not be sufficient to pay even the interest on the national debt.

To reduce the pressure on the administration, Jones proposed a virtual shutdown of the country's military, and a corresponding overhaul of priorities.

> *Our policy, as regards Mexico, should be to act strictly on the defensive. So soon as she finds we are willing to let her alone, she will let us alone.*

> *The navy should be put in ordinary; and no troops kept in commission, except a few Rangers on the frontiers.*

The Indians should be conciliated by every means in our power. It is much cheaper and more humane to purchase their friendship than to fight them. A small sum will be sufficient for the former; the latter would require millions.

By a steady, uniform, firm, undeviating adherence to this policy for two or three years, Texas may and will recover from her present utter prostration. It is the stern law of necessity which requires it, and she must yield to it, or perish!

Jones concluded with a direct attack against the national preoccupation with adventure, stating bluntly that Texas "cannot afford to raise another crop of 'Heroes.'"

Houston proposed drastic cuts in the national budget. The navy, cruising the Bay of Campeche to support insurgents in Yucatán, was to be brought home and laid up. New peace emissaries would be sent to the Indians. Government departments would be consolidated, and many positions established under Lamar would be eliminated. Inflated paper money would be recalled, and replaced with a strictly controlled currency.

The president believed if the Texas Congress adopted his recommendations he might "yet save the country." Nevertheless he was uneasy about troubles on the Indian frontier, and the Mexican attitude plainly worried him. The Santa Fe Expedition had infuriated Mexico, as did the Texas Navy's presence in the Bay of Campeche. More than anything else, however, the Mexicans were enraged because some of the "cowboy" gangs of the Nueces Strip had joined an ill-fated effort by rebel leader Antonio Canales to establish an independent republic of Mexican states along the Rio Grande. Despite Jones's wait-and-see position, on December 29 Houston wrote his wife, "Our chance . . . for invasion by Mexico is greater than it has been since 1836."

Houston's fears were realized. In March 1842, the Mexican general Rafael Vásquez invaded Texas and occupied San Antonio. The city was largely deserted, because Rangers had shadowed the invading force and the citizens were more or less prepared for evacuation. After two days of plundering, Vásquez freed three of Hays's Rangers whom he had captured and started back for Mexico.

Throughout the spring and summer, fear mounted over the prospect that Vásquez's incursion was only a prelude. By August, the Texans in San Antonio were unable to obtain ammunition locally, because it had all been sold to Mexicans. Ranger William A. A. Wallace, called "Big Foot" because his feet were outsized even for his six-foot-two-inch, 240-pound frame, told Hays he had seen "at least a dozen strange Mexicans in town . . . who did not live there." Because Wallace knew virtually every *tejano*, this was ominous.

Hays sent Wallace and another Ranger to Austin to obtain ammunition. Upon arriving, they found the capital in an uproar over an Indian raid and were pressed into service to hunt down the marauders. When they finally headed back to San Antonio, they encountered a couple of Hays's men, who told them the city was occupied by a large Mexican expeditionary force under Gen. Adrian Woll.

Woll's invasion caught San Antonio completely off-guard. Hays and most of the Rangers were on a scouting expedition, and those who had remained in town barely escaped the Mexican cavalry. The Mexicans found the district court in session, and judge and attorneys were among the prisoners marched in chains back to Mexico. Besides the immediate blow to the legal system in San Antonio, the threat of a repeated invasion canceled courts in at least four other western counties over the next several months. Austin was only sixty miles to the north, and Houston, who despised Lamar's artificial capital almost as much as he despised Lamar himself, used the invasion as an excuse to relocate the government to Washington-on-the-Brazos. It remained there for over two years until returning permanently to Austin.

Woll held San Antonio until September 20, when he started back toward Mexico. In November a force of 750 Rangers and militia under Gen. Alexander Somervell marched toward Laredo on a retaliatory raid. They occupied the town on December 8, then continued down the Rio Grande, and on December 19, the force was ordered to return to Gonzales. A retaliatory blow—however minor—had been struck in Laredo, and as Jones had warned, Texas could not afford more heroes.

Hays and many of the other ranking Rangers joined Somervell in obeying the order. But some three hundred men, including prominent Rangers Big Foot Wallace and Samuel Walker, refused. Organizing themselves into a separate command under Col. William Fisher, they started toward Mier, southwest of the Rio Grande, about ten miles from the present city of Roma, Texas. The ensuing debacle, known to history as the Mier Expedition, was an act of sheer mutiny not involving Rangers in any sort of legitimate capacity. However, the roster included former and future Rangers, and the fate of the expedition had a far-reaching impact on Texan-Mexican relations. For those reasons, some discussion is in order.

The three hundred Texans seized Mier, but soon found themselves surrounded and vastly out-numbered by Mexican regular troops. After a desperate battle on the town square, the survivors surrendered and were marched south into the Mexican interior. At Hacienda Salado, south of Saltillo, they overpowered their guards and escaped. Some died in the wastes of northern Mexico, and others simply disappeared. A scant handful, including Ranger Nelson Lee, man-aged to reach Texas and safety. The remainder, unfamiliar with the country, were rounded up and returned to Salado, where Santa Anna ordered them decimated by firing squad. There being 176 prisoners, a jar was filled with 159 white beans and seventeen black beans. A white bean meant life; a black one death.

The drawing was in alphabetical order, and when it reached *W*, Big Foot Wallace found only a few beans left on the bottom of the jar. His hand, which was as outsized as his feet, barely fit in the neck, and he had to feel around for a bean with two fingers. It was white. When he gave it to the Mexican officer supervising the drawing, the latter grasped his hand and called the other officers to come look at its size. Wallace would remember the man because of that incident.

The men who had drawn the black beans were shot immediately after the lottery, and an eigh-teenth man, Capt. Ewen Cameron, was later shot near Mexico City on special orders of Santa Anna because Cameron had led the initial break at Hacienda Salado. The remainder, including Wallace and Sam Walker, joined Woll's prisoners from San Antonio in the grim fortress of Perote on the road between Mexico City and Veracruz.

While the San Antonio and Mier prisoners sat in Perote, waiting repatriation and nursing their hatred toward Mexico and all things Mexican, life at home returned to normal. Texans are a resilient people, and Houston, eager to reestablish some semblance of peace, confined his efforts against Mexico to diplomacy. As early as September 14, 1842, with Woll in San Antonio, the president had written Jack Hays:

> The situation of our frontier is very unhappy in its influence upon the prosperity of individuals, as well as upon the general interests, settlement and growth of our country. To remedy existing evils is a matter of primary importance to our situation. You are so situated [in San Antonio] that you can determine what course will be proper and safe to pursue. I have thought that advantage might result to us if trade were opened to San Antonio and to such other points as would be safe. In 1838 we had friendly relations and commerce with Mexico, so far as the frontiers were concerned, and had it not been for the cow boys and Canales and his gang, we would never have had any further troubles. . . .

Hays himself appears to have been willing enough to comply. He realized that his Rangers were primarily scouts and mounted riflemen, more adept at fighting Indians and keeping an eye on Mexican movements than provoking an open conflict with Mexico. Most of his efforts continued around his Indian expeditions.

Between these expeditions the Rangers passed their time amusing themselves with the social and sporting life of San Antonio. Their profession was dangerous, and about half of all Rangers were killed every year. The life expectancy of the average Ranger upon joining the service was two years. and they intended to make the most of their leisure time. Cockfighting was a major event in San Antonio on Sundays. After church everyone, including the priest, joined in the sport. Most nights, the *tejanos* held dances and the Rangers attended. Hays himself "was sometimes seen whirling around with some fair señorita."

Economics still plagued Texas, and eventually the Ranger companies authorized under the 1841 defense acts were disbanded. Houston, however, was certain the Texas Congress would authorize a new peacekeeping force, and when Hays called on him in January 1844, the president suggested he arm his men from the Texas Navy's supply of Colt's revolvers. From his own experience, Hays knew the value of the weapon. After getting an order from the secretary of war, he went to the naval depot at Galveston, where he drew the revolvers, extra cylinders and bullet molds, and other accessories. The Colt's revolver's time had come.

As anticipated, the Texas Congress approved a new defense act, designating Hays by name to command a Ranger company of forty privates and one lieutenant. They were to be enlisted for four months, although this could be extended by presidential order in an emergency. And, thanks to Houston's foresight, they were armed with revolvers. As a frontier weapon, the Colt's had its baptism of fire on June 8, 1844, after reports arrived in San Antonio of Indian depredations along the Guadalupe River northwest of the city. Hays, who was now a major, took fifteen of his new Rangers, including Sam Walker, who had returned to Texas following his release from Perote. They hunted for the Indians as far as the Pedernales River west of Austin and, finding nothing, were returning home when they discovered the Comanches had crossed their trail and were following them.

A small group of warriors taunted the Rangers, retreating when the Texans started toward them. Surmising this was a decoy party trying to lead him into a trap, Hays ordered his men to take cover in a stand of timber. As the Rangers neared the woods, however, the main band of Comanches emerged from the trees. Hays estimated "some sixty-five or seventy warriors . . . led by two especially brave and daring chiefs."

The Rangers charged, and after a vicious hand-to-hand fight, the Indians slowly began falling back. One of the chiefs, however, started exhorting the warriors, raising himself up in his saddle and gesturing to hit the Rangers one more time.

"Any man who has a load, kill that chief," Hays ordered.

"I'll do it," Richard Addison (Ad) Gillespie answered, and, taking careful aim with his long rifle, he shot the chief out of his saddle.

The Indians charged a second time. The Rangers used their revolvers, "two cylinders and both loaded," one survivor recalled.

"The repeating pistols, the 'five shooters' made great havoc among [the Indians]," Indian Superintendent Thomas Western reported to Houston, "some 30 or more were the killed and wounded, finally they fell back carrying off their dead and wounded and encamped in sight, where they remained, the belligerent camps in sight of each other. . . . "

Sam Walker was badly wounded—at first the Rangers feared mortally—and Gillespie was severely injured. Hays was afraid to move them, so he sent one of his men into San Antonio for help. The Indians were too badly battered to travel far, and the two camps glared at each other across the prairie until Ben McCulloch arrived with twelve more men. The Indians departed, and the Rangers remained in place until Walker and Gillespie were well enough to be moved.

Walker recovered from his wounds and drew a sketch of the fight showing a small band of pistol-packing Rangers chasing a horde of Indians. He sent the sketch to Sam Colt, who had artist W. L. Ormsby engrave it on the cylinders of the heavy .44-caliber six-shooters introduced in 1847. Ormsby's imaginative interpretation erroneously depicts the Rangers as uniformed soldiers, but this does not detract from the cold, functional beauty of the weapon.

Family, Religion, and Music:

"The Strength to Endure"

Randolph B. Campbell

Randolph B. Campbell is Professor of History at the University of North Texas in Denton. From 1993–1994, he served as President of the Texas State Historical Association. His studies include *A Southern Community in Crisis: Harrison County Texas, 1850–1880* (1983), *An Empire for Slavery: The Peculiar Institution in Texas, 1821–1865* (1989), *Grass-Roots Reconstruction in Texas, 1865–1880* (1998), and *Gone to Texas: A History of the Lone Star State* (2003, 2012).

On the eve of the Civil War, the state's slave population approached 200,000. Denied their freedom, Black Texans faced lives of "harshness and hopelessness." Dr. Campbell argues, however, that three important factors—family ties, religious faith, and song— helped "slaves survive the psychological assault of bondage." ❦

★　★

His wife having been sold, and facing punishment himself, a slave who belonged to Irving Jones in Anderson County committed suicide. He "stood it as long as he could," said the bondsman who told the story. Slave suicides were not at all common, however. Bondsmen, although most faced a lifetime of manual labor with at best adequate material conditions while subject to punishment largely at the whim of their masters, very seldom took their own lives. Their

"Family, Religion, and Music: The Strength to Endure" by Randolph B. Campbell from *An Empire for Slavery: The Peculiar Institution in Texas, 1821-1865,* 1989, pp. 153-176. Reprinted by permission of Louisiana State University Press.

instinctive will to live was threatened by the harshness and hopelessness of bondage, but at the same time it was encouraged by several institutions that mitigated the psychological conditions of servitude. What aspects of Texas slaves' lives contributed to the mental and emotional strength to endure, and what behavioral adjustments did bondsmen make in order to survive? These questions serve as a focus for the next two chapters.

Sizes of slaveholdings affected the psychological as well as physical conditions of servitude. Approximately one-third of Texas bondsmen belonged to small holders, whereas the great majority were on farms and plantations having at least ten slaves. Those who lived in smaller holdings, especially the few who resided in towns, benefited mentally and emotionally from having greater control over their own working and living conditions than did their plantation counterparts. Some may have had an advantage also in that closer daily contact with their masters led to greater recognition of their humanity. At the same time, these bondsmen, particularly those on small farms, were likely to spend most of their time under the close supervision of their owners with only a few other people who shared their situation. The presence of as many or more whites than blacks probably served as an oppressive reminder of their inferior status as slaves while reducing their opportunity to share the support that bondsmen could give each other. These slaves endured, but only the plantation majority had an opportunity to demonstrate the truth of an old adage about strength in numbers. They were in a better position to create families, worship according to their own religious ideas, and have their own music.

Slave families had no legal existence in Texas. A treatise on the state's laws affecting married women, written in 1901, concluded that "since there can be no valid marriage between persons who are incapable of assenting to any contract, it follows that slaves could not marry, even with the consent of their master, so as to constitute them husband and wife. . . . Contubernism was their matrimony; a permitted cohabitation not partaking of the nature of lawful marriage, which they could not contract." Since slave marriages had no standing under the law, it followed that fathers and mothers had no legally protected relationship with their children. The state supreme court demonstrated this in 1849 when it ruled that a district court jury had erred in assessing the value of a woman and her child together in determining the damages due for the theft of the two bondsmen. The two had to be assessed separately, the court said, since they were distinct pieces of property. Obviously, slaveowners had no legal compulsion to create or respect family ties of any sort.

A few masters went to the extremes possible under these circumstances and forced their slaves to reproduce without regard to any family relationships. Women were put with men, Annie Row remembered, like "the cows and the bull" and bred for "bigger niggers." Other former slaves spoke of "breeding," "traveling," or "stud" Negroes who in some cases went from one plantation to another to sire slave children. Fannie Brown said that although she had children before 1865, "I never did have no special husband before the war. I marries after the war." Children who were simply "bred" as animal-like property could be treated as such as they grew older. "We mostly were like cattle and hogs are today," said Jane Cotten.

Some owners, unwilling to "breed" their slaves but determined to insure reproduction, forced "marriages" between their men and women. Seventeen-year-old Rose Williams, for example, did not understand what was expected when her master told her to move from her parents' cabin and live with one of his male bondsmen. She fought back at first and drove the man from her bed and the cabin. Finally, however, after remonstrances and threats from her owner, she gave in. The circumstances of this "marriage" marked her for life. When asked by a WPA interviewer if she had married after slavery, she replied: "Married? Never! No sir! One experience enough for this nigger. After what I'se do for the master, I never want any truck with any man." Other former slaves indicated that Williams' "marriage" was not an isolated case. Betty Powers, for example, fairly snorted when her WPA interviewer inquired about slave marriages. "Did we'uns have weddings?" she said. "White man, you know better than that. Them times colored folks am just put together. The master say, 'Jim and Nancy you go live together,' and when that order give it better be done."

Most masters, however, did not interfere in the sexual lives of their slaves to the point of "breeding" or forcing "marriages." Instead, they permitted the formation of families and the bearing and rearing of children within a family setting. In some cases, a woman and her children were referred to as a "family." In 1860, for example, when Reuben Hornsby, Jr., of Austin bought a woman and her seven children, the bill of sale described his purchase as "a family of eight Negroes." A Johnson County bill of sale referred to "a certain family of Negroes, Viz Emily aged about twenty-six years and her four children." Such records suggest that the female-headed black family at least existed during slavery. Generally, however, the word *family*, as it was used by slaveholders and slaves alike, meant the nuclear social unit—a man, his wife, and their children.

Texas bondsmen themselves provided extensive evidence concerning the existence of nuclear families. In a sample of 181 slave narratives, 60 percent remembered living with both parents on the same home place and another 9 percent recalled that their fathers lived nearby on a neighboring farm or plantation. Inventories from probate records also provide numerous examples of nuclear families existing among bondsmen. Jared E. Groce's Austin County estate, for example, had sixty slaves when it was inventoried in February, 1840. Kinship ties were specified for forty-four bondsmen, while sixteen were not identified with a particular family. Most of the families consisted of a man, his wife, and their children, and others, while not "complete" in this way, gave evidence of long-term kinship ties. One, for example, was made up of an "old woman" (age fifty-eight), two of her sons aged twenty-eight and eighteen, and a six-year-old granddaughter. Another was headed by a fifty-two-year-old blacksmith who had five children aged sixteen to three but no wife. The Joseph Mims estate in Brazoria County had seventy-two slaves in January, 1845. Fifty-nine of these lived in twelve family units, only one of which was headed by a female. John Millican of Brazos County owned sixty-seven slaves at the time of his death in 1859. Ten were not identified with particular families, but the others lived in twelve families, eight headed by husbands with wives, three by women, and one by a man with no wife. William Ward of Brazoria County had eighty-two slaves in 1864, and only two did not belong to one of the nineteen families on his plantation. Eighteen of these families were headed by men. Abram Sheppard of Matagorda County owned only ten slaves in 1856, but eight of them belonged to one family headed by a fifty-year-old man. In Cass County in 1849, eight of W. M. Freeman's thirteen bondsmen belonged to one family. Two of the other five slaves were a sixty-year-old woman and her sixteen-year-old son, but they were not designated a "family" in the inventory. In short, the evidence from slaves and slaveholders alike strongly suggests that the majority of bondsmen in Texas lived at least part of their lives within a traditional family setting.

Masters had good reasons for permitting and even encouraging their slaves to live in families. Treating bondsmen with humanity and having them reproduce within a secure family setting, regardless of what the law allowed, was more socially acceptable than "breeding" or forced "marriages." Moreover, owners recognized how determined slaves were to have families and how important family ties were to the mental and emotional state of their bondsmen. Masters could see that the family led both to children and to ties and obligations that made their bondsmen more controllable in servitude. Considerations of humanity aside, few would deliberately deny an institution that served their own purposes so well. Masters were advised that "marital rights and conjugal ties ought to be scrupulously respected." Nevertheless, there was noticeable variation in what they were willing to do to permit and preserve slave families.

When a man and woman on the same place wished to marry, they had to get their owner's permission. This was generally no problem, but the wedding ceremonies that followed varied markedly from one master to another. Some couples, once they had permission, simply moved into a cabin together, whereas others had elaborate wedding ceremonies with ministers presiding. The most common celebration was a "broomstick wedding" in which the bride and groom literally jumped over a broomstick together. According to one legend, the first one over would "rule" the family. In any case, such weddings essentially amounted to, as one former slave said in disgust, "no ceremony, no license, no nothing, just marrying."

A good many families began when men and women from neighboring farms made matches and asked their respective masters for permission to marry. For example, J. W. Devereux's diary for January 25, 1846, noted a marriage between one of his females and Sam Loftus "by consent of all parties. Sam brought a consent and good recommendation from his master." Henry Lewis who lived in Jefferson County described such a match from the slave's point of view: "My first wife named Rachel and she lived on Double Bayou. She belong to the Mayes place. First time I see her I was riding the range seeing about cattle. I was living on Master Bob's place in Jefferson County and I have to get a pass to go to see her. I tell Master Bob I want to get married and he say, 'all right.' Then I have to go and ask Mr. Mayes and he say, 'all right.' Us had a big wedding." When slaves on different farms and plantations married, they generally had to remain apart during the week and be together only on weekends and special holidays such as Christmas week. Such arrangements were far from ideal for the bondsmen, and they were not good business for the owner of the husband either, in that children born to such unions generally belonged to the owner of the mother. It was not uncommon, however, for one slave or the other, usually the man, to be bought or traded so that the couple could live together. For example, Hattie Cole, George Sells, Martha Spence Bruton, and Gill Ruffin all remembered their fathers being bought from other masters in order to unite them with their wives and children. At times, women were sold for similar reasons. When, for example, George Scott prepared to buy a slave named Liddy from Thomas

B. Huling in 1860, the latter wrote his mother, "I have no objections to sell her as she has her husband belonging to Scott."

Slave families tended to be large, since, after all, children were valuable, and reproduction was encouraged. Women often had their first child while in their late teens and then had another every two years until they were in their forties. Even with the very high infant mortality of that age, many women had four or five living children by the time they reached the age of thirty, and some had spectacularly large families. For example, in 1859, a forty-five-year-old Brazos County woman named China had children aged twenty-eight, twenty-four, twenty-two, twenty, eighteen, sixteen, fourteen, twelve, ten, eight, seven, six, four, and an infant. Of course, white families also tended to be large during this era.

Slave families, regardless of how they were created or their size, played a vital role in providing the mental and emotional strength necessary to endure bondage. Family ties gave slaves love, individual identity, and a sense of personal worth—all from relationships with people like themselves, not from their masters or from others of a clearly superior status. "If you love me like I love you," a Harrison County slave woman wrote her husband in 1862 while he served his master in the Confederate army, "no knife can cut our love into [sic]." Judge John Scott wrote to Ashbel Smith about what happened as he prepared to ride his circuit in 1839 and take a hired slave with him as a body servant. "I agreed with Dr. Anderson for his man Thornton," he wrote, "but the rascal runaway, & will not go with me, alleging that he wishes to sleep with his dear wife, etc." One of Smith's own slaves also objected to leaving home even briefly. "Albert got home, safely, on Monday night," M. S. Tunnell informed Smith. "He takes the separation from his family to heart considerably. He said he would rather be set up and shot, then the trouble would be soon over." Clearly the relationships between these men and women were vital parts of their everyday lives.

Slave husbands and wives apparently wanted to divide responsibilities as much as possible along the lines that were traditional in mid-nineteenth-century families. Men, for example, hunted and fished when they could in order to provide additional food. Women kept their homes and took care of the children.

Slave children received love, support, and discipline from their parents. Delia Barclay, for example, remembered how weekend visits from her father who lived on a nearby plantation were a special part of her life. On one occasion, she became so excited at his arrival that she ran across the porch, caught her toe in a crack between the planks, and nearly pulled it off. Martha Spence Bruton told her WPA interviewer that after her mother died her father had to be "mammy and pappy." On Sunday morning, she said, "He'd get out of bed and make a big fire and say 'Jiminy cripes! you children stay in bed and I'll make the biscuits.'" Mollie Dawson described the way children who misbehaved got a good spanking. All most parents had to do, she said, "was to look out the corner of the eye at the kids and they got good right now." Mandy Morrow recalled what happened when she decided to sneak off to the barn and try smoking a pipe. Her mother missed her because things were too quiet and found her in the barn. "She pulled me out of there. Now, white man, there am plenty of fire put on my rear and I see lots of smoke." Finally, the experience of Hannah Mullins at the time of emancipation showed the meaning of her family. She had been living at her master's house as a playmate for his children, but at freedom "my pappy comes after me and we'uns all live together in the cabin instead of me living in the master's house with the kids."

Families were one focal point for survival for many slaves, and yet, paradoxically, families also could bring almost unbearable pain. Husbands generally could not protect their wives from whippings or from sexual abuse by white men. Wives at times saw their husbands beaten and humiliated by overseers and masters. Children had to see their parents unable to protect each other or themselves. Jacob Branch, for example, remembered how awful it was to see his mother whipped. "Many's the time I edges up," he said, "and tries to take some of them licks off my mama." The greatest pain from family relationships, however, came from the fact that they were always subject to disruption by the actions of slaveowners.

Some owners showed notable concern that the family ties of their bondsmen not be disrupted. These masters not only kept husbands, wives, and children together while they lived, they also wrote wills directing that family ties be respected in the settling of their estates. John J. Webster of Harrison County, for example, wrote: "It is my further will that my Negroes be so distributed as to allot the families by families in the partition, that members of the same family may remain together." Dr. E. Stevens of Brazoria County directed his executors to sell all his property for cash but added the proviso that "the slaves shall be sold in families." Richard Carter of Brazos County left all his slaves to his wife. At her death, one large family (a man, his wife, and their eight children) plus four "orphan" Negroes would become the property of his daughter. The other slaves were to be sold, provided that another large family of eight "shall all be sold together to a purchaser, so that they may not be seperated." Samuel McGowen of Polk County bequeathed all his sixtyfour slaves in family units, adding a special instruction that two of the families "shall choose for themselves whichever of my children they may like to live with (the one chosen paying the other a fair consideration)." These masters, and the many others who gave similar directions concerning at least some of their bondsmen, obviously appreciated the strength and importance of the slave family.

Estate administrators and the guardians of minors with slave property also expressed concern at times for the preservation of families. One guardian in Colorado County asked the probate court's approval for hiring to herself the seven slaves belonging to her wards because "it would be painful to separate Negroes united by ties of blood." Rebecca Hagerty proposed to buy part of a Cass County plantation as a place to work the slaves under her care as guardian of Anna Hawkins. This was best, she told the court, because the bondsmen "consist of famillies, say, men, women, and children all of which are unsuitable to hire out." Other guardians and administrators went ahead and hired out slaves but kept families together in the process. For example, the administrator of William A. Nail's Colorado County estate sought and obtained the court's permission to hire out a family together for 1856. David G. Mills, as administrator of Sterling McNeel's huge Brazoria County plantation, hired out six families in 1857. Several large families belonging to William Routt's estate in Washington County were hired out for 1858, although the administrator reported that John, his wife, and their five children were "not hired no one wanting them."

While some owners and estate managers made notable efforts to keep slave families together, others went only so far as was not terribly inconvenient. The will of Dr. John L. Graves is a good example. His wish was that "in making a division the Negroes shall be so divided as to avoid as far as practicable consistently with a just apportionment the separation of the persons constituting a family." Amelia Swanson of Harrison County directed that her slaves' families be kept together as much as possible. The administrator of Susan A. S. Gardner's estate in Colorado County petitioned to hire out two families of slaves for 1857. He kept one family together but hired three members of the second to one hirer and two to another.

Thus, many Texas slaves belonged to masters or came under the control of estate managers who made at least some effort to preserve families; many others, however, were the property of owners who showed absolutely no concern for family ties. In some cases, relationships among husbands, wives, and children were disrupted by the move to Texas from older southern states. For example, Ben Chambers of Jasper County remembered how the move to Texas from Alabama had disrupted his family. He and his mother belonged to Lazarus Goolsby who migrated, while his father's master remained behind. Chambers never saw his father again. John Bates told a similar story: "My mother belonged to Harry Hogan and my father belonged to Mock Bateman . . . I don't know much about him [father] because we moved to Limestone County Texas while I was small leaving my pappy in Arkansas. I never saw him no more." Eli Davison's owner decided in 1858 to leave his own wife in Dunbar, Virginia (now West Virginia), take a few slaves, including young Eli, and begin anew in Texas. Davison was permanently separated from his mother and father. Some young slaves were not even fortunate enough to come to Texas with one of their parents or their original owner. Instead, they were bought elsewhere and brought to the Lone Star state by a new master. Sarah Perkins and her brother, for example, traveled from Tennessee after being sold to Charlie Jones. The boy died en route and was buried beside the road; Sarah was so sickly that she was given away in San Antonio. Ashbel Smith bought three slaves, aged ten, twelve, and seventeen, in 1838 in New Orleans and shipped them to Galveston. Smith's bill of sale and shipping manifest provide no evidence, of course, on the family relations of these young bondsmen, but it is obvious that they were purchased and brought to Texas without their fathers or mothers.

Slave families that survived migration or were formed in Texas also were subject to disruption at any time. Contemporary observers, newspaper advertisements, and former slaves all provide evidence that masters could and did sell bondsmen without regard to age or family ties. Nicholas Doran P. Maillard described an auction during 1840 in Fort Bend County in which a family of four was sold to three different purchasers—the father to one, the wife and an infant to another, and a boy to a third. The Clarksville *Northern Standard* carried an advertisement in 1857 offering a thirteen-year-old girl for sale or barter for a boy or cattle. Lizzie Atkins remembered having two brothers and a sister sold from her family when she was six or seven years old. James Brown described slave families being broken up on the auction block, and Josie Brown saw "children too little to walk split from their mammys and sold right on the block in Woodville."

Perhaps the ultimate example of selling a young slave occurred in Austin County during May, 1859, when James Strawther, who was in severe financial difficulty, sold a six-week-old female for $75. Strawther warranted the infant a slave for life, but did "not warrant her soundness in any manner." The purchaser was Strawther's sister, who soon became the administrator of his estate and a partial heir of his property, so perhaps the infant was never separated from her mother. Nevertheless, the transaction reveals that there was no limit on the age at which slaves could be, and were, sold.

Slave children sometimes were given away as well as sold. Sarah G. Burleson of Hays County, for example, gave her daughter-in-law, Louisa, "a certain negro boy named Phillip of copper complexion and about six years of age." The boy's mother had already been given to one of Burleson's sons (not Louisa's husband). Minerva Bratcher at age six was part of the "dowry" accompanying one of her master's daughters who married in the mid-1850s. The 1862 will of David Barton of Burnet County directed that a girl named Caroline be given to the yet-unborn child being carried by his wife.

Slave families were broken up by migration, sales, and gifts. However, the death of a master created an even greater likelihood of disruption. In many cases, immediately after an owner died, his farm or plantation came under the management of an administrator who then hired out the bondsmen belonging to the estate and in the process often broke up slave families, sometimes year after year. For example, William Steen's De Witt County estate included four nuclear families when it was inventoried in January, 1847. The estate's administrator immediately hired out its slaves for the remainder of that year and in the process disrupted all four families. In Rusk County, six slaves belonging to one estate, including a forty-year-old man, a thirty-year-old woman, and her three children aged fourteen, twelve, and six, were each hired to different renters each year from 1859 to 1862. The boy was separated from his mother and served four different masters before he reached the age of ten.

Hiring out constituted a temporary disruption, but final estate settlements, some of which took place soon after a slaveholder's death and others not until after years of administration, often resulted in the permanent breakup of slave families. Although some slaveowners in their wills sought to protect families, many others made no such provision or even directed the separation of husbands, wives, and children. William C. Sparks of Bell County, for example, left his ten slaves to his six children "share and share alike." Robert O. Reeves of Grayson County and Thomas H. Snow of Polk County also wrote wills that left slave families at the mercy of an equitable division of their estates. Lewis M. H. Washington of Travis County left one slave couple to his wife, but his will also directed that a woman named Charlotte be sold and that each of his four stepchildren be given one of Charlotte's five children. The fifth child went to Washington's wife. Ephraim D. Moore's will bequeathed one slave to each of his seven children. Any slaves born before the will took effect, Moore wrote, will be "kept by them that may have their mother." In similar fashion, John Robbins divided six slaves among his five heirs. The youngest bondsman involved was only four. Isaac Vandorn of Matagorda County wanted his wife to keep all his slaves together during her lifetime. At her death, however, each of his three children was to pick one slave, and the others were to be divided equally. Clearly, these wills permitted or necessitated the disruption of families.

In cases where slaveowners died intestate, settlements partitioning estates according to state laws on the subject often broke up slave families. William Steen's estate again provides a good example. When this estate was partitioned into eight "lots" of approximately equal value in April, 1848, all four families were disrupted in some way. For example, Armystead, a thirty-four-year-old blacksmith, saw his wife Aggey and three children combined with another man to create Lot #3, while he was placed in Lot #6 with a fifteen-year-old girl. Peter W. Gautier, Sr., of Brazoria County had fifteen slaves who comprised six families when his estate was inventoried and partitioned in 1848. In the partition, four of the families were kept intact but two were disrupted. Sancho and Lucy, who were both thirty-three, had their nine-year-old son placed with another family. The Polk County estate of Nicholas M. Callahan had such extensive debts that seven slaves including a twenty-two-year old woman and her four children aged six, four, two, and one, were sold in 1849. The same man bought Letty and her youngest child, but the other three children went to three different purchasers. Probate records provide case after case of this sort, but the point is obvious—estate settlements constituted a major threat to slave families in Texas.

The breakup of a slave family was heart-rending. When eight-year-old Charlie Sandles was traded to a new master, he cried for a week. Tempe Elgin's master moved from Arkansas to Texas, taking her mother and sister, and leaving behind her father who belonged to a different master. The man ran away and followed them for sixty miles, urging his wife to run away and live with him. She, however, would not leave her children, so he gave up. His family never saw him again. Albert Henderson, drawing an analogy from his rural background, said that slaves when sold from each other "bawled" like cattle that had lost their calves. James Brown remembered seeing "them cry like they at the funeral when they am parted, they has to drag them away."

Many slaves demonstrated a willingness to sacrifice virtually everything else in their lives in order to preserve their families. Millie Ann Smith described how she was brought to Texas with her mother and two sisters. Her father, who belonged to a different master, ran away, followed his wife and children to Texas, and begged their owner into buying him so that he could be with his family. Wash Ingram of Panola County told a similar story. His family lived in Virginia, he said, and his father ran away but remained in the neighborhood. Then his mother died, and he and the other children were sold to Jim Ingram from Texas. His father followed the children all the way to Louisiana before catching up with them and becoming Ingram's slave also in order to be with his family. Walter Rimm told his WPA interviewer a story that, he said, "makes the impression on me all my life." At a slave auction on his master's place, a man from "outside" put a fifteen-year-old girl on the block. Suddenly, there was a scream from an older woman who had features very similar to the girl: "Ise will cut my throat if my daughter am sold." The owner talked to the woman, failed to calm her, and took the girl off the auction block. Her threat had preserved a family relationship, at least for the time.

When slave families were disrupted, fathers, mothers, and children did the best they could to stay in contact and visit each other. The Christmas holidays were an especially likely time for families to be reunited, although many were able to get together more often. Charlie Sandles, for example, visited his parents from Saturday night until sundown on Sunday. Mollie Dawson's father lived on a neighboring plantation, and at times she left her home to visit him at his. One of Preston R. Rose's slaves went to California with him during the early 1850s, and somehow managed to obtain freedom and stay in the new El Dorado. In May, 1851, he wrote Rose, saying "I cannot come home this season, but would like much to have my family with me, if any arrangement could be made. Please let me know how much money it will be necessary for me to send you for their freedom." W. Steinert, a German visitor to Texas in 1849, traveled from New Braunfels to Austin by a stagecoach that included a slave woman and child among its passengers. To his surprise, when the stage reached Austin a Negro woman ran up and almost literally pulled the child from the coach, crying, "My baby, my little baby." Steinert then found that "the very happy woman was the mother of the child. The christian whites had torn mother and daughter apart by a sale. On the other hand they were humane enough to permit the visit."

Some efforts to renew family ties after long periods of disruption were truly heroic. Mary Armstrong's mother was sold from her home in Missouri to Texas before the Civil War. Upon being manumitted in 1863, Armstrong decided to go to Texas in search of her mother. She was almost returned to slavery in Austin, saving herself only with her manumission papers, before finally locating her mother in Wharton County after the war. Louisa Picquet was born in South Carolina, the child of a mulatto slave named Elizabeth Ramsey and her master. Eventually a man from Texas bought the mother, and Louisa was sold to a man in New Orleans and became his concubine. Upon his death, she was manumitted and given enough money to move to Cincinnati, where she married a mulatto named Henry Picquet. Louisa then continued a search for her mother that had begun almost as soon as they were separated. Finally, a friend who traveled to Texas told her of a Mr. Horton who fit the description of the man who had bought her mother. This was Albert C. Horton, a former lieutenant governor and acting governor of Texas and one of the state's largest slaveholders. She began a correspondence with her mother and with Horton in 1858 or 1859, seeking to buy her mother's freedom. Horton asked $1,000; Picquet convinced him to take $900 and raised the money through severe personal economies and a public request for funds. A note in the Cincinnati *Daily Gazette* of October 15, 1860, thanked everyone who had contributed to purchasing the freedom of Elizabeth Ramsey and invited them to call at the Picquets' home to be thanked personally by mother and daughter.

Following the Civil War, the Freedmen's Bureau in Texas received numerous inquiries from blacks in other states concerning family members. A letter of July 20, 1866, from Topeka, Kansas, for example, contained a request from David Barber for "information concerning his wife Sophia Howard, who with her 6 children were sent to Collin Co., Texas in 1861." Charles White of Elizabeth City, North Carolina, wrote in June, 1867, asking that the bureau "procure and return to him his wife and two children John Westley & Florence who before the war were sent to Victoria, Tex." These men were attempting to restore families that had been disrupted for more than five years.

No more eloquent testimony to the vital importance of the slave family can be imagined than the determination of the bondsmen themselves to form and preserve bonds between husbands/fathers, wives/mothers, and children. A few may have sought to escape the heartbreak of family disruptions by avoiding such ties. William Byrd told of slaves who tried not to let children know who their parents were, and Lu Lee said women sometimes forced themselves to miscarry by taking calomel and turpentine. But this was not typical. "Nobody can tell me now," wrote Steinert after witnessing the joyous reunion of a mother and her child in Austin, "that the Negroes do not have fatherly and motherly love in their hearts." The bonds of love and support between the men, women, and children who created slave families, in spite of the fact that a majority of those families probably faced disruption at some time, provided much of the emotional strength necessary to endure servitude.

Religion appears to have been second only to the family in helping slaves survive the psychological assault of bondage. Its role, however, depended on how spiritual instruction was given and how slaves heard and received the various articles of faith and religious precepts. Religion could be highly supportive of slavery when it taught that men had to obey their temporal masters in the same manner that they served their spiritual ruler. Bondsmen were instructed to be loyal, virtuous, and industrious, with the idea that, as one traveler put it, "a good christian is not a bad servant." On the other hand, Christianity could be subversive of slavery when it taught that all men, black and white, stood on an equal footing before God and were equally capable of attaining eternal salvation. Most Texans, while they certainly did not mean to undermine their Peculiar Institution, did not deny this most fundamental Christian assumption. At least, then, religion offered many slaves the promise, as Mary Gaffney put it, of an eternity "where they would not be any more slaves." At best, there was the hope for deliverance as the Bible told of people delivered from bondage and sin. Many years later, Ellen Ford remembered how her family had prayed for freedom and insisted that "emancipation wouldn't have come if it hadn't been for the prayers of my mother and grandmother."

Slaveholders probably had fewer reasons to encourage or even permit religious instruction and worship among their bondsmen than they had for allowing slave families. Religion was not generally as vital to the slaves' emotional well-being, and it involved nothing of such practical value as procreation. Under these circumstances, some masters did their best to prohibit all religious activities. They did not allow their bondsmen to attend church or even to worship on their own. According to Sarah Ashley, who belonged to Mose Davis near Coldspring, "there wasn't any meetings allowed in the quarters. The boss man even whip them when they have the prayer meeting." "Sometimes," she added, "us run off at night and go to . . . camp meetings, but I was plumb growed before I ever went to church." John Bates's Uncle Ben read the Bible and told the others on his place that some day they would be free. Their master heard and said, "Hell, no, you will never be free, you ain't got sense enough to make the living if you was free." He said the Bible had put bad ideas in people's heads and took it away from Ben. Bates remembered, however, that his uncle got another Bible and "he keeps this one hid all the time." In 1857, Ashbel Smith's overseer refused the slaves permission to attend services on Sunday, which they, as was their practice in all such disputes, protested to their master.

Preventing religious activity was thus virtually impossible. Most masters, therefore, did not attempt to prohibit worship, and some actively encouraged it. Their purposes ranged from the cynical view that Christian virtues made better slaves to the sincere conviction that the souls of all, black as well as white, should be saved. Wes Brady complained that he heard only about obeying and not stealing. There was "nary a word about having a soul to save." But Albert C. Horton, a Baptist deacon and one of the largest slaveholders in Texas, took a genuine interest in the spiritual welfare of his bondsmen. He built a church, employed a minister, and personally read the Bible and prayed with his servants. Most slaveholders probably had mixed motives. As one Harrison County minister said of the slaveholders in his area, "all seem to understand, that while the Gospel qualifies their servants for immortality and eternal life, at the same time it makes them better servants here—better to their earthly masters—more obedient, industrious, trusty, and faithful."

Bondsmen on some places simply held local services that created as little bother as possible. Charlotte Beverly said that her master sometimes allowed one of the slaves who was "a sort a preacher" to speak to the others. However, he had to preach with a tub over his head, because if he got too "happy" and loud someone would come from the big house and end the "disturbance."

It was common, however, for slaves to belong to organized churches and attend regularly scheduled services. Most Texan slaveholders who attended church belonged to one of the "standard" Protestant denominations—Methodist, Baptist, Presbyterian, Episcopal, Cumberland Presbyterian, and Disciples of Christ (Christian church)—and all these churches baptized slaves. The Methodist church, the largest denomination in antebellum Texas, claimed 1,000 blacks by the mid-1840s and reported nearly 7,500 Negro members and probationers in 1860. Complete membership statistics for the Baptist church, the second largest in the state in 1860, are not available, but clearly thousands of slaves belonged to it, too. In 1861, for example, the Colorado, Austin, Little River, and Grand Cane Baptist associations, which represented fewer than half of such associations in Texas, reported 1,087 Negro members. The other denominations were far smaller, but they, too, baptized slaves. Caleb Ives, the Episcopal minister who organized Christ Church at Matagorda in 1839, accepted "colored" members, and when Texas became a separate diocese in 1859, its first bishop, Alexander Gregg, ministered as regularly to slaves as to whites. The Cumberland Presbyterians accepted Negroes as full members of their local congregations. The Colorado Presbytery, for example, reported 256 white and 44 black communicants in 1860. The Disciples of Christ's pioneer "Old Liberty" Church in Collin County was founded by 16 whites and 5 slaves. In short, only a minority of Texas' slaves actually belonged to organized churches. But thousands had been baptized, many others doubtless attended services, and a good many more worshipped on their home places. Certainly most had access to some form of religion.

Some of the slaves attended worship services with their masters, sitting in pews especially designated for them. Far more common, however, were special meetings for black church members on Sunday afternoon or night. In some cases, the Methodists and Baptists permitted even more separate worship through the formation of all-black congregations. By 1860, for example, the Methodist church had thirty-seven "missions" to the slaves with a total membership of 2,585 bondsmen. The Colorado Baptist Association at its 1854 meeting permitted the "Colored Church on J. H. Jones' plantation, Matagorda County" to join as a separate congregation. The next year, however, the Union Baptist Association rejected a similar request by the "Africa Church at Anderson" on the grounds that "the establishment of independent Churches among our colored population would be inconsistent with their condition as servants, and with the interests of their masters." Separate worship services were acceptable, the association said, "but always to be aided in this work by the presence and counsel of some judicious white members."

The matter of separate slave congregations raised a more fundamental question—who was to minister to the bondsmen? Obviously, the slaveholders intended that white preachers provide religious instruction, but, as slavery matured in Texas, black ministers were not uncommon. In Washington County during the 1840s, a slave named John Mark preached so well to white and black alike that, when his owner moved, local planters bought and deeded him to three ministers in trust for the Methodist church. In 1853, the Texas Conference of the Methodist Episcopal Church, South, elected John Mark "to deacon's orders as a local preacher." The Trinity Presbytery of the Cumberland Presbyterian church in 1848 authorized a man called "Brother Henry," the property of William Roberts, to preach, to baptize other blacks, and to "administer the sacraments of the supplies" to them. Slaves in the Indian Creek community of Jasper County built the Dixie Baptist Church in 1853 with the aid of Joshua Seale. One of Seale's slaves, Richard, was the church's founding minister. Bondsmen in the area reportedly "flocked into the wooden church every Sunday and dared not think of missing." Some black preachers, of course, ministered without the formal approval of any denomination. Some were recognized locally and preached on their own places and adjoining plantations, while others repeated and interpreted what they heard from white ministers. In any case, extensive evidence from church records and from the slaves themselves indicates that many and probably most had the opportunity to hear a religious message presented by a fellow slave. Indeed, black ministers were numerous enough by 1860 that the Texas Conference of the Methodist Church received a recommendation from its committee on African missions to withdraw approval from meetings "conducted by colored men" and stop "licensing or renewing the licenses of colored men to preach."

What did bondsmen hear when they attended worship services? White ministers, as noted above, generally told the slaves to be loyal, honest, and industrious in order to attain ultimate salvation. Blacks who led worship services often had their words carefully monitored by slaveowners or other white supervisors. Nancy Jackson and Simpson Campbell, for example, both remembered how their ministers were instructed to preach obedience to earthly masters. Josie Brown said that the slaves on her place had to hold their church meeting "in the yard, so the white folks could see the kind of religion expounded." Those who preached "wrong" views were likely to have short careers. Sarah Ford told about a preacher named "Uncle Lew" who said that the Lord had created all men equal. "Uncle Jake," the black driver, told the master, and "Uncle Lew" found himself a field hand again the next day. And yet, in spite of all efforts to insure that slaves heard only the "right" religious message, those who worshipped were well aware of the other implications of a belief in God and Jesus. Even without an "Uncle Lew" to tell them, they understood that all men stood equally before their creator. This meant, at the very least, the promise of salvation for all, and, at best, it was a promise of redemption. Religious faith helped many thousands of slaves to endure.

In Texas, as elsewhere across the South, slaves' music contributed significantly to their adjustment to servitude. Music was an acceptable form of expression that served the needs of blacks in a variety of ways. Slaves sang to set a pace for their work and to express their emotions. As

Vinnie Brunson told a WPA interviewer, "the Negro used to sing to nearly everything he did. It was the way he expressed his feelings and it made him relieved, if he was happy, it made him happy, if he was sad, it made him feel better, and so he naturally sings his feelings." Slaves also used music as a deceptive form of communication. Richard Carruthers of Bastrop County remembered how, as a youth with the job of managing livestock, he watched for the overseer, Tom Hill, and used a song to warn his fellow bondsmen in the cotton field. When Carruthers sang "Hold up, hold up, American spirit," the field hands knew that they were about to receive a visit from "Devil Hill." In a similar vein, when one of Rosina Hoard's owner's sons tried to teach some of the slaves the ABCs, lookouts stood ready to give a musical warning if the master approached. Above all, slave music contained protests against bondage and expressions of the dream of freedom. One song protested:

> Master sleeps in the feather bed,
> Nigger sleeps on the floor
> When we all get to Heaven,
> They'll be no slaves no more!

"We hummed our religious songs in the field while we was working," Millie Ann Smith of Rusk County said. "It was our way of praying for freedom, but the white folks didn't know it." Slave music was thus a means of expression, communication, and protest. Bondsmen often said a great deal more through song than their masters knew or cared to recognize, and in the process they exercised one more means of withstanding the psychological pressure of slavery.

Many Texas slaves had some opportunity for education in reading and writing because the Lone Star state had no laws intended to prevent slave literacy. Some owners deliberately sought to prevent any education of slaves because it would lead to running away and other expressions of discontent. Even in some of these cases, however, members of the white family, usually children, ignored the objections of the master and mistress and tried to teach young slaves to read. Susan Merritt, for example, remembered being hit with a whip when her mistress caught her being taught to read by one of the family's daughters. Many owners, however, had no objections if their slaves were taught, and others sought deliberately to give a minimal education and take advantage of it. Andrew Goodman's master, for example, urged his bondsmen to learn all they could, and Robert Prout attended a Sunday morning "school" taught by his owner. W. L. Sloan of Harrison County educated some of his slaves to the point that they could keep records on cotton picking and other plantation work. Others had similar opportunities, although not all cared to learn. Liza Jones, for example, said that she cried to go out and play when one of her master's daughters tried to teach her to read and write. Such reluctance may have been nothing more than the expression of a child's desire to play rather than work, but it may also have been an indication that formal education was relatively unimportant to slaves. It seems that literacy did not confer any special status, unless combined with preaching, and had no particular mental or emotional benefits. No doubt informal education—the knowledge of what it meant to be a slave and how to get along in the system—was more important than formal learning. This type of education, however, was provided by families and other slaves in the quarters and cannot be documented.

Texas slaves, as they endured bondage, generally gained mental and emotional strength from their families, religion, and music. Still, however, they had to adjust their attitudes and day-to-day behavior to the pressures of bondage. How Texas blacks behaved as they faced the widespread harshness and essential hopelessness of slavery constitutes another vital aspect of the psychological conditions of servitude.

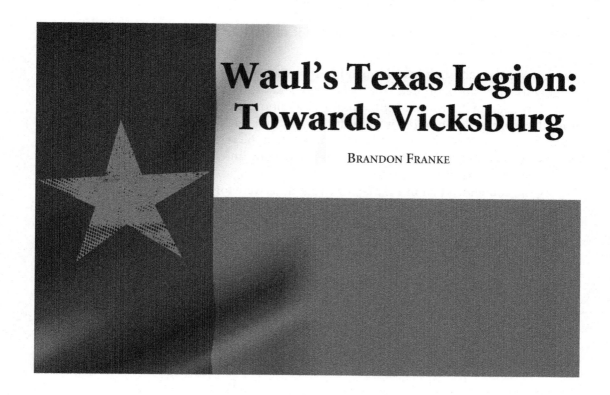

Waul's Texas Legion: Towards Vicksburg

BRANDON FRANKE

Brandon Franke serves as Assistant Dean of Social Sciences at Blinn College in Bryan. In addition to teaching history and government, he is the coeditor of *Inside Texas Politics* (2002).

When the Civil War began, numerous Texas Confederates joined local units. Raised in the vicinity of Brenham in 1862, Waul's Texas Legion, one of the more celebrated Lone Star units, courageously defended the key Southern city of Vicksburg, Mississippi, which fell to Union forces on July 4, 1863. In this selection, Franke examines the history of the Legion in the period leading up to Vicksburg. ✍

★ ★

On 13 May 1862, Thomas Neville Waul received his commission as Colonel in the Army of the Confederacy and was given orders to organize a legion from and around Washington County, Texas. A military designation of legion mixed the best of all three types of units, infantry, artillery and cavalry. The purpose was to establish an independent command with the advantages of all three branches in one fast moving unit, although in practice this proved often unmanageable due to the inherent difficulties of coordinating all three. The ultimate destination for this new unit was to engage the enemy on the eastern side of the Mississippi River, if that river, Waul wrote to his wife "was deemed passable."

Thomas Waul established his command post at Camp Waul, on the Glenblythe plantation roughly six miles north of Brenham, Texas, and began recruiting from other nearby counties, including adjacent Austin and Lee Counties. In addition to new recruits, the Legion also drew from the reorganization of other units during this time such as the "Galveston Boys" of the Ninth Texas Infantry, who constituted the majority of the veterans in Waul's unit. On paper, Waul's Legion numbered 2,000 soldiers with twelve companies of infantry, six of cavalry and a six gun battery under the command of Captain William Edgar. Robert Hasskarl, in his study of the Legion, contended that in Texas, only two legions were formed during the Civil War, and Waul's Legion was the only one that met the true requirements of this designation. However, Captain Edgar's First Texas Field Battery only served under Waul until it was transferred to the command of Brigadier General Henry McCulloch in the fall of 1862, who at the time was organizing a new division for the Trans-Mississippi department.

Orders to proceed to Little Rock, Arkansas, arrived at Camp Waul in early August, 1862. Companies A, G, H, K & L along with Captain W.R. Sullivan's Company E of cavalry left for Clarksville, Texas. Company K under Captain Henry Wickeland refused to leave with the rest of the troops as they believed they had not been issued enough blankets. They soon changed their mind however, as members of the Texas Lone Star Rifles "encouraged" them to depart.

The rest of the Legion departed on 18 August from Camp Waul, marched to Carthage on the way to rejoin the detachment at Clarksville through summer winds and storms. On the way Colonel Waul received orders to join Major General Earl Van Dorn in Jacksonville, Mississippi. Waul dispatched orders for the Clarksville detachment to rendezvous with the rest of the Legion there.

On Friday 12 September the Legion crossed into Louisiana and made camp for the first time in what for many of the soldiers was their first time out of the state. Two days later, Private Edwin Rice saw his first wounded veterans, and was shocked to see "[t]wo of them had their right arms shot off."

On the march to Jacksonville, orders were received on 23 September from Major General Van Dorn to depart with fifteen days' rations and travel to Holly Springs, Mississippi. Van Dorn's orders assigned the previously unattached Waul's Legion to a new division under the command of Major General Mansfield Lovell.

Reaching Monroe, Louisiana, on 28 September, the infantry boarded trains to Tallulah, a distance of 55 miles, while the cavalry protected the wagon train traveling overland on its journey to Vicksburg. Two days later, they crossed the Mississippi River at Vicksburg on the steamers *Desoto* and *Paul Jones* and made camp in the southwestern part of the town. Here the Legion remained, and the soldiers were paid ten cents per mile traveled. Private Rice received $116.68 for his journey from Brenham to Vicksburg. Other detachments held elections for officers. Jonathan Duff Brown, who had been commissioned by Waul as a Captain of cavalry at Camp

Waul was asked by a fellow member of Company D to allow his name to be considered for the rank of Lieutenant Colonel for his battalion. His companion, a Dr. White:

> insisted that there was not the slightest doubt of my election. I thought him correct, but declined from a purely patriotic sense of duty, thinking it best for my country. The battle between desire for position and duty to my country was a strong one, and I have ever since regretted that I did not accept; because, for reasons that I do not think it wise to write, I believe it would really have inured to my country's good.

The infantry departed for Holly Springs via train on 8 October, while once again the cavalry trotted along and protected the wagons. News of the battle of Shiloh fought on 6–7 August arrived bearing with it news of the loss of Albert Sidney Johnston, who had bled to death after being shot. This led Jonathon Brown to lament the loss of "our loved Sidney Johnston".

Upon arriving in Holly Springs, the Legion was presented with new arms, which were for the most part were flintlock muskets converted to use percussion caps. They also received 40 rounds of ammunition, cartridge and cap boxes, and a belt with a scabbard for the detachable bayonet. Three days before arriving at Holly Springs, Union forces under General W.S. Rosencrans defeated the Rebel forces commanded by General Van Dorn at Corinth on 4 October. Although the Confederates were defeated, McNemar wrote to his wife that "we did no[t] loose [sp] one forth the men that we first thought we had." At Holley Springs, McNemar estimated that the Confederates at Holley Springs were faced with forces under "a Ripley twenty miles above here. They are estimated at from fifty to sixty thousand."

As a result of the Confederate loss at Corinth, a reorganization of the army occurred. On 28 October, Waul was stripped of his cavalry and would not see service with the Legion again. Now a Legion in name only, the unit was assigned to Russels' Brigade. This brigade was part of Tilghmans' Division of Terrell's Corps of the Army of West Tennessee commanded by General Earl Van Dorn. That same day they broke camp and marched to Camp Cold Water, seven miles from Holly Springs and forty miles south of Memphis, to join with the army encamped there.

The next day, General Rosencrans received a missive from General William T. Sherman congratulating him on his victory at Corinth. In this letter, Sherman warned Rosencrans that through his sources he had learned that Van Dorn was to receive reinforcements, including Waul's Legion from Texas to arrive with forces numbering four thousand.

From Cold Water, the Legion marched to camp at Tippah Ford on the Tallahatchie River on 11 November. Two days after arrival they broke camp once again and prepared to return to Holly Springs. On their way back, orders arrived informing Waul that Yankee forces were marching down an adjacent road, and that he was to intercept them at Goodman's Mill, approximately seven miles from their current location. Upon arrival, they found, to their ire, no targets to attack. Next, they were ordered to defend a crossing on the Tallahatchie River named Rocky Ford. After marching 13 miles on November 13, they constructed breastworks.

Still unblooded, the Legion experienced their first engagement on December 1, 1862, when they received a message from Van Dorn ordering them to break camp before daylight and destroy all of their stores and provisions. The Legion retreated twenty miles, believing themselves to be outflanked. On the way, they engaged Union forces outside of Oxford, Mississippi, but broke off the fight. Unfortunately, the result of torrential downpours and the lack of adequate roads in the region forced them to throw away even more of their supplies.

The reason for the retreat was a withdrawal of forces bordering the Tallahatchie River by General Pemberton wished to contract his lines of communication as Grant's forces approached from the east. On the night of December 3, the Legion continued its retreat towards Coffeeville, crossed the Yacona River but were met by Union forces at Water Valley. Defeated by the Union forces, they trudged throughout the night through mud that reached up to their calves, which only added to their misery.

Waul's Legion arrived in Coffeeville the evening of December 4 and made camp. There, they would have their first real meal in five days. With less than a full day of rest, the Legion would be sent after Union general Alvin P. Hovey's seven regiments of cavalry. Hovey had crossed into Mississippi from Helena Arkansas on November 27 with seven thousand infantry and cavalry. Hovey's infantry experienced the same marching conditions as Waul's Legion, their movements were slow, and therefore Hovey ordered his cavalry to locate and destroy the Mississippi Central Railroad line that ran from Holly Springs to Jackson, and served as a vital artery to keeping Vicksburg supplied. Hovey's forces would have a bit of success in this regard; they would destroy several miles of rail north of the Yalobusha River, but were unable to burn it as the continuing rain precluded a fire. The Rebels engaged Hovey's forces and lost 7 with 43 wounded according to Davis, and Hovey would suffer 32 or 34 cavalrymen killed and another 27 to 35 captured. Hovey's forces retreated to Oakland Mississippi, and crossed back to Helena, fatigued, injured, and ultimately unsuccessful.

On 6 December 1862, Waul's Legion arrived at Grenada and erected breastworks for a Union attack that never came. The Legion was reviewed by Generals Van Dorn and Pemberton at camp. Davis was thrilled on 14 December when the quartermaster issued new tents to replace those destroyed in the hectic retreat from Water Valley. The next day, Van Dorn left on a "secret mission" with 3,500 cavalry to attack the Union supply depot at their former camp at Holly Springs. Colonel Robert C. Murphy, after very little defense, would surrender the depot and troops under his command at this supply depot, numbering 1,500. When news of the surrender reached Grant, he stalled his westward march and marched his men overland through northern Mississippi, subsisting off of the land, which he would later recall was "amazed at the quantity of supplies the country afforded". He would remember this the next year when he would launch another assault on Vicksburg.

Seeking to finish what General Hovey's cavalry had started at the end of 1862, Grant launched another assault to destroy the Mississippi Central bridge over the Yalobusha River at Grenada. To aid in this endeavor he sought to reopen a levee that divided the Mississippi River from Moon Lake known as Yazoo Pass. The pass was given this name due to the connection of Moon Lake to the Coldwater River, which fed into the Tallahatchie which itself was a tributary to the Yazoo. Confusingly, all three were collectively known as the Yazoo. The Yazoo in turn fed into the Mississippi just north of Vicksburg. Historically, the Mississippi had flooded yearly into this pass, and saturated the diamond shaped delta between the two rivers. The pass had been closed when the Southern Railroad built the levee to protect their rail line six years previously.

Digging began 2 February 1863 on the eighteen foot high, hundred foot long levee and the next day a mine was detonated in the remaining gap between the Mississippi and Moon Lake. The pass was opened in a thunderous explosion and Grant wrote that this new passageway to Vicksburg would open up new avenues of attack, and would "prove a perfect success." Water flooded into the pass through a gap forty feet wide, but the difference between the levels of the Mississippi and the pass was estimated at eight or nine feet, too great to allow an ironclad through without substantial damage. By 24 February, enough water had passed to allow a Union flotilla under the command of Lt. Commander Watson Smith to pass. The length of time would prove part of the Yazoo Pass Expedition's undoing, as the onslaught of water into the diamond shape delta between the two rivers would saturate the land to such an extent to make an assault by infantry untenable.

The ironclads with fourteen transports loaded with 4,500 soldiers led by Brigadier General Leonard F. Ross steamed into the lake at a snail's pace towards their target downstream. Whatever element of surprise they hoped to find was dashed at the leisurely pace at which they proceeded. To add to the misery of the Yankee passage, the rivers they traversed were filled with debris washed into the region from the levee breach, and with low hanging branches on each side of the river, the transports and warships soon experienced damage to their upper works.

While Union forces took four days to proceed fourteen miles to the Coldwater, Waul's Legion was in the midst of fortifying a crucial pass where the Tallahatchie and the Yalobusha Rivers merged. Pemberton had learned early in the New Year that Yazoo Pass had the potential to be a dangerous backdoor to Vicksburg, and had ordered all of his troops, except those under Major General William W. Loring's division to remain on the Yalobusha River as a bulwark against attack from western Tennessee. On 24 January, alerted to the danger of Yazoo Pass, Pemberton ordered Loring to "[s]end Waul's Legion by railroad to Vaughan's Station. Direct him to march to Yazoo City; there take steamboat to Snyder's Mills." The Legion arrived in Yazoo City on 26 January, and boarded the steamer *Parallel*. The next day the Legion debarked at Snyder's Bluff, north of Vicksburg and begun building earthen ramparts they dubbed Fort Pemberton.

Scarcely higher than the river, the ramshackle fort was located in a strip of earth that separated the Tallahatchie and Yazoo Rivers. Its width ran no more than 400 yards. Ernst Knolle recorded that "on this places breastworks were made by putting from 3 to 5 cotton bales on top of one another, and some 4 or 5 bales wide. After this, then dirt was thrown on the bales, which made very good breastworks." In his dispatch to Pemberton upon arrival at the fort, General Loring praised Waul in that "Colonel [T.N.] Waul with his troops is encamped here. He is judicious in his arrangements, and I would recommend that he be kept in command of this position."

Loring led 120 members of the Legion under the command of Major Cameron on the *Hope* up the Tallahatchie to Coldwater to look for Union forces the day before Yazoo Pass was opened up. Failing to find any, Loring returned on 24 February. A foraging expedition on March 1 aboard the *Prince of Wales* up the Tallahatchie returned with no sign of Federal encroachment. Finally, on 8 March, a dispatch reached Fort Pemberton alerting the Confederate forces therein of the approach of four gunboats and thirteen transports fifteen miles below the mouth of the Coldwater on the Tallahatchie. In actuality, Smith had two ironclads, the *Chillicothe* and the *Baron DeKalb*, and fourteen transports. Smith's armada had taken four weeks to traverse the 200 miles from the Yazoo Pass to the Fort Pemberton.

While Smith steamed south, Fort Pemberton received two "large" guns and had brought in the disabled steamer *Star of the West* to sink in front of the fort. Due to the confines of the Tallahatchie, with the *Star of the West* located as it was, any approach from the river required an approach from the bow on, allowing unobstructed cannon fire from the fort, while Federal response would be limited to any cannon they had mounted on the bow of their gunboats. As the Union forces approached the fort, the Confederates burned the *Parallel* loaded with cotton twelve miles above the fort on the Tallahatchie on March 10. The steamboat had broken her wheel and was unable to get away.

Edwin Rice and his compatriots were ordered to fall in before sunrise on 11 March and take their places on the breastworks of Fort Pemberton. At 11 A.M., the fort opened fire as the first enemy gunboat came within range of their "large cannons". According to Rice, this battle amounted to the Union gunship firing "4 or 5 times and we 10–12." At first, the *Chillicothe* and *Baron de Kalb* acted independently of each other in firing upon the fort. This engagement, Ernst Henry Knolle recorded in his diary, lasted "half an hour before they retreated. The Legion suffered no injuries in this skirmish.

On the Union gunboat *Rattler*, Lt. Com. Watson Smith was so shaken by the ensuing racket from the shells hitting his ship that he fainted. When he recovered, his men thought him insane as he began speaking gibberish and giving orders that were unintelligible by his men. One set of orders, issued before his men realized the depth of their commander's mental difficulties, ordered the *Chillicothe* to withdraw from action. Unknown to the Confederates, the builders of the *Chillicothe* had aided their cause unknowingly, like many second generation ironclads; was poorly designed and shabbily constructed, either by intent or neglect. After receiving a few hits from the cannon at Fort Pemberton on her gun ports, the iron casing buckled and the wooden doors cracked, rendering them unable to be opened.

The swampy conditions of the land around Fort Pemberton also precluded an approach from the land side as General Ross's men discovered when the federal transports attempted to disembark his men. Several of the Federal transports had landed troops a mile or more above Fort Pemberton earlier in the day, and at 1 P.M., Rice recorded that Captain L.D. Bradley's Second Infantry Company, and a detachment under Captain Wickeland, marched to meet them and drive them back. When they returned towards evening, they were in a jubilant mood, their band playing, as they had received no injuries. In fact, the closest a Confederate soldier came to an injury in this skirmish was Captain Wickeland, who had a button shot off of his cap. Although the Union forces were stopped in their advance on Fort Pemberton, they were not driven back to their transports.

The gun port problem fixed, and Smith presumably having recovered his senses, the *Chillicothe* returned to action around 4 P.M. This time Watson ordered the *Chillicothe* and the *Baron DeKalb* into a slight bend that provided a bit of protection, moored them together, and fired on the fort while a mortar boat, the *Petrel*, launched shells over them.

Soon after they were attacked by Loring's forces, this time from behind the breastworks at the fort as well as from the trees. "They fired 9 times," Rice recorded in his diary, and "[w]e made a large hole in their boat when they withdrew." Again, the builders of the Union gunship helped the Rebels, as cannon shot striking the hull drove out rivets into the men inside her, resulting in the deaths of four and 15 injured sailors. The first defense of Fort Pemberton was a success, and Grant's Yazoo Expedition was defeated, although the Union forces continued to press the Rebel forces here until early April.

12 March passed fairly uneventful for the soldiers in Fort Pemberton, Rice reported "At the breastworks all day but had no engagement with the enemy. We fired twice at their pickets but they did not reply" and Knolle's entry for the day reads, "March 12-no fighting on either side except a few shells thrown."

The next day the battle returned in earnest. The first shot was fired from the land battery in the Federal works. "For an hour or two from the commencement it was very hot work," related Rice. "They fired 11 & 13 inch ball & shell and injured out batteries considerably." The Federal ironclads returned and shelled the fort. By 3 o'clock, the gunboats retreated from the vision of those in the fort, but continued to lob shells into the fort. "We hit their boat a good many times, and set the cotton bales on fire," Rice wrote that evening. The *Chillicothe* returned to the engagement but withdrew when her ammunition was exhausted.

Shots from the Federal land batteries penetrated the earthen ramparts of Fort Pemberton and dismounted one of the two largest Rebel guns. At noon, a shell passed through the breastworks and struck the magazine for one of the three inch Whitworth guns, causing an explosion that wounded 20 men. Rice recorded in his diary that evening that "Three men had a leg shot off; two above the knee and one below. One of them has since died. Several others were wounded in the arm." The fighting between Fort Pemberton and the Yankees lasted all day."

As the day drew to a close, Davis and his fellow soldiers expected to be shelled throughout the night but were not. Davis wrote that after dark the *Prince of Wales* arrived from Yazoo City with a new 8 inch Columbiad naval gun and ammunition for all of the guns at the fort. "It relieved us a good deal as all of our ammunition for the 32 pdr. had given out." The men worked throughout the night mounting the new gun and rebuilding the breastworks and building a new magazine. Hostilities on the 14th did not commence until the afternoon, this time from the Federal land batteries. "Our guns, however, made them quit that fun less than an hour," Knolle later wrote in his diary." One Confederate was injured in the thigh in this exchange.

"Not a single gun was fired" on March 15, wrote Edwin Rice in his diary. "Both parties seem to have agreed to let each other alone to fortify." The Yankee forces were observed building a fortification in the heavily timbered bend across the river from Fort Pemberton. A deserter from the Federal camp arrived at the Rebel fort and informed Loring "that we killed 8 men in one shot on the gunboat" in the exchange the previous day. Rice would confidently write that "our 8 inch Columbiad is mounted and we feel confident of whipping them in the next engagement." During the day the *Hope* arrived, delivering more ammunition and two 18 pound rifled cannons.

At day break on 16 March, the Legion received orders to march down the Tallahatchie to contest an attempt to cross the river by Yankee forces. "It was a false alarm," recounted Rice. "40 or 50 had crosse[d] in the night but returned." The soldiers marched the two miles back to camp and were safely ensconced behind the breastworks of Fort Pemberton before Federal forces on the land and river opened fire at noon. "[A] brisk cannonading was kept up for two or three hours but not as heavy on Friday." Perhaps this was due to the creation of a new battery built, as Rice reported "two or three hundred yards below our fortifications, opposite the Yankee battery in the woods." This battery's crew would be the target of Union snipers throughout the rest of the day, one of which was Rice. The *Chillicothe* returned to engage the forts, but was so damaged by shot that she retreated from the battle and sought repairs at Mound City, Illinois.

March 18 and 19 passed without a shot fired by both sides. A false alarm on midnight 20 March resulted in "a good many guns and muskets" being fired towards the Union works. As would be expected without a response from the enemy fortification across the Tallahatchie after so long, rumors of the Yankees retreating circulated throughout the Rebel camp. A detachment of 200 soldiers under Lieutenant Colonel Timmons was sent to reconnoiter the Union camp. Upon arrival, they discovered "the Yankee fortifications and camp deserted. 15 graves were found. One of them was the chief gunner of the gunboat Chillicothe." More encouraging to the morale of the Rebels within Fort Pemberton were letters found from Union soldiers "despairing of ever taking 'Fort "Greenbush,'" the Union name for the Rebel fort. In addition to the letters, Rice reported that Timmon's forces captured "bacon and crackers by the quantity." During this lull in battle, Loring again wrote to Pemberton heaping praises on Waul and his command:

> *While I am thankful for the perfectly successful result of our labors here, I wish to express my obligations to Col. T.N. Waul, Texas Legion for his energy, promptness, and good judgment in the discharge of this duty with his Legion in the fortifications during the engagements. I was greatly indebted to him for the assistance he rendered on so many occasions, and which he contributed to our frequent successes . . .*

On 23 March word from upriver reached Fort Pemberton that the retreating Yankee forces numbering 4,500 had met reinforcements under the command of Brigadier General Isaac Quinby and had been ordered to attack the fort again. "About 3 p.m. they announced their arrival by firing three shots at the [Steamer] "Gay" at her landing," wrote Rice. "We fired several small guns at them during the afternoon." Second Lieutenant W.A. Huckaby of Bradley's Company B, Second Infantry under Waul recorded that the Union soldiers took up position near "their old breastworks." Rice reported that the Yankees were repairing their abandoned fort while under attack from Fort Pemberton. "Rained all day. Most of us got very wet—had almost 20 men taken prisoners."

No fighting between the two forts occurred before evening on the 24th and both Rice and Huckaby wrote in their diaries that night that skirmishes between the two camps erupted later in the day "N.E. of camp between the 2nd Texas infantry and the enemy." In this engagement, one Union soldier was killed, one taken prisoner, and six rebels were lost.

The next day Waul's Legion was ordered down to the lower breastworks to defend, and returned to the fort four days later on the 29th. On 1 April Captain Bolling's Company A of First Division was sent out as pickets in advance of the fort to protect it from arriving reinforcements for the Union soldiers across the river. These reinforcements included a small battery of six guns under the command of General D. H. Maury. These cannon did remarkably little damage to the dirt covered cotton bale breastworks of Fort Pemberton. Without siege guns, the Union forces had little hope of defeating the roughly 1,500 rebels ensconced inside.

Union forces on 2 April began to construct a new battery nearer to the fort than the previous one had been. According to Rice, forces at Pemberton fired around 9 P.M. at this battery. The attack continued intermittently into the next morning. 5 April saw two Yankee deserters brought into the camp. With them they brought the news that the Federals had given up attacking the fort and had ordered a withdrawal.

It was true. Grant had finally realized his Yazoo Expedition would not be a success and ordered this troops dug in across from "Fort Greenwood" to return to the Mississippi. In a letter to General Halleck, Grant wrote that he had done so because of information he had received about "other and greater difficulties would be found in navigating the Yazoo below Greenwood." Men crowded the decks of the surviving transports and gunboats for the trip upriver. Officers received cabins, but enlisted men had to fend for themselves. Fires were not permitted to cook or keep warm, and the elements beat down on them as they slowly made their voyage back to the Mississippi. They arrived five days later across from Helena where the levee had been blown two months after beginning their voyage Moon Lake. The flotilla commander, Lieutenant Commander Watson Smith of the *Rattler* died shortly after the withdrawal was complete.

The Legion stationed at Fort Pemberton remained there until April 14, when they received orders to depart and regroup at Point Leflore, two miles northeast of Greenwood. By the middle of May, the Legion was divided, one third returning to Fort Pemberton, and the rest marching to Vicksburg to protect this bastion from Grant's assault. There, the Vicksburg Legion would fight gallantly in the siege and would be surrendered into the custody of Grant on July 4, 1863.

Confederates and Cotton in East Texas

JUDY GENTRY

Judy Gentry, Professor of History at the University of Louisiana—Lafayette, served as President of the Louisiana Historical Association. Her books include *Louisiana Women: Their Lives and Times* (2009) and *I Cannot Forget: Imprisoned in Korea, Accused at Home* (2013).

In this essay, Dr. Gentry examines the significant challenges faced by East Texas cotton producers during the Civil War. ✍

★ ★

The Union naval blockade of the Confederate coastline severely disrupted existing marketing practices. Cotton producers east of the Brazos found their efforts to market their crops disrupted by the unavailability of shipping and the accelerating breakdown of the factorage system that had served their needs since the 1830s. The Union blockade, distance from the Mexican border and the main blockade—running port at Galveston, and the unavailability of enough wagons and teams for overland transport of crops kept the gold value of their cotton in the low range.

Government policies originating from the Confederate capital in Virginia and implemented by the Confederate army also affected the production and marketing of cotton in Texas east of the Brazos. The Confederate Produce Loan in 1861, a government cotton purchasing agent in 1863, Cotton Bureau policies in 1864 and early 1865, and in the last few months of the war, new Confederate Treasury Department rules greatly impacted the lives of cotton producers. Texas east of the Brazos did not share in the large profits that cotton producers in western Texas enjoyed during the war, but planters were able to survive economically despite the blockade and despite the coerced sales of half their crops. Some large planters successfully resisted both coerced sales and impressments, thereby preserving their ability to benefit from the short-lived high prices for cotton that prevailed in the third quarter of 1865.

Students of the Confederate Army's Trans-Mississippi Cotton Bureau have generally concluded that the Bureau failed to achieve its mission to acquire cotton to pay for imported supplies required by the army. They have focused on the cotton that crossed the Rio Grande in payment for supplies and concluded that only a small percentage of the cotton that crossed the Rio Grande was government-owned. This study of Cotton Bureau actions east of the Brazos demonstrates the complexity of Cotton Bureau success in utilizing cotton in support of the war effort. Some of the cotton was indeed sent across the Rio Grande, but, in an effort to reestablish the government's credit, most of the government-owned cotton in Texas east of the Brazos was paid in eastern Texas to firms that had delivered goods to Confederate military officials in advance of payment. Another large portion went to Houston to purchase supplies run in through the blockade or to be exported to England to pay Confederate debts and build a fund for further purchasing. All the cotton acquired by the Cotton Bureau was used for the needs of the Confederate army, but little of it reached the Rio Grande as army property. This study also throws light on a second issue about the Cotton Bureau that has been controversial: To what extent did the Cotton Bureau impress (commandeer) cotton for government use, when farmers and planters refused to sell for the price the Bureau offered? The evidence is very strong that in this region, almost all producers sold the Bureau half their cotton because Cotton Bureau agents threatened to impress all of their cotton if they would not sell half, but no actual impressments of cotton took place.

Students of the private cotton trade or the government acquisition of cotton in Texas have traditionally looked at the Rio Grande area from Brownsville to Eagle Pass. They have also studied the transport of cotton southward from San Antonio and Alleyton (below Houston); the conflict between Texas Governor Pendleton Murrah and the Confederate Commander of the Trans-Mississippi Department, Edmund Kirby Smith; the effort of the Texas government to acquire and transport cotton in western Texas; and the political response in Texas to Confederate cotton policies. Other than one small book that focused on one Confederate quartermaster operating in the northeastern most part of Texas, historians have totally ignored operations of the TMD Cotton Bureau east of the Brazos River.

Texas Civil War historians have long lamented the lack of attention to the economic history of Texas, especially its agricultural aspects, but few scholars have responded to the challenge. Historians of agriculture have especially neglected the marketing of cotton. Morton Rothstein pointed out in 1970 that few studies addressed the "transportation, marketing, or banking relationship to cotton culture" in the nineteenth-century South. Again, few have responded.

As recently at 2003, Gavin Wright included government regulations of agricultural marketing among sadly neglected topics in agricultural history. Harold D. Woodman's path breaking study of cotton factors limits his discussion of Civil War cotton marketing in the Trans-Mississippi area almost exclusively to New Orleans. In 1965, Paul Gates—another of the few exceptions—devoted one-third of his highly respected *Agriculture during the Civil War* to the South, but two of his main conclusions—that the war devastated the South and that King Corn displaced King Cotton during the war years—do not appear to be accurate for Texas. Richard Lowe and Randolph Campbell's 1983 *Planters and Plain Folk* added considerably to our understanding of antebellum Texas agriculture but lacked a discussion of marketing networks. John Solomon Otto's short 1995 book on southern agriculture, 1860–1880, does address marketing as well as government agricultural policies during the Civil War, but mentions Texas only in his closing chapter. This study's focus on the impact of government cotton policy in a major cotton-producing area of Texas—the area east of the Brazos River—where the Union naval blockade had severely disrupted marketing practices contributes to our understanding of the Texas economy during the Civil War.

An outline of the major events is useful. Many cotton producers east of the Brazos patriotically pledged to lend part of the proceeds of the sales of their 1861 crop to the Confederate government, but when it came time to market their crop they found that the blockade prevented exports and had depressed cotton prices well below pre-war levels. Neither factors, other private buyers, nor government purchasing agents, were interested in buying their cotton until the winter of 1862–1863, and then only in the westernmost parts of the region. Cotton could only reach Galveston to run the blockade or the Rio Grande to cross into Mexico by wagon transport, and there were too few wagons, teams, and drivers. Finally, when all the cotton of western Texas had been exported, private buyers and Cotton Bureau agents competed to buy cotton farther and farther east. By 1864, the Bureau required all owners of cotton in Texas to sell half to the government, and almost all producers east of the Brazos complied with the requirement. They then could sell the rest to private buyers or hold it until after the war ended, when they expected the blockade to end and cotton prices to rise.

For at least the first eighteen months of the war, cotton traders in Texas acquired cotton only west of the Brazos and transported it to the Rio Grande for export. Texans, Mexicans, and some others attempted to export cotton across the Rio Grande because the Union blockade of the Confederate coastline made exports from seaports risky. The blockade created a shortage of cotton and high cotton prices in Europe and in the North, as well as a surplus of cotton and low cotton prices inside the Confederacy. Overall, the Union blockade of Confederate ports reduced the commerce into and out of the Confederacy to about 1 percent of the pre-war trade. Although many vessels entered and left Confederate ports during the first year or two of the blockade, these were small vessels with limited cargo space. The large sailing vessels that had carried cotton to England, Europe, and New England could not get insurance to run the blockade and abandoned the trade for the duration of the war. Confederate army officers, in their official capacities, began to purchase cotton in western Texas with quartermaster and ordnance funds for transport to the Rio Grande where it would pay for arms, ammunition, and quartermaster stores available there.

Cotton producers east of the Brazos found the marketing and transporting of the fall 1861 crop (which would normally would have been exported during the winter and spring of 1861–1862) disrupted by the unavailability of shipping and the accelerated breakdown of the factorage system that had served their needs since the 1830s. Most plantations were located on or near navigable rivers and, before the war, transported their crop on steamboats to the coast where it was loaded in small vessels, which carried it to Galveston or New Orleans. Some cotton went by wagon short distances to rail heads that connected to Shreveport or Houston for forwarding to New Orleans or Galveston. The blockade closed these routes. The high cost of transporting cotton the long distances from northern or eastern Texas to the Rio Grande discouraged exports from the area so much that cotton prices remained low there, and the 1861 crop remained, for the most part, where it had been grown, harvested, ginned, and perhaps baled. The well-established marketing patterns had been disrupted.

The Confederate government in 1861 urged planters throughout the Confederacy to subscribe to a Produce Loan, pledging to lend the government part of the proceeds of their crop. The Confederate Treasury Department intended to use the loan's certificates as security for borrowing in England or France pounds or francs to purchase supplies to be run in through the blockade. However, the large ships, which left in May 1861 with remnants of the 1860 crop did not return until the blockade was lifted four years later. Southern debtors refused to reimburse Northern creditors until the war ended, causing Northern credit, which was essential for factors to conduct their business, dried up. Cotton factors soon understood that only small amounts of cotton would get through the blockade and that the port warehouses would overflow. The New Orleans cotton factors placed a notice in the newspapers, to the effect that they would not accept cotton shipments that they could neither ship nor store. This decision affected part of the crop in east Texas that previously had been marketed through Shreveport, Louisiana to New Orleans factors. More importantly, all factors in the major Confederate seaports faced the same problems as their New Orleans colleagues. When export proved to be almost impossible, the Confederate government accepted in the summer of 1862 the cotton itself in return for Produce Loan bonds; when necessary, it would pay for up to half of the cotton in Confederate currency rather than in bonds. Some Texas planters subscribed to the Produce Loan, giving the Confederate government ownership of 25 % to 100 % of their crop; this cotton remained on the plantations and eventually became the security for a major bond issue in Europe that raised over $8 million (specie value) for the Confederacy. Produce Loan records show that producers in Texas, mostly east of the Brazos, subscribed over 14,000 bales of cotton. The producers were paid primarily in Confederate bonds that promised 8 percent interest twice a year in specie. (The government, however, actually paid the interest in Confederate notes.) Some producers may have demanded and received partial payment in cash instead of bonds. In mid-1862, it took $1.50 Confederate dollars to equal $1.00 in gold; by mid-1863 it took $9.00. After the fall of Vicksburg in July 1863 cut the Trans-Mississippi off from the Confederacy east of the river, it is unlikely that enough Confederate currency reached the TMD to pay this interest. Nevertheless, the interest payments to bondholders may have provided a small income from mid-1862 through mid-1863. Those who got some of their subscription in Confederate dollars could have spent them in 1862 without much loss, but would have lost five-sixths of their value if they held them until 1863.

At cotton planting time in early spring 1862, Confederate hopes for a quick victory were still high. Many cotton planters optimistically planted a full crop, or nearly so, with perhaps more acreage than usual devoted to food crops. After the Confederacy quickly won the war, it would be good to have a large crop growing in the fields. The Confederate defeat at Shiloh in April and the fall of New Orleans in May came after planting. In April 1862 the Confederacy began conscripting young white men who had not volunteered for military service. The small family farms east of the Brazos, which produced about 20 percent of the total cotton crop, lost virtually their entire labor force. Some enrolled in the Texas militia but were soon sent to the western frontier; others avoided the Confederate troops that hunted down draft evaders, but few were able to continue their normal labor. The production of cotton and food crops by small farms necessarily declined. During 1862, the Confederate government was increasingly unable to meet the army's needs. In Texas, as well as in the entire Confederacy, military commanders short of food, draft animals, wagons, and forage authorized impressment from the local population. It had long been the practice of Europe and the United States to authorize impressments necessary to keep an army functioning. Officers supervised the seizures and gave detailed receipts. Impressment of draft animals and wagons interfered with the moving of cotton to market.

Because of their distance from the Mexican border and from the main blockade-running port at Galveston, producers east of the Brazos found that the gold value of their cotton remained in the low range (in comparison to 1860 prices) throughout the war except for a short-lived rise in 1863. In November 1862, the Confederate authorities in Richmond attempted to prevent competition among quartermasters in Texas by appointing Major Simeon Hart, an El Paso merchant, as the only quartermaster in Texas authorized to import supplies and acquire and transport cotton to the Rio Grande to pay for them. By the time Hart took charge, cotton prices in western Texas were so high that he used most of his limited fund of Confederate currency to purchase cotton in eastern Texas. Some businessmen also began to buy cotton in the area, causing real (gold equivalent) cotton prices to rise. Hart struggled for the next year and a half to move that cotton to the Rio Grande. Small amounts reached the Rio Grande border in the summer of 1863, but some of his East Texas cotton was still on the plantations in the summer of 1864.

Because Hart's cotton would not be available soon enough, Kirby Smith created in August 1863 a Trans-Mississippi Department Cotton Bureau to acquire cotton to pay for imported supplies arriving in Mexico. Colonel William A. Broadwell, a prominent New Orleans cotton factor, headed the new agency, and by November 1863, Lt. Col. William J. Hutchins headed a sub-unit, the Texas Cotton Office. Hutchins' charge was to acquire cotton in western Texas for forwarding to the Rio Grande. He was also to buy cotton near Houston to pay for supplies arriving at Galveston through the blockade or to send to the Rio Grande. To avoid impressment of all of a producer's cotton crop, he had to sell half to the government and deliver it to Cotton Bureau depots. To a large extent, the Bureau acquired cotton under this plan only near Houston or in the area between the Brazos and Trinity rivers.

The army quartermasters were busy in late 1863, setting up depots to collect a tax-in-kind the Confederate Congress had passed in April. By October 1, 1863, agricultural producers had to pay ten percent of the 1861 and 1862 crops not yet sold, and by February 1864, they owed ten percent of their entire 1863 crop. The tax applied to virtually all agricultural products, including cotton. For goods already impressed or sold to the government, the tax was ten percent of the sale or impressments price. Congress later extended this "tithe" to the 1864 and 1865 crops. The dried peas, grains, hay, and bacon were consumed by the troops nearby. Quartermasters delivered the cotton to Treasury agents, who at first held it as security for potential foreign loans but later exported some to England to buy supplies. The farmers and planters apparently did not have to provide an additional ten percent of their cotton after selling half to the Cotton Bureau.

Unlike cotton growers elsewhere in the Confederacy, Texas cotton producers never experienced occupation by Union troops during the war. Their slaves may have known about the Emancipation Proclamation but had no opportunity to escape to Union lines. Their masters knew better than to send them near the Mexican border, where they could easily slip to freedom across the Rio Grande. The Confederate armies sometimes impressed slave labor, and slaves sometimes acted as teamsters hauling government cotton. Because fewer white men supervised their labor on plantations, the slaves could slack off in their work. They experienced deprivation, since planters could not import cloth, clothing, and shoes for their use. Since the Texas antebellum planters generally produced all the food needed for their families, laborers, and animals, slaves probably did not see a decline in their diet. All in all, Texas planters encountered far fewer problems controlling their slaves than those in other parts of the Confederacy. The war only minimally affected cotton production of plantations east of the Brazos.

Texas planters also enjoyed at least the possibility of selling their cotton for export across the Rio Grande. Consequently, producers in western Texas experienced rising prices for their cotton as businessmen, state agents, army quartermasters, and eventually the Cotton Bureau competed to buy their crop. By 1863, that competition for cotton reached the area between the Trinity and Brazos rivers, and by early 1864 it had penetrated even east of the Trinity, where the prices were limited, however, by the costs of transporting cotton greater distances.

After the fall of Vicksburg, Kirby Smith ordered the removal of government-owned cotton (mainly Produce Loan cotton near the Mississippi River) to safety farther west. As Produce Loan agent and then Cotton Bureau agent, Andrew W. McKee worked from July until the end of December 1863, moving 3,600 bales of government cotton from Louisiana south of the Red River to Niblett's Bluff on the Sabine River. Captains W. W. Barrett and Noble A. Birge, Cotton Bureau agents, hauled 7,000 additional bales from Louisiana to the Sabine River from August through December 1863. They also transported cotton from northwestern Louisiana or points on the Sabine River by wagon train to Waco for eventual shipment to the Rio Grande. Barrett and Birge were extremely efficient at hiring drivers with their teams and wagons, organizing trains, repairing wagons, managing the livestock, selecting routes with adequate forage, and personally supervising the trains en route. Within a few months they had 350 loaded wagons on the road to Waco. The wagons returned to departmental headquarters at Shreveport, Louisiana with quartermaster, ordnance, and medical stores imported across the Rio Grande. These wagon trains made regular round trips, except when diverted for other military purposes. By

November 1864, Barrett and Birge's trains had hauled 6600 bales to Waco or San Antonio, had 965 bales on wheels to those places, and had delivered almost 1100 bales of cotton to other depots—for a total of 8,660 bales transported westward through Texas east of the Brazos.

The Cotton Bureau also arranged to move cotton from farther east in Louisiana to Pulaski, Burr's Ferry, and Sabinetown on the Sabine River. Broadwell then contracted with Moore and Smoker, and later Davenport and Burns, Captain B. H. Perry, and Captain J. W Polk, to build sheds to protect the merchandise on the Sabine, build flatboats, put the cotton in order (it suffered from deteriorating bagging and rope and lack of shelter during transport and to some extent while on the plantations), and at the first rise of the river to ship it to Orange, Texas. From there it could be shipped by steamboat and then rail to Houston or even southwest of Houston to Alleyton, a depot for wagon trains to Brownsville on the Rio Grande. Altogether 12–14,000 bales of cotton accumulated at the Sabine River from Louisiana or nearby areas of Texas, on their way to Houston and beyond. Minimal rises of the Sabine River in the drought of 1863–1864 delayed shipping. Other delays included the need to buy cotton presses and import bagging and rope to put the cotton into good order, the need to load it on steamers or wagons at Orange for transport to the railhead at Beaumont, and the paucity of labor available to accomplish these tasks. The first Sabine cotton arrived at Orange in July 1864, and some was still at Pulaski when the war ended. Some reached Houston by rail in the late winter and spring of 1865 and some was delivered at Sabinetown in payment on a huge debt owed to R. King & Company. Although the agents and government contractors had many advantages, including freedom from impressments of their equipment or transport and an occasional work detail from the military, moving fewer than 14,000 bales of cotton overland to the Sabine River and then to the railhead at Beaumont highlight the difficulties private businessmen and producers encountered in moving cotton to market.

Once established in August 1863, the Cotton Bureau took over existing government cotton contracts and cotton operations, most of them in Texas west of the Brazos or near Houston. By November Hutchin's Texas Cotton Office expanded the purchasing effort to east of the Brazos. The TCO directly administered the area between the Brazos and Trinity Rivers, the area surrounding Houston, and an area eastward along the coast to the Sabine. The TCO area to the east of Houston extended northward about 90 miles on the Sabine River end and about 125 miles northward on the Trinity River end, encompassing Orange and Beaumont in the southeast and Crockett in its northwestern corner. Soon the TCO established major depots at Waco, Marlin, and Mosely's Ferry on the upper Brazos River, and Navasota, Magnolia, and others between the Brazos and Trinity rivers north and northwest of Houston.

In January of 1864, the TMD Cotton Bureau required planters to sell half their cotton to the Confederate government or have all of it seized. Broadwell directed Barrett and Birge to purchase cotton in a large area of northern and eastern Texas—north and east of a line drawn diagonally along the eastern boundary of Anderson County, to Dallas County at the northwestern end and Sabine County at the southeastern. The western boundary of the area bordered on the upper Trinity River, and the southern bounds met the TCO-administered area that stretched eastward along the Gulf Coast. Barrett established his headquarters at Henderson and Birge operated from Jefferson. They attempted to buy half the cotton of their districts. They could offer the schedule price for half, and exemptions from impressments for the rest if the producers hauled the government half to depots within twenty-five miles of their plantation. For permits to export their half, producers had to deliver the Cotton Bureau's half the longer distances to Marlin on the upper Brazos River or Magnolia (nearer to Houston), for instance. Barrett and Birge were only minimally successful until the system was reformed five months later. Five factors limited their success. Entrepreneurs who had previously confined their activities to western Texas began buying cotton during the winter of 1862–1863 not only between the Brazos and Trinity rivers but also in the western parts of Barrett's and Birge's districts, pushing prices up. From early 1864 to the end of the war, Governor Henry W. Allen of Louisiana employed agents to buy cotton in Louisiana and northeast Texas and move it to Waco and then through San Antonio to the Rio Grande. There, his agents exchanged it for medicine, cotton cards for the hand manufacture of cloth, and other civilian necessities. Allen's operation seldom came into conflict with Cotton Bureau agents, and when it did, Broadwell quickly negotiated mutually acceptable solutions. More importantly, by March 1864, Texas government agents offered growers who sold cotton to the state protection from impressment for an amount equal to the amount sold to the state. State agents offered higher prices than the Cotton Bureau. They also claimed that the Cotton Bureau was not legally authorized to impress cotton and denounced its agents as corrupt. Most planters therefore preferred to sell to the state. A fourth factor was a February 1864 law of the Confederate Congress that transferred control of cotton exports to the Treasury Department. But, a key reason the Cotton Bureau's January 1864 plan failed was the simple fact that growers did not have the teams and wagons to transport more than a few bales, and the January 1864 Bureau plan relied on producers to take the initiative to deliver the cotton to get exemptions from impressments and export permits.

In June 1864, Broadwell and Kirby Smith designed a new plan for acquiring cotton and by early July Governor Murrah agreed to no longer oppose the Bureau cotton purchasing program. Again, the threat of impressments was at the heart of the plan. Cotton Bureau agents visited every farm and plantation and offered to buy half the crop at the schedule price in return for exemptions from impressments for the rest. An officer with the authority to impress all their cotton visited producers who did not sell half to the government. Usually, at that time, the producers agreed to sell half to get the other half exempted. Everywhere east of the Brazos except in Barrett and Birge's districts, producers also got export permits for delivering the government bales to nearby depots. In 1864, cotton with export permits sold for almost twice as much as other cotton, but permits were out of reach for most of the producers east of the Trinity River. To obtain export permits for their half, they would have had to haul the cotton they sold to the Bureau from 120 to 200 miles cross country to points on the Brazos River or near Houston. The value of cotton in these easternmost areas was only 2 to 3 cents (specie), because buyers deducted the cost of transport to market. Broadwell used export permits to encourage producers to bear the cost of transport at least as far as the Brazos. Barrett and Birge proved unable to convince Broadwell that the producers simply lacked the means to move their cotton that far.

Whereas almost all producers east of the Brazos sold half their cotton to the Bureau, in several counties the largest owners refused to sell even when the impressment officers arrived, claiming the Bureau had no authority to impress cotton. Kirby Smith based his authority on directives from the Secretary of War and President of the Confederacy when the surrender at Vicksburg brought about a separation of the Trans-Mississippi states from the Confederacy east of the Mississippi River. They instructed Kirby Smith to exercise the civil and military authority of the Confederate government in the Trans-Mississippi and do what was necessary to supply the army in that area. In August 1863, Trans-Mississippi governors agreed to cooperate with Kirby Smith and most often did so. (The exception was Texas governor Pendleton Murrah, from early March to early July 1864.) Kirby Smith also pointed out that the Confederate Congress had confirmed that traditional military authority for impressments. When in early August 1864, new regulations arrived from Richmond with an order to turn control of cotton over to the TMD Treasury agent, Kirby Smith convinced him that the Overland Regulations were impractical and received permission to continue as before until February 1, 1865. Cotton Bureau agents corresponded regarding the desirability of impressing cotton. Most agreed that there was no way to keep the army supplied without acquiring cotton and that the army had no money to pay for cotton or supplies. Because of that necessity, many believed it important to demonstrate the resolve of Kirby Smith and to make an example of the few large planters who refused to sell. They argued that fairness to the smaller planters and farmers who had sold cotton to the Bureau required impressments. Others suggested that while impressments of supplies was lawful, impressment of the wherewithal to pay for imported supplies might not be. Since the Texas legislature had passed laws requiring full payment at the time of impressment and requiring Texas authorities to arrest anyone who attempted illegal impressment, officers in the field tried to shift responsibility up the chain of command but could not obtain a clear order to impress particular cotton. The correspondence of the Cotton Bureau indicates that no impressments of cotton took place in Texas east of the Brazos.

Although in January 1865 some large planters successfully defied Cotton Bureau threats to impress their cotton, the June 1864 program to coerce sales through threats of impressment had made it possible for the Bureau to acquire nearly half the cotton east of the Brazos. When Governor Murrah agreed in July 1864 to stop opposing the Bureau purchasing program and officers began arriving on farms and plantations to impress all of the cotton of those who were slow to sell, almost all producers sold half their cotton to the Bureau. The growers believed impressment was imminent and needed the promised payment. Moreover, those west of the Trinity River got permits to export the other half. Even in Barrett and Birge's districts, producers sold half to the government, in the hope that the exemptions would allow them to sell the rest. Private buyers, some of whom brought wagons and Mexican drivers into eastern Texas, could get the export permits for the other half (which increased its value considerably) if they hauled the government half to the Brazos River.

Cotton Bureau agents east of the Brazos used the large amounts of cotton they purchased from June 1864 through January 1865 in various ways. They transported some to Waco or San Antonio for reshipment to the Rio Grande and some to Navasota (at the junction of the Navasato River with a short rail line to Houston) or other depots for shipment to Houston, to pay for goods being run in through the blockade at Galveston. Hutchins paid 13,700 bales of cotton at Houston, from July through October 1864, for goods run in through Galveston, or to creditors of the Cotton Bureau. After the last blockade-running port on the east coast fell in mid-January 1865, Hutchins could export larger amounts of cotton on blockade runners that shifted their operations to Galveston. This cotton was shipped to Havana, to pay creditors or to Liverpool for sale on government account. During the last five months of the war, the Texas Cotton Office exported 7100 bales of cotton from Galveston on government account.

But most of the cotton purchased by the Bureau east of the Brazos appears to have been used to pay for army stores delivered during the preceding two years. To improve government credit, to maintain their honor and the government's, and to induce contractors to continue importing army supplies, Broadwell and Kirby Smith directed that cotton be paid to Bouldin and Newell, R. King and Company, Bouldin, Riggs and Walker, Governor Morehead, and a few others who had delivered supplies when needed instead of demanding payment before delivery. In the spring of 1865, Bouldin, Riggs and Walker was still awaiting payment for thirteen tons of lead delivered to the arsenal at Marshall in January of 1864, and R. King and Company awaited payment for supplies delivered in June 1864 and advances made to Broadwell at that time so that the Cotton Bureau might sustain its cotton acquisition and transport program. In some instances, the Bureau delivered cotton to contractors at depots east of the Brazos. Eventually, the Bureau transferred to King and Company, and others to whom cotton was owed, the government half of the cotton of entire counties where it lay on the plantations. The contractors' agents then took possession of the cotton directly from the producers and attempted to transport it to the Rio Grande or run it out through the blockade at Galveston or the mouth of the Sabine River.

Few buyers in Barrett and Birge's districts, however, could obtain Cotton Bureau export permits, because most did not have wagons and teams to deliver cotton to the Brazos River. Those who wished to sell their cotton could sell it to private buyers who brought teams and wagons into the district. Generally, private buyers paid in Confederate currency equivalent to the specie value. Thus, if Broadwell's upper estimate that cotton in Barrett and Birge's districts was worth 3 cents per pound (specie) was correct, the buyers would pay 60 cents per pound in Confederate dollars in July 1864. The Bureau, on the other hand, paid a set price, 20 cents per pound in early 1864 (and 25 cents in late 1864) in certificates that could be exchanged for Confederate dollars when the currency became available and, moreover, was dilatory in providing certificates. Bureau buying of cotton and issuing of exemptions and export permits ended February 1, 1865.

Through coerced sales, the Bureau's effective cotton-buying program in Texas east of the Brazos—under the authority of Kirby Smith as Commander of the Trans-Mississippi Department—lasted seven months. In that time, it had acquired nearly half the cotton of the area for the use of the Confederate Army,

Congress's February 1864 law mandated that importers and exporters make available to the government half of their cargo space and effectively transferred control of cotton exports from the army to the Treasury Department. Treasury Department regulations under the new law envisioned exporting to England half the cotton of the Confederacy and prohibited both payment in cotton for purchases of supplies in the Confederacy and contracts providing for payments in cotton in the Confederacy for imported supplies. All cotton would go to England to purchase supplies there at wholesale prices. The Treasury Department planned to acquire cotton from exporters at the ports (and, in Texas, also at Alleytown and Waco), since the exporters could ship cotton only if half the cargo was government owned.

The Treasury Department developed regulations for exports by sea and by overland transport in April 1864. They reached Kirby Smith in early August 1864. Peter W. Gray, former Confederate Senator from Texas, had become the Treasury agent for the Trans-Mississippi Department in February and soon established his headquarters at Marshall, Texas. When Kirby Smith and Broadwell pointed out to him the impracticality of the overland regulations, Gray allowed Cotton Bureau operations to continue while he requested modification. He allowed the Cotton Bureau to buy and transport cotton, and issue exemptions and export permits until February 1, 1865. The Cotton Bureau and those with export permits could continue to export cotton without Treasury Department interference until May 1. From early August on, however, Gray refused to provide any new issue Confederate dollars for cotton buying and directed that payment be made in certificates, or old issue currency that the Cotton Bureau might have on hand. When the modified regulations arrived in early October 1864, Gray published them but did not gain control of Cotton Bureau staff until mid-November. Gray slowly familiarized himself with the practices of the Bureau and in the meantime allowed the June 1864 plan to continue for the overland trade. By December 1864, Gray regretted having agreed to the permits for export and indirectly approving impressments. In early January, Gray published a notice that he had never approved impressments of cotton, and soon after, Kirby Smith withdrew his authority for impressments of cotton, thus undercutting the threat of impressment that was at the heart of the June 1864 program. But by that time, the Cotton Bureau had already acquired a large part of the cotton of the region.

Although the June 1864 Cotton Bureau program had been in effect for seven months, for the last three and a half months of the war the threat of impressments was gone. Cotton producers could freely sell cotton they had not previously sold. The buyers would then attempt to transport it to the Mexican border or Galveston. In either case, buyers intending to export cotton eventually would have to sell half to the government because half the cargos leaving the Confederacy had to be government-owned. Similarly, wagon trains carrying cotton past Alleyton or Waco toward the Rio Grande had to provide half the cargo space to the government, so the traders had to sell to the government half of their stock. Given the time it took for wagon trains to move cotton from northern and eastern Texas, few if any cotton buyers were able to export cotton from east of the Brazos under the Treasury Department plan. An unexpected obstacle appeared when the drought that had plagued Texas since early 1864 broke with drenching rains in the winter of 1864–1865 and spring of 1865, producing mud that bogged down wagon trains across the state.

By late 1864, realizing that the Confederacy had lost the war, some planters became unwilling to sell to private buyers at any price, expecting lifting of the blockade and reopening of the traditional routes. They hoped that the specie price of cotton would then rise considerably. At the time of the surrender, much cotton remained on the plantations. Indeed, many factorage firms returned to business soon after the war ended and exported large amounts of cotton in late 1865 and early 1866. The specie price of cotton at Galveston in the summer of 1865 was 50 cents, more than seventeen times the price east of the Brazos during most of the war. Although the price at Galveston quickly fell to a high of 31–32 cents during 1866 (the 1865 crop marketing year), that was ten times the price that Texans east of the Brazos could get during the war and five times the usual pre-war price.

Texas east of the Brazos did not share in the large profits that cotton producers in western Texas enjoyed during the war, but the planters survived economically despite the blockade and the coerced sales. Although for thirteen months (January 1864 through January 1865), cotton producers faced government policies that demanded that they sell half their cotton or have all of it impressed, producers could, after complying, then sell the other half at higher prices, since it was exempt from impressments. Some major producers apparently successfully held out against this government coercion and probably sold their cotton to private buyers during the summer or fall of 1865, taking advantage of much higher prices once the blockade was lifted.

This study illuminates two important aspects of the economy of Texas east of the Brazos River during the Civil War: the economic lives of cotton producers, as the Union blockade disrupted well-established marketing arrangements for cotton; and the Confederate Cotton Bureau's efforts to acquire half the cotton of Texas.

After the people of eastern Texas found it almost impossible to export or sell their cotton during the first year and a half of the war, the revised Produce Loan provided a little relief in late 1862, and some buyers appeared in the western part of the area in 1863. In early 1864, the demands of the Confederate Cotton Bureau that they sell half their cotton at low prices or have the entirety impressed dashed local hopes to sell cotton at good prices. Private buyers in some areas paid higher prices for the other half but struggled to get permits to export it. By late 1864, many producers preferred to hold their half in anticipation of higher prices after the war was over. It was not until the war ended, the army disbanded, and the blockade was lifted that cotton marketing could hope to return to the pre-war routes and practices.

The TMD Cotton Bureau was successful in the last year of the war in acquiring in eastern Texas large amounts of cotton to pay for military goods imported into Texas. This success was based on coercion by threats of impressing all of a producer's cotton if he or she would not sell half to the army. As a few influential Texans refused to comply and a much larger number protested to the state legislature and Confederate Congress, Kirby Smith withdrew his authorization for impressing cotton. The army, however, required the overwhelming majority of producers who had signed contracts under that threat to deliver their cotton as contracted. Clearly, if the war had continued for another year, the unwillingness of Texas citizens to sell cotton at low prices to the Confederate army would have prevented the army from continuing to import essential military supplies.

This study also demonstrates the complexity of the Confederate use of cotton to pay for imported goods. The Confederate Treasury Department used Produce Loan cotton where it lay on the producer's land as security for borrowing in England and Europe. The Confederate

Army in Texas paid cotton on delivery of imported goods on the Rio Grande and at Galveston, delivered cotton at depots along the Brazos River to contractors who had delivered goods in advance of payment, and delivered half the cotton of entire counties to contractors who had advanced huge sums of money to the Cotton Bureau. Finally, in 1864 Confederate Treasury agents exported large amounts of cotton for sale in England.

The Confederate army in Texas increasingly understood the importance of cotton in its ability to protect Texas from Union forces. The inability of producers of cotton in Texas east of the Brazos to export or sell their cotton eliminated their main source of income. The resulting tension was one example of a weakening of support for continuing the war that was evident by late 1864 in most parts of the Confederacy.

The Prolonged War: Texans Struggle to Win the Civil War during Reconstruction

Kenneth W. Howell

K enneth W. Howell, Executive Director of the Central Texas Historical Association, teaches history at Blinn College in Bryan. A prolific author, his works include *Henderson County, Texas: An Antebellum History, 1846–1861* (1999), *Texas Confederate, Reconstruction Governor: James Webb Throckmorton* (2008), *The Seventh Star of the Confederacy: Texas during the Civil War* (2009), *Still the Arena of Civil War: Violence and Turmoil in Reconstruction Texas, 1865–1874* (2012), and the popular textbook *Beyond Myths and Legends: A Narrative History of Texas* (4th edition, 2013).

In this selection, Dr. Howell contends that the Civil War did not truly end in Texas in 1865. During Reconstruction—really the war's second phase—federal troops, Unionists, and freedmen faced brazen intimidation and brutal guerilla raids by embittered Confederates. Howell also asserts that some violence committed during this tumultuous period was simple banditry carried out under the guise of defending the "Lost Cause." ❧

★ ★

Traditionally, historians have viewed the American Civil War (1861–65) and the Reconstruction era (1865–77) as two distinct and separate periods in US history. Though this approach provides a convenient way to understand two very complex eras, it tends to skew the general understanding of the violence that remained commonplace in the South during Reconstruction. Scholarly celebrations of the Union victory in the Civil War tend to ignore the fact that the US government ultimately failed to rehabilitate southern society in the decades following the war. A more con structive way to study these two periods is to examine them as two distinct phases of a continuous conflict between the northern and southern states lasting from 1861 to 1877.

In the first phase of the war (1861–65), the US and Confederate governments used conventional military forces to achieve their respective goals: Federal troops fought to preserve the Union, and after the Emancipation Proclamation went into effect in January 1863, to end slavery. The Confederate military fought to win southern independence and to preserve the institution of slavery. The larger population, greater industrial capabilities, and naval superiority of the northern states dictated almost from the very beginning that the Union would win what became a war of attrition.

During the second phase of the war (1865–77), sometimes referred to as the War of Reconstruction, whites organized terrorist groups and initiated a prolonged guerrilla war against Republican governments in the southern states that sought to force political and social change. Given that Radical Republicans supported federal and state legislation that would guarantee African Americans suffrage rights and other freedoms, white southerners became concerned about potential changes to their political institutions. They believed that suffrage for former slaves would ultimately lead to complete social and political equality for southern blacks. Perhaps more than any other southern state, Texas became a bloody battleground during this second phase of the struggle between North and South.

Shortly after the fall of the Confederacy, most Texas unionists hoped to cooperate with federal authorities and bring positive change to their state. They believed cooperation was the only way to escape punitive actions such as treason trials, martial law, and a lengthy period of military occupation. On July 17, 1865, a group of North Texas unionists met in convention at Paris, in Lamar County, to swear loyalty to the national government and to vow their willingness to follow the law. The delegates elected W. B. Gray of Titus County as their president; T. G. Wright of Red River County as their vice president; and E. L. Dohoney of Lamar County as their secretary. Gray impressed upon all the importance of cooperating with the US government. He told his fellow delegates that such cooperation might eliminate the need for military occupation and for coercive legislation. Being a realist, he counseled obedience and submission for the good of Texas. Shortly afterward, Rice Maxey motioned that the convention should create a resolutions committee to draft a document to explain their views and that copies of such a statement should be forwarded to Washington. Additionally, Maxey suggested that they should distribute copies to newspapers and to the public. The delegates agreed and voted in favor of the motion; Gray appointed Maxey as chair of the committee. Other committeemen included R. H. Taylor and Sam G. Galbraith of Fannin County; William M. Ewing, L. A. Lollar, and Joseph Smith of Hopkins County; Hardin Hart and M. H. Wright of Hunt County; Henry Jones of Titus County; and W. H. Johnson, G. W. Wright, and E. W. Miner of Lamar County. The committee produced a document stating that military rule was accepted until such time that the provisional governor was satisfied that Texans would "give evidence of their loyal dispositions to the Government of the United States, and a willingness to yield obedience to the Constitution and laws there of."

It was probably fitting that such a proclamation came out of Northeast Texas, where a majority of the citizens of many counties had voted against secession. But the unionists' dreams of a peaceful reconciliation with the federal government proved to be just that—dreams. The plan of those men was the best hope for an alternate history, one that would have led to a constructive rather than destructive Reconstruction, but forces at work at the end of the war dashed all their hopes. Instead of making progress, Texas became a dark and bloody ground—the home of terrorist groups and outlaw gangs that were supported by the Democratic Party so long as the malefactors fought for the goals of the party. Even before the Paris meeting, Texas was spinning out of control.

Following Gen. Robert E. Lee's surrender to Lt. Gen. Ulysses S. Grant at Appomattox on April 9, 1865, the local and state governments in Texas collapsed, leaving vast regions in total chaos. Armed bands of former soldiers, deserters, and common criminals swarmed though various areas. For example, in Tyler lawlessness became commonplace. During the war, the town was home to various Confederate installations, including a post commissary, a wartime prison, an armory, a pharmaceutical laboratory, and a quartermaster's warehouse. Immediately following the war, local women forced their way into the laboratory, taking whatever they wished; also, desperate people with hungry families tried but failed to break into the commissary. Some local men tried to steal the horses on the post, but the commanding officer held them off, while Confederates blew up the armory rather than let panicky men, who could not be trusted, secure arms and ammunition. Many area women were afraid to leave their homes for fear of robbers. Nevertheless, some did so, but most went armed and rode in groups of three or more for collective protection. Worse developments were averted when a company of Union troopers temporarily stopped in Tyler. But even as the cavalrymen tried to restore order, Kate Stone, a transplanted Louisiana aristocrat temporarily living in town, reported that there were "four or five men shot or hanged within a few miles of us in a week."

On June 11, unknown parties even looted the state treasury in Austin, much to the disgust of officials who vainly tried to protect the treasury and restore order to the capital. The robbers successfully made their move in the middle of the night, disappearing in the cover of darkness before anyone could react. As happened in Tyler and Austin, all across Texas mobs of men and women looted places such as Confederate commissaries, stealing all things of utilitarian value. Men swarmed over supply depots, looting them for arms, ammunition, and anything else useful. Some even robbed private homes, threatening the owners with death should they resist. This early mayhem was ongoing even though Confederates still controlled the state, suggesting that this violence was not part of any organized attempt to continue the war against the federal government. Instead, locals were attempting to survive the failed economic and political systems left behind in the wake of the fallen Confederacy. Nevertheless, events would quickly unfold that would cause the southern states, especially Texas, to renew their fight against the national government.

On June 19, 1865, Maj. Gen. Gordon Granger landed in Galveston and was welcomed by area unionists. Commanding 1,800 men, the general announced that Lincoln's Emancipation Proclamation would be enforced in Texas. From the moment he reached Galveston, Granger's command was a difficult one. Given that the troops at his disposal did not even have the strength of two full regiments, he could only send small detachments to the interior, though they did go to Tyler, Marshall, Austin, and San Antonio. The general, like other commanders who were later stationed there, never had enough troops to adequately police the state, a fact that doomed would-be Reconstruction reformers like the men of Northeast Texas. Despite the fact that Union forces in Texas rose to a high of 51,000 in 1865, the number of soldiers in state drastically fell to a mere 3,000 by the end of 1866, with most of them defending the western frontier from Indian raids.

Meanwhile, violence continued unabated, undercutting reformers' hopes for the era and pushing Reconstruction policies along a path bound for failure. By the late spring and summer of 1865, whites were beating, whipping, and killing black Texans. Most of the freedpeople became victims of crimes because of their new status in society; they became victims of irrational racial hatred. In many cases the perpetrators were young men, most Confederate veterans. They hated the Yankees and the outcome of the war, and in their frustration they targeted freedpeople and white unionists, the very groups that supported Reconstruction policies and who were least able to protect themselves. One historian listed the reasons why Anglos killed freedmen: "[F]reedman did not remove hat when he passed him [a white man]; Negro would not allow himself to be whipped; freedman would not allow his wife to be whipped by a white man; he [a freedman] was carrying a letter to a Freedmen's Bureau official; [one murderer killed] Negroes just to see them kick; [one white killed] because he wanted to thin out niggers a little; [freedman] did not hand over his money quick enough; [freedman] would not give up his whiskey flask. Even though rational minds today consider these explanations absurd, the majority of white Texans during the late nineteenth century believed in the absolute right of white supremacy. In an atmosphere of racial hatred in which the least provocation could lead to an uncontrollable riot, whites waged war against black Texans and their white allies. Contemporaries often commented about the treatment of freedpeople and unionists.

From Paris, Mrs. L. E. Potts wrote to Pres. Andrew Johnson providing personal testimony to events unfolding in her area of the state. She reported, "I wish that my poor pen could tell you of their [freedpeople] persecutions here. They are now just out of slavery only a few months, and their masters are so angry to lose them that they are trying to persecute them back into slavery." She continued by stating that "there have never been any federal troops in here, and everything savors of rebellion. I wish we could have a few soldiers here just for a while, to let these rebels know that they have been whipped." Potts concluded her letter with a plea for the president to take some action to save the freedpeople, stating: "your good heart and wise head know best what to do. I have stated only facts; the negroes need protection here. When they work they scarcely ever get any pay; and what are they to do?" Potts, however, placed too much faith in Johnson, for he simply turned the matter over to Maj. Gen. Oliver Otis Howard, the head of the Bureau of Refugees, Freedmen, and Abandoned Lands, giving little more thought to the suffering African Americans in Texas.

At about the same time that Potts wrote her letter, Bvt. Maj. Gen. George Armstrong Custer observed the activities of unrepentant rebels in East, South, and Central Texas. In the summer of 1865, General Granger ordered Custer and his regiment of cavalry from Alexandria, Louisiana, to Houston to help support his efforts in Texas. After suffering organizational problems, Custer's regiment left Alexandria on August 8, crossed the Sabine River, and made its way into Texas. While in route, Granger ordered Custer to bypass Houston and march directly to the rural community of Hempstead, where the troopers would find an abundance of grass and forage for their horses. The regiment remained stationed just outside of the small Texas town until the end of October, when it moved westward to make Austin its new headquarters.

Following his service in the Lone Star State, Custer reported to the Joint Committee on Reconstruction at the first session of the Thirty-Ninth Congress in March 1866. Congress created this special committee in an effort to learn more about conditions in the South. After extensive inquiry, the committee's final report aided law-makers in establishing more-effective policies to bring the embittered South back into the Union. Custer, like many of those who testified before the legislators, reinforced the idea that certain areas in Texas were still in a virtual state of war. He stated, "[I]n Texas it would hardly be possible to find a man who has been strictly faithful to the Union, and remained in the South, during the war. They [rebels] forced all who were truly Union men to leave the state. Those who did not were murdered. The people of the north have no conception of the number of murders that have been committed in that state during and since the war." Custer was certain that it would not be "safe for a loyal man to remain in Texas [once] . . . troops were withdrawn." When asked if he knew of any organizations there that were attempting to thwart the actions of the federal government, the officer replied: "[I]t was reported to me frequently that such organizations did exist, and I have no doubt in my mind that they have existed in the northern part of the state. I was so thoroughly convinced of the fact that I sent a considerable force into that section of the state to disperse them. The fact that such organizations did exist was confirmed by the statements, written and oral, of loyal men, and by the reports of officers sent there on duty." Perhaps the most revealing aspect of Custer's testimony came when the joint committee inquired whether Texans, if offered the opportunity to secede without war, would stay in the Union or would leave. Custer simply replied, "I think they would prefer to go out." His insights were correct. Ex-Confederates, former secessionists, and conservative Democrats wanted to remain as far removed from federal control as possible, and many were willing to continue to wage guerilla war to accomplish their purpose.

Custer also made lengthy comments regarding the conditions of freedpeople in Texas, revealing that blacks suffered even greater atrocities than loyal (white) Union men. "There is a very strong feeling of hostility towards the freedmen as a general thing," stated the general. He continued, "There are exceptions, of course; but the great mass of the people there seem to look upon the freedmen as being connected with, or as being the cause of, their present condition, and they do not hesitate to improve every opportunity to inflict injuries upon [them] in order, seemingly, to punish [them] for this." According to Custer, freedpeople could not find justice in Texas courts. Whites frequently murdered the ex-slaves for the slightest provocations, and in some cases, they killed blacks for no provocations at all. The murderers were rarely brought before a judge for their heinous crimes. Even in the cases where the killers were tried, white juries acquitted them. Because of such harsh treatment, Custer surmised that the freedpeople would remain "loyal without a single exception" to the federal government. He further stated that "they realize, as all Union men in the state do, that their only safety and protection lies in the general government; and they realize too, that if the troops are withdrawn, they will be still more exposed than they are now."

One might wonder why whites felt that they could, with impunity, whip or kill freedpeople. After all, the South appeared to have lost the Civil War. Explanations are not that complex, and one need only look to Presidential Reconstruction to find answers. White Texans after the Civil War were afraid of northern revenge. Some who supported the Confederacy believed that they might be held accountable for their treasonous acts against the federal government. A few of the larger slaveholders, high-ranking state officials, and Confederate officers chose self-exile and left the country, some going to Mexico or Brazil, while others went to Europe.

Both their fears and their escapes were premature, however, for under Abraham Lincoln and Andrew Johnson, the government's position was not to pursue charges of treason against those who voluntarily sought to destroy the Union and the Constitution by force. Additionally, the Lincoln and Johnson administrations pursued a lenient policy toward southerners. Lincoln's prescription for renewing the Union was called the "Ten Percent" plan, which required almost nothing of the defeated South. The president was willing to restore the former Confederate states to the Union when just 10 percent of their voters swore allegiance to the United States and their state governments had ratified the Thirteenth Amendment, which abolished slavery. After John Wilkes Booth murdered Lincoln, the new president, Andrew Johnson, initiated his own lenient policy of reconciliation. Both men made the decision that race relations were to be best managed at the state level; consequently, the presidential plans included few if any safeguards for the new freedpeople.

The former Confederates, including those in leadership positions in Texas, interpreted these "lenient" plans as signs of presidential weakness, for many whites began to obstruct federal operations in the South. With a newfound confidence, they began to seek ways to retain as much of the Old South's traditions as possible, including white supremacy short of reestablishing slavery, which most people considered a dead issue after 1865. In Texas various newspaper editors even predicted that it might be possible to replace slavery with a new labor system that would retain many of the old attributes of involuntary servitude. They were correct. The answer turned out to be sharecropping, an economic institution that entrapped most poor blacks and thousands of poor whites in a state of permanent poverty, that lasted well into the twentieth century.

While Mrs. Potts and General Custer both witnessed racial atrocities after the fall of the Confederacy, economic circumstances also served as an underlying cause of violence in 1865. High prices on cotton led many planters and yeoman farmers to borrow heavily to get back into cotton production. But agrarians were too successful; a glut developed that drove prices down to approximately 50 percent of peak prices in early summer. Rather than suffer loses, many planters and farmers passed the loss down to their laborers (sharecroppers). Early Freedmen's

Bureau figures suggest that about 90 percent of employers simply refused to pay wages to their workers. If the laborers complained, the landowners drove them off their property, especially when the share-croppers were freedpeople. In most of these cases, the landowner claimed that the black workers had "run off and had therefore broken the provisions of their labor contracts, surrendering their wages in the process. When trouble with disgruntled laborers continued, the employers often paid outlaw gangs to force them off their land at gunpoint—or if that failed, to kill them. Some of the more notorious bands of outlaws engaged in this type of activity operated in Northeast Texas and were led by ruthless men such as Ben Bickerstaff, Bob Lee, and Cullen Montgomery Baker.

As part of Johnson's plan of Reconstruction, he appointed provisional governors in each of the southern states to oversee the process establishing new loyal governments. Accordingly, he selected a pre—Civil War unionist, Andrew Jackson Hamilton, as the provisional governor of Texas. Hamilton's primary assignment was to call a state constitutional convention. As part of Johnson's plan, the president required each southern state to create a new constitution before it could be readmitted to the Union. Yet before a governor could call for a convention, he had to make sure that enough Union men were in place at the local level to register loyal voters. Given the true nature of anti-government sentiments in Texas, Hamilton found his job near impossible, especially considering the widespread violence waged against loyal Union men. Nevertheless, on November 15, 1865, he issued a proclamation that called on Texas voters to go to the polls on January 8, 1866, to elect a slate of delegates to a constitutional convention that would convene in Austin on February 7. Political strife soon engulfed the state as election day approached. In Ellis County one candidate stated that "if he had the power he would have swept the last Northerner off the face of God's Earth." It was reported that after these comments, the crowd cheered so loud that "glass fell out of the windows." In the same county another prominent citizen stated that "if he now had the power he would sink the entire [national] Republican party forty thousand feet below the Mudsills of Hell." Such political vitriol was commonplace in January 1866, and it carried over into the constitutional convention that met in February.

Delegates to the constitutional convention met between February 7 and April 2, creating a new system of government for the state. In the process they declared the secession ordinance null and void, repudiated the state debt, and recognized the end of slavery, even though they refused to officially ratify the Thirteenth Amendment. In an effort to thwart Hamilton's plan to provide the freedmen limited rights, delegates denied blacks the right to vote, hold political office, serve on juries, or give legal testimony against whites in court cases. Before adjourning, convention members set June 25 as the date for the referendum on the newly created state document and for election of new officials under its provisions.

Undoubtedly, many ex-Confederate and conservative Democrats celebrated the outcome of the June 25 referendum; the voters overwhelmingly approved the new constitution and elected James Webb Throckmorton as governor. The people of Texas also elected a slate of conservative Democrats, ex-Confederates, and former secessionists to the legislature. The election of these men meant that Hamilton's plan for reconstructing the state, in essence, had failed. With conservative Democrat and ex-Confederates in office, anti-Union forces now controlled the state. The only obstacle that prevented them from absolute authority was the US military still stationed in the state, agents of the Freedmen's Bureau, and a handful of loyal unionists who were not yet willing to concede victory to pro-Confederate Democrats.

Once the state government was in place, the public waited to see how a conservative legislature would deal with the new realities in Texas. Among the assembly's first actions was to create the infamous 1866 "Black Codes" that returned the freedpeople to a status that resembled antebellum slavery. Now codified, black Texans could not vote nor hold political office, could not serve on juries nor testify in cases involving whites, could not marry whites nor claim land under the Texas Homestead Law, and could not escape segregation on common carriers nor share in public school funds. An apprenticeship law potentially gave whites control of under-age blacks either with parental consent or by the order of a county judge. Also heinous was the Contract Labor Code, which forced blacks to sign twelve-month contracts for jobs lasting more than one month. The labor code gave employers certain judicial rights. They could fine workers who failed to perform their work, who damaged tools, who left without permission, or who were generally disobedient.

Related was the Vagrancy Code. Local authorities could issue fines to blacks who were deemed vagrants, especially if they did not have a steady job or any money in their possession. Those who could not pay the fines (which most could not) were arrested and contracted out to local businesses or landowners until their bogus "debt to society" was paid in full. The Convict-Lease Code entrapped blacks whom judges and juries sent to county jails or to the state prison. Such unfortunates could be contracted out to private employers and forced to work for little except room and board. Thus whites effectively had imposed a type of semi-slavery upon the black community, reducing the status of freedpeople to second-class citizens.

By the time the legislature passed the 1866 codes, it was clear that many white Texans had not given up on the Civil War. They continued to fight it, though in a new guise: a guerrilla war in which partisans had both a military and a political role to play. Over time, from 1865 to around 1874, seventy-seven Texas counties gave birth to terrorist groups that went by many names: the Ku Klux Klan, the Knights of the White Camellia, the Knights of the Rising Son, the Red Hand, and the Ku Klux Rangers. The formation of several of these groups even preceded the founding of the historic Ku Klux Klan in Tennessee in 1866. Regardless of their chosen name, these terrorist organizations had the same goals: enforce the doctrine of white supremacy by any means necessary, including violence, and assist former Confederates in the redemption of the state, using the Democratic Party as their vehicle. Indeed, many of the terrorist groups became an informal paramilitary arm of the Democrats.

Outlaw gangs also were legion and did much damage. Some became an informal second para-military force that used the Democratic Party and in turn were used by the party. The members of many criminal gangs wrapped themselves in the Confederate flag, proclaimed loyalty to the Lost Cause, and then proceeded to do their worst. Former Confederate Democrats tended to look the "other way" so long as such gangs only targeted freedpeople, native unionists, and the federal troops who eventually occupied various parts of the Lone Star State. For example, in Northeast Texas, gangs coalesced around such desperadoes as Benjamin Bickerstaff, Cullen

Montgomery Baker, Bob Lee, Elisha Guest, Ben Griffin, Henry Farrar, John "Pomp" Duty, "Indian Bill" English, George English, John Marshall, Tom Emmitt, and a host of others. Each of these men claimed to be fighting for the Lost Cause while truly seeking plunder. Indeed, Bob Lee was once heard to say that he would fight the Yankees "from the thickets and canebrakes of Texas for a hundred years if necessary" if that is what it took to win the Civil War. Their claims of fighting for the Lost Cause resonated with people in the communities where the gangs traveled, providing them with a shield of protection against federal authorities.

Terrorist Klan groups and many—but not all—outlaw bands had common characteristics. The major goal of such groups was to thwart the Reconstruction process because it threatened the antebellum status quo by raising the status of freedmen. Rampant racism was a major factor, for the majority of whites believed that blacks had no rights at all and should still show much deference in all matters involving whites. Such people were willing to use persuasion, intimidation, and violence when necessary to achieve this goal. They were most willing to kill if that is what it took to defeat the proposed reforms that Reconstruction was meant to impart. The groups objected greatly to the federal government's decision to abolish slavery, Aristotle's mudsill for Western civilization of which the slaveholders of the Old South had made maximum use. Indeed, the existence of southern slavery—and the strident demand that the national government protect its expansion—was the major cause of the Civil War. The Union's victorious armies, of course, meant the end of slavery.

Beginning in December 1866, congressional Republicans declared Presidential Reconstruction a failure and took steps to seize control of the process from Johnson by passing the Civil Rights Act of 1866, the Freedmen's Bureau Act, and the Fourteenth Amendment over the president's veto. In an effort to solidify its control of Reconstruction, Congress next passed the Reconstruction Acts. The first of these measures, passed on March 2, 1867, abolished the existing state governments in the former Confederate states except in Tennessee, where the state legislature had ratified the Thirteenth Amendment. Subsequent legislation divided the southern states into five military districts, instituted martial law, disenfranchised former Confederate leaders, and established procedures by which these states would create new constitutions and ensure the protection of African American civil rights.

As Congress gained control of the process, white Texans claimed that Radical Republicans in Washington were attempting to dominate their state through Negro-Carpetbag-Scalawag rule. "Carpetbagger" and "scalawag" were derogatory terms: A carpetbagger was a northern migrant who came to the South after the war. Scalawags were native southerners who remained loyal to the Union and supported federal policies, especially those of Radical Republicans in Congress. In southern newspapers and posted broadsides, Texas politicians outlined how congressional Republicans intended to impose military rule over the South and to force black domination on them, changing the system of white supremacy that had been in place prior to the establishment of the Republic of Texas. In response to these perceived threats, ex-Confederates and conservative Democrats joined forces to expand the already violent guerilla war that had plagued the state.

As Texas became increasingly involved in this second phase of the Civil War, many northern newspaper editors and their correspondents reported on the runaway violence in the state between 1866 and 1869. For example, New York newspapers labeled the violence in Texas as "THE NEW REBELLION" along with other headlines that read "Sulphur Springs—armed desperadoes scouring eastern Texas—a reign of terror." The story that followed the headlines was based on a report by Lt. Charles Vernou, who was sent to Northeast Texas to investigate the rampant violence in that region. Vernou reported that on August 30, 1866, Cullen Baker and a party numbering at least thirty men, including Bickerstaff and some of his men, attacked him in the Bois D'Arc Creek bottoms. The lieutenant rode away, but the desperadoes chased him for several miles before he reached a farm in Lamar County that he had bought earlier that year, escaping them by riding into some dense woods and hiding in a thicket. Not finding him, the attackers beat a black sharecropper in an attempt to force him to tell them where Vernou was. Next the brigands ordered all other sharecroppers off the place after they had gathered their portion of the crops in the field, leaving Vernou's portion to rot. The raiders then ordered all the freedmen to return (within thirty days) to their old masters and to serve them, else, as Bickerstaff threatened, they would die. Vernou said that the renegades came and went in and out of Paris as they pleased and that they intended to kill white Union men, Yankees (especially Freedmen's Bureau agents), and leading black men.

Two years after the New York papers were writing about the "New Rebellion," a correspondent of the *Cincinnati Commercial*, who toured Northeast Texas in 1869, wrote: "You cannot pick up a paper in East Texas without reading of murder, assassinations, and robbery . . . and yet not a fourth part of the truth has been told; not one act in ten is reported. Go where you will, and you will hear of fresh murders and violence. . . .The civil authority is powerless—the military insufficient in number, while hell has transferred its capital from Pandemonium to Jefferson, and the devil is holding high carnival in Gilder, Tyler, Canton, Quitman, Boston, Marshall, and other places in Texas." Other contemporary observers commented that Texas was among the most lawless and most violent of the southern states during Reconstruction. Maj. Gen. Phillip Sheridan, who commanded the Fifth Military District from 1866 to 1867 and who was angered by the unabated violence taking place in the state, was not as eloquent as the northern reporters, muttering once that if he owned both hell and Texas, he would rent out Texas and live in hell. Republican governor Edmund J. Davis was clearer, stating that all the turmoil throughout the state amounted to a "slow" Civil War, while District Judge A. B. Norton agreed, claiming that if "it [the violence] was not a war, he wondered just what would constitute war."

Perhaps the clearest evidence supporting these contemporary assessments between 1865 and 1868 is found in the Report of the Special Committee on Lawlessness and Violence in Texas. The members of the Texas Constitutional Convention of 1868–69 created the special committee to examine and compile statistics on the violence taking place in the state during that time. Its final report, which was forwarded to the US Senate during the Fortieth Congress in July 1868, reveals that freedpeople and white unionists still remained the primary victims of criminal activities taking place within the state. Most of the murders in Texas between 1865 and 1868 were committed by desperadoes "who were either Confederate officers or soldiers, or bushwhackers, during the late war, and now constitute one of the legitimate entailments of secession and rebellion." Of the 939 murders committed in the state, whites had killed

373 freedmen, while only ten whites had been slain by freedmen. This fact alone led members to conclude that whites were involved in a race war against blacks.

The committee further stated that the ex-Confederates were engaged in a war against loyal unionists of both races, believing that the "multitudes who participated in the rebellion, disappointed and saddened by their defeat, are now intensely embittered against the freedmen on account of their emancipation and enfranchisement, and on account of their devotion to the Republican party, and against loyal whites for their persistent adhesion to the Union; that they are determined to resist by every means promising success the establishment of a free republican state government; that is their purpose even by desperate measures to create such a state of alarm and terror among Union men and freedmen as to compel them to abandon the advocacy of impartial suffrage or fly from the state." In this condition of lawlessness, the committee found that free speech had been abandoned and that Republicans could only hold meetings in areas where adequate troops or armed men were stationed. In essence, former Confederates did not tolerate free discourse. As evidence to the fact that men were murdered for their political convictions, committee members made reference to the killings of prominent unionists in Uvalde, Blanco, Bell, Lamar, and Hunt Counties. Just who was committing these murders? According to the report, there were "organizations of disloyal, desperate men in several sections of the state, leagued together for the purpose of murdering prominent Unionists." In fact, Texas became the murder capital of the United States. For two years in a row (1868–69), the state led the nation in the number of homicides, far ahead of the runner up, Louisiana.

Between the years 1865 and 1867, there were 249 indictments for murder before the district courts. In those, only five men were convicted, and only one received the death penalty, a black man from Harris County. In many cases local law enforcement found that they were outgunned and outmanned by the terrorists in their jurisdiction. In other cases the local officers were themselves involved in the acts perpetrated against the unionists. Together these cases illustrate that animosity toward the federal government and its friends was pervasive throughout the state, and the victims frequently were unionists, federal troopers, and agents of the Freedmen's Bureau.

Professional armies typically find it difficult to effectively wage a war against terrorists. Such was surely the case during Reconstruction. Professional armies are trained to fight other professional armies that follow conventional military strategy and tactics. But guerrillas and terrorists play by no rules of engagement, and their tactics vary with each new situation that develops. Able to strike quickly and then disappear, they play hell with military commanders trying to restore order. Just like the Plains Indians that caused havoc in West Texas, terrorist groups and outlaw gangs in the interior of the state used hit-and-run tactics to defeat federal forces stationed in their regions of the state. Even when law enforcers identified criminals, it seemed most easy for such people to commit devilry in one county and then vanish into another, disappearing into the state's vast landscape. Even when criminals were apprehended by local sheriffs or military commands, they were often jailed in porous buildings. Untold numbers of felons escaped incarceration and continued their criminal activities. Even when local law enforcement was able to detain the outlaws long enough for their date in court, white juries often set them free, especially in cases where the victims were African Americans or white unionists.

During the second phase of the Civil War, many areas of settled Texas experienced widespread disturbances. Military commanders had difficulty in obtaining enough soldiers to deal with the terrorist groups and the various outlaw bands. Eventually, these guerillas were able to suppress Republican voters, both black and white, contributing in part to the end of Reconstruction. Widespread violence in the state did not abate until conservative Democrats, also known as Redeemers, regained control of the state government during the early 1870s. Once the Republicans had been defeated and blacks had been relegated to second-class citizenship, terrorist groups no longer found it necessary to organize. Additionally, once Democrats took office, they began to enforce the law. Though the Democratic Party generally favored the use of violence during the early years of Reconstruction as a method of wrenching control away from the Republicans, its members now felt pressure from their constituents to bring an end to the violence. All realized that they had won the second phase of the Civil War and that they could not expect any better terms. Their task complete, Texas guerrillas and terrorists slowly melted into the landscape—hidden but not forgotten. Their victory lasted until the middle of the twentieth century, until finally the federal government resumed its original mission of reconstructing southern society, making it a place where equal rights and justice was not a dream but a reality.

William R. Shafter:

Commanding Black Troops in West Texas

PAUL H. CARLSON

Paul H. Carlson is Professor Emeritus of History at Texas Tech University in Lubbock. A member of the Texas Institute of Letters, his studies include *The Plains Indians* (1998), *Deep Time and the Texas High Plains: History and Geology* (2005), *Amarillo: The Story of a Western Town* (2006), *Myth, Memory, and Massacre: The Pease River Capture of Cynthia Ann Parker* (2010), and *Dancin' in Anson: A History of the Texas Cowboys' Christmas Ball* (2014).

Black troops, known as Buffalo Soldiers, served bravely on the Texas frontier. In this selection, Dr. Carlson discusses the career of Lieutenant Colonel William R. Shafter and examines the white officer's relationship with his African American command. ᕦ

★ ★

From the West Texas Plains in the mid-1870s Captain Theodore Baldwin complained to his wife, "I do not think you would like to scout with Colonel Shafter." The note was understated indeed. A martinet of force and persistence, Lieutenant Colonel William R. Shafter of the Twenty-Fourth United States Infantry Regiment always drove vigorously the black troops of his command. Many young officers, such as Captain Baldwin, grumbled about his dogged determination.

Paul H. Carlson, "William R. Shafter: Commanding Black Troops in West Texas" from *The African American Experience in Texas*, Bruce Glasrud and James Smallwood, eds. © 2007 Bruce Glasrud and James Smallwood. Reprinted by permission of the author and Texas Tech University Press.

Typical of Shafter's drive was an episode in 1875. Upon leaving Casas Amarillas Lake, near present Littlefield on the Llano Estacado, in a southwesterly direction, Shafter had hoped to find sufficient water for his men and horses in the large circular depressions characteristic of the High Plains. During the first two days he was successful, but having found no water by the expiration of the third day, he concluded that he must either strike for the Pecos or turn back. Characteristically, the resolute officer ordered his African American command to make for the Pecos some eighty miles distant. During the following two days and one night of marching, the troops suffered desperately from heat dust, and thirst. On the last night out, many of the officers, having lost all hope of reaching the river, wrote messages to be taken home by those fortunate enough to survive. Worn men were tied in their saddles; others at gun point were forced to keep up. Shafter cajoled, wheedled, and drove his men. After great hardship and privation, everyone safely, but exhaustively, reached the river. In such aggressive style, for more than a decade, Shafter directed black troops.

His black infantry in West Texas, however, was not the first that Shafter had led. During the Civil War he had enjoyed command of a volunteer unit and afterward in Louisiana with the colorful Ranald Mackenzie had organized and trained one of the regular army's first all-black regiments. In 1867 with his troops he had been ordered to the lower Rio Grande and the following year moved to West Texas at Fort Clark.

As a subaltern to Ranald Mackenzie, Shafter at first had few field assignments. But with each opportunity to command he relentlessly pursued horse thieves, cattle rustlers, desperadoes, or Indian raiders who were ravaging the West Texas frontier. As one result he quickly became recognized as the most energetic man of his rank in the Department of Texas. As another he was soon considered a rough, insensitive commander of black troops who, to achieve a sense of discipline, did not hesitate to exert extraordinary and ruthless power. In 1870 his reputation followed him to Fort Concho, at present San Angelo.

Here, the post surgeon was amazed at the energy and restlessness with which Shafter attacked his garrison chores. In his report for January 1870, the surgeon wrote that Shafter "has displayed an abundance of energy, devoting the first days of arrival to thoroughly policing the post . . . [and] seeing a large corral . . . in the process of construction." In the weeks that followed Shafter continued to push his African American command in construction activities. The next month, the surgeon reported that "work upon the guard house and corral is progressing with unprecedented rapidity."

Vigorous and efficient in his post command, Shafter likewise was energetic in the field. In mid-August, after being ordered to Fort McKavett, he planned to scour thoroughly the lower Pecos River. Taking 6 officers and 128 enlisted men of the Ninth Cavalry and Twenty-Fourth Infantry, he marched southwestward to the river, reaching it at a point about twenty miles below present Sheffield.

Here, Shafter temporarily divided his command. Leaving most of it in camp at the Pecos, he and Captain Edward M. Heyl, Ninth Cavalry, with fifteen men crossed to the west bank of the river, climbed up onto the table lands, and marched due south for twenty miles, keeping all the time within four miles of the river. Using his field glasses to examine each ravine, Shafter discovered no indications of Indians. There, he left the river and rode southwestward for six or seven miles to Painted Rock Arroyo, only ten miles from the Rio Grande. Again finding no signs of Indians, with his patrol he returned to the rendezvous camp.

For nearly a month afterward the command scouted in the vicinity of the lower Pecos. The hard-driving Shafter ordered his men to check every ravine. It was monotonous, exhausting work. No Indians were seen, neither were there trails nor other indications of Indians having passed through the country recently. Nevertheless, Shafter doggedly pushed his men to the task. The persistence brought some luck: eight Indian ponies, which Shafter estimated had been near the Pecos for six months, were caught.

In mid-September, unable to locate either Indians or recent signs of them, Shafter finally directed his tired troops back toward Fort McKavett. While returning, his scouts located several abandoned Indian villages, about thirty-five miles west of the headwaters of the North and South Llano rivers. One had contained possibly as many as 150 Indians. Nearby they discovered a large, permanent body of water about two hundred yards long and deep enough to swim horses. For years the army had heard reports of the water pond, but its location had been known only to the red men. Consequently the pond was a favorite and secure place for Indians who committed depredations in the country near the headwaters of the Nueces.

The Pecos River campaign proved significant. Having marched nearly five hundred miles, the scout showed that no Indians were lurking in the vicinity of the Pecos and the headwaters of the Llano rivers. Eight horses had been captured. A strategic and favorite Indian camping place had been located, and no longer would the Indians be able to use the water hole as a safe rendezvous. Moreover, in the psychological warfare that figured vitally in Indian fighting, the expedition demonstrated to the Plains warriors that bluecoat troopers could campaign successfully in an area that Indians previously had thought inaccessible to the army.

Twice the following year Shafter led black soldiers into such supposedly impenetrable lands. In June 1871 with a command totaling eighty-six officers and enlisted men, he turned a routine pursuit of Comanche horse thieves into a major exploration of the Monahans Sand Hills and across the Llano Estacado. He destroyed an abandoned Indian village, two dozen buffalo robes, skins, and a large supply of provisions. He captured twenty horses and mules. He discovered that Comanches and Lipan and Mescalero Apaches, longtime enemies, had concluded a peace in the Sand Hills and that Comancheros used the area as a place of barter.

A month later Shafter penetrated another Indian sanctuary. This time he drove his black command from Fort Davis on an exhausting five-hundred-mile scout into the torrid Big Bend region of the Rio Grande. Here with his troops he explored the country, crossing and recrossing trails, noting important water holes, and marking the sites of old Indian camps. At San Vincente he discovered an important Apache crossing on the river. He reported abandoned Indian encampments twenty-five miles southwest of Pena Blanca. The grass along his line of march was excellent, but the only wood he found was very large cottonwood trees along the streams. Where he struck the Rio Grande, there was no timber.

Although it had killed no Indians, the expedition had found abundant evidence that Apaches used the Big Bend as a sanctuary. Perhaps more important, Shafter added considerably to the geographical knowledge of the Chihuahuan deserts and Big Bend mountains. Indeed, the information he gained about their nature and resources enabled the army later to maneuver more confidently in the region. In addition, it smoothed the way for later settlement.

No sooner had Shafter returned to Fort Davis than an Apache chief, who frequented the Big Bend and who had gone to Presidio to negotiate with the Mexican authorities for release of some children captives of his band, sent word from Presidio del Norte that he wished to surrender. Shafter sent Lieutenant Isaiah H. McDonald to receive the surrender. But perhaps because the Mexican residents there, who gained their living largely by supplying United States Army posts, did not welcome complete harmony between Indians and Americans, the *alcalde* of Presidio warned the chief that his departure would prejudice release of the children. Whatever the reason, McDonald returned to Fort Davis empty-handed. Shafter agreed with his lieutenant that "the local authorities at Del Norte do not want [the Apache] to make or keep peace with the United States."

Meanwhile, at Fort Davis Shafter was active. He supervised the repair of buildings, the construction of corrals, and the remodeling of the hospital. In addition, whenever necessary, he protected his black troops against racial injustice and discrimination. In one incident he took the stage coach lines to task. The infantry in the West was often assigned to guard stage lines. At the end of such a tour of duty men usually returned to the post on an inbound stage. Unfortunately, Shafter's black troops at least once were kept off the stage and forced to walk back to the barracks. Indeed, the El Paso Mail Lines station keeper at Leon Hole refused to provide food and shelter for the station guards. The tempestuous Shafter became incensed and immediately warned the stage company officers against further discrimination toward his men. When the black guards were put off the stage, he wrote, they were obliged to walk to Fort Stockton and along the way to obtain their rations "by their wits." He demanded that his troops should "be fed by the company or allowed facilities at the stations for cooking their own rations." He would "be glad to furnish mail escorts as long as they are wanted," he concluded, "but they must be properly treated." Apparently his letter got results for the records show no further complaint against the stage company.

In another incident Shafter challenged civilian authorities. When the volatile sheriff of Presidio County injudiciously entered Fort Davis to arrest a black soldier for public drunkenness, Shafter, aware that the bluecoat would be summarily prosecuted, would not allow the officer to remove the trooper. Although such belligerency represented a serious breach of military discipline, Shafter refused to subject his troops to what he regarded as legal hazing.

The consequences proved critical. Although the trooper was never arrested, Shafter was immediately removed from Fort Davis. Later, the incident may have been included as evidence to deny him an early graduation to the rank of colonel. Much later, in 1887, after he had obtained the colonelcy, the incident apparently was offered as one excuse to block his promotion to the rank of brigadier general.

Although temporarily rebuked, Shafter was not forgotten. Since the Department of Texas needed durable, effective officers, in the summer and fall of 1872 with his crack command of black troops he teamed for three months with Ranald Mackenzie on the Llano Estacado. While Mackenzie with one force scouted the Palo Duro and crossed the High Plains to Fort Sumner and beyond, Shafter with another examined the Caprock escarpment along the Salt Fork (Main Fork) of the Brazos. His black command made certain that there were no Indians lurking at the foot of the Staked Plains, although it found abundant evidence of old Indian camps near all the springs it visited. In addition, the command located water and fuel supplies and for future operations in the vicinity of present-day Slaton and Lubbock made a map of the country scouted.

The following year Shafter with his black troops aided Mackenzie again. This time he helped during preparations for the celebrated raid into Mexico against the Kickapoos. Although he did not cross into Mexico with Mackenzie, Shafter performed valuable service for the expedition. He provided important information on the Mexican population, the location of villages, and the whereabouts of Mexican troops. Mackenzie stated that he was under great obligation to Shafter for his cordial cooperation and active support throughout the 1873 expedition.

In 1875, after a lengthy stint in New York to study infantry equipment, Shafter led a huge command of African American troops for six months on the Staked Plains of West Texas and Eastern New Mexico. The Llano Estacado campaign, as it was called, proved grueling. At one stretch during the wearisome expedition Shafter in ten days marched his men nearly three hundred miles. Since they were seldom in camp for more than one night, the men, in addition to marching thirty miles a day, had to pack their tents and other field equipment each morning and unpack it again each night. The subsequent wear and tear on both men and animals prompted one officer to complain that "our horses will go to the devil very fast at the rate Col. Shafter charges the whole command."

The comment could not have been more pointed. In the field Shafter demonstrated an unsurpassed ability to get the utmost out of his soldiers. During the agonizing 1875 expedition, in which his command covered over 2,500 miles of the High Plains, many of Shafter's men returned from the first crossing of the Plains without shirts or shoes, most were missing some article of clothing, and all were exhausted. Nevertheless, only two weeks later, Shafter started back across the Plains again, and hardly had he completed the second crossing when a third was commenced. The Llano Estacado campaign was as successful as it was difficult. It swept the Plains clear of Indians, destroyed completely the dreary myth of the Plains as the dreaded Sahara of North America, and paved the way for settlement, which quickly followed.

Even more arduous and successful was Shafter's 1876 expedition to the mouth of the Pecos River. Three times during the strenuous, five-months-long campaign, Shafter marched his well-disciplined black troops across the rugged Coahuila deserts of Mexico. In each instance the troops rode in over 100 degree heat, and on one occasion they went sixty-five miles through the parching desert without water. During the summer his men twice engaged and defeated

Indians. Two large camps of hostiles were completely destroyed, another in the Carmen Mountains was discovered and its location noted, 137 horses and mules and much stolen stock was recovered, and an estimated eighteen Indians were killed or captured.

Shortly after the close of the Pecos River expedition, Shafter became commander of the District of the Nueces. Embracing the upper Rio Grande border area from Laredo to old Fort Leaton, the region was a natural haunt and even a highway for roving bands of Lipan and Mescalero Apaches who slipped across the Rio Grande to prey upon the abundant cattle and horse herds along the upper reaches of the Nueces. Any luckless cowboy or traveler who got in their way, the Indians killed. One raid in 1878 resulted in the death of eighteen citizens, including some women and children.

Protecting the Rio Grande frontier was no easy task. Not only was the topography of the territory on both sides of the river barren and waterless, but Mexican troops resented the presence of American soldiers south of the border. As a result, relations between the United States and Mexico were strained, and Mexican leaders protested each American violation of their country's soil. Moreover, by criticizing the border crossings, Democratic leaders in Washington hoped to embarrass the Rutherford B. Hayes administration. Consequently, Lieutenant Colonel Shafter needed to act with astute diplomatic good will and with the consummate skill demanded of desert campaigning.

Shafter was not timid in his new task. The audacious commander kept his bluecoats in the field. Small patrols suffered through December's cold, scouting relentlessly each trail and vigilantly watching for evidence of raiding parties from Mexico. The perseverance paid dividends. In January 1877, after some marauders were seen, Shafter from his headquarters at Fort Clark quickly dispatched Lieutenant John L. Bullis of his regiment and Captain Alexander B. Keyes, Tenth Cavalry, and over one hundred officers and men some 125 miles deep into the Santa Rosa Mountains of Mexico. The Bullis-Keyes raid recovered much stolen stock and led to the return of several horses and mules.

Additional border crossings followed. In March Shafter waded the Rio Grande with a large detachment of black troops, but too late to rescue from jail two men, who had guided his troops the year previous, sentenced to die as traitors. In July Bullis splashed across the river but with little luck in striking Indians or recovering stolen stock. In the fall, as raiding increased, Shafter twice directed well-armed expeditions to pursue hostile Indians to their sanctuaries in Mexico.

Indeed, Shafter took personal command of the first expedition. The raid into Mexico began near the end of September after black scouts reported to Bullis, scouting along the Rio Grande near the mouth of Las Moras Creek, that marauders had entered Texas. Bullis immediately sent word by courier to Shafter at Fort Clark. In turn the district commander ordered the scrappy lieutenant with his force of ninety men to cross the river on the twenty-eighth and wait for Shafter who, with about three hundred troops of the Eighth and Tenth cavalries, was on his way to join him. When he rode into camp about 2:00 p.m. the same day, Shafter ordered Bullis to start after dark for the Indian village near Saragosa. He promised to protect Bullis's rear in the event that there were wounded soldiers who might slow the retreating command. Both officers were well aware that a Mexican force of some two hundred soldiers, as well as dozens of thieves and desperadoes in the vicinity, would be watching for a favorable opportunity to strike the exhausted invaders.

About 11:00 p.m. Bullis started. Alternating his pace between a trot and a gallop during the long night ride, he reached Saragosa, about forty miles distant, at sunrise. Marching up Perdido Creek, he caught by surprise at about 8:00 a.m. the Lipans and Mescaleros who fled for safety upon sighting the charging American troops. Bullis's scouts and troops chased the terrified Indians for four or five miles, capturing before reining to a halt four women, one boy, twelve horses, and two mules. After burning the small village and destroying the camp equipage, Bullis, turning his troops due north toward the head of the San Diego River where he was to meet Shafter, marched at a fast walk or trot until he reached the appointed rendezvous about 9:00 p.m. His troops, who had been in their saddles continuously for twenty-two hours, rolled from the horses in exhaustion. The support troops were nowhere in sight.

Meanwhile, Shafter had waited until morning before starting for the rendezvous. After moving slowly up the San Diego River, he encamped a few miles from its head. On the following morning, September 30, a little after sunrise, he spied Bullis, who had had an apprehensive, but undisturbed, night's rest, moving northeastward toward the Rio Grande and not far behind a column of approximately ninety Mexican troops from Saragosa under Colonel Innocente Rodriguez. Immediately, he broke camp and joined his trusty subordinate.

The combined command, nearly four hundred troops, continued toward the river at a brisk walk all day and late into the night. Colonel Rodriguez cautiously followed about a mile behind for a distance of ten miles, but then suddenly disappeared when Shafter began to maneuver his troops in preparation for battle. No engagement took place, nor were any shots fired, and, when Shafter again headed for the Rio Grande, some of the officers grumbled about running from "a handful of Mexicans." After wading the river at Lasora Crossing near San Felipe about midnight, Shafter rested his command for two days before returning to Fort Clark, where he arrived on October 4.

The raid brought unfavorable reaction in the capitals of both countries. In Mexico City, the newspapers, exaggerating its significance, indicated that the American troops had flagrantly violated international law. They also boasted of how a small Mexican force of only ninety troops had easily repelled an American force four times its number. In Washington, the raid became an important factor that influenced the decision of Congress to investigate the Texas border troubles.

The Congressional investigations revealed the need for additional troops in the District of the Nueces. Accordingly, in February 1878, when Colonel Ranald Mackenzie arrived with his Fourth Cavalry, Shafter was relieved of his command. Still assigned to the district, however, he once again found himself closely teamed with his former colonel.

With adequate troops to end the depredations, Shafter and Mackenzie wasted little time in bringing peace to the border. In April and May they planned and organized a major raid to destroy in Mexico hostile Indian lairs, and in June, with the army's approval, they carried it out.

Twice during the bold assault there were confrontations, but not clashes, with Mexican troops who turned away after first challenging the Americans. Perhaps embarrassed that his troops had backed down in the face of the hated gringos, Porfirio Diaz, President of Mexico, took steps to cooperate with the United States in haulting depredations north of the Rio Grande. Consequently, no further border crossings were necessary and by the end of 1878 tension along the river had relaxed demonstrably.

Early the following year Shafter left Texas. In March his long-awaited promotion to colonel came through, and he was transferred to the First Infantry Regiment stationed in Dakota. He returned to Texas in late 1880 to pursue followers of Victorio, the marauding Apache. Later he moved to Arizona to help pacify Apache renegades. In 1891, following the Wounded Knee incident, he participated in the Siouan Campaign, and in 1898, during the Spanish-American War, he led the American Expeditionary force to Cuba.

The techniques of command vary, of course, with the personality of the commander. While some men prefer to lead by suggestion or example or other methods, Shafter chose to drive his subordinates by bombast and by threats, and he believed that profanity was the most convincing medium of communication. Although his mannerisms achieved spectacular results, they did not win affection among his men. Good-humored, even jolly, in his intimate personal relationships, he was likely to give short, blunt answers to his subalterns, he would never allow his orders to be challenged, and he always demanded the same dogged determination from his men that he himself gave to field maneuvers.

Clearly, as a commander of black troops in West Texas, the volatile Shafter was tough and aggressive. Energetic, resourceful, and courageous, he possessed initiative, looked out for the welfare of his men and animals, and was utterly unafraid of responsibility. When he thought that they were not being treated properly, he vociferously defended his African American soldiers, and he always spoke highly of their ability. Most officers learned to like him and his men, although he rarely enjoyed their affection, always remembered him as a zealous and forceful commander.

Conquered

DAVID LA VERE

D avid La Vere teaches history at the University of North Carolina—Wilmington. A leading authority on Native American history, his books include *The Caddo Chiefdoms: CaddoEconomics and Politics, 700–1835* (1998), *Life Among the Texas Indians: The WPA Narratives* (1998), *Contrary Neighbors: Southern Plains and Removed Indians in Indian Territory* (2000), *The Texas Indians* (2004), and *The Tuscarora War: Indians, Settlers, and the Fight for the Carolina Colonies* (2013).

In this selection, Dr. La Vere provides an overview of Native Americans in the Lone Star State from the Civil War until January, 1881, when the final Indian battle in Texas occurred. Now conquered, Indians found themselves confined on reservations, forced to submit to the white man's culture. La Vere examines such important events as the Red River War of 1874–1875. He also discusses Satanta, Victorio, Quanah, and other hard-pressed Native American leaders. ✒

★ ★

The Indians of the now-defunct Brazos and Clear Fork reserves barely had time to get settled in southwestern Indian Territory before the Civil War thundered to life. The withdrawal of U.S. troops from forts in Texas and Indian Territory left the line of white settlement unprotected.

"Conquered" reprinted from *The Texas Indians* by David La Vere, 2004 by permission of Texas A&M University Press.

Frightened settlers, who earlier had demanded the extermination of the Reserve Indians, now begged them to ally with Texas and serve as a buffer against both Comanches and Union forces. By late 1861 Texas and Confederate diplomats were fanning out to Indian villages and soon the Indians found themselves just as divided as the United States. Among the Five Civilized Tribes, the Choctaws and Chickasaws, closest to Texas and with many of their leaders slave owners as well, sided almost wholly with the South. The Cherokees, Creeks, and Seminoles split and engaged in their own bloody civil war, with some factions remaining loyal to the Union and others to the Confederacy. Many of the wealthier proConfederate Indians moved their families, livestock, and slaves to North Texas, which they hoped would be out of reach of Union raiding parties. Down in Texas, a few Alabama-Coushattas served briefly with the 24th Texas Cavalry but by late 1862 had left the service and returned to their homes in East Texas.

The former Brazos Reserve Indians, now on the Wichita Reservation in Indian Territory, also split. Some Caddo and Wichita bands went to Union-held Kansas. Others moved farther west, willing to brave the plains, the Comanches, and the Kiowas to get away from the war. A large faction stayed put and sided with the South, especially when their Indian agent, Matthew Leeper, accepted a commission in the Confederate Army. The turmoil of the war years provided an opportunity for old enemies to even old scores. On October 23, 1862, a large band of Indians attacked the Confederate-allied Wichita Agency. They burned the agency headquarters, killed some Confederate officials, but concentrated mainly on the Tonkawas, killing Chief Placido and about a hundred of his people. The Wichitas, Caddos and other Indians at the agency scattered. No one could say exactly what instigated the Tonkawa Massacre, as it has come to be called. Some said it was an attack by pro-Confederate Wichitas, Comanches, Shawnees, and Delawares on the pro-Union Tonkawas. The Wichitas and Comanches blamed the Shawnees and Delawares, saying they were taking revenge for Tonkawa cannibalism. Others said it was a Union attack on the Wichita Reservation and the Tonkawas just happened to be in the way. Whatever the reason for the attack, the few surviving Tonkawas fled back to Texas, settling around Fort Belknap, not far from their old reserve at Clear Fork. There they served as scouts for Confederate Texas forces. Only years after the Civil War, would the government step in and provide a reservation for the Tonkawas in the northern part of Indian Territory, well away from their old Texas Indian neighbors.

In Texas, the Civil War brought more raids and violence. Comanches, Kiowas, Kiowa-Apaches, Kickapoos, and others, their supplies of manufactured goods severely curtailed by the war, stepped up their raids into Texas in hopes of replenishing their supplies. For Texans, this could not have come at a worst time as there were fewer people to give chase. Federal troops had been withdrawn to Union territory, while the Confederacy stripped Texas of many of its fighting men, leaving fewer Ranger companies, most of these undermanned. With raids on the increase, the line of settlement halted its westward march and even backtracked about a 150 miles. Nevertheless, Ranger companies, such as those led by Sul Ross, attacked as they always had. Ross's company had attacked a Comanche camp in December, 1860, and come away with Cynthia Ann Parker, who had been taken by the Comanches in 1836. By this time, Cynthia Ann had become a Comanche. She spoke no English, had a Comanche husband and family, and was the mother of the soon-to-be-famous Comanche chief Quanah Parker. So for the second time in her life, she was stolen away from her family. Brokenhearted, she did not live long after.

MEXICAN KICKAPOOS AND SEMINOLES

While Comanches, Kiowas, and Kiowa-Apaches struck from the north, Kickapoos out of Mexico raided across South Texas. Kickapoos were immigrant Indians, a band of which had settled in East Texas in the early nineteenth century. After the Kickapoo War of October, 1838, most Texas Kickapoos moved beyond the line of settlement or to Indian Territory. However, a small band of about eighty immigrated to northern Mexico and settled around the town of Morelos in the State of Coahuila. Mexico warmly welcomed these Kickapoos and soon the men were serving as scouts and auxiliaries for the Mexican army in their pursuit of Comanches, Kiowas, and Apaches.

In 1849 the number of Mexican Kickapoos increased with the arrival of Seminole chief Coacoochee and his band. Coacoochee, better known as Wild Cat, had fought the United States during the Seminole Wars. Forced to move to Indian Territory, he wanted as little to do with Americans as possible and so determined to move to Mexico. Many Kickapoos agreed with Wild Cat's assessment of Americans and about 250 Seminoles, Kickapoos, and African Americans decided to join him. The next year, Wild Cat was again recruiting in Indian Territory and convinced another 250 or so to immigrate to Mexico. About half the Kickapoos returned to Indian Territory the next year, however most Mexican Kickapoos and Seminoles were again serving as auxiliaries, turning back raiding parties that crossed into that part of Mexico. Though most Seminoles would eventually return to Indian Territory, the remaining Mexican Kickapoos became so successful in battling Indian raiders that Comanche and Kiowa attacks in Coahuila dropped off considerably. During the 1850s, while Mexican Kickapoos battled Indians south of the Rio Grande, Kickapoos in Indian Territory joined with their Comanche and Kiowa trade partners and heavily raided Texas settlements along the upper Colorado and Brazos Rivers and as far west as the Pecos. In 1858 even the El Paso mail route was threatened and several California-bound immigrant trains in West Texas were attacked.

Several incidents during the Civil War served to increase Kickapoo raids. As the Civil War divided the Kickapoos and other peoples of Indian Territory, a band of about six hundred Kickapoos under Chief Machemanet decided to immigrate to Mexico in December, 1862. Wanting to avoid Texas settlements, Machemanet's village swung wide into West Texas, but in Tom Green County near present-day Knickerbocker, a Confederate patrol spied the Indian horse herd, shot down three Kickapoo peace emissaries, and attacked the immigrants. The Kickapoos held their ground, retook their horses, and sent the patrol reeling, with sixteen cavalrymen shot out of their saddles. The Kickapoos resumed their journey and joined their kinspeople in Mexico. Word of Machemanet's village's prosperity soon reached the remaining Kickapoos in Kansas and Indian Territory, and in September, 1864, seven hundred Kickapoos under Chiefs Pecan, Papequah, and Nokoaht began their own migration to Mexico. As before, they swung wide to avoid Texas settlements. However, on January 8, 1865, while camping on Dove Creek near present-day Mertzon, they were attacked by a detachment of Confederate scouts and militia. Once again, the well-armed Kickapoos held fast and aimed a devastating fire on the charging Confederates. In an all-day fight, the Texas Confederates had twenty-six men killed, sixty wounded, and sixty-six horses killed. The survivors barely managed to escape during the night, while the victorious Kickapoos, losing a total of fifteen warriors, continued their move into Mexico. Once there and settled, the Kickapoos determined to take revenge on Texas for twice attacking peaceful migration parties.

During the next two decades, the Mexican Kickapoos certainly took their retribution. Over the years, as the Mexican Kickapoos battled Comanche, Kiowa, and Apache raiding parties, a benefit had been the horses, mules, and goods they acquired in battle. These items found ready markets in Mexico and brought prosperity to the Kickapoos. After the Civil War, as raiders struck less frequently into northern Mexico, the Kickapoos were deprived of these commodities. While supplies dwindled, the demand remained; so to acquire the ever-wanted horses and goods, the Kickapoos began raiding ranches and farms on the Texas side of the Rio Grande. A great semicircle, curving from Laredo in the south up to San Antonio and then west to Terrell County, became the Mexico Kickapoos' area of operations. Atacosa County, just south of San Antonio, became a favorite raiding ground. South Texans demanded protection, claiming the Kickapoos were much worse than the Comanches and Kiowas North Texans faced. A government commission investigating the Kickapoo raids in 1872 calculated that between 1865 and 1872, Kickapoo raiders had taken five hundred thousand head of cattle and fourteen thousand horses, most making their way to markets in Mexico. No count was given of the number of women and children taken captive nor the number of ranches burned and men killed.

Finally, in 1873, the government ordered Colonel Ranald S. Mackenzie and the U.S. Fourth Cavalry to deal with the problem. Mackenzie and his four hundred men rode into Mexico without Mexican permission and on May 18, while the Kickapoo warriors were away hunting, attacked their village at Remolina. Though the women, children, and old men fought back as best they could, the Fourth burned the village and supplies and killed an untold number of Indians. They also took forty women and children captives, who were quickly herded up to Fort Gibson, in the northeastern part of Indian Territory.

Mackenzie's raid had the desired effect, rapidly pushing along the Kickapoo removal plan the government had sought. Authorities believed the best way to stop Kickapoo raids was to get them to return to the United States and take a reservation in Indian Territory. Several approaches had been made but each had been rebuffed. With some of their villages destroyed, the realization that the United States would cross into Mexico if need be, and the knowledge that forty of their kinspeople were being held in Indian Territory, many Kickapoos agreed to return to the United States. In August, 1873, 317 Mexican Kickapoos moved back to Indian Territory, reaching Fort Sill in late December. The next year they were assigned a reservation in the central part of Indian Territory, just east of present-day Oklahoma City. In 1875 another 114 Kickapoos returned from Mexico, leaving about 100 Kickapoos along the Mexico-Texas border. Many of their descendants still live in Mexico, but a few crossed the Rio Grande and settled around Eagle Pass, where they became the Texas Band of Kickapoo Indians and remain there to this day. While Mexican and Texas bands of Kickapoos sporadically raided into Texas over the next few years, counterattacks by U.S. cavalry had the desired effect, and by 1880 the Kickapoos had ceased being a threat to Texas.

RAIDS AND RESERVATIONS

The Civil War provided opportunities for Kickapoo raids into Texas, and it did the same for the Comanches, Kiowas, and Kiowa-Apaches, who seemed to grow ever more powerful. By 1864 they threatened the Santa Fe Trail, the supply route to Union-held New Mexico. To protect the trail, on November 25, 1864, Union colonel Kit Carson and his New Mexico Volunteers attacked a series of Comanche, Kiowa, and Kiowa-Apache camps near Adobe Walls. These were the ruins of an old Bent–St. Vrain trading post built in 1840 on the Canadian River in the Texas Panhandle. Though Carson's men managed to destroy one Indian camp, unexpectedly strong resistance from the Indians forced the troops to retreat to New Mexico, barely getting away with their lives. Though the battle secured the trail, it did not deter Comanche and Kiowa raids on Texas farms and ranches.

Four days after Kit Carson's attack, not far to the northwest at Sand Creek in southeastern Colorado, the Colorado militia attacked Chief Black Kettle's peaceful Cheyenne village, killing and scalping well over a hundred Indian men, women, and children. The Sand Creek Massacre shocked both the eastern establishment and Washington officials. When the Civil War ended five months later, Congress turned its attention to the Plains Indians and determined to bring about what they hoped would be a lasting peace. In October, 1865, government representatives met with various Comanche, Kiowa, Kiowa-Apache, Cheyenne, and Arapaho chiefs in Kansas. After several days of negotiations, feasts, exchange of presents, and the restoration of captives, they hammered out the Treaty of the Little Arkansas River. Essentially, the treaty provided for the Comanches and Kiowas to receive virtually all the Texas Panhandle and western Oklahoma as a reservation. Even better, they could hunt outside the reservation boundaries, south of the Arkansas River until the buffalo were gone and the area settled. They would also receive between ten and fifteen dollars per person annually for the next forty years. In return, the Indians were to allow the government to build forts along the Sante Fe Trail and refrain from raiding U.S. citizens and Indians people friendly to them.

While certainly Indian-friendly, the treaty was dead on arrival in Washington. Texans protested bitterly and would have none of it. Similarly, cost-conscious senators severely amended it, making renegotiation virtually impossible. Many individual Kiowas and Comanches also opposed the treaty, refusing to be fenced in or fenced out of lands they had long called home. In the end the treaty was not ratified and raids continued into Texas, with Texans complaining that between May, 1865, and July, 1867, Indians had killed sixty-two people, wounded forty-two, and taken another forty captive.

Help for Texans was not long in coming. With the Civil War over, the U.S. Army now reoccupied Texas forts. Immediately after the war, the United States sent more than fifty thousand troops to Texas, most stationed on the Texas-Mexico border to prevent any spillover from the French invasion of Mexico. Others served on Reconstruction occupation duty. By 1867 their numbers had been reduced to three thousand but with a good number of these now stationed farther west in forts guarding the line of settlement. Texas now hosted the 17th Infantry, 19th (Black) Infantry, 38th (Black) Infantry, 114th (Black) Infantry, 117th (Black) Infantry, 6th

Cavalry, and 4th Cavalry. Later would come the famous 9th and 10th (Black) Cavalry. None of these units remained congregated at any one place. They were divided into company-size units, usually of about ninety to one hundred men, and distributed among various forts. For example, the 4th Cavalry was headquartered at Camp Sheridan in San Antonio, where its headquarters and B, C, D, F, L, and M companies remained. But Company A was stationed at Fredericksburg; Company G, at Clinton; Company H, at La Grange; Companies E and P, at Fort Brown; and Company K, at Fort Inge. In time, other units would come and go, but as always, they gave chase whenever raids were made.

Most of these encounters were small unit actions, such as running battles or brief skirmishes, rarely involving more than a score or two of men on either side. And though cavalry troopers and Texas Rangers often served together, there was little love between them. As one soldier believed, the Rangers were far superior to the army in the field but their tendency to "kill every Indian on sight without pardon" made them less civilized than U.S. troops, who "endeavored to kill as few as possible and to capture alive if possible."

As before, the army turned to the reservation Indians for help. Tonkawas from around Fort Griffin, along with Caddos, Wichitas, and Delawares from the Wichita Reservation in southwestern Indian Territory served as scouts and auxiliaries for the Rangers and cavalry. In December, 1866, Toshaway and a few other Penetaka Comanche chiefs, as well as Caddo chiefs George Washington, Tinah, and Jim Pockmark all agreed to serve as scouts. The number and variety of Indian scouts serving with the army grew considerably. By late 1874 one cavalry officer reported his detachment of scouts included Wichitas, Tawakonis, Wacos, Kichais, Caddos, Delawares, Shawnees, Pawnees, Arapahos, and Comanches.

The continued raids, the good example of the Indians of the Wichita Reservation, and the failure of the Little Arkansas treaty made Congress redouble its efforts to get a workable treaty with the Southern Plains Indians. In October, 1867, government negotiators met with various Comanche, Kiowa, Kiowa-Apache, Cheyenne, and Arapaho chiefs at Medicine Lodge Creek in southern Kansas. By this time, many more chiefs were open to the reservation idea. Buffalo on the Southern Plains were fast disappearing, a crippling blow to people for whom it was the staff of life. The attacks and potential attacks by Rangers and cavalry often meant life had to be lived on the run. Hunger, warfare, disease, as well as the steady westward migration by non-Indians made many chiefs realize that times were changing and their people now had to walk a different road. They advocated peace, if at all possible. Twenty Comanche and Kiowa chiefs signed the Treaty of Medicine Lodge Creek, which stipulated peace between their people and the United States. The Indians gave up all claims to lands in Texas and accepted a much smaller reservation between the Red and Washita Rivers in the southwestern part of Indian Territory. They agreed to adopt "civilization" by sending their children to school and becoming farmers. The United States pledged to build the schools and provide teachers, blacksmiths, carpenters, instructors, clothing, farming implements, and even agricultural instruction. The Comanches, Kiowas, and Kiowa-Apaches still had the right to hunt on lands south of the Arkansas River as long as the buffalo ranged there. Their reservation lands were guaranteed to them, none of which could be taken without approval of three-fourths of the adult male population. In return, the Indians were to receive annual clothing distributions as well as twenty-five thousand dollars a year for thirty years, sometimes in cash, sometimes in goods. To ensure the peace, just over a year later in 1868 the government built Fort Sill almost dead center in the new Comanche-Kiowa reservation.

Just to the north, the former Texas Reserve Indians on the Wichita and Affiliated Bands' reservation set an example of acculturation. With the end of the Civil War, scattered bands of Taovayas, Tawakonis, Wacos, Kichais, Nadacos, Hainais, Cadodachos, and Delawares returned to their reservation and settled down to farming. The Penetaka Comanches of the old Clear Fork Reserve settled nearby. Now able to live in peace, their lands guaranteed and their persons protected, the Wichitas and Affiliated Bands, as they were collectively called, seemed to prosper, growing large crops of corn and melons, raising small herds of cattle and pigs, even building a sawmill. Young men might divide their time between hunting, farming, and scouting for the government. "Progressive" chiefs, such as Guadeloupe and George Washington of the Cadodachos, José Mariá of the Nadacos, Black Beaver of the Delawares, Toshaway and Esahabbe of the Penetaka Comanches, along with Tawakoni Dave and Tawakoni Jim, urged their people to settle down, send their children to school, and peacefully walk this white man's road. On the reservation, a curious melding of cultures began taking place. Through proximity and intermarriage, the many different bands began to form into one. Where there had been Taovayas, Tawakonis, Yscanis, and Kichais, soon there were only Wichitas. Similarly, the Cadodachos, Nadacos, and Hainais became collectively known as the Caddos. While the Indians themselves still recognized traditional bands and lineages, most non-Indians in Texas and Indian Territory now just saw Wichitas, Caddos, Delawares, Comanches, Kiowas, and Apaches. Adding to this melting pot, Wichitas, Delawares, and Caddos sometimes intermarried, as did some whites who settled nearby.

PEACE POLICY AND THE RED RIVER WAR

Of course, not all Comanches, Kiowas, and Kiowa-Apaches wanted to settle down to farming as the Wichitas and Caddos did. Nor did they accept their "progressive" chiefs' willingness to live on a reservation. Many chiefs and warriors, particularly younger men, refused to give up the culture and lands they valued. They determined to resist at all costs. The Kwahadi Comanches absolutely refused to settle on the reservation, while other bands might drift on and off at will. Most men still saw raiding as the road to individual status and power. Fueling their fire were failures and missteps by the U.S. government. Despite all its promises of clothes, blankets, and food, government indifference, bureaucratic foul-ups, corrupt contractors, and a primitive transportation system meant that supplies often came late and were usually short and substandard. Food supplies were inadequate, and though the Indians could leave the reservation to hunt for food, the buffalo were quickly disappearing. Already starvation stalked the Comanches and Kiowas. Discontent with the treaty increased as many Indians believed the government only fulfilled those treaty stipulations that worked to its favor. Some chiefs who had signed the treaty, such as the Kiowas Satank and Satanta, now turned against it. By the early 1870s Comanches, Kiowas, even Cheyennes, in search of food, goods, status, and revenge, rode into

North Texas, hitting cattle herds, stagecoaches, wagon trains, isolated ranches and farms, and virtually anybody who crossed their path.

President Ulysses S. Grant's "peace policy" did nothing to stop the raids. Looking for scapegoats for the United States' disastrous Indian policy, eastern churchmen pointed to corrupt, spoils-system Indian agents, accusing them of cheating the Indians of their due and so causing much of the conflict. When Grant became president in 1869 he began appointing churchmen and missionaries as Indian agents, which everyone hoped would bring about peace, hence the term "peace policy." The Comanche-Kiowa reservations came under the authority of Quaker missionary Lawrie Tatum. Tatum was honest and his heart was in the right place, but he was naive when it came to Indians. Kiowa chiefs Satank, Satanta, and Big Tree, who had grown up in the rough-and-tumble world of Kiowa politics, easily manipulated Tatum and played to his sensibilities. Comanche and Kiowa raiders found they could strike into Texas and then take refuge back on the reservation in time to receive their share of allotment goods, boasting of their exploits and unpunished by Tatum who wanted to believe the best of everyone. Each successful raid emboldened the young men. They even raided the Fort Sill horse corral as well as that of the agency itself. Army officers fumed over Tatum's reluctance to arrest and punish them. Texans complained loudly, demanding the government do something about the raids stemming from Tatum's slipshod reservation. As one Texan wrote, "Give us Phil Sheridan and send Philanthropy to the devil."

Then, in mid-May, 1871, the Kiowas overplayed their hand. Satanta, old Satank, Big Tree, and more than a hundred other Kiowas rode down into North Texas and set up an ambush on Salt Creek Prairie, along the Fort Richardson road not too far from Jacksboro. A small wagon train appeared that was escorted by a few cavalrymen, but as the Kiowas prepared to attack, the shaman Mamanti urged them to let it go as another, far better wagon train would soon appear. The Kiowas allowed the wagon train to pass. They did not realize that in the train was General William Tecumseh Sherman, general in chief of the United States, who was personally investigating the validity of Texas' complaints. Not long after, as Mamanti predicted, a second train of ten freight wagons loaded with supplies clopped by and the Kiowas attacked. Of the twelve teamsters, five escaped; seven were killed, some tortured to death, all mutilated. The wagons were plundered and burned, and the Kiowa raiding party made off with all the supplies they could carry, as well as forty-one government mules.

Word of the wagon train attack quickly spread. Sherman, now at Fort Sill, was determined to capture the raiders. The Kiowa raiding party returned to the reservation to receive their ration allotments, and when Tatum asked Satanta about the attack, the chief readily admitted it. He had lost three men, so was willing to call it even. Still, he boasted to Tatum, "If any other Indian claims the honor of leading that party he will be lying to you. I led it myself." Tatum now had to forget his Quaker sensibilities. With Satanta's boast as proof, he determined to arrest the leaders of the raiding party. Tatum, Sherman, and Colonel Benjamin Grierson stood on Grierson's porch at Fort Sill; troopers were concealed around the quadrangle and inside the house. When Satanta, Satank, and several other chiefs arrived to "size up" Sherman, the troopers sprang the trap. For a tense moment it was touch and go, but the chiefs surrendered without a shot being fired. Satanta, Satank, and Big Tree were arrested and sent to Texas to stand trial. En route to prison, Satank was killed while trying to escape. But his death seems more like suicide, with the old man not willing to be imprisoned. In Texas, Satanta and Big Tree were tried and sentenced to death. However, public opinion suggested that keeping them in prison might be a better way to end the raids. The idea seemed valid, so Satanta and Big Tree were imprisoned at the Texas State Penitentiary at Huntsville. And it did seem to diminish Kiowa raiding into Texas. Nevertheless, many people, particularly the Five Civilized Tribes in Indian Territory, called for clemency and begged Texas to eventually release the two chiefs.

While the imprisonment of Satanta and Big Tree may have caused the Kiowas to think twice about raiding into Texas, it made little impact on the Comanches and their strikes continued. Then, on September 29,1872, up in the Texas Panhandle, Colonel Ranald Mackenzie and his Fourth Cavalry attacked a large village of more than 260 lodges of combined Kwahadis, Kotsotekas, Yamparikas, Noconis, and Penetakas. The Fourth Cavalry killed twenty-four Comanches, burned the village and its utensils, and took 124 women and children captives. These were taken to Fort Sill, essentially hostages to ensure the good behavior of the Comanches. They remained prisoners until June, 1873. During this time, Comanches raids slackened considerably. The women and children were later returned to their families and a few raids took place. Without the woman and children in custody, the government tried to tie Comanche behavior to the impending release of Satanta and Big Tree. It demanded that at least five Comanche raiders be turned over for punishment or the Kiowa chiefs would not be released. The Comanches refused and in October, 1873, its bluff called, the government finally released Satanta and Big Tree as it had promised, despite demands from Texans and Sherman himself to keep the two in prison.

The spring of 1874 saw tensions at near breaking points across the Southern Plains. Texans had no illusions about the freeing of Satanta and Big Tree and prepared for more raids. The Comanches and Kiowas were angry. Angry at their chiefs' imprisonment and the short rations; angry about American horse thieves out of Kansas who stole Indian ponies and peddlers selling cheap whiskey to the Indians on credit, often getting them so deeply in debt that they had to forfeit what little cash they received from their annuities. But what really enraged them were the buffalo hunters. In the late 1860s American buffalo hunters armed with high-powered rifles began invading the Great Plains. By 1870 they had wiped out the buffalo on the Central Plains, taking only the hide, maybe the tongue, and leaving the rest to rot. Now they cast greedy eyes toward the few remaining buffalo south of the Arkansas River. By 1874 buffalo were almost impossible for Comanche and Kiowa hunters to find. With government rations often late or short, the reservation Indians began to starve. Ignoring Indian complaints, the government did nothing to stop the buffalo hunters, in fact, some officers encouraged them, realizing that killing off the Plains Indians' main source of food was the best way to defeat them. With the government turning a blind eye, by the summer of 1874, a number of hunters had banded together and were killing off the buffalo in the heart of the Comanche and Kiowa hunting grounds in the Texas Panhandle.

Now many Comanches, Kiowas, and Southern Cheyennes had had enough. On June 27, 1874, about three hundred Comanche and Cheyenne warriors attacked a band of buffalo hunters at Adobe Walls, the site of Kit Carson's fight ten years earlier. And so began the Red River War, the last desperate fight of the Southern Plains Indians to remain free. Not all Comanches, Kiowas, or Southern Cheyennes wanted war or joined it. A good many chiefs and their followers had long recognized that their way of life was changing and so had grudgingly accepted the white man's road. War, they understood, would be a disaster and could not be won. Still, fiery young chiefs, such as Quanah Parker of the Noconi Comanches, who led the attack on the buffalo hunters, and Isatai, a young shaman who urged the war, were determined to try. From the first, the Indians experienced mixed results. The hunters, with their high-powered rifles, held off the Indians for several days, suffering only a few losses, and killing at least fifteen warriors, maybe many more. Nevertheless, the hunters quickly abandoned the area once the Indians withdrew. On July 12, a large party of Kiowas successfully ambushed a troop of Texas Rangers at Lost Valley, west of Jacksboro and not far from where the wagon train had been ambushed three years earlier.

The attacks drove a stake through the heart of President Grant's "peace policy." Those Indians siding with the war factions left the reservation to try to live on the Southern Plains as they once had. Given the okay by Washington, army troops out of Fort Sill marched onto the reservations where they made lists of "friendly" and "hostile" Indians. The friendlies, consisting of a majority of Kiowas, as well as all the Penetaka Comanches and about half the Yamparikas and Noconis, were rounded up and placed on Cache Creek within the reservation boundary. As it always had with Indian peoples, family came first and hostiles were able to take advantage of the confusion. They often slipped in to the friendly area for food and rest. At the same time, hostiles posing as friendlies sometimes left the camp and made raids of their own.

By late August several hostile factions of Comanches and Kiowas, many of whom had participated in the Adobe Walls or Lost Valley fights, settled around the Wichita Agency at Anadarko, using the peaceful Wichitas, Caddos, and Delawares as protection. On August 22, when the army demanded the Comanches and Kiowas give up their weapons, a battle broke out at the Wichita Agency. Over the next two days, a fierce firefight raged. About seven non-Indians were killed; the Comanches and Kiowas lost around fourteen. The agency store was looted, and many of the farms of the peaceful Indians were burned, including that belonging to Delaware chief Black Beaver. Starting a grassfire to cover their retreat, the Comanches and Kiowas made their way to the safety of the breaks of the Red River.

The army was already on the offensive, putting more than five thousand men into the field. Columns out of Kansas, Indian Territory, Texas, and New Mexico all converged on the Texas Panhandle. Once again, the Wichitas, Caddos, Delawares, and Penetaka Comanches served as scouts and auxiliaries. Though parties of Comanche, Kiowa, and Cheyenne warriors raided ranches and small wagon trains when they could, they soon found themselves on the run, constantly hounded by army detachments and the Indian scouts. On August 30 cavalry under the command of General Nelson Miles defeated a large camp of Cheyennes at the Battle of the Cap Rock on Prairie Town Fork of the Red River. To escape, the Indians burned their lodges, abandoned their camp utensils, and scattered into the scorching Llano Estacado. A month later, on the night of September 28, Colonel Ranald S. Mackenzie's Fourth Cavalry, along with Tonkawa and Seminole scouts, surprised and destroyed a large camp of Comanches, Kiowas, and Cheyennes inside Palo Duro Canyon, just south of present-day Amarillo. Though the Indians only lost three men killed, they were totally routed. Mackenzie captured more than 1,400 Indian horses and the entire camp of tepees and utensils. Understanding the importance of both to the Indians, Mackenzie kept 350 of the horses and mules for his own men and methodically killed the remaining thousand-plus animals. He then destroyed the entire village and its contents.

For the Indians, the loss of so many horses and tepees, as well as winter food and clothing, proved a crushing defeat. Even the elements turned against them. The horrendous 100-plus-degree heat and drought of the summer now gave way to incessant rains and autumn chill. Constantly harried by the army in what has come to be called the "wrinkled hand chase," many cold, wet, hungry, shelterless hostiles opted for reservation life. Slowly, bands of defeated Comanches, Kiowas, and Cheyennes made their way back toward Fort Sill. Blue northers and blizzards of December sent back more until only a few bands remained at war. On February 25, 1875, the last 250 Kiowa holdouts, led by Lone Wolf, surrendered. Finally, on June 2, the last Comanche warriors under Quanah Parker came in, bringing an end not only to the Red River War, but also to the free life the Southern Plains Indians had always known. Seventy-four Comanche, Kiowa, and Cheyenne warriors, some of them not involved in the war at all, were imprisoned for three years at Fort Marion, Florida. Satanta was sent back to the Texas State Penitentiary in Huntsville. Despondent, he committed suicide in March, 1878, by jumping from an upper-story window. Now all Texas Indians were on reservations.

APACHE INCURSIONS INTO WEST TEXAS

By the 1870s the Lipan Apaches, whose heyday in Texas had been in the seventeenth century, and the Kiowa-Apaches, who had migrated south with the Kiowas in the late eighteenth century, had largely disappeared from Texas. The Lipans had been pushed ever farther south by the Comanches, and by the 1870s, the Lipans, as a recognized division, had ceased to exist. What few remaining Lipans there were had either integrated with other more numerous Apache bands in New Mexico and Arizona or become hispanized peasants living in northern Mexico. During the latter part of the nineteenth century, when Texans mentioned the name "Apache," most were thinking of the Kiowa-Apaches. The Kiowa-Apaches had been defeated along with the Kiowas and Comanches during the Red River War of 1874–75 and took their place on the reservation around Fort Sill. On the reservation, the Kiowa-Apaches dropped the term "Kiowa" and became known just as the "Apaches," or more specifically, the Apache Tribe of Oklahoma.

Then, in 1881, the very last Indian raids ever made into Texas took place. They came from the Chiricahua Apaches, a band not previously known for venturing into Texas. The Chiricahuas mainly confined their activities to the mountains of southern Arizona, southern New Mexico, and northern Mexico. During the 1870s, as the U.S. government tried to concentrate the many different and often antagonistic divisions of Apaches onto the San Carlos Reservation in Arizona, some Chiricahua leaders, such as Naiche, Geronimo, and Victorio, resisted. Geronimo and Naiche never made it to Texas, at least as warriors, but Victorio and his band of Chiricahuas put a scare in West Texans.

In 1877 the government tried to move Victorio and his band of Chiricahuas and Mescaleros away from Ojo Caliente in central New Mexico to the huge San Carlos Reservation in Arizona. Victorio refused, pointing out that he and his people had been living at Ojo Caliente peacefully for the past decade. When the government insisted, Victorio, an excellent tactician, began raiding into Mexico, New Mexico, and West Texas, mainly in the area between Fort Davis and El Paso. The government ordered two African American cavalry units, the Ninth Cavalry and Tenth Cavalry, to give chase. The Tenth recruited Tigua Indian scouts to lead them. In early 1880 the Tenth Cavalry, which had been moved from Fort Concho to Fort Davis, went after Victorio and found itself being led on a fifteen-hundred–mile wild-goose chase. They returned to Fort Davis in May without ever catching a whiff of Victorio. Sent back on the Apache's trail, the Tenth Cavalry caught up with Victorio's band. On June 11 Tigua scouts and the Tenth Cavalry "buffalo soldiers" slugged it out with the Apaches just west of Valentine. Twenty Apaches and four Tiguas were killed. In August, at Rattlesnake Springs in the Guadeloupe Mountains, the army and Apaches met again in a three-hour battle. Once again, Victorio and his band managed to slip away and headed toward Mexico. In September a detachment of Texas Rangers joined the chase and illegally entered Mexico during their hunt. They also had no luck in catching up with Victorio. As one writer calculated, during fourteen months of raiding in Mexico, New Mexico, and Texas, Victorio's band, "seldom more than seventy-five strong, had taken the lives of more than one thousand whites and Mexicans while eluding three American cavalry regiments, two American infantry regiments, a huge number of Mexican troops, and a contingent of Texas Rangers."

However, Victorio's luck was quickly running out. In October, 1880, he and his people took refuge in a mountainous area of northern Mexico called Tres Castillos. On October 15 a detachment of Chihuahua State Militia managed to surround the band and in an all-day battle defeated the Apaches, killing Victorio and all his warriors. The women and children were taken captive and held in Chihuahua City for the next several years. However, though Victorio was dead, some of his band who had not been at Tres Castillos were roaming far West Texas. In January, 1881, at the Sierra Diablo Mountains of West Texas, the last Indian battle in Texas took place. Tigua Scouts fighting alongside Texas Rangers caught up with the last Apaches and routed them. With this, the Indian wars in Texas came to an end, as did the freedom of any and all Indians who had once called Texas home.

RESERVATION LIFE

By 1881 only two small recognized Indian "tribes" remained in Texas: the Alabama-Coushattas, with their tiny reservation in Polk County of East Texas, and the Tiguas near El Paso. In the late 1860s Texas tried to get the federal government to take over administration of the Alabama-Coushattas but nothing came of it and for the next several decades the state virtually ignored the small group of Indians. As for the Tiguas, though Texas had granted them about thirty-six acres of land in 1854, through actions by the Texas legislature and unscrupulous whites, they lost virtually every inch of it. Finally in 1871 the Incorporation Act restored about twenty acres to the Tiguas. The remainder of the nineteenth century saw the Tiguas ignored by the state and federal governments and left to their own devices. None of the other Texas Indians, such as the Comanches, Kiowas, Apaches, Caddos, and Wichitas, lived in Texas anymore. They were on reservations in southwestern Indian Territory.

Defeated and virtually prisoners on their reservations, these Texas Indians in Indian Territory relied on government allotments of cattle, flour, and clothing, though some did try to plant crops and raise cattle. Many Comanches and Kiowas shrewdly learned how to make do on the white man's road. The Kiowa-Comanche reservation contained huge expanses of lush grasslands, excellent for fattening cattle. The Comanches, under the leadership of Quanah Parker, and the Kiowas to a lesser extent, now began leasing their lands to Texas cattlemen for cash payments called "grass money." By 1885 Texas cattlemen were running 75,000 head of cattle on the Kiowa-Comanche reservation, using 1.5 million acres and paying only six cents an acre per year. Though less than market value, grass money did provide about $55,000 a year for the Kiowas, Comanches, and Apaches. Twice a year the cattlemen distributed the grass money. In the summer of 1885 the companies paid each Indian on the Kiowa-Comanche reservation $9.50, all in silver dimes. Many government officials disliked the idea of the Indians leasing their lands, rather than farming them, so in 1890 the United States declared the cattle leases null and void and ordered the cattle off the reservation. Making matters worse, whites living near the reservation often targeted its resources. For example, white settlers often slipped onto the reservation and stole Indian timber to be used as fence posts, housing, and firewood. As one settler recalled, a local missionary had been caught stealing wood by a Kiowa. "White man talk heap Jesus on Sunday," the Kiowa commented, "and steal Kiowa's wood on Monday." It got so bad that an Indian police force had to be created to keep white thieves out of the reservations.

During the twenty-five-odd years of the reservation experience in Indian Territory, the Indians not only had to adjust to farming and ranching but also got "heap Jesus." By the late 1870s Roman Catholic, Presbyterian, Methodist, and Baptist missions had been founded in Anadarko, Oklahoma, and around Fort Sill, where they experienced varying degrees of success. Although many Indians might have gone to church on Sunday, most still attended their traditional ceremonies and dances, at least when they could, as reservation agents normally banned these as "uncivilized." Quanah Parker, who became the main spokesman for the Comanche people, and a few Caddo chiefs founded the Native American Church, which blended traditional Indian beliefs, peyote use, and Christianity. While agents, white churchmen, and even some "progressive" Indians condemned the "peyote road" as mere drug use and a throwback to tribal days, the adherents advocated a peaceful, harmonious, industrious life, and their ceremonies were always quiet and dignified. The church spread rapidly and soon had adherents across Indian America. In 1944 the Native American Church received a charter, with its stated purpose to "promote morality, sobriety, industry, charity and right living." The Native American Church still exists and many American Indian people across the United States are quite active in it. Other religious movements, such as the 1890 Ghost Dance, touched reservation Indians in Indian Territory, but this passed peacefully without causing the bloodshed it brought to the Lakotas at the Battle of Wounded Knee in that year.

Along with religion, the United States also forced American-style education on the Indians. Schools, such as the Riverside Indian School at Anadarko, taught Indian girls and boys domestic and mechanical arts. Besides English, basic reading, writing, and arithmetic, the girls were taught how to sew, cook, and clean. Boys learned how to be farmers or carpenters. Little effort was made to prepare the students for the modern industrial world nor were they given courses that would lead them to universities. Many children were sent to boarding schools far away from their families, such as Rainy Mountain Boarding School near Gotebo, Oklahoma; Chilocco Indian School in northern Oklahoma; Haskell Institute in Lawrence, Kansas; or the most famous of all, Carlisle Indian School in Carlisle, Pennsylvania. At these schools, boys had their hair cut; their old "Indian" clothes were burned; and they were prohibited from speaking their native tongue.

While the government and the churches actively tried to erase traditional Indian culture, the Comanches, Kiowas, Apaches, Wichitas, Caddos, and others also found themselves changing by virtue of the ever-increasing number of Americans around them. White and black store-keepers, teachers, preachers, government officials, cowboys, and ranch hands lived on or around the reservations and came into contact with the Indians in a variety of ways. Many non-Indian men married Indian woman, "squaw men" as they were called. Some of these were loving hus-bands and from the union came children who lived with a foot in both the Indian and Ameri-can worlds. Other "squaw men" were opportunists who hoped to get their hands on as much Indian land and resources as they could. Claiming they were now a member of the "tribe," they demanded every benefit they could, but then turned to the U.S. government when tribal govern-ments attempted to control their activities. Indian culture changed rapidly. As Indian women came into contact with white women, dress styles and cooking methods changed. Although some people remained committed to the past, others learned how to walk the white man's road.

Still, by the mid-1880s many government officials and philanthropists believed the Indians were not "civilizing" fast enough. Seeing only reservation poverty and not the community it contained, these "friends of the Indians" felt that communal reservation land was hampering Indian "progress." The key to Indian "civilization" and prosperity, they believed, was to break up the reservations, give each Indian family its own plot of land, teach them to become small farmers, and force them to swim in the ocean of profits and losses. This approach ignored several realities. The Caddos and Wichitas had been successful farmers for hundreds of years and had their own ideas of farming. The Comanches and Kiowas never possessed any form of agriculture nor had any desire to learn how to plow a field. Cattle leasing was rather profitable and more conducive to reservation geography than farming. And finally, small farms in America were on their way out, being replaced by agribusiness, and the United States was fast becoming urban and industrialized. But as Merrill Gates, a "friend of the Indian," saw it: "To bring [the Indian] out of savagery into citizenship we must make the Indian more intelligently selfish before we can make him unselfishly intelligent. We need to awaken in him wants. In his dull savagery he must be touched by the wings of the divine angel of discontent. Then he begins to look forward, to reach out. . . . Discontent . . . is needed to get the Indian out of the blanket and into trou-sers,—and trousers with a pocket in them, and with a pocket that aches to be filled with dollars!"

So despite almost unanimous protests by the Indians, the U.S. government passed the Dawes Severalty Act of 1887, which would give 160 acres of land to each head of an Indian family and lesser amounts to unmarried or orphaned Indians. Excess land would be sold off by the government, with the proceeds going into Indian accounts to pay for their education and the purchase of stock and farming implements. Most whites, especially land-hungry settlers, small ranchers, railroad companies, and oil companies strongly supported the Dawes Act. Only the big cattle companies of Texas protested, and not because the Dawes Act was bad for the Indians but because they would lose their cattle leases.

Gates said of the Dawes Act, it would be "a mighty pulverizing engine for breaking up the tribal mass." It was. The Dawes Act finally caught up with the Comanches, Kiowas, Apaches, Wichitas, Caddos, and Tonkawas in the 1890s as the Jerome Commission began negotiating the reservation allotment process. In June, 1891, the commission managed to get the Wichitas, Caddos, and Delawares to accept $715,000 for their 574,000-acre reservation, about $1.25 per acre. Congress approved the plan in 1895 and shortly thereafter the reservation was broken up and the Indians began receiving their individual plots of land. In October of that same year, the commission pressured the Tonkawas to give up their 90,000-acre reservation for $30,600 and take individual allotments. In October, 1892, after much arm-twisting, the commission managed to get the Kiowas, Comanches, and Apaches to sell their several-million-acre reservation for $2 million. Congress ratified the agreement in 1900 and the allotment process began soon after. The Tonkawa reservation was thrown open to white settlement first, in September, 1893. A few years later, on August 6, 1901, the surplus land on the Kiowa-Comanche-Apache and the Wichita and Affiliate Bands reservations were sold off to white buyers.

The negotiation and ratification process was not without controversy. According to the 1867 Medicine Lodge Creek Treaty, the government could not take any of the Kiowa-Comanche-Apache reservation without approval of three-fourths of its adult male Indian population. There were grave doubts as to whether three-fourths of the reservation Indians actually approved the Jerome Commission agreement in 1892, but the government ignored these concerns. Showing a shrewd understanding of American society, Kiowa chief Lone Wolf field suit on this point to prevent the allotment from taking place. *Lone Wolf v. Hitchcock* wound its way through the court system and in 1903, the U.S. Supreme Court rejected Lone Wolf's arguments, ruling that Congress could make any law it wanted for the Indians and was not bound by previous treaties. If Indians had any doubt that they were conquered, the ruling in *Lone Wolf v. Hitchcock* put those doubts to rest. Before allotment, many reservation Indians had prospered as ranchers by running their cattle on the communal lands. They now found themselves in bad shape, their allotment too small for ranching and the land too poor for small-scale farming. Within just a few years, many Comanches, Caddos, Kiowas, Wichitas, and Apaches had lost their allotments to whites and sunk even deeper into poverty.

Tiguas around El Paso had their own land problems during the last half of the nineteenth century. In 1871 the State of Texas, with the urging of unscrupulous Anglo land speculators, incorporated the Tigua's town of Ysleta. On paper, the new city was the largest in the state at the time—thirty-six square miles. Suddenly, the Tiguas found their property heavily taxed, and when they could not pay it was confiscated and sold to Anglos. Much of their land had been taken from them by 1874 when the incorporation was declared illegal. Just as bad, in 1877 the

Tiguas were barred from using the salt beds near the Guadalupe Mountains that had attracted the Jumanos in years past. For centuries the Tiguas, as well as the Jumanos and Pueblos, had gotten their salt from these dry lakebeds. They were considered communal property. Local speculators at El Paso, including Judge Charles Howard, tried to gain control of the salt beds and prohibited the Indians from using them. This began the El Paso Salt War in which the Tiguas and nearby Hispanic settlers rose up and attacked the Anglos, killing five, including Judge Howard. Troops had to be sent in to stop the violence. In the end, the Tiguas still lost access to the salt beds.

By the turn of the twentieth century the Indians of Texas, both those living in and out of the state, had been defeated. It had not taken long, just under 400 years from the time Cabeza de Vaca washed ashore at Galveston; about 180 since Spain established a firm presence in Texas; only 64 years since the Texas Revolution; and a mere 35 since the end of the Civil War. Despite a valiant defense, people who had once fearlessly roamed the Southern Plains and whose lands had stretched from the piney woods of western Louisiana to the Rocky Mountains of New Mexico found themselves confined to tiny reservations or land allotments. Nor were they free to live their lives as they wanted. Traditional religious ceremonies were banned. Certain types of clothing were too. They could not do with their allotment as they saw fit and were even told how they must slaughter cattle. Government officials forcibly interfered in the lives, politics, and religion of these Indians to a degree that other Americans would never have tolerated. Even the education provided for them was second-rate and did not prepare them for the modern, industrialized twentieth century.

The Trail Towns

Don Worcester

D
on Worcester (1915–2003), a distinguished scholar in the fields of Latin American and Western history, taught at the University of Florida and Texas Christian University. A prolific author, his books include *Brazil: From Colony to World Power* (1973), *Bolivar* (1977), *The Apaches: Eagles of the Southwest* (1979), *The Chisholm Trail: High Road of the Cattle Kingdom* (1980), *The Spanish Mustang: From the Plains of Andalusia to the Prairies of Texas* (1986), and *The Texas Longhorn: Relic of the Past, Asset for the Future* (1987). Dr. Worcester also served as President of the Western History Association and Managing Editor of the *Hispanic American Historical Review*. In addition to his scholarly pursuits, he raised Arabian horses on his ranch near Fort Worth.

Between 1867 and 1884, Texas cowboys drove over five million cattle from San Antonio to Kansas on the legendary Chisholm Trail. In this selection, Dr. Worcester discusses the history of the colorful, and frequently rowdy, trail towns. These included Abilene, Ellsworth, and Caldwell in Kansas and Fort Worth—known as "Cow Town"—in Texas. ❧

★ ★

Before the Civil War, Baxter Springs, Kansas, and Sedalia, Missouri, had a brief reign as the principal end-of-trail towns. Both exhibited some of the rough characteristics of the later

Kansas cowtowns, but they did not handle large numbers of huge herds and hundreds of trail hands like those that reached Abilene after 1867.

Abilene became a trail town overnight, but its decline was equally rapid. It began as an Overland Stage station which received rare but favorable notice in 1859 when Horace Greeley announced that it was there he ate the last square meal on his trip across the plains. That, and the fact that Abilene had a biblical name, were its sole claims to distinction. In 1867, when Joseph McCoy stopped there in his search for a suitable railhead for Texas cattle, he found only a dozen families living in simple cabins, a post office, a store, and a saloon or two. On September 5 of that year the first trainload of Texas cattle was shipped to Chicago from McCoy's pens.

That first season 35,000 cattle reached Abilene; the following year around 75,000 head arrived; in 1869 the number rose to 160,000. Not all were shipped to market, for many were sold to ranchers in Nebraska. By that time some of the regular residents of Abilene were concerned over the saloons, gambling houses, and dance halls that lined Texas Street. Their efforts to clean up the town were frustrated by the fact that peace officers had a short tenure when the boisterous trail hands were in town. When the Texans saw a stone jail being erected, they happily tore it down.

In 1870, Marshal Tom Smith tamed Abilene somewhat by posting an ordinance against carrying guns. Because Smith enforced the law with his fists rather than with guns, he gained some grudging respect from trail hands before he was murdered while helping the sheriff arrest a couple of killers.

Joseph McCoy, who had brought prosperity to Abilene, purchased cattle on credit in 1869 and lost heavily when the market fell. When the railroad reneged on its agreement to pay him one-eighth of the freight he processed to be shipped from Abilene, McCoy lost everything, even though the courts eventually ruled in his favor. He was able to pay off his debts and he remained closely connected with the cattle business, but he was never again a big operator.

Abilene became famous all over the West, so well known it was natural that people would suppose that it was a city of substance and size. A Texan rode into the center of the town and asked how far it was to Abilene. When told he was there, he replied, "Now, look here, stranger, you don't mean this here little scatterin trick is Abilene." He was told it was. "Well I'll swar I never seed such a little town have such a mighty big name." More important than its size, Abilene's cattle business produced three million dollars a year.

Opposition to the sinful activities on Texas Street intensified, and the permanent residents insisted that the fleshpots be moved to the Devil's Addition outside of town. The saloons along Texas Street remained, and dissatisfaction continued to grow.

In 1870, Abilene had some five hundred residents—the transients who were after the cowboy trade vanished with the last herd of the season and returned before the first herds arrived in the spring. By the trailing season of 1871 Abilene was thoroughly prepared, with ten saloons, five general stores, two hotels, and two so-called hotels in which patrons did not necessarily spend the entire night. The Drover's Cottage, which McCoy no longer owned, catered to trail bosses and cattle buyers; cowboys stayed at the Merchant's Hotel. The men who drove most of the six hundred thousand cattle north swarmed into Abilene in such numbers the saloonkeepers, gamblers, and pimps rejoiced, but the rest of the people had seen enough of Texas cattle and their keepers.

That year was Abilene's most active, but it was also its last year as a trail town. By summer the Atchison, Topeka, and Santa Fe had extended its rails to Newton, near the Chisholm Trail south of Abilene. When the railroad brought Joseph McCoy there to supervise the building of loading pens, a collection of rude shacks was hastily erected. By mid-August 1871 the first train-load of cattle was shipped from Newton to Kansas City. Around forty thousand cattle passed through Newton that year, but its career as a trail town was short as well as violent. By 1873 its trailing days were over, for the Wichita and Southwestern Railroad had reached Wichita.

Early in 1872, before herds had started north, a circular printed in Abilene by the Farmers Protective Association of Dickinson County was circulated widely in Texas. It stated that members of the association "most respectfully request all who have contemplated driving cattle to Abilene the coming season to seek some other point for shipping, as the inhabitants of Dickinson will no longer submit to the evils of the trade." McCoy and others launched a counter-campaign to persuade Texans to bring their cattle to Abilene, but in vain.

The Kansas and Pacific Railroad, which had treated Abilene rather cavalierly and had actually tried to cheat McCoy, suddenly awakened to the fact that it was losing the lucrative cattle-hauling business to the rival Santa Fe Railroad. It decided to provide Texans a new railhead that was easily accessible and without the irritations they had suffered from the farmers surrounding Abilene. The new shipping point was Ellsworth, about seventy miles west of Abilene. The railroad hired Shanghai Pierce and Colonel W. E. Hunter to supervise the building of pens, and sent men to mark out a route from the Chisholm Trail to Ellsworth.

The railroad also sent Shanghai Pierce to Texas to persuade cattlemen to send their herds to the new shipping point. With both Newton and Ellsworth offering inducements to trail men, Abilene was ignored. Many Abilene businessmen quickly loaded their wares on wagons, said good-by to deserted Texas Street, and headed for Ellsworth. The new owner of the Drover's Cottage even moved part of it to the new railhead. For a time Abilene was little more than a ghost town, but it soon became the center of a prosperous wheat-growing business. A stone marker was all that reminded people of the town's former days as "Abilene—The End of the Chisholm Trail."

Ellsworth was an instant success as a trail town, for it took over much of the enormous trade that had previously gone to Abilene. From the start it could truthfully claim to be the leading cattle market of Kansas. In its first season, 1872, at least one hundred thousand cattle reached Ellsworth.

Aware of Abilene's troubles with lawlessness, Ellsworth established a police force and confined the "soiled dove" population to the Smoky Hill bottoms outside the town, a district soon known as Nauchville. The police force concentrated on the town proper, leaving Nauchville wide open. Ellsworth's efforts to control violence were no more successful than those of other trail towns. Its police force proved corrupt and adept at cheating Texas cowboys with false arrests and illegal fines. Some men feared that the Texans' resentment would result in an uncontrollable eruption.

John Montgomery, editor of the *Reporter,* tried to avoid the impending blowup by suggesting raising money by licensing the "fair Cyprians" of Nauchville. "If it can't be rooted out," he wrote, "the vicious vocation should be made to contribute to the expense of maintaining law and order." Although respectable citizens were shocked at this suggestion, the town council agreed to it, and the licenses provided Ellsworth's main source of revenue.

Ellsworth lasted only a few years as a railhead for Texas cattle, for competition among railroads resulted in the establishment of newer and more convenient outlets. Ellsworth's only big year was 1873, but when the financial panic began in September there were many herds in the area awaiting buyers who never came. Of the thousands of cattle that had to be wintered there that year, fewer than twenty thousand "made it through to grass." No herds arrived in 1874.

The extension of the Santa Fe's subsidiary line, the Wichita and Southwestern, to Wichita in 1872 brought four hundred thousand Texas cattle to that town in 1873. Joseph McCoy had completed the shipping pens in time for the 1872 season. It was at Wichita that the buying of cattle for the northern Indian reservations reached its peak. When the Wichita market opened, some of the merchants who had deserted Abilene for Ellsworth loaded their wagons once more and headed for the new cattle center.

By 1873 Wichita was clearly the major cattle market in Kansas. The town enlarged its shipping pens and built a toll bridge across the Arkansas at Douglas Avenue, which was also designated as the official route for driving cattle through town to the stockyards and shipping pens. Most of the dance halls and saloons were located in the quarter called Delano across the river from the rest of the town, but around the intersection of Douglas Avenue and Main Street saloons and brothels were plentiful.

Wichita had been the northern terminus of Jesse Chisholm's wagon road, for his trading post was near where the town was later built. As a result, in the years of Wichita's preeminence as a trail town—1872–76—the herds followed the original Chisholm Trail a greater distance than at any other time.

Those who bought cattle at Wichita or elsewhere were of three main categories: ranchers from the area from Colorado to the Dakotas in search of stock cattle, feed lot owners from corn belt states, and packing house agents who were after fat cattle. During Wichita's years as a trail town, cattle prices reached their highest level for the whole trailing era. A nine-hundred-pound steer that sold for eleven to fourteen dollars in Texas brought twenty to twenty-five dollars in Kansas, and ten dollars more in Chicago or St. Louis. The same animal might net seventy dollars or more in New York City.

When Tobe Odem sold his herd at Dodge City in the spring of 1877, he told his cowboys their pay would continue until they got back to Goliad with their horses and the lead steer, Old Tom. When they reached Goliad, another herd would be ready. Then he invited them to town for "some fun and few drinks." Dodge City's reputation for wickedness, young cowboy Jesse Benton decided, was undeserved.

"Dodge City were a sight to see: saloons, gambling houses, dance halls on every corner," Benton remembered. There were around five hundred cowboys and buffalo hunters in town, "everybody there to have a good time and blow off from the long trail. I've read some of the most exaggerated things about Dodge City. But they are wrong." Most of the cowboys were goodhearted young fellows with money to spend; if they didn't have any, their boss would furnish it. And, he added, Dodge City knew how to treat them right.

"I walked up to the dance halls and looked in. What a sight to anyone, the prettiest gals from all over the world, dressed like a million dollars, was all there. If you did not come in to dance, they would grab you and pull you in, whether you wanted to dance or not. All the girls acted glad to see you. Round after round of drinks, then all would dance."

Odem bought all the drinks for his men; they didn't return to camp until daybreak. After breakfast they rolled up in their blankets, for no one thought of starting for Texas that day. The following day they didn't feel much better.

By 1876 farms and fences had virtually cut off access to Wichita, and cowmen turned to Dodge City, which had handled some trail cattle from 1872 on. Dodge City would continue to be a major cattle center to 1885–86, the longest existence of any of the Kansas trail towns. This "Queen of the cowtowns," this "wickedest little city in America," this "Beautiful Bibulous Babylon of the Frontier" boasted a saloon for every fifty residents. Perhaps Dodge's earlier history as a center for buffalo hunters and shipping point for buffalo hides had a lasting influence on its character. The other Kansas trail towns all started full-blown as cowtowns.

Because of the profitable hide-shipping business, Dodge largely ignored the possibilities of handling cattle until 1875, although some herds had passed that way as early as 1872, when the Santa Fe tracks reached Dodge. Since there were no loading facilities, herds to be shipped were driven on to Great Bend or elsewhere.

For nearly fifteen years Dodge City was considered the wildest town in the West. By 1875 cattle were regularly trailed there, and it was on its way to becoming the "Cowboy Capital" of the nation. Dodge continued to flourish until 1886, when the quarantines against Texas cattle put an end to the declining trailing business. In its heyday Dodge was the location of the original Boot Hill cemetery, resting place for dozens of men who died with their boots on. It also boasted the Cowboy Band, which helped publicize the city.

The continued spread of farmers and barbed wire pressed a greater and greater percentage of trail cattle on Dodge, but in the end the herds stopped coming. The 1884 quarantine law, which prohibited Texas cattle from crossing Kansas between March 1 and December 1, meant that any herds moving north thereafter would have to keep west of the Kansas line. Many herds made it through in 1884, but none did after that. Kansas cattle were still trailed to Dodge for shipment, but after the big freeze of 1886–87 the Cowboy Capital could no longer be considered an important cattle market.

The last of the Kansas cowtowns to figure prominently in the trailing era was Caldwell, the "Border Queen" on the Chisholm Trail just north of Indian Territory. Caldwell was settled in 1871, but it had no railroad. During the winter of 1873–74, however, when thousands of cattle had to be wintered on the plains, many herds were held near Caldwell, and it served as a supply center and also as the place cowboys went for a spree.

Even before the railroad reached it in 1880 Caldwell already had a reputation for violence and killings. The sight of a horse thief "idling his time away under a cottonwood tree" (at the end of a rope) was not unusual. A marshal's term in office in Caldwell was about two weeks on the average. There was a saying, "In Caldwell you're lucky to be alive."

When the railroad reached Caldwell, it gave the Chisholm Trail a slight but temporary advantage over the Western Trail to Dodge City, but the rapidly spreading farms were making it increasingly difficult to move herds without trouble with grangers, and 1884 was the Chisholm Trail's last year.

As the demand for stocker cattle or young steers blossomed in the North, most of the herds sold in Kansas were delivered to ranches in Wyoming, Montana, or the Dakotas. Ogallala, Nebraska, rose as a new cattle center, and many herds not sold in Kansas found buyers among cowmen assembled there. By the mid-1870s Cheyenne, Wyoming, was another important cattle center where many Texas herds were sold. Ogallala and Cheyenne became as important to Texas cattlemen as the Kansas railheads had been. Cheyenne was, in addition, headquarters for all the cattlemen of the North and Northwest. In 1877, Miles City, Montana, became the cattle center for that region.

The town that benefited most and longest from the Chisholm Trail was Fort Worth. In 1865, as a result of the exodus caused by the Civil War, Fort Worth had more houses than people, for the inhabitants of all ages numbered no more than 250. The empty town made, as newcomer K. M. Van Zandt remarked, "a gloomy picture." The town had a blacksmith shop, a flour mill, and a cobbler's shop, but lacked such vital institutions as a post office and a saloon. As the Longhorn was the economic salvation of Texas, the Chisholm Trail was the savior of Fort Worth, which owed its favorable location on the cattle trail to accident. At least in the early days it was the last place for making purchases before reaching central Kansas.

Before its revival Fort Worth was not impressive. "We went by Waco, Cleburne, and Fort Worth," George Saunders wrote of his first trip up the trail. "Between the last named places the country was somewhat level and untimbered. . . . When we reached Fort Worth we crossed the Trinity River under the bluff, where the present street car line to the stockyards crosses the river. Fort Worth was then but a very small place, consisting of only a few stores, and there was only one house in that part of town where the stockyards are now located. We held our herd here two days."

Other men on the early drives noted that Fort Worth was a small village with few stores, but as the purchases of supplies for trail herds infused new life into the town, the population doubled between 1865 and 1868. It continued to grow because of rumors that a railroad line would soon be extended there.

When Colonel John Wien Forney visited Texas in 1871, Fort Worth's population had grown to upwards of twelve hundred. It was, Forney noted, beautifully situated on a broad plateau. "Fort Worth is a city set on a hill, and as the point of junction between two branches of the Texas and Pacific, is particularly enviable, inasmuch as from this locality the Grand Trunk line to the Pacific will be projected and pushed…. During the last year 500,000 head of cattle were driven through Fort Worth on their way to Missouri and Kansas, and as we left the town we met a single drove containing 1250 head."

In anticipation of the coming of the railroad others flocked to Fort Worth, doubling the population again in 1873. Around four hundred thousand cattle had been trailed to Kansas that year, but the financial panic beginning in September left thousands of cattle unsold. What hurt Fort Worth even more was that railroad construction everywhere was suspended. The city's population immediately declined to about one thousand, and "grass literally grew in the streets. This was not a metaphor to indicate stagnation, but a doleful fact" said the editor of the *Democrat*. Former Fort Worth lawyer Robert E. Gowart informed the *Dallas Herald* that Fort Worth was such a drowsy place he saw a panther asleep in the street near the courthouse. To Dallasites, Fort Worth was thereafter Panther City.

Like Abilene's city fathers, Fort Worth officials had to cope with the problems caused by overly exuberant cowboys as well as gamblers, pimps, and prostitutes. In 1873 they passed a number of ordinances prohibiting gambling, prostitution, and the wearing of guns. Because it was soon clear that these regulations were harmful to business, however, the orders were suspended and Fort Worth was again known as a "tolerant" town.

Most of the gambling dens and dance halls were confined to Hell's Half Acre around the intersection of Rusk (later Commerce) and Twelfth streets, and in this district Fort Worth was considered wide open. Like other trail towns that attracted lawless elements, Fort Worth needed some fearless man to keep the peace, and for a time Marshal "Long Hair" Jim Courtright filled the job effectively. When he was hired, his duties were made explicit—he was to keep the peace, not clean up the town.

In 1876, Fort Worth residents turned out, boy and man, to complete construction of the Texas and Pacific track to the city limits. The first train reached the city on July 19, and the expected boom began. By January 1877 all dwellings were filled and an estimated one thousand people lived in tents around the city limits. Fort Worth residents, now confident of their city's future, happily named everything "Panther."

Although some cattle were shipped out of Texas by the various railroads, such shipments posed no immediate threat to the trailing business. It was still far less expensive to trail cattle to Kansas than to ship them by rail.

In 1878, Fort Worth launched a cleaning-up program, and word soon spread among cowboys that a visit to the town likely meant a stopover in the jail. Trail crews now shunned it. In April citizens and businessmen placed an ad in the *Fort Worth Democrat* calling attention to the cost of strict enforcement of laws against drinking, gambling, and other cowboy amusements.

"The cattle season beginning, we think more freedom ought to be allowed as everyone is aware of the amount of money spent in this city by cattlemen and cowboys, thus making every trade and business prosper. We notice especially this year that contrary to their usual custom, almost all of them remain in their camps a few miles from the city and give as the cause the stringent enforcement of the law closing all places of amusement that attract them."

The city council yielded to public pressure, to the great dissatisfaction of Marshal Courtright. As merchants recovered their trade with trail men, the *Democrat* noted that the dance halls were "in full blast again."

By 1880, when the Missouri-Kansas-Texas Railroad reached Fort Worth, the town had a population of 6,663. A year and a half later the Santa Fe also laid tracks through the town, so it had ample rail facilities for serving as a trade and cattle center. It was evident that the city needed to expand its economic base, for the Chisholm Trail would eventually be obliterated by the spread of farms and the increasing use of barbed wire by ranchers.

Former Confederate captain B. B. Paddock, who began editing the *Fort Worth Democrat* in 1872, constantly prodded local businessmen into promoting the city and chided them mercilessly when they let opportunities pass. In the spring of 1875 he had written: "This city is on the nearest and best route. . . . Fencing will be a serious obstacle to herdsmen in many places. This route also allows owners and herdsmen a better opportunity of securing supplies than is afforded by any other route." By 1875 cattle buyers were already coming to Fort Worth to contract for herds moving up the Chisholm Trail.

Looking ahead to the day when the northern trails would be closed, Paddock predicted that Fort Worth would become a center for the meat-packing industry. He chastised the Texas and Pacific Railroad and others for making no effort to develop the shipping of live cattle by offering reasonable freight rates. He pointed out that to ship two thousand head, or one hundred carloads, of cattle from Dallas to St. Louis cost $11,500. The same herd could be driven to Ellsworth, Kansas, for only $1,000; and it cost only $7,500 more to ship them from Ellsworth to St. Louis—a total of $8,500, or $3,000 less than shipping directly from Texas. Eventually the railroads would begin to compete for the cattle business by lowering their freight charges.

Fort Worth continued to grow. In 1877 construction began on the courthouse and the three-story El Paso Hotel, and a slaughterhouse shipped its first carload of refrigerated beef to St. Louis in March. Even though some herds were following the new Western Trail by way of Fort Griffin to Dodge City, many still came up the Chisholm Trail, and the owners bought provisions and equipment at Forth Worth. The cowboys kept the Tivoli Hall, Trinity Saloon, and the various dance halls busy. That same year the Texas and Pacific Railroad shipped more than fifty-one thousand live cattle from Fort Worth.

Although herds continued to pass through or near Fort Worth in the spring of 1878, many turned off the Chisholm Trail at Belton, owing to the blandishments of agents the Fort Griffin merchants sent there to persuade trail bosses to use the Western Trail. Paddock reprimanded Forth Worth merchants for supinely allowing so much business to be siphoned off by rivals from Fort Griffin. "That our merchants should have lost sight of the importance of having a representative to offset the influence of Fort Griffin's enterprise at Belton," he wrote "is singular indeed."

When it was known that only 100,000 cattle had followed the Chisholm Trail, while 150,000 had taken the route past Fort Griffin, Paddock renewed his attack: "Had our businessmen been equally active in securing this immense drive, the season drive would not have fallen short of 200,000. Experience is a dear teacher. We hope that their eyes will be opened to their best interest next year." The Fort Worth merchants responded by sending their own agent to Belton to persuade trail bosses to stay on the Chisholm Trail. This effort succeeded, for by late June of 1879 more than 135,000 cattle had passed by Fort Worth, while a little over 100,000 had gone up the Western Trail.

By the early 1880s trailing cattle to or through Kansas was becoming so difficult that Texas cowmen launched a campaign to have a national cattle trail set aside from Texas to Montana. Northern ranches were now well stocked, and northern cowmen refused to encourage competition from Texas. The project was never approved.

Because of cordial relations already existing between the businessmen of Fort Worth and the cattlemen of northern and western Texas, "Cow Town" remained a cowmen's headquarters even after the Chisholm Trail was only a memory. As the trailing era ended, the railroads began competing for the cattle traffic, and Fort Worth's position as a rail center enabled it to continue to play an important role in the beef cattle business. This role was enhanced by the coming of the packing houses.

In April 1875 the editor of the *Fort Worth Democrat* had written, "There is no reason why Fort Worth should not become the great cattle center of Texas, where both buyer and seller meet for the transaction of an immense business in Texas beef. Fort Worth promises every advantage required in doing a very heavy beef packing business. With an abundance of pure water, ample herding grounds and soon to have shipping facilities by rail to all markets of the East and North, it would seem an admirable point for packing beef."

It was not until 1890, when the Fort Worth Dressed Meat and Packing Company was established, that this advice was followed. In the next few years Swift and Armour opened packing plants in the city. These plants and the business they brought were at least partly responsible for the city's increase in population from around twenty-seven thousand in 1900 to more than seventy-three thousand in 1910.

Trail towns had profited from the trailing business for from several years to a decade or longer. Some declined drastically in population when the herds stopped coming. Although this often meant a distinct improvement in the quality of the local citizenry, it also meant a substantial loss of income. In the more forward-looking or fortunate towns, like Wichita and Fort Worth, other economic activities were quickly developed, and these towns continued to grow on the foundations the trailing era had provided.

A Wild Time in the Old Town Tonight, 1875–1879

TY CASHION

Ty Cashion teaches history at Sam Houston State University in Huntsville. A member of the Texas Institute of Letters, his studies include *A Texas Frontier: The Clear Fork Country and Fort Griffin, 1849–1887* (1996), a revisionist examination of Old Northwest Texas, *Pigskin Pulpit: A Social History of Texas High School Football Coaches* (1998), *The Human Tradition in Texas* (2001), *Sam Houston State University: An Institutional Memory, 1879–2004* (2004), and *The New Frontier: A Contemporary History of Fort Worth & Tarrant County* (2006). Currently, Professor Cashion is writing an intellectual history of Texas.

In this selection, Cashion vividly describes life at Fort Griffin, a rough and rowdy settlement of saloons, dance halls, brothels, and gaming establishments. Soldiers, buffalo hunters, and cowboys populated the Northwest Texas outpost, and lawless acts were common. Still, Dr. Cashion points out, "gratuitous killings were rare and violence was never taken lightly" by local authorities. ✍

★ ★

One summer day in 1877, Charles Bain's stage delivered the *Jacksboro Frontier Echo* to Fort Griffin. Between the headlines and the local news, the paper dedicated an entire page to a

'ng railway strike that had left much of Pittsburgh "in ashes." Pennsylvania militia-
and to preserve the peace, instead provoked a riot by turning their rifles and Gatling
unsuspecting crowd of factory workers and curious spectators who had gathered
..d roundhouse. Later that day and throughout the night several thousand civilians
,unded by attacking the troops with any kind of weapon they could find. The mob pillaged
the city and destroyed buildings, railroad cars, and other property. A month later the *Echo*
reported that "forty persons killed and two-thousand six-hundred cars destroyed are among
the fruits of the late strike at Pittsburgh."

About the same time as the riot, news coming out of Northwest Texas created the impression that keeping order was beyond the ability of civil authorities at Fort Griffin as well. In
December 1876 the *Fort Worth Democrat* reported that vigilantes in Shackelford County had
just hanged almost a dozen horse thieves, adding: "Their bodies will make good food for the
vultures." And only a month earlier the *Frontier Echo* vividly recounted the brutal slayings of
two freighters by a pair of outlaws who had hired their team. After departing the village, the
murderers marched the drivers into the brush; one of them shot his man point-blank in the
head, the other pistol-whipped his victim to death. The *Dallas Daily Herald* covered an equally
violent incident. This time it was a gunfight inside a Griffin saloon, where the sheriff and county
attorney left one reckless cowboy dead and another wounded. Two bystanders had also been
killed—one "with his brain oozing from the hole in his forehead."

While the strikers at Pittsburgh erupted as one body protesting their intolerable conditions,
Griffinites acted as individuals, seemingly resorting to violence in the normal course of their
affairs. Compared with other frontier communities, Fort Griffin was a bloody boomtown,
but the sensational reports emanating from the little outpost did not always paint an accurate
picture. Such incidents were infrequent but widely reported, giving the impression of lawlessness out of proportion to daily life. Travelers, in fact, frequently expressed surprise at finding
Fort Griffin so peaceable. Editor Robson wrote tongue-in-cheek that a number of itinerant
prospectors thought they would "see nearly every citizen a walking arsenal"; they also expected
to "hear of at least one man being killed here regularly each day in the week and several killed
on Sunday." Wildness was nevertheless ever present in the whiskey houses and brothels lining
Griffin Avenue, and the volatile environment indeed invited occasional violence.

Griffin's "heyday" began about 1875, shortly after D. M. Dowell reopened the Flat to settlement. The socially deprived enlisted men welcomed the development, and despite the efforts
of everyone concerned with maintaining military discipline, the army had little success keeping the soldiers away from the rough-and-tumble little town. The fort's medical officer noted
that "the habits of the men might be materially improved by the removal of a number of lewd
women living in the vicinity of the post." He also complained that recently a soldier had been
wounded by a "pistol ball" in one of Griffin's "drunken haunts." Inspector General N. H. Davis
resigned himself to accepting the "nuisance under the bluff," remarking that "this kind of
evil . . . will follow the troops to any locality they may go."

Colonel Buell did not surrender so easily; in February 1875 he ordered his men to stay out
of the Flat. The enlisted men openly flouted him, however, and several of them even erected

shacks in the village. To the colonel's consternation, the situation further degenerated. In October a dispute over sectional differences resulted in a bloody row between drunken soldiers and civilians. When the troops threatened to burn the settlement, the townsmen vowed they would march on the fort. A few weeks later the colonel removed one of the worst offenders, a man named Krause, even though he held a legal lease for what Buell described as a "grog shop and gambling hole." Ill feelings lingered, and in January an infantryman on sentinel duty fired a round into the Flat, mortally wounding a civilian.

When the first session of the district court met in recently organized Shackelford County during June 1875, Judge J. P. Osterhout dealt severely with lawbreakers. In thirty-seven cases during the five-day session he found a dozen men guilty of gambling and selling liquor illegally, and although the fines ranged from only $10 to $15, some of the accused faced multiple counts. Many of the same men who sold illegal spirits were also pandering prostitutes, a more serious crime that cost the guilty parties between $100 and $150. In many instances attorneys for the defendants got cases discharged or transferred to the more lenient county court. The signal was nevertheless unmistakable: the legal community would hold miscreants accountable for their actions. Many petty delinquents such as those listed on the court docket as Banjo Bob, Curley, Smokey Joe, and Frenchy skipped town rather than face Judge Osterhout. Among them was Doc Holliday, whose single crime at Fort Griffin resulted in a gambling and liquor charge.

Osterhout also presided over more serious cases. He issued warrants for two suspected murderers who fled Fort Griffin before Sheriff Henry Jacobs could apprehend them. Several men facing assault charges also eluded the court. W. L. Browning was not as lucky. He was convicted of trying to murder an acquaintance, John Jackson. According to the testimony of Jackson's sister, the two men were sharing a watermelon outside a picket residence when they suddenly began arguing. As Browning pulled a gun, Jackson hit his arm with a shovel and then bolted indoors to get a shotgun. The defendant also ran to the house and began shooting through a crack in the wall, firing so close to the witness that she suffered powder burns. Browning, by then outgunned, retreated across the river. The Court of Appeals in Austin upheld Osterhout's verdict after the defendant contested the decision of the local jury.

Despite its earnest efforts, the court could not stem the proliferation of vice and violence at Fort Griffin. As the activity in saloons, gambling dens, dance halls, variety theaters, and brothels grew with the great bison hunt and cattle trail traffic, increasingly prosperous merchants and businessmen convinced officers of the court to wink at the "victimless" crimes. A more tolerant climate indeed existed when citizens in Northwest Texas elected J. R. Fleming to the district court bench in 1876. A resident of the frontier town of Comanche, eighty miles southeast of Fort Griffin, he understood loose social conditions. Judge Fleming concentrated on controlling violence and let the justices of the peace work with local people to set community standards. During two terms that year he issued a lone indictment for "selling liquor without a license" and a single charge against one "Swayback Mag" for prostitution. Even into the 1880s visitors who remained within the wide latitude of acceptable behavior at the Flat could enjoy a spree without running afoul of the law. "Old Griffin had its night life," remarked one-time resident "Jet" Kenan; "everything went but murder, arson, and burglary."

A ride down Griffin Avenue provided visitors an indelible impression of the little village. Smells, sounds, and sights assaulted the senses. The putrid odor from thousands of buffalo hides rotting in great stacks started many a horse to reeling. More pleasant was an impromptu concert that greeted a transient as he passed by York's store; there he saw a black man holding the reins for a mounted fiddler grinding out "Arkansas Traveler" to the delight of a crowd. Loitering cowboys occasionally passed around Jew's harps, and when stabler Pete Haverty got his organ, the music could be heard throughout the valley between the fort and the river. Rollie Burns described his first visit to Griffin in 1877, while on a cattle buying trip. On the main street were freighters, some unloading wagons, and others starting for Fort Worth with mountains of hides; trail outfits, too, were taking on supplies. "Alongside this busy element," he remembered, "was another, half drunk, boisterous, and bent on raising hell." One visitor recalled that the business district "was a Babel of boisterous talk, whoops, curses, laughter, songs and miserable music." The passing of time no doubt sweetened the memory. Cowboy Ken Cary more accurately declared that "Fort Griffin was more disgusting, after first glance, than alluringly picturesque."

Inside the dives lining Griffin Avenue the coarse scene of filthy transients enjoying a visit to the Flat was even more primitive. "I've seen men and women dancing there in the dance halls without a bit of clothing on," remarked one visitor. Another man affirmed that indeed "the women were scarcely dressed"; they also danced with the patrons, and when the music stopped, "you bellied up to the bar, took a drink and paid fifty cents for it." Animating the drab adobe and picket hovels were women known only by names such as Polly Turnover, Slewfoot Jane, and Monkey-face Mag.

Despite the wide-open conditions, not more than a handful of saloons ever opened their doors at the same time. Many tried to enter the lucrative trade, but the few proprietors lucky enough to gain a foothold connived with the legal community to limit competition. No one was above the law. Even Frank Conrad once had to climb out of a jury box to fight a charge of "selling spirituous liquors without a license." At the peak of the buffalo slaughter a Stribling and Kirkland circular advertised only five Griffin bars; Henry Herron later recalled that as many as five more operated for various periods. Among the lucky owners was Mike O'Brien, who came to hunt bison but quickly found serving drinks more profitable and infinitely more entertaining. Few of his former associates passed through town without stopping at the Hunters' Retreat; Charley Meyers's Cattle Exchange drew much of the drovers' trade. Under one sprawling roof "Uncle Billy" Wilson ran a beer and dance hall, variety show, restaurant, and lodge called the Frontier House. A frequent patron commented that "a blueprint would have been interesting."

None, however, was more popular than Donnely and Carroll's Bee Hive. The saloon gained notoriety as the scene of at least one fatal gunfight and one unprovoked murder. English drifter Jim Grahame, otherwise known as *Dallas Daily Herald* correspondent "Comanche Jim," claimed credit for naming the place. He also asserted that over the entrance he painted a "rough representation of a beehive" under which he scrawled a rhyme that had the drunken inhabitants beckoning visitors to "come in and try the flavor of our honey."

The seasonal nature of hunting and trailing also drew professional gamblers who made Fort Griffin an important stop on their "circuit." Reportedly, a game could be found in the back room of any saloon. The weakly regulated activity invited the use of marked decks, loaded dice, and other aids. "The ordinary fellow did not have the ghost of a show," commented Henry Herron. "I saw a buffalo hunter come to town one day and market his season's kill for $1,500.00," he continued. "The next morning he had to borrow money for his breakfast. The gamblers had gotten all of it."

Prostitutes also scrambled for the money of free-spending transients. In 1877 the *Dallas Daily Herald* reported that "Griffin, which has long been the roost of a large quantity of 'soiled doves,' can now boast of a larger flock than any other town on the frontier." According to Jet Kenan, "Fort Griffin would not have been Fort Griffin" without its "red light district." For about two blocks the brothels extended in a broken line down each side of the main street near the river. The women worked with the blessings of saloon keepers and merchants alike. During the day prostitutes "boldly and openly took their 'friends' around from bar to bar and store to store"; together with the shopkeepers, Kenan claimed, they would "bleed them of every possible dollar in every conceivable manner." At night women worked the saloons, "drinking, cursing, smoking, and contributing greatly to the loud hilarity."

The prostitutes, who added so much color to the stories that men told, led anything but glamorous lives. Low pay and high expenses kept them in poverty. Their fondness for gaudy clothes, material possessions, and alcohol and drugs further drained their earnings. The degrading conditions of prostitution, moreover, elicited the most wretched of human qualities, producing hardened, cynical, grasping women. Among themselves, any number of negative forces—competition, suspicion, jealousy, and petty incidents—checked the bonds that mutual privation might have formed. And because their profession rested outside the law, they were at the mercy of the legal system. The justice of the peace set the rules for the illicit trade, and the women normally observed them. The local court, they knew, provided their only protection against the abuses of an uncaring and often hostile society. For example, Griffin's justice of the peace, who usually ignored petty crimes in the black community, came to the defense of some African American prostitutes harassed by a group of drunken black cowboys. He promptly had the men arrested for brandishing their weapons "in a private house" and fined each of them. Rarely did the county and district courts become involved in the prostitutes' affairs.

The profiles and experiences of prostitutes along Griffin Avenue were neither flattering nor heartening. Although many were youthful, some stayed in the profession long after their looks had faded. Two of the nine women who listed their occupation as "courtesan" for the 1880 census were in their mid- to late thirties; others, who had been teenagers during the town's heyday, had reached their early twenties and looked forward to middle age with few prospects for improving their social condition. Some were married, such as Minnie Delno, who got the sobriquet "Hurricane Minnie" for her forced union with "Hurricane Bill" Martin. But marriage did not add stability to their lives; instead, it made them even more disreputable. A society that already frowned on the trade held a special contempt for a married prostitute. Their husbands, moreover, represented the dregs of society, assuring that the women would remain at the bottom of the social ladder. Bill Martin, for example, became legendary for his frequent brushes with the law. Few women escaped this miserable environment. Griffin resident George Newcomb claimed that a local man had once tried to marry a particularly striking young prostitute—"white and fair"—but authorities supposedly refused him a license because she "had some Negro blood." The sorry legacy of a broken life was often passed down to the children of prostitutes as well. In the same house that Sarah Dickinson operated, her twelve-year-old daughter also entered the profession.

Beyond Griffin Avenue was a more conservative society that frowned on the dissolute life-styles of its neighbors. The occasional trial for adultery and the formation of a temperance union in 1875 demonstrated the rigid moral standards that governed the rest of the community. Only the economic force behind the vices of prostitution, gambling, and unbroken revelry kept the local dives in business. Early in 1876 the *Dallas Daily Herald* reported that some upset citizens chased several of the most disreputable prostitutes out of town, "this done on the principle that bad meat draws flies." In June, when several more arrived to take their places, townsmen threatened them, too. A prominently posted notice, signed "Vigilance," read: "Leave or you are doomed." Evidently merchants checked their zealous neighbors; in September, a docile Griffinite registered a complaint in the *Fort Worth Democrat*, feebly pleading with the sheriff to appoint a deputy to control the rampant vice. The "hard-visaged," part-Indian Kate Gamel was certainly not intimidated by hollow threats. At her cramped adobe brothel that Henry Herron called "a known rendezvous for criminals," officers laid an ambush one dark evening. The outlaws reportedly escaped by spurring their horses over the bluff and into the swollen Collins Creek.

In this pitiable environment Charlotte Tompkins briefly enjoyed part control of a boarding house, the Gus, as well as a saloon. But even though she transcended the normal sphere of her gender, Tompkins could not escape the degrading consequences that attended a woman's entry into this male-dominated environment. More widely known as "the poker queen" Lottie Deno, she gained a reputation for her ladylike dress and the cool manner in which she relieved her rough patrons of their money. Yet just as men mistakenly attributed the raucous gaiety of prostitutes' lives for insouciance, they also misinterpreted Tompkins's aloof demeanor. She certainly shared the desperation of other women who worked on Griffin Avenue. Whether by dint of business acumen or simply because she had accumulated some working capital, Tompkins managed outwardly to earn a more honorable living. But where other saloon owners such as Hank Smith, Owen Donnely, and Charley Meyers were accepted socially, Griffinites shunned Charlotte Tompkins. On one occasion she registered her defiance by staging a "masque ball" while other townspeople gathered at a nearby hotel for a dance. Several old-timers nevertheless asserted that such strength of character was only superficial.

The tragic and impenetrable life of Tompkins invited speculation. Former sheriff John Jacobs called her "unapproachable" and claimed that "she had nothing to do with the common prostitutes." Just before she arrived at the Flat, however, a Jacksboro court had fined her $100 and costs for running a brothel. Supposedly she had worked other "fort towns" on the Texas frontier as well. Her circumstances at Griffin began to sour about the same time as the apparent murder of a tawdry young drifter, Johnnie Golden. Henry Herron commented that Golden was a "nice looking boy, had a little money to spend, and spent it freely." And although little evidence supported his claim, Herron asserted that "Lottie fell for him." Equally dubious was a rumor that she was the unwilling paramour of saloon keeper Dick Shaughnessey. Old-timers nevertheless asserted that the whiskey peddler became jealous and paid Constable Bill Gilson and an accomplice, Dan Draper, $250 to kill his supposed rival. The circumstances of Golden's death certainly implicated them. The pair claimed that they had served him an arrest warrant and were taking him to the post guardhouse, even though the local "calaboose" was only twenty yards away. Gilson and Draper further maintained that Golden's death came at the hands of "rescuers" who fired on them from a ravine; the powder burns on the dead man's body, however, cast doubt on the alibi. In any event, the citizens of Shackelford County "ran Gilson off" after a brief inquest.

Shortly afterward, Tompkins's business situation also deteriorated, forcing her hasty departure from Fort Griffin. For a woman to obtain a mortgage on a bar or brothel was really not so unusual, and neither were the consequences when she could not meet her financial obligations. Typically, courts in tolerant frontier towns overlooked illegal activities as long as participants squared their own affairs discreetly. But in January 1878, shortly after George Matthews brought suit against Tompkins for a $290 debt, she found herself fighting a second charge of "keeping a disorderly house." At first she refused to acknowledge the local court. Her stubbornness cost Owen Donnely and Charley Meyers five hundred dollars—the price of her forfeited bail. An arrest warrant soon compelled her to appear for trial, where a jury found her guilty on both counts. Tompkins appealed the pandering charge, but mounting attorneys' fees and the considerable sum that she still owed to her former confederates prompted her to take expedient measures. Rather than wait for the outcome of the new trial—which, ironically, cleared her—she simply fled.

Stribling and Kirkland, representing George Matthews, later traced Tompkins to Bracketville, adjoining Fort Clark. Unknowing sympathizers believed that Tompkins, still grieving over Johnny Golden, had finally had enough of Fort Griffin. Although the sketchy details surrounding her life as Lottie Deno eventually grew to mythical proportions, her departure was no more mysterious than that of any number of men and women who left town owing money or evading the justice system.

Just as the so-called "lady gambler" inspired exaggerations and even outright fabrications, other dubious tales circulated that probably had just enough basis in fact to seed Griffin's reputation for unequaled violence. Gunman Jeff Milton claimed that as he tried to break up a bar fight between two buffalo hunters, one of them shot the other, splattering Milton with "blood and brains." Jeff, according to his biographer, "learned right there the importance of tending to his own business." On another occasion, an inebriated "tough" supposedly killed a Tonkawa Indian and was simply thrown in the calaboose "until he sobered up." Another time a drunken Lipan Apache was said to have stumbled into a Griffin hotel, where a woman killed him for his disruptive behavior. And when a partially deaf man refused to acknowledge a deputy's order to halt, the lawman reportedly emptied his pistol into the man and then offered to bet that he could cover the bullet holes with a silver dollar. Soldiers also contributed to the list of unprovoked and uncorroborated killings: a post guard murdered a buffalo hunter; a lieutenant, who had lost all his poker money to an enlisted man, shot him in the back; and a recently discharged "Scotty" killed a soldier even as the victim's wife fell to her knees, begging him not to shoot. In each case nobody seemed particularly interested in bringing the killers to justice, nor did anyone mention that any of them ever served a day in jail.

In contrast to these doubtful reports, the court strove assiduously—but seldom satisfactorily—to bring murderers to justice. Between 1875 and 1881 the 12th District Court, which included the counties administratively attached to Shackelford, issued eleven warrants for suspected killers. No case better illustrated the court's persistence than a bill against J. E. Kennedy, who was jailed at Fort Griffin for the 1877 killing of a man on the buffalo range. When he escaped, Texas Rangers recaptured him. After a mistrial, a new jury sentenced him to hang; upon appeal he won a new trial and a change of venue. Finally, after two years of legal maneuvering, he received a sentence of ninety-nine years.

Some other cases, although ending badly, still merited the earnest attention of the court. When a man fired a shot through a saloon window, killing Thorndale man Andrew Brownlee, a coroner's inquest swiftly rounded up witnesses and conducted a thorough interrogation. Narrowing their list of suspects to drifter James Oglesby, a posse combed the town and surrounding area for him. Soon the pitch blackness of night ended the search, and Oglesby escaped, leaving a fugitive warrant on the docket along with an underlined notation left by the court's transcriber—MURDER!

Three years later the court was again unsuccessful when it tried Henry Cruger for killing quartermaster clerk June Leach. The case dragged on for more than a year before jurors finally issued a verdict of not guilty. The slaying evolved out of an argument at a billiard table when Leach accidentally stepped on Cruger, who rebuffed an apology with the admonition that he would "whip him" if it happened again. To the good fortune of the accused murderer, testimony conflicted about what happened next, but witnesses—subpoenaed from as far away as Mason County—agreed that after a brief fight Leach fell dead from Cruger's gunshot.

Even after the Flat's heyday waned, the court still had trouble securing murder convictions. The shooting of Jewish merchant "Cheap John" Marks in 1879 nevertheless stirred the court to conduct a scrupulous investigation. The "pesky drummer," as editor Robson once called him, had left town for the Panhandle owing money to Griffinite Frank Schmidt. Special deputy William King, accompanied by the creditor, went after Marks, and upon apprehending him about fifty miles from town, camped for the night. Schmidt claimed that while King was hunting turkey for their dinner, Marks had somehow secured a gun. When Schmidt supposedly attempted to seize the weapon, it discharged, fatally wounding Cheap John in the back. Hearing the shot, King raced back to camp. Skeptical over Schmidt's story, he left him to care for the unconscious and dying man and then went on to Fort Griffin, where he notified Texas Rangers. After Marks died, four Griffin-bound waggoners happened upon the scene and helped bury him, then carried Schmidt with them. A jury—after hearing the testimony and cross-examination of both Schmidt and King, as well as the statements of the four travelers—returned the supposed murderer his $5,000 bail and set him free.

Contrary to the perception of the Northwest Texas frontier as a place where violen[ce was]
accepted casually, gratuitous killings were rare and violence was never taken lightly. [For exam-]
ple, Griffinites held a public meeting in January 1877 to express sympathy to the [families of]
two bystanders who were killed in a senseless crossfire. Several months later, at iso[lated Rath]
City, hunter Tom Lumpkins shot an unarmed man who had taken exception to h[is constant]
carping. As another man tried to subdue Lumpkins, bartender "Limpy Jim" Smith [stepped up,]
jerked him aside and then shot Lumpkins point-blank. The surly hunter, still firing, stumbled
backwards out of the saloon, followed by Smith, who reportedly kept a stream of bullets flying
as he came. At the bartender's insistence a group of men accompanied him to Fort Griffin,
where he surrendered himself to authorities. With the sympathetic testimony of the other
hunters, a grand jury decided not to prosecute.

While assiduously attempting to bring "deserving" killers to justice, local courts did not overlook the petty crimes that plagued the unstable frontier society. Many were the reports of minor
thefts and the records of prosecutions. During the hot summer of 1875, for example, traveler
Billy Smith, overcome by heat, awoke to discover that someone had gone through his pockets,
robbing him of a lottery ticket, some tobacco, and his keys. County Clerk J. N. Masterson
recounted another typical incident, complaining that a thief had broken into his office and
stolen $4 in change. Another time a man named Christianson was arrested for breaking into
the home of Mrs. Mary Mitchell and taking $165 in greenbacks and some silver. The court at
all levels—justice of the peace, county, and district—prosecuted such indignities zealously.
Thieves seemed always to be sitting in jails at Griffin and Albany or working on roads between
the two towns. County Judge W. H. Ledbetter normally assessed sixty days to nine months
for petty thefts. Judge Fleming was even harsher. In 1876 he sentenced one George Robinson
to two years at hard labor in the state penitentiary for taking clothing valued at $49. The next
year he meted out the same punishment to a man for stealing almost $500 and a butcher knife.
Fleming prosecuted cases of swindling, forgery, and other non-violent crimes as well.

Still, the legal community was sometimes frustrated. Hurricane Bill Martin, for example, was a
one-man crime wave. He constantly sparred with the courts but was seldom held accountable
for his many illicit activities. He reportedly loaded wagons with buffalo hides from stacks lining
the river bottom, then rode into town and sold them to the very men whom he had "fleeced."
He was also believed to have been the leader of a gang of horse thieves, and ironically he was
the only one who survived a vigilante roundup. A deposition recorded that after Sam Stinson
accused him of stealing a watch and chain, Martin pulled out his army Colt and "dropped it
down on his [Stinson's] head saying, 'You can't give me any such game.'" Somehow Martin
was again found innocent. Extenuating circumstances in another case forced the court to try
him for "discharging a firearm" instead of attempted murder. In several other cases he was
charged with assault, forfeiting bonds, and trying to enter the underworld of gambling, liquor,
and prostitution.

While the resolute efforts of the court faded in the minds of former Griffinites, memories of
killings and the tales of men such as Hurricane Bill seemed to grow. One-time sheriff John
Jacobs related to fellow officer Henry Herron that "conditions got so bad . . . he could not feel

sleeping in the same place two nights in succession." Fort Griffin was "a veritable robber's hole," according to rancher Emmett Roberts. "They would throw a blanket over your head and take your money in a flash." A surveyor, C. U. Connellee, recalled that "of all the places I have ever been, that was the worst." Long familiar with the frontier, he asserted that "men who had committed crimes, and fleeing from the law often went as far as they could from civilization, and that was the end."

Nothing did more to burn indelibly the image of Fort Griffin as a violent frontier town than a fatal gunfight at Donnely and Carroll's saloon. The "Shooting Bee," as the spontaneous incident came to be known, emanated from a poorly handled confrontation between Griffin authorities and local ranch hands Billy Bland and Charley Reed. Befitting the image of drunken cowboys, the pair raced their horses down Griffin Avenue, guns ablazing. Entering the Bee Hive, they interrupted dancers by trying to shoot out the lights. As Bland was taking aim on another fixture, Deputy Bill Cruger, accompanied by County Attorney Robert Jeffries, barged into the saloon and demanded that the revelers "put up their hands." The abrupt order provoked Bland into wheeling around and firing in the deputy's direction. When Cruger started shooting, both Jeffries and Reed joined the sharp firefight. The lawman and attorney sustained minor wounds; two bystanders were less fortunate. Newlywed Dan Barrow, shot through the forehead, died instantly. As a Lieutenant Myers tried to flee, he suffered a mortal wound in the back. As for the instigator, Billy Bland, a bullet passed completely through his body, leaving him writhing on the floor. Some men took him to the Occidental Hotel, where "Aunt Hank" Smith said "the poor fellow begged to be killed." According to Phin Reynolds, "Reed left the country that night."

For such a wide-open town, the legal system generally executed its duties in a credible manner. Few times did peace officers experience such mortal tumults as did Deputy Cruger. In fact, a former Griffinite recalled that "no man ever became so bad but that he might land in the 'calaboose' if the marshal so decided." Zeno Hemphill, a would-be badman, might have agreed. In 1878 he and some other cowboys had reportedly planned to kill special deputies Henry Herron and Dave Barker for nothing more than the notoriety. The two officers, appointed to help keep order during a meeting of the Northwest Cattle Raisers' Association, learned of the plot and waited in a crowded saloon for their supposed executioners. When Hemphill knocked a woman backward with the intention of starting a brawl, Herron grabbed the man's six-shooter and "whacked him over the head." Barker then pulled his own gun and covered the crowd while Herron hustled Hemphill off to jail.

Henry Herron, reflecting on his Griffin days, remarked that the calaboose was always occupied. "They were in there for every kind of offense, ranging from fighting to horse stealing and murder, but not many for murder." A jailer normally escorted prisoners to a blacksmith, who fit them for shackles; at night they were chained to the wall. If assaults were common, so were assault charges. The justice of the peace did not keep records, but the district court issued twenty-four warrants for such crimes between 1875 and 1880. Many of the accused simply fled town, and the legal community was probably satisfied to be rid of them. And while a few fought the charges and won, most lost and faced fifty-dollar to one-hundred-dollar fines. Still others earned jail time. Robert Brown, for example, was sentenced to two years' hard labor at the state penitentiary for "assault with intent to kill."

Despite a generally credible record, the law at times was ineffective. Vigilantes, composed of both court-appointed officials and respected citizens, ran amok during 1876, executing almost a score of suspected horse and cattle thieves. A succession of sheriffs, responsible for the entire county, did not often have the time nor the inclination to concentrate on controlling Griffin's transient revelers. Townspeople begged in vain for the court to appoint a deputy to control the gangs of raucous buffalo hunters and trail drivers, but finally had to hire a local officer at their own expense. Jet Kenan remarked that even then "a man had to act very, very badly to be molested by the 'marshal.'" Certainly the violent death of Johnny Golden undermined the reputation of the local legal community. His killers were never brought to trial. The elaborate story that Gilson and Draper told of a "lost" warrant and a three-o'clock-in-the-morning shootout kept the officers out of jail, but also made the court appear indifferent.

Where African Americans were concerned, the law also broke down, but only because it reflected the attitude of the Anglo-dominated society. Joe McCombs claimed that a drunk hunter once burst into the mess hall at the post and fired over the heads of some buffalo soldiers, prompting them to flee. When troops cornered the hunter, Sheriff John Larn convinced the commander to release the man into his custody and afterward let him go. Another time, when a black soldier full of "tarantula juice" shot his gun in the street and declared that he could "smash any 'white descendant of a female canine' in town," officers allowed some irate townsmen to take care of the matter. In buoyant prose a correspondent for the *Fort Worth Daily Democrat* wrote that "by careful maneuvering he at length succeeded in acquiring a 'head' of gigantic dimensions, and was forced to make a retrograde movement on the Fort." The dispatch ended with the comment: "No arrests."

Regarding violence that occurred entirely among African Americans, local authorities throughout Texas routinely turned their backs. Fort Griffin was no exception. For example, an exchange of gunfire between two black men at the Clear Fork crossing went unaddressed, even though one of them, Joe Brandt, was gravely wounded.

Another racial incident, although it occurred after Griffin's wildest days had passed, demonstrated both the court's insistence on following "proper legal procedure" and its attitude toward African Americans. In 1879, Captain S. H. Lincoln, on the eve of his transfer to another post, shot and killed black infantryman Charles McCafferty. The private had escaped the guardhouse, where he had been confined for habitual drunkenness, and headed for town. He promptly became inebriated again, and upon spotting the captain at Conrad and Rath's, he unleashed a verbal assault that ended when the army officer physically removed him from the store. The drunken soldier—in front of everybody in town—then knocked the officer off the sidewalk with a roundhouse punch to the jaw. The ignominious blow prompted Lincoln to draw his pistol and shoot the impudent McCafferty, who died the next day. Despite being released on a two-thousand-dollar bond, the captain left Fort Griffin for his new assignment, forcing Texas Rangers to bring him in. A preliminary hearing bound him over for the "felonious" murder of Charles McCafferty, but in the civil trial Judge Fleming reminded the jury that murder was distinguished from manslaughter by "malice aforethought." The lesser charge, he advised, could also be mitigated by "provocation." In his own defense, Lincoln reportedly declared that his action was "the only dignified course to pursue." Evidently, the jury agreed and found the captain "not guilty."

Certainly, violence and any number of petty crimes and vices underscored the instability of Fort Griffin's boomtown environment. Nevertheless, rough but otherwise unmenacing people and a lighter side of life also represented "wildness" in this frontier society. Buffalo hunters and cattle drivers, little concerned about manners and morals, descended in raucous packs upon Fort Griffin after long periods with little human contact. More frolicsome than reckless, they typically spent a few harmless days and nights of unbridled revelry before resuming their monotonous routines. Skinners and nonprofessionals among the hunters and a handful of "maverick" drovers caused most of the trouble that gave the two groups their undeserved reputation for violence. Rootless opportunists, itinerant pioneers, and people from the interior who ached for a little excitement and some quick money also contributed to occasional lawlessness. Yet even among these largely anonymous men and women, very few came West intending to launch a career outside of the law.

Typical of many buffalo hunters was "Charlie," who traveled to Griffin at the head of his crew when the season ended in 1875. After cashing a large check at Conrad's store, he paid his men, and they camped with about thirty other outfits under the big pecan trees lining the Clear Fork. "I never intended to get drunk," he said, "but what could a fellow do?" According to a friend, Charlie "had a glorious spree"—twenty-one days long, in fact. Once, after he had passed out, some of his men set a stuffed panther over him. When the hunter awoke and saw the beast staring down at him he lurched backward into the river and had to be "fished out."

Cowboys had their fun, too. Frontiersman Jim Gordon recounted that a pretentious Englishman once arrived at Griffin and hired two men to escort him to the ranch of a countryman. Word reached some herders farther up the trail, who prepared a reception as the "lord" and his guides made camp for the evening. With whoops and gunshots, the cowboys pulled the Englishman's well-appointed wagon into a creek. Boldly he emerged in cap and gown, brandishing a small pistol, only to face a dozen gun-wielding "desperadoes" trying hard to suppress an explosion of laughter. After reaching his destination, the Englishman endured further indignities such as affectedly rough language and manners and the sight of the cook dishing out supper in a pair of the visitor's own kneepants. "He was mad as a hornet," Gordon recalled fondly. "Many were the tricks we played on him but eventually he came to be naturalized and proved a jolly good fellow."

Such earthy amusements were typical in an environment where large numbers of unattached men did "manly" things together. Few places gained a greater reputation than Fort Griffin as an oasis where frontiersmen could enjoy themselves unencumbered by conventional social pressures. And not all the fun was just drinking, gambling, and prostitution. Jet Kenan recalled that "many times saloons sent for me to participate in boxing matches . . . or to preside over a 'Kangaroo Court.'"

Dancing and "varieties" were more common forms of entertainment. "Frank Smith & Co. have completed their music hall in Fort Griffin and have secured the services of ten or twelve well known *artistes*," the *Echo* reported in 1876. "They are performing nightly to crowded and delighted audiences."

Concerning a prominent local merchant, Captain Robson chided: "We noticed Caleb Cupp one day this week amusing himself by holding two Tom-cats up by their tails, while the cats amused themselves by picking fur from each other." Pitting animals against each other was always a crowd pleaser. Another time the editor noted that "next Saturday there will be a fight at this place, between a young black bear and Hemphill's two bull dogs, for $50 a side." He did not follow up the report, but presumably the dogs won. A few weeks later the *Echo* reported that Mr. Chifflet, the local tanner, "has a bear skin robe which is a beauty."

Another favorite diversion was horse racing. Stabler Pete Haverty often staged contests at a track across the river. Like many of his patrons, however, he was often in debt because of his losses. In the fall of 1876 the *Fort Worth Daily Democrat* reported that local tough John Selman and bootlegger Jack Greathouse had declared John Larn the winner in a close race—by precisely three inches. "Some dissatisfaction was manifested at the decision," reported the correspondent, adding that bettors were incredulous at the judges' "being endowed with vision of such mathematical nicety, as to be able to determine the exact number of inches the winning horse was ahead at the string."

Like the cowboys who found sport in the Englishman's misery, men who idled countless hours at Fort Griffin found that a ruse or practical joke could provide an amusement that demanded repeated tellings long after the event. "Uncle Billy" Wilson seemed always to be working on a scheme. Jet Kenan claimed that Wilson once concocted a "wonder cement" that he matched against all comers—"Old Hickory, Spauldings, and others." He appeared to patch up some broken dishes with the competing glues and then dropped them all into boiling water. Soon every dish had come apart—except those mended with Uncle Billy's secret compound. According to Kenan the trick was that a friend of Wilson, an accomplished engraver, had etched matching lines on the top and bottom of some china that looked remarkably like cracks. Since few people washed china in boiling water, his scheme worked.

On another occasion Edgar Rye, editor of the *Albany Tomahawk*, fell for a practical joke that Captain Robson could not resist reporting. Rye, upon learning that a woman from Fort Worth had just arrived in town searching for another woman's husband, wrote a few indignant lines, ending with the demand, "Explain!" A few days later the supposed out-of-towner confronted Rye, demanding that *he* explain. As the editor rose to offer an alibi, he looked up into the muzzle of a gun. Aghast, the floundering Rye lost his hat and glasses, then tripped over his stool. Rising to his knees, he begged her not to shoot. Suddenly the "woman" and a group of men standing at the window burst into laughter. His antagonist, it turned out, was a townsman "in drag."

As Rye could attest, Fort Griffin was not the only Texas frontier town to see bawdy action, and neither did it have a corner on lawlessness. Pranksters at the county seat exploded a barber pole with gunpowder, to which Captain Robson lamented: "the old striped sign is seen no more in the land." And, as Albany began to intercept some of the trailing business in the spring of 1879, it also reaped some of the unpleasantries. "Every day or two," the *Echo* reported, fistfights had erupted. "Someone would appear on the streets with a black eye or banged up nose," but as in Fort Griffin the law swiftly put an end to it.

Ironically, Frank Conrad's daughter had left the county before she became a crime victim. Between Fort Worth and Weatherford stage robbers relieved her of one hundred dollars. Virtually every edition of the *Echo*, the *Fort Worth Daily Democrat*, and the *Dallas Daily Herald* carried stories from around the state that comprised a woeful record of crime. Robson complained that Northerners viewed Texas as a "community of murderers and robbers." Blaming frontier conditions and the ubiquitous carrying of weapons, he admitted that his fellow citizens were a law-breaking people "to a fearful extent." B. B. Paddock of the *Democrat* was more defensive, asserting that Texas was not alone in experiencing violent acts. Economic times, he declared, had "thrown upon the country hundreds and thousands of men who, having no families or homes, become reckless and careless, and are wandering over the country depredating upon the rights of others and committing acts of violence."

In the public perception, as in fact, Fort Griffin was nevertheless among the toughest spots on a tough frontier. To contemporaries, distance and unfamiliarity no doubt caused imaginations to magnify the image of lawlessness. The tunnel of memory likewise inflated the level of violence, the colorful descriptions, and fond reminiscences of an otherwise bleak and harsh environment. Fort Griffin in part earned its reputation; violence touched nearly every segment of society, and when trailers hit town, no one could avoid hearing hoots, hollers, and gunfire as they spurred their frenzied horses up and down Griffin Avenue. But revelers most often knew how far they could push local authorities, and more violent offenders knew that when they acted, consequences would surely follow.

Annie Black
and the Soiled Doves
of San Angelo

SUZANNE CAMPBELL

S uzanne Campbell is Head of Special Collections and Programs at Angelo State University Library in San Angelo.

In this selection, Campbell discusses the history of prostitution in San Angelo. She details the careers of successful mother and daughter madams Annie Black and Birdie Ayers. ᢒ

★ ★

Conditions in early day San Angelo have been the subject of numerous stories. John A. Loomis, Concho County rancher, wrote one such account in his memoirs, a place he described this way: "As a natural (of being near the Fort) the saloons, gambling houses and houses of prostitution catered to the army . . . Killings were so common that they occasioned little comment."

Loomis also described early attempts at law enforcement and judicial practice. The first courts were crude at best. Some of the early elected officials were illiterate and without any knowledge of the law. Dr. Escal Duke, long time member of this organization, once related the story of the first lawyer to hung up his shingle in San Angelo. Not smitten by the prospects of law and order, a group of cowboys and gamblers held a kangaroo court and decided the lawyer had

"Annie Black and The Soiled Doves of San Angelo" by Suzanne Campbell from The West Texas Historical Association *Year Book* Vol. LXXXIII, Oct. 2007, Volume 83, pp. 45-53.

fifteen minutes to leave town. When the attorney learned of the decision, he told the "jury" he would give them back five of the fifteen minutes.

The first sheriff of Tom Green County, Frank LaMott, was a popular gambler and "a gentlemanly fellow" according to Loomis. A few citizens of the county complained about his profession and suggested he should quit gambling or resign. LaMott resigned—gambling was much more profitable.

Loomis described J. G. Preusser, an early county judge, as intelligent saying his decisions were "just, if somewhat 'illegal' at times." Once when he made a decision that the officer of the court said was not in accordance with the law, Preusser allegedly answered, "Damn the law . . . It's justice we want."

Little wonder prostitution went unchecked in San Angelo for years. With the establishment of Fort Concho in 1867, the first of San Angelo's soiled doves arrived. They were the women who accompanied the military to the frontier—camp followers and laundresses.

Each troop at the post was allowed four laundresses who received government rations and were paid for washing men's clothing. Dr. W. F. Buchanan, post surgeon, reported problems with several of the black laundresses in the summer of 1875. He filed on three for what he considered their "utter worthlessness, Drunkness [sic], and Lewdness."

The women removed from the fort grounds frequently found their way across the river to San Angelo where they mixed with others who gathered to relieve soldiers of their pay. There was no effort in Tom Green County to control any of the previously mentioned vices until 1880, and that effort seemed to be based more on economies than morality.

In his book, *The Gentle Tamers*, Dee Brown described how the women of easy virtue filled a void on the frontier where women were scarce. The saloon and the ladies who frequented them were often the only home many of the men knew. They provided a modicum of civilization "whether the males were aware of it or not."

District Court Case No. 22 of Tom Green County, filed at Benficklin on 25 August 1880, is the first surviving case lodged against a group of females for vagrancy. Vagrancy was the legally accepted term for prostitution. In April 1892, the *San Angelo Standard* published City Ordinance No. 14 defining vagrancy. Among those considered vagrants were: a person who "strolls about to tell fortunes, exhibit tricks not licensed by law;" a common prostitute; a professional gambler; any person who goes about the streets begging alms but is not afflicted or disabled; and an habitual drunkard. Punishment for any of the above was a fine of not less than $2.50 or more than $10.00. The majority of the early charges of vagrancy can be traced back to one of two offenses—prostitution or gambling.

Court Case No. 22 listed the sixteen ladies who were picked up and charged. Of these, two were or had been married, at least one was black, and one was the well known "Rowdy Kate." The case charged that they were idle persons living without any visible means of support, and "being then and there common prostitutes against the peace and dignity of the state." From then until the turn of the century, the ladies of the evening, along with the owners of gaming tables, were routinely picked up twice a year and fined. Once they paid their fines, all returned to work. The fine was viewed in much the same manner as the occupation tax imposed on business men and women in the county.

To give an idea of the scope of taxable vices, in September 1885, the *Standard* reported on the Grand Jury indictments for Tom Green County. The list included twenty-five charged with unlawfully exhibiting a gaming table, twenty-nine for vagrancy, and thirteen for keeping a disorderly house, defined as a place where prostitutes or lewd women were allowed to enter. It was also reported that all vagrancy cases would be transferred to the Justice Court, and all gambling cases to the County Court.

Into this den of iniquity came a woman, a wife and mother, whose "working name" was Annie Black. Her legal name, according to family sources, was Rachel Angelyne Francis or Franca. She married John Ayers and had four children: Alfred, William, James, and Birdie. What happened to John Ayers is unknown, nor do we know why Rachel turned to prostitution. Rachel appeared in Tom Green County as Annie Black on July 29, 1891, when she was picked up and charged with vagrancy.

In a rather unusual action, Peter Crane was called as a witness for the State against Annie Black. He was asked by the county attorney whether or not in the past ten years he had had "carnal intercourse with the defendant Annie Black which question Peter Crane refused to answer and for which offense said Peter Crane is fined by the court for contempt of court and his punishment assessed at a fine of twenty-five dollars, and one days imprisonment." Interesting enough, no further mention was made of Annie Black or the charges against her!

Annie must have been a good business woman. On September 16, 1899, Annie Black bought, for $600, Lot 6 of Block 10 on West Concho Avenue in the town of San Angelo. She paid $50 cash and financed the remainder with eleven promissory notes of $50 each. The property was paid off by April 1902. This lot corresponds to the home where Annie and her girls lived on West Concho Avenue. Exactly one year later in 1900, Annie purchased the lot next door for $200.

Located directly behind this portion of West Concho was an alley known locally as "The Alley of Ill-Fame." For two blocks, lots were divided in half: those lots facing the street and those facing the alley. Obviously, the alley lots were much cheaper to buy. It was along the alley that transients and poorer prostitutes lived and worked. The majority of San Angelo's brothels at this time were located in these two blocks of West Concho. The soiled doves were "encouraged" to stay in this general area, and proper ladies never ventured in their space. Despite this unwritten law, there were sections of town where the two did mix. For instance, in the 1900 census, the enumerator listed Crickett Guess, a twenty year old white prostitute, living next door to J. W. Timmons, the district judge.

For Bennie Miskimmon, the ladies were an important source of revenue. In 1893 Bennie opened a millinery and dressmaking business when the family ranch was in jeopardy due to drought. She developed a system for taking orders from the ladies of Concho Avenue. She sent pictures and scraps of material, and the ladies chose what they wanted. A young African

American boy took the orders and delivered the goods since it would have been improper for her to do so. According to Bennie, "Their money was as good as anyone else's and they had a lot of money."

The 1900 census listed Annie operating a boarding house at the West Concho location. Her two boarders, however, were listed as prostitutes. One was her daughter, Birdie, who went by the name Clarence Rose.

Annie Black was arrested and charged with vagrancy on numerous occasions despite the fact that she would have been considered a madam. Apparently, she was a "working madam" since most of the other ladies operating boarding houses in the same block were not picked up. After the turn of the century, the round ups of ladies and gamblers became quarterly. The fines remained the same, but the county doubled its revenue.

Other than her arrests, Annie Black remains unknown to history until 1906. On April 16, 1906, Annie Black sold her property on West Concho to her daughter, Birdie Ayers, a.k.a. Clarence Rose, and signed her will on the same day. The deed record states that Annie Black, "of Tom Green County for $6,000 paid in hand by Birdie Ayers (who is commonly known as Clarence Rose)" sold Lots 5 and 6 in Block 10 "together with the house and all improvements situated on said lots on either of them, and also all of the furniture, household furnishings and fixtures in said building, of every kind, character and nature what so ever, save and except the personal effects of said Annie Black."

Annie Black was arrested during the first three quarters of 1907. The next time Annie appeared in the records of Tom Green County was on January 28, 1909, when she died and was buried in Fairmount Cemetery in San Angelo. At the time of her death, Annie Black had real and personal property of $1,000. Wright and Wynn, San Angelo attorneys, indicated that she was "indebted to divers parties, for expenses of her last sickness and her funeral expenses." The exact amount of her debts were unknown at that time. Clarence Rose, not Birdie Ayers, filed application to probate the last will and testament of Annie Black on February 20, 1909. Clarence Rose was named executrix without bond.

By April 5, 1909, opposition had mounted to the will of Annie Black. The first to file was Mrs. Allie E. Cox and husband, Arthur. She produced documents in court showing that she was the daughter of Annie Black. In addition she had a will she claimed was written by Annie Black. Through her attorney, John J. Cox of Goldthwaite, she claimed that Annie Black had been induced to sign the will filed by Clarence Rose. The court rejected her claim.

A few weeks later on April 23, 1909, Alfred Moses Ayers, William Wallace Ayers, and James Madison Ayers, children and heirs of Annie Black, opposed the will. First they denied she had executed the will. Then, they claimed Birdie Ayers had coerced Annie to sign the document in question since their mother was not of sufficient mental capacity to understand.

The two men who witnessed the signing of Black's will, Clarence Smith and S. B. Runyon, both testified that indeed the mark on the paper, along with their signatures, were made when Annie, about age fifty-five, was of sound mind. Throughout the will Annie Black referred to Birdie Ayers as her good and faithful friend. There was never any acknowledgment that Birdie was her daughter. In a statement given in June 1927, Birdie stated "That she was well acquainted with Annie Black from 1895 to long after April 16, 1906." She, too, gave no indication of their relationship.

Three men appointed by the court appraised the personal property of the deceased. Their inventory included a diamond ring valued at $125, a diamond broach for $100, and six suits of clothing valued at $100. The total value of the estate was $835, and her expenses were $557 leaving $278 for her daughter.

Annie Black's daughter, Birdie Ayers, followed in her mother's occupation. Birdie was born May 4, 1880, to John D. and Angelina Ayers. Her first arrest in San Angelo came in February 1900, under the name of Clarence Black. From that point on she was listed in court documents as Clarence Rose. Her last arrest in Tom Green County was in July 1907.

The social standing of the women on the frontier was basically divided into two classes: those who were soiled doves and those who were not. There was no mingling of the two. But from time to time in most communities across the West, a lady of the evening married a local man. Sometimes the marriage proved successful, but at times they were cut short by divorce or death. For example, the *Standard* on July 30, 1887 told of the suicide of one Henry Dierks who had married Mrs. Anna Pierce only days before. The new wife was described as "a nymph du pave." The day they married, the bride went to the fort to ply her trade. The groom went after her and took her home. The next day Dierks told her he would take poison if she went back. She did and he did.

Family stories say Birdie married a well-to-do store owner who died and left her some money with which she bought property. No records have been found to support this notion. After buying Annie's property, Birdie began acquiring other real estate in San Angelo. Her first purchase was three lots in the Park Heights Addition for $800. The only condition to the purchase was that any house erected on the property could not cost less than $1,500.

The next year Birdie purchased two additional lots and part of another on West Concho for $3,000. These lots were located on the south side of the avenue, ran to the bank of the Concho River, and faced the original property bought from Annie Black.

In July 1909, Birdie leased her property that included a two-story frame home with twelve rooms to Bobbie McGregor. McGregor, like Birdie, was a madam and operated the house as a brothel. The lease ran from July 12, 1909 to July 11, 1911, for a price of $1,800. McGregor paid $150 at the signing and $75 per month. At the time Birdie signed the lease she was a single woman. Apparently, she was thinking ahead because by September of 1909 she had married John Walter Reese of El Paso. Reese served as a Texas Ranger (Special Enlistment) and was also a police inspector in El Paso.

The marriage did not last long, and their divorce was granted on March 24, 1910, in El Paso. Their property was separated. Included in her property was a black mare named "Ruby" and her eight month old colt. These were to be delivered from the property at Columbus, Texas, owned by Reese, to Birdie's brother William at Clairmont, Texas.

Birdie returned to San Angelo and resumed her business. However, in October 1914, in Los Angeles, California, she married Joyce A. (Curley) Shield, the son of Tom Green County Sheriff, Gerome Shield. This was an abusive marriage, and they separated March 1, 1915. The couple had a four month old son, Champ B. Shield, born in Del Rio, Texas. The divorce was granted February 1, 1916, and she received custody of the child.

Sometime after the divorce, Curley Shield and Birdie Ayers had a daughter, Angelyne Shield, born in April 1917, in San Angelo. It is not known if they were married at the time. Though unsubstantiated, the family said that Champ, while a toddler, became ill and died. Birdie blamed Curley for his death, which caused the divorce. Angelyne continued to live with her mother, although she remembered as a child going to visit the Shield family who were not particularly cordial.

Prior to 1920, Birdie Ayers married Hubert Wolters of San Angelo. They had one daughter in 1920 and in 1925 were living in the house where Annie and Birdie had worked. In 1927 Birdie and H. E. Wolters, who were then living in Lomita, California, sold property in San Angelo. Birdie bought two lots in the Miles Addition of San Angelo in February 1928, but sold them in December of that same year.

During the Depression Birdie lost her remaining property in San Angelo, divorced Mr. Wolters, and moved in with her brother, William and his family, who then lived in Yuma, Arizona. He worked for the Bureau of Reclamation. Birdie spent her remaining years in California near her two daughters and her brothers. She spoke little of her early life in San Angelo. She died January 22, 1958, in Los Angeles.

San Angelo never dealt harshly with her soiled doves. In fact, in 1914 the newspaper reported that the court system had "difficulties in getting up juries on account of the unwillingness of men to serve with the prospect of having to decide in favor of the law in prostitution cases." The number of ladies fluctuated with the economy of the city. Boom periods such as the fort days, World War I and II, and the oil boom, all saw an increase in the number of soiled doves. Today, one of the city's favorite tourist attractions is Miss Hattie's Brothel Museum. It is a monument to a portion of history that is often overlooked. The red light districts and the ladies who inhabited them are just as much a part of the history of the frontier as the soldiers, buffalo hunters, cowboys, outlaws, and ordinary citizens who made San Angelo and West Texas what it is today.

The Livestock Lobby: Murdo Mackenzie, Railroad Reform, Cattlemen's Associations, and Progressive Legislation

LELAND TURNER

D r. Leland Turner teaches history at Midwestern State University in Wichita Falls. A Fulbright Fellow, he has written on West Texas agriculture and ranching.

Murdo Mackenzie (1850–1939), a successful businessman born in Scotland, moved to the United States in 1885 to direct a cattle enterprise in Trinidad, Colorado. Six years later, the Matador Land and Cattle Company, a Scottish owned joint-stock company, hired him to oversee their investment in the large Matador Ranch on the South Plains of Texas. Mackenzie brought his traditional business acumen to the job of stock raising, influencing a generation of ranch managers. He served as president of both the Texas and Southwestern Cattle Raisers Association (1901–1903) and the American Stock Growers Association (1905–1911). Concerned with railroad reform, Mackenzie played a significant role in bringing about the 1906 Hepburn Act. ✑

★ ★

President Theodore Roosevelt once said of Murdo Mackenzie: "During my term as president, he was, on the whole, the most influential of the western cattle growers. He was a leader of the far-seeing, enlightened element. Mackenzie did not exercise that influence individually, but he did so through participation in several cattlemen's associations during his long career. Mackenzie, a Scottish immigrant, came to the American West in 1885 and in 1891 became general manager of the Matador Land and Cattle Company, an extensive operation stretching from the Texas Panhandle to the Canadian plains.

Meanwhile, in 1884, Roosevelt took up ranching in North Dakota. The paths of Theodore Roosevelt and Murdo Mackenzie crossed when each shouldered the mantle of reform and pressed for railroad regulation in 1905 and 1906. Additionally, Texas Governor James Hogg, who assumed office the same year Mackenzie took over the Matador's management, had campaigned for office on a platform that called for railroad reform legislation. He saw a powerful railroad commission as the key to reform. All three men were progressive activists and played an important part in pursuing legislation important to cattlemen of the American West. Mackenzie and his ranching colleagues were active on a front new to the independent cattlemen—politics and lobbying, the attendant persuasive process.

Historians of ranching and the American West have acknowledged that cattlemen were remotely involved in advocating legislative reform during the late nineteenth and early twentieth century. But most of them had been content to concentrate on heroic imagery and the myth of the ruggedly independent cowboy/cattleman. Few have sufficiently analyzed the importance of cattlemen's associations in the legislative process. In fact, Charles Burmeister, in his 1954 article addressing the history of the American National Live Stock Association, focused on individualism when in actuality he wrote about a group effort. In his 1964 book, *The Matador Land and Cattle Company*, William M. Pearce acknowledged Mackenzie's position as an important national leader among cattlemen but concentrated on his role as an effective and innovative manager.

Economic historians of the era have treated Mackenzie and his association colleagues no better. Important works addressing the history of railroad rate regulation such as Albro Martin's *Enterprise Denied*, Gabriel Kolko's *Railroads and Regulation, 1877–1916*, and William Ripley's *Railroads: Rates and Regulation* hardly acknowledge the part played by the several cattlemen's associations. Robert Wiebe in *Businessmen and Reform* credited "well-organized agricultural groups such as the stockmen" with helping business shippers garner lower railroad rates through the Interstate Commerce Commission (ICC) regulation. He did not mention any of the associations by name or analyze their activities. Instead, Wiebe concentrated his study on Midwestern and Eastern organizations such as the National Association of Manufacturers (NAM). Further, in discussion of pure food and drug legislation, he analyzed the actions of Chicago packers and NAM food producers but did not mention the cattlemen's lobbying efforts on behalf of the Meat Inspection Act.

Cattlemen obviously played a larger role, and like businessmen nationwide and members of the National Association of Manufacturers, they participated in the movement for state and federal railroad rate regulation and other reform legislation. In a 1904 speech, Texas Senator J. W. Bailey made clear the importance of the cattlemen's associations in making railroad reform a major political issue. He gave the cattle raisers credit for raising the issue through petitioning Congress to grant the ICC authority over railroad rates. Further, President Roosevelt, Bailey said, made the association's railroad reform position a plank in the 1904 Republican platform. The cattlemen association's influence was at least understood by their contemporaries.

Murdo Mackenzie believed in, and actively promoted, involvement in cattlemen's associations. He once said that Matador money spent on association dues and activities was probably the best investment the ranch could make. He also took on leadership positions within the organizations and served as president of the Cattle Raisers Association of Texas (in 1901 and 1902) and the American National Live Stock Association (in 1905 and again in 1911). In every instance, he lobbied state and federal governments on behalf of western ranchers. Mackenzie, as an association leader, endeavored to involve government and influential government leaders in policymaking that benefited him and his industry, or business, colleagues. He was, in fact, a businessman rather than social progressive.

Early in his career, Mackenzie exhibited a propensity to exercise influence at the federal level. In 1888, A. P. Hill, president of a regional Texas cattlemen's group, chose Mackenzie to travel to Missouri along with Charles Goodnight and other influential Texas beef producers to meet with Senator George Vest of Missouri. Subsequently, the Vest Committee Report charged four major packing companies with price fixing and dividing up business in territories—the report contributed to passage of the Sherman Antitrust Act.

When Mackenzie first associated with the Cattle Raisers Association of Texas (CRT), the organization's main function was its detective and protective services. Cattlemen's associations were typically formed for the mutual benefit of members, and detectives and inspectors apprehended thieves and enforced quarantine lines in order to deter the spread of disease. The association employed brand inspectors to check all cattle moved from one range to another or shipped to market. It also bore the expense of prosecuting all persons attempting to "unlawfully handle member's cattle." Because of the association's efforts, between 1877 and 1893 unlawful traffic in cattle belonging to members steadily declined.

The organization that was to become the CRT was founded in 1877 at Graham, Texas. Members of the Stock Raisers Association of North West Texas, the organization's original name, called the meeting to set out procedures for cooperation during annual round-ups. The group was also concerned with rustling and illegal branding, and its members approved a fifty dollar reward for anyone furnishing evidence that resulted in conviction for stealing or illegally marking cattle. The cattlemen's initial impulse to protect their herds and their land would slowly change. Two years later in March, 1879, the Northwest Texas Association passed its first resolution to lobby a government body. The resolution was not an attempt to influence railroad rates; it was an attempt to convince the Texas Legislature to raise the penalty for burning certain woodlands and prairies in West Texas. Cattlemen, however, soon turned their attention to railroads.

On December 22, 1879, the Northwest Texas Association called a meeting that was to deal specifically with the railroad question. The object was to get less expensive rates for the transportation of cattle from West Texas to market centers. The men elected a committee of five influential stock raisers to confer with railroad authorities in St. Louis. The cattlemen were not yet ready to call on the government for legislation to control rates. At the annual meeting in 1880 C. C. Slaughter, in a speech "received with enthusiasm," pressed the importance of organization in obtaining better rates. The original railroad committee was largely unsuccessful, and there is no record of its meeting after 1879. In 1886 cattlemen at a meeting in Weatherford, Texas, continued to grumble about the combination between railroads and commission merchants in an arrangement that granted rebates to the merchant rather than the shipper, or cattlemen.

Texas Governor James S. Hogg took office in January, 1891, with a clear mandate for reform. Although not part of the more radical Farmers Alliance movement in Texas, Hogg and his allies favored conservative businessmen, such as Mackenzie and his associates, and conservative practices that benefited Texas. But, Hogg intended to impose railroad regulation. At the time, such regulation was not high on Mackenzie's priority list, but as the years passed railroad regulation moved toward the top and in response Governor Hogg took measures to break railroad price-fixing. He won the 1890 gubernatorial election largely because of a promise to regulate railroads. In the 1890 election Texans voted to amend the Texas Constitution to allow for a railroad regulatory agency. Because the Texas Traffic Association, a powerful combination of railroad traffic managers, united to fix rates, discriminated between shippers, and used their economic and political resources to prevent legislation which would end such abuses, Hogg and the Texas Legislature in 1891 established the Texas Railroad Commission. The new state agency held regulatory power over railroad rates and operations.

Despite shipping rates that many considered prohibitive, Texas cattlemen, when Hogg took office, were not ready officially to embrace government railroad regulation. Thus, once again they tried group negotiation. At their annual meeting in 1892 the Northwest Texas Association voted to send a committee to Chicago, Kansas City, and St. Louis to seek fair prices. The convention also created a committee on railroad rates, but Murdo Mackenzie was not one of its five members. In fact, after the brief involvement with the Vest committee in 1888 Mackenzie was notably absent from association proceedings, and his name was not listed on any committees or in any leadership role until 1893.

Rather, Mackenzie was involved with quarantine line disputes. The activities contributed to Mackenzie's early role as a leader among cattlemen and eventually thrust the Matador leader onto the national political stage. Because of the myriad of quarantine lines set by individual states, the federal government stepped in and established a federal line along the southern borders of Cochran, Hockley, Lubbock, Crosby, and Dickens counties in Texas. Cattle from south of the quarantine line, enforced by the Department of Agriculture, were prohibited from crossing between February 15 and December 1. When discussing the quarantine in 1891 with a group of cowmen in Childress, Texas, Mackenzie suggested they convene a meeting. The purpose, according to Mackenzie, was to "show southern cattlemen, we [Panhandle ranchers] are in earnest about this [quarantine issue]."

When it convened just weeks later, the convention appointed a committee to lobby Governor Hogg to go to Washington to negotiate a quarantine line agreement with the federal government. Getting no satisfactory action out of Hogg, committee members, Mackenzie among them, took it upon themselves to travel to the nation's capital to present their case to Secretary of Agriculture J. M. Rusk. The committee remained there a week longer than expected because when it sought to move the quarantine line farther south, fierce opposition from Plains states representatives appeared. Mackenzie supported the Department of Agriculture's right to quarantine southern cattle and expressed his belief that the federal government should maintain the right to interfere inside the state of Texas, an early indication of Mackenzie's growing endorsement of federal intervention.

In 1893 Mackenzie joined the executive committee of the Texas association which, notably, changed its name in that year to the Cattle Raisers Association of Texas. He served along side such legendary cattlemen as C. C. Slaughter, Samuel Burk Burnett, and James C. Loving. Beyond the detective and protective function of the CRT, Mackenzie's association activities revolved around his executive committee responsibilities and a growing interest in exercising influence over railroad rates and policy. Without a doubt the zeal and success of the Hogg administration in regards to railroad reform influenced a growing change in attitudes among Mackenzie and his colleagues. The cattlemen soon looked to the state and federal government for assistance.

In 1895, when the association formed legislative and transportation committees. Mackenzie became a member of the transportation committee. His appointment to the committee proved a harbinger of things to come. In the mid to late 1890s, he focused on influencing railroad rates and policy through negotiation as opposed to legislation. On April 27, 1895, for example, he backed a proposal encouraging cattlemen to ship exclusively on association endorsed railroads. Slowly, attitudes were changing, and Mackenzie and his fellow cattlemen, having successfully influenced quarantine line legislation, gradually embraced government intervention.

Mackenzie did not join trade associations and assume leadership positions for simple egotistical reasons. Rather, he understood that combined action in favor of western cattlemen was also good for the Matador bottom line. Unlike the populist movement of the 1890s, he and his contemporaries were not radical in their demands.

Mackenzie attended a convention of stock growers on January 24, 1898, in Denver. At the convention, 1,500 delegates from across the country formed the National Live Stock Association (NLSA). Mackenzie's colleague, S. J. Springer of the Continental Company, was elected president. Mackenzie said of the meeting, "I don't know what they can accomplish, but I know they can't do any harm [and] it costs us nothing to speak of." "I think a meeting of this kind does some good," Mackenzie wrote to the Matador board of directors, "it brings people together and you get an opportunity of meeting men who may be of some use to us in the future." He was certain of the importance of individuals but was yet uncertain about the effectiveness of a national cattlemen's organization. His experience had proven, however, that the Texas cattlemen's association was an effective group, and he continued his active involvement with that organization.

The railroads, on the other hand, were an altogether different story. After he was elected first vice president in 1899, Mackenzie continued to serve on the traffic committee. The committee's

1899 report called for settlement of the question concerning terminal charges in Chicago and recommended that the association immediately take the issue to the Interstate Commerce Commission. The railroads, according to the traffic committee, were determined to keep unreasonable and unjust charges. The committee recommended that the association file suit in federal court.

To exacerbate problems, in January 1899, railroads in New York had raised rates on cattle from all Texas points 2.5 cents per 100 pounds. The increase amounted to about six dollars per car. In light of "the railroads never being more prosperous and [realizing] unprecedented earnings" association members protested the higher rates. At the same time railroads raised the feed-in-transit charge five dollars per car. Together the two rate hikes amounted to about fifty cents per head.

After presenting the report, Mackenzie encouraged all association members—1,200 in attendance at the 1899 convention—to stand behind the committee in its battle with the railroads. Two years prior to the convention, CRT dismissed its traffic manager, and consequently, railroad rates continued to rise. The committee recommended that the association reinstate a traffic manager to deal with high rates. It noted: "We feel that the railroads are not justified in thus raising the rate, and the question again arises whether it would not be well to again secure the services of a competent traffic manager to aid us in securing more just rates." Railroads rates were the only issue Mackenzie, never one to give superfluous speeches, deemed important enough that he should personally address the 1899 convention. He continued to believe that the concerted effort of cattlemen would eventually prevail on railroads. His beliefs were soon put to the test.

In June, 1900, Mackenzie, along with other CRT members, traveled to St. Louis for a meeting. Traffic managers from various railroads were also in attendance. Recently, railroads had again raised rates. This time charges from Texas to Kansas City and Chicago went up such an extent that cattlemen could no longer bear the expense. For example, the rate from Pampa to Kansas City rose from 26 cents to 31.5 cents per 100 pounds, amounting to about $13.20 per railroad car. Mackenzie felt it unfair to pay a higher rate than Colorado shippers. The rate from Las Animas, Colorado, to Kansas City, a twenty-five mile shorter trip, cost Colorado cattlemen only 23.5 cents per century weight.

Mackenzie and traffic committee members met with about fifteen railroad representatives. The group "went into the whole question (concerning rate schedules) with them . . . they admitted we had a strong case but were not certain how to resolve the issue being reluctant to reduce rates." When the meeting concluded, Mackenzie believed that some concessions would be forthcoming from railroad officials. The cost for Texas cattle to reach market, because of the higher rates, was approximately $1.00 more per head than Colorado cattle. "We cannot stand to be handicapped to this extent," wrote Mackenzie. His initiative to use association management and pooled resources to counter railroad rate hikes was largely unsuccessful.

At the twenty-sixth annual meeting of the CRT, the first year Mackenzie presided over the convention, Texas cattlemen urged Congress to pass a bill, the Elkins Act, giving the ICC more power over interstate railway carriers. One association lawyer said, "We have given the matter attention and we recommend that if this association desires protection in the matter of freight rates it should lend its influence in a substantial way to aid that legislation." The convention subsequently passed a resolution stating, "Whereas, the operations of the ICC under the present law are absolutely worthless, for the reason that they have no power to enforce their decisions," we endorse a bill giving the ICC power to enforce its ruling. Representative of the changing attitudes among cattlemen towards government economic intervention, S. J. Springer, President of the National Live Stock Association stood before the March, 1901, Texas cattlemen's convention and proclaimed, "The American Congress has got to come to our rescue."

Mackenzie changed the focus of the Cattle Raisers Association of Texas. As indicated, it was conceived of, and operated as, a detective and protective agency complete with a legal department for the prosecution of thieves. Under Mackenzie's influence, the association gradually migrated toward legislative matters. Shortly after his departure, an association official reported: "Today the association is foremost in questions of legislative interests, and as a representative of the industry in Texas and neighboring states, has been successful in preventing adverse legislation, increased freight rates, and other matters of material concern to its members."

In the beginning, Mackenzie negotiated with railroads as an individual cattleman. When that proved ineffective, he utilized the association as a negotiation tool. His growing belief in the effectiveness of associations was obvious in his approach to railroad rate regulation. His emerging inclination to endorse government as the vehicle by which to effect change revealed his progressive streak.

In his role as general manager of the Matador, profitability and long term viability were always Murdo Mackenzie's first priority. When in 1903, drought, rangeland availability, and poor markets threatened his systematic beef production, Mackenzie resigned the presidency of the CRT to devote his full attention to the Matador. The resignation, however, may well have been his own well orchestrated segue onto the national scene, a stage on which he could more effectively influence national policy pertaining to the western cattle industry.

In that same year, 1903, Mackenzie and his fellow cattlemen abandoned attempts to influence railroad policy through direct negotiations. As a group, they petitioned the federal government to pass legislation addressing their grievances, especially concerning railroad rate regulation. Mackenzie and members of various national cattlemen's associations successfully lobbied Congress to pass legislation favorable to the cattle industry. The year 1906 found the cattle associations at the height of their collective power. The Hepburn Act was their most important success, but the group also influenced other legislation.

Railroad rate expenses remained at the core of cattle industry profitability, and Mackenzie's renewed association activities consequently focused on railroads. Cattle shipments to Matador ranges in the Dakotas in 1903 cost the Matador three dollars per head. The charge was "entirely too high," Mackenzie wrote, but "we are at the mercy of the railroads unless we resort to trial again." Additionally, Mackenzie was anxious to keep rate regulation decisions out of the courts saying, "if they ever once get us into court they can keep us there indefinitely." Rather than depend on litigation, he and his contemporaries embraced government regulation of railroads.

When the National Live Stock Association (NLSA) formed in 1898, Mackenzie expressed doubts about the effectiveness of a national group. But, as railroad rates soared, he championed federal intervention. He and his western cattle industry colleagues endeavored to influence President Theodore Roosevelt and Congress to act in their collective favor.

Foreshadowing his role as an influential national leader, Mackenzie became a member of an NLSA committee to discuss transport grievances, such as slow transport, uncertainty of car availability, and rate discrimination, with railroad traffic managers. "We expect to hear from them soon," he exclaimed, "and if not satisfactory we are to press the matter before Congress. We may be able to get a bill passed regulating freight on livestock." The Interstate Commerce Commission had certain powers, he believed, but not enough, and he was intent on empowering the committee to regulate freight and commodity rates.

The business of making money was always at the forefront of Mackenzie's agenda. He was careful to explain his association related expenses and wrote the Matador board saying, "As you are aware, for the past fourteen years I have been very prominent in the affairs of the Association (CRT), and I claim that part of its present satisfactory condition is due to my efforts." Having proven himself with the CRT and with an emerging national reputation, he strove to use his influence to effect national policy.

Within just a few years of its founding, the NLSA experienced internal discord. Many cattlemen were unhappy with the authority exercised within the association by packers, railroad officials, commission men, and various outside interests. They were also unhappy with the influence of such groups in association affairs. Conflict over what factions should wield influence within the organization led several important cattlemen, Mackenzie included, to form a new organization.

Confident in their ability to influence national policy, the ranchers formed an association that admitted only cattle producers to full membership. Having failed in almost every attempt to redress issues with railroads, the men realized that a new organization combined with reliance on the federal government to combat the corporate strength of railroads was their only effective defense. Mackenzie, in a rare speech once said that organization gave "each member of the body the entire power and influence of the organization, with the greatest amount of efficiency at the least possible cost."

"There has been an Association formed," Mackenzie reported, "called the American Stock Growers Association (ASGA) with an object in view of getting cattle men from all the Western states interested and joined together so as to be in a position to insist upon legislation with the end in view of protecting our interests." Cattlemen from all parts of the country asked Mackenzie to lead the new organization. Their reasoning was that he was more familiar with the status of contemporary political issues and legislative possibilities than most anyone in the business. He had "been in this fight," by his own admission, "longer than anyone and [was] more familiar with present affairs than anyone." But, Mackenzie always returned to the bottom line, saying "sometimes you can scarcely avoid making a sacrifice for the sake of the general business." Thus, believing that "if he could do anything to help that I should do so because in helping others we are helping ourselves," he accepted the presidency of the new organization.

Suddenly, Mackenzie found himself in a politically powerful position. President Roosevelt appeared at the May, 1905, convention where Mackenzie was elected president of the American Stock Growers Association. When speaking to the assemblage, Roosevelt reiterated his determination to help, saying he was in "perfect accord" with the cattlemen's goals. His growing influence was apparent when Roosevelt, traveling through Trinidad, Colorado, recognized Mackenzie among a crowd gathered on the railroad platform there and called him over. On the occasion, Roosevelt assured Mackenzie that everything would be done to help the cattlemen get a bill through Congress, one that would enlarge the ICC's power to regulate railroad rates.

In January 1906, two competing national cattlemen's groups, the NLSA and the ASGA, were reorganized under the banner of the American National Live Stock Association (ANLSA). Mackenzie won election as president of the reorganized group. As president, Mackenzie immediately implemented a structured lobbying system. Indicative of his motivation to sustain business through organization were his early appointments. He first asked Sam H. Cowan, a Fort Worth attorney previously retained by the CRT, to challenge railroad rates and seek ICC intervention. Judge Cowan, in Mackenzie's estimation, was a "very capable and energetic man" who would look after the association's work in Washington. Mackenzie put a proven lobbyist to work on behalf of western cattlemen. Incidentally, Cowan won every rate case he presented to the ICC before his 1916 retirement.

Next, he hired T. W. Tomlinson, a Chicago railroad expert, as the organization's secretary and manager in charge of the Denver office. Tomlinson, Mackenzie reported, had for years been associated with the railroad industry and was familiar with every aspect of the business. Particularly, he had assisted cattlemen when they resisted the two dollar per head terminal charge on all cattle shipped into Chicago. Tomlinson was also part of the CRT when it challenged the railroad's rates on shipments originating in Texas. "I know Mr. Tomlinson well," Mackenzie wrote, "and I have the utmost confidence both in his integrity and ability, and for that reason I was very anxious to secure [Tomlinson's] services." Some competent person, Mackenzie concluded, must do the work in order to keep the railroads in check, or the Matador Land and Cattle Company might as well go out of business.

Mackenzie believed the national organization put cattlemen in a position to "hold the railroads in line." It was the railroads that the cattlemen were most dependent upon and which consequently drew their greatest criticism. Railroad rates were the paramount issue concerning cattlemen during Mackenzie's tenure as president of the national association in 1905–1906. Mackenzie suspected that the railroads had even greater power than the packing consorts and certainly more than cattle producers. In March 1903, Mackenzie exhibited his distrust of railroads when he accused the railroad interests of influencing the passage of a bill which prohibited the issuance of free passes to important customers, passes on which Mackenzie normally traveled, or any other concessions to shippers. Mackenzie, however, appreciated the role railroad officials played in regards to the Matador's economic well being and playing the role of a crafty businessman he suggested, during the battle over railroad rate legislation, that the Matador procure some fine scotch whiskey—two casks at ten gallons each—for two specific Santa Fe Railroad managers.

It was in the passage of the Hepburn Act, however, that Mackenzie and the ANLSA realized their most significant victory. Hiring Judge Cowan as a full time Washington lobbyist paid off for Mackenzie and the association. Cowan not only testified before the ICC Senate committee in June of 1905, but had three "perfectly satisfactory" meetings with Roosevelt. In fact, Roosevelt was so pleased with his recommendations regarding rate regulation that "the President . . . asked [Cowan] to prepare and send to him a bill which [Cowan] felt would be a proper one." In effect, the Hepburn Bill was largely written by Sam Cowan, Mackenzie's hand-picked Washington lobbyist and ANLSA representative. Mackenzie then traveled to Washington in November of 1905 to make certain the bill he wanted was presented.

The Hepburn Act empowered the ICC to define and enforce an issue at the heart of cattlemen's grievances: railroad shipping rates. The law authorized the commission to prescribe railroad bookkeeping methods and to determine, upon a shipper's complaint, just and reasonable rates. Mackenzie had long advocated such a bill and was busy in early 1905, just months before the ASGA was formed, to ensure passage of the bill. In one report Mackenzie said, "The lower house of Congress passed a bill such as we wanted, giving the ICC the necessary powers to regulate railroad rates. We are now waiting with interest to see what the Senate will do.

In February, 1905, Mackenzie was in Washington. He appeared "before the Committees of the House and Senate with the view of having the Interstate Commerce Law amended," granting the Commission power to regulate railroad rates. While in Washington, he testified before the committees on several different occasions and discussed the matter with its members for nearly two weeks. He left Washington confident that as a result of their labors a bill would pass giving the Commission the powers requested. He reported:

> *While in Washington I had the pleasure of an audience . . . with President Roosevelt and he expressed himself as highly pleased with our demands and the conservative manner in which we had gone about it. The President promised me that unless Congress passed a bill, such as indicated in his message, giving the Interstate Commerce Commission the powers asked for, he would call a session of Congress for this purpose and keep on calling special sessions until they would pass a bill to please him. It was very gratifying to us to have this assurance from the President.*

Mackenzie believed Roosevelt would press the matter with the Senate, and, if he did not get the desired legislation, the President would take the fight directly to the people. Mackenzie said, it is possible that Roosevelt may "reconsider his decision not to run again and ask the people to give him the proper Senate and he will give them a bill to protect them from the ravishing of Wall Street." It was not only possible that Roosevelt would run again, Mackenzie argued, but also probable if the railroads "through paid agents in the Senate defeat a reasonable bill to protect the shipper and consumer."

Railroads, Mackenzie reported, had over the last six years raised rates on all cattle shipped from Texas by about one dollar per head. Alternately, railroad traffic managers testified before

Congress that railroad rates probably remained insufficient to provide acceptable service. Convinced that railroads intended to continue regularly raising rates, Mackenzie stated that in the "opinion of a great many other people, the only reason the rates were not raised last year and this, is that the agitation made by the cattle men scared the railroads out." He defended the time and expense the battle cost the company and reassured board members that he and other leading cattlemen expected to win their battle for regulation. He wrote:

> This is to be the hardest fight we will have. We are making a strong fight, and we have the President right with us, and I feel that when the matter comes up, we can scare some of the senators at least, into line. We have had Judge Cowan in Washington for the past month, and I am pleased to say that the President is working with us hand and glove, and he is to do everything in his power to force this matter on the Senate.

Cattlemen, intent on having rate regulation, in the fall of 1905 organized an Interstate Commerce Law Convention while Congress debated the Hepburn bill. Their stated goal was to get "every organization desirous of the enactment of the [railroad rate] legislation recommended by the President" to attend the convention in order to effect influence on Congress.

Mackenzie and his colleagues were not alone in their battle. They had a powerful ally in President Roosevelt. "There is a man in the President's chair," stated influential cattleman R. H. West while arguing for railroad regulation, "who has the people behind him to the extent that has never been seen." Roosevelt used that power to the benefit of his fellow cattlemen.

Mackenzie reported that a bill which set "forth exactly what we want, . . . will go before the Senate with full knowledge that is backed by the President." He and Roosevelt were in absolute agreement concerning the power of the ICC as a regulatory agency. Roosevelt, one colleague reported, was "utterly opposed to putting the power [of rate regulation] into the hands of the courts." "This has been a tedious fight," Mackenzie reported, "but success [is] now in sight."

Following twelve weeks of debate, the Hepburn measure, in May, 1906, passed both houses of Congress, and President Theodore Roosevelt signed it into law. It was arguably the most significant accomplishment of Mackenzie's years of industry service and political activism. The Hepburn Act strengthened the ICC's power to determine and enforce "reasonable rates" and was an important step toward effective regulation of industry. Shipping costs were a major Matador expense, and in 1906, after the bill became law, the Matador raised dividends by 1.25 percent.

Other legislation occasionally threatened the economic livelihood of cattlemen. In 1905, for example, Congress passed an act which required that cattle, if even a spot of mange was found within a herd, be dipped twice within ten days before receiving a bill of health. If carried out, in Mackenzie's opinion, the act would be ruinous to the cattle business. Consequently, a deputation of cattlemen, Mackenzie included, went to Washington and succeeded in getting the order modified so that cattle, if free of mange at the point of shipment, could be shipped to market. "I wish to say to you," Mackenzie wrote, "that this modification of the Department's order is one of the most important which we have been able to attain for many years." He was also beginning to understand his national prominence in the beef cattle industry and made certain the Matador directors, who often complained of his expenses, understood the influence he wielded. He wrote them saying. "The reason why they wanted me to be along was that I had considerable influence . . . [and can] get the ear of the President" and subsequently influence the Secretary of Agriculture's decision.

Shortly thereafter, because of his connections and influence, leaders asked Mackenzie to support a change in a U.S. statute concerning cattle shipments. He agreed and subsequently arranged a meeting in Chicago with the Secretary of Agriculture. The issue involved a law that the Humane Society championed. The measure prevented shippers from holding cattle in railroad cars for more than twenty-eight hours unless the cars were equipped with water troughs and feed racks. Previously shippers were allowed to hold cattle in cars for up to 40 hours. The law also reduced the number of cattle that could be shipped in each car by seventy-five percent, which in effect, raised shipping costs significantly. Mackenzie prevailed on the Secretary to rescind the order, which he did, and as a result cattlemen could ship cattle much as they had on previous occasions.

The national association was also successful in regards to the Meat Inspection Act of 1906. The act authorized the Secretary of Agriculture to inspect meat coming under the purveyance of interstate commerce laws to determine whether it was healthy and packed under sanitary conditions. Roosevelt remained by the cattlemen's side. "There were many other things that we did in connection with corporations" he later wrote, "one of the most important was the passage of the meat inspection law because of scandalous abuses shown to exist in the great packing-houses in Chicago, and elsewhere." The association backed the bill because it forced packers to maintain sanitary facilities and encouraged consumer confidence in beef products, resulting in increased sales of beef. Packers opposed the bill. It subjected their product to the possibility of being condemned as unfit for human consumption and detrimental to packing company profits. Cattlemen were also unhappy with parts of the act. Inspection created expense and the act charged that fee to the packers, who openly made known their intention of passing the fee onto the producers. Ultimately, the cattle association prevailed and convinced the government to bear the cost of inspection.

Mackenzie, upon accepting the presidency of the American National Live Stock Association, identified railroad conglomerates as one of the largest threats to the future profitability of the beef cattle industry. When he surrendered the office in 1907, he reported that the association under his leadership and with the passage the Hepburn Act (1906) had realized important successes.

Above all other legislation, leading cattlemen desired railroad regulation, but they did not embrace the Populist idea that railroads should be federally owned. They were, after all, businessmen, as opposed to agrarian homesteaders who raised stock. Cattlemen, in general, did not desire that the federal government suppress private enterprise; allegedly they only desired a level playing field and Roosevelt helped them get just that. An empowered Interstate Commerce Commission, Roosevelt argued, "became a most powerful force for good . . . [the bill] hurt only those who were not acting as they should have acted."

Mackenzie, for his part, was never an ardent crusader for the Progressive movement that embraced government as the vehicle by which all American lives could be improved. On one occasion he assured Matador board members that the association was in good and experienced hands and was not some group of radical reformists. He was simply interested in the economic health of the Matador and the western cattle industry as a whole.

Historian Robert Wiebe called the Progressive Era an "age of organization" and identified the proliferation of reform organizations and associations with Progressivism. Those organizations, according to Wiebe, "carried the message of collective action to save the individual." Cattlemen founded the American National Live Stock Association with the specific intent to influence national legislation, and the several other associations with which Mackenzie associated were certainly pressure groups. And, Mackenzie's firm, sometimes overbearing, leadership brought discipline to a diverse group of individuals and in the process exerted powerful influence on Congress and the federal government.

Historians have long been enamored with the "rugged individualism" of the western cattleman. That personality trait, individualism, was evident in Mackenzie's management of the Matador but, he embraced association membership and activism throughout his career. In a 1911 speech before the Cattle Raisers Association of Texas, shortly before he left for Brazil to tackle the largest cattle operation in the world, Mackenzie summarized his many years of association involvement. The speech was entitled "The Benefits Derived from Organization." In the speech he defined organization as a systematic way to use action to benefit an entire body. He mentioned the importance of the association's detective and protective services but focused on legislative successes. Most important among the success was the cattlemen associations' important part in influencing the passage of the Hepburn Act. Without organization, Mackenzie asserted, no individual association or single cattleman could wield the influence of the stock associations and were powerless in getting laws passed. He concluded his speech by saying, "If you concentrate your forces and go to [Congress] . . . I will risk assertion that there is no body of men in this country that will get as patient a hearing [as] the stockmen of the West."

Mackenzie's assertions were supported by Ike T. Pryor, an influential sheep and cattle rancher. Pryor, in a speech welcoming the 1911 CRT convention to San Antonio reinforced the heroic imagery of cattlemen when he said the typical American citizen recognized the Texas cattlemen as "direct descendents of the heroes of the Alamo, San Jacinto, and Goliad." He acknowledged the detective and protective role of the CRT by saying that "the cattle rustlers of Texas have stopped their vocation . . . . and they will always shy around the brands of the Cattle Raisers Association of Texas." But most significantly he recognized the importance of the cattlemen's lobbying efforts. Pryor said, "the ICC will listen to the [cattlemen's] representatives, . . . and as long as you keep Judge [Sam] Cowen[sic] at the head of that department, [Congress and the railroads] will always take off their hats to you and be willing to treat with you.

Cattlemen like Murdo Mackenzie and the organizations of which they were a part played an important role in Progressive Era reform. As business progressives with an eye on profits, Mackenzie and his colleagues in the Cattle Raisers Association and the American National Live

Stock Association were instrumental in promoting reform legislation—especially railroad rate legislation such as the Hepburn Act.

What historians in their pursuit of the independent cattleman of western mythology have tended to ignore is that when profits were on the line, most ranchers and cowmen set aside personal predilections and joined cattlemen's associations. When Mackenzie and his associates put the weight of their national coalition of several associations, or the livestock lobby, behind an issue, the federal government, in particular, listened and often took action favoring the cattlemen. Murdo Mackenzie, although often cited as a typically independent cattleman, should not be overlooked as an important livestock lobbyist who contributed to significant reform legislation in the Progressive Era.

The Great Storm

GARY CARTWRIGHT

Legendary Lone Star writer Gary Cartwright earned his journalism degree at Texas Christian University in Fort Worth. His articles have appeared in such publications as *Life*, *Esquire*, and *Harper's*. Over his long and distinguished career, Cartwright worked for the *Fort Worth Press*, the *Dallas Times Herald*, the *Dallas Morning News*, and *Texas Monthly*. A member of the Texas Institute of Letters, his books include *Blood Will Tell: The Murder Trials of T. Cullen Davis* (1979), *Galveston: A History of the Island* (1991), and *Turn Out the Lights: Chronicles of Texas During the 80s and 90s* (2000). In 2015, Cartwright published his memoir, *The Best I Recall*.

The Great Galveston Storm of 1900 still ranks as the worst natural disaster in American history. The devastating hurricane killed at least 6,000 people and countless homes, schools, churches, and businesses were demolished. In this selection, Cartwright provides a compelling account of the savage storm and its terrible aftermath. ◦⟋

★ ★

Friday, September 7, 1900, started out oppressively hot, then turned into one of those seemingly perfect days when the wind swings around and blows out of the north and the heat of summer starts to retreat. Frayed strings of clouds stitched a satin blue sky, promising the relief

Chapters 15-16 from *Galveston: A History of the Island* by Gary Cartwright, 1991. Reprinted by permission of the author.

of rain. Long swells broke on the beach, and young sports who should have been tending to business on the Strand took off early to frolic in the breakers. This was a day for getting out, for experiencing life.

Isaac Cline saw the surf, too, but wasn't amused. Cline, the chief of the U.S. Weather Bureau's Galveston Station, had been plotting a storm that had started days earlier in the Cape Verde Basin, off the western coast of Africa. Swept along by the easterly trades, the storm had blown just north of Cuba on Tuesday. By Thursday it had passed through the Straits of Florida and was traveling across the Gulf of Mexico in a northwesterly direction, headed toward the Texas coast. On its present course it would likely make landfall well to the east of Galveston, which would put the Island on the comparatively safe left side of the storm's vortex. Cline dutifully hoisted storm-warning flags on the pole above the Levy Building, where the Weather Bureau was located.

Later in the day Cline walked along East Beach, feeling uneasy and trying to put things into logical order. He was a practical man, a scientist, and a physician, and he had a low tolerance for inexactitude. Something didn't add up. The barometer was falling slowly, as one might expect, and the wind was blowing out of the north at a brisk fifteen to seventeen miles per hour. And yet the tide was four and a half feet above normal and rising; it had already inundated the Flats on the Island's east end. That was what worried Cline. The tide was rising even though the wind was blowing directly *against* it. Normally, a north or offshore wind meant a low tide—on such occasions, Islanders joked that you could walk halfway to Cuba. The phenomenon of high water with opposing winds was an uncommon occurrence, but Cline knew its name: it was called a storm tide.

Cline had been with the Weather Bureau for eighteen years, eleven of them in Galveston, and in all that time the only severe hurricane to hit the Gulf Coast was the one in 1893 that drowned 2,000 people on the Louisiana, Mississippi, and Alabama coasts. The 1886 hurricane that wiped out Indianola was a trifle by comparison. In 1900 there was little information available on the habits of tropical storms, but Cline knew that under the right conditions they were capable of devastation beyond belief. The sixteen-foot storm tide that swept over the Ganges delta and blasted Calcutta in 1864, for example, drowned 40,000 people. All that afternoon Isaac Cline and his brother Joseph, who was also a meteorologist with the Weather Bureau, distributed information about the storm's movement and warned people to move away from the beach.

Rain started just after midnight and fell steadily all night. At one in the morning Joseph Cline finished up at the bureau and went home to bed. Joseph lived four blocks from the beach, in Isaac's two-story frame house at 25th and Avenue Q. It was a sturdy house, constructed to withstand any storm in memory, and it was raised on pilings well above the high-water mark of the 1875 hurricane. Nevertheless, Joseph slept fitfully until four, when some "sense of impending disaster" awakened him. He went to the south window and looked out. In the few hours that he had slept, the backyard of the Cline home had become part of the Gulf of Mexico. "I shook my brother awake and told him that the worst had begun," Joseph Cline said. Joseph hurried back to the Levy Building to file a report over the bureau's national circuit, and Isaac Cline harnessed his horse to a two-wheeled cart and drove along the beach from one end of town to the other, warning people of the approaching storm.

By nine o'clock rain was running calf-deep down the street in front of Louisa Rollfing's house, a few blocks from the beach. People in her neighborhood were enjoying the downpour. Children and even a few housewives removed their shoes and stockings and waded amid pieces of driftwood and clumps of seaweed. On the beach, waves crashing against the streetcar trestle shot into the air high as telephone poles. Everyone was having fun until someone came up from the beach and told them that the bathhouses were breaking to pieces. "Then it wasn't fun anymore," Louisa recalled. Her husband, August, was working with a paint crew downtown, and she sent her eldest son by streetcar to tell August to come home immediately. Her son reported back later with this message: "Papa says, 'You must be crazy,' he will come home for his dinner." Water was already coming in over the doorsill. Louisa began packing.

Two competing forces were tearing at the Island. Far out at sea the storm was piling up walls of water and pushing them toward shore, and on the mainland a north wind was pushing in the opposite direction. The tide had forced itself steadily into the harbor, raising bay waters six feet, and the north wind drove angry brown waves against and over the wharves and railroad tracks. By one in the afternoon the wagon bridge and the three railroad bridges across the bay were all submerged. If anyone had thoughts of escaping to the mainland, it was too late.

Rabbi Henry Cohen was returning from temple when he noticed a long exodus of people moving up Broadway from the east end, carrying odd pieces of household goods and armloads of clothing. Broadway was the Island's highest point, a sort of continental divide, 8.7 feet above sea level: from there the Island tapered down to the bay and the Gulf, where the distinction between sea and land was measured in inches. But there was no record of a flood tide seriously threatening Broadway. Though the rain was pounding down and the sky was dark as twilight, the rabbi observed among the refugees something resembling a holiday mood. Children ran ahead, sliding on the mud slicks. The rabbi found spare umbrellas and blankets and passed them out, and Mrs. Cohen gave apples to the children.

Mollie Cohen finally persuaded her husband to come inside and put on some dry clothes. The electricity was off, and they sat down to lunch by candlelight. "We had a storm like this in "86," she told the children as they ate. "My father's store on Market Street was flooded." At that moment a gust of wind shook the house, causing plaster to shower from the ceiling. "It's just a little blow," she tried to assure them. Presently, the rabbi went to the door and looked out. He couldn't see the boulevard through the dark curtain of rain, but he could see water lapping over the first step of his front porch. "It looks as if the water has reached Broadway this time," he said, gathering the children and steering them away from the door. "Come in the parlor, Mollie, and let's have some music."

August Rollfing had finally realized the seriousness of the situation and sent a wagon from Malloy's Livery Stable to fetch his family and take them to the home of his mother on the west end. "It was a terrible trip," Louisa Rollfing recalled. "There were electric wires down everywhere and we had to go slow. The rain was icy cold and hurt our faces like glass splinters, and little 'Lanta pressed her face hard against my breast and cried all along the way." By the time they reached 40th and Avenue H, their horse was up to his neck in water. They were only a block from their destination, but when they tried to turn down 40th, a man shouted for them to stop. "You can't get through," he said. "There's a deep hole ahead." Louisa made a desperate decision: their only hope was to try and reach her sister-in-law's home at 36th and Broadway.

The tower that Nicholas Clayton had built above St. Mary's Cathedral began to lurch and sway—and the statue of Mary, Star of the Sea, placed there to protect, now threatened to crash through the ceiling and crush the people who had taken refuge beneath. The lower apartments of the rectory had already flooded, forcing Father James Kirwin and other priests and members of the household staff to move to the second floor. The cathedral and the rectory seemed about to disintegrate. Windows exploded, shooting shards of glass across the room. Cornice work tore lose and rambled down the seashell pavement like concrete tumbleweeds. Father Kirwin observed, "Slates from roofs were flying more thickly than hail and more deadly than Mauser bullets." Ironically, slate shingles had been a safety precaution mandated by city ordinances after the great fire of 1885. Now they were cutting people in half.

Through broken windows priests witnessed the tableaux of death, conscious, perhaps, that there was something almost biblical in the strength and random cruelty of the storm. A family of four, desperately trying to reach the cathedral, appeared for an instant, then vanished in the darkness. A panicking horse galloped through the surging waters of 21st Street, on a rendezvous with death. At that exact moment the wind ripped an enormous beam from a building and launched it, end over end, as casually as an Olympian might toss a baton, killing the horse in his tracks. Above the fury they could hear shotgunlike explosions as the iron bands and clasps that anchored the two-ton tower bell began to break free. A second tower at the front of the cathedral groaned, then its iron crosses toppled and crashed through the roof. Moments later the tower itself gave way and pitched forward into the racing brown torrent that used to be 21st Street. The bishop touched Father Kirwin's arm and told him; "Prepare these priests for death."

A German servant girl working in the home of W. L. Moody, Jr., was sent outside on an errand, and returned to report that the water standing in the yard tasted salty. Salty? How could that be? Then Moody began to understand, and ordered his servants to evacuate his wife and children to the home of his father, a block west on 23rd Street. The unthinkable had happened—the entire Island was covered by water. The Gulf and the bay had converged, and for the time being, Galveston was no longer an island, but merely part of the ocean floor, its houses and buildings protruding like toys in a bathtub.

By three-thirty Isaac Cline had recognized the scale of the disaster and drafted a final message to the chief of the Weather Bureau in Washington, D.C., advising him that great loss of life was imminent and the need for relief was urgent. Joseph Cline waded through waist-deep water to deliver the message to Western Union, only to discover that all the telegraph wires were down. He was able to get a telephone message through to the Western Union office in Houston, but he had no sooner delivered his report than the line went dead. Now Galveston was completely cut off from the outside world, alone with the fury of the gale and the rage of the tide.

Having done his duty, Isaac Cline left the bureau in the hands of assistants and waded nearly two miles to his home, thinking of his pregnant wife and three young daughters. Because of complications with the pregnancy, he had been unable to move his wife to a more secure place in the center of town. The wind wasn't yet constant—Cline estimated the gusts at between sixty and a hundred miles per hour—and by waiting for the lulls between gusts he was able to make headway. He had never seen anything like this: nobody on the Island had. Entire roofs were sailing through the air like discarded pages of newspaper. Timber and pieces of brick rocketed out of nowhere, splitting the paling and weatherboarding of houses. Nothing was where it had been that morning. Homes were gone. Streets had disappeared. Waves had washed wreckage against the pilings of his own home, creating a dam and backing up water to a depth of twenty feet: Cline's house was now in the center of a small lake.

Issac Cline found his family and about fifty neighbors huddled together on the second floor, frightened but apparently well. Joe Cline, who had made one last attempt to warn people to seek shelter in the city's center, arrived a few minutes later, badly shaken. "I tried to tell them that the worst was yet to come," he said. "I saw a family trying to reach the Catholic Convent, but they never made it. I saw people killed by flying debris and people drowned." Isaac began to realize that they were witnessing a sort of cataclysmic chain reaction. As buildings nearest the beach were wrecked, the wreckage was collected by winds and waves and driven against other buildings, which in turn collapsed and joined the grinding, swelling, insatiable mass. The storm was creating a battering ram of debris, mowing down everything in its path, scraping the earth clean. Soon it would be their turn.

The storm was intensifying with each minute. At five the anemometer at the weather station recorded a two-minute gust at 102 miles per hour. Fifteen minutes later the wind carried the instrument away. By six the tide was swelling at an incredible rate of 2.5 feet an hour, and the wind was shifting around to the northeast. At about seven-thirty, in a single enormous swell, the tide rose four feet in four seconds. The center of the hurricane apparently passed west of the Island between 8 and 9 P.M. By then the velocity of the wind was estimated at 120 miles per hour. The tide on the side of the Island nearest the Gulf was at least 15 feet, and breakers 25 feet or higher crashed over the beachline.

Every church, hospital, business building, or home still standing became a shelter for the homeless. Sailors tied boats to the fence in front of the Sealy mansion at 24th and Broadway, and pulled people out of the storm surge and onto the porch: more than four hundred found shelter at Open Gates that night. In a frantic effort to do what they could, against a force nobody could comprehend, workmen braced walls with beams, and nailed shut doors and windows. Holes were drilled in floors, inviting floodwaters to enter, in hopes that the water would help anchor houses and keep them from floating off. From one end of the Island to the other—in their instinctive struggle to survive for even one more minute—people committed astonishing, desperate, heroic, and sometimes foolish acts.

A nurse on duty at a home near the beach wrapped the body of a stillborn infant in a blanket, administered a sleeping potion to the helpless, pain-racked mother, and then, as the house began to disintegrate, calmly made preparation for her own escape. She put on a man's bathing suit, cut off her hair with scissors, and plunged into the sea. From eight in the evening until two in the morning, she clung to a piece of driftwood, finally washing ashore on the mainland. Naked, bleeding, and shivering in the cold rain, she found a shaggy dog and snuggled up against him until daylight.

The highest structure on the Island, the 220-foot tower above St. Patrick's Church, crashed unceremoniously into the street. But the storm was so loud nobody heard it. By seven in the evening the church was rubble. More than a thousand refugees took shelter at the Ursuline Convent and Academy, including several hundred blacks. When the north wall collapsed, the blacks began to sing and pray. "They shouted and sang in true camp-meeting style," wrote Father Kirwin, "until the nerves of the other refugees were shattered and a panic seemed imminent. Mother Superioress Joseph rang the chapel bell and caused a hush of the pandemonium. When quiet had been restored the mother addressed the negroes and told them that this was no time nor place for such scenes."

On the beach three miles west of town, the sisters of St. Mary's Orphanage herded their ninety-three children from room to room as the storm worsened. Their final refuge was the second-floor girls' dormitory. A caretaker brought a coil of clothesline from a store room, and the sisters wrapped the ropes around their own waists and then around the children's. A short time later the roof caved in, and all the nuns and all of the children except three were crushed or washed to their deaths.

When the front section of YMCA secretary Judson Palmer's house on Avenue P1/2 washed away, Palmer, his family, and fourteen others crowded into an upstairs bedroom and began to pray. Palmer's young son, Lee, prayed for the safety of his dog, Youno, and asked Jesus to "give us a pleasant day tomorrow to play." One room after another collapsed and disappeared, until all that remained was a room at the north end, part of the roof and the bathroom. As water continued to rise, Palmer and his wife and child climbed onto the edge of the bathtub. When the water reached their chins, the boy put his arms around his father's neck and asked if everything was all right. Palmer never got a chance to reply. At that moment the final section of the house gave way, hurling everyone into the roiling current. For three hours Palmer drifted on a floating shed. Eventually, he was rescued, but he never saw his wife or little Lee again. Of the fourteen neighbors who had taken refuge in the Palmer home, only one survived.

Far down the west end of the Island, Henry R. Decie, his wife, and baby boy took shelter in the home of a neighbor. The Decies were resting on the end of a bed, the baby between them, when the water began to rise "four or five feet in one bound." At that same moment a wave slammed into the side of the house and took it off its blocks. "My wife threw her arms around my neck," Decie recalled, "and kissed me and said, 'Goodbye, we are gone.'" The house shook violently, dislodging a beam that came crashing down. Decie tried to scoop his son into his arms, but the heavy timber caught the child and killed him instantly. "Another wave came," Decie said, "and swept the overhanging house off my head. I looked around and my wife was gone. Catching a piece of scantling, I held on to it and was carried thirty miles across the bay, landing near the mouth of Cow Bayou."

Though the front and rear porches of Isaac Cline's home had been smashed to sticks, the fifty refugees inside told themselves that the house was secure. Joseph Cline remembered feeling strangely calm. He kept thinking of an uncle who, alone of all those aboard a sinking ship, saved himself by hanging onto a plank and riding it five miles to shore. Around him, people were singing or praying or crying—or wandering about aimlessly, looking for some place that might give them an advantage when the end came. "I knew the house was about to collapse," Joseph Cline said, "and I told my relatives and friends to get on top of the drift and float with it."

The storm had been pounding against a quarter-mile-long section of streetcar trestle, built out over the Gulf. Suddenly, the trestle pulled loose from its mooring—rails, ties, crosspieces, and all. The storm surge and the 120-mile-per-hour winds carried a 200-foot trestle section like a scythe out of hell directly toward Isaac Cline's home. A fraction of a second before the collision, Cline felt his house move off its foundation. Then it began to topple and break apart. Cline tried to wrap his arms around his wife and six-year-old daughter, but the impact threw them into a chimney and swept the three of them beneath the wreckage, to the bottom of the water. Cline lost sight of his daughter. A dresser pinned him against a mantel, and his wife was trapped nearby, her clothing tangled among the wreckage. It's over, Cline thought. Surrendering to the inevitable, he told himself: "I have done all that could have been done in this disaster, the world will know that I did my duty to the last, it is useless to fight for life, I will let the water enter my lungs and pass on. . . ." Then he lost consciousness.

Joseph Cline had been standing near a window on the windward side. When the house began to capsize, he grabbed the hands of Isaac's other two daughters, smashed the window glass and storm shutters with his back, and let the momentum carry the three of them through the window. The building settled on its side, rocked a bit, and then rose to the surface of the floodwaters. Joe Cline and his nieces were alone on the top side of a flotilla of wreckage, momentarily safe and drifting with the tide. Rain was driving down, and pieces of timber went by like swarms of giant insects. A dim moon shone through broken clouds, making it possible for Joseph to see a short distance. Heaving masses of debris, like the one that served as their rescue ship, stretched for blocks. Cline and the two youngsters were the only humans in sight.

In a night of catastrophic losses it was impossible to separate coincidence from miracles, but there was an abundance of each. Isaac Cline regained consciousness to find himself hanging between two timbers: the wave action against the timbers had apparently pressed the water out of his lungs. There was a flash of lightning and Cline saw his youngest girl, alive and floating on the wreckage a few feet away. A short time later another flash revealed his brother and his other two daughters, still riding their raft of debris. "I took my baby and swam toward them," Isaac Cline recalled. "Strange as it may seem these children displayed no sign of fear, as we in the shadow of death did not realize what fear meant. Our only thought was how to win in this disaster."

For four hours they drifted through endless darkness and despair. Over the downpour and the wail of wind, they heard houses being crushed, and the screams of the dying. Isaac and Joseph Cline turned their backs to the wind, placing the children in front to protect them from flying debris. To shield their own own backsides, they gathered planks from the float-ing wreckage and propped them up like chairbacks. "The wind-driven debris was showering us constantly," Isaac Cline wrote. "Sometimes the blows were so strong that we would be knocked into the surging waters, but we would fight our way back to the children and con-tinue the struggle to survive."

Periodic flashes of lightning added to the surreal specter, and revealed the terrible carnage—and sometimes the approach of new danger. At one point they saw a weather-battered hulk that had once been a house, streaming in their direction, one side upreared at a forty-five-degree angle. The hulk towered six or eight feet above them, and was bearing down like a derelict freighter, crushing everything in its path. Joseph Cline retained sufficient presence of mind to leap just as the monster reached them, gaining a grip on the hulk's top edge. His weight was enough to drag it lower in the water, and with his brother's help he pulled the upper side down. They climbed on top with the children, just as the drift upon which they had been floating went to pieces under their feet.

For a time their new makeshift raft was swept out to sea, but then the wind became southerly, indicating that the storm's center was bending northward and heading inland. Gradually, they could see the lights of shore. They were drifting toward a steady point of light, and as they got closer, they realized that it was a house on solid ground. Battered and exhausted, they climbed through an upstairs window, into a room where a group of refugees were huddled. This house, they learned later, sat at the corner of 28th and Avenue P, only five blocks from where Isaac Cline's home once sat. Their journey through hell had delivered them close to the place where they started.

By midnight the storm had passed over the Island, and the tide was falling rapidly. In the backyard of the Kempner home at 16th and Avenue I, the water dropped from more than eight feet to less than six feet in the time it took Ike Kempner to swim from his back porch to the stable and back. Kempner had gone in search of his coachman, who had been sent to release two carriage horses. When the coachman failed to return, Kempner tied a rope to his belt and went looking for him. As it turned out, the coachman and horses were safe: they had found a high, dry spot on the porch of a neighbor. "After that, I needed a stiff drink," Kempner recalled. Since the flood was obviously receding, Kempner and his friend Safford Wheeler started on foot to inform their neighbors. "In our dripping clothes and shoes, we were cordially received at four or five residences. In each, we were promptly tendered refreshments, and after imbibing several we found the 'spiritual courage' to continue spreading the good news."

In high fettle, Kempner and Wheeler began to wade in chest-deep water in the direction of the Tremont Hotel, their mission being to toast the renewal of life with whoever was there. Unfortunately, they found the hotel doors locked. They rang the bell but got no response. Undeterred, the two millionaires gathered paving blocks they found floating along Tremont Street, and used them to smash hotel windows. They were so engaged when a security officer from the hotel appeared and placed them under arrest.

August Rollfing was frantic. At the peak of the storm he had stood on the counter of a store with eighty strangers, holding a small boy he had never seen before on his shoulders and praying that his own family had somehow survived. When the water began to recede, Rollfing ran toward the west end neighborhood where his mother lived. He was relieved to see her house still standing—it was the only one on the block that was—but when he got inside and asked about Louisa and his children, his mother just shook her head. "They are not here, my boy," she told him. "I haven't seen them." She begged August to wait until daylight, but he bolted out the door and disappeared into the rain.

His throat dry and his chest burning, August raced along 23rd Street in the direction of Broadway, thinking that his family might have taken shelter at his sister Julia's house. A faint moon broke through the clouds, and August saw some sort of gigantic shadow stretching across Avenue N, blocking his path. It looked like a levee, or a small mountain range, and it stretched from east to west, as far as he could see. August was nearly to the base of the shadow when he realized that what he was looking at was a monstrous wall of wreckage. It was taller than a two-story building, and six to eight blocks wide. It started at the Flats on the far east end of the Island and ran all the way to 45th Street. In its relentless, grinding fashion the battering ram that Isaac Cline described had rumbled across 1,500 acres of the Island, finally playing itself out against a break-water of its own creation.

August Rollfing stood looking up at this grotesque monument to death, trying to comprehend. "It seemed endless," he said. "House upon house, all broken to pieces, furniture, sewing machines, pianos, cats, dogs . . . and what was underneath? How many people had gone down with their houses? And behind the wall of debris, nothing! Absolutely nothing! The ground was as clear as if it had been swept, not even a little stick of wood. For blocks and blocks, nothing, and then that terrible pile of debris . . . and what was in and under it."

By the time August Rollfing reached his sister's home, the rain had almost stopped and a fresh breeze was whipping straight out of the south. In a few hours it would be light. Julia's home was still standing, more or less. There was a twenty-foot hole in one wall where the kitchen had broken loose, and the house had been lifted off its brick pillars on two sides so that it leaned like a house in a child's drawing. When August saw that his wife and children were safe and well, he collapsed in a heap on the stairway.

Sunday morning was a scene out of hell, played against a brilliant blue sky and a drowsy sea. At low tide the Gulf seemed as peaceful as a sleeping teenager, spent and unaware of its night of murderous violence. Small groups of people began to appear in the streets, tentative at first, as though they didn't want to disturb anything. Bruised and stunned, wet and chilled to the bone, they stumbled about, trying to assimilate the scope of this tragedy.

Those who had stoves and chimneys standing did what they could to cook breakfast. Others looked for dry wood. The entire Island was water-logged and covered with an inch-thick layer of foul-smelling slime. Still others dared to survey the damage. It was worse than anyone imagined—far worse. In the blackest hour no one had conjured up a vision like the one that spread before the survivors this Sunday morning. One-third of the Island was scraped clean, and the other two-thirds battered almost beyond recognition. In the Sunday morning stillness people climbed on top of the debris and looked around. They heard faint cries from people buried alive. At first, their impulse was to attempt rescues, digging with their bare hands or whatever tool they could find, but it was hopeless. No human effort could alter the inevitable or limit the final suffering of those who were trapped and waiting to die.

A more urgent concern was aiding the injured and homeless. There wasn't a building on the Island that escaped damage. More than 3,600 houses were totally destroyed, as were hundreds of buildings and institutions. Like an avenging angel on a special mission, the storm had been coldly selective in its choice of targets. Sacred Heart Catholic Church was in ruins, while just across 14th Street the mansion of Walter Gresham had escaped with only damage from the high water. The fourth floor of the Moody Building was gone, sheared away as though by a giant knife. St. Mary's Cathedral was nearly destroyed, but miraculously the tower that Nicholas Clayton built survived, and Mary, Star of the Sea, continued to stand watch. The east wall of the Opera House had collapsed, and the interior was coated with slime the consistency of axle grease. Except for a few scattered bricks, there was no trace of St. Mary's Orphanage. Railroad tracks were buried or twisted into hideous forms, trees uprooted, telephone poles flattened, streets and sidewalks buckled or washed away, wires ripped loose, gas and electric lines ruptured, sewers plugged with vegetable, animal, and human remains. Huge oceangoing ships had torn loose from their ropes and cables and had been swept across the bay and deposited on the mainland. The British steamship *Taunton* was carried from its anchorage at the mouth of the ship channel to a thirty-foot bank at Cedar Point, twenty-two miles from deep water. Household items, clothing, trade goods, machinery, almost every material possession that wasn't stored higher than fifteen feet was saturated with salt water and scum, and either ruined or badly damaged. Weeks and even months later, bicycles that seemed no worse for the experience suddenly fell apart, rusted from the inside.

There were so many bodies that after a while the senses numbed, and the corpses seemed to be merely some sort of demented design. They were heaped together in the streets, strewn across vacant lots, sticking from mounds of wreckage, floating in shallow pools of water, scattered along the beach, bobbing in the filthy backwash of the bay. Most were naked, mutilated, and dashed beyond recognition. They hung like macabre ornaments from trees, trestles, and telephone poles. One observer counted forty-three bodies dangling from the framework of a partially demolished railroad bridge. The horror and the unspeakable suffering of the victims' final moments were often preserved in ghastly frescoes of death. The body of twelve-year-old Scott McCloskey, son of a sea captain, was found with his left arm shattered, his right arm still wrapped protectively around the body of his younger brother. A woman, her long blond hair entangled in barbed wire, reached back in death as though to disengage it. Miles down the beach from the orphans' home, the bodies of a nun and nine children, still tied together with clothesline, lay half-buried in sand and seaweed.

For days survivors continued to search among the ruins, hoping to find some trace of loved ones. Most of the dead were so badly battered they couldn't be identified. Father Kirwin, who had waited out the storm in St. Mary's Cathedral, told of seeing a man going from corpse to corpse, looking into their mouths, hoping to recognize his wife's bridgework. Twenty days after the storm Isaac Cline found the body of his wife, under the wreckage that had carried the rest of her family to safety. He knew it was she because of her diamond engagement ring.

Late Sunday morning Mayor Walter Jones called an emergency meeting at the Tremont Hotel. Most of the city's leading citizens were there—Ike Kempner, John Sealy, Rabbi Henry Cohen, members of the Deep Water Committee. Not a single department of city government was functioning, so the mayor appointed these men to an ad hoc Central Relief Committee, with the power to do whatever they believed necessary. Looters were already roaming the Island, stripping the dead and ransacking shops, banks, and warehouses. The mayor declared martial law, and local militiamen were ordered to shoot looters on sight. By one account as many as seventy-five "ghouls" were summarily gunned down.

The Central Relief Committee in effect assumed the monumental job of governing the Island for the duration of the emergency. There was no communication with the mainland, except by boat. The three railroad bridges and the wagon bridge had been destroyed. The only city-owned craft afloat that could navigate the shallow waters of the bay was a twenty-foot steam launch, and even that was badly battered. Nevertheless, a crew and messengers volunteered. After a perilous journey across the bay, they scrambled ashore at Texas City, ten miles to the north, and made their way overland, across a flooded prairie littered with debris and corpses. At a railroad they found a handcar and pumped along the tracks for fifteen miles until they met a train that took them to Houston. The journey took sixteen hours.

The committee decided that every able-bodied man would be required to work on cleanup squads. Everything had to be rationed—food, medicine, water, transportation. Commissaries were set up in each of Galveston's twelve wards, dispensing supplies to those with no money. Hotels and restaurants accommodated all who applied, with or without money, and shop owners handed out canned goods as long as their supplies lasted. Galveston got its water from artesian wells eighteen miles from the city, and though the thirty-six-inch main under the bay survived the storm, the pumping station did not. Most residences still retained cisterns from the old days, but only a few were positioned high enough to escape contamination. It was almost a week before the pumping station was repaired, and in the meantime supplies of water came from these few cisterns, and from water barrels shipped from the mainland.

The homeless took refuge anywhere they could—in the train station, at city hall, in commercial buildings, in warehouses, in hotels and private homes. Saloons, gambling halls, and whore-houses were either closed or turned into temporary shelters. Churches that were still standing welcomed worshipers from those that were not: four Protestant denominations worshiped in Rabbi Cohen's temple. Most Islanders willingly opened their homes and shared what they had. But when the relief committee asked W. L. Moody, Jr., to take in a group of orphans, he refused. "We had no place for them," his daughter Mary explained later. "We had no water, no food. We couldn't take care of orphans. It would have been impossible." Will Moody, Jr., and his family had waited out the worst of the storm in his father's mansion. The colonel and his wife were in New York at the time—it was Moody company policy that Will Junior and his father couldn't both be off the Island at the same time. Moody did permit the relief committee to use his father's yacht, but only after his wife and daughter had been ferried safely to the mainland.

At first, the number of dead was estimated to be no more than five hundred, and some members of the relief committee insisted on the legal formality of a coroner's inquest. By Monday morning, however, that suggestion was dismissed as ludicrous. The death count was running into the thousands. Funeral homes and improvised morgues were already overflowing with corpses uncomfortably close to putrefaction. Work crews attempting to load bodies on carts reported that the corpses were falling to pieces. The only solution, it became apparent, was immediate and wholesale burial at sea. All day Monday and Tuesday carts and wagons full of corpses plodded along the ravaged streets of Galveston, in the direction of the wharves, arms and legs protruding under tarpaulins. The job of loading the bodies onto barges and taking them to sea was so abhorrent that recruits had to be rounded up at bayonet point and plied with whiskey. "An armed guard brought fifty negroes to the barges and went on with them," wrote Father Kirwin, who had helped supply whiskey to the white volunteers. "The barges were taken out into the Gulf and remained there all night, until it was light enough for the negroes to fasten the weights and throw the bodies overboard. When the barges returned those negroes were ashen in color."

Two days later Father Kirwin's face was similarly ashen. A member of his congregation came to the cathedral and told the priest: "My mother-in-law is back." "That's impossible!" said Father Kirwin, reminding the man that they had dumped his mother-in-law's weighted body eighteen miles out to sea. But she *was* back, as were the bodies of hundreds of others: they had washed up on the beach overnight. The committee had to rethink its strategy. Since it was no longer possible to haul decaying bodies through the streets, the committee decided to burn corpses on the spot. The bodies, and the mountain of debris created by the storm's battering ram, were burned in sections. From one end of the Island to the other, funeral pyres burned night and day: at night you could see their glow from the mainland. No one alive during that terrible time would ever forget the sight, or the smell.

In her report to the Red Cross, a volunteer named Fanny B. Ward recorded a conversation with a custodian of one of the bonfires.

"This here fire's been going on more than a month," the fireman told Miss Ward. "To my knowledge, upwards of sixty bodies have been burned in it—to say nothing of dogs, cats, hens, and three cows."

"What is in there now?" she asked.

"Well, it takes a corpse several days to burn all up. I reckon there's a couple of dozen of them— just bones, you know—down near the bottom. Yesterday we put seven on top of this pile, and by now they are only what you might call baked. Today we have been working over there (pointing to other fires a quarter of a mile way) where we found a lot of them, eleven under one house. We have put only two in here today. Found them just now, right in that puddle."

"Could you tell me who they are?"

"Lord no," he said. "We don't look at them any more than we have to, else we'd been dead ourselves before today. One of these was a colored man. They are all pretty black now, but you can tell them by the kinky hair. He had on nothing but an undershirt and one shoe. The other was a woman; young, I reckon. At any rate, she was tall and slim and had lots of long brown hair. She wore a blue silk skirt and there was a rope tied around her waist, as if somebody had tried to save her."

With a long pole the fireman poked an air hole near the center of the smoulder heap, and Fanny Ward stepped back from the unearthly smell and took a new position windward. Sparks showered the ground, leaving bits of bone and singed hair. She stooped and picked up a curling yellow lock, tears in her eyes as she wondered what mother's hand had lately caressed it.

"That's nothing," remarked the fireman. "The other day we found part of a brass chandelier, and wound all around it was a perfect mop of long, silky hair—with a piece of skin, big as your two hands, at the end of it. Some woman got tangled up that way in the flood and just naturally scalped."

No one would ever know for certain how many Islanders died, but the most reliable estimate was somewhere between six and seven thousand. Since the population of the city in 1900 was 37,700, that meant that in the hours between Saturday afternoon and Sunday morning one out of every six citizens of Galveston perished. Thousands more were killed on the mainland. The storm was recorded as the worst disaster in the history of the United States. An article a month later in the *National Geographic* described Galveston as "a scene of suffering and devastation hardly paralleled in the history of the world."

One reason the death count was so inexact was the massive migration that followed the storm. In the immediate aftermath people were playing huge sums for boat passage to the mainland. Once rail service was restored, railroads gave victims free transportation anywhere in the United States, and hundreds of families took advantage of it. Many never returned. So great was their suffering and grief—so terrible the memory of that night—that they didn't even bother to go back for their possessions, or to look for or bury their dead.

Many predicted that the city would never be rebuilt, or if it was rebuilt, it would be relocated on the mainland. But Joseph Cline reminded skeptics that Galveston was the only city on the Gulf west of New Orleans. "Commerce always takes precedence over life," Cline said. He was right. Within eleven days one of the railroad bridges across the bay had been repaired, and rail service restored. There was talk of a new causeway, ten feet higher than before. Repairs and extensions to the wharves were pushed forward. Saloons, gambling joints, and whorehouses reopened. The streets hadn't yet been been cleared of the dead, but already the electric trolley was running again. Cotton arrived by rail and barge, was processed, and then loaded aboard oceangoing ships. On October 14, 30,300 bales cleared port.

When Will Moody, Jr., told the colonel that people were leaving the Island and that business was bound to suffer, the colonel uttered one of the best-known and most cynical remarks in Galveston lore. "Good," he declared. "Remember, we both love to hunt and fish. The fewer people on the Island, the better the hunting and fishing will be for us."

The colonel was speaking metaphorically. The Island would recover—there was no doubt about that—and in the meantime it was a buyer's market. Property values had dropped drastically. Indeed, prospects for hunting and fishing hadn't been this good since Samuel May Williams and other founders of the original Galveston City Company began dividing up the Island in 1838. The colonel returned from New York convinced that the eastern press had greatly exaggerated the damage done by the storm—he'd even brought a stack of newspapers to show his son—but when he saw with his own eyes that the devastation was even worse than reported, the Moody Family made plans accordingly. Two weeks after the hurricane, Will Moody, Jr., purchased a thirty-room mansion at 2618 Broadway, for ten cents on the dollar.

The Western Front, October 13–30, 1918

GREGORY W. BALL

Military scholar Gregory W. Ball serves as Command Historian for the 24th Air Force in San Antonio. In addition to *They Called Them Soldier Boys: A Texas Infantry Regiment in World War I* (2013), he contributed an article on the Denton County draft during the Great War to *This Corner of Canaan: Essays in Honor of Randolph B. Campbell* (2013), edited by Richard B. McCaslin, Donald E. Chipman, and Andrew J. Torget.

World War I was a significant event in the lives of Texans, many of whom served courageously in the armed forces. In this selection, Dr. Ball discusses the combat experiences of the 142nd Infantry, 36th Division, during the Champagne Offensive in France. ✧

★ ★

As the 142d Infantry filtered into the lines on the night of October 13, 1918, they were certainly not aware that in several weeks they would have to attack such a strongly fortified position as Forest Farm. Lieutenant Sayles' weapons platoon dug in on the side of a hill and managed to bring up straw from Vaux to line their holes. Several soldiers also found doors to use as roofs over their fox holes, but it turned out they had taken the doors from regimental headquarters and Sayles ordered them to return them. For the most part, the soldiers waited and tried to stay comfortable and warm. Whenever he went to sleep, Sayles wrapped his scarf around his stomach and wrapped his feet in a rain slicker and slept in the same hole as another man so they could keep each other warm. Over the next several days, Sayles's platoon dug a "long gallery" into the side of the hill, covered the floor with straw, used branches to keep the sides from caving in, and created an "arbor" that kept some of the rain out, although the "roof always dripped somewhere, and little rivulets broke out under the deep mat of fallen leaves that covered the ground." The dugout was large enough to hold half of his platoon, who would crowd into the dugout to eat. At the top of the hill, above their "gallery," he placed two 37mm cannon, ready to fire across the river on German positions to the north. Not everyone had it so great, as part of Company I dug into an area that was "so flat it was nearly a lake," and the soldiers lived "in the slush," trying to keep the rain away with half tents stretched over their holes, and covered the bottoms of their holes with blankets and overcoats scrounged from dead Germans. Still, as one man commented, "Everything oozed water."

Sometimes the men ate well. Occasionally, field kitchens got them a hot stew of dried potatoes and carrots mixed with corned beef, and infrequently they received sugar, which they ate on bread and considered a "rare delicacy." As for the bread, Lieutenant Sayles recalled that each loaf had the date stamped on it and that it was so tough it could be stockpiled, covered with a tarpaulin, and last for days. As he recalled, the bread "always tasted good when it could be dried out over a fire," and it was "fine with jam." Besides eating the bread, some soldiers found creative uses for it, such as sticking it on their bayonets when marching, calling it a "practical method for carrying the dishpan sized hunk of fodder," and that "it also would keep rain drops out of" rifles. Other foods the soldiers devoured included condensed milk on bread and "oleomargarine cut in thick slabs which was eaten like cheese." Just as often, the food did not keep warm on its way to the front and the men received cold coffee and stew which congealed into "a solid mass with a hard layer of grease on top."

When the regiment moved into the line south of the Aisne River, the front stabilized and the four regiments of the division dug in. General Smith organized the 36th Division's lines into an outpost zone, a support zone, and a reserve zone. Within each regimental sector, one battalion held the outpost and support zone, and the other two battalions occupied the reserve zone. The battalion in the outpost and support zone pushed forward listening posts and patrols into the outpost zone which extended five kilometers from the Aisne River and back. Despite the static nature of the front, combat continued. From October 14 through October 26, the 142d stayed in front of the Aisne River, trying to get a feel for the enemy, who posted snipers in Attigny and remained in force north of the river. Cloudy and cold weather prevailed and it rained more often than not. The rain and fog often reduced visibility and made it difficult to detect enemy movements. The regiment's daily operations report frequently described the gloomy weather during the last two weeks of October using terms such as, "very dark and rainy," "raining," and "dark and cloudy, observation poor." Indeed, during this period on the front the regiment reported only two periods of clear weather, October 18 and October 23–25. There were, however, things much more dangerous than the weather.

Artillery fire remained a constant threat. For example, out of thirty-seven operations reports filed during the period October 16 to October 27, twenty-four reported enemy artillery fire somewhere in the regiment's sector. Sometimes reported as light or "desultory" fire without a particular target, such as "occasional shells fell in Attigny between 17:30 and 18:30 o'clock," or "harassing fire on Vaux and advanced positions," at other times the shelling was more purposeful, such as on October 17, when German observers may have spotted American soldiers "attempting to reach a station in church steeple at Attigny," and brought down high explosive shells on the area. By October 25, artillery barrages were so commonplace that the operations report considered 100 high explosive shells falling in the area to be "light," although on October 27, the commander's younger brother and operations officer Captain Bertram Bloor reported that nearly 200 shells fell in the regimental area. Finally, there existed the danger of being shelled by gas. On the afternoon of October 25, the enemy shelled the regiment's support battalion with high explosives and mustard gas. The attack lasted into the evening, and when the shelling ended, regimental personnel estimated 2,000 shells had impacted the area. Still, soldiers seemed to handle the gas situation calmly as Captain Bloor reported that "when these shells land near positions the men move away from it. The general dispersion of gas is not strong and continued wearing of gas masks in not necessary." Nevertheless, the next day 100 rounds of mustard gas fell around the village of Mery during a twenty-four-hour period resulting in thirty-two "inhalation" casualties. While artillery was a constant danger, the regiment also exchanged sniper and machine-gun fire with their adversaries across the river.

On the morning of October 16, a German sniped fired on a regimental patrol, land the next day, Captain Bloor reported "enemy snipers were active this morning, the least exposure of members of our patrol bringing shots. Snipers still located on strip of land between canal and river" referencing a canal that paralleled the Aisne River. On October 24, he again reported that "enemy snipers are very active along front" and reported that "owing to the bright moonlight and clear days action above ground north of Chufilly is practically prohibited. Small parties using cover move at night." Captain Bloor concluded his report with "our snipers returning fire shot for shot." By October 26, Captain Bloor noted that "enemy activity decreased to practically nothing during the night," although American snipers remained active. Lieutenant Sayles and his 37mm cannon also sought targets, at one point firing thirty-two rounds at an enemy strong point which succeeded in reducing the enemy machine-gun fire from that location. Of course, with such threats, it remained very dangerous for soldiers to be seen out in the open, although during this two-week period the regiment could not afford to simply wait and watch. It had to gather intelligence, and did so by sending out patrols.

For example, on October 17, a small patrol of one officer and three men crossed the Aisne River at 8:30 pm, and took two prisoners in a clump of woods to the north. The Germans resisted being captured, so the patrol opened fire, wounding one. Tearing that the firing had disclosed their location, the patrol hustled back across the river with the two prisoners. Later the same evening, the regiment sent out another patrol, although it could not cross the river because of a "lack of facilities to cross." The patrol then came under "heavy artillery fire" and retreated. In another instance, a patrol advanced to the Attigny canal because of reports of moving trucks.

When the patrol got close to the river, they realized the truck sounds were coming from the north side of the river but could not determine the purpose of the movement. Other patrols tested the enemy's defenses, such as one that approached the bridges crossing the Aisne River only to report that the "bridge sites remain covered by enemy machine guns and snipers." Such patrols were obviously dangerous and stressful to those who went on them. In one case, Lieutenant Sayles sat in regimental headquarters when a lieutenant returned from a patrol in which he lost three men. The lieutenant came in "wet, muddy, and blubbering," and after explaining what had happened to his patrol, began to cry.

In another instance, on October 14, a patrol moved toward the town but during their approach came under fire. One of the men, Sergeant Ormsby, was wounded by a sniper and could not walk. The patrol leader, Sgt. Charles Lydell, normally in charge of the 1st Battalion intelligence section, placed Ormsby in a protected area and made his way back to Vaux Champagne for help. Lydell managed to convince an ambulance to return to the town with him to get the wounded Ormsby. The ambulance made it part way before the shelling became so intense that the driver turned back to Vaux Champagne. Sergeant Lydell then approached Colonel Bloor and asked him to provide a detail of men to help him get Ormsby out of the town. Because of the artillery fire, Bloor believed he was not justified in endangering a group of men to rescue one wounded soldier, and declined to provide the detail. However, he offered Lydell the use of his motorcycle and sidecar, which the intelligence sergeant accepted. The motorcycle driver, Jesse Morrison, agreed to the mission. Under constant artillery and machine-gun fire, the men dashed into the town on the motorcycle, put the wounded Ormsby in the sidecar, and got him back to Vaux Champagne.

On October 19 and 20, the regiment made efforts to improve its positions, sending out numerous patrols in their sector in order to get a better feel for the ground to strengthen their own positions "for defensive action." On October 21, however, the regiment received word from division headquarters that the enemy "had evacuated the territory to our front." Although Colonel Bloor disagreed, he nevertheless ordered two patrols to "gain contact with the enemy." Neither patrol advanced very far. One made it seventy-five meters beyond the river crossing before it was "fired upon by machine guns and snipers." Two men were wounded, and the patrol sought cover. The second patrol fared even worse, being stopped by enemy fire as soon as it crossed the river. After both of these patrols returned south of the river, a third patrol went out. This patrol, consisting of a corporal and three men, reached the river and attempted to cross a German foot bridge. In the attempt they were fired on and "rushed by about twenty-five or thirty infantrymen." The Germans captured three of the four, and the last escaped by swimming the canal. Finally, two officers, Major Nelson and Captain Barth, took a motorcycle and sidecar in broad daylight and "under direct enemy observation" into the town to verify the enemy remained north of the river and had not withdrawn. Under artillery and machine-gun fire, the two officers moved by foot to the canal, having already accomplished their mission. They were back at the regimental command post in one hour. In the operations report's section titled "general impression of the day," Captain Bloor laconically observed that "enemy is still holding river bank to the north of our sector with a number of machine guns and probably one hundred infantrymen. It is inadvisable to attempt to patrol strip of land between canal and river without considerable artillery support." Indeed, as if to prove that the Germa̶ area, the next night soldiers spotted a patrol estimated at fifty Germans crossi̶ several flares were shot from the general location of the German patrol but ̶

Patrols also went out to maintain liaison with units to the right and left. T̶ the 141st and the 142d was about 1,200 yards, and only the 142d patrolle̶ friendly fire accidents. However, Captain Bertram Bloor believed this g̶ isfactory" and worried that Germans could easily infiltrate the area: "̶ us," he wrote, referring to the 141st Infantry. The situation along the front rema̶ made worse because of rumors passing back and forth from division to regiments. Soldiers on the front saw and heard unusual things. For example, Lieutenant Sayles awoke one night to the sound of music. At first he believed he was dreaming, but other members of his platoon heard it as well. The last thing he remembered before falling back to sleep was "the sound of the liveliest tunes coming clearly through the cold night air." One night, men at sniper posts reported "a great deal of talking, barking of dogs and noise of motor trucks" across the river, and at one point a fire of unknown origin burned in front of the lines. Finally, a soldier in an observation post saw a "brilliant light" opposite his position, and had no idea what it was. However, intelligence officers believed it might have been a "projector gas attack." Captain Bloor also expressed concern about officers visiting front line positions. Apparently, officers occasionally approached front line positions by "observed routes" which brought enemy shells crashing down. In one day, for example, the regiment lost five men wounded and one man killed after receiving an estimated 2,000 shells, including 100 that fell on an "unimproved road" near Company M's position, perhaps brought on by an unwary officer.

The period from October 14 to October 27 in front of Attigny and the Aisne River passed in a dangerous, wet, and cold haze for many of the regiment's soldiers, and many felt the stress of their position. Lieutenant Sayles often surveyed the area around the village of Voncq to the north. Because of its elevation, the village served as a prime area for German artillery observers. Sayles nervously and constantly watched the area through his binoculars and although he never saw movement, he knew the "Germans were there and no doubt watching us with more powerful glasses, and possessing more information of us than we had of them."

Toward the last week in October, however, things began to change. While senior officers discussed the best ways of attacking across the Aisne River, the French and Americans agreed they needed to take the horseshoe bend area south of the river. French units had earlier attacked Forest Farm twice, only to be repulsed with heavy losses. Now Whitworth's 71st Brigade sat directly across from the bend, and on October 24 word arrived from the French XI Corps, to which the division was now assigned, that the Forest Farm area would again be attacked, this time by General Whitworth's brigade. The men of the old 7th Texas who still remained with the regiment would be among those who found themselves preparing to go "over the top" once more.

On October 24, 1918, General Whitworth submitted his plan for the capture of Forest Farm. In his memorandum, titled "preparation for minor offensive," Whitworth stressed a massive artillery preparation, followed by a frontal assault, in which the "infantry should go over the ack formation, using the lanes cut through the wire by the artillery and such other gs as they may be able to make by wire-cutters the night before the attack." Although xperience with tanks had not turned out well at Saint Etienne, General Whitworth suggested that five or six light tanks could crush the barbed wire and aid in "destroying machine gun nests." Also, and perhaps most importantly, General Whitworth pointed out that to take the Forest Farm position, the town of Voncq, situated northeast of the horseshoe bend on a slight hill that commanded the area, had to be taken or else enemy artillery could devastate the attackers. Finally, if they were not careful, German troops in Attigny would be able to fire into the left flank of the attacking soldiers and present significant problems. In other words, the Forest Farm operation required advanced planning and preparation and had the potential to turn into a disaster, such as had occurred with the previous two attacks. To succeed, the 141st and 142d Infantry would have to overcome severe obstacles, and the soldiers were well aware of the failure of the French to capture the position several weeks earlier. Indeed, several of Whitworth's points so concerned General Smith that he wrote a letter to the commanding general of XI Corps, stating several objections to the attack, primarily that the area would be subject to enfilade fire from the north bank of the Attigny and second that the brigade was scheduled for relief immediately after the attack. General Smith believed that could cause problems in evacuating casualties, collecting the dead, and getting the brigade to its assigned area in the rear. Despite the formal protest, the French Corps commander, General Prax, ordered the attack to proceed, and division historian Captain Spence later wrote that "no satisfactory reason for the attack was ever received." General Prax wrote to General Smith: "It will succeed, and will thus give to the brave American troops that I have the honor to have under my command, the occasion of a glorious victory, which will be the crowning of their participation in the great battle of CHAMPAGNE in 1918."

Because of the possibility that the attack could go badly, General Smith wanted to ensure that the preparations for the attack went undetected. Indeed, General Smith and his commanders knew that the Germans tapped into the division's telephone wires and listened to their communications. As Colonel Bloor wrote after the armistice, "There was every reason to believe every decipherable message or word going over our wires also went to the enemy." In fact, at one point the division tested the theory by passing along false coordinates of an imaginary supply dump on the telephone, and in thirty minutes "enemy shells were falling on the point." While it is not clear who thought of the idea, the regiment's officers concluded that they might have a significant advantage over the Germans by using Choctaw Indians from the old 1st Oklahoma Infantry to transmit messages. According to Colonel Bloor, "There was hardly one chance in a million that Fritz would be able to translate these dialects, and the plan to have these Indians transmit telephone messages was adopted." The regiment successfully tested the process on October 26 and then used Choctaw soldiers to relay messages during the assault on October 27.

To lead the attack, Colonel Bloor selected an officer who had been in the thick of the fighting around Saint Etienne and an original member of the 7th Texas, Capt. Steve Lillard. Still with 3rd Battalion, Lillard spent several days in divisional reserve after the fighting around Saint Etienne while the 72d Brigade continued the advance to Attigny. On October 22, Lillard's battalion went into the line near the village of Roche, near the southeastern edge of the Forest

Farm horseshoe bend and just across the river from Voncq where the Germans maintained observation of the surrounding countryside. On October 25, Lillard assumed command of the battalion. The battalion was to be relieved after four days in the outpost and supporting zones. The next day, after reporting to Colonel Bloor's command post, he learned of the upcoming attack. According to Captain Spence, Lillard asked permission to lead the assault because his troops were familiar with the enemy positions and the ground they would cover. Bloor granted the request and selected Lillard's battalion to lead the attack on the twenty-seventh.

The final plan called for the 141st and 142d Infantry to assault Forest Farm. In the 142d's zone Lillard's 3rd Battalion led the assault. The battalion included Company I under Lt. Rudolph Fried, Company M under Lt. John Douglas, Company M under Lt. Verne Hillock, while Company L under Lt. Alvin Leubke remained in support. The command arrangements illustrated the regiment's casualties: not one of the assault companies was led by a captain, the normal rank of a company commander. Of the three companies in the assault battalion commanded recently by members of the old 7th Texas, only Lillard was available for the assault. However, there were other 7th Texas officers, including Lt. Nat Perrine, Lieutenant Sayles, who had just found out he had been promoted to captain, and the Stokes mortar platoon commander, Lt. George O. Thompson.

The assault battalion had several days to observe the enemy positions around Forest Farm, and with adequate planning and preparation, Lillard's battalion was ready. As Lillard later wrote, "we had had 24 hours advance notice of this attack, with maps and definite orders. Every man in the organization knew just what he was going to do." Lillard also stressed the cooperation of senior commanders and plenty of artillery support. Such circumstances, he believed, "made it impossible for anything but success." Finally, on October 27, 1918, a day that began clear and sunny, the remaining members of the old 7th Texas waited to go "over the top" across muddy fields and into the teeth of the German main line of resistance blocking the horseshoe bend of the Aisne River.

Lillard's soldiers knew that the enemy barbed wire was thick, the strong points covered by at least three belts of wire that were twelve yards wide, while other areas were blocked by one or two layers of wire. The front itself was approximately two kilometers wide. To overcome those obstacles, Bloor assigned engineers to Lillard's battalion who would advance with the infantry. Lillard's men also knew that the main objective was the trench line cutting across the horseshoe bend. The attack was scheduled to begin with an artillery preparation at 4:00 pm followed by the assault battalions of both regiments moving out at 4:30 pm. As the men waited through the day, the clear skies gave way to clouds and rain. The soldiers ate their usual meal of bread, beans, and coffee several hours before the attack. Somewhere along the line, two soldiers of Company I, Ira Shockley and Sgt. Albert Robinson, talked over the coming battle. Robinson, who had been on duty for the previous four days and four nights, told Shockley that this would be his last battle "for I expect to get killed today." Soon, a lone gun of the 2d Field Artillery Regiment signaled the start of the artillery barrage on the enemy strong points. The Stokes mortars fired on the enemy trenches and tried to cut the belts of barbed wire, a smoke screen was laid, and other artillery units fired barrages against Voncq, Attigny, and north of the Aisne River in an effort to disrupt German observation areas and destroy machine-gun nests which could fire across the river at Lillard's attacking soldiers. Close to the assault battalion, Lieutenant Sayles's 37mm cannons "were firing as fast as they could be loaded." Sayles saw the engineers pass him by with "rifles slung, each man carrying a pair of long-handled wire-cutters."

At 4:30 pm Lillard's battalion moved out and discovered that the artillery preparation had not only cut the barbed wire but succeeded in keeping the enemy in their dugouts. Although the enemy attempted a counter barrage, it did not stop Lillard's men, who moved forward in a "single line of skirmishers" armed with "rifles, Browning Automatic Rifles, pistols, trench knives [and] grenades." Lillard's attackers stayed close behind the rolling barrage, advanced quickly through the wire, and were waiting for the Germans as they began to come out of their dugouts. As the enemy scrambled to man their weapons, Lillard's men either captured or shot them. Lieutenant Sayles recalled the sound of Browning Automatic Rifles firing from the front as he advanced with his cannons, while "machine gun bullets were still cracking overhead" from an American machine gun barrage. Indeed, Sayles believed the sound of the bullets was so close overhead that it "caused many a man to hesitate at first, thinking that he was being fired on by the enemy." The soldiers did not hesitate for long but continued the advance. A shell hit near Sayles, knocking him down and blowing his helmet off. He managed to get back to his feet and continued to direct his platoon. Lt. Nat Perrine, with a platoon of about twenty-eight men, continued to advance and captured a trench. His leadership that day earned him a promotion to captain. Sergeant Albert Robinson, who expected to meet death that day, instead kept his platoon so close to the rolling barrage that they captured a German machine-gun nest before the soldiers could get their guns into action. He survived the day and was recommended for the Distinguished Service Cross.

Less than an hour later, it was over. The attack had gone off almost without a hitch. The only major mistake occurred to Company M, whose men scattered for cover after they ran into their own rolling barrage when it inadvertently fell short of its intended target. Otherwise, the regiment overran the main German line in about forty-five minutes. Lillard's men entered 16 German dugouts and captured 109 prisoners from the 3d Prussian Guard Division, most of whom they captured "as they came out of dug outs and trenches," after the artillery barrage passed. The Germans "seemed to be glad to be taken prisoners and offered no resistance." The attackers also captured German equipment, including twenty-one examples of the Maxim machine gun, known as the "Devil's Paintbrush."

Once Lillard's men captured the German positions, two patrols advanced to the river and rounded up twenty-seven more prisoners. The patrols also reported signs of "enemy confusion" along the north bank. Lillard brought machine guns up for support in case of a counterattack, and mopping up parties "threw grenades into dugouts and trenches, doing excellent work." Captain Lillard wrote that by 6:00 pm, maps had been drawn showing the location of all friendly troops and by 9:00 pm Lieutenant Hillock passed word that "our line would withstand any counter attack of the enemy's, should he dare to make one."

Although the operation went smoothly, it was not without cost to the 141st and 142d regiments. The initial reports estimated that the 142d killed forty Germans in the assault while suffering eight killed and twenty wounded. In total the two regiments lost eleven men killed and thirty-six wounded. Several members of the old 7th Texas lost their lives at Forest Farm, including Pvt. Oscar Fry of Company K, who was knocked down by an artillery shell. Corporal Hart, who was thrown in the air by the same shell, asked Fry if he were hurt and Fry replied that he was not. Hart urged him to keep moving, but Fry "kindly laughed and said that he couldn't go any farther." Hart left him behind and kept on. He later learned that "the shock of the explosion" killed Fry. A sniper shot another Company K veteran, Cpl. Bruce Cobb, in the chest, although one of his fellow soldiers, Pvt. Robert Lynch, saw the sniper's location and shot him in return. Company M lost Pvt. Will C. Curtis at Forest Farm as well. Curtis was struck in the right temple by a large shell and sank slowly to the ground without uttering a word. While they were perhaps grateful for the minimum number of casualties, the violent deaths that some of their comrades suffered weighed heavily on the survivors' minds.

In the operations report prepared after the battle, Capt. Bertram Bloor wrote that "operations were carried out exactly as planned. The plan was good. The morale of the men was good . . . The operation was not difficult." At least one officer of the regiment, Capt. Rudolph E. Fried, believed that much of the credit belonged to Captain Lillard. In written observations shortly after the battle, Fried pointed out that when Lillard took command of the 3rd Battalion, all "confusion ceased and from that time on until we were relieved the battalion functioned as smoothly as a well trained organization would at home in peace times." According to Fried, this occurred because Lillard inspired "mutual confidence between battalion and companies," something that arguably only the commander could instill, and Corporal Hart believed that Captain Lillard was as popular in Company K as he was in his own company. Nevertheless, Captain Lillard could not keep the men from hunting for souvenirs as they settled into their new positions that night. Officers engaged in souvenir hunting as well, as Lieutenant Sayles found a heavy cane he believed would help him navigate shell holes as well as a pair of green cloth mittens and a "knitted bellyband" that he wore on his head and over his ears.

On October 28, the Germans began shelling the regiment's position in the horseshoe bend, but it was "without material effect." More importantly for the soldiers, however, they knew that their time in the line was coming to an end. Following a plan developed prior to the attack on Forest Farm, French troops relieved the 1st Battalion, in brigade reserve, and the 2d Battalion, in regimental reserve, on October 28. Both battalions marched south toward Somme-Py, where three weeks earlier they had arrived as inexperienced troops awaiting their first combat experience. However, in accordance with the plan of relief, Lillard's 3rd Battalion remained in position in the horseshoe of the Aisne River for an extra day. This did not sit well with Captain Lillard, who later wrote that "all of our supporting troops, including the artillery were withdrawn and we were left to the mercy of the German artillery with French infantry to support us and with French artillery to give excuses for not firing when we called upon them to do so." The Germans shelled the 3rd Battalion all day on October 28 and into the early morning hours of October 29. While waiting to be relieved, Sayles studied the terrain behind him, trying to memorize it so he would be able to lead his platoon out that night. The stress of waiting for relief increased as each round fell. Every time he heard a shell on its way in, Sayles closed his eyes "so tightly that the sound was partly drowned out." After the shell exploded, he "relaxed until the next one came over."

At approximately 3:30 am on October 29, the French relieved Captain Lillard's 3rd Battalion, including Sayles's 37mm platoon. The battalion marched south to the village of Marchant. Shells continued to fall along their route, and during brief stops, soldiers tried to lighten their packs by dropping some of the souvenirs collected earlier, including Sayles, who dropped a "small automatic pistol and had emptied my pockets of brass belt buckles and red and black decorations." In Marchant, trucks took the 3rd Battalion the rest of the way to the "old artillery camp" just south of Somme-Py, where the remainder of the regiment waited. On their way to Somme-Py, they rode through Saint Etienne. Sayles noticed that the streets had been cleared of "loose stones and timbers," and that several elderly people watched them drive by. As they left Saint Etienne, east of the village they passed the enemy trenches they had fought over several weeks before. Now filled in, a long line of crosses marked the final resting place of many of their comrades killed in the fighting. In fact, as each unit passed through Saint Etienne, they found time to "halt and permit the men to look at various points where comrades had been killed and to clear up hazy impressions that existed about the lay of the land during the fighting." The weather was clear and the daily operations report, for the first time in weeks, made no mention of casualties or enemy machine-gun operations, or the status of patrols. On October 30, the 142d Infantry Regiment marched from the artillery camp to the town of Valmy, arriving in the late afternoon. The weather had become cloudy again, but that probably did not matter much to Colonel Bloor's soldiers. The daily operations report did not take long to write that day, as it contained just four words: "Not in the line."

Although the war continued for almost another two weeks, and the 36th Division received assignment to the American First Army, there would be no more fighting for the 142d Infantry Regiment. At least thirty-five original members of the old 7th Texas had lost their lives in the twenty-three days their regiment spent on the Western Front, and dozens more wounded. Those who survived witnessed the horrors of combat and felt the loss of their comrades keenly. Perhaps for most, their ideas of what war really consisted of had forever changed. Now that they were out of the line, their thoughts would turn to trying to describe and understand what they had experienced. Their thoughts would turn to home.

Yet Another Look at the Fergusons of Texas

JANE BOCK GUZMAN

J ane Bock Guzman serves on the Board of Directors of the Dallas Historical Society
and the Dallas Jewish Historical Society.

Jim and Miriam Ferguson, known by Texans as "Pa" and "Ma," governed the
Lone Star State in the early decades of the twentieth century. In this selection, Guzman
examines the careers of these two colorful—and controversial—politicians. ∞

★ ★

Texas politics and politicians have always been interesting, and James E. (Pa) and Miriam A. (Ma)
Ferguson were among the most engaging characters in Texas political history. They both were
elected governor, although most observers believed at the time that only one of them, Pa, actually
performed the duties of the office. He was the only Texas governor ever to be impeached; she was
the first woman elected to the highest office in the state.

James Edward Ferguson was born on August 31, 1871, near Salado in Bell County. His father
died when he was four years old. After being expelled from school for disobedience, he left
home at sixteen and wandered through the West, working as a miner and on a railroad gang.
He returned home two years later to study law, and was admitted to the bar in 1897. His law

practice was not lucrative enough, so he turned to real estate, insurance, and banking. He married Miriam Amanda Wallace on December 31, 1899.

Miriam and Jim had probably known each other all their lives. Her mother, Eliza Garrison Wallace, was a widow with two daughters when she married Joseph L. Wallace. Her first husband was Wesley G. Ferguson, the brother of James Edward Ferguson, Sr., and the uncle of James Jr. The two daughters from her first marriage were his first cousins, as well as Miriam's half-sisters; therefore, Miriam's mother was Jim Ferguson's aunt. Miriam was born on June 13, 1875, in Bell County, four years after Jim. Unlike her future husband, she had the benefit of higher education; she attended two colleges, Salado College and Baylor Female College at Belton, although she did not graduate from either.

The Fergusons held an interest in the Farmers State Bank of Belton for several years, and Jim, who managed the concern, was a member of the Texas State Bankers Association. In 1907 the Fergusons sold their share of the bank and moved to Temple, where Jim organized the Temple State Bank and became its president. He became involved in local politics, opposing prohibition even though he was a teetotaler. His position on this, one of the most pressing political issues of the era in Texas, put him in direct opposition to the Ku Klux Klan, a powerful force throughout the state that was promoting prohibition. Not only did Ferguson's stance distance him from other Texas politicians, it gained him the support and friendship of Texas brewers, who stood to lose their businesses if prohibition became law.

In 1914 Jim Ferguson decided to run for governor. Although never before holding elective office, he won the Democratic nomination when other "wets," or anti-prohibitionists, withdrew from the race to avoid dividing the vote. Ferguson found his calling in politics, employing a time-honored practice of appealing to the "common man." He wore a frock coat and deliberately used poor grammar, despite the fact that he was well read, to appeal to his "boys at the forks of the creek," as he called the tenant farmers. He frequently criticized "city slickers" and "educated fools who know nothing of the farmer's problems." Building on this populist theme, he usually added that he "warn't no college dude, and durned glad of it." This tactic—portraying himself as one of the people—was quite a leap, considering his presidency of a bank, his financial interest in ten others, and his ownership of 2,500 acres of black farmland—but it worked. Ferguson called for state regulation of rental fees landlords charged their sharecroppers and opposed bonus payments attached onto customary rent charges. He proposed laws limiting the amount of rent that landlords could demand from tenants, one-fourth for cotton and one third for grain crops. Ferguson insisted that by improving the lot of tenant farmers, the entire Texas economy would be strengthened. He also supported organized labor, which made him unpopular among business owners, and apologized for the fact that his mother had been educated by Ursuline nuns, explaining that she had been orphaned at an early age and that the nuns had taken her in. He added that she had married a Methodist minister and had never set foot inside a Catholic church. Fergusons appeal to tenant farmers succeeded; after capturing the Democratic nomination in the primary, he easily defeated his Republican opponent in the general election and took office.

Ferguson's apparent disdain for education was not universal, nor was it apparent in his early policy decisions. He often asserted his desire to improve the condition of rural schools in Texas, and during his first term in office textbooks were supplied free for the first time to children enrolled in Texas public schools. Despite his rhetoric to the contrary he also supported higher education, urging generous appropriations for colleges and making provisions for eight new ones. In fact, during his first term, the legislature authorized agricultural colleges at Stephenville and Arlington, appropriated funds for West Texas A&M, and established colleges that later became East Texas State University, Stephen F. Austin State University, and Sul Ross College.

Ferguson did, however, have personal issues with administrators at the University of Texas. Rumors abounded that the UT appropriations bill of 1915 had a number of items that would be vetoed. Ferguson, however, signed the bill without a veto after having discussed it with the University's acting president, W. J. Battle, and several members of the Board of Regents. But because of a recent change in administration at the state's flagship school, there had been no time to prepare a proper itemized budget. Therefore, what Ferguson and the legislature authorized was a proposed budget for the preceding biennium, with an addendum requesting that they be permitted to make such changes as might prove necessary. This was explained to Ferguson and to members of the legislature; the bill specifically stated that the regents might make necessary "changes and substitutions within the total"—in other words, shift money around—as long as they did not exceed the amount appropriated.

Changes were made, which the governor protested. He sent a letter to the regents asserting that Battle was not qualified to be president of the University. Although Battle was assured by the regents that he had their support, he withdrew his name for consideration after Ferguson challenged his ascension to the leadership position. Ferguson insisted that an auditor be appointed for the University, and the auditor found a few minor accounting errors. The governor used these as evidence of a widespread pattern of wrongdoing.

The Board of Regents elected R. E. Vinson to serve as president of the University in 1916. Ferguson, however, had his own candidate in mind, and was displeased with their decision. He believed that, as governor, he should have been consulted about the filling of such an important office, and he made his views plain to several of the regents. Shortly before Vinson's inauguration, he visited the governor along with Regent George W. Littlefield. During this meeting, Ferguson restated his opposition to Vinson and told the two men that he had inflammatory information about five faculty members. In September Vinson, now the President of the University, asked Ferguson to share this information so that he might submit it to the Board of Regents for evaluation, but the governor declined. He added that in the future, it "would be better for us to remain in our respective jurisdictions and no good purpose can be served by any further relation between us."

Ferguson decided that what he needed was a Board of Regents whose members would follow his wishes. He had already appointed Maurice Faber, a rabbi living in Tyler and the first clergyman to serve in such a capacity, to the board. Ferguson now demanded either Faber's complete support or his resignation. Faber refused to comply with either choice, so Ferguson wrote that he "did not care to bandy words with him, and that if Faber wanted Ferguson to remove him from office, he could rest assured that he (Ferguson), would not shrink for the task."

Apparently changing his mind about involving himself in university affairs, Ferguson attended a Board of Regents meeting in October 1916 to present his evidence against five faculty members and to show the extent of the graft he claimed infected the University. The governor's case was weak, but he insisted that Vinson and the board members should remove these faculty members. After investigating Ferguson's charges they refused to act. Their report was made public and led the governor to declare that the entire issue was "becoming more clearly defined as to whether the University shall run the people of Texas or the people of the state run their own University."

Ferguson must have been surprised at this turn of events; he had just removed three members of the San Antonio State Hospital and encountered only token resistance in replacing a member of the staff at Prairie View A&M College. As a result, he believed that he had more power than he actually did as governor. Ignoring the advice of his wife, who pleaded with him to drop the matter, he pressed onward with his vendetta. Meanwhile, during the legislative session of 1917, several legislators introduced resolutions asking that Ferguson be investigated, and several legislative committees censured the governor for misdeeds.

When the special session of the legislature adjourned in 1917, Governor Ferguson had to decide whether or not to sign the generous appropriations authorized for different state institutions, including the University of Texas. He asked the UT Regents to meet in his office on May 28. Rumors abounded that the governor would demand the removal of five faculty members and the expulsion of fraternities from the university. Fraternities were a favorite target of Ferguson, the populist; he declared that they drew a line between wealth and poverty at the university, and that their members lived in "stately mansions," while the poorer students lived in "crowded boardinghouses." He added that the university as a whole was an institution "of fads and fancies, grossly mismanaged."

The regents realized that if they followed the governor's wishes, the appropriations bill would be signed. The Ex-Students' Association issued a statement saying that it would be better to close the university rather that submit to the governor's demands. Ferguson vetoed the university appropriation on June 2, saying that he thought the bill was excessive. He made no mention of an injunction issued by a district court in Austin that had intended to prevent Dr. Fly of Houston, a new Ferguson appointee to the board of regents, from taking his seat. The district court also granted an injunction that enjoined the regents from removing any members of the faculty.

The regents met in Austin on June 5, hoping to compromise since the governor's veto had not been filed with the secretary of state. However, Ferguson then took an even stronger stand and demanded that nine members of the faculty, as well as all lawsuits and injunctions, be dismissed. No compromise was reached, the veto was filed, and the university was allowed the use of its available money and the salary of only one dean.

In July 1917 the injunctions were lifted, and six of the faculty members mentioned by the governor were removed. Ferguson believed he had won, and continued to ridicule the school in a speech he delivered at an Old Settlers' picnic at Valley Mills on July 13. He took a number of swipes at the university, ending his diatribe by declaring "I say that not only are too many people going hog wild over higher education, but that some people have become plain damn fools over the idea that we ought to have an army of educated fools to run the government."

This speech aroused the wrath of Will C. Hogg, secretary of the Ex-Students Association and the son of former governor James S. Hogg. The Ex-Students Association had been organizing opposition to the governor, encouraging former students to monitor the governor closely for any indication of misdeeds—which they soon discovered. Ferguson was indicted by a Travis County Grand Jury and later impeached by the Texas House of Representatives, meeting in a special session on August 1, 1917. The House impeached him on twenty-one charges of misconduct: these included findings that Ferguson juggled state accounts to serve his private financial interests; that he lied to the legislature earlier concerning the bad state of his personal finances; that he had secured a mysterious personal loan for $156,500, (rumored to have come from Kaiser Wilhelm of Germany—this was, after all, the early days of American involvement in WWI—but later found to have been made by San Antonio brewers); that he tried to become the dictator of the university; that he tried to bribe government officials; and finally, that he had intermingled his own and the state's accounts at the Temple State Bank to make money for himself. Ferguson excused himself on the last day of the trial before members of the Texas Senate and went to Fort Worth to attend a livestock show. The vote was twenty-five to three to convict Ferguson and remove him from office. William P. Hobby, the president of the senate, succeeded Ferguson as governor and called a special session of the legislature to appropriate new monies for the university, and things returned to normal. As a result of the conviction, Ferguson lost all his civil rights, including the right to hold office. He claimed that he was a martyr, put to death by the university clique and the newspapers.

Jim and Miriam Ferguson left Austin in disgrace and moved back to Temple, where the former governor started a weekly newspaper, *The Ferguson Forum*. He liked to call it "my little Christian weekly," and used it to communicate with his supporters, especially in East Texas, who waited eagerly for their papers every Friday. Ferguson used his paper to launch a diatribe against the Ku Klux Klan and the University of Texas, to lobby for repeal of the prohibition laws and elimination of the poll tax, and occasionally to slur Jews. He endorsed Henry Ford for president in 1924, saying, "He is the living personification and perfection of the principle of a dollar's worth of services for a dollar paid," and even sold subscriptions to the *Dearborn Independent* in his newspaper. Ferguson ran for governor again in 1918, against Hobby, despite being legally barred from doing so, and lost by a landslide. In 1920, he left the Democratic Party to run for president on the American Party ticket.

Ferguson's main political thrusts were against the Ku Klux Klan and prohibition. The Klan was founded after the Civil War by Confederate veterans, as a means of keeping former slaves "in their place." It collapsed early in the 1870s but was revived in 1915 by Dr. Hiram Evans, a Dallas dentist. In its early years the new Klan was an object of ridicule to some; invitations to a party honoring an engaged couple, Beatrice Wertheimer and Herbert Mallinson, asked guests to dress in Klan attire, which the society columnist of the local paper described as "grotesque." Despite such derision, the organization's membership grew in strength, especially in Dallas:

October 24, 1923, was Ku Klux Klan Day at the State Fair of Texas. The Fergusons moved to Dallas briefly in 1923, but were unhappy there and soon moved back to Temple. One reason could be the fact that *The Ferguson Forum* did not flourish in Dallas. A lack of advertising from Dallas merchants led Ferguson to print his most infamous column in the March 15, 1923 issue. "The Cloven Foot of the Dallas Jew" was a diatribe listing the evils of the Jewish merchants of Dallas. This column was so extreme that Klan editors reprinted it in their paper one week later to expose Ferguson as an anti-Semite. The gist of his complaint was that the "Big Jews," i.e Alex Sanger, Herbert Marcus, etc., refused to advertise in *The Ferguson Forum*. The fact that these same individuals did not advertise in either the local Jewish paper or the Klan paper was a fact Ferguson either chose to ignore or deemed unimportant. Frustrated, and finally acknowledging that he was ineligible for state office himself, Ferguson decided to run his wife for governor in 1924. Miriam Ferguson was, by all accounts, a private person who was mainly interested in her home and family, but declared that she was running for office "for the vindication of our family name." When asked about her qualifications for office, she replied, "I know I can't talk about the Constitution and the making of laws and the science of government like some other candidates, and I believe they have talked too much, but I have a trusting and abiding faith 'that my Redeemer liveth,' and I am trusting to him to guide my footsteps in the path of righteousness for the good of our people and the good of our State."

The Ferguson campaign slogan was "Two governors for the price of one." Because Mrs. Ferguson had spent her first forty-nine years as a housewife and mother of two daughters, Dorrace and Ouida, and because her initials were M and A, she soon became known as Ma Ferguson. After finishing among the leaders in the Democratic primary, her campaign began to attract national attention. Reporters wanted human-interest stories, so Ouida Ferguson persuaded her mother to let the press photograph her peeling peaches in the kitchen of her birthplace, the Wallace family farm eleven miles outside of Temple. She was also photographed feeding a flock of white leghorn chickens, hoeing her garden, and standing beside a brace of mules. The caption of the picture showing her peeling peaches called her "Ma" Ferguson, and her husband automatically became "Pa." Pictures showing her wearing a bonnet were circulated widely, and led to her campaign song, sung to the tune of "Put on Your Old Grey Bonnet."

> *Get out your old time bonnet*
> *And put Miriam Ferguson on it*
> *And hitch your wagon to a star*
> *So on election day*
> *We each of us can say*
> *Hurrah, governor Miriam, Hurrah.*

Mrs. Ferguson won the Democratic run-off election in August of 1924, and easily defeated her Republican opponent in November. Posters and stickers appeared claiming "Me for Ma . . . and I ain't got a durned thing against Pa!"

Mrs. Ferguson was elected for several reasons. The Klan, though strong in membership, aroused fear in many due to the appearance of its hooded members. One of Mrs. Ferguson's first campaign promises was to see that an anti-mask law was enacted (which the State

Supreme Court soon found unconstitutional). Klansmen inspired terror by beating, whipping, and tar-and-feathering individuals they deemed immoral, including pimps, murderers, child-molesters, straying husbands and wives, abortionists, bootleggers, and gamblers, as well as African-Americans who did not "keep in their place." In addition, the Klan newspaper, *The Texas 100 Per Cent American*, was a continuous diatribe against the evils of Roman Catholicism. Many of Mrs. Ferguson's supporters were those who were weary of the constant fear the Klan inspired. Texas had a considerable Catholic population, as well as a number of those wishing an end to prohibition. They were among her voters, as were feminists who voted for her because she was a woman. Prominent business and political leaders around Texas endorsed her candidacy, including John Nance Garner, the vice-presidential candidate, who promised that a Democratic victory would mean a return to state and national prosperity. In an August 17, 1924 editorial, George Dealey, the editor of the *Dallas Morning News*, stated that Miriam Ferguson's election would "sound the death knell of the Klan as a political power base in the State." He was correct.

The Fergusons returned to Austin in the same 1917 Packard Twin-Six in which they had driven away in disgrace. Since Jim had never learned to drive, Miriam was at the wheel. When they had departed Austin several years earlier, Miriam had declared that a brighter day would dawn for them, and that they would return in the same Packard. It had been stored in a Temple garage until the governor-elect remembered her prediction and had it repaired, polished, and fitted with new tires for the triumphal return. As she pulled the car under the *porte cochere*, she exclaimed, "Well, we have arrived!" While walking around the old familiar grounds, she was aghast to discover that her name had been removed from a block of concrete at the threshold of the greenhouse she had built during her husband's administration. She immediately called a concrete worker to restore her name and date to the greenhouse.

Her administration operated smoothly at first. In addition to the anti-mask bill targeting the Ku Klux Klan, the chief legislation passed was a tick eradication bill crucial to the cattle industry of the state. However, controversies arose, usually centering around the governor's husband. For the most part, she governed in name only. Jim Ferguson's desk was next to hers (similar to those of Queen Victoria and Prince Albert), and everyone knew that he was the real power. He attended meetings of state boards, commissions, and agencies, with or without the governor, and received personal callers.

Jim's "little Christian weekly" was still going strong. There was no standard rate for advertising during this period, but those wishing for favorable attention from the Ferguson administration paid exorbitant prices for the privilege of promoting their concerns. For example, a special edition of the paper appeared on December 18, 1924, just before Miriam's inauguration. It contained more than twice as much advertising space as editorial copy—2,674 inches v 1,246 inches—and all but nineteen inches of advertising space were for firms wanting favors from the new administration. As a result, contracts were awarded for the building of highways to individuals or firms that had never built or maintained roads, including doctors, ranchers, politicians, and lawyers. The one thing they all had in common was that they either were loyal friends of the governor's husband or they had advertised in *The Ferguson Forum*.

The Ferguson's older daughter, Ouida Ferguson Nalle, had worked in the insurance business before her mother's inauguration. She then became an agent for the American Surety Company and wrote surety bonds for road and other contractors. Her clientele was strictly limited to those seeking business with the state. She was also a partner in a real-estate firm that promoted development at the Colorado River Dam near Austin. Her husband, George S. Nalle, promoted stock in a company that had a twenty-year lease on land containing lead ore. Nalle corresponded with friends of the administration, including several legislators, inviting them to buy stock and to send their checks to him in care of the governor's mansion in Austin.

Controversy also surrounded textbook contracts. Jim Ferguson was elected clerk of the Textbook Commission, and one of the pending state contracts was with the American Book Company. It called for the state to purchase thousands of copies of a spelling book at a price a nickel a copy more than it would have cost in Ohio, but the State Supreme Court found the contract valid. The biggest controversies, however, stemmed from the number of pardons criminals received during Mrs. Ferguson's administration. Rumors abounded, but no proof has ever surfaced that pardons were sold, although it seems unlikely that anyone who bought one would ever admit it.

During his wife's administration Jim Ferguson continued his law practice, and was counsel and advisor to several railroads. The newspaper prospered as well; a *Ferguson Forum* was launched in Austin, for which Jim solicited advertising on the governor's official stationery, and state employees were among the subscribers.

The proudest moment for the Ferguson family was the Amnesty Act for James E. Ferguson that Miriam signed into law with a gold pen on March 31, 1925. In the fall of the same year, however, several members of the House of Representatives began an abortive attempt to impeach Mrs. Ferguson, citing several irregularities in her administration. But the legislature was not sitting, and the governor would have had to call a special session, so nothing came of this.

Miriam Ferguson had declared she would only seek one term, but either she or her husband had changed their mind as her term neared its end. She lost to fellow Democrat Dan Moody in the primary, then completed her term. The Fergusons remained in Austin afterwards, living first in the Driskill Hotel, then a rented house, and finally settling into a home on Windsor Road they had built for them. While Miriam lived quietly, Jim kept up his opposition to Moody through his newspaper. In 1928, for the first time since 1914, no Ferguson name appeared on the ticket of any political party. However, with the coming of the Great Depression, the Fergusons saw an opportunity, and Miriam ran again in 1932, becoming the first Texas governor elected to two nonconsecutive terms. Miriam was not a candidate for re-election in 1934, but she ran, unsuccessfully, against W. Lee (Pappy) O'Daniel in 1940, an old enemy of her husband. She came in fourth in that race, her last.

On June 13, 1955, the Austin Junior Chamber of Commerce held a dinner in honor of Miriam Ferguson's eightieth birthday. Approximately 300 people attended the event at the Driskill Hotel, including former governor James V. Allred and Senate Majority Leader Lyndon B. Johnson. Governor Allen Shivers served as Master of Ceremonies. President Dwight D. Eisenhower sent his felicitations, and as a salute to her, the entire gathering sang her old campaign song, "Put on Your Old Gray Bonnet." Jim had died more than a decade earlier, in 1944, and Miriam Ferguson passed away in 1961 and was buried next to her husband in the state cemetery in Austin. There is no doubt that their administrations were colorful. However, together they were responsible, more than any other politicians, for offering Texans a viable alternative to the Ku Klux Klan. While some of their actions may have benefited themselves or special interests more than the state or its residents, they never encouraged the violence and hatred that the Klan endorsed. Considering the climate of the day, Texas could have easily been governed by worse people.

Life in the Shadows of Oil Derricks

ILTA S. HALL

I ndependent historian Ilta S. Hall is a member of the East Texas Historical Association.

In this selection, Hall, using family reminiscences, discusses working class life in the East Texas oil fields during the 1920s and 1930s. ✦

★ ★

Without a doubt, my grandmother was a colorful character. As a child, I can recall my Granny recounting stories from her childhood through the time she moved to Houston in 1946. These stories, filled with adventure, tragedy, and humor, astonished me as a young girl. On many occasions my mother would add her memories of the same incidents, tamed down, yet still exciting. Some of my favorites among Granny's recollections involved her early married years living in the East Texas oil fields. With much assistance from my mother, I have recorded these wonderful memories of life in the shadows of the oil derricks.

My Granny was born Elsie Lesteen Vest on July 28, 1906, in Dawson, Texas, which is located twenty-one miles southwest of Corsicana. She was the first child of her sharecropper parents, Eula Florence Cagle and Thomas (Tom) Franklin Vest. She endured a childhood typical of

"Life in the Shadows of Oil Derricks" by Ilta S. Hall from *East Texas Historical Journal;* XLVI, No 1, 2008, pp. 41-50. Reprinted by permission of East Texas Historical Association.

most poor children; she worked long hours picking cotton, attended school sporadically, and helped her mother care for four younger siblings. Between growing up with a harsh father who demanded arduous work and often doing without basic necessities, Elsie emerged with a strong, survivalist personality and a desire for recognition and appreciation for her accomplishments.

Granny's family moved to Raleigh, Texas, when she was twelve years old. Her father worked as a blacksmith and on farms owned by others, hoping to save enough money to get into the cattle business. Tom went broke when his previous herd had to be destroyed due to blackleg disease. He could not get another loan at the bank to buy more cattle because he already owed too much, and the bank foreclosed on his land and his home. The only other occupation that Tom knew was farming, so he had to resort to sharecropping to provide for his family. As the oldest girl, Elsie was needed at home, making school attendance low on the list of priorities. When she was fourteen, Elsie played on the girls' basketball team and met a handsome twenty-year-old spectator named Robert Price. He was a cousin of her friend and he worked on his family's farm a few miles down the road from Raleigh.

Elsie and Robert (called Ott by his family) both attended the local Methodist church in Raleigh, and they soon fell in love. It was not unusual for teenaged girls of Elsie's age to get married because they were mature enough to handle a household on their own. Elsie was also anxious to get away from her father's harsh rules and the hard work on the farm. Elsie's parents agreed to the young couple's plan to marry because it meant one less mouth to feed. Family members and friends attended Ott and Elsie's wedding at the preacher's house on June 19, 1921. There were so many people in the house to witness their vows that the wooden floor fell in from the weight!

The newlyweds moved into a two-room wooden shack near Raleigh. Ott worked in the fields while Elsie stayed at home keeping house and canning. On June 18, 1924, the day before their third anniversary, Elsie and Ott became the parents of a baby girl. Elsie wanted the baby named after her, while Ott wanted to name the baby Pauline because he liked the name Paul. After much discussion, they named their daughter, my mother, Elsie Pauline, but Ott always called her Pauline.

The young family struggled to make ends meet and farming work for Ott was slow. Many northeast Texas folks were farmers and the competition triggered low agricultural prices. Also, many people had no money to buy food and grew their own crops. Elsie and Ott helped their families on their farms often, especially during cotton-picking time. Elsie grew tired of the laborious life and just scratching out a living. She wanted a better life for herself and her daughter, so she pressured Ott to get a better job, one that paid more money. A few of his unemployed friends were hired in the oil fields. Ott had grown up around Corsicana where oil was discovered in 1894 as contractor's drilled artesian wells to help the local farmers. He had seen oil derricks all over the town, as well as a refinery that produced kerosene and later gasoline for automobiles. To please Elsie, Ott began to look for a manual labor job in the oilfields.

When Pauline was three months old, Ott heard that drillers were hiring workers in the oilfield in Mexia. The discovery of oil in Mexia four years earlier had created a massive growth spurt for the little town in Limestone County. The population increased from near 3,500 to almost 35,000 in a few years, and the frenzy caused martial law to be established there for a short time.

Ott landed a job stacking pipe in the derricks. Drill pipe came in thirty-foot joints that were connected as the bit drilled deeper, pulled out and stacked when the cuttings needed to be removed from the hole, and then rejoined as drilling continued. The job was considered dangerous and most workers did not want to take such a risky position. Ott accepted the risks since it paid well. Elsie later boasted that it paid much more than what her brother Roy made working for the Works Progress Administration (WPA). With their few belongings. Ott brought Elsie and Pauline to the Wortham lease, where they lived in a tent house, a one-room structure with walls three-foot-high topped by a tent. They joined other former sharecroppers who set up tent cities or "rag towns" to call "home." Here, the family celebrated the baby's first Christmas.

Not satisfied with living in a tent, Elsie persuaded Ott to move to a small house located next to the railroad tracks in the middle of the Wortham Oilfield in February 1925. A big oil strike there the previous November led to the drilling of 300 wells in one year. Production and profits were high. Ott made enough money to purchase a used Buick touring car with a canvas top. Elsie learned to drive and visited her family in Raleigh to show off her new car and baby, let them see how well she was doing. She packed up and, in her ignorance, placed Pauline on the floorboard so that she would not fall off the seat. Upon their arrival at the Vest farm, Elsie's family reprimanded her for subjecting the baby to gas fumes. Undaunted, she paraded Elsie and the car in front of all her relatives before returning to Wortham.

Many oilfield workers, including Ott, found that when the oil drilling began to decline, they had to look for other work, any work. In August 1926, Ott took his family back to help with the harvest at the Price's family farm between Frost and Raleigh. They rented the old Vincent place and tried to make another go of sharecropping. After the harvest, the landowner kept most of the profit and refused to honor the deal he had made with the farmers. Unhappily, Ott and Elsie had to depend on help from their families to keep going.

Work in the oilfields picked up again in early 1929, but the closest employment that Ott found was near Luling. For a short while, the family lived in a two-room yellow house next to a house where Elsie's cousin and his wife were renting. Young Pauline received a little broom for Christmas. When she was sweeping the porch one day, the landlady's donkeys came up next to the house and frightened her. Instinctively, she poked her little broom at them; one of the donkeys grabbed it and ate it, causing Pauline to cry for hours.

There were only a few other children to play with Pauline. The landlords' children were occasional playmates but much of the time she played alone. When Pauline went with her mother to visit Ott on the derricks, her father would let her climb on the drill pipe and play in the "doghouse" where the workers changed clothes. The only place where she was not allowed to play was on the rig floor. Elsie boasted that Pauline spent more time in the oilfields than most workers.

When the stock market crashed in October 1929, the country's economy suffered. Many Texans became unemployed and families were hungry. The Great Depression had little effect on Elsie and Ott, who managed well enough since they had little money anyway. Many people were desperate after the stock market crash, but oilfield labor was about the most lucrative work to be found. Ten major oil companies operated in Texas in 1929, and many independent oil companies also employed oilfield workers. Also, there were important refineries in Port Arthur and Baytown. Ott continued to get steady work in the oil patch.

Elsie's talents and ingenuity helped her manage during the Depression. She made Pauline's clothes on a borrowed sewing machine. Outgrown clothing was sent to her brother Roy's daughter. There was no problem getting food on the lease because Ott had steady employment. He and Elsie bought coffee, flour, sugar, and other things that could not be grown on the farm to send back to their families along with some money.

When the wells were all completed, Elsie and Pauline stayed with the Vests a few weeks until Ott found another job in Van, twenty miles northeast of Tyler. The Pure Oil Company used seismograph soundings to direct their drilling and discover oil in Van in October 1929. This find attracted several oil companies that signed a joint agreement with Pure Oil for unitization to reduce competition and promote conservation. Ott took a position as a roustabout, tightening and loosening the joints of the drill string.

Shortly after the move to a boarding house, Elsie received a message that her mother was ill and in the hospital in Corsicana. Elsie took Pauline and drove to her mother's bedside. That day, Elsie's mother passed away at the age of forty-two from a ruptured appendix and gangrene. Her death was a blow to a family with two children still at home. Elsie tried even harder to send any extra funds home to her little sisters.

In the fall Pauline began attending kindergarten and gave Elsie the opportunity to seek her own job rather than spending her days at home canning fruit and vegetables. Elsie had never enjoyed staying at home. It was unusual for a wife to be employed and no other females in Elsie's family had ever worked outside the home, but she was bored there. A job gave her a chance to get out of the house, find adventure, and earn money of her own. She worked at Thompson Commercial Company in Van in the dry-goods department. She enjoyed meeting people and saved some of her money to buy her own car. She could buy fabric at a discount and sew for Pauline. The little girl was dressed well, with bloomers to match every dress. Having only one child, which was uncommon for most families, Elsie kept up her duties at home while enjoying her job. Most wives of oilfield workers stayed at home on the lease to raise their children and perform household chores. Many of the workers were young men who had not yet married. These single men found accommodations at "cot houses" or boarding houses.

Employment in Van began a period when the family moved wherever Ott could find work for independent contractors on another well. He heard about an Oklahoma promoter named "Dad" Joiner who spudded wells in Rusk County. Joiner, using only his intuition, had leased 10,000 acres in East Texas and began drilling, on his third attempt, the Daisy Bradford #3, he struck oil in October 1930. His discovery was followed by two tremendous strikes and the vast East Texas oilfield began production of over six billion barrels of oil in the next few years. Joiner attracted investors to the area and many independent drillers, called "wildcatters," began their own wells in search of a big strike. Ott worked as a roustabout whenever and wherever he could find work.

For the first two or three months, the Price family lived in a rooming house and ate meals with the owners and other boarders. The family had to move often because the rigs were drilled in a set number of days and when they were completed, the crews moved on. Wherever the next contract required them to drill was where they would live, sometimes in the same town, other times twenty or thirty miles away. A possessive woman, Elsie never wanted Ott out of her sight when he was not working. This attitude drove her to follow him to every oil lease. Elsie and Pauline would trail the group of roustabouts in their car, find a place to spend the night, and then locate a place to live. Because of the hard economic times, most people with a spare room would rent it, whether in a rooming house or a private home. Such frequent moves meant that Ott and Elsie had no furniture of their own. Nothing could be accumulated because they did not stay in one place long enough. Perhaps this was the reason that my Granny amassed so much "stuff" in her later years.

Every place the family lived, Ott planted a garden. They often had to move before anything was produced, but Ott enjoyed growing food. It gave him pleasure to give produce away and he enjoyed leaving the garden for the next renters. Between the garden and the lease store, food supplies were not a problem, although there may not have been a big variety. When Ott, Elsie, and Pauline visited the Vest farm, Grandpa Vest slaughtered hogs and sent them home with ham, bacon, and sausage from the smokehouse. On occasion, they bought chickens to add to the staples they purchased at the lease store.

Pauline went to school wherever they lived. During one four and one-half month period, she attended seven different schools, each one not long enough to learn the teacher's name or get a report card. Most of the schools were two rooms, one for first through third grades and the other for fourth through sixth grades. Teachers were available but some were not well educated. Children such as Pauline, who come from the oil leases, were put in the grade that their mothers thought they should attend. Pauline would find a chair and follow the other children's lead until it was time to move again. She learned to read, and Elsie listened to her read aloud and help her with the more difficult words if she knew them. The children were taught phonics and their books usually consisted of a reader, speller, and a math book.

Ott continued to work wherever he could. The East Texas oilfield was the largest oilfield in the United States, covering parts of Gregg, Rusk, Upshur, Smith, and Cherokee counties. Ott found employment on the Cook #2, owned by Mr. W. H. Cook, in December 1930; then for the Sun Oil Company at the J. W. Akin #1 site, and later on the T&P RR Company's Fee #1 site, among many others. He worked as a roustabout on several wells but because of his experience, he held the position of derrick man on a wildcat well near Troupe, Texas. He stood on crossed boards on the derrick where he grabbed a snap hook, pulled up a link of pipe, stacked it, and continued the process in and out of the hole. On one well between Gladewater and Longview, Ott assumed the position of driller. He always worked on rotary rigs, which were becoming more common than the traditional cable rigs. Rotary rigs required a minimum of five workers per shift. The "boss" of the rig was the tool pusher, followed by the driller, the derrickman, and two roughnecks.

The more Ott worked, the more Elsie hounded him to make more money, putting stress on their marriage. Occasionally, Ott went to local beer joints with co-workers at the end of the day, only to come home to Elsie's fury. Elsie gave up her job at Thompson's in Van to stay in closer proximity to Otto. They lived in several communities, including Troup, Arp, Overton, Henderson, Greggton, and Gladewater.

When the market became flooded with East Texas oil, prices fell from a dollar a barrel in 1930 to eight cents a barrel the following year. Also, because small producers controlled the East Texas oilfields, the major oil companies called on the Texas Railroad Commission to limit oil production. The independent producers countered by marketing "hot oil" in defiance of the Railroad Commission's limitations. "Hot oil" was a term used to describe oil that was produced beyond the restrictions of the Railroad Commission or obtained illegally by siphoning from pipelines. A volatile situation existed in the East Texas fields, and jobs with independent producers were harder for Ott to find, so he took whatever positions were offered to him in order to provide for his family, even if they involved "hot oil."

When Pauline started the third grade, Ott got a job as a lease foreman for Stroube & Stroube, turning wells on and off as the Railroad Commission would allow. This independent company had made a tremendous strike in 1930 only 600 feet north of "Dad" Joiner's Daisy Bradford well, when oil prices were high and large profits common. Ott received top pay and he performed his duties independently of any crews. The family moved into a company house on a lease in White Oak, located east of Gladewater near Kilgore. This allowed them enough stability and purchased their first pieces of furniture. Elsie and Ott opened a charge account at the grocery store and could pay at the end of each month. Then Elsie could buy groceries without having cash and she allowed Pauline to buy ice cream or milk on their account, but never candy. The family never worried about what they did not have and they were relatively happy, except for incidents involving Ott's "drinking with the boys," which collided with Elsie's aspirations for a better life.

In 1933, Elsie's youngest sister Mackie came to live with the family and go to school because their father had remarried. She stayed until another sister, Evlin, got married and settled and Mackie went to live with them so that she could be closer to the rest of the family and her friends. With Pauline and Mackie attending school in White Oak, Elsie became involved with the Parent Teacher Association. The PTA put on plays and sold tickets to the community to raise funds for school projects. Elsie found her place in the limelight by acting in the plays and occasionally forcing a reluctant Pauline to take part. A highlight for Elsie occurred when Mackie won a trip through the 4-H Club to A & M College in College Station. Elsie accompanied Mackie as a representative from Gregg County.

On a visit to Grandpa Vest's farm, Pauline fell in love with a little brown goat. She begged to take it home, so Grandpa Vest put it in a gunny sack with its head sticking out and Pauline rode home sitting on the floorboard of the backseat, holding the goat she named Billy. Pauline played with the goat after school. They chased each other across the long front porch. One day, Elsie hung a pair of blue rayon pajamas she bought to wear on the College Station trip on the clothesline to dry and Billy ate one of the pajama legs. Elsie was so angry that she called a man to come and get Billy and barbecue him. When the man returned with a large pan of barbecue, the family, along with cousin David, who was staying with them, sat down to eat. Suddenly,

David said "Baaaaa" and Pauline burst into tears. She felt betrayed by her mother, but Elsie felt no remorse. The meat was returned to the man and no one ate that night.

Ott and his family spent almost three years in White Oak. Other oilfield workers and their families continually moved on and off the lease, living wherever space was available. Oilfield boomtowns rarely had paved streets. The streets turned to mud whenever it rained and the big trucks transporting pipe kept the roads in a quagmire. In the leased company home, Ott, Elsie, and Pauline adjusted well. Many of the larger oil companies provided housing for their workers on their leases. These homes were rented to employees for a nominal costs and encouraged company loyalty and discouraged labor union support.

At the lease house, as usual Ott planted a garden. They had no running water, but there was a well on the end of the porch. There was an outhouse in the back and Pauline was assigned the job of scrubbing it with hot water and a broom every Saturday. Pauline despised the job, especially with the spiders.

At White Oak School, there was no electricity, and the children pumped their own water in the front yard into tin cups brought from home. One day, a boy who did not have a tin cup of his own tried to pump water into a snuff glass. In the process, the snuff glass broke so the boy threw the pieces and one hit Pauline in the arm, causing a surge of blood. The boy's father paid to get the wound stitched and Elsie sent Pauline back to school the next day.

Often guests or family members came to visit Ott and Elsie. Adults spent the evening playing dominoes or talking. The children were shielded from most "grownup talk." Most of the crime in the area was limited to petty thefts, but they never talked about crime, sex, or having babies around children. Elsie and Ott bought a radio, first with earphones and then later one without them to hear the latest broadcasts. Every Sunday the family attended church, returned home, and killed a chicken. They cleaned and fried it, accompanied by potatoes, and ate lunch around 2 P.M. They killed additional chickens when anyone else showed up for a visit.

As Pauline progressed in school, she enjoyed the traveling shows that performed at the schools once a month. Children could attend the shows for ten or fifteen cents admission, depending on the performance. Sometimes they would be entertained by bands or minstrel shows. Once, an expert archer demonstrated trick shots, including one where he shot objects out of a child's hand. The most memorable visits for Pauline were a performance of Shakespeare's "As You Like It" and an appearance by some members of Admiral Richard Byrd's expedition.

Elsie became more involved with social activities in White Oak. In addition to working with the school PTA, she joined the local Rebekah Lodge, which was the women's division of the Oddfellows. Because Elsie would not leave her daughter alone at the lease house, Pauline went along to all the meetings and sat in the anteroom with other members' children. Out of boredom during the two-hour meetings, they "hollered" at people who passed the window and Pauline stayed in constant trouble with Elsie.

Elsie did a great deal of community service work. She sewed dresses for neighbors and clothing for their children if they purchased the cloth, usually at a nickel a yard. She cut up worn men's shirts and made clothing for babies. She cooked meals and took them to those in the area who were in need. Elsie's humanitarian and social pursuits took up much of her time, so naturally, she could not handle all the duties of the household. A local black man told her that he had a daughter that needed to work and Elsie agreed to let Geneva do her housework and live with the family. She placed a cot in the corner of the garage for Geneva to sleep. Elsie treated Geneva well otherwise and enjoyed her cooking and cleaning abilities.

After Geneva arrived, one of Pauline's school friends showed her some white rabbits. Pauline asked Ott if she could have some rabbits since she was the only child on the lease and had no one to play with. He bought her two pairs and a double hutch. The rabbits multiplied so Ott bought another hutch. Elsie insisted that Pauline be in charge of their care since they were her pets and she did not want them to be eaten. When there were more rabbits than the hutches could hold, Ott built a pen on the ground for them. Elsie got angry with her daughter for trying to get Geneva to help her clean the pen, so she went out in the yard, lifted the side of the pen, and herded all the white rabbits, about seventy-five of them, into the nearby woods. Their descendents probably still live in the forests of East Texas. Pauline cried, but Ott was not concerned because the cost of feeding the rabbits was taking a toll. After this incident, Geneva's father discovered that his daughter was sleeping in a drafty garage, so he told Elsie that Geneva's mother needed her help and he took her home.

Working on the oil derricks had many dangers. Several times there were oil well fires on the leases. Ott and other workers took great risks in controlling the fires. Once while in White Oak, there was a heavy rain and the runoff flowed into a slush pit that contained oil from a well that had just come in. A bolt of lightning struck near the pit, igniting the oil. The water began to boil and the burning oil overflowed. Pauline followed her father as he and other workers heard the calls for help and tried to extinguish the flames by shoveling dirt over them. As the streams of overflowing oil and fire ran downhill, Ott called for Pauline to get back. The fire grew so fierce that it blocked her view of the men. Pauline watched with increasing uneasiness, then panic, fearing that the inferno had engulfed her father. Eventually, she could see Ott and the others through the flames that surrounded them as they continued shoveling dirt on the fire. Pauline believed that she saw angels in the sky above the flames and that God had sent them to save her father from harm. None of men suffered major injuries that night.

By 1934, the Great Depression had begun to have negative effects on the oil industry. Prices for petroleum continued to decline and oilfield jobs were scarce. Ott was temporarily promoted to a position reading gages for Stroube and Stroube Oil Company. He gauged oil in the tanks and turned valves on when required, running oil in the pipes to the refinery.

Disagreements between Ott and Elsie grew, and Ott's drinking increased. This brought the fragile marriage to the breaking point and Ott and Elsie separated. Ott had learned that he would lose his job, so he helped Elsie move into a rental house across the highway. Ott packed his duffle bag and joined some of his friends at a rooming house. Within six weeks, Elsie packed her car and moved their furniture to a four-room, yellow rent house on Eastview Street in Longview. Wasting no time, she went to work at K. Woolens in dry goods and enrolled Pauline in the fourth grade at the elementary school. Elsie's cousin, Dora Cagle, came to live with them for a short time and shared expenses.

Shortly after their divorce was final, Elsie began dating again. When a gentleman came to the house for dinner, Pauline was instructed to be on her best behavior. But, in the middle of the meal, Pauline got tickled at something that was said and strangled, spitting tea all over the table. The suitor never came back.

Elsie would not let Ott see Pauline often unless he brought money to help her. He went back to work on the derricks again, often as a driller, whenever he could find work, and he brought money to Elsie whenever he could. Elsie and Pauline lived in Longview for a year and a half until Elsie remarried. Her new husband, George, provided plenty of food for them because he owned an interest in a butcher shop at Greggton. The new family rented a house close to Pine Tree School, where Pauline attended the sixth grade. Unfortunately, George and his partner lost their lease on the butcher shop, so the family relocated to Overton for a short time, and then to Kilgore when George took a job at the Wickham Packing Company processing meat, including wild game.

George bought Pauline a horse because of their joint love of animals. The bay had been a bucking horse in the rodeo in Fort Worth that had lost his desire to buck, so he was a good deal. George and Pauline both enjoyed riding him while Elsie had a cow for milk. A few years later, Elsie had to have all her teeth pulled, so Pauline was allowed to drive her mother's car to school. Pauline attended Kilgore High School and was graduated in 1940, just before her sixteenth birthday. She sold her horse to help finance her first year at Kilgore Junior College. Then George accepted a job in Tyler at Rose City Packing Company, and the family moved into a nice brick house.

When Pauline completed her education at Tyler Junior College, she became a telephone operator for $15 a week. She lived at home until she moved to Georgia to accept a job making $50 a week and to experience freedom and adventure. After a while, Elsie joined her there. She and George had divorced, for which she offered Pauline no explanation.

With the beginning of World War II, Elsie and Pauline returned to East Texas. Elsie got a job at the Post Exchange at Camp Fannin and Pauline worked in a grocery store there. Elsie pretended that she and Pauline were sisters to meet soldiers at the camp at a dance featuring Ozzie and Harriet Nelson and their orchestra. One evening, Pauline went to the Post Exchange to have dinner with her mother. While waiting, Pauline met a wonderful young soldier from Louisiana. Pauline and John, the young soldier, fell in love. They married and moved to Houston after John's discharge in 1945.

Pauline and John are my mother and father. They raised four children who were entertained by Granny every day after she bought a house two doors away and married a soldier who grew up in Chicago. Granddaddy Ott and his new wife lived in East Texas, Midland, and Louisiana, where he continued to work for oil companies, lastly as a tool pusher, until his retirement in 1962. We grandchildren heard many stories about the oilfields whenever he visited, but none could compare with the tales with which Granny amused us. They have both passed away now, but their stories of life in the shadows of the East Texas oil derricks live on as we share their experiences with our children.

1920–1929:
The Texas League during
the Golden Age of Sports

BILL O'NEAL

B ill O'Neal taught history for many years at Panola College in Carthage. In 2012, Governor Rick Perry appointed him Texas State Historian. Professor O'Neal's numerous books include *Encyclopedia of Western Gunfighters* (1979), *The Texas League, 1888–1987: A Century of Baseball* (1987), *Tex Ritter: America's Most Beloved Cowboy* (1998), *The Johnson County War* (2004), and *Reel Rangers: Texas Rangers in Movies, TV, Radio & Other Forms of Popular Culture* (2008).

Major League Baseball came to Texas in 1962 when the National League Houston Colt .45s (later renamed the Astros) played their inaugural season. The American League arrived in the Lone Star State ten years later with the relocation of the Washington Senators to Arlington, where they became the Texas Rangers. Prior to the arrival of the big leagues, however, the Texas League had a long and illustrious history. In this selection, O'Neal discusses the Texas League during the Roaring Twenties. Under the leadership of W. K. Stripling, Paul LaGrave, and Jake Atz, Fort Worth's Panthers dominated the period from 1920–1925. The Dallas Steers and Wichita Falls Spudders surpassed Fort Worth in the decade's latter years. Such legendary players as "Big Boy" Kraft, Joe Pate, Paul Wachtel, and Ike Boone thrilled Lone Star baseball fans, and from 1920–1929, the Texas League champion defeated their Southern Association rival eight times in the Dixie Series. ◅

★ ★

"1920-1929: The Texas League During the Golden Age of Sports" from *The Texas League, 1888-1987: A Century of Baseball* by Bill O'Neal, 1987, pp. 51-66. Reprinted by permission of the author.

The decade of the 1920s is regarded by many as the Golden Age of Sports in America, and baseball enjoyed a heyday as the most popular professional game in the land. The ball was livelier now, and Babe Ruth led the sport into an exciting era of home run sluggers and high-scoring games. The day of tight pitchers' duels—contests which featured hit-and-run, stolen bases, and bunting to play for one run—faded rapidly under a barrage of home runs as batters swung from the heels. Fans responded eagerly to a more electric style of baseball that proved perfectly suited to the accelerated pulse rate of the Roaring Twenties.

Babe Ruth was a sensation in 1920 when he walloped an astounding 54 roundtrippers (he duplicated this total in 1928, but in 1921 he hit 59, and in 1927 he slugged 60 homers). Prior to the 1920s, the Texas League home run record was 22, set by San Antonio first baseman Frank Metz in 1911. The next season Metz hit 21 homers, but until the 1920s no other Texas Leaguer had ever hit more than 18 home runs.

The Texas League wasted little time in joining the power parade. Scores went up dramatically, as did batting averages and, of course, ERAs. The leading team batting averages during the previous decade had ranged from .240 to .270, but in seven of the ten seasons of the 1920s the team batting average leaders hit over .300, and in 1927 the Waco Navigators established a league record .316 team mark. A record 3,778 extra base hits were pounded out around the league in 1925, and 7,044 runs were scored that year. In 1926, 1,024 home runs were hit, and in 1929 Texas League batters rapped out a record 12,711 base hits. In 1921 "Hack" Eibel, a strong Shreveport first baseman who, like Babe Ruth, also was a lefthanded pitcher, blasted 35 home runs (and led the circuit in triples) to set a new Texas League record. But the mark did not last for long.

During the next three seasons, the home run leader was Fort Worth first sacker Clarence Otto "Big Boy" Kraft. The veteran slugger hit 32 homers in 1922 and 1923, then poled 55 in 1924—the highest total in organized baseball that season and a record which would stand for 32 years in the Texas League. Kraft retired after the 1924 season, but his place on the Fort Worth roster was capably filled by longtime major leaguer "Big Ed" Konetchy, who led the Texas League in 1925 with 41 roundtrippers and 166 RBIs. By this time every team in the circuit was on the prowl for sluggers, and hitting exploits continued through the decade. Indeed, in 1929 an all-time total of 17 players scored 100 or more runs during the season.

For the first six years of the 1920s, the Fort Worth Panthers dominated the Texas League with an awesome combination of power hitting and overwhelming pitching. The architects of the most sustained team success in league history was a management trio: two men who became part owners in 1916, W. K. Stripling (team president, 1917–1929) and Paul LaGrave (team secretary and business manager—equivalent to a modern general manager—in 1916–1929), and Jake Atz (field manager, 1914–1929). Stripling and LaGrave collected fine players and paid them so well that they stayed in Fort Worth, even after stellar performances brought offers to play in higher classifications. Of course, independent minor league owners were under no obligation to sell outstanding players, which is a major explanation for the Texas League dynasties of the period.

An infielder by trade, Jake Atz found himself in Fort Worth in 1914 as a 35-year-old player-manager. He did not manage a complete season until 1917, when he won 91 games for a second-place finish. He brought the Panthers (soon they were being called "Jake Atz's Cats") in second again in 1918, and the next season won the most games — 94 — but lost in the playoffs to Shreveport. Then Atz's Cats hit their stride, winning six consecutive Texas League pennants. Atz's victory totals during his string of championships were: 1920 — 108; 1921 — 107; 1922 — 109; 1923 — 96; 1924 — 109; 1925 — 103. The 109 wins in 1922 and 1924 set an all-time Texas League record.

In each of the six years, Fort Worth far outdistanced the closest challengers. Although each season except 1923 was split (a ploy to create playoff competition), Fort Worth won both halves every year. The only playoff the Panthers had to face occurred in the second half of 1925, when Fort Worth tied with archrival Dallas. But Atz's Cats triumphed over Snipe Conley's Steers in three straight, and Fort Worth had won the second half as well as the first half, thus guaranteeing their sixth straight flag without a playoff series. In 1923, with no split season, Fort Worth finished thirteen and a half games ahead of second-place San Antonio.

Five players were on the Panther roster during all six championship seasons. Lefthander Joe Pate was a 20-game winner in each of the six flag years, and in 1921 and 1924 he won 30. Paul Wachtel, the righthanded spitballer, also was a six-time 20-game winner for the Panthers (he won 21 in 1919 and 19 in 1923). Pate and Wachtel won 26 apiece in 1920 to start the pennant run, and over the six years they made a combined contribution of 292-121 Ponderous Possum Moore caught for Fort Worth from 1919 through 1926; his best seasons were 1921 (.298) and 1924 (.311). Ziggy Sears, who spent 11 seasons in Texas League outfields, hit .304 in 1922, .323 in 1924, and .321 in 1925. Dugan Phelan, a five-year National League veteran, played 13 seasons in the Texas League; with Fort Worth he was a third baseman and pinch hitter who batted .300 in 1922.

Pate and Wachtel had impressive pitching support throughout the string. In 1920 and 1921 there were four 20-game winners on the staff: Pate and Wachtel won 26 each in 1920, while curveballing Buzzer Bill Whitaker was 24-6 and control artist Dick Robertson was 20-7: in 1921 Pate won 30, Wachtel 23, Whitaker 23, and southpaw Gus Johns won 20. There were three 20-game winners—Pate, Wachtel and Johns—in 1922, and in 1923, when Wachtel "slumped" to 19 victories and Pate won 23, Ulysses Simpson Grant "Lil" Stoner took up the slack with a 27-11 season (then he went directly to the major leagues). In 1925 Pate, Wachtel, and Johns won 20 or more, and southpaw Jim Walkup was 19-7. It was the greatest pitching staff in Texas League history.

The Panthers' leading slugger was Big Boy Kraft. He played seven seasons in Fort Worth (1918–1924), and in 980 Texas League games his batting average was .317. In 1921 he won the batting title with a .352 percentage, and he also led the league in at bats, runs, and hits. Kraft established the Texas League lifetime records for the most consecutive years scoring 100 or more runs, most years scoring 100 or more runs, making 200 or more base hits, making over 100 RBIs, leading in extra base hits and home runs. His finest season was 1924, when he hit .349 and belted 55 homers and an all-time record 196 RBIs.

The dominance of Fort Worth for the first six years of the decade overshadowed various heroics by players on other teams. Twenty-six-year-old Ike Boone, a six-foot, 200-pounder with three years' experience as a minor leaguer, signed on with San Antonio for 1923. It was to be his only year in the Texas League, but Boone had an unforgettable season, leading the league in batting average (.402), runs (134), hits (241), doubles (53), triples (26), RBIs (135) and total bases (391—the next year Big Boy Kraft established an all-time record 414 total bases). Boone also pounded 15 home runs and hit safely in 37 consecutive games—still the longest hitting streak in Texas League history. Boone finished the season with the Boston Braves, but he had enjoyed the most productive offensive year in modern Texas League play. Two seasons later San Antonio fans watched infielder Dan Clark flirt with .400 before finishing at .399. Wichita Falls Spudder fans cheered four batting champs during the decade: Red Josefson (.345 in 1920), Homer Summa (.362 in 1922), Arthur Weiss (.377 in 1924), and Tom Jenkins (.374 in 1926). Waco produced back-to-back batting champs: former major leaguer Del Pratt (.386 in 1927, plus a league-leading 32 home runs) and outfielder George Blackerby (.368 in 1928, plus a home run championship the next year).

A notable team exploit of the 1920s was Wichita Falls' impressive 1922 winning streak. On July 21 Victor Keen outdueled Snipe Conley and the Dallas Steers, 2-1 in 17 innings. Then the Spudders returned to Wichita Falls for a four-week home stand. During the streak Keen won seven games (he went 13-4, then finished the season with the Cubs), while Floyd "Rip" Wheeler also won seven (he was a 22-game winner in 1922 and again in 1923), including complete game victories in both halves of a doubleheader against San Antonio on August 3. On August 12 Keen squared off against Snipe Conley again. By the middle of the game spitballer Conley was complaining of burning lips, and soon his lips and tongue were so swollen that he could not talk. One of the Spudders—an aggregation notorious for their addiction to practical jokes—had applied colorless creosote to the game balls, and as Conley wet his fingers throughout the contest he severely burned his mouth. The Spudders won the game, 4-3, for their twenty-fifth consecutive victory. Spudder hopes of surpassing Corsicana's 27 straight in 1902 were thwarted the next day, when Roy Mitchell (who had beaten Wichita Falls the day before the streak started) pitched the Steers to a win. Dallas protested the Conley loss, however, and when the league upheld complaints over the "Creosote Incident," the official total stood at 24 consecutive victories—the second longest skein in Texas League history. But even after winning 24 in a row, the Spudders still trailed mighty Fort Worth by half a game. At season's end the Spudders were 94-61—good for second place to Fort Worth's 109-46 record.

A significant innovation of the 1920s was the Dixie Series, which became the most popular baseball event in the South for nearly four decades. As far back as the 1890s, Texas sportswriters had urged a post-season playoff series between the champions of the Texas League and the Southern League, forerunner of the twentieth-century Southern Association. But the Southern Association was more advanced in classification than the Texas League and had nothing to gain and a great deal of prestige to lose by such a series. In 1920, however, when Fort Worth and Little Rock clearly dominated their respective leagues, Paul LaGrave contacted R. G. Allen, president of the Little Rock club, and reached an agreement for a seven-game series after each team wrapped up its regular schedule. Little Rock, managed by Kid Elberfeld (who had played the 1896 season for Dallas en route to the major leagues), did not officially represent the Southern Association—which proved convenient for the association, since the powerful Panthers won the series. But the seven games had attracted 36,836 ticket-buyers and nearly $50,000 in gross receipts, and the opportunity for future profit was obvious.

In 1921 the Texas League was elevated to Class A status, and the two now-equal circuits made formal arrangements for the Dixie Series. Fort Worth prevailed again, this time over Southern Association winner Memphis, and the next year Panther fans chartered a "Dixie Special" and brought along a Dixieland band, cowbells, and raucous enthusiasm. Fort Worth lost to Mobile in 1922, but during the next three years Jake Atz's Cats beat New Orleans, Memphis, and Atlanta in succession. By this time the Dixie Series had attained the status of a "little World Series," and was avidly followed across the South and Texas.

In 1926 Fort Worth's long monopoly over the Texas League championship finally was ended by archrival Dallas. Panther ace Joe Pate at last went up to the major leagues, while Paul Wachtel, now 38, slipped to 16-19 (Wachtel could not advance to the majors during the 1920s because the spitball, his most effective pitch, had been outlawed). The league did not declare a split season, and the resulting 156-game pennant race proved to be the closest since before World War I. Galveston had dropped out of the Texas League in 1924, replaced by Waco, and the eight member cities in 1926 drew 1,159,906 paid admissions—an attendance record that stood for two decades.

Dallas attracted 286,806 of those fans. Snipe Conley had become a playing manager during the 1925 season, and in 1926 he pushed his team relentlessly toward a pennant. Snipe no longer pitched regularly, but 6'6" Slim Love (21-10) and southpaw Dick Schuman (17-5) led a solid mound corps, while R. L. Williams (.369), E. J. Woeber (.330 and 25 home runs), J. N. Riley (.329), and Charles Miller (.321, 30 homers and 118 RBIs) added lethal bats. Dallas battled for the lead throughout the year, but when Fort Worth dropped a late-season doubleheader, Conley's Steers took a stranglehold on first place. Then the Steers went on to beat New Orleans in six games for a Dixie Series triumph.

During league meetings preceding the 1923 season, circuit executives determined to follow the example of the rest of organized baseball and eliminate spitball pitching. Like the majors and other minor loops, the Texas League permitted current spitball practitioners to continue business as usual. Nine spitballers were sanctioned by the Texas League: Snipe Conley, Paul Wachtel, Slim Love, Ed Hovlik, Dana Fillingim, Hal Deviney, Larry Jacobus, Tom Estell, and Oscar Tuero. Most of these men were veterans nearing the end of the line; Estell and Tuero pitched until 1932, the last pitchers to *legally* throw a loaded baseball in the Texas League.

Edward Hock, who spent nine years in the Texas League, usually as a third baseman, was at shortstop for Houston when the Buffs lined up against Dallas on May 5, 1927. In the bottom of the third Dallas outfielder Rhino Williams walked. Fred Brainard dropped a sacrifice bunt, but both runners were safe when the ball was bobbled. Then Jodie Tate lashed a line drive up the middle. Moving to his left, Hock speared the ball, stepped on second for out number two, then chased down Brainard as he tried to scramble back toward third. It was the second unassisted triple play in Texas League history, following Roy Akin's unique effort from third base in 1912. Overall, there were six triple plays during the 1927 Texas League season.

Another remarkable fielding performance of the 1920s was turned in by Frankie Fuller, who played second base for San Antonio from 1920 through 1924 and for Houston in 1925. In each of the six seasons he led all pivot men in double plays, participating in a total of 531 double plays during the six years. Twice, Fuller took part in more than 100 double plays per season, and in 1922 he led the league in starting double plays—the only time a second baseman has surpassed all shortstops in that category.

The Wichita Falls Spudders proved to be the class of the league in 1927. The Spudders won their opener, and never relinquished the lead during the season. Third baseman Walter Swenson hit .300; second sacker Pete Turgeon, the Spudder leadoff man, hit .305, scored 115 runs, hit 31 doubles, 11 triples, 18 homers with 94 RBIs; center fielder Howard Chamney, an ex-University of Texas great who averaged .308 in 1,129 Texas League games from 1924 to 1932, hit .306; right fielder Lyman Lamb hit .314; even the utility man, Stanley "Rabbit" Benton, hit .322. But the offensive star of the team was left fielder "Tut" Jenkins, the defending champ (.374 in 1926) who hit .363 with 25 homers, 147 runs scored, and 129 RBIs.

Spudder pitching matched the explosive attack. At 23-9, old pro George Washington Payne led the league in victories; Frederick Fussell led the league in winning percentage (.724) at 21-8; Joe Kiefer was 20-9; spitballer Tom Estell was 16-7; and Milton Steengrafe was 15-6.

This powerful club overwhelmed the Texas League, finishing 102-54 (second-place Waco was 88-68), then swept New Orleans in four straight in the Dixie Series to complete a splendid season. It was the only time during the first 16 years of the classic that a team from either league took the Dixie Series in four games.

During the Texas League meeting in February 1928, it was decided to divide the season at mid-summer; 1928 would be the first time the league had ever determined beforehand to have a split season. Houston ran away with the first half, opening a lead of seven and a half games by June 29. Right fielder Red Worthington (.353 on the season) and catcher-manager Frank Snyder (.329) led the attack. "Pancho" Snyder had just finished a 16-year major league career, and he expertly handled a superb pitching staff that boasted no fewer than four 20-game winners: James Lindsey (25-10), Wild Bill Hallahan (23-12, with a league-leading 244 strikeouts and 2.25 ERA), Ken Penner (20-8), and Frank Barnes (20-9).

In the second half Wichita Falls aggressively defended their title. Although some of the big guns of 1927 had moved up, Tut Jenkins (.348 with a league-leading 27 homers, 121 runs scored, and 122 RBIs), Rabbit Benton (.324) and catcher Pete Lapan (.324) generated considerable offense, while Milt Steengrafe (22-8) and big league veteran Mike Cvengros (21-8) headed a pitching staff that was not up to the previous year's overall quality. But the Spudders dominated the second half, finishing with a margin of seven and a half games over second-place Houston. It seemed as though Wichita Falls would provide yet another dynasty for the 1920s.

In the best-of-five playoffs the Buffaloes won the first game in Wichita Falls, then dropped a decision to the Spudders. In the opening contest at Houston, Hallahan beat Cvengros, 1-0, on a two-hitter, and the Buffaloes wrapped up the series the next day. Having regained early-season form with their first flag since 1914, Houston downed Birmingham in the Dixie Series.

Competition was fierce throughout the Texas League in 1929. Fort Worth led in team batting (.303), but finished fourth; Waco led in home runs (188), but ended up fifth. During the year, Paul LaGrave died, and longtime Fort Worth president W. C. Stripling and the LaGrave estate sold their interests in the Panthers. Jake Atz, the brilliant field general who had served since 1914, including the past 13 consecutive years, left the team. The splendid management combination that had fashioned the Panther dynasty was dissolved before season's end.

Dallas, sparked by the explosive bats of outfielder Randy Moore (.369) and Simon Rosenthal (.339), took the first-half championship by merely a half game over Shreveport. Bridesmaid Shreveport finished second again in the last half, this time to Wichita Falls. The Spudders were led by George Washington Payne, who pitched in 55 games and finished at 28-12. As usual, Wichita Falls fans enjoyed a number of fine hitters: left fielder Fred Bennett (.368 and 145 RBIs); catcher Pete Lapan (.367); infielder Rabbit Benton (.327); and almost everybody else in the lineup.

The race for the batting title went down to the last day of the season. Randy Moore won by a single percentage point and established an all-time league record for base hits (245). Fort Worth center fielder Eddie Moore, a speedy ball hawk and baserunner, set the all-time mark for triples (30). Texas League fans enjoyed the aggressive baserunning of Houston outfielder Pepper Martin, who led the league in stolen bases both years (1927 and 1929) he played for the Buffs.

Wichita Falls ended 1929 with the best record in the league, but the Spudders lost out to Dallas in the playoffs. Although Payne pitched in three of the four games, the Spudder ace ironically could not gain a playoff win. The Dallas Steers, with their second title in four seasons, were defeated in the Dixie Series by Birmingham—snapping a six-year losing streak inflicted by the Texas League on their Southern Association opponents.

By the time the season closed, the New York stock market had begun to wobble toward its disastrous collapse. The 1920s had been a period of unparalleled fan interest and attendance. The decade had exhibited great teams, a number of admirable pitching performances, and, above all, unprecedented hitting. It was the most exciting, explosive baseball that had yet been played in the circuit. But the 1930s would bring the Great Depression to the cities and ball parks and club offices of the Texas League.

Red Burton and the Klan

Ben Procter

Ben Procter (1927–2012) taught for over forty years at Texas Christian University in Fort Worth. From 1979–1980, he served as President of the Texas State Historical Association. Procter's studies include *Not Without Honor: The Life of John H. Reagan* (1962), *The Battle of the Alamo* (1986), *Just One Riot: Episodes of Texas Rangers in the 20th Century* (1991), and the two-volume biography, *William Randolph Hearst* (1998, 2007).

The Ku Klux Klan was a formidable force in the Lone Star State during the 1920s. In this selection, Dr. Procter recounts the violent confrontation between a Klan mob and two intrepid Texas lawmen—Red Burton and Bob Buchanan—in McLennan County.

★ ★

A wave of fear swept across Texas in the summer and fall of 1921. Masked men in white robes paraded triumphantly; flaming crosses illuminated the sky, eerie and ominous in the darkness; and bands of nightriders, vigilante style, tortured or murdered their victims in the name of law and order. At crossroads and in Texas towns, billboards demanding "One Hundred Per Cent Americanism," "Booze Must and Shall Go," "Love Thy Neighbor as Thyself but Leave His Wife Alone," "Keep This a White Man's Country," apprised citizens that a new force, supposedly

"Red Burton and the Klan" from *Just One Riot: Episodes of Texas Rangers in the 20th Century* by Ben Procter, 1991, pp. 44-58. Published by Eakin Press. Reprinted by permission.

patriotic, most assuredly moralistic, definitely restrictive, was moving into their community. Preaching racism and religious bigotry, the Invisible Empire of Kleagles and Imperial Wizards and Grand Dragons called for a war against malevolent groups such as radicals, foreigners, and "niggers" to keep them from undermining "pure" American institutions. And how? The Ku Klux Klan had the answer. The best element of society must purge all "alien" forces, no matter how great the cost, no matter what the method.

For $10 "true" Americans could join the Klan; for $10 they could help save the United States. At last they had found an effective vehicle for alleviating the frustrations of a rapidly changing world, for fighting against conditions both disturbing and startling. To them it was shocking how much society was degenerating, how immoral people were becoming. The family, with its spiritual and moral base, was showing signs of fracturing, even of disintegrating. Some women were choosing a career instead of marriage; divorce in preference to self-sacrifice for their children; plunging necklines and rising skirts in defiance of modesty and decency. Yet political leaders on both the national and local levels, although staunch advocates of law and order, were apparently helpless to combat trends toward the disruption of society. Prostitution and gambling were increasing; "racketeer" and "speak-easy" and "booze" were becoming familiar terms in the English language; and that "Noble Experiment," the Eighteenth Amendment, was ineffective—and laughable.

To make matters worse, American institutions seemed to be under heavy attack. Since the Bolshevik Revolution of 1917, "true" Americans believed that Communists and radicals were trying to undermine the American system. United States Attorney General A. Mitchell Palmer had moved in the right direction by ferreting out those "traitors" in the government and bringing them to trial. But this "witch hunt," as the radical press called his actions, had definite limitations; in no way could he noticeably affect local situations. At the same time, the New Immigration, alien and Catholic, spouting strange political philosophies that were often critical of the American way of life, was also weakening this nation by its "mongrelizing taints." Those dark-skinned peoples, who lived in slums and tended toward vice and corruption, usually could not speak English, much less understand how democracy functioned. Equally alarming were attempts to paralyze the economy, to engulf the United States in depression. And who was to blame? Obviously, the "true" Americans agreed, it was the alien element, such as the "Uncle Shylock," the avaricious Jew who kept prices high and wages low.

So in October 1921, Klansmen were marching in Texas almost 100,000 strong, raising the fiery cross and the American flag in unison, denouncing the cancerous evils and corrupting vices in their midst, then enrolling "good solid middle-class citizens" in their ranks: lawyers, doctors, bankers, businessmen, even ministers and policemen. Already they had organized and paraded in Houston, Beaumont, Dallas, Fort Worth, Waco, Austin, and San Antonio. Now they were moving into rural communities. In East Texas and along the Gulf Coast their gospel spread like wildfire; on the Black Prairie in North Texas they were equally successful. The next region to "educate" lay in the center of the state, a land of rolling prairies dotted with small, fairly prosperous farming villages. But here the Invisible Empire hit a snag in the form of two law enforcement officers, Red Burton and Bob Buchanan.

Born on August 10, 1885, near Mart, Texas, Marvin "Red" Burton was the youngest son of John F. and Alice Cubley Burton. Originally from Montrose, Mississippi, his parents had migrated to Texas in the early 1880s and bought a farm between Mart and Waco. In that locale Red Burton grew to manhood, a typical product of his environment and of the era. Like most farm boys in Central Texas, he had specific family chores, helping his father in the fields and his mother around the house. Whenever possible he went to school, but scholastic endeavors did not prevent him from learning to fish, ride, and shoot well. Overall, life was not easy for Red; work hours were long and tasks often tedious. The span from childhood to maturity was brief.

Consequently, when only eighteen, Burton married a local girl and assumed the more difficult responsibilities of making a living. Starting without "a dollar in the world," he worked wherever possible, but essentially his life was without purpose or direction. In 1905 he landed a job on a ranch near Wortham, Texas. Then, in 1913, he returned to the Waco area and, with the savings of the last eight years, purchased a lot and built a house. Once again he was penniless and out of work, lacking even "money enough to buy . . . groceries."

But in 1914, after pouring concrete for stormsewers (and not too regularly), Burton informed his wife one morning: "I'm going to work at somethin'. I don't know what it does; I don't care what it pays. I'm going to work." Determined and almost desperate, he applied for a position with the Cleveland Construction Company. When the foreman sarcastically announced, "Sonny, we have work to do here but you wouldn't do it," Burton bristled, "You don't know me, man; I'll do anything honorable." And looking at the lean-muscled, 6'2 farm boy, almost skinny at 180 pounds, the foreman suddenly changed his mind. Perhaps something in Burton's voice, his clipped, terse comments, his firm, positive tone, carried conviction. Or possibly his appearance—light blue eyes, sandy red hair and ruddy complexion, a mask of defiance and resolution, huge hands, noticeably scarred and calloused, hanging like ham-hocks from his shirtsleeves—made the foreman recognize a difference in this applicant. But whatever the reason, he found himself saying: "I'll tell you what, Sonny. You come over here tomorrow morning and . . . we'll run you off." That was one thing no one ever did. Burton stayed three years.

After that day, Red Burton never went hungry again; he was too much in demand. Within three weeks he was elevated to foreman, even though obviously inexperienced. When he expressed feelings of inadequacy, his boss explained the promotion this way: "I know you don't know a whole lot but you will work. I'll help you if you get in trouble." He never had to, however, for Burton learned his trade well. But even more importantly, he won the respect of the men under him. Those who met his standards could count on steady employment, while those who were "toughs" or troublemakers (and there were plenty of that sort in construction work) learned to steer clear of him or quit. He would—and could—back up his decisions.

In August 1917, Burton decided to change jobs, but not because he was unhappy. It was a matter of economics. The United States government, upon entering World War I, contracted the Grace Construction Company to build an airfield at Richfield, a few miles west of Waco. Since thousands of men were enlisting or being drafted into the armed forces, labor was hard to come by and even more difficult to keep. The Grace Company officials therefore offered

Burton a job as foreman at double his present salary. They knew his reputation: that he was a tough taskmaster, that he inspired loyalty, that his men were ready to fight for him.

For two and a half weeks at Richfield, Burton measured up to all advance notices. Then, in an unexpected turn of events, the Waco Police Department drafted him into its ranks. Although the city council could in no way enforce such an act, Burton decided to serve for six months. He liked the idea of public service, of doing "things for other people." Besides, he was overworked, almost exhausted, and here was a chance, he reasoned, to "rest up" before returning to his old job.

How wrong he was! At nearby Camp MacArthur thousands of soldiers, mostly from the Midwest, had arrived and were inundating Waco, causing the usual problems between townspeople and the military. For the first few months, therefore, Burton had his hands full directing traffic as well as learning police procedures and gaining an understanding of the problems and techniques of law enforcement. Then he was assigned to night duty, patrolling residential and outlying districts on a motorcycle—and the orientation process began all over again. Gradually, as the months rolled by and as he became more involved, thoughts of returning to construction work faded away; each day he found "policing" more and more fascinating.

But in 1919, with the passage of the Eighteenth Amendment, Burton was caught in a situation which law officers have always dreaded. Besides having to enforce an unpopular law, he watched it corrupt some of his colleagues, thereby placing him in a difficult position. Because he was not "on the take," word went out to "get Red Burton lined up." After all, contraband liquor was bringing high prices and police salaries were low. Yet in spite of all inducements—promises of money, promotion, and favors—he steadfastly refused. So one morning in September his chief informed him that "for the good of the department" he was transferring him to a daytime schedule. Incensed over this roundabout way of curtailing his effectiveness (most of the contraband arrived at night), Burton replied: "Well, sir, if I thought it was better for the department, I wouldn't say a word"—and he quit.

Actually Burton only changed jobs, not professions. Because of his fine record, Bob Buchanan, the sheriff of McLennan County, offered him a deputy's commission. What a lucky break it was for both men. Besides seeing eye-to-eye concerning law enforcement, they became close friends. And on October 1, 1921, at Lorena, Texas, approximately thirteen miles south of Waco, they had need of each other. Together—and alone—they faced the Klan.

Robert "Bob" Buchanan was a rugged law-enforcement officer and a formidable opponent, cut from the same mold as frontier marshals and Texas Rangers. Although fifty years old, he looked much younger, possibly because of his smooth, tanned face and black, wavy hair. Physically he was an impressive man, carrying 225 pounds easily on a sturdy 6'1 build. A huge Colt .38 "thumbbuster" on a .45 frame strapped to his left hip made him even more imposing. Yet his eyes, coal-black, piercing, at times ominous and unfathomable, were his dominant feature. When someone challenged him, they were like gale warnings, prominent and threatening. No one was going to run over Bob Buchanan. He represented the law—and that meant fair, impartial enforcement. Never did he allow political pressure or expediency or friendship to interfere with duty. Of course, this strict adherence to the law, this tough application of justice, was also an Achilles' heel. But he knew no other way; to him any other conduct was unthinkable.

Even with law officers like Burton and Buchanan in McLennan County, the Klan leaders decided to act on October 1. Having already organized thoroughly in Waco, they planned a Saturday evening rally at Lorena, where they would march with fiery crosses through the black section of town and then convene, ironically enough, at the Baptist Church for an ice cream supper. Throughout Waco and the surrounding areas they tacked up notices, announcing in bold black type: "The Ku Klux Klan Will Parade Tonight at 8:30."

Surprisingly, neither Buchanan nor Burton was aware of these arrangements. Both were busy investigating a cotton theft in the nearby towns of Leroy and Mart. Yet while on the job they came to an understanding concerning the Klan. Each soon discovered that the other was not a member. In fact, they both voiced grave misgivings as to its purpose and activities, especially since a demonstration in Mart the previous Saturday had caused considerable damage. "If there is ever another parade in McLennan County while I am sheriff, I intend to find out who is responsible," Buchanan asserted emphatically, "and if I am out of the country, I want you to do it." Burton agreed. The matter was closed. Both sensed, however, that a "bad situation" might soon develop.

The two men had no idea that a confrontation was imminent. Upon their return to Waco that afternoon, however, several citizens from Lorena were waiting in Buchanan's office to inform him of a scheduled mass meeting and to appeal for help. Within a few minutes they had their answer. Turning to Burton, the sheriff asked, "Will you go down there with me?" And when Red replied he would, they were on their way.

It was a beautiful autumn afternoon as they rode to Lorena. The air was crisp, the sun bright, the countryside a greenish-brown, not quite ready to succumb to winter. With approximately 350 inhabitants, Lorena resembled many other Central Texas farm communities in the 1920s. Situated on a rolling black prairie, it rose into view easily, the spires from its several churches and the roofs of rambling two-story frame houses surrounded by large shade trees, obvious landmarks. Like so many small towns it had two principal avenues: Main Street, comprising most of the business district, and Highway 81, cutting through the best residential area. Where these two thoroughfares intersected, townspeople had built a funeral parlor, bank, Ford agency, and combination drug and general store, symbols of a permanent and growing community. Except for market day, Saturday mornings, and holidays, the atmosphere was always easygoing, relaxed, often phlegmatic.

But by the time the two lawmen arrived that evening, Lorena had changed dramatically. On the outskirts hundreds of cars, surreys, and wagons were parked haphazardly along the highway or in nearby fields. Along the streets vast throngs, estimated at 15,000 to 20,000 people, were milling about restlessly, though apparently in a festive mood. And as the sun quickly receded and the evening shadows lengthened, they eagerly anticipated the forthcoming events, for less than half a mile to the north hundreds of hooded, white-robed figures were assembling in a cotton field.

In order to maintain some semblance of authority and keep the peace, Buchanan promptly sought out the town leaders. Although known to be "pretty hotheaded" at times, he was extremely calm and "reasonable" that evening. Carefully, he explained his position. He had not come to stop their parade; on the contrary, as far as he was concerned they could march all night. But as sheriff of McLennan County, he announced, "I think I'm entitled to know who's responsible for it, so if anything happens I can know who to look for." For instance, he explained, whenever a circus came to town, the owners always made arrangements with him and the police regarding the parade. Consequently, if the leaders would identify themselves to him by raising their hoods when marching by, he would be satisfied.

Within thirty minutes, after much huddling and conferring, two McLennan County officials who were well-known to both Buchanan and Burton stepped forward to assume responsibility. Jovially the sheriff remarked that they need not lift their hoods because he would "know either of their hides in a tanning yard." So the matter was resolved—but not for long. A majority of the Klan leaders would not accept this agreement. Unhappy with the two officials for violating one of the basic rules of membership—that of secrecy—they rejected Buchanan's proposal, confident that their decision would cause no significant reverberations. After all, what could two law officers, alone and without public support, do? How could they prevent thousands from parading? The answers were obvious, the questions rhetorical. After taking precautionary steps, just in case the lawmen should react foolishly, the Klansmen quickly formed into lines of white-hooded figures, raised several American flags, lit huge crosses (one man, however, had wired one electrically), and began the march.

Meanwhile, Buchanan and Burton were chatting amicably and visiting with friends at the main intersection, unaware that the Klan was not going to cooperate. Then the situation changed dramatically. Out of the crowd the two county officials emerged in front of Burton, told him what had just happened, and rather fearfully asked if the sheriff would "think hard of them" if they did not participate. Rushing across the street, Red was repeating the conversation to Buchanan, who was listening silent and grim-faced, when a resounding roar announced the beginning of the parade. Out onto Highway 81 the Klansmen came, a sea of white-clothed figures outlined against the night. Without a word to anyone Buchanan, with jaw set, and wearing a mask of determination, began walking toward the marchers. Burton, remembering that the sheriff had earlier told him to "stay close" in case of trouble, followed some fifteen to twenty feet behind. Nearer and nearer they moved toward the mass of white, the crowd closing in behind them, both hostility and fear apparent in the expressions of the people.

Now the antagonists were face to face, just a few feet apart; yet Buchanan never hesitated or wavered. Whether unafraid of the consequences or feeling that he had no choice, he reacted bravely, even heroically. Confronting the first two leaders who were carrying a flaming cross, he reached out and slammed it to the ground, then raised up the hood of the nearest figure and resolutely declared: "I don't know you, but if I ever see your face again I will."

As Buchanan moved toward the second man, all hell broke loose. Stealthily, a robed form, later identified as a Waco policeman, crept up behind him and either with a blackjack or billyclub knocked him to the ground. Then, upon seizing the sheriff's pistol, the outraged Klansmen swarmed over him as he lay prostrate in the road, hitting and beating him repeatedly. At the same time Red Burton "was completely covered with men," two or three holding him while others pounded at his face and body. Physically powerful and doubly so because he was fighting for his life, he repeatedly broke away from one group only to be grabbed by another. Suddenly, two pistol shots rang out, startling the melee into silence. Buchanan, hurt and bleeding, yelled out: "Red, they've shot me."

Now the action became deadlier. Flicking out a pocketknife with a four-inch blade, the sheriff, even though badly wounded, slashed and stabbed two of his antagonists. Then Burton, like a man possessed, wild and uncontrollable after seeing his comrade fall, reacted almost unbelievably in the next few minutes. Never losing sight of the man who had shot Buchanan, he managed to pull a small .38 Colt automatic from his left pants pocket and fired two shots. The would-be killer dropped. Oblivious to the punishing blows from men who were still pommeling him, Burton fired the remaining seven bullets at Klansmen near the sheriff, definitely hitting one and possibly several others. For some reason the mob had failed to take his holstered single-action .41 Colt; but in his highly excited state of mind he had no time to ponder such an oversight, for he needed the weapon. Wrenching his pinned right arm free, he unsheathed the .41 Colt and stuck the barrel into the stomach of a prominent Lorena businessman, T. C. Westbrook, who was still trying to hold him. In a cold, deadly voice he said: "Mr. Westbrook, I love you like a daddy, but if I am not released I'm going to kill you." And for the first time since the fight began he was free of fists and arms and bodies.

Bruised and blood-smeared, Burton quickly assessed the situation as he stood in the highway exposed and unprotected—and it was not to his liking. In front of him, some ten yards away, the sheriff was staggering but on his feet, bleeding profusely from wounds in his right chest and leg. Approximately fifty feet to his left a robed Klansman was leveling a pistol at Buchanan, while at about the same distance on his right someone was also shooting at the sheriff.

Instinctively, Burton swung into action. With two shots he ended the threat to Buchanan, the man crumpling to the ground in a heap. Then he whirled to face his own assailant. In haste he fired several times, missing on each attempt but causing the man to flee. In fact, upon realizing that Burton could not be stopped and with bullets hitting indiscriminately in their midst, the crowd had dispersed, men and women scattering frantically in all directions.

Burton then turned to help Buchanan, but during the last exchange of gunfire someone had carried him to the drugstore at the intersection. So Red Burton hobbled and stumbled down the highway, unaware that he had been wounded in the right thigh. All about him was confusion. In a few short minutes Lorena had become a hate-filled disaster area. The town was a shambles, white robes and debris strewn everywhere, the streets spattered with blood, Klansmen confused and disorganized, their leaders striving to regroup. In the middle of the intersection a former Waco judge was damning and cursing the two lawmen at the top of his lungs, encouraging the apprehensive to more violence. For a fleeting moment Burton had "an evil thought," but with only one bullet left in his .41 Colt he decided not "to waste it on the old son-of-a-bitch."

After considerable physical exertion, Burton finally reached the front door of the drugstore, fearful that his comrade was mortally wounded because boastful Klansmen were shouting that they had killed Buchanan. Once inside he took command, threatening and cursing those who seemed to be more afraid of the Klan than of him. To Wiley Stem, a Waco policeman, he gave specific instructions to bolt the door and let no one in "unless someone had been injured." At the same instant he flipped back Stem's coat, grabbed his .45 Colt automatic, and grimly said, "Wiley, I need this and you have no use for it, so I'm taking it." Then he hurried over to Buchanan, who was sitting upright in a chair, obviously in pain and having difficulty breathing, blood flowing profusely from his chest. "Burton, they've killed me," the sheriff weakly exclaimed, to which Red replied: "No, Bob, those sons-of-bitches can't kill you; you just can't die."

But for the moment Burton could not be sure that anyone would not die. Outside the building Klansmen were milling about, venting their hate and frustration by angrily shouting: "Get a rope! Get a rope! Let's hang 'em." Inside, the foul stench of sweat and blood grew stronger, the moans of suffering men reverberating through the room as more and more wounded were brought in. Among them were Louis Crow, a prominent Waco businessman and ironically a close friend of the sheriff, with a deep stab wound in the chest; Ed Howard, a Waco policeman, knifed in the stomach; Carl West of Lorena, shot in the neck; and at least five others suffering from bullet or knife wounds. Already medical assistance was on the way, for Burton had summoned ambulances from Waco. But with the mob threatening to break in at any moment, and with an enraged Red Burton fingering a fully loaded gun and ready to kill anyone who threatened the wounded Buchanan, the chances of another bloodbath seemed definite.

Buchanan, however, realizing that trouble would continue as long as he and Burton were in town, repeatedly pleaded with his "friend" not to wait for the ambulance. Unsuccessful at first, he used the one argument which Burton could not resist. "I have always thought you were the best friend I had in the world," the sheriff declared, "and if you are, you will take me to the hospital." To that plea there could be only one answer. So Burton instructed Wiley Stem to "get a car" and bring it to the side entrance on Highway 81. Then he asked for someone to help him with the sheriff, but everyone shied away, fearful of what the Klan might do. He therefore draped Buchanan across his shoulder and back, holding him with his right hand, and dragged him across the room and out the side door through the crowd to the waiting car. Just in case the Klansmen intended to carry out their threats, he had Stem's .45 Colt automatic in his left hand, cocked and ready for action. But they had had enough of Burton for one night; they wanted no more. In silence they let the lawmen depart.

At breakneck speed Burton drove along the narrow winding highway to Waco, his thoughts a mass of mixed emotions. Worried and increasingly concerned, he kept checking on Buchanan, who was coughing spasmodically and sometimes gagging, watching him push a forefinger into the chest wound to stop the flow of blood. As ambulances passed by, clanging and screaming in the night, he bitterly reflected upon the events of the evening, the threats and violence, the unreasoning hatred of the mob, the feeling of loneliness when no one would help him. Suddenly, robed figures appeared on his right, running across a cotton field, and instinctively he reached for his .45 Colt automatic, feelings of vengeance and retribution welling up inside him. As if reading his mind, Buchanan spoke out almost pleadingly: "No, Burton, I think they whipped us; let's not have any more trouble."

So onward they raced toward Waco, Burton blaring the car horn to clear the way after reaching the city limits. Upon arrival at the Colgin Hospital, just across from the county jail (which was also the sheriff's home), they proceeded with the help of an attendant to the second-floor emergency room. Then events quite similar to the drugstore scene at Lorena happened all over again. With the Buchanan family and Burton standing guard at the door, doctors worked feverishly on the wounded and suffering men who streamed into the operating room. In the corridors, newspaper reporters and law officers, as well as county and district officials, were trying to piece together from the participants exactly what had happened, while outside in the street, thousands of people began gathering, surly and hostile, threatening to storm the hospital and lynch the two lawmen.

In all this frenzied commotion Burton remained calm and seemingly unmoved. Now painfully aware of both the multiple bruises on his body and the gunshot wound in his leg, he slumped into a chair to rest while listening without comment as I. Mac Wood, Buchanan's office deputy (and a Klansman), told what the mob was plotting. To pleas that he sneak out the back way and barricade himself in the county jail, Burton replied: "No, Mac, I have never had to be locked in jail yet." If, however, the Klansmen wanted trouble, he would accommodate them, Burton informed Wood, because he intended to come out soon.

At 4:00 Sunday morning Burton left the hospital. Although limping badly, he opened the front door, hobbled down the steps, and moved defiantly through the crowd, never speaking to or noticing anyone, yet expecting a confrontation each step of the way. After a few hushed, extremely tense minutes he had run the gauntlet and was safe within the county jail. For the moment he had faced the mob and had backed them down.

But the issue was by no means resolved, for the Klansmen were determined to win out. With Buchanan incapacitated, Burton was now in charge and therefore the key to the situation. Yet every attempt to outwit, pressure, or scare him failed miserably. When a fellow deputy, with whom he had worked closely, told him "to line up with the Klan" or "be a damn fool," Burton grabbed him by the back of the neck and the seat of the pants, unceremoniously dragged him into the county clerk's office, and ordered one of the secretaries to stamp "Canceled" across his commission as a deputy sheriff. Later the same day, two county commissioners tried still another approach, offering him a thirty-day paid vacation (to begin immediately) because they were afraid for his safety. Thanking them for their concern, he resolutely announced that he had "no intention of leaving." And if Klansmen wanted him, they would find him "in the sheriff's office," he asserted, "eighteen or twenty hours each day."

For over a week the pressure continued to mount, but Burton remained adamant. No matter that friends and prominent citizens asked him to submit to the Klan, no matter that public opinion was overwhelmingly against him and the sheriff, he would not back down, even after Crow died on October 4 and most of Waco turned out to mourn a "fallen hero." Scornful of hundreds of posters offering a "$5,000 Reward for Red Burton, Dead or Alive," he purposely appeared more prominently in public, challenging the Klan by his presence. Against a barrage of threats on his life, he countered with equally violent actions and statements. Whenever drivers happened to pull up beside him in a car, they found an automatic shotgun pointing out the window. During one difficult day after visiting Buchanan, who was still on the critical list, he bitterly and unwisely declared: "My greatest desire is that I may live to see . . . the streets of Lorena grow up in weeds."

Consequently, the Klansmen realized that only one course of action was left: Kill Red Burton! Throughout McLennan County and Central Texas word went out for Klansmen to assemble in Waco, whereupon they would march on the county jail and lynch Red Burton. On Wednesday afternoon, October 10, men began gathering on the city street corners, whispering their thoughts and plans. But as their numbers increased into the hundreds and then thousands, they boldly announced their intentions. Under the cover of darkness, with fiery crosses illuminating the sky, they were going to demonstrate what would happen to those who opposed the Klan.

By late afternoon Red Burton recognized the full extent of the danger. Yet he could do nothing. The Klansmen had the offensive; it was their move. That was the worst part—the feeling of helplessness, the loneliness, the waiting. To say the least, Burton was "considerably worried"; he knew that his opponents were deadly serious.

Darkness came quickly that October night in Waco. A light, cold mist was falling, the dampness bringing shivers to those in the streets. At approximately 8:00 p.m. three prominent citizens entered the county jail to see Burton, and to his surprise they wanted to help. "If you knew what all we know, you couldn't be in Waco, let alone sitting here in the sheriff's office alone," one of them began, because "[the Klan is] coming over here . . . to kill you." Under no circumstances could they condone such behavior; therefore, they were offering their services. They had already decided to hide him in one of their homes, to protect his family, and if necessary to stand with him against the mob; for, as one of them put it, "We need you, but we need you alive."

To accept their aid was definitely the sane choice, the human one; to reject it seemingly foolhardy. But Red Burton, even though deeply moved by their concern, would not run. After all, if the Klansmen really wanted to kill him, they would "finally do it," he explained, "so they had just as well get through with it tonight." He was not certain, however, that when actually facing him—and also the possibility of his retaliation—they could do murder. "But I am going to give them a chance," he told his startled friends. Presently he intended to make his usual nightly check around town.

As Burton recalled later, the next thirty minutes were a nightmare. Almost instinctively he reached for a sawed-off shotgun and placed it under his raincoat. Then over "strong protests" he opened the door and stepped out onto the street. With the sidewalks jammed with people, he had to push through the crowds, his ruddy face reflecting his grim determination. Up Austin Avenue to the Raleigh Hotel, then back to city hall and the police station he walked, catcalls and threats of violence all about him, a mob of people following and closing fast behind him. Crossing over to Sixth Street, he stopped at the Riddle Cafe for a cup of coffee. Sitting at a table near the back, he readied his shotgun as the angry crowd pressed against the large glass window panels. At that moment Mrs. Riddle hesitantly approached him, tears running down her cheeks, and whispered: "Mr. Burton, when you get ready to leave, my car is at the back door and . . . I am going to drive you away from here, because if you don't, those people are going to kill you." Burton again refused help. "Those men think they want to kill me but they don't," he replied, "because they realize that . . . some of them will be killed." Besides, he announced, while rising to pay his check, "I didn't come in your back door. I am going out . . . just as I came in." And he did, with no one challenging him or even attempting to slow him down en route to the sheriff's office.

Later, Burton readily admitted that he "really had no hopes of returning to the office alive." But now he felt safe. Perhaps his three friends, jubilantly returning to the jail, most accurately assessed what had just happened. As one of them put it: "Burton, you have done the smartest thing that a man ever did . . . we thought you were crazy but . . . if you had run as we advised you, this thing would have never ended; but now they have gone home with their tails tucked like a bunch of whipped puppies."

The violence was over; however, the evil effects, the cancerous suspicions, the hatreds and animosities, lingered. When Texas Governor Pat Neff ordered an immediate investigation, the Klansmen in Lorena and Waco withheld information and obstructed justice, threatening anyone who might think of testifying against them. Consequently, the McLennan County grand jury returned no indictments but issued "a sweeping rebuke" to Bob Buchanan for his actions. The citizens of Lorena acted in the same spirit; approximately 300 of them signed a petition, vindicating the Klan of its part in "the trouble" and damning the lawmen "for the blood that was spilled." So the bitterness would continue in the county, with people blaming one another for what had happened. And even though the Klan would continue to thrive in Central Texas for several years, the Lorena affair alarmed many thoughtful citizens and thereby aroused staunch opposition against the organization.

No one was a more outstanding opponent of the Klan than Bob Buchanan. A constant reminder of that terrible night, he continued to live for seven years, somewhat crippled by the bullet still in his right leg and physically unable to run for sheriff again. But he never apologized for his actions; instead he battled the Klan, whenever possible showing people what it really stood for. During the next few years he also fought several civil suits brought against him by those wounded at Lorena—and each time he won. In fact, so great was his reputation, so dominant his presence, that the Klan did not parade in Waco until after he retired from office on January 1, 1923.

As for Red Burton, Lorena was just the beginning of a long career in law enforcement. Because of Burton's dedication and valor as a chief deputy in McLennan County, Governor Neff appointed him a Texas Ranger in 1922; he was never disappointed. During the next eleven years Burton became almost a legend in the Ranger service, especially in cases concerning bootleggers, oil boomers, and Klansmen. Then, in 1933, he returned to Waco to serve as chief of detectives and later as chief of police. Upon retirement in 1951, despite all his many contributions to law enforcement over a thirty-five-year span, he would best be remembered for that night in Lorena—for the example that he and Bob Buchanan had set, where two peace officers, disregarding personal safety, faced the Klan and fought it to a standstill.

Dashed Hopes and Gained Opportunities: Mexican American Educational Experiences in Lubbock, Texas, from the 1920s through the 1960s

SCOTT SOSEBEE

Scott Sosebee, Executive Director of the East Texas Historical Association, teaches history at Stephen F. Austin State University in Nacogdoches. His publications have appeared in the *East Texas Historical Journal*, the *Journal of Southern History*, and the West Texas Historical Association *Year Book*. He also contributed an essay, "Agriculture, Ranching, and Rural Life in West Texas," to the anthology, *West Texas: A History of the Giant Side of the State* (2014), edited by Paul H. Carlson and Bruce A. Glasrud.

This selection, based largely on interviews, examines the struggle for educational equality in Lubbock, a city where Mexican Americans faced entrenched racism. Dr. Sosebee discusses the tremendous sacrifice made by Tejano parents, resolutely determined to end segregation in the public schools. ⋖

★ ★

The Mexican American educational experience in Lubbock, and in Texas as a whole, is one mixed with great injustice as well as significant accomplishments. In the twentieth century alone Mexican Americans have had to battle legal segregation and societal discrimination, in addition to Anglo perceptions of inferiority and a lack of intellectual acumen. While many

Mexican Americans were denied equal access to educational opportunities, others did break through the barriers and, largely through educational achievement and personal initiative, did attain some measure of economic and societal advancement.

The conviction that the Mexican American people could succeed only through education has a long history. Historians have tended to focus solely on the post World War II period, but as George J. Sanchez observes in his work *Becoming Mexican American,* education was an important part of many Mexican American organizations' agenda before the war years. For example, the Mexican American Movement (MAM) identified education as the key for success in the 1930s. The League of United Latin American Citizens (LULAC) made educational opportunity their primary objective and understood that any political, social, or economic advancement depended almost solely on an educated populace. Given such a strong heritage of educational importance, it is little wonder that Mexican Americans possessed a deep respect for and commitment to education and made concerted efforts to increase their children's educational opportunities.

Despite the importance of education within the *barrios,* until recently historians have often neglected the role of education in the field's historiography. Guadalupe San Miguel, in his work *Let All of Them Take Heed,* specifically points out the exclusion of studies that detail the ambitions of Mexican American students, their perceptions of the educational experience, and the impact of the public schools on their lives. For San Miguel, this has led to a lack of historical knowledge concerning Mexican Americans and education, as well as a definite dearth of interpretative insight into the experiences of Mexican Americans in school and the schools' response to this segment of the population. Little is known about their educational aspirations or the extent to which they have participated in influencing the support, structure, processes, and content of public education.

The few historical studies that exist on Mexican Americans and education have focused on what schools and educational policy have done to these children. Without a doubt, there is a large body of evidence that shows how Mexican American schoolchildren were more often than not subjected to ethnocentric curriculums and "tracked" to vocational programs that developed cheap labor for the low-skills industries of the Southwest. Such a paradigm tends to relegate Mexican Americans into a "history of victimization," which ignores human agency. Despite the enormous barriers placed before them, Mexican Americans have not been passive victims of racist school policies nor have they willingly succumbed to assimilationist policies. Rather, they have actively sought educational equality and continue to strive for academic attainment.

In such a vein, a primary focus of this article is to first examine the barriers that restricted Lubbock's Mexican American population and then explore how some of the city's Mexican Americans overcame or dealt with the restrictions on their educational advancement as well as their aspirations and accomplishments. Lubbock serves as an excellent locale for study; by the mid twentieth century it had developed as the largest city in Northwest Texas and its centrality made it a hub a for the agricultural community of the region. Thus, a significant Mexican American population grew within the city, drawn to the region for work in the cotton-growing industry as well as employment with the area's railroad and construction sectors.

Although Texas always had a significant Mexican descent population, in the nineteenth century most of those numbers were concentrated in areas along the border. The advent of commercial agriculture and the upheaval of the Mexican Revolution during the early twentieth century, led to substantial increases in the numbers of Mexicans throughout Texas. The increase in the population also led to a natural increase in the numbers of Mexican school-age children. The new development presented Texas education officials with a unique quandary; would Texas continue with its traditional concept of racial and ethnic segregation or would new conditions (principally economic, but there was the state's reliance on the southern tradition of white superiority to consider) mean the need for new policies and adjustments? Initially, state officials ignored the phenomenon; the state's strong local school autonomy tradition combined with the historically spartan state spending on education led to policies that left the schooling of Tejano children at the discretion of local officials. What developed was a patch-work system of education for Mexican Americans. In urban areas, such as El Paso and San Antonio, there was some access to schools and an opportunity for at least a high school degree. In other more rural areas, in South Texas for example, education was often rudimentary at best or non-existent.

Lubbock resident Roberto Lugo recalled his father's recollection of his experiences in the San Benito area. Lugo's father attended school sporadically due to his obligations in helping his family work in the Rio Grande Valley's agricultural fields. He left school permanently at the age of thirteen with only a fourth grade education. Mr. Lugo was taught exclusively in Spanish in a segregated "Mexican" school. "My father told me that the teachers did not seem too concerned whether or not the children were learning or not," said Roberto, "and when he left school he could neither read or write English and could barely do either in Spanish." The elder Lugo was probably a victim of the ideology of the period. Within Texas, and particularly within the state's agricultural regions, there existed the idea that any advanced education would "spoil" the needed Mexican laborer. In simpler terms, an educated man did not pick vegetables or fruit for living.

Despite his father's negative experience in Texas' public school system, he still stressed the value of education to his son. Roberto remembers his father emphasizing his attendance in school and telling him that if he did not further his education he would never be anything more than "a cotton-picker." "After we moved to Ballinger, my father would not let me miss school to help in the fields; in twelve years of school I only missed two days," recalled the younger Lugo.

Lugo's school days were not without hardships. Grades one through six were segregated and he felt that he was not given the same level of education that the white children received. The pattern continued even after elementary school. Upon completing the sixth grade, Ballinger's Mexican American students attended the small West Texas city's only junior high, attending classes with white children for the first time. Lugo felt that he was "behind" his white classmates—in fact he failed the seventh grade. But with his father's persuasion and his determination to "leave the cotton fields," Lugo graduated from Ballinger High in 1952 and eventually attended Texas Tech University. But he was the exception to the rule. He began elementary school with thirty Mexican American classmates, but he was the only one to graduate high school; in fact, Roberto Lugo was the first Mexican American to ever graduate from Ballinger High.

Lubbock's burgeoning cotton industry began attracting Mexican migrant workers in the early part of the twentieth century. By 1920, a *barrio* located on the northeast fringes of the city had formed, an area that became known as the Guadalupe (after the Catholic Church that served the region) neighborhood. Lubbock's educational experiences mirrored that of other Mexican Americans in the state. Until 1922 the city did not provide any sort of educational facility for Mexican American children. In that year, the school board appropriated funding for a tiny one-room school exclusively for the residents of the *barrio*. This "Mexican" school employed a single white teacher and all lessons were taught in English. In 1924, Lubbock Independent School District (LISD) reported thirty-one students attending the school.

By the late 1920s, Texas officials could no longer ignore the presence of Mexican American children in the state's schools. Educational researchers discovered that children of Mexican descent were now present in virtually every district in the state and they were also increasing at a rate much more rapid than the white or African American populations (a trend that continues to the present). Furthermore, the studies indicated that the majority of Mexican American children were non-English speakers and predominantly from lower socioeconomic stratas. Another finding was that Tejano children were largely denied equal educational opportunities, including inferior and substandard facilities, textbooks, and curriculums. In some predominantly white counties, over seventy percent of Mexican American school-age children were not even enrolled in school. School officials could no longer ignore Tejano students and were forced to deal with the issues raised by the increasing population.

Lubbock's segregated school reflected the conditions detailed in the reports. Throughout the 1940s there were never more than forty students enrolled in the school. Still, classes were conducted in such a small building that overcrowding was a constant problem. Catholic missionary nuns assigned to St Joseph's Church reported that the *barrio* school was "deplorable," and expressed astonishment that the school district would force Mexican American students to attend school under such conditions. The students never graduated, but then they were not expected to. Many parents seemed resigned to the situation, feeling powerless to change the status quo. One parent summed up the feelings with an exasperated, "you know how once they reach a certain age, they no longer want to continue in school." It would not be until the 1940s that Lubbock would have its first Mexican American high school graduate.

LULAC was one Mexican American organization which did stress the importance and value of education. The organization's stated goal was to end racial discrimination in Texas and obtain equal access to legal, economic, and educational opportunities. LULAC, which consisted mostly of the Mexican American middle class, also stressed more assimilation for Mexican Americans while maintaining a cultural sense of pride and responsibility. Educational achievement was their key to such goals. In the years before World War II, LULAC concentrated on a wide-range of educationally related activities. They conducted back-to-school campaigns and attempted to overcome segregated schools, inferior equipment, and the lack of qualified teachers. In LULAC's eyes, such conditions were seen as the primary obstacles to the full economic and social assimilation of the Mexican American and the only true pathway to full participation in America's social, economic, and political systems.

LULAC members did not wholly blame whites for the deficiencies in the *barrio* schools. According to some LULAC officials white discrimination and segregation certainly was a factor, but "[the] . . . Latin American often does not understand his rights and does not demand his rights nor does he try to find solutions to these problems which serve as obstacles for his children." Of all the obstacles facing Mexican American schoolchildren, most "LULACers" saw one glaring barrier that became the most difficult to overcome—the inability of a majority of Mexican American children to speak English. LULAC as an organization emphasized the importance of all Mexican Americans to learn English, but they gave particular urgency to teaching their children the language of the American majority. For them, English proficiency, in addition to education, was the key to assimilation and full participation in American society. It was this fundamental belief that led LULAC to declare English as the official language of the organization and began to advance the notion that Mexican American education be conducted solely in English.

While LULAC may have stressed English-based education, in Lubbock's schools through the 1930s instruction continued in Spanish. Following the St. Joseph's nuns' 1930 report (although there is no evidence that the report played a role), Lubbock's school board did appropriate funding for a new *barrio* school, the first brick building in the Guadalupe neighborhood. In 1935 the Public Works Administration granted money for improvements to the structure. While the building's facilities improved, instruction remained substandard. Augustin Estrada, who attended the facility in the 1930s related that his education was, except for grammar, in Spanish. He never remembered a teacher encouraging him to learn English and he completed his education only through the sixth grade. "It was never considered that we would go any further. We were only going to be working the fields or in garages anyway, so I guess they figured that there was [no] use for us to learn much," recalled Estrada. Hector Gonzalez also attended the *barrio* school in the 1930s. He remembered the great pride the community took when the new school was built, but also recalled that the quality of education did not change. He attempted to attend junior high school after he left elementary school, but dropped out when he realized he would never complete his studies. "I was way behind the white kids and would never catch up because the teachers were not interested in teaching me," said Gonzalez, "so I left to help father."

Lubbock's Mexican American community also underwent changes in the 1930s and early 1940s. After shuttling back and forth across Texas and the Southwest in the early years of the Depression, a large number of Mexican American migrants realized that Lubbock's economy could support permanent settlement and thus many decided to make Lubbock home. In a one-year period between the 1940 and 1941 cotton seasons, there were more land tracts bought in the Guadalupe neighborhood than any purchased in a similar prior period. The result was an expansion of the *barrio* with the beginning of the Wayside and Rio Vista additions. The Mexican American population continued to increase throughout the 1940s and the traditional *barrio* expanded west of Avenue Q, in effect doubling in size and expanding the population density of Mexican Americans in the city.

Population expansion only exacerbated Lubbock's Mexican Americans' educational problems. The *barrio* school (now renamed Guadalupe) quickly outgrew its facilities, but due to continued segregation policies, Mexican American children were still restricted from attending white elementary schools. The residents of the Guadalupe neighborhood no doubt realized the gravity of the situation, but they were also largely powerless to change the educational conditions. A particular problem was the recalcitrance of Lubbock's white farm owners to help alter the school schedule. Since entire *familias* worked the cotton fields, farm owners expected the Guadalupe School to suspend classes during harvest and planting seasons. When parents either tried to fashion a compromise or petition the school board to keep the school open and their children in school, farm owners used their influence with the school board to ensure that the school remained closed and then threatened parents with the loss of jobs. Bonifacio Delgado's father was a proponent of his son receiving as much education as possible and worked within the community to try to keep the school open and on a regular school year calendar. In response, Delgado's employer threatened to fire him if he continued his "agitation." The younger Delgado recalled that most of the other residents were afraid of the same type of response and ignored his father's pleadings. Predictably, Bonifacio Delgado soon left school after the seventh grade, regrettably, saying it "is the worst decision I have ever made in my life. I don't think my father ever forgave himself for not trying harder."

The end of World War II and the return of veterans from Europe and the Pacific would prove a watershed event for Texas' and Lubbock's Mexican Americans. The organizations that saw their nascent beginnings in the 1920s and 1930s would begin to grow stronger, more forceful, and more aggressive in pushing for civil rights in all areas of society—and educational access and opportunity would rightfully assume a prominent position in such campaigns. Tejanos in the coming decades would boycott schools, seek relief from the nation's courts, and begin to make real and concrete demands of local and state institutions. Much of this new activism was due to a change in attitude. During World War II, Mexican Americans had actively participated in the country's war efforts and now saw the contradictions of fighting abroad for American principles (including equal opportunity) while discrimination and a lack of opportunity was still the norm at home.

One of the new organizations that began in the immediate post-war years was the American G. I. Forum (AGIF), a group that would, along with LULAC become a leader in the campaign for equal access, opportunity, and civil rights. Organized initially as a veteran's organization in 1948, the AGIF soon became interested in much more than veterans affairs. It became an advocate for issues of interest to all Mexican Americans and, like LULAC, education became a top priority for the AGIF. An AGIF pamphlet described the organization's position on education: "Education is the principal weapon to fight the many evils affecting our people." In fact, education occupied such a prominent position for the organization that its motto became, "Education is Our Freedom and Freedom Should Be Everybody's Business."

The end of the war also brought great changes to Lubbock. As Mexican American veterans returned to their hometown they realized that conditions in the *barrio* had improved little since the beginning of the war. Their livelihood still depended on work in the cotton fields and the continuing social condition of discrimination and segregation made it difficult for them to make any improvement and advancement Housing conditions were deplorable and educational attainment was still relegated to, at most, completion of the elementary school.

Lubbock's first Mexican American high school graduates began appearing very infrequently in the early 1940s. But the activism of groups such as LULAC and AGIF, as well as favorable court decisions at the federal level would begin to bring changes and opportunities to Lubbock's Mexican Americans.

The lack of educational access (to both secondary and higher education) and continued school segregation became priorities for Mexican American civil rights groups. Such lack of access was probably the most virulent form of discrimination and social barrier for Mexican Americans. It branded almost all Mexican American children as inferior and the lack of a quality education in the state's deplorable segregated schools denied them access to social, political, and economic equality. A campaign to eliminate segregated and inferior schools had emerged during the war, but it gathered more force, and perhaps more importantly more influence, with the return of Mexican American war veterans. A 1946 California court decision, *Mendez v. Westminster School District*, which ruled against California's practice of segregating Mexican American students, established a precedent that could be used to fight Texas' practice of school discrimination. Texas state officials understood the ramifications of the case and in response state Attorney General Price Daniel issued a legal opinion on behalf of the state that seemed to forbid the segregation of Mexican descent school children if such segregation was based solely on race. Daniel's opinion was probably deliberately ambiguous since it went on to state that separate schools and classrooms could be maintained based on "language deficiencies and individual needs," and left such discretion to individual school boards. The state of Texas had found a seeming loophole to exploit. Some school districts began to segregate Tejano school children in separate "language instruction" classes and buildings although many of those children were perfectly proficient in English. In effect, Texas had found a way to maintain Mexican American segregation.

Given the ambiguity (and perhaps duplicity) of Daniel's opinion, enforcement was ineffective. In order to force the issue, LULAC sought a clarification and Daniel responded to the organization's lawyers that the "law prohibits any discrimination or segregation of citizens of Mexican or Latin descent." Daniel had to issue such a statement—anything less would mean he was refusing to comply with a Supreme Court ruling. But he also had to know that local school districts were continuing to segregate Tejano public school students and his office was refusing to enforce the ruling. LULAC then had no choice but to seek relief from the courts. In January 1948, with assistance from LULAC's legal team, Minerva Delgado filed suit against the Bastrop Independent School district asking the court to end the central Texas school district's practice of segregated "Mexican" schools. Two months after Delgado filed suit, the American G. I. Forum joined LULAC in providing support for the case and also began a campaign of raising funds from Mexican American communities throughout the state to help pay the legal costs of the action. Eventually, the U. S. Supreme Court ruled in *Delgado v. Bastrop* that Texas' system of Mexican American school segregation was illegal under the Fourteenth Amendment and restrained the school district, as well as any district in Texas, from continuing the practice.

Delgado v. Bastrop was followed with keen interest throughout many Mexican American communities. Johnny Ramirez, Jr., currently of San Angelo, remembered the importance the case and school segregation had in his household. Ramirez's father was a World War II veteran and an active member of both LULAC and the AGIF in Victoria. Texas in the immediate post-war years. "*Mi padre* lived through the war as a tail-gunner on a B-17, but he always told me that doing away with the "Mexican" schools was a far more important battle than any he had ever fought," said Ramirez, Jr. in 2001. "When the local chapter [AGIF] heard about the case they organized bake sales and other activities to raise money and my Dad actually took vacation from work to follow the case in court." Ramirez, Jr. was nine years old when the case was filed and, although he did not attend a segregated school in Victoria, he understood the consequences for others who did. "I had cousins who went to a 'Mexican' school in Abilene and they did not receive the same education that I did." His father had attended a segregated school and still recalled the bitterness he felt when he was in high school. "My Dad was a good student and really wanted to be an engineer," recalled Ramirez, Jr., "but in the tenth grade a counselor told him that he was 'wasting his time in school,' so he left and went to work for a plumbing company. He never forgot what [had] happened to him."

According to Ramirez, most of the Mexican Americans in Victoria felt as his father did and hoped for the day such practices would end. Ramirez felt that the most important result of desegregation would be the opportunity for higher education. While he did attend college after high school, primarily because his father insisted, most of his friends did not. "I don't think they were pushed enough and I think that was because the parents knew how hard it was to simply graduate from high school and that was enough. And the white teachers were not preparing us for college." Ramirez did encourage his children to pursue a higher education, but he thought the fact that they had attended an integrated school in San Angelo also helped.

The *Bastrop* decision, increases in Mexican American population, and the growth of Mexican American owned businesses and middle class, combined with the 1954 *Brown v. Board of Education, Topeka* ruling began to erode Lubbock's policy of segregation. The Guadalupe School closed in 1949, but more due to the fact that the *barrio* had outgrown its original area than LISD policy. Also, during the 1940s, Mexican Americans began to move into areas of the city away from the traditional *barrio* and strict segregation became less practical. LISD was also struggling with plans and schemes to implement the *Brown* decision and integration of Mexican Americans into the district's schools might help stop any legal oversight of the district's racial practices. LISD officially integrated in 1955 and reported few problems.

While Mexican American school segregation was no longer *de jure*, it was still, for the most part, *de facto*. Since most Mexican Americans continued to live on the east side of the city, the new schools in this area were still predominantly Mexican American. To its credit, the LISD did seem to make a concerted effort to construct first-rate facilities and there is no record of discriminatory funding for the new schools. Still, *de facto* segregation still separated Lubbock. The concentration of Mexican Americans into one section of the city represented the situation, a process that historian Albert Camarillo has termed "barrioization." For Camarillo, barrioization was both a defense against white oppression and an attempt to maintain a cohesive, distinctly Mexican descent culture. Often relegated to a "neighborhood" through segregation, political gerrymandering, and economic circumstances, Mexican Americans often responded by insulating themselves in the *barrio* and modifying and adapting their community to the new circumstances they faced. While Camarillo's specific study dealt with Santa Barbara, California, Lubbock also underwent a similar process. In the 1920s through the 1940s, Lubbock's Mexican American citizens were isolated in the Guadalupe area of the city, politically powerless and socially segregated.

"Barrioization" created a distinct Mexican American neighborhood in Lubbock. When, in the late 1930s and through the 1950s the neighborhood expanded, it kept fairly distinct borders. Mexican Americans, for the most part, were concentrated east of Avenue Q, some voluntarily, others through various processes of social coercion. The Guadalupe neighborhood's residents, paralleling the *barrio's* attitude toward education, developed immense pride in their place of residence. Salome Morales described how the residents felt in a 1979 interview. "We (Lubbock's Mexican American citizens) thought of our neighborhood as something that was ours. Nobody gave us anything there and we looked out for each other." Antonio Villareal explained the attraction of the *barrio* in another way. "I guess we were comfortable there [in the neighborhood]. We could have moved to another area of the city many times, but we *chose* [emphasis mine] to remain here. This is where we wanted to raise our children." Lubbock County Commissioner Gilbert Flores believed that the strength of the Mexican American community was reflected through its neighborhood. He laments the fact that in the last twenty years a number of prominent community leaders have left the *barrio,* saying that the loss "has destroyed some of the cohesiveness and togetherness the community felt for each other. Now we are more out for ourselves than for each other."

While some Guadalupe residents chose to remain, others were barred from leaving. "Redlining," the process of denying home ownership on the basis of race or ethnicity was a practice in Lubbock. A perusal of Lubbock real estate contracts from 1955-1970 reveals that the practice was fairly widespread. One such contract, dated 1956, expressly forbids "sell of said house to any person of the Negro or Latin American race." Others were more subtle. One, from the South Overton area, required any purchaser to be approved by the neighborhood association. Lubbock's real estate agents practiced the most predominant form of "redlining." They would not show a home to a minority outside of the east side. Roberto Lugo experienced the practice firsthand. In 1963, the successful Lubbock businessman decided to buy a new home. He located a house on 22nd and Memphis and contacted a real estate agent. The agent insisted on showing Lugo homes on the city's east side and made a number of excuses on why the house on Memphis was not available. Lugo insisted on seeing the property. The agent refused and Lugo sought another agent who agreed to show Lugo the house. He bought the property and reported that he suffered no repercussions from neighbors. He was incensed with the agent's actions and began to probe similar practices. He found that his experience was not unique.

As Lubbock's Mexican Americans began attending formerly segregated schools, they still experienced problems. Most Mexican Americans continued employment in the region's agricultural industry and local farm owners were dependant on entire families, including the school children, during harvest season. In 1949, the Federal Fair Labor Standards Act was amended to make illegal use of child labor under the age of sixteen during school hours. Area farmers protested the law and successfully sought a suspension of over half of Lubbock's schools until the harvest was completed. Not surprisingly, the schools affected were predominantly Mexican American.

But not all the blame for the situation could be placed at the feet of farm owners facing a harvest without workers. Since working the harvest was of such economic importance to many Mexican American families, a number of parents chose to not even enroll their children in school. In 1951 over five hundred Mexican American children of junior high age were not enrolled and almost eight hundred who should have been in high school did not appear on the school enrollment records. The trend did not alter much in the next decade, creating a further obstacle for Mexican Americans to overcome—with access to education becoming more widespread, parents had to allow children to take advantage of the new opportunity. Julio Luchara provided insight on the condition when he related that many of his neighborhood friends did not attend school because "their parents did not see the point; they didn't go to school so they didn't send their kids."

Cultural differences also hindered Lubbock's Mexican American school children. Some white children taunted Mexican American students' poor use of English. Some Lubbock teachers actually punished students for speaking Spanish in class or on the playground. Nephatali DeLeon attended Lubbock High School in the early 1960s and reported that his educational experience was generally negative. He was "scared to death" to read before a class because he was unsure of his English usage and knew that his fellow classmates "would make fun of him." DeLeon, who in his 20s would become a Chicano activist, believed that Lubbock was "one of the worst kind of racist places because the racism was not overt, but you knew it was there." He could not recall specific instances, but that "is because I am sure that I have blocked them from my mind." He felt that it was the teachers' responsibility to become bi-cultural and bilingual, not the student. In his view, "If a teacher was hired to instruct and his or her classroom included Chicano children, they should be able, in fact required, to instruct both bi-culturally and bilingually." In the end, DeLeon was convinced that he "just was never very comfortable as a Chicano in Lubbock's schools."

DeLeon's experiences may not have been the norm. Other Mexican Americans reported a positive experience in Lubbock's school system in the 1960s. Leonel and Arrora Galindo saw three of their children progress through Lubbock schools in the 1960s and 1970s. They reported that their children encountered no real discrimination or prejudice from teachers or students at Lubbock's Monterey High School. The Galindos moved to Lubbock in the 1950s from Falfurrias, Texas and they "had heard that Lubbock was a bad town for Mexicans," but they found it a very enjoyable place to live. Their children had attended a predominantly Mexican American elementary school, but they moved to the south-central portion of the city when the kids were in junior high specifically so their children could attend Monterey High. According to the Galindos, their children's teachers were attentive and interested in their children's education and encouraged them to attend college after high school. Two of their children went on to receive M. A. degrees from Texas Tech and the other a B. A. in education from West Texas State University (now West Texas A&M). The Galindos did make it a point to stress education in the home and realized early that education "was the key to overcoming discrimination." Mr. Galindo explained his ideas bluntly — "the only color that is never discriminated against is green [money]."

Benito Perales reports a somewhat similar experience while he attended Lubbock High School in the mid-1960s. "I guess I have no complaints about attending Lubbock High School," said Mr. Perales in a 1999 interview. "I made some good grades and some bad grades; the bad were my fault and the good ones were too," Perales offered that the he was the object of some prejudice, but it was isolated and "didn't amount to much." He said that the most difficult aspect of his experiences was there were not more Mexican Americans in school at the same time he attended. But he did not believe that racism was the reason. Instead, in his mind, most Mexican American peers "just thought they could do better if they went to work and began making money." Manuel Gonzalez believed that there was a degree of racism in Lubbock's schools during the 1960s, but "it was mainly among the 'old folks' who didn't know the times were changing." Gonzalez believed that the resistance among some of the teachers to accept Mexican American students in Lubbock High contributed to some of the high drop-out rate among Mexican Americans. "Oh we talked about it, how some teachers didn't seem to care whether we did good [sic] or not and some of my friends just decided that it was just not worth it [to continue in school] so they left."

The perceptions of Lubbock's Mexican Americans relating to their educational experiences may be more important than the actual realities. While no one who scrutinizes the accounts of Lubbock's Mexican Americans and the city's schools in the 1920s through the 1960s can deny that racist practices did exist, it was the determination that many Mexican Americans showed in obtaining education that allowed them to overcome those barriers placed before them. Groups such as LULAC and the AGIF recognized that education was a key to success in American society as early as the 1920s and the 1940s. LULAC and other organizations waged pitched battles so that Tejano children would have the same access to educational opportunities as white children, battles that eventually ended in some victories despite virulent opposition. If there is a theme that runs through the perceptions in this narrative, it is that many of Lubbock's Mexican Americans understood the importance of those battles and waged their own fights to attain an equal education. For many of these people, that fight has produced measurable results. Leonel and Arrora Galindo's children overcame obstacles and currently enjoy economic and social success. Roberto Lugo's father instilled in him the importance of education and he used that lesson to acquire a successful business career. Even Nephalti DeLeon, who described his school experiences as far from the best time in his life, overcome the prejudice he perceived and became an outspoken proponent for Mexican American civil rights.

While Lubbock's Mexican Americans overcame the barriers placed before them from the 1920s through the 1960s, Mexican Americans still face a number of educational problems. The drop-out rate among Mexican Americans remains alarmingly high and the proportion of Mexican Americans who enter college lags behind that of almost all other American ethnic groups. Linda Chavez, in her book *Out of the Barrio,* speculates that Hispanic parents must encourage their children to pursue education if Latinos can ever hope to narrow the socio-economic gap that exists between them and whites. She postulates that Hispanics must invest the same amount of years in school as other American groups do. Governmental action can only go so far and at some point personal responsibility must be used to attain full economic and educational equality. The accounts included in this study come to the same conclusion. When parents stressed education in the home, success generally followed. Lubbock's Mexican American community has progressed from an unheated, dilapidated one-room school house to inclusion in a cross-section of Lubbock's schools. LULAC, the AGIF, and the federal government played a part, but progress was attained when the parents and children of the community pursued their dreams, and outlasted the nightmares that dashed their hopes. Then, they gained educational opportunities despite the barriers placed before them.

Newspapers and the 1936 Texas Centennial

PATRICK COX

P atrick Cox, retired Associate Director of the Dolph Briscoe Center for American History at the University of Texas, presently heads a public history consulting firm. His books include *Ralph W. Yarborough: The People's Senator* (2002), *The First Texas News Barons* (2005), and *The House Will Come to Order: How the Texas Speaker Became a Power in State and National Politics* (2010).

In 1936, Texas commemorated its one hundredth year of independence. Across the state, proud Texans threw festive celebrations. While Dallas hosted the official Exposition, Fort Worth offered the competing Texas Frontier Centennial. Dallas businessman Stanley Marcus asserted that "modern Texas history started with the celebration of the Texas Centennial, because it was in 1936 . . . that the rest of America discovered Texas." The 1930s also witnessed a change in the Lone Star image. Texas moved away from its Southern Confederate identity and embraced, instead, its Western frontier heritage. In this selection, Dr. Cox analyzes the important role newspaper publishers, such as George B. Dealey of the *Dallas Morning News* and Amon G. Carter, Sr., of the *Fort Worth Star-Telegram*, played in the great Centennial celebration. ᥍

★ ★

The 1936 Texas Centennial joined the ranks of four other major expositions in the nation during the years of the Great Depression. Preceded by Chicago's Century of Progress Exposition (1933) and San Diego's Panama California International Exposition (1935), and followed by the Golden Gate International Exposition in San Francisco (1937) and the New York World's Fair (1939), the Texas Centennial Exposition was a celebration of U.S. history, knowledge, and commercial enterprise. As *Business Week* magazine described the Texas centennial celebrations of 1936, the festivities blended "patriotism and business." Promoters intended to attract outside capital and visitors and provide them with exposure to the Lone Star State. The exposition spread far beyond the fairgrounds in Dallas to become an exercise in redefining the state's character and its institutional memory. The state's newspaper publishers served as a driving force in the creation and promotion of centennial events. As they debated the course between tradition and modernization, the publishers also cemented the new western image of Texans, a legacy that was carried forward for the rest of the twentieth century.

The new Texan mythology—the western, cowboy mystique—owes much to the newspapers and publicists of this era. Myths are not entirely fiction. They represent historical events and people that are re-created and turned into legends. These mythic events and figures illustrate the central feature of the romanticized past. In the Depression of the 1930s, western images came to represent "individualism, self reliance, and integrity in the face of a corrupt world." The image of cowboys and outlaws was well defined by the 1930s. Dime novels, films, magazines, music, and newspapers utilized western figures as heroic characters. Billy the Kid, Buffalo Bill Cody, Frederick Russell, Owen Wister, and Theodore Roosevelt came to represent distinct figures in popular memory of the idealized West. Outlaws, cowboys, artists, writers, and politicians provided a grand tapestry upon which popular memory of the Texas past arose. Popular media helped define the image of the western cowboy and played the significant role in vitalizing Texas of the past.

Texans also continued to glorify their southern background. As Paul Gaston stated in *The New South Creed*, myths "are not polite euphemisms for falsehoods, but are combinations of images and symbols that reflect a people's way of perceiving truth . . . they fuse the real and the imaginary into a blend that becomes a reality itself, a force in history." Glorification of the antebellum South and the Confederacy in the six decades following the Civil War served as the central theme for public memory in the region. The entire fabric of southern history became woven into what became known as the Lost Cause interpretation. The motivation for the Lost Cause mythology came from the desire of southerners to cope with the seemingly un-American experience of defeat and at the same time to rationalize slavery, secession, and the failures of the Confederacy. Advocates successfully introduced a "correct" version of history that allowed for a southern bias in interpretation. Many historians now agree that "[i]n terms of how Americans have assessed and understood the Civil War, Lost Cause warriors succeeded to a remarkable degree."

Through the 1920s, Texans interpreted their history as viewed through the southern lens. From the 1870s through the early twentieth century, former Confederate leaders rose to dominant positions in the state's business, political, and educational centers. This legacy helped southerners justify their clouded past as they prepared for the future in a nation dominated by northern capital and enterprise. Newspapers recounted stories of Confederate veterans and eulogized their deaths. Associations of former Confederates gained widespread coverage and support for philanthropic efforts. Supporters downplayed slavery or the South's long record of racial violence, characterizing both issues—and African Americans themselves—as irrelevant. Reunions, meetings, commemorative events, statues, and buildings were a tribute to the Lost Cause and the southern interpretation of history. Little of past suffering, deprivation, death, and destruction made its way into print.

The Lost Cause provided more than a patriotic reinterpretation of the past. In the view of some historians, at its fruition, allegiance to the Lost Cause "elevated it above the realm of common, patriotic impulse" and made it the equivalent of a state religion in the South. Southern adherents created a mythological past that raised individuals to saintly positions who lived a godlike existence. "Lee and Davis emerged as Christ figures, the common soldier attained sainthood, and southern women became Marys who guarded the tomb of the Confederacy and heralded its resurrection." The Civil War became a sacred event with inviolate doctrines: the war occurred for the right to self-government, not slavery; and Confederates were not traitors but acted against a corrupt northern society bent on imposing its will on the South.

As the last generation of Confederate veterans died out and the grand reunions held their final parades in the 1920s, a successor movement made its way into Texas in the 1930s. The seeds of the Texas creation myth fell on well-prepared ground. Just as the Lost Cause found its impetus in the tumultuous decades after the Civil War, the rise of the new Texan mythology occurred during the nation's worst economic depression. The Texas myth followed the same pattern as the earlier New South construction. The unpleasant realities of the past were obliterated, while the pictures of pride and progress were displayed for all the world to see and read.

Since the 1930s had no revitalized economy or boom like the 1920s, urban promoters sought to provide the public with a past that they would feel proud of, one in which they had faced challenges fearlessly, so they would look beyond their existing problems and focus on the future. By utilizing traditional values associated with nineteenth-century rural principles, business and the media reassured people that they acknowledged and respected their honored past. As situations arose in the Great Depression that questioned the foundations of U.S. capitalism, its value was reaffirmed by recognition of a heroic past and its challenges, recalled through a history where individuals were able to overcome great odds and adversity. The promoters of this new heroic Texan image recalled earlier generations who seemingly made clear-cut decisions when confronting a common enemy. The pioneer Anglo Texans and creators of the Republic of Texas appeared as ready-made historical actors to replace the Confederates enshrined by the Lost Cause mythology.

Texas declared its independence from Mexico in 1836. After a series of disasters at the Alamo and Goliad and during a long retreat, a force led by Sam Houston defeated Santa Anna, the president of Mexico and leader of its army, at San Jacinto on April 21, 1836. The Republic of Texas existed for nearly a decade prior to its annexation into the United States. The infant republic endured and awaited admission to the United States as the nation debated over the extension of slavery and the admission of slave and free states. The state's revolutionary heritage, along with its colonial and Native American history, suddenly ascended in the 1930s as a rival to the celebration of the Confederate past.

How this spirited image of Texas' past became part of the collective memory of the state and the nation derived from the centennial celebrations of the 1930s. As John Bodnar explains concerning public memory in the United States, collective ideas originate from "a political discussion that involves not so much specific economic or moral problems but rather fundamental issues about the entire existence of society: its organization, structure of power, and the very meaning of its past and present." The Texas Centennial certainly occurred during one of the most economically trying times in the nation's history. Many civic leaders joined with the newspaper publishers to extol the financial benefits of these large-scale celebrations. "Texanism," the rise of a Texas heritage and associations, assumed a new mantle of importance. The beliefs, symbols, stories, language, images, and physical structures that encompassed this new public memory originated in this centennial era. Furthermore, the image of Texas as a distinct region apart from the Old South gained its impetus in the public sphere during this period. Much of this improvised cultural heritage (which maintains a presence to this day) originated with the ideas and promotions of the Texas daily newspaper publishers.

In 1936 Texas celebrated the one-hundredth anniversary of its independence with centennial activities across the state. The state and federal governments each provided $3 million to kick off the events. Local communities also sold bonds to finance construction of new projects. To prime the pump, Washington provided money for many of the buildings and Centennial projects, which provided thousands of jobs for Texans.

For more than a decade, Lowry Martin, advertising manager of the *Corsicana Daily Sun*, served as the workhorse of the centennial movement. A central part of Martin's strategy was to obtain massive support from the Texas newspaper industry and the endorsement by the state's political establishment. Themes focused on the individuality and frontier spirit of nineteenth-century Anglo Texans. During the years of planning, Jesse Jones served on the statewide coordinating committee, but his tenure was marked by uncertainty as to the scope of the centennial celebration. Competing business and political activities also distracted Jones from the task. Jones maintained reservations about the feasibility of having only one primary exposition site modeled after world fair expositions of the early twentieth century. The onset of the Depression and his appointment to the RFC brought an end to his leadership on the Centennial Commission, but Jones eventually played a role in obtaining federal government financing for many centennial-related projects during the 1930s.

Lowry Martin and the Texas Press Association kept the centennial celebration effort alive after Jones' departure from the board in 1930. Martin provided an ongoing stream of information, surveys, and promotions to newspapers. As economic conditions worsened throughout the state, the concept of a statewide commemoration of its birthday began to gain momentum. Many civic and political leaders viewed a centennial celebration as a potential stimulus to revive the flagging economy. The campaign resulted in a constitutional amendment passed by the state legislature and submitted to the voters during the November 1932 general election. The amendment, which called for a celebration combined with an unspecified commitment for funding by the state, passed during the same election in which Texans overwhelmingly voted for Franklin Roosevelt and John Nance Garner.

Houston's civic and political leaders believed the competition for the main exposition came down to a battle between Houston and Dallas. If the selection involved only historic considerations, Houston would have been a natural choice because of its role in Texas independence and the early republic. "But that equation is entirely eliminated by the centennial law," the *Houston Post* editors wrote. "It is now simply a matter of which city makes the highest bid."

A state commission selected Dallas as the location for the official exposition. Not to be outdone, Houston, San Antonio, and Fort Worth scheduled their own celebrations. Neighboring Fort Worth created the Texas Frontier Centennial and a "Winning of the West" celebration. San Antonio and Houston hosted events to commemorate battles of the Texas Revolution. The newly completed San Jacinto Monument and Historical Museum opened on the anniversary of Sam Houston's victory over Santa Anna's army in April 1836. Numerous events throughout the state extended the celebration to nearly every county. Huntsville, Sam Houston's hometown, featured the initial sale of the Texas Centennial postage stamp. Stamford held a cowboy reunion and roundup. Crystal City hosted a spinach festival and proclaimed the cartoon character Popeye as honorary mayor. Every major daily in the state published a special centennial edition, sometimes totaling more than 100 pages, stocked with history, anecdotes, and ads.

Centennial editions, similar to anniversary and other special commemorative publications, served newspapers and the larger community. These highly publicized newspapers validated the publication as the official collector and interpreter of historical memory. Centennial publications enhanced the role of cultural authority and opened the door for other businesses and individuals to enlist in the narrative effort. Editorial content and the selection of historical articles remained the prerogative of the editorial staff. The presentation was nearly as important as the content of these commemorative issues. Large, eye-catching print and artwork such as photos and other illustrations formed an essential part of the grand exposition that unfolded throughout the edition.

In 1934, on the *Houston Post*'s fiftieth anniversary, the newspaper featured a front-page reproduction of a congratulatory letter from President Roosevelt. Vice President John Nance Garner and other Texas political leaders sent messages commending the *Post* on its anniversary and civic leadership. *Fort Worth Star-Telegram* publisher Amon Carter proclaimed the *Post* to be a newspaper whose influence in Texas politics "at all times has been statewide." *Dallas Morning News* editor Ted Dealey noted the *Post* "grew with the city" and won for itself "respect and honor."

As a premier example of the commemorative editions of this era, the *Dallas Morning News* celebrated its 1935 golden anniversary in grand style. Alongside stories of the dedication of Boulder Dam and the discovery of a lost manuscript of Sam Houston's account of the Battle of San Jacinto, the *News* published congratulatory letters from President Roosevelt, Vice President Garner, and many other state and national leaders. Congratulatory messages from officials and other newspapers occupied several pages. The majority of the paper featured local histories and stories that accentuated the growth of Dallas and Texas—accounts of organizations, construction, industrial expansion, and the 1936 State Centennial—and photos from the previous fifty years. *News* president G. B. Dealey highlighted and recounted important stories of the previous fifty years of national and local importance. One story featured W. D. Austin, an original subscriber, who had read "every copy" of the newspaper since its initial publication in 1885.

Dealey's page one editorial on the fiftieth anniversary of the *News* amplified his philosophy and expounded on the role the newspaper had played in Dallas' development and growth. The *News* began when Dallas was "an overgrown, Topsy-like town, unkempt, with little paving." In working with civic leaders, the *News* "exerted all its power to lead and to co-operate with the thousands of men and women who are responsible for the Dallas of today." Dealey stated he intended to have the influence in promoting civic development expand statewide. "Always it has spent time, thought, money and effort in printing matter to inculcate a desire for attractiveness and beauty of every kind in its urban centers and countryside. It has desired to be the champion of all kinds of wholesome education and to develop the finer things of life." He also attributed the paper's success to "the efficient, ever-faithful and loyal interest of and work" of the *News* employees. Dealey planned to pursue the same course in the following years—striving to make the daily a respected and influential regional publication. The golden anniversary edition served as a prelude to even loftier plans for the *News* in the upcoming centennial year. The commemorative issues of that year provided the standard for other newspapers, from the hectic daily publications to the smallest weekly tabloids.

John Bodnar states in his analysis of collective memory that civic leaders select commemorative events for a number of reasons. These include events that calm anxiety and evoke change, and efforts to solicit support from the general citizenry and to promote exemplary behavior. The special editions of newspapers and centennial promotions in 1936 clearly supported each of these criteria. Anxiety over the ongoing economic depression maintained its hold over the population, and one of the stated goals of centennial proponents was to have a celebration that would improve the collective outlook of the citizenry. As evidenced by the intense competition among the large cities for the coveted centennial headquarters, widespread support from the major urban communities existed. In the promotions for all the celebrations, proponents urged citizens to participate and extol the virtues of a past built on traditional American ideas—independence, liberty, freedom of expression, and the desire to establish a better society.

As the leading proponents of the centennial, the state's major newspaper publishers reaffirmed their position at the center of cultural and political leadership. They recognized that their individual positions as community leaders, along with their role as newspaper publishers, depended on the success of the centennial-related activities. In addition, growth and financial success depended on the continuation of the daily newspaper as the focal point of communication in the community. As the centennial events gained acceptance and achieved regional and national recognition, the newspapers and their publishers reached the apex of approval by the citizenry.

Publishers also contributed to what may be termed the origin myth, which took firm root in the collective memory of Texans. *Fort Worth Star-Telegram* editor J. M. North described these sentiments in a 1935 letter to *Dallas Morning News* editor Ted Dealey. "The history of Texas began 100 years ago," North stated, which conveniently ignored the entire history and role of Native Americans, Spain, Mexico, France, and the United States prior to 1835. The historical interpretation promoted and distributed during the centennial provided an explanation that accommodated the racial and economic views of the state's hierarchy. Briefly, Texas fought for its freedom because of Spanish and Mexican misrule and oppression. These hardy Anglo-Saxon pioneers created a land of opportunity after the conquest of the native populations and the government in Mexico City. The state's business and political leaders combined forces to forge a new frontier and began promoting new communities where life would peacefully progress and where conflict would be downplayed and avoided. These themes accommodated the prevailing racial stereotypes, class distinctions, and cultural prejudices of the era. Mexican Americans were associated with barbarism and hostility. African Americans were viewed as inferior and uncivilized. This interpretation ignored cooperative efforts and public/private cooperation in favor of private initiative. The Populists, Socialists, and other political movements outside of the mainstream were conveniently ignored.

Once it was chosen as the main site for the state celebration, Dallas acted as a magnet for the state's celebration. Planning and promotion for the main event took place in Dallas. News of the event was disseminated from Dallas through special publications and the pages of the *Morning News* and the *Times Herald*. Newspapers throughout the state received *Centennial News*, a weekly publication with information on the progress of the event, and *Texas Centennial Review*, a newsletter with ideas and information on local events. From the largest cities to the smallest communities in the state, the centennial emerged as the leading issue of the day. Its patriotic message moved into diverse areas and populations, with its unifying themes of Texas history and view of Texas as a state that stood separate from the others in the nation. As the *Dallas Morning News* reported on April 1, 1935, "every progressive community in the state, it would seem, is busy" with a centennial program.

The selection of Dallas embarrassed and frustrated major daily newspaper publishers in Fort Worth, Houston, and San Antonio. Amon Carter, the *Star-Telegram*, and Fort Worth civic leaders moved to close the gap after learning that Dallas had the winning bid for the state centennial. As they worked to secure state funds for their own celebration, the *Star-Telegram* moved to quench some of the fire that burned in the competition for the centennial competition. The two newspaper enterprises, which often threw barbs at one another through their editorial pages, realized the centennial offered a potential economic boom in the midst of the Depression. "We can't conceive of people coming to see the Livestock Centennial and not seeing the main Centennial at Dallas," *Star-Telegram* editor J. M. North wrote to Ted Dealey of the *Morning News*. "We believe that two attractions will supplement and benefit each other and that neither can possibly be hurt by the other."

A number of precedents of cooperation between the Fort Worth and Dallas publishers existed before the centennial projects. The newspapers and civic leaders had cooperated to form the Trinity River Canal Association in 1930. The Trinity River flowed through both cities and several hundred miles later emptied into the Gulf of Mexico. Community and business leaders had sought millions of dollars in federal funding to dredge the Trinity River and open the waterway for commercial shipping and barge traffic. In support of the joint project, the *Morning News* stated, "[T]here need be no uneasiness about Fort Worth in the matter." For the first time, the *News* acknowledged Carter's motto for his newspaper and community. The *News* also acknowledged Carter's vision and political prowess. " 'Where the West Begins' looms now and aims to loom considerably more," the editorial stated. Carter's friend and Trinity River Canal booster Silliman Evans wrote, "[T]here can be no further doubt but that the Dallas Morning News has officially accepted Fort Worth as 'Where the West Begins.' "

Editor and Publisher magazine noted the centennial promotions were a boon to newspaper businesses in the state. While the promotions yielded increased employment, more advertising, and a jump in the tourist trade immediately, the benefits of these "farsighted newspapermen" would also accumulate in subsequent years. "The more people who visit Texas and see its wonders and get acquainted with its citizens, the more people will invest their capital and their lives in Texas, according to the shrewd judgment of Texas publishers," the article stated. George Dealey immodestly predicted that the exposition would create "more development and greater posterity in the state of Texas than have the last 25 years." Amon Carter, *Fort Worth Star-Telegram* publisher, Tom Gooch, editor of the *Dallas Times Herald*, James Pollock, business manager of the *Fort Worth Press*, and John Payne. *Houston Press* business manager, joined in the rosy predictions. For emphasis, the article included a cartoon of a cowboy wearing a large western hat with "Texas" on the brim and a basket over a candle that proclaimed "Texas Billion Power Candle Light."

With their rival expositions, Dallas and Fort Worth gained national headlines as evidence of a "major outbreak of exposition fever." In June 1936, *Business Week* magazine described the festivities as "an amiable blend of patriotism and business." The competing shows may have appeared to be a tribute to the rivalry between the two cities, but the magazine reasoned both communities would enjoy the "chime of cash registers" from crowds, anticipated to number in the millions, making their way to the two Texas cities. The article noted the substantial contribution from the federal government and the local and state contributions. It also lauded the two expositions' success in attracting large corporations such as the large automakers, for which each city constructed its own multimillion structures at the Dallas fairgrounds. The *Dallas Morning News* attempted to downplay the rivalry. In a July 15, 1936, editorial, the *News* stated, "In the Frontier Centennial our neighbor to the West preserves the tradition of the Old West in the spirit of the jazz age." The "highly publicized notion" of the competition between the Dallas and Fort Worth exhibitions was a "press agent's dream. It has no real bearing on the success of either the Centennial Central Exposition in Dallas or the Frontier Centennial in Fort Worth."

Centennial funds provided construction and landscaping for Fair Park in Dallas. Construction provided much-needed jobs, but labor strikes by Dallas building trades union members slowed down construction. The state contributed over $1 million, while the federal government contributed $1.5 million and funded more than fifty Dallas mural projects as part of the Public

Works of Art Project. The Texas Hall of State, a million-dollar building to honor Texas heroes, became the center of the permanent buildings. The park site included museums and exhibition buildings for petroleum, industry, communications, agriculture, and transportation. Centennial visitors enjoyed rides and entertainment on the Midway, as well as a re-creation of Judge Roy Bean's courtroom in the Jersey Lily Saloon and Admiral Richard Bird's Little America camp in Antarctica. President Roosevelt, hosted at a dinner by R. L. Thornton and other Dallas bankers, appeared in Dallas amid great fanfare. The Dallas newspapers carried many positive promotional stories for the event. Few stories appeared that involved labor strife during the construction appeared in the dailies. The special centennial editions of the Dallas newspapers completely omitted any news of labor problems.

The main exposition also contained the Hall of Negro Life, the first time that African Americans were recognized at a national exposition. African American business and community leaders worked with centennial promoters for this landmark appearance. The *Dallas Express*, which had a history of attacking lynching, voting restrictions, and segregation, advocated inclusion of the hall in the centennial fairgrounds. The newspaper and local black leaders obtained entrance to the state fair in Dallas on a single day, designated "Negro Day." African American business leaders saw a greater opportunity for themselves through the Centennial. Once Dallas won the selection for the main centennial celebration, the *Express* told its readers that the Negro Chambers of Commerce was working with the Dallas business community to participate in the events and gain a share of the anticipated business. The *Express* stated that the "Dallas Negro Chamber of Commerce has sought to assure for the Negroes of Dallas suitable accommodations and participation in all of the departments of this celebration."

After agreeing to support the Dallas exposition and participate in the bond campaign, the Hall of Negro Life received $100,000 as part of the $3 million federal appropriation. The centennial exposition received support from African Americans in Texas despite the fact that unemployment and poverty ran much higher in black communities than white communities in both rural and urban areas. In Dallas, African Americans represented half the city's unemployed in the mid-1930s. Only one major African American business, the Excelsior Mutual Insurance Company, managed to survive to 1937. Thus the Hall of Negro Life represented a symbol of hope and accomplishment for the black community. Included in the hall were murals of African Americans providing contributions of music, art, and religion to the nation. The exhibit also represented a small achievement in opposition to the segregated life of the 1930s. A. Maceo Smith, an African American insurance executive, led a concerted effort to have the Hall of Negro Life included at the exposition. Smith's early work with the Dallas NAACP and white business leaders established a pattern that was expanded in the coming decades as the African American community began to increase its efforts to combat segregation.

At the dedication of the centennial exposition on June 7, a host of dignitaries and thousands of visitors attended. As Sam Acheson of the *Dallas Morning News* wrote, the festivities opened "before the largest crowd ever gathered in the Southwest." An estimated 250,000 people attended, "making it the greatest occasion in the history of Dallas and the most notable event in Texas since Sam Houston and his men changed the course of the New World at San Jacinto."

Extensive coverage over radio stations and the state's newspapers heightened the enthusiasm for the great event. Texas governor James Allred introduced Secretary of Commerce Daniel Roper. As he inserted a gold key and unlocked the ceremonial gate, Roper proclaimed, "Texas welcomes the world."

Secretary Roper escorted a delegation of officials, some of whom were descendants of Stephen F. Austin, and other state and local leaders. Later that day, Roper dedicated the Federal Building and visited the Hall of Negro Life. In his speech that evening, entitled "Texas and the Nation," Roper surprised many by praising the progress of African Americans. "No people in all history can show greater progress in their achievement in seventy-three years than the American Negro," the Commerce secretary said. "This is traceable to their patient, loyal, patriotic attitude toward their country and to their gifts of soul and song." The Dallas newspapers carried the remarks as part of the coverage of the opening ceremony. But later, the *Dallas Morning News* carried more critical stories that depicted African Americans in a less flattering light. "History of Negroes from Jungles to Now" and "black faces deep into slices of watermelon" were among the racist, condescending phrases used in coverage of the Hall of Negro Life. The statements undoubtedly provided some comfort to fair organizers who acquiesced to the demands of African Americans. But to make sure that no one would overlook the state's Confederate heritage, a statue representative of the Confederacy stood in the center portico of the Centennial Building. Confederate leaders appeared prominently in murals in the Great Hall of State. President Franklin Roosevelt dedicated a statue of Robert E. Lee on his horse Traveler as one of the centennial highlights. Allegiance to the Old South and Confederacy remained strong, even as civic leaders elevated the Texas Lone Star alongside the Stars and Bars.

As mentioned earlier, Amon Carter pushed for a separate centennial site for Fort Worth. Following the untimely death of Will Rogers in 1935, Carter urged a memorial coliseum in honor of his friend. Rejected by the PWA, the plan was reborn in the form of a Frontier Centennial Exhibition. A 135-acre tract west of downtown Fort Worth, formerly occupied by the military, became the chosen site. The Fort Worth Frontier Centennial Exposition emerged as Amon Carter's cause célèbre. Carter united the Fort Worth business community behind the promotion as the western alternative to the Dallas celebration. The venue would offer the entertainment and lavish productions that Carter believed that the Dallas venue omitted. The *Fort Worth Star-Telegram* declared that Fort Worth would become the beneficiary of increased jobs and would receive favorable publicity for the city's businesses. Carter's newspaper and WBAP radio carried daily stories and promotions of the event. A series of front-page editorials in 1935 boasted of the benefits. "Fort Worth can stage a show that in appeal to visitors will equal that of any other city or the main Centennial itself at Dallas," Carter wrote. The benefits would bring "large and immediate cash-drawer returns to every businessman, professional man and property owner in Fort Worth."

Carter lobbied his friends in Washington to assist with the funding. After obtaining a loan and grant from the PWA along with privately funded bonds for the multimillion dollar project, Carter learned in early June 1936 that funds were insufficient to complete construction. He wrote Vice President John Nance Garner, only days prior to the dedication, that the Fort

Worth production needed more money. "Costs have exceeded estimates thirty to forty percent." He claimed that the project provided jobs for more than 3,000 people. "Can you not see your way clear to giving us some relief immediately," Carter said. "I assure you that it would be a Godsend to us." Carter wrote RFC Chairman Jesse Jones soliciting loans up to $500,000. "There would not be a Chinaman's chance for you to lose a penny on this note," Carter stated. If Jones faced any legal problems, Carter observed, "[Y]ou would be fully justified in waiving them, as no doubt you have found necessary in many cases where you have rendered emergency financial assistance." Carter concluded that everyone would be protected in the investment and would be amazed at the "magnificent" production. "Nothing like it ever has been shown in America." Eventually, another $50,000 in federal money found its way to the Fort Worth promoters.

When Carter obtained funding for the Fort Worth exposition, he and fair organizers raced to open before their Dallas neighbors, but delays forced the Fort Worth exposition to open a month after the one in Dallas. Carter utilized the staff of the *Star-Telegram* and WBAP for publicity, planning, and accounting for the Fort Worth production. Prior to the official launch, Carter invited hundreds of newspaper publishers and editors to attend a preview. WBAP radio provided an hour-long show that fed to network radio around the nation. At the July opening, news reports stated the production was "a startling blending of Texas longhorns, cowpunchers, chuck-wagons, six-pistols and naked Indians, with show girls, Billy Roseian scenic effects, Paul Whiteman's music and Sally Rand's bubbles." President Roosevelt telegraphed congratulations to Carter from the schooner yacht *Sewanna* off the coast of Nova Scotia, "Best of luck to you all," the president wrote.

Governor Allred and other state political and business leaders officially launched the opening. New York director Billy Rose featured a highly anticipated floor show, the "Frontier Follies," at the Casa Mañana. One of the attractions of the show was a "chorus of some 500 beautiful girls." Rose also brought his acclaimed *Jumbo*, a one-ring-circus musical production, to the theatre. "The atmosphere of a Texas town of 1849 will be perfectly re-created," one account stated. "There will be soldiers, Indians, Mexicans, cowboys, wagon trains, stage coaches, buffalo, all the frontier business enterprises, such as trading posts, saloons and dance halls—all open for business." The floor shows and the liquor attracted the crowds. According to Carter's biographer, "[I]llegal liquor was served everywhere" because Amon had made a deal with the state's Liquor Control Board. The summer heat often made the Fort Worth exposition unbearable, but throngs of people continued to appear. Critics and visitors praised the productions for months.

The Texas Centennial Exposition in Dallas closed in November 1936. The Fort Worth Frontier Centennial suspended most operations by Thanksgiving. More than 6 million people attended the six-month-long celebration in Dallas and an estimated 1 million visited the Fort Worth show. Visitors included President Franklin Roosevelt and his wife, Eleanor Roosevelt, Vice President Garner, and a host of national and federal officials. Over 350,000 schoolchildren from Texas and other states attended the centennial celebrations. The Dallas and Fort Worth events, especially when combined with others around the state, expanded the national awareness of

Texas. The festivities laid the foundations for a growing tourist trade. The centennial events also provided economic relief in the form of thousands of jobs and substantial improvements in many communities around the state. Finally, the celebrations offset some of the concerns about the ongoing economic depression and lifted the spirits of many of the state's citizens. For newspaper publishers, the increased revenues, circulation, and recognition provided welcome relief in the difficult years of the Great Depression. Publishers whose proclamations appeared extravagant in 1935 actually achieved many of their goals.

In Dallas, the closing of the fair led to a monumental decision: to create the Dallas Citizens Council, chartered in 1937 to plot the city's future. Charter members in the elite group included independent Dallas publishers G. B. Dealey and Edwin J. Kiest. The group embraced business-men, insurance and utility executives, and bankers drawn from the city's civic leadership. No reporters, educators, attorneys, women, minorities, or members of the clergy were included in the original council. The organization sought to influence the course of business, civic projects, local politics, and major organizations such as the chamber of commerce. The group's membership changed, but the Council successfully controlled Dallas for the next fifty years. The Council accepted the premise that Dealey in particular had advanced for many years: Dallas, as represented by the business community, should speak with one voice and offer a business-oriented agenda for the people of Dallas. The insecurity created by the Depression, the success of the centennial celebration, and the near unanimous conviction that the city's business leadership provided the best direction created the glue that held this group together for years to come. The insular, self-perpetuating, confident organization best resembled the *Dallas Morning News*, which, under Dealey's leadership and with its consistent policy of promoting business, survived the economic challenges of the Depression and remained a closely held family operation with a secure base of longtime loyal managers and employees.

In another sense, the centennial events and their promotion by the state press illustrated the desire to accept Washington's expanded presence, especially in the form of federal dollars. As long as the social and political order remained in place in the state, Texans maintained their allegiance to the traditional one-party Democratic system. Projects such as those represented by the centennial allowed Texans to boast of their individuality which, on the surface, set them apart from the rest of the South and the nation. The New Deal projects and the expanding role of the federal government sometimes produced criticism and divisions within the business and political leadership of the state. Although some grew increasingly nervous about President Roosevelt's policies and the direction of the Democratic Party, Texas editors took solace in the knowledge that friendly Texans still commanded major positions in the legislative and executive branches. Even with their power and influence in Washington, newspaper publishers and Texans from all walks of life realized the Depression retained its grip over the region and the nation.

Kenneth Ragsdale, author of a history of the centennial, reports that many out-of-state visitors "expressed their praise for the 'new Texas'; they found not the 'countrified folks' they had expected, but an 'ultramodern' culture. This changing attitude among non-Texans ultimately created a great cultural impact on the state, negating the 'pride with shame' syndrome and instilling a new sense of state pride in Texas." Regional self-consciousness was, after all, not a congenital deformity. Dallas retailer and civic stalwart Stanley Marcus reflected on the impact of the centennial on his city and the state. "I've frequently said that modern Texas history started with the celebration of the Texas Centennial, because it was in 1936 . . . that the rest of America discovered Texas. The spotlight was thrown on Texas and people from all over the United States came here."

Labor strife also became a concern during the centennial celebration, and Texas newspaper publishers became more critical of organized labor by 1937. The sit-down strikes that closed many coalfields and manufacturing plants in 1936 garnered headlines and criticism from southern politicians and newspapers. Many believed that the strikes violated property rights, and that President Roosevelt and his administration provided tacit support to the unions. Sentiment against organized labor in Dallas among the business community discouraged union organizing, especially after the closing of the centennial expositions. But violence and death erupted during an especially bitter strike at the Dallas Ford Motor Company plant in 1937. Ford, long known as a bastion of antiunion sentiment, retaliated against organizers and workers in the summer and fall of 1937. The victims of Ford's hired thugs included plant workers, CIO organizers, and Dallas residents who expressed sentiments in favor of the employees. The enforcers attacked over fifty individuals and killed one man. In scenes reminiscent of the Klan activities of the early 1920s, targeted Ford employees were "taken for a ride" to an isolated area away from town, where they were beaten. The Ford gang seized Barto Hill, a labor organizer from Tennessee, and administered a beating, then stripped and tarred and feathered their victim, much as the Klan had done a decade earlier. They dumped Hill in front of the *Dallas Morning News* office. A photo of the victim appeared the following day in the newspaper. Governor Allred called in the Texas Rangers, and the National Labor Relations Board (NLRB) eventually conducted hearings on Ford's activities in Dallas.

Labor organizers claimed Ford's violent acts would end only when the business establishment and the daily press criticized the automaker's tactics. Unlike their reporting of the earlier Klan-orchestrated violence, the Dallas dailies downplayed the incidents and provided little coverage of the NLRB hearings and investigation. The dailies' concern over labor strife mirrored that of the Texas congressional delegation of this period. The national press, which included the *New York Times*, reported Ford's antiunion activities and the labor board's actions; it also noted the city's growing reputation for hostility to groups that opposed large businesses. After World War II began, Ford workers nationwide became members of the United Auto Workers as a result of federal court action and a national agreement between Ford and the unions.

Texas newspapers aligned with most Texas businesses in the 1930s in expanding their opposition to organized labor. In this case, the probusiness bias of the publishers clearly outweighed their editorial assessment of community living standards and working conditions. As in other southern cities, the dominant leadership accepted federal assistance to provide unemployment wages and other relief efforts. But they resisted any challenges to the prevailing wage schedules or large-scale efforts at unionization. Many business and political leaders also feared unionism, especially the CIO, as an open door to racial integration. The Dallas Open Shop Association, organized in 1919, opposed union activities in the city and subjected members who knowingly hired union workers to a $3,000 fine. The members represented the city's chamber of commerce, which worked closely with the Dallas newspaper establishment. The local AFL leadership cooperated with businesses that resisted CIO organizers, and the labor leaders refused to publicly condemn violence and atrocities. In 1937 the *Nation* called attention to the city's antilabor positions in the critical story "Dallas Tries Terror." Based on the resistance in the South to CIO organizing attempts in cities like Dallas, historian George B. Tindall concluded that the "South remained predominantly nonunion and largely antiunion."

Daily newspapers showed evidence of prosperity as a result of the 1936 centennial celebration. But the recession of 1937 hit Texas and the nation with a vengeance. The *Morning News* closed its long-running *Semi-Weekly Farm News* and merged it with the daily. Dealey complained in his annual report that with the exception of radio station WFAA, all of the Belo Corporation publications lost money in 1938. Dealey sold the afternoon *Dallas Journal* to Houston businessman James West. Commenting on the sale, Dealey reported that the corporation received only twenty cents on the dollar, "but we were perhaps lucky to receive anything."

Even after World War II began in Europe, publishers still faced difficulties in maintaining their newspapers as a profitable enterprise. George B. Dealey turned over the presidency of the *News* to Ted Dealey, his son. The Belo Corporation annual report disclosed that advertising rates still fell short of supporting the newspaper operation. The report stated that both "leading newspapers" in the city, the *News* and the *Times Herald*, lost money. However, the Dallas corporations survived, as they were "supported largely by radio revenues." Belo owned WFAA, while the rival Times Herald Corporation owned KRLD. Ted Dealey stated, "We have the modest conviction that the *Dallas News* is being managed more sanely and more wisely than is the business of our nearest rival" and that the "competitive situation will adjust itself." With this disclosure, he asserted, "[W]e confidently anticipate that, in the long haul, we will come out 'at the top of the heap.'"

Historian Dewey Grantham surmises that by the end of the 1930s, the New South formula won the debate over the character of the southern economy. The New Deal provided a source of new capital with few strings attached in the form of the federal government. Along with regulations for industry, finance, agriculture, and labor, some of the old walls of resistance and blame that Texans and other southerners hurled at the rest of the nation came tumbling down. The metropolitan newspapers of the state took the lead alongside Texas politicians who formulated these fresh ideas. Differences continued to exist and lead to conflict and criticism, especially when issues involved a challenge to the status quo, that is, when they related to segregation and the region's labor system. While displeasure with the Democratic Party increased in the years prior to World War II, the disputes failed to completely dampen loyalties to the national Democratic leadership. Publishers retained their close connections to the federal leadership and relied on the entrenched Texas congressional delegation and their allies in the government to offset any serious challenges to the dominant coalition back home.

While historians agree that the federal presence expanded in the South during the 1930s, disagreement exists on the extent of its impact on the region and its meaning for this generation of Americans. For many, especially the rural poor, African Americans, and Mexican Americans, their suffering continued and conditions sometimes deteriorated during the 1930s. Yet life for many rural and urban dwellers, including some minorities, showed some degree of improvement. Texas and the South were not entirely agrarian. Urban communities expanded and their workforce increased, due in part to widespread urban support for federal initiatives. These programs, aided and abetted by the urban daily press, provided an alternative to the poor tenant farmers of the region. Although they criticized many federal programs and only offered lukewarm support for others, Texas daily newspaper publishers acknowledged this shift in alignment and advocated the establishment of federal programs in the region. Public power, minimum wage, work standards, relief programs, federal loans to business, improvement of public education, and other New Deal programs found fertile ground and editorial support from the state's leading newspapers.

The Texas publishers adhered to their consensus philosophy that had carried them forward from the early years of the twentieth century. This approach continued in the difficult years of the 1930s when debate finally moved from disagreements over Prohibition to substantive issues that involved business expansion, labor and race relations, support for public education, and improved health services. The publishers also helped set a tone of race accommodation and tolerance, albeit within a segregated system. The newspapers remained opposed to federal anti-lynching legislation and affirmed their support of the poll tax. They steadfastly refused to carry news of accomplishments by African Americans and Mexican Americans. They tolerated the discrimination exercised in most of the New Deal programs in Texas and the rest of the South. Yet by the 1930s, the major dailies in the state refused to enter into the vile, race-baiting tirades to which many southern politicians and newspaper publishers subscribed. They endorsed the very programs that were to provide a seedbed of expanded opportunity to all people, regardless of their skin color or background. The differences in the racial communities remained wide, but some bridges were established through the support of the New Deal and its promise of a better life. The era marked the beginning of a period when the southern press would have to recognize a need for reshaping the region's economic and social structure.

Reviewing the accomplishments of the centennial year, the editors of the *Texas Almanac* believed the events signaled a "return of prosperity" and "served the purpose of bringing full realization that the old Texas had passed—that the centennial event meant more than the passing of a mere historic milestone." The soil and natural resources still held great wealth for the state's citizens and businesses. After 1936, proponents believed that expanded opportunities in the form of manufacturing would supersede agriculture and extractive industries that relied on natural resources. In the midst of the Great Depression, Texas had finally passed "into cultural and economic adulthood."

Operation Texas:
Lyndon B. Johnson,
the Jewish Question
and the Nazi Holocaust

JAMES SMALLWOOD

James Smallwood (1944–2013) taught at Oklahoma State University and authored such books as *The Great Recovery: The New Deal in Texas* (1983), *Struggle for Equality: Blacks in Texas* (1983), *Murder and Mayhem: The War of Reconstruction in Texas* (2003), *The Indian Texans* (2004), and *The Feud That Wasn't: The Taylor Ring, Bill Sutton, John Wesley Hardin, and Violence in Texas* (2008).

In this selection, Dr. Smallwood examines Operation Texas, Congressman Johnson's covert attempt to save European Jews from Hitler's clutches. Because of LBJ's bold and humane efforts, hundreds of Jews—many smuggled into the United States through Galveston—escaped the Holocaust. According to the *Houston Chronicle*, numerous "Jews have Johnson to thank for their lives because of his display of moral courage" during the dark days of Nazi Germany. ❧

★ ★

Charles Marsh, a powerful Austin, Texas, newspaper tycoon, and Alice Glass, his future wife, attended the Salzburg, Austria, Music Festival of 1937. They then took a side-trip to Germany. While in the country of Kant, Beethoven, and Goethe, they found time to attend a meeting of the Nazi Party and to hear a speech by Adolph Hitler, who would soon be responsible for the deaths of millions of people. Marsh and Glass immediately understood what a menace that Hitler was to peace, to Western Civilization, and to the sanctity of human life.

Their young congressman, Lyndon B. Johnson, had arrived at a similar view in 1934, the year he became engaged to Claudia Alta "Lady Bird" Taylor. On their first encounter, they discussed European affairs, the Nazi rise in Germany, and the potentially disastrous fate of the Jews. Both were concerned. One day later, Lyndon gave Lady Bird a gift, a book which he inscribed "To Bird–in the hope within these pages she may . . . find reiterated some of the principles in which she believes and which she has been taught to revere and respect." The book was *Nazism: An Assault on Civilization*, edited by Pierre Van Paassen and James Waterman Wise. Published just one year after Hitler assumed power, it predicted the coming Nazi terror and the not-too-distant Holocaust in which millions of Jews, Slavs, numerous gypsies, and other "undesirables" would be murdered.

The prescient work also predicted Hitler's seizure of Austria, and attacks on Czechoslovakia, Poland, and the Soviet Union—in proper order. In March 1934, co-editor van Paassen made a speech that he titled "Every German Jew Doomed to Death, Slavery, or Exile." Again, van Paassen predicted the Holocaust, only to be laughed at and ridiculed.

Johnson did not laugh; rather his wide reading of European affairs led him to some conclusions. LBJ could not stop the coming Holocaust, but he recognized the Nazi menace to Western Civilization and he knew that millions of lives were at stake. He determined at that point to do what he could to help the world cope with such insane aggression and murder.

Regarding his concern for European Jews, Johnson had to vote his convictions only five days after taking office in 1937. The Omnibus Immigration Bill came before the House on May 18. The heart of the bill could be posed in a question. "Should the United States deport or naturalize aliens, mostly Jews, from Poland and Lithuania who had entered the country illegally on false visas?" Aligning with most Republicans and the "Dixiecrats" of the South, LBJ voted with the majority—naturalize the Jews and save them from Hitler's executioners.

In March 1938, after Hitler seized Austria, thousands of Jews from Germany and Austria sought safe haven, many of them hoping to come to the United States. Would America accept them? This time the answer was "no." A significant number of Americans, including many national politicians, were anti-Semitic and had no desire to increase the Jewish population of the country. Some people feared that more Jewish immigrants would lengthen unemployment rolls, become public charges, and bleed away precious resources during the Great Depression. The American government turned a "deaf ear" to the Jews. But some people did not close their hearts to Jewish suffering and Lyndon Johnson was among their number. Although LBJ represented approximately 400,000 people in his district, only about 400 were Jews. Although they were but a tiny fraction of his Hill Country, the congressmen had developed pro-Semitism early in his lifetime.

LBJ's interest in the national and international Jewish community can be traced, in part, to his early religious upbringing, which included exposure to Christadelphian doctrines. In the 1860s or 1870s, a Christadelphian preacher remembered only as Oatman visited the home of LBJ's paternal grandfather, Sam Ealy Johnson, who lived in central Texas town of Johnson City. The two men engaged in an informal debate about religion, a debate that Sam Johnson relished. The elder Johnson knew his Bible, but he could not answer several of the Biblical questions posed by Oatman. Impressed, Johnson arranged a public debate between Oatman and Johnson City's Baptist preacher. With several of his relatives in tow, Johnson attended the debate, which Oatman won, to hear the locals tell.

Won over by Oatman, Johnson and some of his relatives became Christadelphians, whose doctrines had originated in the 1820s when physician-preacher John Thomas left the Christian Church and founded his own Brethren of Christ. Thomas taught the literal exegesis (meaning) of the Bible, with Jews and Israel having a special place, for they were the "People of the Book." In Christadelphian eschatology, Christ's second coming would be signaled by a return of the Jews to Palestine and the recreation of the Jewish state of Israel. Christian millennists, Christadelphians believed that the Jews must return to Israel and that they had a duty to help them fulfill the Bible's prophecy. Sam Johnson taught young Lyndon these doctrines. As one author put it, the youngster "was raised in a pro-Jewish household . . . he was fed pro-Zionist propaganda along with his Pabulum and milk." Although the mature LBJ did not become a Christadelphian, he remained a member of the Christian Church, he internalized his grandfather's charge to "take care of the Jews, 'God's Chosen People.' Consider them your friends and help them in every way you can."

When Sam E. Johnson was in the twilight of his years, still passing life's lessons on to his grandson, events in Georgia made a permanent impression on both grandfather and grandson. In 1913, a twenty-nine year old Jewish businessman, Leo Frank, who managed a pencil factory in Atlanta, was accused of the mutilation of Mary Phagan, a thirteen-year-old girl whose body was found in Frank's factory. Although he was likely innocent, police arrested Frank who, as events proved, had little chance of justice. Frank was a Northerner, he represented industrialization, and he was a Jew. As his case developed, Sam Ealy, Sam Ealy, Jr., and young Lyndon Johnson followed the four-week trial. The nation as a whole was also experiencing a wave of ugly anti-Semitism in the same year as the Frank trial. Jewish immigration was at an all-time high and a number of demonstrations and magazine articles fueled anti-Jewish sentiment. Congress even passed an immigration bill complete with a literacy test, although President William Taft vetoed the measure.

Bigots aimed death threats at Frank's attorney, the trial judge, and the jury—if they did not find Frank guilty and sentence him to death. After only four hours of deliberation, the jury found Frank guilty and the judge did sentence him to die. The evidence in the case was so flimsy that many humanitarians protested. During two years of appeals, Albert D. Lasker, a wealthy American Jew and later a friend of LBJ and Lady Bird, led a campaign for clemency. Touched by public protests, petitions, and appeals from other governors, Georgia chief executive John M. Slaton commuted Frank's sentence to life in prison. Enraged, a group calling itself the Knights of Mary Phagan entered Georgia's Milledgeville Prison where Frank was incarcerated, seized him, drove across the state to Mary's hometown, and hanged him in Marietta, Georgia.

With Sam Johnson Sr. reporting the events surrounding the Frank case to the Johnson family, Lyndon learned the facts of the case and all the race hatred involved in the trial and the lynching. He never forgot what harm that racism could do and he remained friendly to Jews throughout his life, in addition to developing concern for blacks, Catholics, and other minority groups. In his political career, LBJ could always count on solid support from the Jewish community in Texas and, later, on the national community as well. Historian Robert Dalleck pointed out that although Johnson occasionally engaged in "rhetorical anti-Semitism," he still had sympathy for the downtrodden. "There was something about him," Dalleck contended, "that made him sympathize with the underdog. It may have been his harsh boyhood in the Texas hill country . . . or there was his sense of emptiness, a hole in his psych that made him identify with the persecuted."

Young Lyndon's grandfather and father also educated him about Tom Watson, a one-time Georgia Populist firebrand with egalitarian views who metamorphosed into a racist and bigot. Watson used his monthly, *Watson's Magazine* and his weekly paper, *The Jeffersonian*, to arouse Georgians against Leo Frank, calling him a "jewpervert," among other derogatory names.

Events away from his Texas home were not all that made an impression on the young Lyndon Johnson. The same year the Georgia mob lynched Leo Frank, LBJ's father had several confrontations with the Texas Ku Klux Klan, a group he condemned on the floor of the Texas legislature. LBJ proudly watched from the gallery as his father called the group "KuKluxsonsof bitches." Later, the Klan made him a target of their terrorist campaign. LBJ's younger brother Sam Houston Johnson remembered one threatening phone call to the Johnson home. After listening to a death threat, Sam Johnson, Jr., boomed, "Now, listen here, you Ku Klux Klan son-of-a-bitch, if you and your goddamned gang think you're man enough to shoot me, you come on ahead. My brothers and I will be waiting for you out on the front porch."

LBJ learned something that night. He learned of fear and terrorism born of racial and ethnic hatred as he and his brother hid in an earthen cellar near their home while his father, uncles, and older cousins—all with loaded shotguns—waited for the Klansmen. The Johnson men stationed themselves at intervals along a front porch and waited until dawn. Apparently losing their nerve, the terrorists never came. Sam Houston Johnson said later, "The Kukluxsonofab-ictches never showed up. But after that my daddy carried a gun wherever he went, even as he sat in the House of Representatives in Austin."

Learning practical lessons from incidents such as Klan threats, and saturated with the news his grandfather and father related—sometimes-current events, sometimes history—young LBJ internalized the lessons. He never gave himself over to irrational racial hatred. As a mature man, he did the opposite; he helped minority groups, advancing their causes whenever he could. According to Horace Busby, a long-time Johnson aide and speechwriter, the mature LBJ often mentioned the Leo Frank case and similar persecutions of others. Johnson said that those kinds of incidents were the sources for his opposition to anti-Semitism and to all other forms of racism. Johnson felt that such events—which led to the Holocaust—were responsible for his internationalism and his opposition to isolationism. He seemed to believe, but left unspoken, that America had a duty to act in the international arena whenever any group carried out genocidal war against another group. Later, another long-time aide, George Reedy, added that LBJ "had less bigotry in him than anybody else I have ever met . . . he was not a racist."

Given Johnson's early religious teachings, when Charles Marsh and Alice Glass contacted him about a matter involving Jews, the young congressman was willing to listen. Marsh already had helped Johnson with good publicity during his victorious congressional campaign in 1937. The young man was willing, even anxious, to please a benefactor. Marsh and Glass explained how they had begun to provide financial resources to Jewish refugees attempting to escape Germany. They had befriended the brilliant twenty-five-year old Jewish musician Erich Leinsdorf, from Austria, who they had met at the Salzburg Festival. In 1938 Leinsdorf came to the United States on a temporary visa to perform with the New York Metropolitan Opera.

Leinsdorf accepted many invitations to visit Marsh and Glass at the tycoon's countryside farm in Virginia. The Austrian was still in the United States when German Nazi forces rolled over his country, and he had no desire to return home where, most likely, he would be persecuted and possibly murdered. Although he applied for an extension of his visa, eight days before it was to expire, he still had not heard from the immigration service. When Leinsdorf told Marsh and Alice Glass about his problem, they contacted LBJ to ask him for help.

On a Sunday morning, Marsh drove Leinsdorf to Washington's Mayflower Hotel where the newspaperman kept a suite. Johnson met them, heard Leinsdorf's predicament, and the next day began solving the problem. Operation Texas was in motion. Johnson learned that the immigration service had rejected Leinsdorf's application because he had asked for a two-year extension, something not possible under existing American law. But, immigration personnel had not notified Leinsdorf of their decision. Johnson used that oversight as ammunition for strongly pressuring the service to extend the visa, and officials granted Leinsdorf a six-month extension. Next, Operation Texas began in earnest. LBJ first worked on having Leinsdorf's classification changed to permanent resident, a possibility only if the musician went abroad and returned as a regular immigrant from a country whose quota of Austrians had not been reached. After contacting the United States Consul in Havana, Cuba, to make sure the office's quota of Austrians still had slots open, Johnson put together the necessary documents and arranged for Leinsdorf to travel to Cuba and the conductor returned to the U.S. as a permanent resident.

Leinsdorf eventually became director of the Boston Symphony Society, but he never forgot Johnson. He contributed to all of LBJ's political campaigns, and at a party in Georgetown in 1960, Leinsdorf told the story of his rescue as plotted by LBJ, a rescue that involved the stopover in Havana that Johnson arranged. Because the rescue included illegal acts, secrecy had to be maintained. After his remarks, LBJ asked, "Now Erich, this is a lovely story and I certainly would like to hear it again, but let me ask you something; what kind of town shall we now put in that story to replace Havana?"

Leinsdorf's rescue was just the beginning of Operation Texas. Even as Johnson was plotting to save Leinsdorf, Jim Novy—a wealthy leader of Austin's Jewish community and a Johnson friend—planned a trip to Palestine to celebrate his son David's *Bar Mitzvah* and his own twenty-fifth anniversary in America. The two also planned to visit Poland and Germany and spend time with relatives that Jim had not seen since he left Europe.

With his brother Louis, Jim Novy had migrated to the United States in 1913 from a small town in what was then western Russia (now eastern Poland). The two escaped on the eve of World War I and both settled in Austin. Louis Novy became a successful scrap metal dealer. As Novy and his son prepared for their trip, the first German-Czechoslovakia crisis occurred and Nazi anti-Semitism was on the march. LBJ learned of the trip and urged Novy to "get as many Jewish people as possible out of both countries" while predicting that "very difficult" times were about to strike Europeans Jews.

Leaving for Europe in July 1938, Novy became a partner in Operation Texas. He had Congressman Johnson's letter of introduction to diplomats in the United States Embassy in Warsaw. Novy also had a large stack of immigration papers signed and counter-signed, to use at the appropriate time. The papers had no names; Novy was to supply the names after he located and identified Jews who wanted out. Johnson's maneuver was the key to success. Ordinarily America's overseas embassies arranged and approved visas, but LBJ had the Department of State in Washington approve them beforehand. Johnson and his staff wrote the appropriate letters, checking and rechecking to ensure that the materials would pass the scrutiny of all immigration officials.

The Novy's hid the papers among their personal possessions. At one point, they rode in a railroad car that had a microphone hanging from the ceiling, probably placed there by the Gestapo. Father and son made innocent small talk but mostly remained silent. When they reached their destination, Germans in Poland called them "dirty Jews," among other things. Once in Warsaw, they went to the American Jewish Joint Distribution Committee and were shocked to learn that the group was spending money on new furniture while more unfortunate Jews were lacking food. Novy became upset and criticized the committee for not doing more. At the American embassy, Navy learned that Johnson had called and asked for the consul's cooperation in processing the pre-approved visas.

Forty-two Jews from Poland and Germany, including four of Novy's relatives, received the documents, fled Europe, and lived while millions more were about to die. The Novys did more than pass out documents. Jim agreed to pay the expenses of Jews who could not afford the trip, and he promised to provide for them until they found jobs and homes. Novy and his son learned of a new threat when they reached Paris, where they stopped before continuing to Palestine. The second German-Czech crisis was in the wind and war might break out at any time. Rumors were rampant that the Germans might even have attacked Alsace-Lorraine, a border province long disputed between France and Germany and the Novy's faced the possibility of becoming trapped in Europe. Believing such a threat possible, LBJ frantically contacted authorities in Europe until he found the Novys in Paris. In the middle of the night, a man from the United States embassy banged on their hotel door and rousted them from their beds. Afraid, they refused to respond until the visitor slipped his credentials under the door. Once inside, the representative relayed Johnson's message demanding that they immediately return to the United States. They booked passage on the next ship bound for America. They never made it to Palestine, but they could celebrate, for, with LBJ's help, they had saved the lives of forty-two human beings.

After Jim Novy returned home, he received a letter from Berlin's Ernst Israel Rychtwalski addressed to the "Jewish Relief Association, Austin, U.S.A." No such organization existed, but a post office worker sent it to Novy, who did not know Rychtwalski but who listened to the man's appeal. He was writing on behalf of Adel and Fanny Gontschar, a Jewish mother and daughter who lived in Berlin. Rychtwalski asked Novy to help them get out of Germany before the Nazis crushed them. Novy's concern for Jews such as the Gontshars meshed with LBJ's continuing concern. Working together, they arranged for the Gontshars to make a sudden dash out of Germany, destination, Texas.

By 1939, Johnson had become more and more distressed about the precarious position of European Jews. Although it was not common knowledge that the Nazis intended to exterminate millions of Jews, Johnson believed that it was only a matter of time before the Holocaust would begin. He knew of the international rejection of Jewish refugee ships, including rejection by the United States, and he knew of England's policy of thwarting Jewish migration to Palestine. Unwilling to stand by while Nazis murdered the "People of the Book," Johnson met with Jewish leaders and said simply, "we must do something to get Jews out of Europe."

So LBJ expanded Operation Texas. Using methods, sometimes legal and sometimes illegal, and using cash supplied by wealthy benefactors such as Jim Novy, Johnson smuggled hundreds of Jews into Texas, using Galveston as the entry port. Money bought false passports and visas in Cuba, Mexico, and other Latin American countries. As Johnson smuggled Jews into Texas, he gave them new names and hid them in the Texas National Youth Administration (NYA), a New Deal agency he had once headed in Texas. Johnson's task was made easier because his longtime friend, Jesse Kellum, directed the NYA in Texas. Although most of the Texas NYA records were later lost or destroyed, Morris Shapiro. Jim Novy's son-in-law, and other sources, verified that many Jews were routed through the state's NYA. Although it was illegal to harbor and train non-citizens in the NYA programs, the refugees were housed at various sites scattered around the state. Novy reimbursed the NYA for all expenses, including room-and-board for the trainees. He also covered the cost of classes for those who did not speak English and for vocational training so refugees could "blend" into American society.

Johnson channeled many men into NYA welding schools since welders were in high demand during the war preparedness campaign of 1940–1941 and then in the war itself. He also took advantage of his close relationship with President Franklin Roosevelt. Although Johnson became the first congressmen to enlist in the service after Pearl Harbor, Roosevelt called him home and put him charge of the Navy's shipbuilding personnel. In that capacity, Johnson made sure that "his" refugees were hired. Other Jews that he aided worked in a strange assortment of jobs, including liquor stores, carnivals, and janitors in schools. Jim Novy's son David estimated that Johnson and his father saved as many as four or five hundred Jews, possibly more.

The rescue efforts were offset by failures. With his wife Lilii, the physician Otto Lippmann escaped after the Nazis revoked his license to practice medicine and he became a target of the Gestapo. Lippmann's mother, who lived in a Jewish ladies home remained in Germany and he appealed to LBJ to help him get her out of Germany. Johnson worked for eighteen months to get her out, but was ultimately unsuccessful. "We tried everything," Lippmann later recounted.

Arrested before she could escape, Mrs. Lippmann was sent to a small death camp in Poland and executed. LBJ also failed to save Herman Winter. Approached by Rabbi Abram Vossen Goodman on Winter's behalf, Johnson tried to extricate him, but the Nazis arrested Winter before he could escape. Like Lippmann's mother, Winter also died in a concentration camp. Despite such setbacks, Operation Texas was for the most part successful.

Operation Texas also included aid to Jews already in Palestine who were "underground fighters." In March 1942, Novy hosted a World War II bond drive party for thirty or so influential Texans and invited Johnson to make remarks. After they raised their quota for the bond drive, Johnson rose, gave his listeners some "straight talk" about the European and Middle Eastern situations, and then raised yet more cash—the new money ear-marked for the Palestine Jewish "underground." While in the midst of Operation Texas, Johnson gave voice to why anti-Semitism was wrong, especially in America. In his remarks, Johnson said, "without tolerance and mutual understanding, without a sincere sense of the rights of our neighbors to differ in their views from us, this nation is endangered. We spring from too many races and nationalities and religions here to find unity in any intolerant theory of race and creed."

Operation Texas continued after the United States entered World War II. Novy reported that in 1942 Johnson sent him on a secret mission to Europe. The Jewish businessman said that the job was so dangerous that he did not tell his family, not even his wife and children what he was doing. Novy knew that he might be caught, identified, and shot by German authorities. Soon after his return, Novy, a civilian, received a Purple Heart, something almost unheard of because such an award normally goes to only members of the military wounded during combat. Years later, in 1958, Novy told a reporter of his mission, but refused to answer specific questions, saying that "only when Senator Johnson says so will I tell the story."

With the conclusion of World War II, LBJ had the sad opportunity to see what he fought against when he took on the Nazis in Operation Texas. With other congressional leaders, Johnson flew to Europe to inspect conditions and visit the horrific death camps. On 4 June 1945, his party visited the concentration camp at Dachau. After passing through the camp's black iron gate with a banner stating *Arbeit Macht Frei* (work brings freedom), the Americans were stunned. They saw death up-close and even smelled the stench of it. Some people in the diplomatic party wept. One of the congressmen, Louisiana's F. Edward Herbert, summed up the feelings of all the observers with, "God, how can men do to other men what these beasts have done . . . [the Nazis have] destroyed the last vestige of decency in the human being . . . [young boys are] emaciated, puny, weak, devastated, some beyond hope of redemption . . . death is their only salvation[,] and they are still dying at the rate of 40 a day."

LBJ agreed with Herbert's views even though he may have remained in Paris. Johnson heard reports from observers, Herbert included, that detailed the murders and torture in the concentration camps. Such cruel scenes were reinforced by the committee's visit to Italy. As Donald Cook remembered, in a comment that also related to the Vietnam War, "The worst [of the poverty] was down at Palermo . . . where there were tremendous lines of people who would form with their pots and pans and dishes to get a ration of soup from the [American] Navy, which was turning out this stuff [soup] out of the garbage from the vessels." It was a saddening episode," Cook continued, "but it kept them alive . . . [Congressmen Johnson] was appalled . . . the realities of war made a very, very, deep impression on him, and I think that a recollection of those realities undoubtedly played a part in his initial opposition to going into Vietnam. That's one of the reasons why I'm sure that a tremendous selling job was done on him [to escalate the Vietnam War]" Lady Bird Johnson later recalled that when her husband returned home he was still shaken, stunned, terrorized, and "bursting with overpowering revulsion and incredulous horror at what he had seen." Linda Johnson Robb, the Johnson's oldest daughter, added, "He came home after that trip, and he wouldn't talk about it. He was just miserable. It was as if he were (sic) struck by some terrible illness . . . Depressed and wordless, he took to his bed."

The horrors of Dachau and other killing fields may help explain Johnson's foreign policy as president. He was a man torn by inner-conflict. Although he questioned the Vietnam War at first, to LBJ, Dachau meant "never again." Never again should unarmed people be murdered by madmen. From the 1940s to the 1960s, Johnson saw the United States as defender of the free world, the defender that could not let Dachau happen again whether by fascists or communists, by the political right or the political left. Such views explain why Johnson bowed to his advisors and reversed his early view on Vietnam, ultimately insisting on "saving" South Vietnam. After much "soul-searching," he cast the Vietnamese struggle as one that could produce another Dachau. He feared that millions of unarmed civilians would be butchered by a powerful, hate-filled foe. Perhaps he wanted another Operation Texas, a chance to save lives by opposing what he saw as the aggression of North Vietnam.

Operation Texas was a secret affair. Some LBJ aides, friends, and associates even denied that it existed. There is no mountain of evidence that divulges all of the specifics of the scheme, but evidence does substantiate that it existed. First, that LBJ was addicted to the telephone is legendary. He seldom wrote things down. Sometimes he made as many as 100 calls a day. Second, certain aspects of the scheme were illegal. Thus, there would not be a "paper trail" that would implicate people in such a plot. A one-time NYA administrator and Johnson friend, Elizabeth Goldschmidt, denied any knowledge of Operation Texas, but she was not stationed in Texas between 1938 and 1943. However, she did offer with a sly grin, "Of course, in those days we all took a loose view of what we could and couldn't do." Jack Baumel, an engineer who worked for the Texas Railroad Commission and who was also one of Johnson's friends, recalled that LBJ once said, "We had to do something to the Jews out of Europe." Baumel added, "There's no question that LBJ was instrumental in helping literally hundred of Jews get into the U.S., especially through Galveston." Jim Novy's son Dave confirmed that the operation existed, as did Novy's son-in-law, Mike Shapiro. Professor David Bell and Barby Weiner, co-chairmen of the Criteria Committee for the selection of the Holocaust Center and Memorial Museum's annual Lyndon Baines Johnson Moral Courage Award, believe that LBJ saved at least two score of Jews in 1938 and, subsequently, likely saved "several hundred [more] through other lesser-known and even riskier means."

The best witness is Jim Novy. The Jewish leader finally made the story public during the 30 December 1963 dedication of Austin's newest synagogue, Agudas Achim. Invited to the ceremonies by Novy, LBJ and Lady Bird were in attendance, with the president scheduled to make remarks. Knowing that the new president was well beyond prosecution for his acts of long ago, Novy told the story to 400 synagogue members and their guests, along with Austin's civic leaders and local newspaper, radio, and television reporters. He did not discuss his secret 1942 mission to Europe, the details of which the public and later historians will never know. Novy's presentation, humorous at times, drew much laughter from the crowd, beginning with his order to President Johnson, then the most powerful man in the world. "If I get mixed up, you help me out!" Even Lady Bird had to cover her mouth and try to stifle her laughter, while the president only smiled and nodded that he would do what Novy demanded.

After Novy finished his story, he introduced LBJ by looking over to him and—trying to hold back tears—said with a breaking voice, "We can't ever thank him enough for all those Jews he got out of Germany during the days of Hitler." Then pointing to the first row where four small boys were sitting, Novy added, "There's the ... current generation, and they'll be watching [out] for you and helping you [while you are president]."

LBJ gave a speech that lasted approximately twelve minutes. He began by saying how glad he was that his first unofficial speech as president was one presented in a "house of worship in my hometown." Continuing, for the first time publicly, he "owned up" to Operation Texas to celebrate human life, to acknowledge Jewish support, and to determine that long before his presidency he had become involved with the Jewish community in a positive way. Humanism shined through in the remarks of both Novy and Johnson. At the end of the ceremonies, the crowd mobbed Novy and both the Johnsons. Lady Bird remembered that "person after person plucked at my sleeve and said, 'I wouldn't be here today if it weren't for him. He helped me get out." Perhaps the testimonials provided the ultimate "truth-test" that Operation Texas was a success. Wrote a reporter for the *Houston Chronicle*, "Johnson was a man who took considerable risk with his political career to uphold the message [racial, ethnic, and religious tolerance] for the future. Thus, many Jews have Johnson to thank for their lives because of his display of moral courage."

Lyndon Johnson is often criticized by many laymen and professional historians. He has been stereotyped as a crude Texan who had few serious beliefs, an opportunist only out for personal political gain. Operation Texas belied that image. The rescue efforts saved hundreds of Jews from the Holocaust. Johnson cared for the "People of the Book," as he obviously revered human life and detested suffering caused by naked aggression and racial and ethnic animosity. While he agonized over the loss of life during the Vietnam War (a war he repeatedly hied to end with secret negotiations), he remained consistent in his attempts to help others. Because of his domestic policies, he became known as the "Education President" and the "Civil Rights President." He fought a "War on Poverty" that reduced the United States poverty rate to eleven percent in just five short years. In his humanism, Johnson tried to help Jews, Blacks, Latinos, or other minorities. He made it to the top, and he took as many people with that he could.

AFTERWARD:

In 1951, Israel needed money and material to help Jewish refugees coming in the new country. LBJ successfully lobbied the Senate Foreign Relations Committee for $150 million to help with the problem.

In July 1956, the Ku Klux Klan burned a cross on the LBJ Ranch to protest his willingness to help minorities. A message with the cross proclaimed, "Our favorite son must serve Texas and America, not B'nai B'rith."

In his speech about the Civil Rights Act of 1964, Johnson said, "Our Constitution, the foundation of our republic, forbids [discrimination]. The principles of our freedom forbids it. Morality forbids it. And the law I sign tonight forbids it."

In October 1965, Johnson signed a new immigration bill that voided the old racist act of 1924.

In 1994, the Holocaust Education Center and Memorial Museum established the Lyndon Baines Johnson Moral Courage Award. The award could be given to someone who committed a single act of moral courage or to someone whose entire career displayed that virtue. LBJ, said the committee, acted by "stretching his authority to its utmost and risking the personal dreams his actions might shatter [if he failed]."

One observer wrote, "John F. Kennedy once said that 'each time a man stands up for an ideal or acts to improve the lot of others or speaks out against injustice, he sends out a ripple of hope . . . these ripples [become] a current that can sweep down the mightiest walls of oppression' . . . Lyndon Johnson chose not to make a ripple. He made a [tidal] wave."

Sam Rayburn

D. CLAYTON BROWN

Clayton Brown is professor of history at Texas Christian University in Fort Worth. His other studies include *Electricity for Rural America: The Fight for the REA* (1980), *Globalization and America since 1945* (2003) and *King Cotton in Modern America: A Cultural, Political, and Economic History since 1945* (2010).

Texan Sam Rayburn (1882–1961) stands as one of the nation's eminent legislative leaders. Known popularly as "Mr. Sam," he served as Speaker of the U.S. House longer than any other individual. Harry Truman praised Rayburn as "one of the greatest and most respected statesmen who ever lived." In this selection, Dr. Brown examines the life and career of the distinguished Democratic politician. ✍

★ ★

When Sam Rayburn died on November 16, 1961, the world knew it had lost a great leader. "Sam Rayburn . . . was the greatest of the great Speakers of the House of Representatives," wrote Harry Truman. "He was the second most powerful person in the United States Government. It is my opinion that Sam Rayburn was one of the greatest and most respected Statesmen who ever lived." Eleanor Roosevelt wrote: "He was one of the finest Speakers and Representatives. My husband at all times had great respect and affection for him." These statements of

"Sam Rayburn" by D. Clayton Brown from *Profiles in Power: Twentieth Century Texans in Washington* edited by Kenneth E. Hendrickson, Jr. and Michael Collins, 1993. Reprinted by permission of D. Clayton Brown, Professor of History, Texas Christian University.

eloquence refer to the political side of Mr. Sam's life, a life that began in the Texas House of Representatives when he was twenty-five and continued until his death at age seventy-nine. Other statements made at the time of his death had a more personal tone. Montana Senator Mike Mansfield wrote: "I feel that I have lost both a father and a brother, but I know that the nation's loss is greater still. He is the last of the old frontiersmen." And from former President Dwight Eisenhower came this short and poignant phrase: "As his friend of many years, I mourn his passing." Journalist Eric Sevareid combined the political and personal nature of Rayburn when he said: "He was the salt, soil and substance of our political system and inheritance. We shall not see his like again in the Speaker's chair, for the old ways, the old image of America are going as the old men go."

This last statement referred to the value system that was so much a part of Rayburn's personality. The longest serving Speaker of the House came from common stock, the class of American yeomen synonymous with self-sufficient farmers whose lifeblood was the soil. The Rayburn class, like generations of pioneer stock preceding them, lived close to nature and the earth, and as was the case of an America of bygone days, they depended on one another and developed a sense of fair play. These people believed in trust and honesty, explaining the pioneer belief that a man was only as "good as his word."

Rayburn, born in 1882 in Tennessee, moved with his family to the high-yield cotton growing area of Northeast Texas in 1887 and settled near the town of Flag Springs. Sam was one of eleven children. Though the family scraped for every dollar, it should not be assumed that the Rayburns were poor. In the agrarian environment in which they lived cash was scarce for nearly all. "We were short of money," Rayburn once recalled, "but we had a comfortable home, plenty to eat. My father couldn't put us all through college, but most of us went anyway." As a boy Sam learned to be resourceful, not to settle for less, and to be ready to make the sacrifices required to achieve a goal. His long days spent working the cotton rows alongside his father and brothers, his observance of the rotation of the year's seasons, and seeing new life come forth each spring gave him patience and taught him that hard labor would, over time, bear fruit. But in this environment of hardship, an environment in which baptisms were conducted in a pond or creek, the young Rayburn learned that money and material wealth were not always labor's reward. Instead one's compensation might be a modest life filled with contentment and satisfaction, or one of public service, as long as it was a life filled with respect for one's self and others. Around the rural town squares of Rayburn's youth, men and women who held this southern agrarian value system were plentiful.

Rayburn's personality at all stages of his career reflected this background. His friends always described him as hard-working, patient, and steadfast to his word. His personal life and business conduct were said to be simple, but he ran the House of Representatives, by everyone's assessment, out of his hip pocket. His refusal to keep notes was famous, and he always explained that when a man was honest he didn't need to worry about what he said. The "Rayburnisms," short quips of personal philosophy, were part of his mode of operation. They included: "Any fellow who will cheat for you will cheat against you;" "Any jackass can kick a barn down, but it takes a carpenter to build it," and his most repeated Rayburnism, "If a man has good common sense, he has about all the sense there is." Such views of life were once heard throughout rural

America, and they endeared Rayburn to his friends and won him respect around the world. At the peak of his power, when he was regarded as second in power only to the president of the United States, he was admiringly and simply called "Mr. Sam."

Rayburn's adult life prior to becoming a member of Congress had both common and uncommon features. In 1900, when he was eighteen years old, he left home in order to attend Mayo Normal College at Commerce, Texas, where he worked as a janitor, dairy-hand and at other odd jobs to pay his tuition. Financial strains forced him to leave Mayo and to teach school for awhile, but he finished the curriculum at Mayo in time to graduate with his class. He returned to teaching in small country schools, but in 1906 he left teaching in order to enter politics. The Texas House of Representatives was his first political goal, and that year he was elected to represent Fannin County.

Only twenty-four years old when he took the oath of office as a Texas legislator, Rayburn kept a low profile during his first year. He entered the University of Texas law school in Austin to take a special three-month review class which proved to be sufficient preparation for Rayburn to pass the state bar exam. During his second term Rayburn chaired two committees and served on four others. Well liked and highly respected, Rayburn was elected Speaker of the Texas House during his third term, an amazing feat for such a young man. His one term as the Texas Speaker was not particularly eventful, but he was remembered as a party loyalist who still managed to be fair and impartial. Rayburn himself said that he had enjoyed being Texas Speaker more than he had enjoyed holding any other public office.

The young Texan's move to Washington, D.C., occurred in 1912 when he was elected to represent Texas's Fourth Congressional District. In a race of eight candidates, Rayburn won by 493 votes over his closest rival. During his campaign he pointed to his clean record in the Texas House and freedom from special interests. He championed lower tariffs, the need for inheritance and income taxes, electoral reform, and the right of workingmen to organize. These issues were popular in 1912, as evidenced by their presence in the platform of the Progressive party, led by Theodore Roosevelt. Rayburn's goal to reach Washington was well known by his friends in Austin, and his decision to run came as no surprise.

Thus at the age of thirty-one, unmarried and free of family responsibilities, Rayburn settled down to a career in the U.S. House that went uninterrupted until his death. He was a strong supporter of President Woodrow Wilson and received an assignment to the Committee on Interstate and Foreign Commerce. He fought for regulation of the railroads and supported the American role in World War I. Rayburn, however, "realized there would be a long, long period of hard work, careful planning, and continual friend-making," wrote one biographer, "before he would be eligible for the final goal: to serve as Speaker of the U.S. House of Representatives." Indeed that was the case. Rayburn entered into a period of quiet and routine work until events turned to his favor in 1931 when he became chairman of the Committee on Interstate and Foreign Commerce.

This period of calm, however, should not be overlooked or relegated to a minor place in Rayburn's career. To begin with, he maintained his personal ethics, which meant punctual attendance at meetings, acceptance of extra work, and a spirit of cooperation. His willingness to accept tasks of drudgery gained favor with senior Democrats who in turn promoted his career. Later, when he was Speaker of the House, Rayburn gave the following advice to freshmen legislators: "Get to know your committee chairman, let him know you want to work and help him do a good job of running the committee so it can make a record, and he'll help you with your problems." Particularly helpful to young Rayburn were John Nance Garner of Texas, who acted as House Democratic whip, William C. Adamson, chairman of the Committee on Interstate and Foreign Commerce, and Tennessee Congressman Cordell Hull.

Democrats were, of course, out of favor during the Republican-party dominated 1920s. Young Democrats were therefore relegated to strengthening the party in their home districts, maintaining ties with House leaders, and gaining seniority. Rayburn was unhappy during these years. His party was in the minority, and he had little chance to promote his constituents' interests or his career. He started reading during his spare time and nearly always kept one book in his office and another in his Washington apartment. It was during this Republican era that his parents died and his attempt at marriage to Metze Jones failed. The marriage ended in divorce after about three months, and Rayburn never talked about it, neither to family members nor political friends. It was always a matter that both he and Metze kept to themselves. Rayburn was greatly disappointed with this failure because he had always wanted a large family and frequently said that he regretted "not having a little towheaded boy to teach how to fish." Therein lay his devotion to the House. A long day for Rayburn was standard; he commonly went into his office on Saturdays and always seemed bored on weekends, restlessly awaiting the arrival of a new week of business. The enthusiasm and love that would have gone to a family went instead to the House and his constituents. His single attempt to marry and have children was opened and closed during the quiet Republican years. Any damage that his divorce might have caused with the voters of the Fourth District did not materialize.

Until the national public sentiment changed, bringing the election of a Democratic Congress, Rayburn had little to do. Like other Democrats, his best friend during these years was time, and hence seniority, and while he kept his seat on the Interstate and Foreign Commerce Committee and continued to work alongside Garner and the Democratic leadership, these quiet years offered little opportunity for legislative activity. He fended off challengers in the Fourth District and solidified his position at home. Until things changed, Rayburn simply had to endure. Nonetheless, during these years Rayburn had managed to become well known in the House and well liked by the Democratic elders and the ranking Democrat on his committee.

The Republican era ended dramatically with the Wall Street crash of 1929: the Democrats won control of both houses in 1930. For Rayburn things started moving quickly. He took over as chairman of the Interstate and Foreign Commerce Committee in 1931, and he played an important role in the nomination of Franklin D. Roosevelt for president in 1932.

The 1932 Democratic convention could have been disastrous for Rayburn. He was indebted to Garner, who had guided him as far back as 1913, and felt that he must remain loyal to a fellow Texan with a chance, albeit slight, to receive the party's nomination. But on the other hand Roosevelt was quite popular, and, given President Herbert Hoover's vast unpopularity, the Democratic nominee was expected to become the next president. Therefore had Rayburn offended Roosevelt, or had Garner fought hard for the nomination, Rayburn might have endangered his career. Garner showed statesmanship; he did not want the convention to deadlock as it had in 1924 and therefore released his delegation after the third ballot. Rayburn had hoped this would happen, and as soon as Garner made the decision, Rayburn swung the Texas vote over to Roosevelt, even though some members of the Lone Star delegation wanted to keep fighting for Garner.

When the New Dealers, with a flurry of activity, descended upon Washington after Roosevelt's victory, Rayburn was in a position full of power and opportunity. As chairman of his committee, Rayburn played a major role in the preparation of several pieces of reform legislation, some of them with far-reaching impact. In these particular battles, as well as in others, he used his middle-of-the-road, or compromise, philosophy in order to strike a bargain that was fair to all.

In 1933, after the Wall Street crash and the resulting revelations of considerable fraud in the brokerage industry, "the reputation of Wall Street for financial wisdom, care of other people's money, and common honesty," wrote one historian, "was never lower." Wall Street investors considered themselves to be responsible members of a private elite, but the general public and the Roosevelt administration had a different opinion of them. The original draft of the Securities Act of 1933, put together by the Roosevelt brain trust, went to Rayburn's committee, but Rayburn felt that the original bill would put too much authority into the hands of the Federal Trade Commission (FTC). The Commission "would become the Czar of American business," wrote one observer, "because it required all companies to get FTC permission before issuing stock."

Rayburn therefore persuaded the brain trust to write a less authoritarian bill and held hearings on it with his committee. Representatives of Wall Street met with Rayburn and tried to kill the bill. He listened to their objections but left the meeting convinced that the bill was fair and operable. He took it to the House floor, where he answered all objections and explained the details of the legislation. It passed. The Senate version was not as well written, so ultimately the House bill became law as the Truth-in-Securities Act. A Rayburn characteristic vital to understanding his success was apparent in this episode. He had refused to hold all brokerage firms accountable for the wrong-doing of some and had refused to go along with the New Dealers' attempt to concentrate complete authority in a government body. On the other hand, he did not yield to the objectionable demands of the industry. His sense of fair play had shone through, and while the press and the general public had not noticed it, his practice of even-handedness had been duly noted by insiders.

The ease with which Rayburn had guided the passing of the Truth-in-Securities bill, however, was not an omen of things to come. Roosevelt wanted to regulate the stock exchanges so as to protect the public interest. Among other provisions of his proposal, he wanted to establish more realistic conditions for buying stocks "on the margin," a practice widely abused and partly responsible for the crash in 1929. Again the measure went to Rayburn's committee, and again it authorized the FTC to regulate the industry. In this instance Wall Street was ready for a fight and "some of the mightiest names of high finance," wrote one observer, "flanked by their legal and financial experts, came swarming into Washington for public hearings before Rayburn's committee." Rayburn faced an array of belligerent witnesses and after several weeks of testimony asked Roosevelt's experts to draft a revision incorporating some of the objections presented to the committee.

Rayburn took it to the floor where critics described the measure as a communistic idea. The industry had rallied considerable opposition, and Rayburn faced tough opponents. Fortunately, senior Republican Carl Mapes of Michigan agreed with Rayburn and provided some help. Support for the bill proved to be stronger than it first appeared. It passed 281 to 84. A similar measure passed the Senate, and in the conference committee Rayburn conceded that a special Securities Exchange Commission should be created to carry out the new law. Rayburn had become identified with one of the most important examples of New Deal legislation, the Securities Exchange Act.

The major battle of Rayburn's career, however, still waited—in the Public Utility Holding Company Act of 1935. It dealt with the pyramiding of stocks, or the creation of holding companies. By the 1930s the practice of stock pyramiding had become a political issue, and the Roosevelt administration sought to stop it. Rayburn had a particular interest in this subject and served as the House sponsor of the regulatory bill. The bill contained one provision that was particularly offensive to the utility companies—the "death sentence," which called for abolition rather than regulation of holding companies. Wendell Willkie, the 1940 Republican candidate for president, led the fight against the bill and exerted considerable pressure against Congress. Rayburn's committee conducted the House hearings on the bill; so great was the pressure that his committee broke rank and voted to remove the death sentence clause despite Rayburn's efforts to keep the measure intact.

Being floor leader of the bill, Rayburn had to fight hard to defend it, but despite his best efforts, he could not persuade the House to reinstate the death sentence provision that had been removed by his own committee. The House vote marked a severe loss for Roosevelt—and for Rayburn. In the Senate the death sentence had remained intact, but the House conference committee refused to budge, forcing Roosevelt to accept a compromise that killed the death sentence proviso.

Despite Rayburn's loss in fighting for the death sentence provision, his role in the passage of the Public Utility Holding Company Act oddly enough brought important developments for him. To begin with, he had accepted the responsibility to defend a piece of legislation that was particularly technical and difficult to understand. (He had, of course, relied on White House assistance in this respect.) Nearly everyone was impressed with his knowledge of detail and ability to counter the charges made by opponents who could be quite adept at exposing flaws in the proposal. At the same time Rayburn had resolutely stood firm. He had refused to back down on the death sentence, even to the extent of being overturned by his committee. This was unusual behavior for Rayburn, who liked to avoid punitive legislation. But his unflinching position in the struggle had endeared him to the president, "a powerful asset," wrote a biographer "when the time came to make his bid for a House leadership position."

Rayburn's legislative style and personal way of dealing with people was best illustrated in the creation of the Rural Electrification Administration (REA) in 1936. By that time most urban residents had electrical service, but only 10 percent of the farms had service, and in many areas the percentage was far lower. Morris Cooke, the "father of the REA," had persuaded Roosevelt to create the agency by executive order in 1935, but its temporary status and lack of dependable funding had thwarted its progress. In 1936, Senator George Norris, "father of the TVA," and Rayburn jointly introduced legislation for a permanent REA. Rayburn's committee held hearings on the measure and Rayburn led the floor fight for its passage.

In this case Rayburn followed his usual practice of taking the middle position. Norris wanted to exclude power companies from receiving REA funds, but Rayburn disagreed, saying that they could be of some help. The goal was to extend service to farmers, he would say, not to punish the electrical industry. Rayburn's provision remained intact in the House bill, but Norris had kept the companies out of the Senate bill. Now the two highly respected members of Congress, anxious to see their people in the countryside enjoy modern conveniences, reached an impasse at the conference committee. "We quarreled for a long time," Norris recalled, "but neither side would yield an inch."

Norris left the room, determined to keep the power industry out of the program. Rayburn immediately followed and, catching up to Norris, said: "Now Senator, don't be discouraged . . . just let it rest awhile. Within a few days we will notify you we are ready to have another meeting."

By the next meeting, the House conferees had developed a compromise. Why not let rural electric cooperatives, or public bodies, have first preference in qualifying for REA loans but still keep the door open to any power companies that applied to the REA? Norris conceded. In 1936 the Rural Electrification Administration, with its new statute of authority, embarked on a program to organize cooperatives and extend electrical service throughout rural America. Rayburn was, of course, the cosponsor of the bill, and the REA was one of his proudest achievements. It proved to be one of the most successful and lasting contributions of the New Deal and remains today a fixture in American rural life.

By 1936 Rayburn had developed into a legislator who clearly disliked punitive laws and preferred compromise whenever possible; he was well known as a man of conviction willing to fight to the end when a fight was necessary. The Texas lawmaker was also well-positioned from a tactical point of view in the House. Roosevelt liked him and regarded him as a firm believer in New Deal reforms. His career was poised for another jump which came in 1936.

That year, while Roosevelt ran for reelection, House Speaker Joseph W. Byrnes died. Rayburn at the time was in Texas and went to Byrnes's funeral in Nashville, Tennessee. The vacancy of the Speakership brought an opportunity for Rayburn to climb higher in the House leadership. Majority Leader William Bankhead quickly replaced Byrnes, leaving open the position of Majority Leader, the position normally presumed to be next in line to that of Speaker. Rayburn committed himself to run for that position against John J. O'Connor of New York, a Tammany Hall Democrat. O'Connor had already announced his candidacy for Majority Leader and had obtained pledges of support soon after Byrnes's funeral.

Rayburn let it be known that he was a candidate but took a slower approach, and while O'Connor appeared to be the front-runner, the president had not indicated his choice. Vice-President Garner stepped into the race and effectively damaged O'Connor by exploiting his reputation as a mouthpiece for Tammany Hall. Roosevelt indicated his preference for Rayburn, and two state delegations, Louisiana and Pennsylvania, announced their support for the Texan. Rayburn was gathering momentum, and when Massachusetts representative John McCormack came out for him, big-city bosses moved their support to him as well. More joined the Rayburn camp, and he wound up winning the job of Majority Leader easily by a vote of 184 to 127 when Congress convened in January 1937. He could now expect to reach the Speaker's chair in a reasonable time unless something went dreadfully wrong. Garner's contribution to Rayburn's success should not be overlooked. As vice-president and as an experienced Democratic politician, his anti-O'Connor campaign obviously had an impact on the race.

Compared with his experience during the early years of the New Deal, Rayburn's stint as Majority Leader was uneventful. However, Speaker Bankhead suffered poor health, requiring Rayburn to preside frequently over the House in the Speaker's chair. This had the effect of conditioning him and his fellow representatives for Rayburn's election to the speakership in 1940. That year Bankhead died, and with no nominee from the Republicans, the House elected Rayburn Speaker. He reached his life's goal, but would always say: "I came within a gnat's heel of remaining a tenant farmer."

As in the case of his ascending to the chair of the Commerce Committee, Rayburn's achievement of the speakership came at a time when events seemed to heighten the responsibility of his new job. Soon after he took over as presiding officer, the House was embroiled in one of its most dramatic debates, one with serious consequences: the extension of the military draft in September 1941. In the previous year the government had established a peacetime draft as a measure of military preparedness, but the conscripts, according to law, were limited to one year's service. As war raged in Europe, however, Roosevelt wanted the period of service extended on grounds that the United States could not afford to be without enlarged armed services as Britain stood alone against Nazi Germany.

The real fight over this request came in the House, where isolationist sentiment was strong. Rayburn took the position that foreign policy should remain largely the prerogative of the president and argued for the extension. Rayburn's biographer stated that the Texan exerted unusual effort to persuade those House colleagues not adamantly opposed to the bill. "I need your vote," he would say. "I wish you would stand by me because it means a lot to me." Members of the Congress faced a heart-wrenching decision: a vote against the bill might imperil the country, but a supporting vote would bring the United States closer to war. American sentiment at that point was leaning toward noninvolvement in the European conflict.

When House debate began, it was emotional. As Speaker, Rayburn had to be fair and could not threaten or pressure anyone opposing him. During the vote, however, he used the weapons of his position to encourage passage. As the clerk called the roll, the count went back and forth, and it was impossible to predict the final tally. As the clerk counted, one member changed his yea to a nay, narrowing the vote to 203 to 202 in favor of passage. At this point Rayburn froze the vote and announced passage of the bill. Some confusion appeared on the floor, as opponents wanted to make a move to recast the vote, but Rayburn informed them that only a person from the winning side could make such a motion. Opponents still objected and wanted to reconsider the vote. Twice Rayburn refused, and he carried the day. His tactics could be interpreted as "strong-arming" the isolationists, but the bill nonetheless became law. When the Japanese attacked Pearl Harbor and Germany subsequently declared war on the United States,

Rayburn's tactics were seen as life-saving measures, and his prestige grew. He was seen as a leader and not a strong-armed politician. "He had pushed the Speaker's powers to the limit," wrote one observer, "and had triumphed, not only for himself but, as later events proved, for the nation as well."

Once the United States entered the war, a strong sense of unity and purpose swept across the country, and that sense of togetherness was reflected in the House. Indeed, a striking example occurred in 1944 when Rayburn became involved with the project to develop the atomic bomb. The Manhattan Project, code-name for the U.S. nuclear weapons development project, had been underway since the nation's entry into World War II, but in 1944 it needed more funding. Until this point the administration had managed to take funds from various agencies in such a way as to avoid a special appropriation. Now, in a dramatic visit to Rayburn's office, Secretary of War Henry Stimson and Army Chief of Staff George Marshall asked him to obtain a $2 billion appropriation for the project without letting the House know the purpose of the money. In other words, to approve the appropriation without revealing the project to members of Congress. In both chambers the congressional leadership managed to get the money without disclosing the secret. Rayburn simply asked, and since the House respected him so much, the members agreed. Not until the bomb was used against Japan did Congress realize what had happened.

As Rayburn settled down in the spring of 1945 with a sense of relief after the hectic events of 1944, President Roosevelt died. Although insiders in Washington knew of his growing weakness, Roosevelt's death still came as a surprise. Rayburn and Vice-President Harry Truman had already become close friends, sharing drinks together in late afternoon sessions at the Speaker's "Board of Education." Like many Americans, Rayburn was shaken by Roosevelt's death. He had felt a sense of closeness to the man who had brought relief directly to his constituents with rural electrification, farm-to-market roads, educational projects in soil conservation, public power, and other sorely needed projects. His grief, however, did not let him slow down because the war was winding down. The United States now had a long agenda of needs, both domestic and international, and Rayburn was close to the new president. He and Truman had a first-name friendship: Harry and Sam.

The 1946 midterm elections gave the Republicans control of both chambers of Congress, and Rayburn had to step back in the line of ascension to Minority Leader. He talked about retiring, but the Democratic leaders persuaded him to accept the lesser post, arguing that no one else in the House could handle it. He detested having to step aside for a party that he considered unsympathetic to the needs of the common man, but for Rayburn a satisfying victory for his party came in 1948 when Truman ran for reelection; the Republican presidential candidate, Thomas Dewey, was favored to win, but Truman's "whistle stop" campaign overpowered him. Democrats regained control of Congress, and Rayburn returned to the Speaker's chair.

In 1952 the Republicans nominated Dwight Eisenhower for president while the Democrats nominated Adlai Stevenson. Eisenhower was so popular in Texas that many Democrats there endorsed him, refusing to campaign for Stevenson. They were known as "Shivercrats" since Texas Governor Allan Shivers led them. Rayburn remained loyal to his party, which meant an open break for him with the Shivers camp. Eisenhower endorsed state ownership of the Texas tidelands, a dispute involving jurisdiction over offshore oil resources, and his victory in 1952 ended the dispute. Congress passed a bill giving Texas its jurisdiction, and Eisenhower happily signed it. Rayburn opposed the measure but was outgunned, particularly in view of the fact that in 1952 Republicans again captured the House, relegating him to Minority Leader for the second time. In the Fourth District the question over the tidelands never became an issue for Rayburn, and his fight with some Texas Democrats had no impact on his constituents. His enormous power and prestige in the House were not tarnished, and when in 1954 the Democrats regained control of Congress, he returned to the Speaker's chair.

Here he stayed, becoming the longest-serving Speaker in American history. Free of serious challengers at home and recognized worldwide as a statesman, Mr. Sam was becoming well known around the country, due in part to the television coverage of the 1952 Democratic convention and also to his reputation as a fair leader of the House. Rayburn had always treated his opponents with respect and avoided exercising his power excessively. "It is a wise man," he would say, "who realizes that the church is bigger than its pastor."

By the mid 1950s Rayburn had become untouchable. His personality and history of leadership, which stretched back to 1931 when he chaired the Interstate and Foreign Commerce Committee, were well known, and among young members of Congress he was an awesome figure, almost a living legend. For the rest of his career, "the golden years," as described by one biographer, he relied to a considerable extent on his persuasiveness to wield power. A combination of circumstances also strengthened his hand. For one thing, he and Eisenhower had similar personalities and philosophies in spite of some obvious differences that each was always quick to point out. Each had a middle-of-the-road philosophy and "a strict sense of national duty. Both understood the necessity of compromise. Both were men of good-will, abhorring venomous personal attacks." And even though they disagreed on specific matters, they created an environment of mutual trust and respect between the House of Representatives and the White House. In this period of "consensus politics," the emphasis should be placed on Rayburn's and Ike's sameness, their similar approach to duty, and their emphasis on good-will. To be sure, partisan politics never disappeared, and each on occasion had sharp criticisms of the other. But they were still much alike. The general public recognized the similarity, extending their trust and dependence to them to work out the daily business of governing. As a consequence, the consensus of the 1950s, at least between Congress and the White House, originated in part from the relationship of the president and the Speaker.

To some extent Rayburn's influence at this point extended to the Senate, where Lyndon Johnson, a fellow Texan and Rayburn protege, was Majority Leader. The Rayburn-Johnson relationship has been the object of several writers, and in some ways it is a perplexing subject. Johnson had come to the House in 1937 as a staunch supporter of Roosevelt, and he worked hard to please Rayburn, who was Majority Leader at the time. Rayburn liked Johnson and through the years had a father-son relationship with him. When Johnson rose to Senate Majority Leader, he and Speaker Rayburn maintained their closeness and worked to achieve harmony. Since both branches of the Congress were led by Texans with similar ideologies who shared a close friendship, the daily business of government flowed smoothly.

Certainly these were Rayburn's best years. His history of service and devotion to civic duty, plus his behind-the-scenes manner of conducting business, explained why *Look* magazine wrote of him: "he is more valuable to have on your side than any other man in Washington, if its pending legislation you have in mind.

In 1957 Rayburn accomplished a goal that originated in the latter years of his life: he opened the Sam Rayburn Library at Bonham, Texas. It was built by the Rayburn Foundation solely with private funding that began with the $10,000 Collier Award which he received in 1949 for outstanding legislative service. He wanted the building to serve as a research center for congressional affairs and named one of his staff members, H. G. Dulaney, as director. Rayburn used the building as his office when he was in Bonham, but he encouraged the facility's use by students, including school children, as a resource center. The library, under the leadership of Mr. Dulaney, has retained the Rayburn personality and style. It is a beautiful marble building that houses Rayburn's papers and other documents and includes a replica of Rayburn's House office. But, most important, the library has an open-arms attitude toward the public and maintains a friendly atmosphere.

Rayburn's library seemed to be the final tribute to a distinguished career, the ending point of his political life. But Rayburn still had energy. In 1960 he backed Lyndon Johnson's bid for the Democratic nomination for president. During the early months of the campaigning, Massachusetts Senator John F. Kennedy worked hard in the state primaries and surged forward after winning the West Virginia primary, while Johnson remained at work in the Senate. Rayburn had originally thought Kennedy was too young and inexperienced to be president, a thought shared by many prominent Democrats such as Eleanor Roosevelt. Kennedy, nonetheless, outmaneuvered Johnson and won the nomination on the first ballot.

Probably the most intriguing part of the 1960 race was Johnson's acceptance of the vice-presidency. Rayburn and Johnson were solidly opposed to it, but Kennedy wanted Johnson, realizing that he needed southern support to win the election. Johnson agreed, but warned Kennedy that Rayburn first had to be convinced. Rayburn remained opposed, but after Kennedy personally pleaded his case and Mr. Sam's own advisors worked on him, the Speaker agreed. Rayburn quickly swung behind Kennedy, frequently saying, "That boy grows on you." Kennedy showed the highest respect for Rayburn and agreed with the *New York Times* when it asserted that Rayburn was "Mr. Everything."

Rayburn now approached the final episode of his career: the fight over the House Rules Committee, one of the "worst fights of my life," he said. At the age of seventy-nine, Rayburn, whose only health problem was failing eyesight, wanted to amend the powers of the Rules Committee, which could keep legislation off the floor. By 1960 the committee was controlled by conservatives who were opposed to the proposals of the Kennedy administration, and Rayburn wanted to keep the Rules Committee from ruining the new president's domestic programs.

He personally took over the battle against Howard Smith, the committee chairman. The Speaker proposed that the committee be enlarged so as to allow the appointment of more liberals to it. In some respects it was a fight over ideology. In an emotional struggle reminiscent of the New Deal battles, Rayburn won by five votes. It was a particularly sweet victory for him, one that put to rest the rumors that he was losing his grip on the House. Again, Rayburn had made the right move. His prestige and command of respect were at that point not exceeded by any public figure. As Rayburn himself put it, "It's easy to be an obstructionist; its hard to be a constructionist."

Time was running out for Rayburn. At home in July 1961, he complained of back pain and went to his local doctor who found nothing wrong. Back in Washington he started losing weight and strength, but still there was no correct diagnosis of his condition. Convinced that he could overcome the mysterious illness, he went home in September for a prolonged rest. Further tests at Baylor Medical Center in Dallas revealed what Rayburn had dreaded: cancer. The disease had already spread and doctors gave him about two weeks to live. He lasted for six weeks before dying at the Risser Clinic in Bonham, on November 16, 1961.

There followed one of the greatest outpourings of public grief ever associated with a legislative leader in American history. His funeral service, conducted at the First Baptist Church of Bonham, was attended by President Kennedy, former Presidents Truman and Eisenhower, and future President Johnson. A crowd of twenty thousand stood outside the church. His biographers, D. B. Hardeman and Don Bacon, concluded that Rayburn's pastor at the Primitive Baptist Church at Tioga best described the Speaker at his funeral: "He has fought a good fight. He has been a fair and loyal man . . . He has kept faith with the democracy of our country." Thirty years later, H. G. Dulaney, when asked to compare other political leaders with Rayburn said, "It can't be done. Rayburn is incomparable."

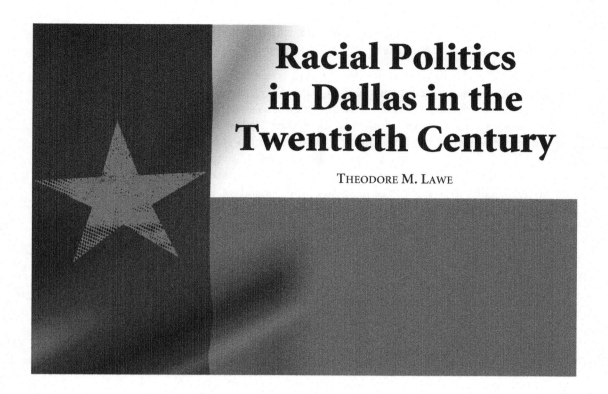

Racial Politics in Dallas in the Twentieth Century

Theodore M. Lawe

Theodore M. Lawe (1942–2015), past president of the East Texas Historical Association, served as historian and curator for the A. C. McMillan African American Museum in Emory, Texas.

In this essay, Lawe provides an overview of African American political history in twentieth century Dallas. Because of the efforts of its stalwart Black residents, aided by Federal judges, Dallas has escaped "its once rigidly segregated past." Lawe contends that the city, at the close of the twentieth century, "was an African American political success story." ⊰

★ ★

At the end of the twentieth century, Dallas was viewed as a progressive city that had made a complete departure from its once rigidly segregated past. The most visible indicator was the election of an African American mayor, Ron Kirk, who claimed victory over an influential white opponent. During Mayor Kirk's two-term administration, he was credited with successful bond elections to build the American Airlines Center, and successfully organized voters and city business leaders in a project to approve the initial planning and construction of the Trinity River Project, a key component for future growth in the city. Several prior attempts

"Racial Politics in Dallas in the Twentieth Century" by Theodore M. Lawe from *East Texas Historical Journal,* Vol. 46, Issue 2, 2008, pp. 27–39. Reprinted by permission of East Texas Historical Association.

to get this project supported had been defeated, which proved Kirk's ability to bridge former divides within the city's structure.

In addition to Kirk's election, at the closing of the twentieth century, four African Americans and three Latinos sat on the fifteen-member Dallas City Council. The nine-member local board of education included three elected African Americans and three Latinos, and the five-person Dallas County Commissioners Court had an elected African American commissioner on that body for over twenty years. The county treasurer, elected at large, was an African American female. Five African Americans served in the state legislature at the end of the century from Dallas County, including one state senator African Americans were also elected judges in Dallas County District Courts, justices of the peace, and constables, along with appointed judges in Municipal Courts and the first African American from Dallas was in the United States African Americans were finally well represented in the local city administration, legislative bodies, the judiciary, county commissioners court, and the board of education. Dallas was an African American political success story; political pluralism had seemingly arrived.

Such political accomplishments were the results of population growth in the African American community and the community's development of sophisticated political skills, which resulted from direct community intervention tactics, federal legislation, Supreme Court decisions, over 100 years of community struggles and demands, and other external influences. But more specifically, African American accomplishments came at a high cost from a long and painful history—they were active actors in their own success, not passive observers depending on external forces. According to the Dallas Black Chamber of Commerce (formerly the Dallas Negro Chamber of Commerce), this success came "from long, patient hours of planning and negotiating by dedicated persons associated with the Black Chamber."

To understand the significance of these accomplishments requires an understanding of the incremental changes in the African American Community that were socially, economically, and politically driven. These changes extended for a hundred years and involved thousands of people and the creation of many committees and organizations.

A look back shows that the early part of the twentieth century found African Americans in Dallas County struggling to survive. Most worked in menial jobs such as maids, busboys, waiters, porters, and in agriculture. The best job available to African Americans was a Pullman porter that required constant travel but at least provided a clean uniform. To help alleviate the lack of economic opportunity, the community organized several self-help groups to promote social and economic progress. The largest African American owned business, organized in 1901, was the New Century Cotton Mill Company, which survived until around 1908. Investors in both Dallas and New England raised $400,000 to finance New Century. Its owner was J. E. Wiley, a transplant from Chicago and the second African American lawyer to organize a practice in Dallas.

African Americans, out of necessity and institutional segregation, also organized their own cultural pursuits. The major annual recreational affair was the Colored Fair and Tri-Centennial Exposition, which began in 1901. Annual Emancipation Day celebrations drew large crowds.

The Dallas Black Giants were active in the Texas Colored Baseball League. *The Dallas Express*, a newspaper founded in 1892 by Mississippian W. E. King, was the recorder and voice for the African American community. *The Southwestern Baptist Newspaper* published by Reverend E. W. D. Isaac, the Senior Pastor at New Hope Baptist Church, was the primary religious organ for Dallas' African American community.

From 1900 to 1910, the African American population in Dallas increased from 13,646 to 20,828—over a fifty percent increase. During this period, several African American professionals moved to Dallas, led by Dr. Benjamin R. Bluitt, who built the city's first "Negro-owned" and operated sanitarium. William M. Sanford and Sandy Jones operated the Black Elephant varieties theater. Dock Rowen founded a successful insurance company, grocery store, and money-lending business. Dr. M. C. Cooper became Dallas' first African American dentist. In 1905, Ollie Bryan became Dallas' first African American woman to practice dentistry. The presence of such prominent professionals was a boon for the community since they provided leadership and served as role models for uplift and economic advancement.

In 1916, the Knights of Pythias built the first commercial building in Dallas for African Americans, designed by architect William Sidney Pittman, the son-in-law of Booker T. Washington. The building, located at 2551 Elm Street, provided office space for doctors, dentists, lawyers, and other professionals. It was designated as a City of Dallas Landmark in the 1980s.

Dallas' African Americans did not passively accept Texas' southern system of institutional segregation. In 1911, J. A. Gilmore refused to give up his seat in the "white-only" section of a streetcar and was ousted from the train by the conductor. The Court of Civil Appeals later ruled that the conductor was lawful in enforcing the "Jim Crow" law, but he used undue force. Gilmore was thus awarded $100.

In 1918, a group of socially sensitive men organized the Cotillion Idlewild Club for the purpose of providing social recognition and presenting young ladies to society. Because of the uniqueness of the club, *LIFE* magazine sent a photographer to Dallas to attend the annual affair. A favorable article appeared in a subsequent issue of the magazine.

The third decade of the twentieth century saw several events that demonstrated growth and maturity on the part of African Americans in Dallas. In 1921, St. James A.M.E. Temple opened a new state-of-the-art church designed by architect William Sidney Pitts. In the same year, Thad Else opened the first hotel in Freeman's Town, an establishment designed and built by African Americans that provided a vital place for a community subject to Jim Crow segregation. In 1928, the African American community raised $50,000 to help fund the proposed $175,000 community based Y.M.C.A. The first two African American Boy Scout troops were organized at El Bethel Church in Oak Cliff and St. Paul A.M.E. Church in North Dallas. In 1934, Father Max Murphy, a graduate of St. Peter's School in Dallas, became the first African American priest to perform a mass in the Dallas diocese.

From a political perspective African Americans more actively participated in the political processes after the 1950s when African Americans in Dallas were no longer willing to ask for a change and wait patiently to see what happened, but to organize for change for themselves.

Until the 1960s, social inequality was mandated by Jim Crow etiquette. Historically, the African American church provided a venue for self-expression and served as an erected shelter against a hostile white community. The political and social issues in Dallas involved both whites and African Americans on the issues of housing, jobs, law enforcement, enfranchisement, and public accommodations. Indeed, no area of life for African Americans in Dallas was exempt from racial discord.

At the beginning of the twentieth century, Dallas was a violent place for African Americans. According to W. Marvin Dulaney, a Dallas historian, in March 1910, Allen Brooks an elderly black man, was accused of abusing a white child. After his arrest (but before he could receive a trial), he was taken from the jail by a mob of approximately 5,000 people and lynched. He was later dragged through the streets of downtown Dallas and pieces of his clothing and parts of his mangled body were handed out as souvenirs. A second case came in 1921 when members of the Dallas Ku Klux Klan kidnapped Alexander Johnson, a bellhop at a local downtown hotel, whose only "crime" was to have supposedly bragged about having sex with white female hotel guests. For such an offense, he was branded with the KKK symbol and killed. In both cases, no one was ever prosecuted. Rumors swirled that Dallas police officers that were KKK members took part in both incidents. The two episodes were emblematic of how violent life was for African Americans in Dallas at the beginning of the twentieth century as well as how racially charged the political environment was. Too often, such lynchings and violence had the intended effect of intimidating African Americans. Approximately 340 African Americans were lynched in Texas from 1885 to 1942. Northeast Texas was one of the most lawless and lynching-prone areas in the state.

Dallas' history is well documented with examples of segregationist and apartheid measures that denied African Americans their constitutional rights. For example early local ordinances barred African Americans access to housing, law enforcement, voting, public facilities, health care, and employment. The Texas Poll Tax passed in 1902 and the Democratic White Primary Law passed in 1903 were major instruments used to disenfranchise African Americans in Dallas and throughout the state of Texas. In 1907, the Dallas City Council revised its Charter to codify rigid segregation of all races in all aspects of city life: public schools, housing, amusements, and churches. The City of Dallas further restricted where African Americans could live by adopting additional Charter amendments in 1916. In the 1930s, the Dallas City Charter was amended to require all candidates for city government offices to run at-large and on a non-partisan basis, which effectively prevented African Americans from holding public offices. Reverend Alexander Stephens Jackson and Attorney Ammon S. Wells voiced African Americans protests to these circumstances through local Republican politics in Dallas County, but given that Texas was a one-party state dominated by Democrats, such actions had very little effect.

During the war years and the out migration of African Americans from the South, African Americans in Dallas, as throughout the South, started to increase their demands for full citizenship by organizing civic and protest groups, community based organizations, and social clubs. In 1918, African Americans formed a Dallas chapter of the NAACP under the leadership of George F. Porter, a schoolteacher, and attorney Ammon S. Wells. Porter was one of the first teachers in Dallas to protest the unequal pay for African American teachers employed in the same job as white teachers. During this time, the KKK-dominated police department intimidated the NAACP by requiring that they have oversight at NAACP meetings. The Dallas Negro Chamber of Commerce (an offspring of the Negro Business League) was formed in 1926 to promote minority owned businesses and to generally improve African Americans' living conditions. The Chamber later hired A. Maceo Smith, a graduate of Fisk and New York Universities, as its Executive Secretary. In addition to re-organizing the Negro Chamber of Commerce in 1933, he became the publisher of the *Dallas Express Newspaper* in 1935. The African American Museum at Fair Park celebrates his contributions to the community with an annual community service awards brunch held in his honor.

In 1935, Ammon S. Wells unsuccessfully ran for state representative for the seat vacated by Sarah T. Hughes, who resigned to become a Dallas County District Judge. In a field of sixty candidates, Wells received 1,001 votes, an impressive showing considering the winner polled 1,844 votes. Well's candidacy signaled to the African American leadership that they could have success in electing their own in Dallas with more attention given to voter registration and voter turnout.

In 1936, a cross-section of the African American community organized the Progressive Voters League under the leadership of the Reverend Maynard Jackson and A. Maceo Smith with the charge to represent the community's interests and recommend candidates for political support. In 1937, the League's agenda centered on hiring African American police officers, low-cost public housing, additional public schools, and municipal job opportunities. Under the direction of the League, the African American community cast deciding votes in the city council election of 1937. Such a show of political strength encouraged the city council to vote to integrate the Dallas Police Department and to encourage building a second African American high school to supplement the existing Booker T. Washington High—Lincoln High School. The City of Dallas Park Board also released plans for a new recreation center in the African American community and, in 1941, construction began on the first housing project in Dallas for African Americans—Roseland Homes. According to Dallas Historical Society's "Portrait of an Educator," Principal John Leslie Patton encouraged the teaching of racial pride through innovative approaches to African American history as early as the 1930s. J. Mason Brewer, a noted African American folklorist, was a part of the school's faculty at the time.

Also, in 1936, the African American community, through the Negro Chamber of Commerce, secured $100,000 in federal funds to build "The Hall of Negro Life" at the Centennial State Fair. Raising the funds proved difficult. A. Maceo Smith, orginator of the idea, was initially turned down for funding by a joint state legislative committee and the City of Dallas. Through the help of John Nance Garner, vice president of the United States, funds were eventually obtained. The money arrived just three months before the exposition opened and on June 19, 1936, The Hall of Negro Life opened in Fair Park. Over 400,000 people visited the exhibit, with an estimated sixty percent being white. Harlem Renaissance painter, Aaron Douglas, painted four large murals in the main lobby; one of the murals is currently in the Corcoran Museum in Washington, D.C. and the Fine Arts Museum of San Francisco owns another. The famous Cab Calloway and his Cotton Club Orchestra, along with the Duke Ellington Orchestra, performed at the celebration. The building was immediately demolished after the Fair; perhaps signifying the white establishment's indifference to African American racial pride, it was the only exhibit hall not a part of the Pan American Celebration a year later in 1937. Sixty years later, the site received its proper reverence when it became the home of the African American Museum at Fair Park, the largest of its kind in the Southwest with 25,000 square feet of exhibit space.

During the 1930s, African Americans symbolically elected a "bronze mayor" to represent their interests. Dr. Edgar E. Ward and A. A. Braswell held this position in the late 1930s. Because no public hotels were available to African Americans, many special guests stayed in the homes of the "bronze mayors."

In 1945, Maynard H. Jackson, one of the leaders in the Progressive Voters League, became the first African American to run for the Dallas School Board, and although he was unsuccessful, its symbolic importance cannot be understated. In 1959, Attorney C. B. Bunkley, another African American, ran for the School Board; he also was overwhelmingly defeated by Nevelle E. McKinney—34,330 to 13,411 votes. By the 1940's, the African American leadership in Dallas realized that real progress would only come from making progressive plans. They set three priorities: to organize campaigns to overturn the Democratic White Primary; to equalize salaries of African American teachers; and to integrate the University of Texas Law School. In 1942, African Americans in Dallas organized the Dallas Council of Negro Organizations. This group retained Attorney W. J. Durham to represent Thelma Paige and to file a lawsuit, *Page v Board of Education, City of Dallas*. In 1943, African American educators finally received a victory when the court held that the Dallas Independent School District had to equalize teachers' pay. This was the first action of its kind in the state of Texas and it forced other Texas cities to follow suit.

Public school access was important, but movements needed leaders and leaders were trained within the world of higher education. African Americans in Texas were banned on the basis of race from most of the state-supported institutions; Prairie View Normal Institute (now Prairie View A & M) was the only state funded school for African Americans, although African Texans did have access to a number of all-black private colleges, including Wiley College in Marshall. But there were no professional or graduate schools or programs for African Americans, which greatly hindered economic and social advancement for the state's minority citizens.

The issue of lack of educational equality due to the "separate but equal" clause was not limited to African Texans—it affected African Americans throughout the nation. In fact, the NAACP had endeavored to overturn this egregious injustice for years. Led by its brilliant legal counsel, Thurgood Marshall, Texas presented the national organization with an opportunity. Heman M. Sweatt, a graduate of Wiley College, applied for admission to the University of Texas Law School in 1946. Although he was qualified in every area, the university rejected his application solely on the basis of race. Sweatt, supported by the NAACP and with Marshall as lead attorney, filed suit and challenged the rejection. The suit was first argued in state court and the trial judge immediately recognized the potential of the case to overturn "separate but equal." Marshall argued that the state was required to admit Sweatt since Texas had no "black" law school and thus did not satisfy "separate but equal."

The presiding judge delayed the case and Texas' officials scrambled to find a solution. State elected officials decided that the only way out of their dilemma was to fund and open a separate school and in February 1947 a temporary law school, The School of Law of the Texas State University for Negroes, opened in Austin. Satisfied with the Texas' response, the state court subsequently rejected Sweatt's suit.

Marshall appealed the decision and in 1950 the United States Supreme Court held that the University of Texas had to admit Sweatt to its law school, ruling that the temporary law school was not an equal facility. The court ruled very narrowly and the decision did not overturn the "separate but equal" clause, but most observers recognized that the end was near for basis of southern institutional segregation. Sweatt enrolled at the law school for the 1950–1951 academic year, along with a few other African Americans. Marshall would use the *Sweatt* decision as a foundation for his monumental argument in the landmark *Brown v. Board of Education, Topeka* decision in 1954.

During the 1940s another milestone in Dallas took place when the first African American, John King, was allowed to serve on a Dallas jury. African Americans had been barred from serving on juries for over fifty years. Political progress also began to pay bigger dividends in the 1940s when an African American became a precinct chair in the Democratic Party and participated in the Democratic County Convention for the first time. During this time, the Dallas City Council also authorized the hiring of fourteen African American police officers with limited authority to patrol the streets in African American communities. The first two officers hired were Lee Gilbert Bilal and Benjamin Thomas, the first hired in Dallas in over fifty years. The city council also authorized the building of several segregated public housing projects in West Dallas for African Americans and a middle-class housing subdivision to maintain racial residential segregation in an area that became known as Hamilton Park, named for Dr. R. T. Hamilton, an influential African American physician. Donald Payton, a Dallas historian, remembers the Hamilton Park community in which he was raised to be one of pride and influence.

In the decade of the 1950s, the African American community was under constant threat of bombings that started as early as 1941 with the bombings of eighteen houses bought by African Americans in then "all white" South Dallas. The Reverend Donald Parish of True Lee Baptist Church vividly remembers his father, who was a member of the special grand jury that investigated the bombings, grabbing shotguns and gathering his entire family on the front porch every time there was a rumor of bombings. Marilyn Mask, a retired school administrator, revealed to a reporter of the *Dallas Morning News* how her employer tried to coerce her into moving from the then all-white Park Row/South Dallas area. The Texas Rangers and the Dallas Police Department investigated the bombing incidents and although they made several arrests, only one man was ever tried and he was found not guilty. Two of the men arrested said that they had been paid by white community organizations to toss bombs at African American homes. The local white religious community was also implicated. Although African Americans had taken the initiative to improve their political, social, and economic conditions prior to the decade of the 1950s, it took the U.S. Supreme Court decision in *Brown v. Board of Education in 1954* to give more muscle and direction to these grassroots efforts. After the *Brown* decision, the political game changed. Racial politics became more confrontational.

Dallas hosted the NAACP National Convention in 1954, and 7,500 conventioneers celebrated the *Brown* victory. Nobel Laureate Ralph Bunche gave the closing address and he forcefully called for full rights for African Americans. During the convention, St. Paul Hospital announced that it was for the first time allowing five African American doctors permission to serve patients at its hospital.

In 1955, in an attempt to implement *Brown v Board of Education*, twenty-eight African American students attempted to integrate all-white schools, but Dallas' school authorities denied them entry. The White establishment continually challenged desegregation within the city. The Reverend C. W. Criswell, the most powerful minister in Dallas and the pastor of the largest Baptist church in America, spoke as a demagogue against school desegregation in 1955. His position was balanced by speeches from Rabbi Levi Olan of the Temple Emanuel, who confronted Dallas and his congregation on the moral demands to end poverty and improve education. Olan was a member of the delegation that greeted Dr. Martin Luther King, Jr. at Love Field in 1963, when he came to speak at a voter registration drive. White city officials successfully dodged segregation for the remainder of the 1950s and through the 1960s. It was not until Sam Tasby, a taxi driver and father of six children, filed a federal lawsuit in 1970 did the school district earnestly begin to desegregate in 1971, under a federal court order with busing as the chosen mechanism. The school district would remain under court order for more than thirty years.

In retaliation for the NAACP's school desegregation suits, in 1956 the attorney general for the State of Texas, John Ben Shepherd (with the acquiescence of Governor Allan Shivers), organized a campaign to outlaw the NAACP and to intimidate its leaders. As in other parts of the state, the Dallas NAACP's records were confiscated, which crippled the effectiveness of the organization. A. Maceo Smith, a local leader who worked for the Federal Housing Authority, was thus forced to resign as state executive secretary of the NAACP and to terminate ties with the local chapter. The NAACP did not come back to its original strength for several years until Minnie Flanagan became president in 1959 and linked the civil rights organization to the local sit-ins movement.

In 1960, the Dallas School Board held an "integration referendum." Dallas' voters rejected integration by a four-to-one margin. The Dallas School Board adopted a plan in 1961 to desegregate the district one grade a year, starting with the first grade in the 1961–1962 school year. Dallas' defiance of the Brown Decision was consistent with other approaches in Texas and throughout the South.

Also, during this time, the State Fair of Texas was under attack from the African American community for only allowing African American entrance to the fair during "Negro Achievement Day." In an attempt to segregate the Fair, in the 1930s fair officials set aside the day as the lone day African Americans could attend the State Fair. After many years of protests, in 1953, African Americans were allowed to attend the full run of the State Fair of Texas with the exception of certain rides and restaurants. Dating back to 1901, African Americans had organized and promoted their own "colored fair." In a *Dallas Morning News* article, Bessie Slider Moody details her involvement at age sixteen with the NAACP Youth Council and their efforts to desegregate the State Fair of Texas and the Dallas Public Library.

On the suggestion of Roy Wilkins, the National Executive Secretary of the NAACP, the Dallas community formed the Committee of 14 (later called the Bi-racial Committee) in 1960 to negotiate and "manage desegregation" in Dallas. The Dallas Citizens Council appointed the seven whites; the African Americans came from the Negro Chamber of Commerce and the NAACP. At the first meeting, A. Maceo Smith (an African American) charged the committee with six objectives:

1. provide integrated food services;
2. provide integrated public accommodations;
3. provide equal employment opportunities for Negroes at City Hall
4. removal of racial designation signs from all public places;
5. provide integrated seating accommodations at sporting events and at other public places; and
6. open accommodations in hotels and motels.

The Committee of 14 was challenged in its approach to "managed desegregation" from various sectors of the African American community that believed in more direct action. Among those who supported sit-ins and more direct action were such leaders as Reverend T. D. R. Thompson, Reverend Aston Jones, Reverend Rhett James, Reverend Earl E. Allen, Dr. Dudley Powell, and such organizations as the Student Non-Violent Coordinating Committee (SNCC) and the Dallas Coordinating Committee on Civil Rights (composed of the NAACP and SNCC). The biggest public demonstration occurred in March of 1965 when an estimated 3,000 people marched and rallied in downtown Dallas. Evidence shows that Black Dallas was divided on strategy for achieving racial integration, but united behind the objective of integration.

Two prominent African American ministers who affiliated with the Committee of 14 harshly criticized those who advocated direct action and called for a "moratorium on picketing" in Dallas. The Reverend E. C. Estelle of the St. John Baptist Church said that "direct action had diminishing returns and public opinion had turned against civil rights demonstrations." The Reverend B. L. McCormick stated, "There was no need for a city ordinance prohibiting discrimination because none existed." It should be noted that Reverend E. C. Estelle was a strong supporter of the Reverend J. H. Jackson, the leader of the National Baptist Convention USA, Inc., who was opposed to the strategy of Martin Luther King, Jr. and promoted "gradualism" to desegregation and knocking down the doors of Jim Crow.

In 1964, African Americans began to receive appointments to civic boards and commissions. Dr. William Flowers was appointed to the Advisory Health Board and John H. Glenn and the Reverend Caesar Clark to the City Planning Commission. Conditions changed drastically when the United States Supreme Court declared the Texas Poll Tax unconstitutional in 1966. Soon after, Attorney Joseph Lockridge was elected the first African American to the Texas legislature from Dallas. The Reverend Zan Holmes later succeeded Lockridge and he remembers being told by the rest of the Dallas delegation never to vote in favor of single-member districts. Holmes disobeyed, and was cursed and called a "nigger" on the floor of the house by the chairman of the Dallas delegation. In 1966, Attorney L. A. Bedford, who had earlier run for the state legislature, was appointed the first African American judge in the Municipal Courts. Judge Bedford remembers those days as being exciting times. He said that he always strived to be a "hard-working judge and fair in my rulings."

A chapter of the National Urban League was organized in Dallas in 1967, with the goal of helping African Americans identify employment opportunities. Also in 1967, Dr. Emmett Conrad was elected the first African American school board member. Latino Trini Garza, was appointed as well. Dr. Conrad's election to the Dallas School Board was in a citywide election and he gained white as well as African American votes. When he was elected in 1967, the school district had failed to follow through on the federal court order to integrate its junior high schools by 1965 and its senior high schools by 1967. Dr. Conrad won his seat on the school board with the support of the League for Educational Advancement. He succeeded in beating the Citizens for Good Schools' candidate, Albert Roberson, by 4,000 votes, even though the Citizens for Good Schools had won every seat on the school board since its inception in 1950. After serving on the school board from 1967 until 1977, Dr. Conrad eventually served on the Ross Perot Committee studying education in Texas and later served on the Texas State Board of Education.

The following year, C. A. Galloway became the first African American to serve an unexpired term on the Dallas City Council when he was appointed to the position. More concrete political progress came in 1968 when George Allen, a former member of the City Planning Commission, was elected to the Dallas City Council in a citywide election with white community support. Lucy Patterson, a social worker and granddaughter of pioneer school principal, Norman W. Harlee, later joined him in 1973.

The killing of nine African American men and the wounding of eleven others by the Dallas police over the course of several months in 1972 brought the two factions of the African American community together. In that same year, A. Maceo Smith led a coalition before the Dallas City Council representing approximately thirty community organizations. He called for establishing a community relations commission and improvements in investigating complaints against the police department relating to the failure to appoint an African American deputy police chief as well as the assignment of more African American officers to African American neighborhoods. Smith's appearance received results. Dallas received an African American deputy police chief in 1973 and an assistant city manager in 1974. As a further indicator of political and social change in 1975, the Dallas Negro Chamber of Commerce changed its name to the Dallas Black Chamber of Commerce and broadened its membership to include African American political leaders.

At the same time, a new generation of grassroots activists such as Peter Johnson, Al Lipscomb, Elsie Faye Heggins, and J. B. Jackson began to take on leadership roles along with Diane Ragsdale, Marvin Crenshaw, and Roy Williams, and others, some of them in prominent positions. All of these people were introduced to politics through participation in the Fair Park homeowners' protests involving eminent domain. The new grassroots leadership approach was to file federal lawsuits aimed at creating more district elections for maximizing grassroots political participation. In essence, their efforts were directed at institutional and systemic changes rather than individual concessions. In the 1970's, the federal lawsuit of *Lipscomb et al v. Wise* (Dallas Mayor Wes Wise) began the process that eventually led to single-member district elections for the Dallas City Council and the Dallas School Board, a key component of increasing African American representation. After several years in federal court and multiple rulings, district elections were finally mandated. In 1991, Dallas instituted a 14-1 political configuration, following earlier attempts to implement an 8-3 Council and a 10-4-1 Council. What this meant was the end of the at-large system, which was the centerpiece of the Dallas Citizens Council political machine. The new council make-up greatly curtailed the business community's control of city affairs and public education issues, another long-time centerpiece of the white establishment's control. Lipscomb, Heggins, and Ragsdale were later elected to the Dallas City Council; J. B. Jackson became active in mass transportation issues through DART and continued his role as a political strategist.

Marvin Crenshaw made several unsuccessful attempts for mayor. Roy Williams' book on Dallas politics, *Time Change*, explains how, because of single-member districts, more than twelve African Americans became members of the Dallas City Council in the last decades of the twentieth century, a numbers serving multiple terms, which indicated growing African American political strength. Among the unsung heroes that worked tirelessly for institutional change were Kathleen Gilliam, then president of the Board of Education, and Yvonne Ewell, who led the East Oak Cliff Sub-District of the Dallas Independent School District. Ewell was also active in bringing about change in the employment practices of the Dallas based major television network affiliates. Iola Johnson was hired as the first African American female news anchor in the Southwest in 1973. According to Al Lipscomb, the dean of African American politicians, "Dallas has great potential to show other cities how the concept of inclusion works.

According to Alwyn Barr in *The African Texas*, African American office-holders in Texas increased from twenty-nine in 1970 to over three hundred in 1990. Within the private-sector, in 1977, a local group known as the Committee of 100, which was comprised of young African American white-color workers in non-traditional jobs, hosted a dinner for seventeen whites and seventeen African Americans to discuss the need for improvements in local corporate hiring and the image of the African American community in the press. The initiative demonstrated new leadership and, in a change from earlier activism, involved no one from the African American religious community. In another radical change, several white bankers and industrial leaders occupied roles, indicating that Dallas' white citizens had finally realized that working with African Americans was the best direction for the future of Dallas. Although no noticeable results came from this pioneering meeting, at least African American and white leaders initiated and began to form a base from which future cooperation could develop.

The decades of the 1980s and 1990s saw the Dallas City Council appoint two African Americans as city manager and the selection of the first African American and Latino as Dallas

Superintendent of Schools. African Americans Sam Lindsey and Shirley Acy also occupied the positions of city attorney and city secretary, respectively. Al Lipscomb fondly remembers the backroom arguments that led to these appointments. President Bill Clinton later appointed Sam Lindsey the first African American federal judge in North Texas. As the twentieth century came to a close, African Americans served in the appointed positions of chairmen and directors of the board of the DFW International Airport, which aided in more construction and concessions contracts awarded to African Americans and Latinos. John Wiley Price was elected also County Commissioner in 1984 and he became one of the most powerful politicians in the city of any race.

Seven African Americans sued the Dallas Housing Authority in federal court in 1975 on the grounds of racial segregation and unequal conditions. The case eventually resulted in improved public housing conditions; a final settlement known as the "Walker Decree" was reached in 2004.

In 1995, Ron Kirk, an attorney, former lobbyist, and Texas Secretary of State, became Dallas' first African American mayor. His election was monumental in more ways than one since it brought together a working coalition between the white business establishment and the African American community. Kirk made a historic appointment when he selected the first African American as the city's police chief. His administration ended in 2002 not because of electoral defeat (he remained popular with all constituents throughout his tenure), but because of term limitations.

As a powerful reminder of the "Old Dallas" that was run as an white business oligarchy, there is a picture prominently hung in Dallas City Hall that includes all of the Dallas decision makers from that era, including the mayor, federal judge, and the business community. There is not an African American face in the photograph.

Clear relationships can be drawn between African American grassroots organizations and political concessions in Dallas. Black Dallas leadership prior to 1950 was vastly different from post 1950 leadership. Before the 1950s, and immediately after the *Brown v. Board of Education* decision, the NAACP dominated African American politics. The NAACP strategy of filing federal lawsuits challenging Jim Crow practices within the context of Constitutional rights, played a pivotal role in implementing court-ordered school desegregation mandates. A. Maceo Smith, Juanita J. Craft, and W. J. Durham led the campaigns and were the key players for the NAACP efforts. Juanita J. Craft, after serving on the Dallas City Council, died in 1985 at the age of eighty-three and left her house to the City of Dallas to be used as a landmark designated Civil Rights House. The house was the historic gathering place for civil rights lawyers such as Thurgood Marshall, who led so many NAACP efforts to end institutional segregation. W. J. Durham, a lawyer who moved to Dallas after the bombings in Sherman, Texas in the 1930s, provided the NAACP with strong analytical legal support. He was reputed to be one of the finest trial lawyers in Texas. Durham, assisted by C. B. Bunkley, Jr., was legal counsel in the historic cases of *Sweatt v. Painter* and *State of Texas v. NAACP*.

Beginning in the 1960s, the federally funded North Texas Legal Services organization assisted African American grassroots organizations in preparing their challenges to unequal political representation on the Dallas City Council, the Dallas School Board, and conditions in public housing. They replaced the NAACP as the legal entity challenging the system for a level playing field.

The progression of African Americans in Dallas does not mean that racism has necessarily ended. The white backlash to the "new politics" was white flight from the city and the school system. A prime example of the phenomenon is statistics from the early 1970s, which show that at least fifty-four percent of the students in the Dallas Independent School District were white. By the end of the twentieth century, white enrollment hovered around ten percent. According to the *Dallas Morning News*' commissioned report prepared by Booz/Allen/Hamilton, "Dallas residents are migrating from the city to the suburbs at a faster rate than anywhere else in the nation." The in-migration to the city is coming from South Texas, Mexico, and other countries in Latin America." In fact, new arrivals in Dallas from 1990–2000 numbered approximately 174,000 people; seventy-five percent of those were Latinos.

Given current trends, the next twenty years will witness more meaningful participation of minorities in the Dallas political process. As the Latino voting base becomes larger and more sophisticated, more Latinos will be elected to public office. Coalition politics in Dallas is the wave of the future.

In summary, the demise of Jim Crow policies and practices in Dallas can be attributed to the efforts of African American plaintiffs and local federal judges in the persons of Judge Jerry Buchmeyer and Judge Barefoot Sanders. These two federal judges made rulings that desegregated housing, schools, and changed the political structure of the local governing bodies; namely, the Dallas City Council, Dallas Independent School District, Dallas County Community College District, and the Dallas County Commissioners Court.

Disney Meets Davy

MARK DERR

Writer and historian Mark Derr is the author of *Some Kind of Paradise: A Chronicle of Man and the Land in Florida* (1989), *The Frontiersman: The Real Life and the Many Legends of Davy Crockett* (1993), and *How the Dog Became the Dog: From Wolves to Our Best Friends* (2011). His articles have appeared in such publications as *Natural History* and *Atlantic Monthly*.

In this selection, Derr, a distant relative of the Tennessee politician and Alamo defender, discusses Walt Disney's Davy and examines the Crockett craze of the 1950s. He also considers the various ways Crockett has been portrayed, from bold backwoodsman to drunken braggart to New Age paladin. ✒

★ ★

On the evening of December 15, 1954, the ABC television network, fighting to establish itself opposite CBS and NBC, broadcast Walt Disney's "Davy Crockett, Indian Fighter" and created a cultural phenomenon that transfixed the nation for nearly a year. By February the final two episodes of the trilogy—"Davy Crockett Goes to Congress" and "Davy Crockett at the Alamo"—had aired before an estimated sixty million viewers. In May, Disney released the three as a motion picture called *Davy Crockett, King of the Wild Frontier*, having shrewdly filmed the programs, which were broadcast in black and white, in color for that purpose. School halls and back yards echoed with "The Ballad of Davy Crockett." By the million, children daily died and rose again from the carnage of their Indian wars, the ruins of their private Alamos. Most of those enthralled viewers—and a large number of people who never saw the programs—can today chant a verse or two of Davy's twenty-stanza ballad, and more than a few remember their first coonskin cap. Even today their children are learning the ballad in school.

Fess Parker, the six-and-a-half-foot tall, thirty-year-old Davy, overnight went from being an obscure character actor, whose sole credit was as a victim of rampaging ants in *Them*, a grade-B science-fiction thriller set in New Mexico, to an international star. In 1955, he toured forty-two cities and thirteen foreign countries, promoting the programs, the film, and an array of "Walt Disney's Davy Crockett" paraphernalia. By a contractual arrangement with Disney that was a rarity at the time, Parker received a 10 percent royalty on the sale of official clothes and toys, which totaled in the tens of millions of dollars and made him a wealthy man. Huge crowds of children greeted him wherever he appeared, often creating dangerous situations. "Crowds would push out windows in store fronts," Parker said. "In Holland I had to escape in a cab because I feared for the kids' lives." Parker became so thoroughly typecast that even in his starring role as Daniel Boone in the long-running television series by that title, which aired several years later, he looked and acted like Davy Crockett.

Watching Disney's Davy on videotape thirty-seven years after its debut, I was struck more by the primitive production values and stunts than by the inaccuracies in the story line, which at least serve dramatic purposes. In the wake of such recent action-adventure extravaganzas as *Star Wars, Indiana Jones*, the two *Terminators*, even the antics of *Baron Münchausen*, the $750,000 Crockett film—not exactly low-budget for the time—resembles a home movie. Punches are clearly pulled, falls padded. The dialogue, like the action, is wooden. The Indians—white men in greasepaint—have their origins in Hollywood studios, not in life. Although the script initially parallels Crockett's biography and more or less serious legends, it departs in significant details—giving him a sidekick named Georgie Russel (Buddy Ebsen, who became more famous in *The Beverly Hillbillies*), leaving him a widower, and finally dropping his family completely. Absent altogether is Crockett the farmer, mill owner, and speculator scrambling to stay ahead of debt, the remarried man with a cabin full of children and a wife who can run the family enterprises better than he. In the third episode, Russel at last reveals that he has been writing pamphlets featuring his friend as a backwoods epic hero, and that the pamphlets have become increasingly popular. It is a clever explanation for Davy's fame, a poetic conflation of the historical process by which he became a legend.

Disney's Davy was the all-American manchild, the buckskin-clad paragon of the values that had won the West and was keeping the world safe for democracy—honesty, courage, and natural nobility. Able to read and write his name only with great difficulty, he was fluent in the ways of the wild, a superb tracker and hunter. The frontier, not civilization, was his true home, yet when duty summoned him to Washington to serve the people of West Tennessee, he willingly obliged. He lived for truth, justice, and liberty. He fought and killed Indians like a good scout when his country called, and then, when Justice demanded, he rode hell-bent-for-leather from

Philadelphia to Washington and stalked into the House of Representatives to deliver a ringing denunciation of President Andrew Jackson's plan to force the southern Indians—the Creek, Cherokee, Seminole, Chickasaw, and Choctaw—to move west of the Mississippi.

In addition to creating the stalwart man, Disney's screenwriters paid homage to the Crockett legend, which had proved so popular over more than a century, by investing their Davy with preternatural power. Throughout the three programs, he practices grinning man and beast into submission, subjugating them by his will alone and good humor. He subdues a bear and later tries to pacify an Indian. Unfazed, his foe attacks, tomahawk raised, and Davy bests him in a bare-knuckle brawl. He wins every fight until the last one at the Alamo, where, swinging his empty gun through the final dissolve, he ascends into the pantheon of great warrior-heroes. He is a nineteenth-century Horatius, guarding the road into Texas, not the bridge to Rome.

Disney's timing was impeccable. Playing before tens of millions of viewers—nearly everyone with a television set—Davy turned ABC into the third nationwide network and did even more for Walt Disney. Davy was the star of Frontierland, one of four theme areas—the others being Fantasyland, Adventureland, and Tomorrowland—in Disneyland, the grandiose amusement park scheduled to open in July 1955 in Southern California. Featuring Crockett, Mickey Mouse, and a host of supporting characters, along with rides and displays, the park captivated the American public and established Walt Disney as the greatest showman of the age. His genius lay in his ability to blend a faith in human progress through technology with an idealized image of nineteenth-century small-town America as an idyllic place of wholesome good times, of families and friends. New machines would make the old home more real and perfect, more harmonious, as they did in Disneyland. The Disney vision offered progress without disruption or pain. His heroes might have difficulty reading and writing, but they were without major character defects that might cause one to question their motives or goodness.

Walt Disney's creations reflected and helped shape the mood of guarded optimism and self-congratulation that pervaded the nation in the mid-1950s. Having come through the Depression and emerged victorious from World War II, only to stumble into a stalemate in Korea, Americans appeared intent on pursuing prosperity and advancement. The popular press, radio, cinematic newsreels, and the fast-growing medium of television, which would collectively become the media, exuded sufficient optimism to take the edge off persistent reports of conflict, famine, a sluggish economy, and epidemics, even to make surviving a nuclear attack seem little more difficult than escaping a tornado—"duck and cover," the Civil Defense planners advised, when you hear the air-raid siren. Along with their advertisers, the media conveyed the message that business and industry would create a world richer in goods—from houses to cars to appliances—and more abundant in leisure than any imagined before. Judicious management of the national economy and control of wages, although the unions disagreed, would ensure the good life. Medical breakthroughs, like the new polio vaccine that would wipe out that scourge, promised to conquer a score of life-threatening diseases.

Political leaders in both parties and national publications like *Time* propounded the view that America's continued greatness was dependent on vigilant men, who would stand firm against Communism abroad and at home, men who not only had the capacity to harness the awesome power of the atom but also the wisdom to decide when and where to unloose it. Only with its defenses up, they argued, its institutions freed from the corrupting influence of subversives— anyone who questioned the existing system and policies—could America enjoy the fruits of its labor. Mainstream politicians who spoke out against the abuses of this red baiting were marked for defeat. In 1955, alienation was not a condition that applied to "decent" young people or professionals. What clouds there were, Davy and his fellow superheroes—strong, courageous, righteous men—could pocket and cart away.

In the first nine months of 1955, neither man nor beast escaped Davy Crockett. He was everywhere, a sudden infestation—the first of a series of "crazes" or fads that would mark the babyboom generation, leading a number of marketing specialists, journalists, and demographers to conceive of that group of postwar children as a single monolithic entity that could be inspired to act en masse. No one had imagined that these children not only would immediately demand an object associated with the celluloid image but also could persuade their parents to go along. By some accounts, the magnitude of the response surprised even Walt Disney, who had planned the release for years and was a recognized master of the medium of television. "The Ballad of Davy Crockett," which jazz trombonist George Bruns and scriptwriter Tom Blackburn penned in twenty minutes as filler for the already completed programs—relying on rhyme, not sense— defined Davy as solidly as the film. Selling 18 million copies and recorded by no fewer than twenty crooners, including Parker himself, it was the number-one song of 1955, going away. A shelf of Crockett books—ranging from juvenile to adult fiction, biography, and autobiography—hit 14 million in sales. *The Story of Davy Crockett*, an indifferent biography by Enid La Monte Meadowcroft containing more fiction than fact—this Davy killed him a "b'ar" when he was all of ten—skyrocketed from a steady 10,000 a year in sales since its publication in 1952 to 300,000. A Crockett comic strip was syndicated in 200 newspapers. Disney distributed, under the title "Davy Crockett Says," newspaper columns featuring a picture of Fess Parker as Davy and homilies regarding honesty, trust, justice, duty, and even frugality. As the demand for coonskin caps outstripped supply, the price of pelts soared from $0.25 to $6.00 a pound. After decimating populations of raccoons, trappers turned to wolves, foxes, skunks, and opossums. Manufacturers sold the substitutes as the genuine item and also bought and recycled old fur coats.

Every child needed at minimum a coonskin cap and some semblance of a flintlock, and parents, with memories of their own Depression deprivations still fresh—many a child in the 1930s missed out on Buck Rogers toys, for example—were eager to oblige. For this Baltimore boy, aged five, a nine-iron made an enduring Old Betsy, a more sturdy long rifle than those bought for hard dollars—and it was more accurate. Parents routinely bribed their children to engage in desired behavior with a sampling of the 3,000 Crockett items—everything from the ubiquitous cap and toy gun to towels, sheets, books, records, lunch boxes, fringed shirts and pants, pajamas, moccasins, soap, balloons, and wading pools—that filled the stores. Adults were not exempt: Offering a free "Davy Crockett" tent—actually a renamed pup tent—to each purchaser of a Norge appliance, Borg-Warner Corporation gave away a total of 35,000 by May.

By then, Crockett paraphernalia had reached $100 million in sales and prognosticators confidently predicted the total would soar to $300 million during the Christmas rush. In some department stores, Crockett accounted for as much as 10 percent of sales. Sensing windfall profits, manufacturers and retailers began mislabeling unsold products with "Davy Crockett" and turning out vast quantities of poorly made goods. In Boston, a shoe store unloaded 3,000 moccasins after placing a "Davy Crockett" sign in front of them. Elsewhere old Daniel Boone caps, assigned a new identity, found buyers. In Albany and Rochester, New York, fake-fur hats proved easily inflammable. F.A.O. Schwarz executive Philip Kirkham sounded a cautionary note, predicting that authentic Crockett toys would last on the market, because Davy was universal, but the rest of the junk would fade away. No one listened.

As abruptly as it had begun, the craze went into free fall. In Washington, D.C., Crockett T-shirts that once sold by the thousand at $1.29 each gathered dust on the shelves when marked down to $0.39. From around the country came equally grim reports. In December, a number of disappointed retailers grumpily declared "kids more fickle than women." *Variety* announced, "Davy was the biggest thing since Marilyn Monroe and Liberace, but he pancaked. He laid a bomb."

ABC's *Disneyland* aired two new episodes—"Davy Crockett's Keelboat Race" and "Davy Crockett and the River Pirates," featuring Big Mike Fink (The King of the River), the Mississippi, and a catchy tune—in November and December. The slapdash programs cleverly played on the legends of the big river, allowing Davy, the masterful Everyman, to best the conniving, unsportsmanlike Fink—a man so locked in legend that his reality has all but vanished—in an epic keelboat race and then to destroy a den of evil thieves. The beaten Mike Fink did not tip his hat to the victor; he ate it, honoring a bet and spreading the fun. Crockett's one attempt at navigating the Mississippi in 1826 had nearly cost him his life, when his boat sank, but that accident was of no interest to Walt Disney, who presented the new programs—released to cinemas early in 1956 as *The Legends of Davy Crockett*—as nothing more than fiction. Eager to cash in on the phenomenal success of the first three episodes, he had turned fully to the tales, even having his screenwriters invent their own. But the King of the Wild Frontier and the King of the River together could not win over an audience that had lost interest. Davy had become ordinary, another program to watch or ignore. *The Wonderful World of Disney* on NBC repeated all five programs (now available on videotape) every three years into the 1970s without fanfare.

Explanations for the collapse were as diverse as those for the beginning of the fad. Some observers blamed the bad publicity attendant to problems with the production and sale of Crockett memorabilia. Others attributed the demise to critics who charged that Disney had made a hero of a reprehensible lout, a besotted liar and clown. While a number of retailers and journalists suggested that the children had grown bored or fickle and turned their short, collective attention span elsewhere, other commentators posited that they had become disaffected after learning that their hero was a fraud. Although some of the hypotheses appear somewhat silly in retrospect, the debate itself was born of genuine interest in the nature of the craze, which was the first with its origins in television. Advertisers, sociologists, marketing experts, and politicians were impressed by the power of television to influence not only public opinion but also mass behavior.

Even as hazardous merchandise drove consumers to other products, a rancorous trademark fight between Disney and a Baltimore garment maker sowed uncertainty and fear among businesses that they might be liable in a lawsuit. The dispute also prevented Disney from exercising the kind of quality control it generally enforced to protect its reputation.

On May 6, 1955, when business was booming, Walt Disney Productions went into U.S. District Court in Baltimore to file suit against Morey Schwartz, his wife Hannah, and their companies—Schwartz Manufacturing Company and Davy Crockett Enterprises, Inc., asking that their trademark, "David Crockett, Frontiersman," be declared null and void and that Disney be granted exclusive rights to its own "Walt Disney's Davy Crockett" and any permutation thereon. Disney stated that its *Davy Crockett* was a fiction, conceived in 1950 "to describe the exploits of the early American pioneer and politician named David Crockett." Over the next five years, it had employed as many as 400 actors, writers, cartoonists, artists, and marketers to develop the films, the promotional material—including books and cartoons—and the merchandise. Disney considered marketing central to the financial success of the project, and so arranged for 125 licensees to produce 1,000 articles under its imprint. For all its obsession with detail, however, Disney failed to register its trademark or even have its lawyers check on other claimants to Crockett.

On the face of it, there was little reason to worry. Since the 1830s, the Crockett name had been used to sell everything from citrus to chewing tobacco and liquor. A legend of enormous proportion, Davy Crockett was fully in the public domain. A clipper ship, *David Crockett*, plied the seas from San Francisco to Wall Street during the 1850s and '60s, promising the most comfortable, fastest delivery under sail. She could make the passage in 115 days, Wm. T. Coleman and Company boasted in its advertisements, which featured a bearded Crockett riding a pair of alligators and a version of the famous Crockett motto: "Be sure you're right, then go ahead." In 1889, Betterton and Company took out a trademark on Davey Crockett Wisky, and in 1906 Union Distilling Company registered Davy Crocket Pure Copper Whiskey. Both companies were playing on Crockett's notoriously poor spelling and his love for alcohol, "arden spirits," as he called it, in which he indulged much of his adult life. The registrations on both trademarks lapsed.

Then, in 1946, Morey and Hannah Schwartz registered the trademark "Davy Crockett, Frontiersman" with the U.S. Patent Office under No. 434,317. A manufacturer of military uniforms, Schwartz was inspired by his frequent visits to San Antonio, home of the Alamo, to shift production to western wear at the end of the war. But as textile mills completed the transition from military production, they began shipping their full runs of "hard-finish worsteds' to large apparel makers, leaving small companies like the Schwartzes' without access to the quality cloth they needed to compete. Their business failing, Morey and Hannah Schwartz transferred their Davy Crockett patent to Henry Kay, who produced western wear through his advance Tailoring Company of Baltimore. When the Disney-inspired craze began, Kay, unable to raise capital to expand his business, sold the trademark back to the Schwartzes, who established Davy Crockett Enterprises, Inc., in their hometown. They began sending letters and telegrams to producers of Crockett goods demanding 5 percent of their net sales as royalties and threatening legal action if they failed to comply.

The manufacturers complained to Disney, to their associations, to each other, and to the press that they feared retaliation if they ignored the Schwartzes' demand. It was then that Walt

Disney Productions sued, seeking to appease its licensees and protect itself from charges of trademark infringement. Disney alleged that Morey and Hannah Schwartz were interfering with the production and marketing of "Walt Disney's Davy Crockett." In a countersuit, the Schwartzes portrayed themselves as small merchants victimized by a huge and powerful company from California named Disney. The press treated the whole affair with a dash of humor. "Old Davy Crockett and his winning ways have a pack of lawyers fussing and feuding and businessmen befuddled," said William E. Giles in *The Wall Street Journal* on May 11. "Hitching up his buckskins, and with his big butcher [knife] in his belt, Disney charged into Baltimore's Federal Court and brought suit against Davy Crockett Enterprises, run by an oldtime Baltimore garment maker . . . ," said *Time*. For the sake of business, if not justice, the two parties settled the suit on July 12, agreeing to split the fast-growing profits through cross licensing.

After news of the settlement broke, a covey of Crockett's direct descendants filed a motion to intervene, claiming that neither Disney nor Schwartz had a right to profit from their forebear's name. Seeking royalties for themselves, the Crockett descendants had organized two groups in Illinois: the David Crockett Descendants' Fund, an educational and charitable trust; and Crockett Kids, Inc., to market the Crockett name. Lawyers for the Schwartzes and Disney united to argue that allowing the fund's trustees—Bourke C. Crockett, Margie Flowers, Pauline Flowers Tillery, Oscar Doetsch, and Albert J. Watts—to break their uneasy truce would be tantamount to bringing mass confusion and ruin on the world of Crockett merchandising. Bloodlines, they said, did not carry a right to monopolize an ancestor's name. The motion to intervene was dismissed on October 6, 1955, with the heirs unrewarded. By then, the buying frenzy was slowing, consumers having received the message that greed mattered more than quality or the safety of their children.

The great success of Disney's Davy set off an intellectual debate as intense in its way as the frenzy for Crockett products. No sooner had the "craze" begun than a number of social critics, journalists, educators, and even politicians began to proclaim that Davy represented values ranging from anti-intellectualism to unbridled individualism that, if followed, would subvert their programs and institutions. Teachers around the country complained that their pupils were uncontrollable, spending more time singing "The Ballad of Davy Crockett" than reciting their ABCs. Invoking their fictional counterparts in a song, Fess Parker and Buddy Ebsen appealed to the kids to "do the right thing" and behave, without visible effect. Educators and journalists also engaged in a running debate over whether Davy subsumed all other frontier heroes—like Daniel Boone and Kit Carson, himself a somewhat overrated figure—thereby impoverishing the imaginations of their students, or inspired them to explore American history, thereby enriching them.

In Washington, D.C., late in the spring of 1955, a group of schoolchildren touring the Capitol asked to see the statue of their idol Davy, which they believed must be prominently displayed. Their teacher pointed to a figure dressed in buckskins, with a cap on his head and rifle in his hand, and called him Crockett. But it was Dr. Marcus Whitman, the Protestant missionary who traveled extensively through the West in the 1830s and early 1840s and helped open the Oregon country to settlement. Crockett does not stand in bronze or marble in the Capitol, where he was a controversial, if colorful figure.

Teachers and students were not alone in their confusion. Texas Congressman Martin Dies asked his colleagues in the House to follow Davy's famous maxim and vote only for what was right, rather than what was expedient. Other congressmen joined the fray and soon found themselves divided along party and sectional lines, with various Democrats from Tennessee and North Carolina seeking a piece of the glory by declaring Crockett a native of their states—although raised in Tennessee, he was born in the independent State of Franklin, which North Carolina considered part of its domain.

Liberal Democrats worried that the Republicans would adopt Davy and his coonskin as their campaign symbol. They over-looked the fact that Tennessee Senator Estes Kefauver, a Democrat, had been campaigning in the famous headgear since 1948, choosing instead to recall that in 1840 the Whigs, the party of the rich and privileged, had successfully, if cynically, employed the cap, the log cabin, and hard cider as symbols in order to prove themselves champions of the "common man" and place their candidate, William Henry Harrison, in the White House. If the victor at Tippecanoe could do it, the Democrats reasoned, why not the allied commander of Europe? Eisenhower hardly needed such help in 1956, but that did little to assuage the Democrats' concerns. In the pages of magazines and newspapers, on radio and television, they launched an ad hominem attack on the fictional Davy Crockett that, while sometimes farcical, had a major, negative impact on the way Crockett came to be perceived and portrayed.

Brendan Sexton, education director for the United Auto Workers in Detroit, opened the campaign soon after the Disney programs appeared. Sexton feared that Republican and anti-unionists, embracing the celluloid Crockett, would use his uncompromising individualism and martyrdom at the Alamo as a club against organized labor. He thought they would say that real Americans, like Davy, had no need or desire for a union because its emphasis on collective action and a strict seniority system for determining promotions and layoffs—the traditional "last hired, first fired" rule—was antithetical to individual opportunity. With the nation's economy in a slump and the campaign against Communism—and by extension, socialism and labor—at a fever pitch, many workers were beginning to believe that they could better serve their interests by dealing directly with management. Deciding to discredit the perceived messenger, rather than address the concerns of workers, Sexton gave a radio talk and interviews charging that Crockett was "a drunk and brawler, a wife deserter, hireling of big business, and shiftless no-account."

Columnist Murray Kempton, who wrote on labor issues for the *New York Post*, picked up the refrain and charged that Crockett could be bought for the price of a drink. His diatribe inspired outraged children to demonstrate in front of his newspaper's office. John Fischer, editor of *Harper's*, one of the nation's most venerable liberal periodicals, was more caustic in his comments. After repeating Sexton's claims, he added that Crockett was "a poor farmer, indolent and shiftless. . . . He was never king of anything, except maybe the Tennessee Tall Tales and Bourbon Samplers' Association." Attempting to turn anti-Communist, red-baiting sentiment against Crockett, Fischer also stated that the myth making associated with Davy most resembled that which created the benevolent image of Papa Joe Stalin.

Conservative commentator William F. Buckley, Jr., tweaked the liberals for their discomfort, announcing on his radio program that "the assault on Davy is one part traditional debunking campaign and one part resentment by liberal publicists of Davy's free approach to life. He'll survive the carpers." The liberals also found themselves criticized by the emasculated American Communist Party for attacking the nation's democratic traditions, an interesting argument grounded to some degree in Karl Marx's conception of the radical way people along the frontier organized their political and judicial institutions.

Underlying the criticism of Crockett was the growing belief that the myths of America and its heroes were at variance with its history, that westward expansion was more the story of destruction of the Indians and nature for profit than of valiant white settlers struggling to survive against the elements, that slavery was a cruel and dehumanizing institution, that democracy and opportunity were not extended equally to all people. As this necessary corrective took hold, the extreme negative views of Crockett gained ascendancy over Disney's Davy. Presenting a rogues' gallery of the "Braggarts of the Backwoods," on April 11, 1960, *Life* declared Crockett "an epic boaster." *People* on January 12, 1987, ran a photo of Fess Parker with the comment that Crockett "was a flamboyant frontiersman who owed his reputation to his ability to tell tall tales. But there were a few facts that even his prodigious fibbing couldn't hide—that the king of the Wild Frontier was a drunk, a carouser, a less-than-honest politician and Army scout who'd hired someone else to finish his term of enlistment." Popular histories began to follow suit, as did film characterizations. In the 1987 NBC television film *The Alamo: Thirteen Days to Glory*, for example, Brian Keith portrayed Crockett as a kindhearted, boastful, ultimately courageous drunkard.

The Disney Company engaged in revisionism of a different sort when, in the late 1980s, it created a new five-part Davy Crockett series, featuring a sensitive, New Age hero in tune with nature, brave, peace-loving, and humorous in a sincere way. One expected the backwoods stalwart to consult crystals. The audience and critics generally nodded through the episodes, which aired on NBC's *Magical World of Disney* and now periodically appear on the Disney Channel on cable television.

The polar images of the fictional Crockett are the negative and positive of a freeze-frame portrait of a four-dimensional man—fixed and predictable, the way Americans too often demand their heroes, and antiheroes, to be. Crockett the legend is plastic enough to adjust to changing fashion and accommodate himself to those who would make him a guardian of the environment or a wild man weaned on whiskey, a braggart, a "screamer," or "ring-tailed roarer," in the language of the nineteenth-century comic fictions. But Crockett the man hangs trapped between those poles, lost in the nation's ambivalence about its past. He is a victim of a collective inability to determine any longer how to define a brave man, by what actions or standards—those of war and exploitation or of peace and caring. Is it necessary that a hero—or public official—be a saint, free of earthly flaws? The only man or woman who can meet that standard is a one-dimensional character in a poor fiction, boring precisely because he or she is perfect. But how many and what kind of failings are acceptable? Where is the line between human frailty and venality? The answer to those questions can only become clear once the individual is freed from the constraints of ideology and viewed in the context of his or her life, aspirations, and accomplishments.

"We Want Aggies, Not Maggies": James Earl Rudder and the Coeducation of Texas A&M University

CHRISTOPHER BEAN

C hristopher Bean teaches at East Central University in Ada, Oklahoma. He has also written on the Freedmen's Bureau in Texas.

Second World War hero James Earl Rudder served as president of Texas A&M from 1959 until his untimely death in 1970. Under his leadership, significant changes occurred at the institution, including the admission of women and minorities and the abrogation of mandatory military training. These moves caused tremendous uproar at the tradition-minded school. According to LBJ, Rudder's "heroism on the Normandy beaches in a time of war was only a prelude to his contribution in peace as an educator, public official, and concerned citizen." In this selection, Dr. Bean discusses President Rudder's tenure at Texas A&M, a period of major transformation. ◅

★ ★

In 1930, when twenty-year old James Earl Rudder enrolled at A&M College of Texas, two Texas institutions converged for the first time—one already established, the other yet to be. For the next four decades, through depression, a world conflagration, and post war uncertainty, an unbreakable bond remained. Late in the 1950s Rudder returned to the school as its president, a second convergence that proved a blessing to the college, because just on the horizon awaited

"We Want Aggies, Not Maggies": James Earl Rudder and the Coeducation of Texas A&M University by Christopher Bean from *East Texas Historical Journal,* Vol. XLIV, No. 2, 2006, pp. 17-27. Reprinted by permission of East Texas Historical Association.

one of the most trying times in the long history of A&MC—the 1960s. With leadership, discipline, and vision, Rudder guided the school through this most turbulent of times. Prior to Rudder's tenure, A&M was an all-male, segregated, provincial military school. Afterward, it became one of the Southwest's premier educational institutions. Although aided and assisted by other administrators and faculty, Rudder remains the seminal figure in this transition.

The Agricultural and Mechanical College of Texas opened its doors in 1876 with a class of 106 students. The school began as an all-male military institution with compulsory participation in the Corps of Cadets, an organization that became the most visible symbol of the school and one that played an integral role in its initial growth. The school consequently developed a strong military character. It regularly commissioned more officers than any of the service academies, including West Point. Former students achieved outstanding records in all of the country's wars from the Spanish-American War to the present. More than 20,000 former students served during World War II, twenty-nine of them at the rank of general.

After the First World War, the A&MC experienced rapid growth and became recognized for its programs in agriculture, engineering, and veterinary and military sciences. The college even branched out, establishing complexes throughout the state. These changes resulted in the organization of limited graduate degree programs by 1936. Driving this growth was the discovery of oil on state lands during the 1920s. Beginning in 1931, A&M received one-third of the income derived from the state's Permanent University Fund. These oil revenues kept costs and tuition down and spurred enrollment growth even during the Great Depression. By the 1950s, A&M College confronted many new challenges: changing population dynamics; decreasing enrollment; and developing fissures between the student body and faculty. "[At this time] Texas A&M confronted change without really changing," wrote historian Henry C. Dethlof, while another historian argued that this was a time of "turmoil, unrest, and lack of progress; indeed, the institution appeared to be in retrogression, with loss of student members, and agitation among the faculty and the student body."

Despite this situation, no leader pushed for change. Various issues loomed ahead for not only the school, but also for the nation as a whole. Coeducation, racial integration, curricular and administrative changes, elective military training, and the admission of civilian students were topics that the college would have to address soon. Furthermore, with explosive growth in the state's population, concerns about a broader university complex and a focus on research and academics surfaced. The future of the college depended on how the administration approached these matters.

This was the situation that faced James Earl Rudder when he arrived as vice-president of the college early in 1958. Born on May 6, 1910, in Eden (Concho County), Rudder was one of thirteen children. From his father he received an indelible work ethic and from his mother a moral compass. After excelling at football for two years at John Tarleton Agricultural College, Rudder transferred to A&MC in 1930, where for the next two years he helped anchor the offensive line for the Aggie football team. After a brief stint coaching at Brady High School, where he met his future wife, Margaret Williamson, and at Tarleton College, Rudder was called to active military duty in the summer of 1941. For the next year or so, he moved from one assignment

to another, advancing to company commander at Fort Sam Houston, Texas, and execu
officer and Army component operations staff officer (G-3) for the 83rd Infantry Division. In the summer of 1943, Rudder received orders giving him command of the 2nd Ranger Battalion.

During the D-Day landings on June 6, 1944, "Rudder's Rangers" scaled the one-hundred-foot Pointe-du-Hoc cliffs and destroyed a German battery that threatened the landing. After the war, General Omar Bradley remarked "No soldier in my command has ever been wished a more difficult task than that which befell James Earl Rudder." In November 1944, Rudder received orders reassigning him to the 109th Infantry Regiment, 29th Infantry Division. Army brass wanted Rudder to transform the 109th as he had the Rangers. Eight days after he took command, the Germans launched what would become the Battle of the Bulge. In spite of the suddenness of the attack, Rudder led the 109th through the battle admirably. By war's end, Rudder had received every military decoration except the Congressional Medal of Honor. After the war, he served as vice president of labor relations for the Brady Aviation Company and three terms as mayor of Brady. While mayor, Rudder befriended several powerful men, including future president Lyndon B. Johnson and Governor Allan Shivers. In 1955 Governor Shivers appointed Rudder Texas Land Commissioner in order to clean up the corrupt mess left by Bascom Giles. With the land commissioner's office restored to its proper place, Rudder, realizing that his work was completed, decided to accept the position of vice president of A&MC.

The title of vice-president made Rudder the principal administrator of the college. Marion Thomas Harrington held the joint title of president of the college and of the college system, but Rudder was, in effect, the real "president." Harrington's position was more like that of chancellor at a modern university system. Regardless of his impressive accomplishments in public service, Rudder appeared to be a questionable choice for the position. "[M]ost academic people counted him at best an 'unlikely' candidate to head a major university," wrote one historian of the school. "Rudder gave every appearance of being an Aggie of the old school, with old-school ties, loyalties, traditions, and basic conservatism. A university in the throes of change, many anticipated, would not be helped along the way by such a man as Earl Rudder." He had reservations about taking the job for this reason. According to his wife, Rudder believed that the "academics" would resent him because he was not one of them.

Prior to Rudder's arrival, the first salvos on several major issues that he would face had already been fired. An internecine conflict had erupted over compulsory military training. In 1957 President David W. Williams, at the request of the board of directors, distributed a questionnaire among the faculty seeking opinions on a variety of policy questions, one of which pertained to compulsory military training. In spite of the faculty's vote (forty-nine to one in favor of optional military training) school officials retained compulsory military training for freshmen and sophomores. The conflict soon became public. What made this quarrel significant was that it involved nearly every constituent body of the university—the president, chancellor, board of directors, and the faculty—plus outside forces such as state officials and local merchants.

The question of coeducation crept into the discussion, and soon the two issues became one. This inevitably brought the student body, which generally held views completely opposite ministrators, into campus politics. Joe Tindel, editor of the school newspaper *Bat-* ...vocated the admission of women to the college. The *Bryan Daily Eagle*, concurring ...del, editorialized, "The world changes and A&M must change with it." The student ... however, voted eleven to five in favor of a resolution calling for Tindel's resignation. ...ispute became violent when William Boyd Metts, creator of the Aggie Association for the ...ancement of Coeducation, was hospitalized after inhaling fumes from a bomb thrown into his room. The controversy expanded when several women filed suit against the college in 1958 and 1959, asking to be admitted into the school. The cases reached the state supreme court and, in one instance, the United States Supreme Court. Both courts, however, refused to hear the case. With each new chapter in the saga, one newspaper noticed that the school appeared to be "redividing like a swirling amoeba."

In an interview with the *College Station Battalion*, Rudder described his position on the issue. "[T]he decision is in keeping with the Board of Directors' desire—it is my job to run A&M as the Board wants it to run," he replied. When the interviewer asked Rudder about the future, he retorted, "I don't have a crystal ball." As a result, Rudder was labeled as wanting to retain the "old school" in spite of changing times. In reality, his authority was limited by the board of directors; rather than dictating policy, he was implementing that of the board.

In a sense Rudder was "*old school.*" He was sympathetic to the college that he remembered—all male and military. Now he was an administrator, partly responsible for the day-to-day activities and future policy of the school, and like any good leader, he did what was best, even if that contradicted his personal prejudices and attitudes.

Almost unnoticed and with little fanfare, Rudder was named president of Texas A&M on July 1, 1959, when Harrington advanced to the position of chancellor. With this promotion, Rudder gained authority and a proximity to the board that he had lacked as vice-president. Now he was "at the helm" with the power and influence to take the school in the direction he desired. Rudder could "batten down the hatches" against the coeducation advocates or accept that the time for coeducation at the college had come. But with the position came sole responsibility for those policy decisions. With the spotlight on him, Rudder was in his element.

On March 26, 1960, when he was inaugurated, Rudder did not directly address the coeducational issue, although he did mention how the school was to provide the young *men* of Texas the greatest of benefits. Instead, he stressed the role of A&M College in the history and future development of Texas and the nation. Rudder also addressed the need for the school to lead the charge in a nation relying ever more heavily on technology, one in which an increasingly higher percentage of people attended college. "This is now the responsibility of our nation," he declared. "It soon will pass to our children. Their ability to assume the task is in no small measure dependent upon the availability to them of higher education, and its quality." He added that the United States needed to redirect its priorities, considering that it spent more on cigarettes, recreation, liquor, and legalized gambling than on education. "The crucial question is whether we will or not," he said. "It will be expensive. Modern education facilities come high; research is especially costly. Our nation can afford it; to survive, we must afford it. We can spend our money for no finer, more fruitful or more deserving endeavor."

Rudder then began the task of mending the wounds of the prior years while trying to [ ] the school in its academic development. Many on the faculty and staff believed that J[ ] would fail. These individuals underestimated him. If they had known Rudder, they wo[ ] realized that in all previous assignments he had succeeded in tense and complex si[ ] "James Earl Rudder was a fighter who never quit anything until it was finished," remarked on[ ] observer. "As many have said since, he turned out to be the right man in the right place at the right time."

Rudder began to quiet the tumultuous situation. In a measure "to define challenges and opportunities anticipated in the future," he and the board of directors authorized a long-range planning study of the college. "This is an event which is an important milestone in the history of A&M College," declared Rudder. The project began in 1961 under the title "Century Study." It called for the participation of practically everyone involved with the university. Rudder asked participants to keep four questions in mind: What kind of graduate and citizen should this college seek to produce? What should be the mission of A&M College during the next fifteen years? To what degree of academic excellence shall they aspire? What should be the scope and size of the school by 1976? Members were told not to "reflect in your report existing traditions or policy." We must, concluded Rudder, let "success fully plan the future of this great institution and effectively project these plans to the citizens we serve."

As he had done on previous occasions, Rudder looked to those who knew more about the situation than he did. Rather than believing that he had all the answers, he sought everyone's opinion and assessment of a problem before he implemented a solution. This was one of the reasons that he was such an effective leader. Rudder entered into a situation knowing that in order to solve problems he had to have the cooperation of the "frontline troops"—those who had been there from the beginning. To obtain this cooperation, Rudder needed his subordinates' confidence and respect. Rudder made them understand that their opinions mattered.

The college evaluation initiated by Rudder resulted in four independent studies. The Century Council, comprising one hundred outstanding citizens from more than 1,200 applicants (some alumni, others not), produced the *Report of the Century Council*. The report sought "to determine those structural and program modifications which would enable the [college] to achieve a position of state, national, international prominence among universities of higher learning and make recommendations." Many of the council's findings were vague, however—the council recommended a "greater emphasis on excellence," for example. The group also recommended that the ROTC program "currently in effect at the college be continued," noting that leaders "produced under this program are of inestimable value to our state and nation." Because the average A&M College student scored slightly below the national average on the college entrance exam, the study advocated a "continuous study of selective admissions policy." The group referred the matter of coeducation to the board. Remarking on its "divided opinion," the council members believed that "the Board will make a wise and effective disposition of this matter."

In another self-study, administrators and faculty produced the *Report to Commission on Colleges, Southern Association of Colleges and Schools*. This report was for the school's major accrediting association. While the other reports issued recommendations pertaining to the student body, curriculum, and school administrators and faculty, this study focused on improving the college's physical facilities. The report proposed a $55 million construction program to build or improve facilities for engineering, biochemistry, oceanography, and meteorology programs, as well as a student center, improved library facilities, a data processing center, and a TV closed-circuit studio.

A committee of faculty and staff also produced a study entitled *Faculty-Staff-Student Study on Aspirations.* "The recommendations of the general report," remarked one historian, "are important in view of what came to be." In addition to suggesting a tenure policy for faculty that conformed to those used at other schools, higher salaries for higher professional ranks, and annual salary increments, the report also recommended merit raises. It recommended other moves to attract and retain faculty, including improved physical facilities, the development of a graduate school, higher admissions standards, endowed faculty chairs, and changing the name of the institution "to foster and maintain a university image." The study further proposed an "end to compulsory military training and all-male admissions policy." According to the report, the Corps of Cadets took precedence over all other aspects of student life, "determining habits, attitudes and ambitions." Furthermore, the school's military emphasis "limited the true pursuit of scholarship and the development of an environment which will contribute to this scholarship." The emphasis on military training caused potential students to select other schools. The group recommended that military training be voluntary for all students, that the Corps no longer exist as a residential organization, and that an adult director reside in each unit.

Treading on the very foundations of A&M College traditions, this report came as a surprise to some, particularly Rudder. But, as he himself had stated, he wanted honest and candid answers. According to rumors his first reaction to the *Faculty-Staff-Student Study on Aspirations* "was a loud exclamation followed by tossing the report into the garbage can." Rudder personally supported the traditions of A&M College, including the all-male admission policy and compulsory military training. What really matters, however, was not his reaction to the study or his personal biases about coeducation or compulsory military service, but rather his ability to set aside such beliefs and "do what needed to be done." He took action when others had resisted or hesitated.

"It [the report] helped to define Rudder's job," said one historian. "Rudder meant to finish the job." He and the board accepted almost all of the findings of the various studies and published them in a summary report entitled *Blueprint for Success.* Despite being broad in its context, "the meaning, purposes, and importance [of the report] . . . cannot be overestimated in its significance" to the development of the university. They "charged all members of the faculty and staff of the Agricultural and Mechanical College of Texas, in whatever capacity they may serve, that their watchword and goal shall be *excellence* [emphasis in original]." In spite of the enormous expenditures, most of the building projects proposed were completed before the centennial and faculty salaries were increased without raising tuition. Enrollment doubled, exceeding 16,000 by 1972.

In conjunction with these changes, two other notable transitions also occurred under Rudder's tenure at the college—the school became coeducational and its name was changed to Texas

A&M University. On April 28, 1963, with support from Rudder, the board unanimously voted that eligible women "would be admitted into graduate programs and veterinary medicines as day students," effective June 1, 1963. The admission of women was on a limited basis for undergraduate courses, however. In addition to the normal requirements for admission, the woman had to be a wife or daughter of an enrolled student, faculty, or staff member. Numerous individuals and organizations favored the move. Some openly displayed their approval of the decision, but others expressed their support covertly—afraid of ostracism and retaliation. "The [decision] proves that the college fathers are willing to act in an objective manner not motivated by tradition for tradition's sake," applauded an editorial in the local paper. "With the board operating in a flexible manner attuned to the changing world we live in Texas A&M is well on its way to the excellence sought by school officials." Another proponent appealed to the proper sensibilities of the men of the school and the state. "It's about time they had some coeds there and started having a little fun," he said. "It might help out football recruiting!" Nevertheless, for many, including members of the Corps, this fight was not over.

In the fall of 1963, fifteen women enrolled. They had to sign a contract stating that they would withdraw if the new policy was reversed. By spring 1964, 183 women had enrolled, and Stella Haupt, the first woman to enroll under the new policy, earned an M.A. degree that fall. A year later, the number of women enrolled had nearly doubled to 321. At long last, the college was coeducational. But for critics of coeducation, Rudder was in their "cross-hairs as the prime culprit."

Rudder and his associates in the college's administration expected the firestorm of criticism and the fears about what the admission meant to the Corps, perhaps even its continued existence. Some feared the abolition of the football team. Rudder realized that his decision would be unpopular among some groups, and that admitting women was a policy that he would have to sell to the students and alumni. The president of the board of directors, Sterling C. Evans, wrote to the Association of Former Students explaining the decision. Evans stated that the board had no intention of making the college an "all-out coed institution." Evans noted, "The admission of women will not bring sudden or drastic change to the school." Nor did he foresee any changes to the Corps, which was the real issue to many of the critics.

To address this concern, Rudder called a meeting of the entire Corps at G. Rollie White Coliseum in April 1963. He informed the crowd of more than 4,000 that the board had absolute authority on this and other matters. Greeted with chants of "We don't want to integrate" accompanied by boos and hisses, Rudder nevertheless explained his position: "If we had not voted to admit women to our school of veterinarian medicine, many students would go to Texas Tech." When asked about effects of the policy on the Corps of Cadets, Rudder replied, "If the Corps of Cadets does what it stands for, its future is bright."

Some in the audience grudgingly accepted the argument, but many of the cadets did not. For had those who booed and hissed really thought about it, they would have remembered that James Earl Rudder was a former member of the *Corps of Cadets* and *old soldier*. He was solidly in favor of the Corps, but he realized that many students who wanted to study at Texas A&M simply did not want to join the Corps. Rudder would never allow a decision or policy to undermine one of the most cherished and storied traditions of the school, especially one so dear to his heart. Despite the justifiable arguments and concerns, he realized the Corps benefited from coeducation.

Those opposed to the decision engaged in the loudest and most obstreperous behavior. "I'm 54 years old and I still like girls," opined one graduate, "but not at A&M." "Big mistake," remarked another critic. Another found a Biblical precedent for not admitting women. "We men know how to appreciate, love and honor our women," he declared, "but we know also what a fix Eve got us in the Garden of Eden. Let us not let that happen at A&M." Several opposition groups formed in response to the decision, including the Committee for an All-Male Military Texas A&M and the Senior Committee for the Preservation of Texas A&M. The Committee for an All-Male Military Texas A&M "marched" on the state capital to oppose coeducation. Chanting "We want Aggies, not Maggies," and claiming women would halt the program of excellence at the school, over 300 members of the Corps, along with several representatives of the A&M Mothers' Club and Aggie-Exes, gathered in the rotunda as State Representative Will L. Smith submitted an anti-coeducation resolution. In addition, one senator submitted a resolution that threatened to cut off state funds if the school admitted women. Despite overwhelming passage in the House of Representatives of a resolution requiring the state to maintain one major university for men and one for women, a senate filibuster killed the resolutions.

The Senior Committee for the Preservation of Texas A&M initiated an intense letter writing campaign to enlist support for their cause. One editor who was solicited for his support noted the futility of it all. He stated that this was:

> a cause every bit as worthy as impeaching Earl Warren or repealing the income tax—and with about the same chance of success, which is a big fat zero. Still, the fool-hardy valor of its adherents . . . commands the same sort of admiration which generations have felt for Giacomo Casablanca, the boy who 'stood on the burning deck, whence all but he had fled; the flame that lit the battle's wreck, shone 'round him o'er the dead.' Giacomo wound up fricasseed, and so, I fear, will the 'no coeds in Aggieland' alumni. You can't fight city hall or the board of directors. Besides, I'm a subscriber to the theory that there is nothing like a dame.

In 1965, A&M's board of directors authorized President Rudder to use his discretion in the admission of women. This had the "overall effect of completely ending the prohibition on coeducation." The full admittance of women, however, happened with little of the bitterness and emotion present a few years earlier—in part because many of the fears never materialized, in part because the country had changed.

Rudder's prediction that admitting women would be a positive change also contributed to the lack of animosity. He repeatedly told students and alumni that the admission of women would strengthen, rather then undermine, the foundations and traditions of the school. Much of the student population believed coeducation beneficial rather than detrimental. In a student poll in 1965, sixty-three percent favored unlimited coeducation over a return to the all-male policy. As a result of Rudder's "discretionary powers," more applications were approved, and by the fall of 1969, applicants "who could meet the same academic qualifications as men were admitted." By 1971, the administration admitted women on an equal basis with men. I₁ 1,700 women attended the school. By 1980 that number had increased to more than By 2006, women made up half of the student body at the school and held many posit the university believed out of reach for women only a few decades ago.

Even the Corps, the most cherished of the school's institutions, was not immune to change. In 1965 compulsory enrollment in the Corps was abolished in favor of a volunteer system. By 1970 only a quarter of the student body remained in the Corps. Four years later, it was opened to women. About fifty women were organized into an all-female unit. The members were called "Waggies." The change made the Corps stronger, but its exuberance and discipline were undiminished. The group had become an "even more elite and selective organization by virtue of its volunteer status." In the end, none of the fears associated with the admission of women came to fruition. The traditions, except female exclusion, remained. "The old school, and the old fraternity, did not die," wrote one historian, "instead they merely changed their complexion." Many of the school's traditions—reveille, Silver Taps, Aggie Muster, and others—remained part of the vibrant spirit of the school.

With little fanfare or turmoil, Rudder also presided over racial integration at Texas A&M in the fall of 1964. The lack of resistance to integration was atypical of other Southern universities, but A&M was an atypical Southern university. Although located in the "more Southern" part of the state, the university differed from other institutions because of its focus on the military. Blacks did not threaten nor offend the social sensibilities at Texas A&M—women represented the *real* threat. The military traditions and structure of the school epitomized masculinity. The admission of minority men never threatened to change the fabric of the school.

By the end of the 1960s the old college had become a new, vibrant, energetic institution with a bright future. With each passing year, women and minorities became more important to the university. Enrollment increases shattered all projections and to accommodate that growth numerous construction projects were completed. And Rudder led the university throughout this remarkable transformation. "[H]e was constantly in the middle of it," wrote one historian. "He never spared himself. He was tough, but fair. Usually congenial, he could be abrasive if he thought it would help. He held an open mind, and would act on advice contrary to his own preconceived ideas when it appeared that such advice was better informed. He was a forthright, vigorous man, whose integrity, personal honor, and dedication were unquestioned."

In January 1970, while at his home, Rudder suffered a partial stroke and was rushed to a local hospital. In his absence, three vice-presidents shared the responsibilities of administering the Texas A&M University system. Doctors transferred Rudder to a hospital in Houston when it appeared at first to be a heart ailment turned out to be a cerebral hemorrhage. To stop the bleeding, physicians operated to remove a blood clot. After improving briefly, Rudder took a turn for the worse. The stress of the operation and the hemorrhage caused a stomach ulcer. More operations were conducted to stop the intestinal bleeding, but his condition worsened, and Rudder passed away on March 23, 1970, at the age of fifty-nine.

Rudder's body lay in state in the rotunda of the administration building on the campus of A&M. A public memorial service attended by such dignitaries as Governor Preston Smith, former governor Allan Shivers, numerous local, state, and national politicians, and many military comrades, including former Rangers, was held at White Coliseum. Those such as Generals Norman D. Cota and Troy Middleton, who commanded the 28th Infantry Division and the VIII Corps, respectively, during the Battle of the Bulge; Senator John G. Tower, and former governor John Connally could not attend, but expressed their condolences via telegrams. Also in attendance was former president and friend Lyndon B. Johnson. "His heroism on the Normandy beaches in a time of war was only a prelude to his contribution in peace as an educator, public official and concerned citizen," Johnson remarked. "Earl Rudder brought Texas A&M University to new heights of achievement, excellence and prestige," said Senator Ralph Yarborough. "He was the best," quoted Representative Olin L. Teague. With military honors, Rudder was buried near the campus.

In some ways Rudder was the most unlikely of candidates to bring about many of the changes at Texas A&M. He was from the South, imbued with military traditions and values, and was, for all intents and purposes, a product of the nineteenth century. But Rudder was the person most responsible for the admission of women and minorities and ending compulsory military training at the school. Not necessarily because of his ideological beliefs as a crusader, but because he knew it to be the right and necessary step to attain particular goals.

Progressive Country and the Austin Spirit

RICK KOSTER

Rick Koster grew up in Dallas and is a former professional musician. Currently, he writes for New London, Connecticut's, newspaper, *The Day*. His books include *Texas Music* (1998, 2000), *Louisiana Music* (2002), and *Poppin' a Cold One* (2012), a novel.

In the early 1970s, Austin became a mecca for musicians seeking to escape the regimented, corporate world of Nashville. Native Texans Willie Nelson and Waylon Jennings were among the first to lead the way back to the Lone Star State, and Austin was well on the road to becoming the "Live Music Capital of the World." During this "Cosmic Cowboy" period, Texas music began to coalesce into a unique genre. ✍

★ ★

Back when Willie Nelson was trying to make it as a country singer—he was already earning a six-figure annual income as a songwriter—he released an album for Liberty (now out on United Artists) called *Country Willie Nelson.* On the cover, clad in faded overalls and a plain white T-shirt, Nelson grins goofily at the camera, looking, perhaps, like a casting call-back for the role of some corn-dusted goofus on *Hee Haw* (a part that would in fact be filled with eerie resemblance by Junior Samples).

The essence of the cover was to type Nelson as a farm-raised good ol' boy, the sort embraced by Nashville and the Grand Ole Opry in the Minnie Pearl mold. The strategy was typical of the Nashville mafia that ran country-and-western music, a disturbing and ruthless operation which nevertheless sought to mold its artists in images that today would be wrought by Tipper Gore.

The problem though, was that Nelson didn't give a rat's ass about the old-line Nashville establishment. And, though the overalls *were* Nelson's, and efforts to fit in on his part indicated an early desperation to "make it" which has been paralleled by countless artists, Nelson and Nashville were ultimately not meant for each other.

It took years for the big split to happen—during which time Willie would struggle with toeing the line—but as his status as a performer grew, so did his penchant for rebellion. An affection for marijuana and certain aesthetics borne of the sixties upheaval in rock 'n' roll were twisting Willie's concepts of art and lifestyle, and few of these character and musical evolutions fit in with the Nashville view of how things should be.

But ultimately, it wasn't so much that Nelson and his renegade pal, Waylon Jennings, were rocking the boat. It was that they couldn't handle the way the actual business of country music was being run by the likes of RCA head and Nashville icon Chet Atkins (for whom Nelson and Jennings recorded). So, at last, Nelson sidestepped Nashville and went to New York and signed with Atlantic Records—becoming the first country artist ever signed by the label.

The resultant album, *Shotgun Willie* (1972), was a radically different record, bursting with kooky energy and exploding in numerous directions, none of which sounded remotely like the glossy product Nashville was famous for cranking out. Nelson's own humorous title track fit in perfectly with cover tunes like Bob Wills's "Stay All Night" and Johnny Bush's "Whiskey River," and the whole package was refreshingly different.

It was followed almost immediately by a concept album, *Phases and Stages*, a wonderfully structured record detailing a painful divorce from the perspective of both husband and wife.

These records were like a creative rebirth for Nelson, and since his Nashville home had burned down shortly before he jumped labels, the time seemed right to move back to Texas. He chose Austin, the laid-back state capital nestled in the Hill Country, home to the University of Texas and center of the fruitful Texas music scene.

Austin in the early seventies was mellow to the third power, a curious amalgamation of students, hippies, ne'er-do-wells, and politicos—characteristics that might frequently be found in the same individual—and if any one location was the symbolic headquarters for the Austin attitude, it was an old national guard armory turned live music cavern called the Armadillo World Headquarters.

The club opened in 1970 under the guidance of manager Eddie Wilson, house artist and general maintenance dude Jim Franklin, and a vague organization of hippie pals, and its booking policy reflected the beatific philosophy of its management (which viewed the Armadillo as less a business venture than a giant playpen for stoners). Blues, rock, country, *conjunto*, folk bands, and musicians of every description played there, and the amazing and utopian result was that all manners of formerly antagonistic subsets— bikers, hippies, rednecks, acid heads—found themselves dancing, drinking, getting high, and laughing together.

It was the ultimate coexistence, lacking only a musical figurehead. Earlier that year, Nelson had headed up an outdoor show at Dripping Springs called the Dripping Springs Reunion, which was a financial disaster, but an eclectic lineup including Loretta Lynn, Tex Ritter, Kris Kristofferson, Waylon Jennings, Billy Joe Shaver, and Leon Russell had created an energy and vibe that seemed to flow promisingly enough. So when Willie played his first show at the Armadillo on August 12, 1972 (with the quintessential Willie Nelson band: his sister Bobbie on piano, bassist Bee Spears, guitarists Jody Payne and Grady Martin, percussionist Billy English, harmonica wizard Mickey Raphael, and drummer Paul English), the spirit of the Dripping Springs seemed to have found a home and, thereafter, the phenomenon known as progressive country, redneck rock, and/or the cosmic cowboy movement began to percolate.

The following year, Nelson staged the first of several annual Fourth of July picnics, again at Dripping Springs (the locations would vary over time). In a little more than a year, the lycanthropic mutation of country and rock had become readily apparent on the streets of Austin. The sight of a longhair wearing a cowboy hat and fine-tuning his Lone Star beer-induced buzz with a joint was not only accepted, it was an image to aspire to. Attendance by said folk at Nelson's picnics would become mandatory, and the event was for years a Dionysian rite of summer that typified the new Austin mentality and its Live Free and Party philosophy.

Of course, by that first picnic, Nelson himself bore no resemblance to the cover of *Country Willie* from years before, and his braided pigtails became as much a symbol of outlaw country music as his effervescent smile and his tattered Martin guitar.

Inasmuch as Atlantic had folded its country department shortly after *Phases and Stages*, Nelson signed with Columbia, and it was at that point that he began to record a string of brilliant albums that typified the entire era. Another concept record, 1975's *Red-Headed Stranger*, a story about the Old West featuring the huge-selling "Blue Eyes Crying in the Rain," was clearly the album that established Nelson as a bona fide country superstar.

The next year, he teamed with several of his Austin and Nashville pals—Waylon Jennings, Jessie Colter, and Tompall Glaser—to release *Wanted: The Outlaws*, which boasted the Nelson/Jennings duets "Good-Hearted Woman" and "Mamas Don't Let Your Babies Grow Up to Be Cowboys." The album went platinum, Nelson and Jennings would win a Country Music Award for Best Duet, and the resultant Outlaws tour blew the doors open for progressive country to "go national."

Being the figurehead of the entire movement was a full-time job, but Nelson managed to handle his duties with grace and admirable goodwill. Throughout the rest of the seventies, Nelson toured constantly, the annual picnics were certifiable big times, and his records were often adventurous and of undisputed quality. He and Jennings recorded *Waylon and Willie* in 1978, an effortless million-seller, and anyone in the contiguous United States who hadn't been aware of the duo's outlaw personas before certainly was by now.

Nelson could do no wrong—a situation strengthened by the consistent high quality of his work and the unerring brilliance of his business decisions. He released two tribute albums, 1977's *To Lefty from Willie* and 1979's *Sings Kris Kristofferson*, and encored with a collection of Nelson's ten favorite songs, *Stardust*. The idea of the latter album was reportedly frowned on by CBS, a situation that bothered Nelson not at all. Including the title song and standards like "Moonlight in Vermont," "Someone to Watch Over Me," "Georgia on My Mind," and "Blue Skies," *Stardust* was stupendously successful, selling over three million copies, and once again demonstrated Nelson's instinctive superiority over the C&W big shots.

In 1979, as the progressive country movement began to burn itself out and the Armadillo World Headquarters eased into its last year of existence, Nelson made his film debut alongside Robert Redford and Jane Fonda in the critically received *Electric Horseman*. Nelson had become bigger than the movement he created, and the only possible solution was to keep moving, artistically and figuratively. He continued to maintain a base of operations in Austin, but he also secured a ranch in Colorado, a golf course and a recording studio on the Pedernales, and continued to dip his fingers into dozens of lucrative pies.

Though he would encounter tax troubles in the eighties, even the wily IRS couldn't thwart the indomitable Nelson, who finally reached a settlement with the agency, and his creative legacy would continue to sparkle. Numerous recording projects have shone in the nineties—none more so than the brilliantly dignified *Teatro*, which came out in 1988 and more than proved the songwriter is still a force to be reckoned with.

The name that kept popping up with Nelson's during the entire progressive country heyday was, of course, Waylon Jennings. Born in the West Texas community of Littlefield in 1937, Jennings was a disc jockey by the time he was twelve and an accomplished guitarist by his late teens. He moved to Lubbock in 1958 to do another deejay gig, and made the acquaintance of Buddy Holly during one of the station's *Sunday Afternoon Dance Party* programs. Shortly thereafter, Jennings signed on as a Cricket, playing bass guitar, and Holly actually produced Jennings's first recording, a take on the Cajun classic "Jole Blon."

It was also Jennings who gave up his seat to J. P. "The Big Bopper" Richardson on the ill-fated flight that killed Holly and all aboard in February 1959. Thereafter Jennings shakily relocated to Arizona and switched allegiance from rock 'n' roll to country.

Blessed with a distinctive and powerful baritone voice which could astonish in its ability to render ballads tenderly or belt out hardcore C&W with an abrasive tequila-and-cactus-needles quality, Jennings formed a backing group, The Waylors, grew a Mephistophelean beard, threw out every item of clothing in his wardrobe that wasn't black, and in the course of a few years acquired quite a reputation as heading up a stone-serious country band. Chet Atkins signed Jennings to his RCA label and brought him to Nashville to record—whereupon Jennings ran into the same attitudinal problems Nelson had encountered. Though a number of releases did respectably enough throughout the balance of the sixties, including two hit singles, "Walk On Out of My Mind" (number 5) and "Only Daddy That'll Walk the Line" (number 2, both 1968), Jennings grew tired of Nashville's cookie-cutter mentality of record making and simply circumvented the bullshit by heading to New York to negotiate his own deal with the label honchos.

In the face of Jennings's reputation for pill ingestion and his stubborn and increasingly adamant insistence that he record with his own band (another Nashville taboo), the Old Guard finally threw up their hands and allowed the black-clad rebel to record his own way. The result was 1973's *Honky Tonk Heroes*, which was, intentionally or otherwise, a spiritual companion piece to Nelson's *Shotgun Willie* and *Phases and Stages* albums.

On *Honky Tonk Heroes*, Jennings utilized the songwriting talents of another Austin songwriter, Billy Joe Shaver, and the focus of the tunes shifted from traditional country fodder to introspective and lonely themes. The connections to the whole progressive country scene were too significant to ignore, and when Nelson talked Jennings into playing at the Armadillo, their status as the dual personifications of outlaw chic was set.

There followed the aforementioned *Wanted: The Outlaws* album, after which Jennings became the closest thing to a rock star working the C&W market. His string of hit singles during that period was astounding, and included "Bob Wills Is Still the King," "Are You Sure Hank Done It This Way?" (both 1974), "Suspicious Minds" (1976), "Luckenbach, Texas (Back to the Basics of Love)," and "Wurlitzer Prize" (both 1977)— all the while interspersing CMA awards, gold, platinum, and number 1 albums (*I've Always Been Crazy, Mamas Don't Let Your Babies Grow Up to Be Cowboys*), and duets and tours with Willie and like-minded mutineers.

At last, though, the "outlaw" tag grew to such outlandish proportions as to embarrass Jennings, at least partially. In 1978, he recorded "Don't You Think This Outlaw Bit's Done Gone Out of Hand," proving that he had a self-effacing sense of humor as well as a propensity for writing the longest song titles on earth (until a British angst-infected pop star named Morrissey would come along in the eighties, anyway).

Still, even with the C&W rebel concept on the wane, Jennings would close the decade as a reliable hit machine, churning out two number 1 songs before the end of the decade with "Amanda" and "Come with Me."

Despite the fact that Jennings's official base of operations had always remained in Nashville, and while he would eventually change lifestyles and settle in the sedentary C&W Social Security haven of Branson, Missouri, Jennings's membership in and contributions to the redneck rock movement are significant and undeniable. Of late, Jennings has been particularly inspired, and his recent CDs *Backtracks* and *Closing in on the Fire* are of competitive quality.

If Nelson and Jennings were the king and jack in the face cards of progressive country, then surely Jerry Jeff Walker was the joker. A transplanted songwriter born in Oneonta, New York, in 1942, Walker (given name: Paul Crosby) spent his itinerant young adulthood as a quasi-folk songwriter, marinating his liver and brain cells in towns across the United States. He played for a brief time in a rock band called Circus Maximus, which recorded an album for Vanguard, but shortly thereafter he decided he wanted to travel the country as a solo songwriter.

It was the same sort of education that seasoned Jack Kerouac's muse, and when Walker wrote a song in the late sixties called "Mr. Bojangles," a wonderful and haunting song about a street dancer he met in the Orleans Parish jail that perfectly captured the innate dignity and humanity found even in society's bottom-feeders, Walker's reputation as a songwriter began to match his legacy as a bacchanalian performer. His material began to take on country characteristics, particularly in his sympathies for drunken losers with starry eyes, and if his voice sounded like it had arthritis—a diametric opposite of the smooth tenors of C&W stars like Ray Price or Jim Reeves—it was instantly identifiable and had a certain dipsomaniacal charm.

Walker had settled in central Texas in the mid-sixties, after hitchhiking through Houston and Dallas and hating them. The Austin music scene and the laid-back nonchalance of Hill Country communities like Fredericksburg, Wimberley, and Kerrville were particularly appealing.

Walker released *Driftin' Way of Life* for Vanguard in 1969 (an evocatively composed set of autobiographical tunes) and, after the Nitty Gritty Dirt Band had a top ten hit with "Mr. Bojangles" in 1970, Walker was signed to MCA. He recorded *Jerry Jeff Walker* in 1972, a slap-dash record relying heavily on the material of West Texas song wizard Guy Clark and a group of studio musicians comprised largely of Michael Murphey's band.

Clark's "L.A. Freeway" was an instant classic, a perfect three-minute tune that captured the essence of the Beautiful Oaf, a fun-time loser always one step ahead of the bill collector and repo man. Along with Walker's "Hill Country Rain," the album was unlike anything recorded by mainstream C&W, a detour from the expected journey-through-life gig bought into by most of young America, and it seemed to emphasize the concept that a beer-drenched holding pattern and a porch hammock weren't bad things.

All the while, Walker was endearing himself to nightclub crowds around Austin with the backing group he'd purloined from Murphey, which would come to be called the Lost Gonzo Band (Gary P. Nunn, Bob Livingston, John Inmon, Kelly Dunn, and Donny Dolan).

In 1973, Walker, preferring the loose and liquid environs of the club experience to the sterility of recording studios, persuaded the label to let him record in the friendly confines of Hondo Crouch's bar in Luckenbach.

The resultant album, *Viva Terlingua*, boasted another Clark classic, "Desperados," and a tune by Dallasite Ray Wylie Hubbard called "Up Against the Wall Redneck Mother," and the LP so perfectly captured the essence of Walker's lifestyle and philosophies—the envy of every young Austinite of legal drinking age—that its status as an indispensable record remains today.

Still, much like the whole Austin scene in the seventies, Walker was about maintaining an easygoing and decidedly nonambitious status quo. He continued his erratic performance schedule—terrific when he was sober, clownlike and occasionally pathetic when he was drunk—and recorded a yearly series of mostly dog-paddling records over the next few years: *Walker's Collectibles* (1974), *Ridin' High* (1975), *It's a Good Night for Singing* (1976), *A Man Must Carry On* (1977), *Contrary to Ordinary* (1978), and *Too Old to Change* (1979).

The records continued to sell moderately well to Walker's hardcore following, and he was able to work his persona on sporadic tours throughout the United States into the early eighties.

Ultimately, Austin's liquid minstrel is doing as well as ever by virtue of two shrewd nods to the future. Walker sobered up and through a craftily managed Web site and a never-ending supply of new and old product, sells a lot of stuff.

By 1974, all of Austin was immersed in the progressive country concept. One radio station, KOKE-FM, was created simply as a soundtrack to the progressive country experience, and along with the Armadillo, clubs like Castle Creek, the Pub, the Cricket, the Texas Opry House, the Split Rail, the El Paso Cattle Company, and the Broken Spoke became live-music hangouts catering to the music. And if it could be said that Nelson, Jennings, and Walker would ultimately comprise the scene's attitudinal holy trinity (and even that is arguable given Jennings's infrequent appearances in Austin), there were several significant artists who certainly qualified as cardinals.

And to belabor the religious analogy, one of the more spiritual of the Austin songwriters was Michael Martin Murphey, who utilized in his tunes the recurring theme that Austin is heaven on earth. Born in Dallas, Murphey at one point studied to be a Baptist minister before opting to write tunes. He plied his trade for Screen Gems in Los Angeles, in Colorado mining towns, and in the record company service in Nashville before he finally brought his family back to Texas in time for the progressive country upheaval. In fact, the title of his second album, *Cosmic Cowboy Souvenir*, lent a phrase to one of many pseudonyms for the music of the time, whose practitioners were called Cosmic Cowboys.

Murphey was something of a hero by the time he moved to Austin; his tunes had already been recorded by the likes of Flatt and Scruggs, the Monkees, Kenny Rogers, and the Nitty Gritty Dirt Band. Too, he bore no small resemblance to *Jeremiah Johnson*-era Robert Redford, sang in a plaintive voice that might crack in the higher registers (but in doing so gave his work a certain earnestness), and his songs combined a hippie spirituality with clever lyrics and pleasant and simple melodies.

His 1972 A&M release, *Geronimo's Cadillac*, worked the honky-tonk country field with a definite left-leaning awareness of environmental and Native American concerns, and 1973's *Cosmic Cowboy* was in itself a paean to the nirvanic qualities of Austin and the Hill Country.

He switched labels in 1974 to Epic, for whom he recorded *Michael Murphey*, and moved back to Colorado. In 1975 he released *Blue Sky, Night Thunder*, which cemented Murphey's movement away from what had already become "traditional" progressive country. Murphey segued into a smoother, more orchestrated sound typified in the monster number 1 hit "Wildfire," a stirring ballad about a girl and a horse—a musical salad made up of the sentimentality of Bobby Goldsboro's "Honey," the sad pet concept of *Ol' Yeller*, and the piano theme from *The Exorcist*.

Murphey has since relocated to Santa Fe, New Mexico, has released several more albums including 1987's terrific *River of Time* and a series of CDs and books of cowboy and Old West-motifed songs and has had huge hits like 1982's "What's Forever For." He also heads up Michael Martin Murphey's WestFest, one of the nation's finest country music festivals, every year in Vail, Colorado.

On the opposite side of the religious coin was Kinky Friedman, a decidedly sacrilegious Jewish songwriter who was a graduate of the University of Texas and particularly popular with a collegiate audience possessed of a certain black humor about the world in general.

With his band, the Texas Jewboys, Friedman danced around the periphery of the Austin scene, preferring instead to hang out in New York and Nashville. He recorded for the Vanguard label, for whom he released *Sold American* in 1971, and while the music was marginally accomplished country, it served as nothing more than structural background for his twisted, hilarious, and often brilliant lyrics—most of which seemed to be contrived to offend people.

Friedman moved to ABC for 1974's *Kinky Friedman*, and then to Epic for 1976's *Lasso from El Paso*, but nothing really changed. "They Aren't Makin' Jews Like Jesus Anymore," "Get Your Biscuits in the Oven and Your Buns in the Bed," "The Ballad of Charles Whitman"—all were calculated to get horrified reactions out of people. But for all of Friedman's sarcasm, he had a following. There was something about his hoarse, Dylanesque voice and leering Groucho mannerisms that were completely different from the longhaired cowboys competing against him in record stores.

In the end, it was the sublime idiocy of the songs that captured a theretofore neglected slice of the progressive country pie: the segment that had stopped taking themselves too seriously. Though Friedman has essentially retired from music to write a series of amusing, quasi-autobiographical mystery novels, a 1992 greatest hits CD, *Old Testaments and New Revelations* (Fruit of the Tune Music) is an excellent collection for the curious.

And inasmuch as artists like Nelson, Jennings, Gary P. Nunn, and Guy Clark had already said everything there was to say about progressive country's lyrical mother lodes (heartbreak, drinking, and loneliness), Friedman had the shrewd wisdom to seek the uncharted territories of redneck rock's outhouse. After all, surely no one will ever top Friedman's "Old Ben Lucas," the greatest country song ever written about snot.

Another subset of progressive country luminaries was the one comprised of the guys who *wrote* a lot of the most famous redneck rock tunes for folks like Waylon and Willie and Jerry Jeff, and occasionally experienced a hit or two themselves—but for one reason or another never became top o' the charts stars.

If he'd never done another thing during his time in our solar system, Ray Wylie Hubbard would forever be famous as the guy who was cursed to write the anthem of the progressive country movement: "Up Against the Wall Redneck Mother."

Hubbard rightly considers it a curse because it doesn't matter how many inspired tunes he might write (and he's written plenty), or if somehow he discovers the cure for AIDS—people will always screech for "Redneck Mother."

In fact, the song was a throwaway tune written before the progressive country movement ever got rolling, based on a true-life exerience in which the longhaired Hubbard tried to buy some beer from a transplanted Okie woman running a store in Red River, New Mexico. She questioned Hubbard's hippie appearance and patriotism (bolstered by the guardian presence of her silent, crew-cut, and absolutely Frankensteinian son), and the songwriter returned from the encounter with a song in his heart and a case of beer under his arm.

At first, Hubbard interspersed the song during performances only when musicians were changing broken strings or vomiting, and it was during one such occasion that Jerry Jeff Walker heard the tune and witnessed the subsequent riot it caused—and insisted immediately on recording the piece.

In spite of the welcome royalty checks wrested from the tune, it still hangs like a decaying albatross around Hubbard's neck, particularly in light of the sluggish pace of his own career. True, back at the dawn of the Armadillo World Headquarters, Hubbard and his country-punk Cowboy Twinkies were quite popular, with Hubbard riding the crest of a wave of alcohol and touring the country with Willie Nelson.

They released a self-titled album in 1975 for Reprise with a fine single, "Bordertown Girl," and followed that with an album for Nelson's Lone Star Records, *1978's Off the Wall*. When that label folded, Hubbard put out *1979's Something About the Night* on Renegade, and though the LP featured what actually may be his best tune, "Texas Is a State of Mind," album sales weren't exactly overpowering.

Hubbard battled gamely throughout the eighties, but when alcohol began to win the day, he had to pull back and sober up. He emerged in the early nineties freshly clean and newly inspired, and released two marvelous independent albums, 1993's independent *Lost Train of Thought* and 1994's *Loco Gringo's Lament* (both now available on DejaDisc). Hubbard continued to work and write steadily, and his material continues to improve. The commitment paid off: Hubbard signed with Rounder/Philo in 1997 and issued two superb CDs for the label: *Dangerous Spirits* and *Crusades of the Restless Knights*.

Billy Joe Shaver, born in Corsicana and raised in Waco, is a songwriter whose acumen utilized the poet-as-drinker motif and has written for a staggering collection of artists: Elvis Presley, Jerry Lee Lewis, the Allman Brothers, John Anderson, Bobby Bare, Johnny Cash, Tom T. Hall, and Kris Kristofferson among them. And of course, every song except one on Waylon's legendary *Honky Tonk Heroes* was written by Shaver.

He was perfect for the progressive country image, including a colorful series of nonmusical background jobs in a sawmill (where he lost a finger-and-a-half), as a farm worker, in the navy, and as a used car salesman. But he wrote songs as well, and eventually tried Nashville, where he slowly earned a reputation as a terrific writer. Songs like "Black Rose," a tune about an interracial marriage, or the lushly evocative "Georgia on a Fast Train," were so much more literate and intriguing than the usual Nashville pap that Shaver should have been a star.

Finally, as the progressive country movement took hold, Shaver signed with Monument Records and, in 1973, released the Kristofferson-produced *Old Five and Dimers Like Me*. He jumped to Capricorn for *When I Get My Wings* (1976) and *Gypsy Boy* (1977), then moved to Columbia for several more albums during the eighties. But although his LPs always received critical hurrahs, none sold particularly well, and his forte has remained song-writing. He was signed to Zoo/Praxis in 1993, for whom he released *Tramp on Your Street* later that year, then followed with a gritty, high-energy look back at his earlier work on *Unshaven*, which was the debut of a country power trio called Shaver that includes his son Eddy on lead guitar. Two scorching CDs, the live *Shaver* and a New West release, *Electric Shaver*, and an acoustic gospel record called *Victory* are well worth owning.

Kris Kristofferson is another brilliant writer whose career hasn't been helped particularly by his decidedly nonangelic voice. Born in Brownsville in 1937, Kristofferson is probably the only important country songwriter to have been a janitor *after* he was a Rhodes scholar. A frustrated novelist who also did time in the army, the oil fields, and flying helicopters, Kristofferson went the requisite Nashville songwriter route—a pursuit he was about to abandon when Roger Miller recorded his song "Me and Bobby McGee."

At once, Kristofferson was an in-demand guy, and wrote particularly literate hangover and loneliness tunes like "Sunday Morning Coming Down" (a hit for Johnny Cash) and "Help Me Make It Through the Night" (big for Sammi Smith). Still, though he hung out with the likes of Nelson and Jennings, and his aura and material fairly reeked of Austin, Kristofferson was never particularly visible on the progressive country scene.

In any case, his albums were cool, particularly 1970's *Kristofferson*, 1971's *The Silver-Tongued Devil and I*, and 1972's *Jesus Was a Capricorn* (all Monument). But when Kristofferson's frog-with-a-four-pack-a-day habit voice kept him from becoming a radio star, he simply channeled his good looks and Mensa brain toward Hollywood and became an actor. He also married country singing star Rita Coolidge, and though their separate and combined careers have ebbed and flowed, anyone with Kristofferson's stark and emotive songwriting ability will never go hungry.

Steve Fromholz will never be called taciturn. A self-described "up and coming, middle-aged stand-up folksinger specializing in free-form, country/ folk/rock, science fiction, gospel-cum-bluegrass opera Cowjazz music," Fromholz is the same guy who defines the difference between a folksinger and a savings bond: after forty, a savings bond matures and starts earning money.

Similarly entertaining are Fromholz's songs. He was born in Temple in 1945, met and played with Michael Martin Murphey while the two were students at North Texas State University, and formed a short-lived duo with Dan McCrimmon called Frummox. They released one album in 1969, *From Here to There* (Probe/ABC), which featured Fromholz's immortal "Texas Trilogy," a three-song mini-opera comprised of "Daybreak," "Train-ride," and "Bosque Country Romance," and which has remained Fromholz's signature piece.

After a stint in Stephen Stills's band and an unreleased solo album for Michael Nesmith's Countryside label, Fromholz moved to Austin in time to become a huge part of the redneck rock agenda. He signed with Capitol and cut *A Rumour in My Own Time* (1976), generally regarded as a classic of progressive country. Two follow-ups, 1978's *Frolicking in the Myth* and 1979's *Jus' Playin' Along* (the latter on Willie Nelson's Lone Star label), fared poorly, and Fromholz began a post-cosmic cowboy career wherein he plays golf, writes plays, acts a bit, and goes whitewater rafting whenever possible.

He still pursues music whenever it occurs to him, and in 1995 recorded *The Old Fart in the Mirror*, a mixture of Fromholz classics and new songs in the same whimsically weary vein revered by his small but rabid coterie of fans.

Rusty Wier, whose Brett Maverick hat, copper beard, and demon's smile were just part of his irrepressible stage presence, came to the Austin progressive country scene through a circuitous series of rock bands. Originally a drummer, Wier, who grew up in Manchaca and went to college at Southwest Texas State, played in two of Austin's seminal sixties rock bands, The Wig and the Lavender Hill Express.

When rock didn't pan out, though, Wier opted to become a folksinger. To his own surprise, by the early seventies, he was enormously popular, on his own and with pals John Inmon and Layton DePenning in the trio Rusty, Layton and John. Building on an enormously likable stage persona, Wier continued to draw crowds even as the progressive country built up around him. Eventually, he formed a band and went to Nashville a time or two on near-miss excursions.

Oh well; back home, his boyish enthusiasm and consummate bar band polish continued to work. By then, the scene was bubbling: Michael Martin Murphey had brought his act to town, Willie was in charge, B. W. Stevenson was recording for RCA, Jerry Jeff could do no wrong artistically, and Steve Fromholz had "Texas Trilogy." Every night was like a musical slumber party, and the consensus was that, for Wier, success was inevitable.

Sure enough, ABC-Dunhill came calling. Wier took Inmon and De-Penning to L.A. and with a variety of session guys recorded *Stoned, Slow, Rugged*, a magical album of country/folk with heavy rock overtones. Bolstered by a Murphey tune, "Five O'Clock in the Texas Morning," the album sold strongly across the country.

Wier jumped to 20th Century for 1975's *Don't It Make You Wanna Dance?*, featuring the hit title song and Weir's personal Austin anthem, "I Heard You Been Layin' My Old Lady." Another label switch ensued, and Weir recorded *Stacked Deck* for Columbia in 1977. It was at that point that the scene began to stagnate, and Wier's contributions became less frequent. Still, he tours with semiregularity, and everywhere he goes they call out for two songs: "Don't It Make You Wanna Dance?" and "I Heard You Been Layin' My Old Lady." Most old folksingers would tell you that that ain't a bad legacy.

The most enigmatic of the redneck rock brigade was bear-sized B. W. "Buckwheat" Stevenson. Frequently clad in overalls and a hillbilly hat, with his pale cherub's features obscured by a werewolf beard, Stevenson sang in a floating tenor voice at once melancholy and sweet, which was particularly incongruous with his hulking presence. And, though he was a frequent performer and collaborator in Austin circles, he actually lived in Dallas.

He was a graduate of Adamson, the same Oak Cliff high school that brought us Michael Martin Murphey and Ray Wylie Hubbard, and after aborted stints at NTSU and in the air force, Stevenson cut his teeth singing folk in Dallas clubs like the Rubaiyat.

A captivating writer from early on, his forte was balladry and soaring melodic sagas of lost and unrequited love. He released an album for RCA in 1972 that contained several terrific Buckwheat originals, including the heartbreaking "On My Own." With typical logic, though, the record company selected "Say What I Feel," an uptempo Murphey tongue-twister, as the first single, and it stiffed.

RCA employed a similar strategy on 1974's *Lead Free*, from which an obscure tune called "Shambala" was chosen as the single. Though it actually dented the *Billboard* charts, Three Dog Night, the biggest-selling rock act in the world (and a band that relied heavily on cover material) needed yet another hit. Upon seeing that "Shambala" actually had legs, the Dogsters rushed out *their* version—which quickly long-jumped past poor Stevenson, who in turn went to Texas to mire in his new obscurity.

But RCA was just taking care of biz, and they still had plans for Stevenson. They kept him away from the degenerate influences of Austin, insulating him in saccharine environs like Hollywood and Nashville, and cranked out product. The next album boasted a hit in the title song, "Maria," which Stevenson at least cowrote, and the damned thing actually went top ten.

There followed 1977's *Calabasas*, which RCA also had big plans for, but somehow they short-circuited. Ever unsure of what exactly he was supposed to be, Stevenson moved to MCA for 1980's *Lifeline*, which was in fact what he would soon need. Stricken with cancer, his health declined rapidly and he passed away shortly thereafter.

If Stevenson was enigmatic and tragic, Willis Alan Ramsey was eccentric and mysterious. A pleasant, handsome recluse, Ramsey was born in Alabama and moved to Austin where he wrote two classic songs, "Northeast Texas Women" and "Muskrat Love." The former is a textbook Austin in the Seventies composition, and the latter is lamentably associated with the treatment given it by the Captain and Tenille (though, face it, it *is* a song about rodents).

Ramsey released one obscure but brilliant record, *Willis Alan Ramsey*, for Shelter in 1972, then drifted into the mists of his own self-induced twilight.

In a scene typified by camaraderie and much musical incest betwixt bands and writers, Gary P. Nunn was absolutely the most important sideman in Austin. Though most frequently associated with Jerry Jeff Walker's Lost Gonzo Band, Nunn is an outstanding singer/songwriter who eventually struck out on his own. And his "London Homesick Blues" (known by feebs as "I Wanna Go Home with the Armadillos") ranks, along with Guy Clark's "Desperadoes" and "L.A. Freeway," just below Hubbard's "Redneck Mother" in the Flagship Song of Progressive Country sweepstakes.

A prolific writer who's had hits for the likes of Willie Nelson and Roseanne Cash, Nunn eventually left the Lost Gonzo Band (after *they* left Walker), and went solo with his own backing unit, the Sons of the Bunkhouse. He relocated to Oklahoma in the late eighties, and independent LPs such as *Border States* and *Guacamole* are still available.

Two other Texan country artists experienced noteworthy success during the progressive country era, but weren't actual members of that fraternity: Mickey Gilley and Johnny Rodriguez.

Rodriguez, who was born in Sabinal, Texas, in 1951, was a former altar boy who formed a rock band when he was sixteen, and was playing lead guitar for Tom T. Hall when he was twenty.

Shortly thereafter, Hall, who was blown away by Rodriguez's voice, got the youngster a deal with Mercury Records, and his first single, "Pass Me By," was a top ten hit in 1972. He was awarded the ACM Most Promising Male Vocalist award, encored in 1973 with three number 1 releases, and suddenly found himself a huge star.

Rodriguez's style echoed the more pop end of the C&W spectrum, and throughout the seventies he scored several hits each year. After a bad fall broke his sternum and collarbone, Rodriguez experienced vocal as well as marital problems, and though he recorded for several labels in the eighties and continued to chart an occasional hit, it was thought that his career was probably over.

Still, in 1993, he released the well-received *Run for the Border*, and with a surge in Hispanic music coinciding with Rodriguez's propensity for singing in Spanish, his career appears to be on the upswing.

Mickey Gilley, notable as Jerry Lee Lewis's cousin and as the former owner of Gilley's (at one time the world's largest honky-tonk), should also be remembered as having sold several million records.

After having been drawn into the music business by his cuz, Gilley recorded for a few small labels as well as for Texas's legendary producer Huey Meaux before opening the Gilley's club in 1970. Four years later, he recorded a single for his own jukebox, and the B-side, "Room Full of Roses," became a hit. Playboy Records, distributed by Epic, picked up the record, which climbed all the way to number 1.

Gilley, whose honky-tonk piano style and warm voice made for a winning combination, began to real off a string of consecutive number 1 singles which was astonishing. The awards swirled like confetti, and Gilley continued to rack up hit after hit, including the chauvinistic barroom verity, "Don't the Girls All Get Prettier at Closing Time."

Despite all the hits, Playboy went under and Gilley jumped to parent label Epic, for whom he recorded ten more number 1 singles by 1986. By mixing pop, classic Buddy Holly-style rock, and mainstream C&W, Gilley had a style that seemed impervious to trends.

Finally, by the end of the decade, Gilley's luck seemed to abate a bit. He closed his nightclub and, though his records continued to sell steadily, the long run of top ten hits came to an end. Ever the visionary, though, Gilley became the first artist to open his own theater in Branson, Missouri, where he continues to thrill fans by the thousands.

All in all, the redneck rock era was a highlight in country music history, for the songs as much as for its colorful, irreverent, and truly free purveyors—and in particular for the camaraderie that wrapped the scene and the entire Travis County community in a decade-long cannabis-smoke cocoon. Besides the aforementioned heroes, artists such as Greezy Wheels, Calico, Commander Cody and the Lost Planet Airmen, Balcones Fault, Asleep at the Wheel, Alvin Crow and the Pleasant Valley Boys, and Mother of Pearl were all active and integral in the never-ending circus.

If, to its participants and admirers, the whole progressive country phenomenon seemed over with too quickly, well, maybe such a movement should, by definition, remain short-lived. Only through brevity can such a happy accident retain its vibrancy, freshness, and spontaneity—and in any event, the sheer pace of the madness would've killed 'em all by now, anyway.

Women in Texas

CARY D. WINTZ

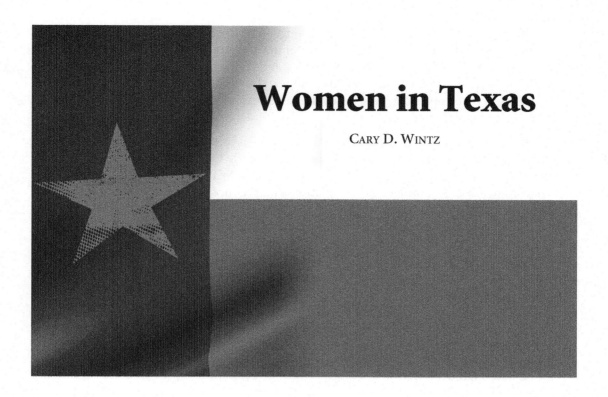

C ary D. Wintz, past president of the Southwestern Social Science Association, teaches history at Texas Southern University in Houston. A specialist in African American and Texas history, his studies include *Black Culture and the Harlem Renaissance* (1988), *Black Dixie: Essays on Afro-Texan History and Culture in Houston* (1992), *Major Problems in Texas History* (2002), *Texas: The Lone Star State* (Tenth Edition, 2010), and *The Harlem Renaissance in the American West: The New Negro's Western Experience* (2011).

Women have played a significant role in shaping Texas. In this selection, Dr. Wintz provides an overview of women's history in the Lone Star State, from the powerful Caddo queen Santa Adiva to such twentieth-century leaders as Oveta Culp Hobby, Barbara Jordan, Ann Richards, and Kay Bailey Hutchison. ❦

★ ★

A cold wind blew across the narrow bay from onshore signaling the arrival of the season's first winter storm. The north winds would bring with them the opportunity to scavenge for oysters in the low tides. The sky was gray, almost the same steel-gray of the gulf waters. Two women and a young child left a crude half-tent shelter that they had rigged at the abandoned stockade and trudged across the dunes to the narrow beach carrying sacks, which they hoped to fill with

"Women in Texas" by Cary D. Wintz. Reprinted by permission of Harlan Davidson, Inc., from *The Texas Heritage,* 3rd ed., by editors Ben Procter and Archie P. McDonald. pp. 185-208. Copyright © 1997 by Harlan Davidson, Inc.

crabs or oysters for their evening dinner. The younger woman, a black in her early teens, led the way, looking carefully up and down the beach for any signs of Indians as she hurried toward the shore. The other, a white woman, barely twenty and visibly pregnant, followed, her progress slowed by her young daughter who was almost hidden by the tall grasses that stretched halfway up the dunes. As she approached the beach, her eyes scanned the bleak horizon looking for a sail that might signal the return of her husband, or at least bring news of him.

Jane Long, accompanied by her young daughter Ann and a young slave woman known as Kian, spent the winter of 1820–1821 on Bolivar peninsula, while her husband, Dr. James Long of Louisiana, conducted his ill-fated military mission against Spanish forces in Texas. Jane Long and Kian contended with hunger, cold, isolation, and the threat of attacks by hostile Indians. Kian successfully nursed Long through illness and childbirth in mid-December; at one point the women went three days without food before Kian managed to find an oyster reef in the shallows of Galveston Bay. On another occasion the women dressed in military uniforms, hoisted a red flannel petticoat up the flagpole of the abandoned fort, and fired off the fort's old cannon in order to convince a passing band of Karankawa Indians that the post was still manned by soldiers. The two women and two children survived the harsh winter through a combination of courage, ingenuity, and luck. Their ordeal came to an end when a Mexican rider appeared on the deserted beach with the message that the Spanish had captured and executed Dr. Long. Unwilling to let matters rest, Jane Long and her entourage traveled by horseback, first to San Antonio de Béxar and then to Monterrey, seeking to have her husband's "murderers" brought to justice. Although her determination impressed Mexican officials, she received no satisfaction, only polite expressions of sympathy. Finally Long gave up and returned to her home in Mississippi. A year later, however, she would return to Texas, along with Kian and her two daughters, as one of Stephen F. Austin's original "old three hundred" colonists.

Jane Long's courage and determination, as well as the fact that she was perhaps the first Anglo-American woman to come to Texas—and the first to give birth there—have earned her a place in Texas mythology as the "Mother of Texas." Kian, who shared all of the original adventures, returned to Texas with Long (as her servant and life-long companion), and raised her own family in and around the lower Brazos River town of Richmond, can claim with equal justice the title "Mother of Black Texas." However, women's history in Texas predates Jane Long and Kian. Spanish women, Indian women, and the women ancestors of the American Indians influenced the history and development of the area that we know as Texas long before the arrival of Jane Long and Kian. Indeed, Texas history may be viewed as a series of migrations that brought people into the region. Women, of course, participated in each of these successive waves of immigration and influenced the culture established by each set of newcomers.

While archaeologists continue to search for the clues that will settle the debate over when humans first arrived in North America and subsequently in Texas, there is no debate over the fact that women played a significant role in Texas's earliest cultures. Whether these first inhabitants came 12,000 years ago or 25,000 years ago, the role that women played in early cultures is fairly well known. (Our knowledge of these first inhabitants of Texas comes from the work of archaeologists and anthropologists who have examined the artifacts of early cultures, and from anthropologists who have studied nineteenth- and twentieth-century cultures with economic, social, and technological practices similar to those of earlier cultures.)

Paleo Americans, as the predecessors of the American Indians are generally termed, lived by hunting and gathering. In the more distant past their livelihoods centered around hunting large game, such as the mammoths, mastodons, and prehistoric bison that once were plentiful in North America; around ten thousand years ago, as these ice-age animals became extinct, the peoples' methods of getting food shifted, first to hunting small game and gathering wild plant food, and then, in most areas, to agriculture or a combination of agriculture, hunting, and gathering. Women performed essential tasks in these early cultures. Generally labor was divided along sexual lines. Among the nomadic hunters of large game, women cared for the children, prepared food, processed meat and hides, prepared clothing, sometimes erected shelter, often made tools, and saw to it that all household possessions were properly packed for transport during seasonal migrations. Meanwhile, men primarily were responsible for hunting. As big-game hunting gave way to hunting and gathering, women generally assumed more responsibility for acquiring food—especially the gathering of wild plant food—and processing and storing food. In these early cultures, women played important and occasionally dominant roles in the ceremonial and religious lives of their people. The transition to agriculture tended to make the division of labor along sexual lines more rigid. For those cultures that remained seminomadic, or combined agriculture with a continued reliance on hunting and gathering, women generally added production of the crops to their other labors, while men continued to hunt (and make war). In those societies that settled down in permanent or semipermanent agricultural villages, women acquired additional duties associated with maintaining the home, food preparation, the manufacture of clothing, and caring for the young. They also helped tend the crops, but by this time men began to assume more of the responsibility for farming and home construction.

By the time that Europeans first arrived in the region that became Texas the various Paleo-American cultures had given way to four major Native-American cultures, plus several other minor cultures. The role of women varied considerably from culture to culture. Among the groups that shared the Western Gulf cultures, along the coastal prairies and in the arid lands of South Texas and northern Mexico, there was little division of labor along sexual lines. Life was so harsh and the environment so unproductive for these hunter-gatherers that all members of the community spent virtually all of their time in the search for food. In contrast, among the Lipan Apaches, who occupied the plains of West and Southwest Texas, the roles of men and women were clearly delineated. While men were buffalo hunters and warriors, women cultivated the fields, butchered the buffalo, dressed the buffalo hides and turned them into the leather used to cover tepees and make clothing. Women also built the teepees, made the clothing, and fashioned tools out of buffalo bone. After the acquisition of horses made buffalo hunting and warfare rich and rewarding professions, the importance of agriculture, and consequently the position of women in the Apache economy, declined, and Apache men frequently made the women abandon their unharvested fields and pack up the village to follow the buffalo herds, or to engage in military activity.

Among the Caddos of East and Northeast Texas, women attained position and influence unmatched in early Texas. Two Caddo confederacies existed in Texas in historic times, the Kadohadacho and Hasinai, as well as related cultures to their south and north. By most standards the Caddo had developed the most impressive civilization in Texas. They were highly skilled farmers, lived in permanent agricultural villages, and participated in an extensive trading network with Indians to the east and west of Texas. The Caddo also maintained a very elaborate political and social system. In addition, Caddo culture, as well as that of related groups such as the Wichitas and Tonkawas, was matriarchal. At the beginning of the world, according to Hasinai mythology, there was one woman, and this woman had two daughters; from these two the human race descended. In historical times the oldest competent woman, the "mother of the house," was the dominant figure in the family; typically the family consisted of a woman, her sisters, her husband, unmarried children, and married daughters and their families.

Caddo women also could hold great political and economic power. Fray Gaspar Jose de Solis, who traveled among the Caddo late in the 1760s, described his encounter with a woman of great wealth and power known as Santa Adiva. Her house, he wrote, "is very large and has many rooms. The rest of the Nations bring presents and gifts to her. She has many Indian men and women in her service called *tamas comas*, and these are like priests and captains among them. She is married to five Indian men." Another early European explorer described a "queen" among the Kadohadacho—a term that probably referred to the mother of the heir apparent, or the sister of the current ruler, but who was herself a person of great power. In other respects the role of women in Caddo life reflected the more structured, hierarchal nature of Caddo society. Labor was divided along sexual lines, with men performing the heavy work of clearing and plowing the fields, building the houses, and hunting, while women tended the fields and harvested the crops, prepared the food, tended house, and gathered wild herbs, fruits, berries, and nuts. Both men and women held positions in the political and religious hierarchy.

The first Europeans in Texas arrived as part of a series of Spanish expeditions in the sixteenth century, and a French expedition in the seventeenth century. These were exploratory undertakings that did not involve European women. However, women were involved in the Spanish settlement of Texas, which began late in the seventeenth century. While the mission, the principal institution for spreading the Spanish Empire north into Texas, was male dominated, the soldiers who manned the presidios that supported the missions frequently brought their families with them, so nearly half of the population of the initial civil settlements at San Antonio and Nacogdoches were women. Even the missions, founded by priests to convert the Indians and transform them into law-abiding Spanish subjects, actually resembled walled villages with a population of Indian, Mexican, and Spanish men, women, and children. A census of the population of the missions in Spanish Texas in 1783 indicated that the population of the five San Antonio missions consisted of 207 adult men, 149 adult women, 123 male and 75 female children. The population was more balanced in the towns of Spanish Texas; in 1783 San Antonio counted 331 adult men and 311 adult women, while Nacogdoches numbered 129 adult men and 104 adult women.

Women also played an active role in Spanish Texas. Although Spanish custom and law, as well as the rules of the Catholic Church, severely restricted women's rights, on the fringes of the Spanish empire women were able to assert themselves fully. Whether the opportunity they enjoyed was due to the "democratic" nature of the frontier, the fact that the strength of traditional restrictions against women was diluted by distance and the necessities of frontier life, or the high mortality rate which often forced widows to take over responsibilities generally fulfilled by men, women in Spanish Texas ran businesses and ranches, received land grants, and occasionally even helped lead settlers into Texas, while still performing their traditional duties as wives, mothers, companions, and helpmates. Though women assumed these many roles and tasks, on the official level Spanish Texas remained a male-dominated society, as evidenced by census reports that listed women separately only if they were widows, and, indeed, that treated widowhood as the principal female occupation.

Nonetheless, the degree to which women found room to assert themselves in Spanish Texas is surprising. Fate—often in the form of the death of a spouse—left many women in charge of property and the heads of households, even if adult sons were present. Other women achieved prominence through their economic achievements or their political skills. María Josefa Granados owned the largest general store in San Antonio in the 1780s, while Doña María Hinojosa de Ballí expanded the landholdings that she inherited from her husband until she owned about one-third of the lower Rio Grande Valley, including Padre Island, and truly merited the designation as Texas's first cattle queen. Doña María del Carmen Calvillo not only presided over the ranch that she inherited from her father in 1814, but she expanded its livestock holdings and built a sugar mill, granary, and large irrigation system. María Betancour earned her fame as one of the early pioneers in San Antonio. In 1731, as a twenty-eight-year-old widow and mother of five, she helped lead thirty-one Canary Islanders to San Antonio, became a fixture in the city's life, and named the main plaza there the Plaza de las Islas in honor of the Islanders' origins. Early in the nineteenth century Maria Cassiano, another descendant of María Betancour, was the wife of the Spanish Governor of Texas who assumed the responsibilities of office whenever her husband was absent.

Of course, for most women in Spanish Texas life entailed neither glamour, wealth, nor power; most worked hard as wives and mothers, farmers or ranchers, or seamstresses, cooks, peddlers, or laundresses. Even on the ranches life was spartan—houses were poorly built and usually consisted of only one room—and women worked from dawn to dusk tending the garden, caring for children, cooking, making household necessities such as soap and candles, spinning, weaving, and fashioning clothing and shoes. The women of Spanish Texas were restricted by Spanish law, which prevented them from voting, as well as by religion, both of which bound them to marriage. On the other hand, Spanish law did give women rights in court, allowed them to sue and be sued, and to enter into legally-binding contracts. Spanish law also protected the property rights of women: it allowed them to maintain property separate from that of their husbands; it protected wives by preventing creditors from seizing their home to satisfy their husband's debts; and it guaranteed women legal right to half-interest in all profits a married couple earned. These latter two rights would persist after the collapse of Spanish rule and provide the basis for the homestead exemption and community-property rights.

The early nineteenth century brought dramatic changes to Texas. First, in 1821, following a ten-year struggle, Mexico received its independence from Spain. As important as this event was, it was overshadowed by an even more momentous development—the Anglo migration to Texas and the demographic revolution that followed. Mexican independence had little direct impact on women in Texas. The legal rights and restrictions women experienced under Spanish jurisdiction did not change substantially. However, some women who lost their husbands to the long struggle for independence successfully sued the Mexican government for survivor's benefits. A few used this income, together with the profits they made from shrewd land dealings, to amass substantial wealth. On the other hand, the revolution did not add to women's political and legal rights or to their social status. The arrival of Anglo-American immigrants, together with African Americans and German immigrants, had a much more profound impact on Texas. By the middle of the 1830s Hispanics were the majority ethnic group only south of the Nueces River and in the Rio Grande Valley, and Hispanic cultural influences, while far from gone, no longer dominated Texas north and east of San Antonio.

Women played a major role in the Anglo migration to Texas. The first Anglo woman known to enter Texas was Jane Long. Almost two years before her adventures on Bolivar Peninsula, she made her first trip to Texas to join her husband, who was attempting to establish a republic for land-hungry Anglos in Spanish Texas. Following the collapse of this expedition and the Bolivar adventure, Jane Long returned to Texas and joined the Austin colony as one of the Old Three Hundred. In 1834 Long and Kian, who would be her lifelong companion, opened an inn at Brazoria; in 1837 they opened another inn, and then a plantation near Richmond. The Long establishments, first in Brazoria, then in Richmond, hosted the most prominent Texans, including Stephen F. Austin and Mirabeau B. Lamar. The latter used the Long inn in Richmond as his campaign headquarters when he ran for president of Texas in 1838. By 1850 Jane Long was one of the sixteen wealthiest people in Texas.

Other women also achieved prominence in early Texas. Mary Austin Holley, a widow who came to Texas from Connecticut, achieved fame by publishing in 1833 a very popular guide for prospective immigrants to Texas entitled *Texas, Observations Historical, Geographical, Descriptive in a Series of Letters*, which provided settlers with detailed and practical advice about what household equipment to bring to Texas and what type of life they could expect to have there. Holley, an avid promoter of Texas colonization and a speculator in Texas land, never achieved the economic security (either from her writing or investments) that she suggested awaited all who moved to Texas and returned to Louisiana, where she worked as a governess. Other women were more successful. Many widows received land grants from Austin and other empresarios in their own right; others, whose husbands died in Texas, managed the lands they inherited and added to their estates.

Most women who immigrated to Texas came with husbands and families. Lucky ones like Mary Crownover Rabb, an eighteen-year-old bride from Arkansas who settled near La Grange in 1823 with her husband and a large group of her husband's relatives, arrived with a ready-made community; other women came only with husband and children; and still others came without husbands, such as Abigail Fokes, a widow with six children who settled on the San Gabriel River in 1835. Stephen F. Austin's 1830 "Register of Families" listed twenty widows, most with children, in his colony. The experiences of these Anglo women on the Texas frontier differed little from those of the Spanish and Mexican women who preceded them. Their life was difficult and the living conditions were primitive. They worked alongside their husbands and older children, clearing the land and planting crops. Like Hispanic women, Anglos found that the social and legal restrictions that limited the rights of women in the early nineteenth century often weakened as one moved west. In the Anglo colonies men outnumbered women in the early years, sometimes as much as two-to-one—a situation which added to the value and influence of women, but one which also could place them under the social and economic subjugation, albeit the loving subjugation, of a male relative. In addition, the social mores of the early nineteenth century still placed married women in a subservient position and expected them to behave in ways that seem strange today. For example, it was not unusual for women in early nineteenth-century Texas to serve meals to their husbands and then retire to the kitchen to eat separately from them.

In spite of the primitive living conditions and the restrictions forced upon their gender, women contributed significantly to colonial Texas. Some successfully managed land or businesses and achieved economic success; others played important roles as community builders. The establishment of schools and churches in early Texas owed much to the work of women. Mary Rabb, Lydia McHenry, and others were instrumental in bringing the Methodist Church to Texas early in the 1830s, while Mary McKinzie Bell was central in the history of the Presbyterian church in Texas. Mexican women worked to overcome the lack of resources that limited the strength of the Catholic Church in Texas during the early nineteenth century. For example, women in San Antonio and Nacogdoches raised funds to repair church buildings in their communities, while Doña Patricia de la Garza de León provided much of the support for the parish Church at Victoria. Most of the work done by Anglo women to bring protestant churches to Texas was done out of public view, because gender restrictions prevented women from assuming formal positions of leadership. On the other hand, women assumed a highly visible role in the early efforts to establish educational institutions, for teaching was one of the few acceptable occupations for women in colonial Texas. Women not only worked as teachers, but they established or helped to establish schools in Independence, Houston, Matagorda, and Washington County. Most of these institutions were private academies or boarding schools that did not survive more than a year or two; efforts to establish public school systems in Texas did not succeed until after the Civil War.

During the turbulent decade of the Texas Revolution and republic, the position of women in Texas underwent a subtle transformation as Anglo culture supplanted Hispanic culture. These changes affected both Anglo and Hispanic women, as well as the growing population of black women. In the second quarter of the nineteenth century, Anglo culture generally placed greater restrictions on the property rights of women than had Hispanic culture; on the other hand, the initial stirrings of feminism and women's suffrage would make their way into Texas from north rather than from south of the Rio Grande.

The mythology of the Texas Revolution, which produced larger-than-life male heroes and tales of heroic encounters between Texans and Mexicans, also encompassed women—most notably Emily Morgan, who reportedly joined Santa Anna's entourage as his army pursued

Texas refugees during the Runaway Scrape, sent word to Sam Houston about Santa Anna's position, and then kept the Mexican general "occupied" as the Texans launched their attack at San Jacinto. Morgan, a mulatto and most likely a slave who was rewarded with freedom for her heroism, was immortalized in the song *The Yellow Rose of Texas*. Less well known are the activities of those women left at home while their husbands fought the Mexicans at the Alamo, Goliad, and San Jacinto. They ran the farms and plantations in their husband's absence and organized the evacuation of their families as Mexican armies approached. Others were more directly involved in the war, including several who survived the siege of the Alamo. One of these, Suzanna Dickinson went to the Alamo with her husband and served as a cook and nurse throughout the battle; another, Andrea Candaleria, served as a nurse for James Bowie during the siege (and was one of the few Tejano women at the Alamo).

In spite of the fact that a number of Tejano men and women supported the Texas struggle against Santa Anna, Texas independence generally had a negative impact on them. Many Anglos were bitter over the atrocities committed at Goliad and the Alamo, some were reluctant to accept Tejanos as equals, and others were determined to eliminate the Mexican influence, if not their very presence, in South Texas. The Anglos' attitudes generated racial conflict that resulted in prejudice against Mexicans in Texas that occasionally erupted in violent acts. Mexican women found themselves victims of both gender and racial prejudice. For example, Doña Patricia de León, who had helped build the Catholic church in Victoria and who had supported the Texas Revolution, was forced to leave Texas and lost control over the extensive property that she had inherited from her husband, empresario Martin de León.

The role of Hispanics in Texas was further diminished by the demographic changes that followed the Texian victory at San Jacinto. Texas independence and then statehood triggered a massive immigration to Texas, the population of which soared: from approximately 50,000 in 1836 to 212,592 in 1850 and to 604,215 by 1860. While a sizeable portion of these immigrants came from Germany, the vast majority came from the United States, especially the southern states, and they helped bind Texas to the United States in general and to the South in particular. The sexual imbalance continued, especially on the frontier, but not to the degree that it had among Anglos in colonial Texas. In 1860 men outnumbered women in Texas by approximately 36,000.

Women's rights during this period included those based on American (and English) law as well as those derived from Hispanic practices. More dramatic, however, were the restrictions Texas society now placed on women's rights. Women could not vote or hold public office, sue or testify in court, or gain entry into most professions; married women did not have full control over their earnings or full guardianship of their children. Women were not permitted to present public lectures or sermons and were shackled by a double standard in morality. The mid-nineteenth century also witnessed the emergence of the "cult of true womanhood," which honored women as the guardians of home and hearth, entrusted them with nurturing the children and with safeguarding the moral values of the community; at the same time it did not view them as mental or physical equals of men. The first half of the nineteenth century, then, confronted American (and Texas) women with severe social, political, and economic restrictions;

however, this same period also witnessed the emergence of the first organized women's rights movement. Women, especially in the northern and northwestern states, defied restrictions on public political expression by becoming actively involved in and even spokespersons for a number of social reform programs. Furthermore, at this time women began to gain entry into a number of professions, achieved greater economic rights and greater control over property, and launched their struggle for suffrage. These reforms, however, made few inroads into Texas in the first half of the nineteenth century.

The influx of Anglo women was not the only demographic change Texas experienced early in the nineteenth century—many migrants from the United States brought their slaves with them. While the Spanish were the first to bring African slaves into Texas, blacks did not comprise a major element in the population until the 1820s, when Anglos began importing slaves as labor for the production of cotton and later sugar cane in the fertile river bottoms of the state. As a result, the black population soared from approximately 450 late in the eighteenth century to about 5,000 in 1836 and to over 182,000 in 1860.

The vast majority of black women in early-nineteenth-century Texas were slaves. While sharing some experiences with Anglo and Hispanic women (such as harsh working conditions and primitive living conditions), black women had their rights restricted far more by slavery than by gender discrimination. Slave codes restricted the legal rights of all blacks, and the lack of legally recognized marriage contracts left slave women with even less legal and social protection than their nonslave counterparts. Slave women, of course, had virtually no voice in the decision to migrate to Texas. While the trip to Texas could be arduous for Anglo women, and while many came to Texas as the result of decisions made by their husbands, fathers, or other male relatives, their immigration could not compare with that of Silvia King, who reported that she was marched in chains from the slave market in New Orleans to a plantation near LaGrange: "it was a horrible time because we were all chained up . . . when one got tired or sick, the rest had to drag and carry him." Once in Texas slave women experienced an equality of sorts in the cotton fields. They did the same work as men, usually six days a week from sunrise to sundown, or, as some put it, from "can see to can't see." Sarah Ashley recalled, "I used to have to pick cotton and sometimes I picked 300 pounds and toted it a mile to the cotton house . . . I never got whipped because I always got my 300 pounds." On some plantations women with young children received less demanding work assignments. In any event, not all black women submitted to slavery without resistance. A number ran away, protesting the violence of the system or the destruction of slave families; some committed acts of violence against their masters or overseers.

In spite of the difficulties that enslaved black women faced and the severe restrictions placed on free blacks in antebellum Texas, some black women achieved a measure of success. A slave woman named Minerva often served as overseer on a Brazoria plantation in the slaveowner's absence. Fanny McFarland, a free black woman, lived in Houston for years, even though she had no legal right to reside in Texas; she worked as a laundress and engaged with some success in real estate speculation. Harriett Reynolds owned and operated a fairly successful ranch in Jackson County.

The Civil War influenced dramatically the lives of all women in Texas, but most especially those of black and Anglo women. Wars consume men, and in the process thrust new responsibilities onto women. The Civil War, by precipitating the abolition of slavery, also bestowed freedom on black women.

As the conflicts over the expansion of slavery, abolitionism, and sectionalism deepened in the 1850s, Texas women were drawn into the political arena. Just as abolitionism drew women into political activity in the North, women's participation in the debates of the day in Texas, first over slavery, then over secession, eroded traditional restrictions on women's involvement in public issues. While most women in the Lone Star State supported slavery, states' rights, and later the Confederacy, some were outspoken unionists, a few were even abolitionists. Melinda Rankin, a Presbyterian missionary who came to Texas in the 1850s, lost her job because of her advocacy of abolitionism and her outspoken unionism. Elise Waerenskjold, an immigrant who settled in North Texas late in the 1840s and became a leader in the Norwegian community, advocated women's rights, education, and abolitionism. Her critique of slavery centered on her conviction that all humans were equal and that slavery was "contrary to the will of God."

Once the war began, Texas women generally supported the conflict in the same manner as did others in the South and those in the North—by filling jobs that men vacated when they marched off to battle. In Texas, women ran the farms, plantations, and businesses. They also wove cloth for uniforms, made bandages, ran hospitals, and attempted to bolster morale among the civilian population and, through their letters, the men on the front lines. In Austin the Ladies Needle Battalion sewed uniforms for soldiers, while in East Texas Harriet Perry reported that the women and the slaves kept busy by making cloth for the army "up to 90 yards of cloth a week" in some households. Some Texas women played an even more active role. Sally Scull ran the Union blockade by shipping cotton overland to Mexico and exchanging it for munitions for the Confederate military. Sophia Porter, the "Texas Paul Revere," rode her mule across the icy Red River to notify Confederate forces of the location of Union soldiers who had quartered at her trading post. Chipita Rodriguez, who ran an inn in San Patricion was as spy for the Union; she was hanged in 1863 after being framed for murder.

While isolation from the major theaters of war spared Texas much of the devastation experienced by other Confederate states, Texans did face hardship. Over 100,000 Texans fought in the Civil War. Women separated from their husbands or widowed by the war not only experienced loneliness but were forced to assume many of the roles that men traditionally served. In addition, although escaping the more direct ravages of battle, they endured shortages that were sometimes extreme. Paper, medicine, and some foodstuffs were in short supply, as was salt, which was essential to food preservation in the prerefrigeration era. In Galveston, when a group of women organized a protest against shortages and the high price of basic commodities, Confederate military leaders arrested them and removed them from the island.

Black women also shared in the hardships of war. Not only did they spin thread to make cloth for Confederate uniforms, but, like Anglo women, many had to endure the absence of their loved ones: some black men were forced to attend their masters on the battlefield, others had run away to join the Union forces. After the slaves were emancipated, black women assumed an even more active role in Texas society. Like Anglo pioneer women, they participated in organizing their communities and played a major role in establishing schools and churches. They also moved quickly into the workforce. Some labored alongside their husbands; single women, including widows, became working single head of households. Black women toiled as agricultural workers, sharecroppers, farmers, laundresses, and domestics. They adjusted quickly to the wage-labor market. Some negotiated their own sharecropping contracts, while others became active in the state's fledgling labor movement. In 1877, under the slogan "we will starve no longer," black laundresses in Galveston organized a strike for higher wage. This labor strike was the first by the women of Texas, and it reflected the growing involvement of women in social and political reform movements in decade following the Civil War.

In these years, Texas again experienced a large influx of settlers. The expansion of agriculture, the spread of the open-range cattle industry, the construction of railroads, and the first stirrings of industrial development attracted hundreds of thousands of new residents to Texas and transformed the state demographically, economically, and politically. The population of Texas increased from about 600,000 in 1860 to over 3,000,000 in 1900, with most of the new residents settling on farms as the Texas frontier moved west. The population of Texas also remained predominantly male (about 110 men for every 100 women) through the end of the century.

Women participated in all aspects of the post–Civil War expansion of Texas. During the heyday of the Texas cattle industry, a number of women, following in the footsteps of successful Hispanic women of the colonial period, achieved success as cattle ranchers. Lizzie Johnson made a fortune by investing in cattle in the 1870s; she was also one of the first women to participate in a cattle drive along the Chisholm Trail. Following the death of her husband, Captain Richard King, Henrietta King ran the famed King Ranch for forty years, from 1885 to 1925. With the help of her son-in-law, she eliminated the ranch's debt and doubled its land holdings to over 1 million acres. She also promoted the development of South Texas by donating land for Kingsville and other townsites and by contributing funds to aid the development of the First Presbyterian Church of Kingsville, Texas A&I University, and other community institutions. Some Mexican women remained active in the ranching industry in the late nineteenth century. Margarita Villareal and several others operated ranches in far South Texas after the Civil War.

Far more women were involved in farming than in ranching. As late as 1940 half of the women (and men) in Texas worked at farming—either on family farms or as tenant farmers or sharecroppers. On the frontier farm there was little differentiation in the work regimen of men and women. Women, in addition to their duties as wives and mothers, participated in planting and harvesting crops, caring for livestock, and even clearing land. On more prosperous farms in settled areas, women's work usually was confined to "household duties," which included planting, tending, and harvesting gardens, canning and preserving foods, assisting in the slaughter of livestock, salting or smoking fresh meat, spinning thread and weaving cloth, making clothes, washing clothes, cleaning house, and raising children. For these post–Civil War pioneers, life on the frontier could be as primitive as it had been for their predecessors fifty or even one hundred years earlier. Generally, new arrivals on the Texas High Plains set up housekeeping in a tent or covered wagon before moving into a frame house of one or two rooms; some spent an extended period of time in dugouts or in sod houses.

Women also continued to be involved in organizing and working with the basic community institutions—home, school, and church. Some, such as Margaret Adams McCollum Mooar, became active in women's clubs. Mooar, determined to inform the women of West Texas about the national issues that affected their lives, helped found the "Up-to-Date History Club" in Colorado City in 1892. For the most part, though, women on the frontier concentrated on recreating whatever life and culture they had left behind. For some this meant organizing schools and churches, working as school teachers or music teachers, and bringing "culture" to the West; others, perhaps those with less formal educations, focused on transplanting their eastern cultural values and basic domestic skills.

The most notable change in the role of women in late-nineteenth-century Texas was that increasingly it expanded to include involvement in political and social reform. As Texas women became more politically active, a second theme would emerge in the history of Texas women—their struggle for equal rights. Women were active in the various organizations that made up the agrarian movement, they played a major role in the prohibition movement, and they voiced concern about other social and political issues. While Texas was not a center of feminism in the late nineteenth century, Texas women increasingly interpreted their responsibilities as the guardians of the home and public virtue under the "cult of true womanhood" as necessitating their active involvement in politics and in social reform organizations.

Since the majority of women lived on farms or in farming communities, it is not surprising that they became involved in agrarian protest movements. Texas farmers did not fare well in the thirty years that followed the Civil War. Continually declining agricultural prices and deflation were especially debilitating to the debt-ridden agrarian class. The shift from subsistence to commercial agriculture left farmers at the mercy of transportation systems, banking institutions, and marketing processes with which they had little experience or understanding, and over which they had virtually no control. And as government fell increasingly under the control of business and industrial interests, farmers became frustrated over their lack of political influence. They responded to the crisis with the formation of the Grange and Greenback parties in the 1870s, the Farmer's Alliance in the 1880s, and the People's party in the 1890s. Texas women participated in several phases of this agrarian protest.

In 1873, when the Grange first appeared in Dallas, it was the first farmer's organization in which women were engaged to any significant degree. The Grange accepted women as members but it generally restricted them to involvement in women's auxiliaries or Grange youth groups. Nevertheless, for the first time Texas women participated openly and in large numbers in a political organization, and although their role was limited they acquired a political consciousness and leadership skills that would be valuable to them in future political efforts. The experience that women gained in the Grange enabled them to assume a far more active role in the Farmer's Alliance. The Alliance, which had been founded in Lampassas in 1875, did not become a significant instrument of agrarian protest until the mid-1880s. More than any other political organization in nineteenth-century Texas, the Farmer's Alliance accepted (indeed, it actively sought) the involvement of women on an equal footing with men. As a result of the opportunity afforded to them, women such as Fannie Moss, Dr. Helen Lawson Dabbs, and Bettie Gay played active roles by writing numerous articles and essays about the Alliance (and about the rights of women) and serving as delegates to Alliance conventions. Fannie Moss served as secretary-treasurer of the Texas Farmer's Alliance from 1892 to 1894; her successor in this position was Dr. Francis Elizabeth Daniel Leak. Bettie Gay, who wrote extensively on the relationship between women and the Alliance, argued that the Alliance would redeem women from the unnatural position of inferiority in which society had placed them and restore them to their proper sphere of equality; she insisted that women could be active in the politics of the Alliance without neglecting their responsibilities in the "home sphere."

The Texas women who were active in the Farmer's Alliance also tended to be active in other reform organizations. A number participated in the St. Louis convention that resulted in the founding of the People's party in 1892, although many Texas women had their enthusiasm for the new party dampened by its failure to endorse women's suffrage. The most popular reform movement among Texas women of the period was prohibition. Many Texans (and Americans) in the late nineteenth and early twentieth centuries believed that alcohol abuse was linked to an array of social and moral problems from crime to poverty, to prostitution, divorce, and delinquency. Furthermore, most advocates of prohibition approached the issue as a moral crusade; they refused to consider compromise, and they branded their opponents as sinners. The debate in Texas over this issue generated excited and heated political conflict, which in the words of former governor Oran M. Roberts "stirred up society to its very foundations with a greater manifestation of universal feeling and interest than had ever occurred before in Texas."

Women emerged as an active force in the debate over prohibition with the establishment of Texas's first chapter of the Women's Christian Temperance Union (WCTU) in Paris in 1882, following a speech there by Frances Willard, president of the national body. The WCTU recruited the wives of a number of prominent Texas political leaders, including Matilda Cassa Denton Maxey, wife of Senator Samuel Bell Maxey. However, its most important Texas recruit was Helen Stoddard, a Fort Worth mathematics professor who joined the organization in 1887. Stoddard served first as the legislative chair of the Texas WCTU, during which time she successfully lobbied for the passage of a series of reform laws, including an act that mandated the inclusion of curriculum material on alcohol and drug abuse in the state's public schools. Beginning in 1891, Stoddard served sixteen years as president of the WCTU.

Women were attracted to the WCTU and the prohibition issue for a variety of reasons. The definition of the campaign against alcohol as a moral struggle fit well with the popular image of the role of women as defenders of the home and of community morality. Also, many women believed that the misuse of alcohol induced men to wife battering and child abuse—issues of great concern to women. Finally, the WCTU was the first organized political association of Texas women; consequently it provided the first political forum for women's issues, including ones that ranged far beyond the scope of prohibition. It was, for example, the first organization in the state to endorse women's suffrage, and its legislative program included the enactment of anti-tobacco legislation as well as a state child-labor and pure-food-and-drug act; the WCTU also championed the creation of a state college for women. In 1903, after a ten-year political struggle, the WCTU saw the establishment of the Texas Industrial Institute for the Education of the White Girls of the State of Texas in Arts and Sciences (now Texas Woman's University); Stoddard, who had directed the campaign for the college, was one of three women named to the institution's first board of regents—the first women to hold such a position in the state.

In spite of their increased activity in politics and social reform, Texas women did not see their overall status change significantly in the latter part of the nineteenth century. Women remained politically disfranchised; they could not serve as lawyers, sit on juries, or hold elected public office, and, except for on the farm and in the home, their presence in the workplace still was rare. The census of 1870 listed only 5 percent of women over the age of ten as employed; by 1900 this figure had risen only to 13 percent. Of those who did work outside of the home (aside from agricultural labor), most found employment as domestics. Other women worked as seamstresses, laundresses, hotel employees, milliners, tailors, and laborers. Only a handful of women managed to gain entry to the professions at this time; the 1880 census listed a few women bankers, lawyers, doctors, and ministers. Even the traditional women's professions, nursing and teaching, still were dominated by males as late as 1880.

The political experience gained by Texas women through their involvement in the Grange, the Farmer's Alliance, and the prohibition movement provided the foundation for their increased political activity and for their greater political success in the progressive movement of the twentieth century. Additionally, Texas women entered the progressive movement through their involvement in women's clubs, which increasingly became centers of social reform, and the women's suffrage movement. Each of these approaches had its roots in the nineteenth century but achieved real success during the Progressive era. The prohibition movement, especially the WCTU, continued to build on the base it had laid in the late nineteenth century. After failing to win referendums on prohibition in 1887 and 1911, the movement successfully lobbied for statewide prohibition and the approval of the national prohibition amendment in 1918. Women's clubs, often dismissed merely as social organizations, in reality became the principle vehicle for the political activism of Texas women. Indeed, women's clubs and prohibition groups were fundamental components of the alliance that comprised Texas progressivism. The clubs channeled women's political energies into community development activities, which left their mark on Texas, and committed themselves to a broad agenda of social reform. For example, following the passage of a resolution supporting public libraries at the first statewide meeting of the Texas Federation of Women's Clubs, in Tyler in 1898, Texas women's clubs began an active campaign to establish public libraries across the state. Over 85 percent of the public libraries in Texas trace their origins to this movement. Prison reform was another issue that women's clubs championed. Many Texas women believed that through their influence the state's prisons could accomplish what they had failed to achieve under male leadership—the social rehabilitation of inmates. As early as 1906 the Texas Federation of Women's Clubs endorsed prison reform, but they did not focus their energies on this issue until after 1918. In that year an investigation of prisons prompted the Women's Clubs to put forth their plan for reform, which included placing a woman on the three-person Texas Prison Board, placing women on the staff of all prisons, and placing the women's prison under the full control of women. Women would not have as much luck with prisons as they did with libraries. They enjoyed limited but short-lived success in prison reform in the 1920s during the administration of Governor Dan Moody (1927–1931), but most of their gains were reversed by his successor, Ross Sterling.

Women's clubs in Texas pursued a broad-based agenda that encompassed self-improvement, community action, social reform, and political reform. The program of the Current Topics Club of El Paso, which included a study of Ibsen's plays and Roman history as well as an examination of the issues of household economy, cooperative living, and the rehabilitation of convicts, illustrates well this scope of interests. The Texas Federation of Women's Clubs, organized in 1897 as the Texas Federation of Women's Literary Clubs, dropped the "literary" from its name in 1899 as it broadened its agenda to include such things as compulsory school attendance, pure food and drugs, and issues protecting children and women. By 1907 they could claim credit for state laws that established a juvenile court system, regulated adoption, and provided for compulsory blood tests for marriage licenses. In 1908 the *Dallas Clubwoman* published a list of the projects that should attract the energies of Texas women. The list included: the improvement of parks, public health, and sanitation; pure-food legislation; civil service reform; laws controlling child labor and improving the status of women workers; and expansion of libraries and public education. These issues were not only important to women's clubs; they also represented the basic elements of the progressive agenda. In no sense were the interests of Texas club women confined to local issues. Under the leadership of Anna Pennybacker, who served as president of the Texas Federation of Women's Clubs from 1901 to 1903 before assuming the leadership of the national body (General Federation of Women's Clubs) from 1912 to 1916, the Texas organization endorsed world peace and U.S. participation in the League of Nations.

In addition to the Texas Federation of Women's Clubs, other women's organizations with more specific interests helped promote social and political reform. Ella Caruthers Porter helped establish the Texas Congress of Mothers (which later became the Parent-Teacher Association—or PTA) in 1909. Local mother's clubs, which first appeared in Texas in the mid-1890s, worked primarily to improve schools and the services they provided. Porter, who had first become interested in issues affecting women and children through her work in the WCTU, used the state organization to lobby for a number of social reforms, including a state child-welfare commission, which was established in 1918 under the direction of Ms. Claude De Van Watts. Black women also established a number of women's clubs during the first quarter of the century that were committed to self-improvement and community service. Since the Texas Association of Women's Clubs was segregated, in 1905 Ms. M.E.Y. Moore founded the Texas Association of Colored Women, and in 1911 Jovita Idar established The League of Mexican Women (*La Liga Femenil Mexicanista*), which advocated education for women and opposed racial discrimination.

In spite of the broad range of concerns of the various women's clubs, the major political goal of Texas women during the progressive movement was women's suffrage. The roots of the Texas suffrage movement reach back to the immediate post–Civil War years when women petitioned unsuccessfully to get women's suffrage included in the Constitution of 1869 and then in the Constitution of 1875. In 1887, following their defeat in the state prohibition referendum, the WCTU endorsed women's suffrage. The first organizations in Texas created specifically to promote women's suffrage appeared in the late nineteenth and early twentieth centuries. In 1893, Rebecca Henry Hayes of Galveston, an associate of Susan B. Anthony and vice-president of the National American Woman Suffrage Association, organized the Texas Equal Rights Association to promote the "industrial, educational, and legal rights of women and to secure suffrage to them;" ten years later Annette Finnigan of Houston, an associate of Carrie Chapman Catt, founded the Texas Woman Suffrage Association. Neither of these organizations survived long. However, a third organization, the Texas Equal Suffrage Association, founded in 1915 under the leadership of Minnie Fisher Cunningham, spearheaded the successful drive for women's suffrage. With effective grass-roots organization, skillful lobbying efforts, and the ability to take advantage of the patriotism generated by World War I and the support of both President Woodrow Wilson and Governor William P. Hobby, suffragettes achieved victory in their long struggle for the vote. Black women, such as Christia Adair, joined in the campaign for women's suffrage, even though the Texas Equal Suffrage Association was segregated and most black men in Texas had been effectively disfranchised by 1915. In 1917 the Texas Federation of Colored Women's Clubs endorsed suffrage, and in 1918 Ms. E. P. Simpson of El Paso unsuccessfully attempted to affiliate the El Paso colored Women's Club with the National American Women's Suffrage Association. In a special session in 1918 the legislature granted women the right to vote in primary elections; at the request of Governor Hobby in 1919, the legislature submitted a state constitutional amendment enfranchising women—an amendment that the voters rejected. Finally, in that same year, the Texas legislature's favorable vote made Texas the ninth state and the first southern state to ratify the Nineteenth Amendment to the U.S. Constitution. One year later, with ratification by the necessary three-fourths of the states, white women had gained the right to vote in Texas and throughout the United States.

The enfranchisement of Texas women removed the final legal barrier to their participation in all aspects of the political process. A few women had held public office prior to 1918, usually on local school boards or in appointed positions, and for several decades they had worked diligently in reform movements and in lobbying efforts. But the acquisition of the right to vote in primary elections in 1918 and in all elections in 1920 allowed women to take an even more active role in state politics. After gaining the right to vote in primaries in 1918, over 385,000 women registered to vote and then immediately elected the first woman to statewide office in Texas when they selected Dr. Annie Webb Blanton as the state superintendent of public instruction.

During the decade following suffrage, hundreds of Texas women followed Blanton's example and ran for local or state office. Many were successful. By the end of the 1920s, 109 of the state's 254 counties had women treasurers; two women, Edith Wilmans (in 1922) and Helen Moore (in 1928), won election to the Texas House of Representatives, and in 1926 Margie Neal was elected to the Texas Senate and became the first woman to serve on the Texas State Democratic Executive Committee. In 1928 Minnie Fisher Cunningham became the first woman in the country to run for a seat in the U.S. Senate; and, in 1924, Texas elected a woman as governor.

In addition to their success at the polls, Texas women also utilized the political skills they had gained through their experiences in reform movements and the suffrage campaign to structure a sophisticated political machine in the early 1920s. Soon after the enactment of the Nineteenth Amendment, the Texas Equal Suffrage Association was reorganized as the Texas League of Women Voters under the leadership of Jessie Daniel Ames. By 1922 the League had allied with the Texas Federation of Women's Clubs, the Congress of Mothers, the PTA, the WCTU, the Texas Federation of Business and Professional Women's Clubs, and the Texas Graduate Nurses Association to form the Joint Legislative Council. This "petticoat lobby," as its detractors labeled it, proved to be an effective force in the legislature in the early 1920s. During the four years of its existence, it saw its entire legislative package enacted into law, including improved funding for public education, public health programs, and new labor laws; it also advocated prison reform and stricter enforcement of prohibition laws.

The most dramatic evidence of the new role of women in Texas politics was the election of Miriam A. Ferguson as governor of Texas in 1924 and again in 1932. "Ma" Ferguson was a controversial political figure. Many Texas women opposed her candidacy on the grounds that she was only a stand-in for her husband, James "Pa" Ferguson, who was ineligible to run for governor following his impeachment in 1917, and because James had been one of the state's most adamant opponents of women's suffrage. On the other hand, Jessie Daniel Ames, former suffragist and first president of the Texas League of Women Voters, campaigned for Miriam Ferguson because of her anti—Ku Klux Klan stance. As Governor, Miriam Ferguson clearly allowed her husband to influence her administration. On the other hand, she supported aid to education and prison reform, issues that the petticoat lobby had endorsed, and she appointed Emma Meharg as Texas's first woman secretary of state.

Whether Miriam Ferguson truly was governor or just a figurehead, her campaign and presence in the governor's mansion reflected the changes that women's suffrage had brought to Texas politics. Recognizing the new power women exercised at the polls, some campaign literature early in the 1920s began to focus its appeal directly to women voters. Women's groups opposed Tom Connally's bid for a Senate seat in 1922, castigating him for opposing the Federated Women's Clubs' legislative agenda in Congress and for failing to support the woman's suffrage amendment. Furthermore, Miriam Ferguson's campaign directly confronted the issue of a woman campaigning for office, as well as her principal opponent's link to the Klan. In a Spanish-language appeal to the Hispanic voter she assured her supporters that "*Yo sere el Gobernador y no Jim*" (I will be the governor and not Jim); another broadside read, "We will vote for a woman with a bonnet and a dress before we will vote for a man with a pillow case and sheet on."

Women continued to be active in Texas politics in the 1930s and 1940s. The victory in the suffrage campaign and occasional victories at the polls did not end the quest for equal rights, for women continued to face discrimination in many areas. Texas women did not gain the right to serve on juries until the 1950s, and they did not gain complete equality in property and contract rights until the 1970s. Efforts to secure the passage of an equal rights amendment in the 1920s were unsuccessful. Although only about one-third of the women had entered the workforce (including a growing number of married women by 1930) and women had found increased employment opportunity as clerical workers and in retail sales, women professionals continued to be confined primarily to occupations that had become stereotyped as "women's work." In 1930 women comprised over 80 percent of the teachers and 90 percent of the nurses and librarians, but less than 2 percent of the lawyers and doctors. During the Great Depression, Texas women experienced discrimination in employment and in New Deal agencies. New Deal agencies that found work or provided job training for the unemployed generally restricted women to "traditional" jobs (sewing, food processing, health care, and domestic service), and some officials did not approve of jobs for married women. In San Antonio, New Deal officials channeled most black women into training programs for domestic service, or into segregated programs. World War II, like other major wars, brought more women into the workforce, and into jobs traditionally held by men.

One political gain that Texas women made in the mid-twentieth century was the increasingly prominent role that they played in national affairs. No Texas woman was more visible during this period than Oveta Culp Hobby. Her career in politics began in 1926 when, at the age of twenty-one, she served as parliamentarian to the Texas House of Representatives. In the 1930s she worked for the Texas State Banking Commission and married former governor William P. Hobby. During World War II she became the first commander of the newly organized Women's Army Corps; then, during the Eisenhower administration, she headed the Department of Health, Education and Welfare, becoming the second woman ever to serve in the cabinet. Following her retirement from politics, she became the publisher of the *Houston Post*.

The political agenda of Texas women had changed somewhat by the middle of the twentieth century from the strong commitment to social reform that had typified their activities in the first quarter of the century. Organizations such as the League of Women Voters focused more on international issues, voter registration and education, and expanding the political rights of women by abolishing the poll tax and overturning the laws that prevented women from serving on juries. The political activities of women became more diversified in the postwar period. Women served as volunteers and held leadership positions in both the Democratic and Republican parties and were especially instrumental in establishing the latter as a viable political force in the state. They also were active in some of the political fringe groups that were common in the state and the nation during the era of political excess that grew out of McCarthyism. In Houston, the Minute Women became a powerful force in local politics, especially school-board politics, as they campaigned to "save" Texas from communism in the early 1950s. In the late 1950s professional atheist Madalyn Murray O'Hair made Austin the home of her campaign to take prayer out of the public schools and to purge religion and religious symbols from all government activities.

But even as Texas approached the mid-twentieth century, African American and Hispanic women were still struggling for their basic political and civil rights. This struggle was initiated largely by women in the second quarter of the century. Black women played a central role in the founding of chapters of the National Association for the Advancement of Colored People (NAACP) in Houston in 1912 and in Dallas in 1918. Lulu B. White, a school teacher born in

Elmo, Texas, in 1898, became active in the Houston branch of the NAACP in the mid-1920s. In 1939 she became president of the Houston branch, and in 1943 she became its executive secretary. An uncompromising foe of segregation, she led the challenge for the integration of The University of Texas that resulted in the landmark Supreme Court decision, *Sweatt* v. *Painter*. Christia Adair, the former black suffragette, also became active in civil rights and in the Houston chapter of the NAACP, campaigning to end restrictions on black suffrage, integrate public facilities, and end racially motivated violence. Juanita Craft did similar work in Dallas; as an NAACP organizer she was credited with establishing 182 chapters of the organization in Texas. In addition she spearheaded voter registration drives, fought discrimination, and organized youth clubs. Following the *Smith* v. *Allwright* decision by the Supreme Court in 1944, which made possible black participation in Texas politics in significant numbers for the first time since the 1890s, voter registration drives and get-out the-vote campaigns became the focus of the political activity of black women. Hattie Mae White was the first to benefit from these developments. In 1958 she became the first black elected to political office in Texas since the early twentieth century when she won a seat on the Houston school board. A few years later Juanita Craft became the first black woman elected to the Dallas city council.

The most significant change that Mexican-American women confronted in the twentieth century was the migration of hundreds of thousands of persons from Mexico to Texas. By 1988, Hispanics were the largest minority in the state, numbering almost 4 million and comprising 23 percent of the population. During the first half of the century, reform efforts in the Mexican-American community were centered in labor organizations. Mexican-American women played a major role in these activities. For example, in 1938 the twenty-year-old Emma Tenayuca organized a strike of 10,000 largely Mexican-American pecan shellers; this was the largest labor action Texas had seen to that time. As the strike dragged on, and as the strikers endured abuse and violence, the action was transformed into a broad-based struggle for jobs, equal rights, and protection against deportation. Tenayuca became a local folk heroine for her fiery leadership and courage. Other Mexican-American women were instrumental in improving the working conditions and wages of garment workers in Dallas and San Antonio.

Women also played a major role in the political organization of the Mexican-American community. In 1929 Maria Hernandez helped found one of the first organizations in the state dedicated to protecting the civil rights of Mexican Americans. After World War II, political energies in the Mexican-American community shifted from labor struggles to civil rights. Women became involved in LULAC and the GI Forum, where they worked to end discrimination and gain equal rights. Mexican-American women frequently faced the same kind of prejudice from men within their community as Anglo women had faced when they had first became politically active in the mid-nineteenth century. Frequently Mexican-American women were forced to limit their political involvement to women's auxiliaries of LULAC and other organizations. Nevertheless, Mexican-American women made political gains. In 1974 Irma Rangel became the first Mexican-American woman elected to the Texas legislature.

The person who symbolized the success of minority women in Texas politics in the second half of the twentieth century was Barbara Jordan. Like Oveta Culp Hobby, Jordan's first political success came in the state legislature in Austin, before she moved on to Washington and the national spotlight. Jordan grew up in Houston's Fifth Ward and attended Texas Southern University prior to earning a law degree at Howard. In 1966 she became the first black elected to the Texas Senate in the twentieth century; six years later she became the first woman from Texas elected to Congress. During the televised Watergate impeachment hearings, Jordan entered the national spotlight as perhaps the most articulate, certainly the most compelling, orator on the House Judiciary Committee. Before ill health forced her to retire from Congress in 1979, some political observers suggested that she had the potential to become the first black and the first woman president.

In the late 1960s and 1970s, inspired by the civil rights movement and the antiwar movement, feminism enjoyed a resurgence in Texas. The new feminist agenda centered on: ending job discrimination for women; eliminating sexism in the media and in education; increasing the number of women in elected political positions; assuring equal status for women under the law; addressing social problems confronting women such as wife battering, rape, and child abuse; and guaranteeing women access to legal abortion. The issue that became the focus of the women's movement in the 1970s was the effort to secure ratification of the equal rights amendment to the U.S. Constitution; in the 1980s the abortion issue dominated the women's movement. Both of these issues (but especially the abortion issue) divided women as had no others. Although the Texas legislature approved ratification of the equal rights amendment, the measure failed to gain the approval of the necessary three-fourths of the states and was not ratified. As of 1997 the right of women to legal abortion had not been restricted in Texas.

Women succeeded in attaining many of their political objectives in Texas. Women's groups set up shelters for battered women and rape crisis centers in most of the state's major communities. In 1972, by an overwhelming majority, Texas voters added an equal rights amendment to the state constitution that eliminated virtually all of the legal discrimination against women. In 1973, a Texas attorney, Sarah Weddington, successfully argued the case for legalized abortion before the Supreme Court. Even though job discrimination did not vanish in Texas, by the 1990s women had gained access to management positions and entry into the professions in unprecedented numbers.

Women's success in politics also was impressive. On the local level, women became a major political force. Beginning with the election of Carole Keeton Rylander as mayor of Austin in 1977, and the election of Kathy Whitmire as mayor of Houston in 1981, women mayoral candidates have had remarkable success in Texas's major cities; in the late 1970s and 1980s Houston, Dallas, San Antonio, Austin, El Paso, Galveston, and Nacogdoches have all had women mayors, and Whitmire of Houston had held the post longer than any other person in the city's history. Indeed, in 1990 the state's largest city had a woman mayor, a woman school superintendent, a woman police chief, an African-American woman as president of its largest university, and a woman as president of its chamber of commerce. Minority women have shared in this political success. In Houston, for example, the mid-1990s saw African-American, Mexican-American, and Asian-American women serving on the city council, and Sheila Jackson Lee, an African-American woman, representing the city in the U.S. Congress.

Women's influence in state politics also increased. Between 1922 and 1985, forty-six women served in the state legislature; in 1985, nineteen women (seventeen in the House, two in the Senate) served there. However, even though women have comprised the majority of the state's population ever since 1960, they still make up less that 14 percent of the legislature. Furthermore, since Miriam Ferguson was elected for her second term as governor in 1932, no woman won election to statewide office for fifty years. In 1972 Frances Farenthold, a two-term veteran of the Texas House of Representatives, made a credible run for the governor's office. She finished second in a field of seven in the Democratic primary before losing to Dolph Briscoe in the run off. Ten years later Ann Richards became only the third woman to win a statewide race when she was elected state treasurer. However, 1990 was the banner year for women politicians in Texas. That fall 21 women were elected to the legislature (as late as 1970 there were only two, Farenthold and Jordan). Kay Bailey Hutchison, a Republican, defeated another woman, Nikki Van Hightower, for state treasurer. And Ann Richards was elected Governor of Texas, the second woman to hold that office and the first to be elected in her own right. Two years later Kay Bailey Hutchison became the first woman from Texas elected to the U.S. Senate.

As Texas approaches the twenty-first century, no one can seriously question the fact that women play a major role in the state. The 1990s not only have witnessed a woman in the governor's mansion and a woman representing Texas in the U.S. Senate, but women administering the government of several of the state's major cities, holding positions of responsibility in corporations, medical institutions, colleges and universities, and the media. Texas women work as physicians, attorneys, accountants, and engineers, as well as in the "traditional" professions of nurse and teacher. As they have done since they first arrived in Texas, women continue to contribute to the task of creating the community in which they live, organizing its principal institutions, and working to ameliorate the social problems that exist there. As new waves of migration bring new groups of residents into Texas, women will continue to participate in the building of new communities. And Texas women will continue to assert their right to an equal partnership in the state that they have helped to build.

CPSIA information can be obtained at www.ICGtesting.com
Printed in the USA
LVOW03s0751110815

449578LV00004B/4/P